WILFRED OWEN

Collected Letters

At Leith, July 1917, with
Arthur Newboult

WILFRED OWEN

COLLECTED LETTERS

Edited by
Harold Owen and John Bell

London
OXFORD UNIVERSITY PRESS
NEW YORK   TORONTO
1967

Oxford University Press, Ely House, London, W.1

GLASGOW NEW YORK TORONTO MELBOURNE WELLINGTON
CAPE TOWN SALISBURY IBADAN NAIROBI LUSAKA ADDIS ABABA
BOMBAY CALCUTTA MADRAS KARACHI LAHORE DACCA
KUALA LUMPUR HONG KONG TOKYO

CONTENTS

PLATES

INTRODUCTION

The survival of these letters throughout the vicissitudes of family life is largely due to Susan Owen's devotion. She kept every word written to her by her eldest son from his early childhood. Other mothers have done the same; the surprise in this instance lies in the casual, even careless manner in which the letters were preserved (together with the few she could glean from other members of the family). For she—and her daughter Mary—were perfect squirrels in the way in which they hid and hoarded all manner of objects and forgot where they were.

Tom Owen died in 1931, his wife in 1942. It was not until after Mary's death in 1956—unmarried, she lived at home all her life—that the family belongings were thoroughly sorted. It was only then that the extent of the squirrel-like hoarding was fully realized. In every room and outbuilding of the little house at Emmer Green, near Reading, bundles of Wilfred's letters and postcards were found. There was no chronological order, no yearly sequence. Tied up with string, wool, odd bits of ribbon or tape, some of these bundles also contained letters from other people and receipted bills, some dating back to the days at Plas Wilmot in the early years of married life. In one packet was the catalogue of sale by auction of the furniture, outdoor implements, and effects of Plas Wilmot on 16 March 1897. Some letters were found in the garden shed in nailed-down boxes and tea-chests, unopened for many years; others had been hidden amidst remnants of materials, oddments of wool, and silk embroidery work. In one box a few letters had been packed with a tea-set. And in another nailed-down box, incidentally, opened by the Emmer Green boy scouts on Mary's instructions, was Wilfred's heavy army revolver, loaded, with a pouch of live ammunition.

From time to time an odd bundle or a single letter had been handed by Mary to her brother for safe keeping; but she, like her mother, had forgotten or did not realize how many letters had been stored in this haphazard way. Only one letter had been carefully preserved, the first; and this was discovered in Susan Owen's jewel-box after Mary's death. Carefully sealed in an envelope, it was inscribed in pencil 'Wilfie's first letter, 1898'.

The family moved house eight times after leaving Oswestry for Birkenhead. There was a move within a few weeks to Shrewsbury; then back to Birkenhead, in three different houses; to Shrewsbury again, and two successive houses; to Norton Fitzwarren, Somerset, on Tom Owen's retirement in 1922; and finally to Wilmot, Emmer Green, in 1925. Wilfred's letters survived, somehow.

Six hundred and seventy three letters[1] have been preserved, and we

---

[1] We have taken the word 'letter' throughout as including postcards and incomplete letters.

1

have printed them all. Publication may bring a few more to light, but it seems likely that the collection is as complete as one could hope for. Some of the letters are, of course, trivial; but there are few that do not have some interest, and publication in one volume being practicable we have chosen to print everything. In addition to all this correspondence, there are a few picture postcards bearing no message and twelve Field Postcards sent from France between 31 December 1916 and 2 May 1917. These have not been included or listed. We have, however, included one communication without written message—a picture postcard—because the word Amiens is underlined, a signal of significance to the family.

The recipients of letters are as follows:

Within the family	Susan Owen	554
	Tom Owen	5
	Mary	41
	Harold	9
	Colin	22
Outside the family	Leslie Gunston (cousin)	30
	Siegfried Sassoon	7
	Osbert Sitwell	1
	Mrs. Bulman	1
	Alec Paton	3

—that is, 631 of the 673 letters are to the family; and the overwhelming majority of the family letters are to Susan Owen.

In essentials, then, this volume is made up of a devoted son's letters to his mother: the first from Birkenhead in 1898, aged 5, the last from France on 31 October 1918, aged 25, four days before he was killed in the assault on the Sambre-Oise Canal. Susan Owen was the centre of her son's life; the recipient of all his adoration, all his youthful confidences, all his anguish of mind. These letters apart, there are affectionate, caustic, or magisterial letters to other members of the family; the group to his favourite cousin Leslie Gunston, the only one with whom, until 1917, he could freely exchange views on poetry and poets; and that, for almost all his life, was all. Determined to be a poet, he knew no poets until he met Laurent Tailhade[1] in August 1914 and Harold Monro at the Poetry Bookshop in November 1915 (and did not greatly take to him). With these exceptions, he knew no one on the literary scene until, in the late summer of 1917, he met Siegfried Sassoon at Craiglockhart Military Hospital, and the initiation began. But now there was little time or opportunity to write letters to his new and still slightly awe-inspiring friends. The hurried pleasures of leave encounters with Robert Ross, Wells, Bennett, Scott Moncrieff, Osbert Sitwell, Robert Graves, Monro, and, of course, Sassoon were over far

[1] After seeing the photograph of Wilfred with Tailhade (see Plate Vb) H.O. asked Wilfred about him. He gathered that after the first enthusiasm over meeting a real poet Wilfred's liking for the older man not only diminished but evaporated; and that he did not greatly admire Tailhade's work. But see p. 278, note 1.

too quickly. He went back to France, sent back occasional Field Postcards to keep in touch, and within weeks he was dead. Sir Osbert Sitwell
has only one letter, which we print here; Robert Graves had two or
three, which he did not keep, and a Field Postcard dated 3 November
1918; Siegfried Sassoon kept seven of perhaps twice that number. None
to Ross, Scott Moncrieff, or anyone else are known to exist. There was
no time to write—except to his mother.

It seems to us necessary to publish these letters, for three reasons.
Firstly, they constitute an autobiography of, we believe, great interest
and great candour; the autobiography of one who now appears, some
fifty years after his death, as not only the most important poet of the
first war, but also one of the major poets in our language. Secondly, they
help to illuminate the poems and reinforce their increasing relevance to
our times. And thirdly, they provide, when read in conjunction with the
poems,[1] published and unpublished, and the three volumes of *Journey
from Obscurity*,[2] the basic material on which an authoritative biography
can one day be based.

The letters must be left to speak for themselves; but we would like
to make one observation. It is not difficult to single out certain moments
or periods of particular significance: the impact of Keats; the misery of
the closing months at Dunsden Vicarage; the gradual realization that
the dream of getting to a university was not going to be realized; the
emotional turmoil of the weeks in the Pyrenees in August-September
1914; the relief of joining up, and the transformation of personality that
begins at this moment; the appalling impact of the Somme; and the final
determination to go back to the front. But to him there was one moment
of supreme importance; and this is made abundantly clear in the letters.
It was the momentous meeting with Siegfried Sassoon at Craiglockhart,
little more than a year before his death, that touched off the great poems
and opened doors hitherto shut. 'Oh! world you are making for me,
Sassoon!' he writes rapturously from Scarborough. Without that recognition, encouragement, and impetus the full flowering might not have
been achieved. Given time, the poems would have come; but time was
the enemy, and death in action was not many months away.

.   .   .   .   .

The letters are set out as they were written. His spelling, punctua-
tion, and paragraphing were accurate, his handwriting clear; all this
has simplified the task of editing, and we have been able to follow him

---

[1] *The Collected Poems of Wilfred Owen*, edited with an Introduction and Notes by C. Day
Lewis, Chatto and Windus, London, 1963.

[2] Harold Owen, *Journey from Obscurity*, Vols. I, II, III, Oxford University Press, London,
1963, 1964, 1965. These three volumes, published before the letters were edited, are now
seen to contain some inevitable inaccuracies of detail and dating. These inaccuracies in no
way affect the validity of the recollections. In the same way, some biographical details and
dates in the Introduction to the *Collected Poems* are wrong; but this does not detract from the
value of the edition. We have appended to this Introduction a Biographical Table summariz-
ing the facts established by the letters. Some new datings of poems, published and unpublished, are included.

faithfully. We have, however, made certain exceptions, as follows:

1 He consistently misspelt wierd, thus; and frequently misused apostrophes in such phrases as 'the Gunston's house'. We have corrected these, not wishing to irritate the reader with apparent misprints. In the first few letters, however, we have preserved the youthful misspellings that are an attractive part of the letters of early childhood.

2 In about half a dozen places we have supplied a missing full point at the end of a sentence where without it the sense was not always clear.

3 A few slips of the pen, common in all hastily written letters, have been silently corrected: most frequently, the repetition of a word or the omission of a letter. Where a word has been omitted, we have supplied it, enclosed in square brackets.

4 Obviously misspelled proper names have been corrected (there are very few instances of this); otherwise correct spellings are given in footnotes.

5 Every address from which he writes is given in full in the first instance and thereafter abbreviated to the essential minimum. It has not seemed necessary to distinguish between written and (very few) printed addresses. Except where they occur within the text of a letter we have standardized the forms of dates, though keeping all idiosyncratic additions (*Tues.*, *Easter Morning*, etc.), and print them on the left, with the address on the right. With postcards, we print the address of the recipient only when it differs from the usual home address.

6 We have standardized titles. Those of short poems and articles are printed in Roman type between single quotation marks, which are used throughout in preference to double; those of long poems, books, plays, journals, newspapers, and ships in italics. All foreign words or phrases are printed in italics (unless the whole letter is in French), as are the occasional sub-headings indicating that a letter has been taken up again after an interval: *Sunday afternoon; after tea*, etc.

7 To avoid confusion with italicized editorial comments, we have reproduced the underlining of words rather than print them in italics. No indication is given of the few double and treble underlinings.

8 Words or phrases struck out by the writer are shown in footnotes where the change of mind is of interest. Insignificant changes of this kind are not shown.

9 Many of the letters were signed with a monogram, thus: ⓦⓔⓞ In all such cases, we simply print W.E.O. Wherever kisses were added, however, thus: x x x, we have retained them.

10 We have made a few deliberate omissions, all unimportant, to avoid hurting the feelings of living people. All such omissions are clearly indicated. The total number of words involved is 229.

· · · · ·

In general, the transcription of the letters presented few problems. Even the hastily written note or card from the front, from hospital, or at the close of a fatiguing period, is admirably legible. His firm, clear, vigorous hand changed hardly at all, with age or circumstance. But there were certain problems of transcription unconnected with the handwriting, with fading, or with staining.

Ten years ago, when it was first decided to transcribe the letters preserved by Susan Owen, certain words and phrases, and some short passages, were inked out, rubbed out, or pencilled over, in the originals. This was done by one of the present editors, in good faith, and without a realization of the difficulties that might arise later. The intention was to remove trivial passages of domestic news of the kind that would certainly be left out in any volume of selected letters—something that was at that time contemplated; to remove names of people whose families might have been upset by some particularly scathing reference, or simply by the unexpected appearance of their names in print; and to remove words or expressions that seemed displeasing or unworthy. In full agreement, we have attempted to decipher and restore all such obliterations, and have largely succeeded. Some passages, blacked out particularly thoroughly with Indian ink, are irrecoverable in places, though we have usually succeeded in recovering the greater part, using infra-red treatment in one or two particularly obstinate cases. All that has been restored is now printed. It all appears harmless, almost comically so. Auntie for Aunt, dinner for lunch, unattractive slang expressions, words with mildly disagreeable associations such as pimples, boils, and so on, disparaging comments on casual acquaintances who cannot now be identified; and some sentences so respectable that the original impulse to obscure cannot now be recalled. In addition, ten years ago, a few short passages, publication of which was felt more strongly not to be necessary, were scissored out of the originals and destroyed. Fortunately, there were few such passages: probably not amounting altogether to more than half a dozen printed pages. We believe that these passages would now appear as inoffensive as those that have been retrieved. They were cut out with the same innocent intention; but cut out rather than inked out, because they displayed a critical or over-emotional turn of phrase that was then found irritating or embarrassing. Disparaging comments on the Royal Navy, for example, were the cause of the present fragmentary form of letter 488.

In addition, it will be seen that opening or closing sheets, sometimes both, are missing in some thirty instances. It is clear that most of these became accidentally detached and lost over the years; but, though the details cannot now be recalled with certainty, a few of these missing pages were deliberately detached and destroyed. This would increase the estimate of six printed pages to about nine.

The exact position, and, where it can be estimated, extent of all obliterations and cuts is shown. In relation to the whole volume, the extent, like the content, is trivial. Indeed, the context is usually the surest indication of triviality. We estimate that approximately two-thirds of all this material has been restored, and that the equivalent of some twenty-four handwritten pages is lost or illegible.

The annotation, which has been kept as factual as possible, excludes the precise identification of some thirty people. These are usually village acquaintances at Dunsden, family friends in Shrewsbury, and fellow officers and other ranks (though the majority of the officers have been identified in the Army Lists). To insert a note reading 'unidentified' in these cases seemed an unnecessary imposition on the reader. Where, however, we have failed to trace a reference that called for clarification, we have said so; and here apologize that there should be any such instances.

In a volume containing a number of different Owens, we have felt it best to avoid confusion by calling the poet Wilfred throughout.

The provenance of each letter is not indicated in the text, for it can be more simply stated here. All the letters to the Owen family are in HO's possession, as are all Wilfred's books and papers. Leslie Gunston, Siegfried Sassoon, Sir Osbert Sitwell, and Alec Paton have the letters addressed to them; Miss Blanche Bulman has the letter to her mother. With the exception of Mr. Gunston's letters, where we were provided with transcripts, and Sir Osbert Sitwell's, where we reproduce the full text as printed in *Noble Essences*, we have worked from the originals in all cases.

The following abbreviations are used after the first reference, which is given in full:

EB   Edmund Blunden and his Memoir for the 1931 edition of the poems
LG   Leslie Gunston
CDL   C. Day Lewis
HO   Harold Owen
SS   Siegfried Sassoon
BM   British Museum
JO   *Journey from Obscurity*
Letters *Letters of John Keats*, Vols. I and II, ed. Hyder Edward Rollins, Cambridge University Press, 1958
Poems   *The Collected Poems of Wilfred Owen*
Welland D. S. R. Welland, *Wilfred Owen: A Critical Study*, Chatto and Windus, London, 1961

Finally, a note about the poems may be helpful here. In April 1934, through the generosity of the Friends of the National Libraries, the British Museum acquired practically the whole surviving manuscript of the poetry. A few manuscripts were known to remain outside this collection, but, as Edmund Blunden wrote in *The Times* on 16 April 1934: 'the nation now owns by far the greatest share of what Owen penned'. Mr. Blunden continued: 'Among the manuscripts now housed at the British Museum some are relics of Owen's earliest poetry and of days when he had little thought of his function except as the rich statement of beautiful details and romantic dreams. From this stage he was bound to advance as life mingled sterner impulse and significance with his luxuriant fancies.' The greater part of this early, minor, or fragmentary material remains unpublished. C. Day Lewis is explicit about this in the Introduction to *Collected Poems*: 'Part III offers a selection of Owen's juvenilia and minor poems, chosen to illustrate some of the things I have said about his youthful work and sensibility.' In the course of preparing the letters for publication we have taken this unpublished material, both in the BM and in private hands, into consideration, and refer to it in the notes. A few minor poems are here printed for the first time as integral parts of the letters in which they appear.

.   .   .   .   .

Our chief debt of gratitude, like Wilfred's, is to Siegfried Sassoon. He did not preserve all the letters written to him between November 1917 and October 1918, but he has freely made available to us all that have survived, and has offered assistance and encouragement throughout. In this he has done no more than continue the generosity of spirit that made his friendship with Wilfred the turning-point in the younger man's development as a poet; a generosity that showed itself again after the war, when his energy and vision, supported by the enthusiasm of Edith Sitwell, led to the publication of *Poems of Wilfred Owen* (Chatto and Windus) on 2 December 1920, with an Introduction that though brief is a noble testimonial from a friend and fellow poet.

Our second debt is to Leslie Gunston, who has been of the greatest help and kindness in providing information on the family background and has permitted us to print the letters in his possession. Without his patient help, a number of references would have eluded us.

We are also greatly indebted to Dr. Charles La Touche and his brother David for giving us, in letters and in conversation, their recollections of the Mérignac period, from Christmas 1914 to the summer of 1915; to Robert Graves, for allowing us to reproduce two letters of his own to Wilfred; to the Rev. Alfred Saxelby-Kemp, who has talked to us of the days when he and Wilfred were together in Dunsden vicarage in 1912 and 1913, sharing (in Wilfred's words) 'the Silence, the State, and the Stiffness'; to Cecil Day Lewis, whose 1963 edition of the poems, the fullest and most detailed yet to appear, has been a vital instrument in preparing the letters for publication; to M. Roland Bouyssou, of Rodez, Aveyron, France, through whose enthusiasm and generosity we have been provided with more photographs associated with the Bordeaux period than, alas, we have been able to include; to

Mr. George Derbyshire, the historian of the 5th Battalion the Manchester Regiment, whose patient research into the histories of the 2nd and 5th Battalions has solved a number of problems for us; to Patric Dickinson, devoted and tireless champion of Wilfred Owen, who has given a special encouragement to the venture; to Robert Gittings, who has helped us over certain Keatsian queries and has given a good deal of support throughout; to Professor Edmund Blunden and Messrs. Chatto and Windus for all they have done to foster the poems over the years, and in particular for allowing us to reproduce the passages first printed in the Memoir in 1931; to Sir Osbert Sitwell, for permission to reproduce the letter first printed in *Noble Essences* (Macmillan and Co., Ltd., London, 1950); to Sir Rupert Hart-Davis, for his example as an editor, his sound advice, and his ingenuity in establishing a connexion with the enterprise by disclosing that his great-uncle was Vicar of Dunsden before the Rev. Herbert Wigan, Wilfred's mentor; to the Rev. Bernard Wigan, whose reminiscences of his uncle are set down in these pages; to the Headmaster of Downside School, Bath, whose enterprising reading of old files on our behalf turned up some useful and entertaining information; to Mr. A. K. Newboult of Edinburgh, the small boy in the frontispiece, and his sister Miss Mary Newboult; and to Miss Anne Harden, who has been an invaluable help in cheerfully and skilfully undertaking research of every kind and ferreting out a remarkable amount of information to assist us both.

In addition we would like to thank a number of others for their help: notably Miss Carol Bourne, Miss Blanche Bulman, Mrs. David Butler, Mrs. Olga Bowditch, Miss Irene Drake, Mrs. Edith Dymott (Wilfred's cousin), and Col. Brian Dymott, Major F. Harden, Miss Cynthia Harnett, Miss H. V. Hart-Davis, Mr. Donald Heatby (Town Clerk of Birkenhead), Professor James Hepburn, Mr. C. Walter Hodges, Mr. Derek Hudson, Mr. George Kimble, Dr. Norman Lansdell, Mr. Conrad Latto, F.R.C.S., Mr. William Mayne, Miss Anne Pasmore, Mrs. Anne de Pass, Mr. Alec Paton, Dr. Rosemary Rostron, Mrs. Leonard Smith, Mr. and Mrs. Angus Stewart (the present owners of the old Vicarage at Dunsden), Mr. T. J. Walsh of the Birkenhead Institute, Dr. A. R. H. Williamson, and Dr. W. B. Yapp.

And to our wives, for their patience during our preoccupations, we are indebted most of all.

H.O., J.B.

June 1967

BIOGRAPHICAL TABLE

We have included in this table only those poems which can be precisely or approximately dated. Poems marked with an asterisk remain unpublished or uncollected

1893	18 March	Wilfred Edward Salter Owen born at Plas Wilmot, Oswestry, son of Tom and Susan Owen
1895	30 May	Mary Millard Owen born
1897	March	Plas Wilmot sold on Grandfather Shaw's death. Tom Owen appointed to supervisory post at Birkenhead with the Great Western and London and North Eastern Railways
	April	Poor accommodation obliges Tom Owen to apply for transfer. Appointed to Shrewsbury
	5 September	William Harold Owen born
1897–8	Winter	Tom Owen reappointed to Birkenhead. The family moves to Willmer Road, Birkenhead
1898–9		Move to Elm Grove, Birkenhead, and further move to 51 Milton Road, Birkenhead
1900	24 July	Colin Shaw Owen born
1901	11 June	Wilfred starts (in mid-term) at the Birkenhead Institute
1905	August	Welsh holiday with Alec Paton
1906	July	Family holiday at Torquay and Carbis Bay, Cornwall
1906–7	Winter	Tom Owen appointed Assistant Superintendent, GW and LNER, Western Region; the family moves to 1 Cleveland Place, Underdale Road, Shrewsbury. Wilfred starts at Shrewsbury Technical School
1908	June	Tom Owen takes Wilfred to Brittany
1909	July	To Brittany again with Tom Owen; then to Torquay
1910	January	The family moves to Mahim, Monkmoor Road, Shrewsbury
	August	Holiday with Harold in Torquay. Calls on Miss Christabel Coleridge
	September	Writes 'Written in a Wood, September 1910'*†
1911	April	To Torquay again. Reads Life of Keats, and visits Teignmouth
	21 April	Writes sonnet 'At Teignmouth, on a Pilgrimage to Keats's House'*‡
	Summer	Works as pupil-teacher at the Wyle Cop School, Shrewsbury, while preparing for matriculation exam

† Reproduced in full by EB. MS. believed lost.
‡ MS. believed lost.

1911	9 September	To lodgings at 38 Worple Road, Wimbledon, to take University of London Matriculation exam, held in the Imperial Institute, Kensington. Visits British Museum to see Keats manuscripts
	28 September	Interview with the Rev. Herbert Wigan, Vicar of Dunsden, near Reading. Is offered an unpaid post as lay assistant and pupil
	Early October	Hears he has matriculated, but not with honours
	20 October	Arrives at Dunsden. During the following sixteen months writes 'The Imbecile' and probably 'Maundy Thursday'; and, among others, 'Nocturne',* and 'It was a navy boy'*
	December	Writes 'Deep under turfy grass and heavy clay'*
1912	16 April	Arranges to attend botany classes at University College, Reading, for six hours a week
	15 May	Completes long blank-verse poem, *Little Claus and Big Claus**
	c. 7 July	Joins family at Pringle Bank, Kelso, for holiday with the Bulman family
	Summer	Writes 'On Seeing a Lock of Keats's Hair'*§
	20–25 July	Attends Keswick Convention
	September	Starts revision of long blank-verse poem *The Little Mermaid**
	December	Miss Edith Morley urges him to sit for a scholarship to University College, Reading, and invites him to attend her remaining classes in Old English free of charge
	Christmas	At Shrewsbury
	28 December	Visits Mr. Morgan, a clergyman at Bordesley, Birmingham, and is offered another post as lay assistant. He does not accept. Returns to Dunsden
1913	Early January	Determines to leave Dunsden. Writes 'On my Songs'
	7 February	Returns to Shrewsbury
	February–March	Ill with congestion of the lungs
	13 March	Harold, joining the Merchant Service, sails for the Mediterranean and India
	18 April–3 May	Convalescent holiday in Torquay staying with his Aunt Anne Taylor at 48 Belle Vue Crescent. Starts to look for a teaching post
	16–19 May	In lodgings at 67 South Street, Reading, to sit for the University College scholarship
	Late May	Harold critically ill with heat apoplexy in Calcutta
	July	Writes 'When late I viewed the gardens of rich men'.* Harold returns to England

§ Reproduced in part by EB. MS. believed lost.

1913	c. 6 July	Hears he has failed the Reading scholarship. Considers taking an assistant mastership at the village school, Dunsden
	August	Holiday with Uncle Edward Quayle's family at Dorfold, Great Meols, Cheshire
	c. 15 September	To Bordeaux, to teach English at the Berlitz School of Languages. Lodgings in rue Castelmoron
	Mid-October	Visited in Bordeaux by Tom Owen
	28 October	Moves to 95 rue Porte Dijeaux, Bordeaux
	November	Ill with gastro-enteritis
1913–14	Winter	Harold again at sea in the South Atlantic, remaining at sea, with occasional short home leaves, until autumn 1916
1914	18 March	Twenty-first birthday
	Early May	Grandfather Owen dies
	18 June	Mme Léger, a pupil, invites him to spend the late summer with her family in the Pyrenees
	25 July	Gives up his job at the Berlitz School
	30 July	To Castel Lorenzo, Gayeste, Bagnères-de-Bigorre, High Pyrenees, as guest of the Légers
	Early August	Writes 'From my Diary, July 1914'
	4 August	War. French Government moves to Bordeaux. Mary joins the V A D. 'The Seed' and 'The Unreturning' written during the following five months
	c. 21 August	Meets the poet Laurent Tailhade
	24 August	Invited by Mme Léger to go with her to Canada in March 1915
	17 September	Returns to Bordeaux with the Légers, and stays with them at 12 rue Blanc-Dutrouilh. Starts to look for pupils as a free-lance teacher of English; plans to return to England by Christmas
	7 October	Moves to temporary lodgings with the family of a pupil, Raoul Lem, at 12 rue St. Louis, Bordeaux
	12 October	Mme Léger leaves for Canada
	19 October	Moves to new lodgings at 31 rue Desfourniels
	4 December	Offered post as tutor to the two elder de la Touche boys at the Chalet, Mérignac, near Bordeaux
	8 December	Accepts post for a month, retaining his private pupils and going to Mérignac in the afternoons. Arranges to return to England in mid-January, taking the two boys back to Downside
	19 December	Moves to Mérignac to live at the Chalet
1915	Early January	Channel unsafe. Invited to stay until the spring
	6 February	Early April settled on for return to England

1915	10 April	Miss de la Touche decides to keep the boys and urges Wilfred to stay. Arranged that he should have three weeks in England in May, returning to Mérignac for the summer. Mr. Bonsall engaged to be tutor in his absence
	18 May	To Imperial Hotel, Russell Square, London, while carrying out a commission at the British Industries Fair for a Bordeaux scent manufacturer; then to Shrewsbury
	13 June	Returns to Bordeaux via Le Havre and Paris. Into new lodgings at 18 rue Beaubadat, continuing to teach the boys (Bonsall teaching Latin and Greek only) while retaining his Bordeaux pupils. Invited by the scent manufacturer to become his agent and travel in the Middle East as soon as the Dardanelles are cleared
	20 June	Considers joining the Artists' Rifles in the autumn, after returning the boys to Downside.
	10 July	Considers joining Italian Cavalry if the Artists' Rifles falls through
	31 August	Gives up lodgings to return to England; persuaded to stay on three more weeks, and finds new lodgings at 1 place St. Christoly, Bordeaux
	14 September	To London with the boys
	15 September	Sees the boys off to Downside from Paddington and goes home to Shrewsbury
	21 October	Joins up in the Artists' Rifles. Into lodgings at Les Lilas, 54 Tavistock Square, W.C.
	27 October	Meets Harold Monro at the Poetry Bookshop, 35 Devonshire Street, W.1.
	2 November	Takes a furnished room at 21 Devonshire Street, opposite the Poetry Bookshop, as a *pied-à-terre* for future leaves
	15 November	To Hare Hall Camp, Gidea Park, Essex, as Cadet Owen, Artists' Rifles
1916		Writes 'Has Your Soul Sipped?' during the year
	c. 1 January	Home on a week's leave
	27 February–5 March	Ten days' course in London. Lodges over the Poetry Bookshop
	4 March	Shows his poems to Monro
	5 March	To Officers' School, Balgores House, Gidea Park
	10 May	Writes 'To—'
	19 May	On leave pending gazette, first in London then Shrewsbury
	4 June	Commissioned into the Manchester Regiment
	18 June	Reports to 5th (Reserve) Battalion, Manchester Regiment, at Milford Camp, near Witley, Surrey

1916	7 July	Attached for a musketry course to 25th Battalion, Middlesex Regiment, Talavera Barracks, Aldershot
	Mid-July	Week-end leave at Alpenrose, Kidmore End, near Reading, home of his cousin Leslie Gunston. To church at Dunsden and sees the Vicar again
	Early August	To Mytchett Musketry Camp, Farnborough, in command of the 5th Manchesters contingent
	Early September	Applies for transfer to the Royal Flying Corps and is interviewed in London. Nothing comes of this
	19 September	Writes 'To a Comrade in Flanders'
	24 September	5th Manchesters move to Oswestry, under canvas
	October	Writes 'Storm'. Harold posted to the Royal Naval Air Service at Chingford Aerodrome, Essex, and stays there till March 1917
	19–20 October	5th Manchesters to Southport, Lancashire, the officers living in the Queen's Hotel. Wilfred has lodgings for a few days at 168a Lord Street
	c. 5 November	To the firing-ranges at Fleetwood in command of the battalion and brigade firing-parties. Lodgings at 111 Bold Street, Fleetwood
	8 December	Back to Southport
	Christmas	Embarkation leave
	29 December	Hotel Metropole, Folkestone
	30 December	To France. Reports to the Base Camp, Étaples
1917	January	Writes 'Happiness'
	1–2 January	Joins 2nd Manchesters on the Somme near Beaumont Hamel, in a rest area. Assumes command of 3 Platoon, A Coy.
	6 January	2nd Manchesters on the move towards the front
	9 January	Into the line at Bertrancourt
	16 January	Battalion relieved
	c. 20 January	Into the line again
	4 February	Arrives at Abbeville for a course on transport duties. During the month writes 'Exposure'
	1 March	Rejoins his battalion at Fresnoy, still on the St. Quentin front. Posted to B Coy.
	c. 11 March	Concussion following a fall at night into a cellar or shell-hole at Le Quesnoy-en-Santerre
	15 March	Evacuated to Military Hospital at Nesle
	17 March	Moved to 13 Casualty Clearing Station at Gailly. In the following fortnight writes 'A Sunrise'*
	23 March	Drafts 'To My Friend'
	4 April	Rejoins his battalion in action. Selency had just been taken, and one company had probed as far as the outskirts of St. Quentin
	8 April	The battalion is relieved, and pulls back to Beauvois

1917	12 April	Into the line again at Savy Wood for twelve days
	21 April	Relieved; into cellar quarters at Quivères. Writes 'Le Christianisme'
	2 May	Evacuated to 13 CCS with shell-shock
	11 June	To No. 1 General Hospital, Etretat
	16 June	To Welsh Hospital, Netley, Hampshire
	25 June	Arrives at Craiglockhart War Hospital, Slateford, near Edinburgh
	Late June	Starts, but does not finish, 'The Ballad of Dame Yolande'*
	Early July	Visited by Susan Owen. During July writes 'The Fates' and 'Antaeus'
	17 July	Writes first contribution to *The Hydra*, and becomes Editor
	August	Writes 'Song of Songs', and—between August and November—'The Promisers'
	Early August	Plays Wallcomb in a production of *Lucky Durham*. Siegfried Sassoon arrives at Craiglockhart
	Mid-August	Meets Sassoon
	21 August	Writes 'The Dead-Beat'
	29–30 August	Writes 'My Shy Hand'
	1 September	'Song of Songs' published in *The Hydra*
	September	Writes 'Anthem for Doomed Youth' and 'Six O'Clock in Princes Street'
	25 September	Gives first of several lessons in English literature at Tynecastle School, Edinburgh. Medical Board
	October	Writes 'Miners'
	13 October	Introduced by Sassoon to Robert Graves, who is shown a draft of 'Disabled'
	15 October	Writes 'Dulce Et Decorum Est'
	18 October	Writes 'Winter Song' and (about this date) 'Sonnet: to a Child'
	20 October	Tea at Swanston Cottage with Lord Guthrie
	Late October	Writes 'The Soldier's Dream', and last draft of 'Music', started a year earlier. Sassoon urges him to collect his poems for publication
	30 October	Medical Board. Three weeks' leave pending return to unit. Sassoon gives him an introduction to Robert Ross
	November	Writes 'Apologia Pro Poemate Meo', and 'The Show'
	Early November	'Miners' accepted by *The Nation*
	9 November	Lunches and dines with Ross at the Reform Club and meets Arnold Bennett and H. G. Wells
	10 November	Lunches again with Ross, Wells, and Bennett and meets A. G. Gardiner, Editor of the *Daily News*

1917	11 November	Visits Leslie Gunston near Winchester
	14 November	Sees Monro at the Poetry Bookshop. Writes 'Asleep'
	24 November	Reports to 5th Manchesters, Northern Cavalry Barracks, Scarborough. Still on light duties, appointed 'major-domo' of the Officers' Mess, Clarence Gardens Hotel
	26–27 November	Writes 'Vision of Whitechapel'*
	December	Writes 'Hospital Barge at Cérisy'
	3 December	Writes 'Wild with all Regrets'
	19–23 December	Short leave. To Edinburgh, revisiting Craiglockhart and Tynecastle School
	Christmas	Sassoon posted back to France
	24 December	Receives warm letter of encouragement from Robert Graves
1918	23 January	Attends Graves's wedding to Nancy Nicholson at St. James's Piccadilly, meeting Edward Marsh and C. K. Scott Moncrieff. Dines at the Reform with Ross and Roderick Meiklejohn, afterwards to 40 Half Moon Street to meet 'two critics', one probably More Adey, Editor of *The Burlington Magazine*. 'Miners' published in *The Nation*
	c. 18 February	'The Last Laugh' drafted
	Early March	Medical Board. Upgraded to Division 5
	12 March	To Northern Command Depot, Ripon
	c. 23 March	Into lodgings at 7 Borage Lane, Ripon
	Late March	Writes 'Insensibility'
	April	Writes 'À Terre'
	9–11 April	Week-end leave in Shrewsbury and last meeting with Harold
	22 April	Upgraded to Division 4
	May	Writes 'The Send-Off'
	10 May	Upgraded to Division 3
	Mid-May	'Song of Songs' published in *The Bookman*
	16–19 May	In London, staying in a flat over Ross's in Half Moon Street. Visits War Office, where Scott Moncrieff was attempting to arrange for him to be appointed instructor to a cadet battalion. Meets Osbert Sitwell at Ross's flat
	21 May	Upgraded to Division 2
	24–25 May	Writes 'Mental Cases'
	June	Writes 'Training', 'Futility', 'Arms and the Boy', 'The Calls', and 'The Roads Also'
	4 June	Graded fit for general service
	5 June	Rejoins 5th Manchesters at Scarborough
1918	11 June	War Office letter holds out possibility of posting to Artists' Rifles as instructor, to be preceded by

		a month's course with the Inns of Court OTC, Berkhamsted. Request from Edith and Osbert Sitwell for poems to include in *Wheels 1918*
	15 June	'Hospital Barge at Cérisy' and 'Futility' published in *The Nation*
	Mid-June	Colin joins the R.A.F.
	July	Draws up contents list of *The Disabled and Other Poems* for 1919 publication
	13 July	Sassoon wounded and invalided home
	Mid-July	Harold sails to join the light cruiser *Astraea* at Simonstown
	30 July	Writes 'The Kind Ghosts'
	12–18 August	Embarkation leave. Sees Sassoon in hospital in London
	31 August	Crosses from Folkestone to Boulogne, reporting again to the Base Camp at Étaples. Meets Conal O'Riordan, former Director of the Abbey Theatre, Dublin
	Early September	Writes 'The Sentry' and 'Spring Offensive'
	9 September	To Reception Depot, Amiens, to await arrival of 2nd Manchesters
	15 September	2nd Manchesters arrive at Amiens
	23 September	Writes 'Smile, Smile, Smile'
	28 September	Battalion moves forward to Vendelles
	29 September	Positions taken up for assault on the Beaurevoir-Fonsomme line
	1–3 October	Objectives gained. Assumes command of C Coy and awarded MC on the field
	5 October	Battalion back to rest area at Hancourt. Robert Ross dies in London
	15 October	Command of C Coy handed over to senior lieutenant returned from leave
	18 October	Battalion moves to Bohain
	20 October	Battalion moves to Bussigny
	29 October	Battalion takes over the line at St. Souplet
	30–31 October	Battalion takes over the line west of the Oise-Sambre Canal, near Ors, in preparation for an attack across the canal at dawn on 4 November
	4 November	Killed on the canal bank
	11 November	News of his death reaches Shrewsbury. Armistice signed
1919		*Wheels* published, containing seven of his poems
1920	2 December	*Poems of Wilfred Owen* published, with an Introduction by Siegfried Sassoon

THE OWEN AND SHAW FAMILIES

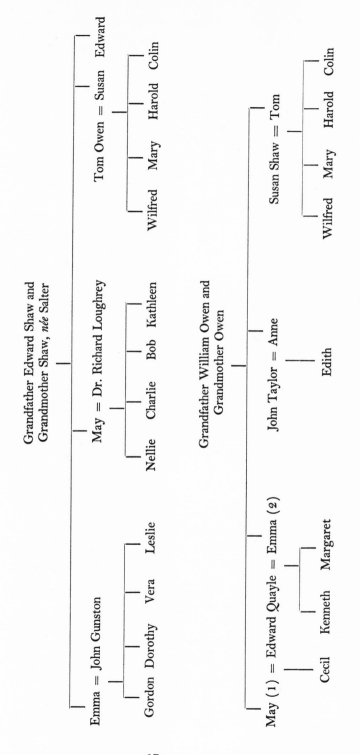

Grandfather Edward Shaw and
Grandmother Shaw, *née* Salter

Grandfather William Owen and
Grandmother Owen

Emma = John Gunston

Gordon Dorothy Vera Leslie

May = Dr. Richard Loughrey

Nellie Charlie Bob Kathleen

Tom Owen = Susan Edward

Wilfred Mary Harold Colin

May (1) = Edward Quayle = Emma (2)

Cecil Kenneth Margaret

John Taylor = Anne

Edith

Susan Shaw = Tom

Wilfred Mary Harold Colin

BIRKENHEAD AND SHREWSBURY

1898–1911

1. To Susan Owen

Addressed *Mary and Mother* with a pattern of kisses

[*1898*]   [*Birkenhead*]

my dear mother

i no that you have got there safely. We are making huts. I have got a lantern, and we are lighting them up to-night.

With love from Wilfred I remain your loving son Wilfred

2. To Susan Owen

Saturday 19th [*April 1902*]   [*Underdale Road, Shrewsbury*]

Dear Mother,

Grandpa[1] has given me as much garden as what you see from the dining room window only where the bricks are and I have got about six potatos planted, I have made another path and on the right side of it is the Vegeatble Garden and on the left is the fruit and the one you saw is the flower. It has just been raining a little for the first time but now it has stopt. We are going to Market this afternoon and I might buy some seeds. I know the children next door they have got a horse and carriage which will fit me comfortably and the path slopes like Grandpa's and I can go down without anybody touching me, I can sit or stand which ever, I like.

I look something like this standing.

I'm glad Mary is better I expect Harold is. Now I must stop, my hands are begining to shake.

Kisses for all.

From your loving Wilfred

---

[1] Grandfather Owen. Wilfred is staying with his Owen grandparents in Underdale Road, Shrewsbury. Early in 1907 the Owen family left Birkenhead for 1 Cleveland Place, Underdale Road, Shrewsbury, a few houses away from the grandparents. See *Journey from Obscurity*, Vol. 1, pp. 122–4.

3. To Mary Owen

[*1903*]

[*Wales*]¹

Dear Mary,

I have really not much to tell you. I went up the hill the day before yesterday, I am afraid you or Colin could not have climbed up it, dear, it was so hard. I hope the young ladies in your school are very good & all your large family is well. I am trying to learn Welsh. I should like to have been with you on Sunday & at our service. Mind you have it next Sunday & I shall think about you. I shall expect you to read more of that story book by the time I am home.

With best love & kisses from your brother Wilfred

4. To Susan Owen

4 January 1904

51 Milton Road, B'head

Dear Mother,

Just a line or two to say we are all-right. Father went to Wallassey yesterday and Uncle Ted² is going to business today. My little thing for my chain has come back. It is a beastly day, it it [is] gloomy, foggy & cold. Cousin May³ is miserable on account of the weather & you would be worse!!!!!! Ceicil was skating all Friday but of course I had none. Harold's cold is better and I don't think I can scrape up any more news. Give my best love to my 'Fair maiden'⁴ and tell her to write to me soon and put some funny drawings in her letter, also to Morris⁵ and Leslie⁶ and 'all the rest of 'em'. Now I must close (I say that to be sociable you know!)

From your loving Wilfred

P.S. It is now afternoon. My report has come. Remarks:—His work is very fair but I expected rather a better place in form; I think his abilities are excellent. J. Smallpage.⁷

Will you please send me Mrs Dale's⁸ address as I can't send her letter until I know it.

---

¹ Staying with a school friend, Alec Paton, whose uncle farmed in Wales. See Letter 9.
² Edward Quayle, tinplate broker of Liverpool, married Tom Owen's eldest sister. On her death, he married her sister Emma, the second of the three Owen girls. See p. 17.
³ Susan Owen's unmarried cousin May Susan Davies, of Filey, E. Yorks., later headmistress of a small private school for girls in Scarborough. See *JO* I, pp. 107–12.
⁴ Mary.
⁵ A school friend of his cousin Leslie Gunston.
⁶ Leslie Gunston, youngest of the four Gunston cousins (Gordon, Vera, Dorothy, Leslie). Their father, John Gunston, married Emma, eldest of the three Shaw sisters. The others were May (Mrs. Loughrey) and Susan. See p. 17.
⁷ Mr. J. A. Smallpage was Headmaster of the Birkenhead Institute, where Wilfred was a pupil 1900–7. See Letter 21.
⁸ A family friend known as Aunt Dale. She lived at Chester (see Letter 213), where she owned a music shop.

5. To Susan Owen

19 September 1904   [*Birkenhead*]

Dear Mother,

I have had no home-work to-night so at last I am writing to you.
Thank Mary for the little fish she sent me, I do like it. I have had some
lessons in short-hand. We are so glad you are feeling better and having
a nice time. Harold and I are very happy but will be happier when you
are home. Father asks you to bring a little toad like Harold's for
Kenneth.[1]

Tell Colin he had better put on armour for I might hug him to death ! !
I took the papers to school, and I gave some to the boys to show their
parents. Colin McHutchon was away last Sunday.

Father says as I have written he will not write again. He sends best
love. So do Harold and I.

We hope to see you on Wednesday. I must now close with love to
all in the house

From your loving Wilfred

6. To Mary Owen

[*?20 September 1904*]   *Birkenhead*

Dear Mary,

Thank you very much for the present you sent me, it will swim very
nicely. I have no present for you now but I may have one when you
come home. Tell Colin I think of him every time I go to school & wish
he was coming up the road with me. I went to Paton's to tea on Saturday.
I am very sorry you could not go to the Cates's,[2] I hope you are better
now. Thank mother for her Post-card. Dickie is well but some of his
feathers are coming off. We hope you are enjoying yourself, Harold &
I are very happy, but we want you all home again. I know my tunes
fairly well now, & I want to hear you play *Bohemian Air*. Thank mother
for the book of Puzzles she sent me, it contains many interesting
sperishuns (experiments.). I think I have scribbled enough now. I got
10 marks for an essay on Becket (I suppose you don't know anything
about him!) Well now I must end up with best love to all

From your loving Wilfred

7. To Susan Owen

28 June 1905   *Birkenhead*

Dear Mother,

Before I begin let me tell you that there will be no composition in
this letter. We have just had an essay on 'Should our streets be paved

---

[1] Kenneth Quayle, elder of the two children of Edward Quayle's second marriage.
[2] The Cates family, Wimbledon friends of the Gunstons. There were at least three sons:
George, Harry, and Geoffrey.

with wood?' So I am quite tired of 'composing!' I have really been so busy that I hardly seem to miss you. I am very sorry to tell you this but I have had only one time free, and then I ought be doing something but I forgot the book. I did not lose any marks though. The garden-party was fine, we found our way quite well. I will give you particulars when you come home. I was not nearly so bad as you think on Sunday I'm sure, only I felt a bit 'queer' all day & in the evening [you] know what happened. I am sorry you have had such bad nights. I can imagine you poking about in the corners, smelling fire!! Thank you for the letter & photograph. I think it did me more harm than good (in case of cheering me up) because every time I look at it, I begin to think about you & forget what I am doing. I don't think I can scribble anything more down now. there are 100s of mistakes, I know, & I doubt whether you will be able to read it.

Love—From Wilfred

OVER PAGE

Dear Mary
    Mr Galloway looked fine at the garden party. I am making just a hasty sketch. Of course it is not a bit like him but it is for you to laugh at.

8. To Susan Owen

29 June 1905   *Birkenhead*

Dear Mother,
    I expect this will be [the] last letter I shall be able to send to you, so I hope you will have a very good journey, and have had very pleasant holidays. I am sending this little bottle of scent for you to sniff when you come across an 'obnoxious effluvia'. Say, perhaps, when you are waiting at some station, 'and the gentle breeze bringeth forth the delicious perfume of . . . fish!'[1] I procured the bottle with much difficulty from school. The scent I put in myself, and the cork, or rather india-rubber, is my own make, I send two in case the one gets lost, or pushed in. I think you will excuse me writing more,*(P.T.O.) for my fingers are aching and trembling with holding the pen. It seems nothing but writing now. I also trust you will not show this to anybody, either, please. There is no grammar nor sense in this letter, I know. I found it rather hard to

---

[1] Uncle John Gunston had delighted the Owen children with this pronouncement, from which Wilfred omits the word 'stinking'—a banned word in the family.

Ia. Plas Wilmot

Ib. Family Group at Plas Wilmot, Oswestry, 1895

Wilfred is on his mother's knee, next to Grandfather Shaw, Aunt Emma Gunston standing, left. In front, Gordon, Dorothy and Vera Gunston. The parrot was called Jubilee

IIa. Plas Wilmot, drawn about 1885 by Susan Owen

IIb. Wilfred and Grandfather Shaw, 1895

part with the wee bottle, but I thought if you get hot or tired in church
you might squeeze a little smelling salt in it, and nobody would see it,
it is so small. Mind you don't bring me anything home from Scarborough.
I don't expect anything, so just a half-penny for chemical-collection is
just what I want. With best love and kisses from

Wilfred

* I find I <u>have</u> written more, but I have no time to write to Mary or
Colin.

9. To Susan Owen

Dear Mother,
    Thank you very much for the boots, which I received this morning.
It has been so wet here that I changed my shoes & stocking 3 times on
Saturday! & Alec & I put our feet in hot water when we went to bed.
Our feet were only just a little damp, & Mr Paton laughed & said
they were all right, but Mrs Paton made us change. (Don't tell anyone
this!) At first, before we got to the farm the place was not what I
anticipated, we had to go <u>through</u>, not along, a dirty, wet, muddy lane.
But the farm is fine. I am very happy but I am not wild. We are both
kept under great restriction. We got up a ladder on to a hay-stack in a
Dutch Barn. In case you don't know what a D.B. is, I will draw one.

Well, we made little nests on the top, but Mrs Paton heard us moving
the hay and soon called us down. (Mr P. laughed.) I am asked to thank
Mr Owen for the f. rod. It is useless now! We cannot fish!! No licence!!!
Is it not sad!!! Alec's Uncle broke my rod. It is mended now. He was
fishing this morning when a river bailiff came up & told him something
about how to fish, thinking he had a licence! You have to pay 15 or 16
shillings for 1 to fish, I <u>think</u>. This is a filthy letter, all blots. Thank
Mary & Colin for their letters. I slept in chair bed 1st night but I do
not now. I sleep with Alec.

From your loving Wilfred

[1] Near Ruthin, Denbighshire, N. Wales, on the River Clwyd. The farm belonged to Alec
Paton's uncle. See Letter 3.

10. To Susan Owen

16 August 1905   *[Rhewl]*

Dear Mother,

I am so sorry you were not well on Sunday. I thought about you very often, nearly all day. We climbed Moel Famma[1] (Varma) on the 14th. I was rather exhausted by the time we reached the top. It was about 4 o'clock, started at 11.30 but when we got home I was hardly so bad as the others were. Alec made a show of sliding down the smooth slippery grass, but he found he could not stop himself. He went bounding on till he was suddenly checked by a sharp stone wall. We thought he had hurt his head, but he had a deep cut on the knee, he said he was able to climb the hill though! I was lying down at the time, resting. Thank you very much for the letter & Turkish Delight. I have had a little bad luck. Up Moel Famma I lost my big fat knife I think. I am very sorry to say I broke the end off your umbrella. We tried to fish with the end of our rods in a tiny stream that runs into the Clwyd. I lent Alec a hook which he lost, & I lost my own, & cracked the tip end of my rod. I have bought a Picture Postcard for Harold which I hope to send tomorrow.

With best love to all from Wilfred

11. To Susan Owen

Picture postcard: women in Welsh dress

[Postmark 19 August 1905]   *[Postmark Ruthin]*

Dear Mother,

Thank you for all the letters I received this morning Alec & I read the portions every night together. We often look out the references too! Tell the children I hope to see some little wee piggies soon I thought they would come last night but they did not. Mr. Jones can hardly speak English at all. I help him to drive the cows & pigs & all he can say is 'good boy, very quick'. It is a lovely farm.

from Wilfred

12. To Susan Owen

Postcard

21 August 1905   *[Postmark Ruthin]*

Dear Mother,

It will soon be time for me to go home again. I shall be very glad to have my own family again. I have new brother & sisters & mother it seems. Alec & I found two little streams; his is the 'Wiswos', & I call mine the 'Fontibel'. How extremely clever of Mary to catch 6 fish. It is more than I did. When I fished in the little 'Wiswos' I caught

[1] Moel Farma (1,823 ft.), the highest hill in the Clwydian range, SSE of Denbigh.

O! (tell her). We went to the Weeest little church you ever saw, on Sunday. About every pew was occupied & there were only 40 people. We counted going out. Looked so pretty was lit only by candles. We did not laugh but felt inclined to because the bell in ringing made a big squeak.

From Wilfred

13. To Susan Owen

22 August 1905   [*Rhewl*]

Dear Mother,

I hope you are all quite well, I am eating tremendously! We went gathering nuts this morning I have got, altogether, 113. I am going to bring them home for the children you must not tell them please. Mr. Jones has bought 120 sheep today. They are so tired after walking 3 days that some will let me stroke them. I can count up to 10 in Welsh, & have learnt a few expressions. It will soon be time to milk the cows now. I can milk a bit. I drink buttermilk for dinner, & have cream on the stewed fruit. Indeed I fare very sumptuously, & wish Mary was here to eat the plums we get off the tree every day.

There are nine little piggies. You would be amused if you saw them. Their heads are too large for their bodies & their tails are like curly bits of string.

We are having fine weather now. I am very glad of the boots, because in the morning the grass is wet. I have not been to Ruthin yet. When I go I want to buy a little tiny boat to sail down the Clwyd. It is nearly time for the post now.

With love love & kisses always from Wilfred

14. To Susan Owen

Postcard addressed to 3 Clement Road, Wimbledon, Surrey

[*Postmark 12 October 1905*]   [*Postmark Birkenhead*]

Dear Mother,

Tea is finished, & we have just had our reading. The homework for tonight is a map, French, but there is no Arithmetic as it is not set! I suppose you are all very happy with father & the G's.[1] But we are quite happy at home so you must enjoy yourself as much as you can. With best love & kisses.

from <u>Wilfred</u>

15. To Susan Owen

[*October 1905*]   [*Birkenhead*]

Dear Mother,

It is Saturday night; struck half past seven this moment, and I have work to do. There is arithmetic to be done, which is out of those 'harder' examples. Dora[2] can understand one of four sums. It is that exercise that dear father helped me to do, one Wednesday night. How I wish he was here now. I have an essay on 'Modes of Travelling' to produce so I have no time [to] waste now.

During tea this afternoon a porter arrived with a brace of pheasants, shot Oct. 13th. (from Mr Melly)[3] It has been very wet here so we could not go out this afternoon. We went to the Seamen's Institute & saw Mr. Grindon.[4] He was very nice and took us round the docks. Well I must struggle on once again now. With my very, very best love, from your loving boy

Wilfred

16. To Susan Owen

[? *Spring 1906*]   *Birkenhead*

Dear Mother,

We went to the Bible party on Saturday afternoon and were not a bit late! In fact we were there at the exact time. We got in the same car that Poole[5] did.

Mr. Thomson was a very nice gentleman, who once lived in the Backwoods of North America, so he had many wonderful stories about himself which I will tell you when you return. He has two fine gardens, one in B'head Park which is almost wild.[6] In it is what he calls his rockgarden. I am sure you would be delighted with it. There are banks of ferns & foxgloves, and it has a little pool in the middle. When we (Colin, Poole myself, & another boy) had passed through the garden we came to his bowling-green. The big boys then had a game of bowls,

---

[1] The Gunstons.

[2] Dora Taylor was one of three children by the first marriage of John Taylor, bookseller, of Torquay, whose second wife was Anne Owen, Tom Owen's third sister. See p. 17.

[3] Unidentified. Tom Owen was Assistant Superintendent of the Great Western and London and North-Eastern Railways, Western Region.

[4] Manager of the Birkenhead Seamen's Institute.

[5] William Poole, a senior boy at the Birkenhead Institute.

[6] On 14 May 1906 the Birkenhead Parks and Cemeteries Committee declined an offer from a Mr. W. P. Thompson to sell to the Corporation for parks purposes an area of land of 18,000 sq. yds.

while Harold with the little boys played golf! (in the other garden) We only had a very short meeting just after tea, & before the games. I only wish you were there to have seen the gardens.

Harold and I are getting on very well, and we hope you will have a very pleasant holiday [*three words illegible*]

From your loving Wilfred

17. To Susan Owen

[*? Spring 1906*]   [*Birkenhead*]

Dear Mother,

I have just had my music lesson & must start to work soon now. I know I have not written to you for a long time but I really have not much time. We went to Elizabeth's[1] house to tea yesterday, & got home about 7 o'clock & I was up late last night working.

I hope you will enjoy yourselves at Wolverhampton.[2] I know you are enjoying Wimbledon.

I think that it would be better to wait till you come home, before buying the Pestle & mortar. I <u>may</u> want something more too instead of it. Thank you very much for the snake it is just what I have wanted for ages! & the parachute I am keeping till you come home to take out. This letter is strictly private, I suppose you know. I shall have to stop now by reason of the valuable time which is going past. I have not very much work to-night, but it is half past seven.

With best love to all at Alpina[3]   from Wilfred x x x x x x

18. To Susan Owen

[*? Spring 1906*]   [*Birkenhead*]

Dear Mother,

I am so glad to hear that you are having a good rest.

Smith's dolls are not quite classical statues, but they certainly bear a resemblance to the human form. I think he bought four of them. Their apparel is of crinkled paper, & tinsel! Well, now to be serious we've had more exams. Results, in short are these.

	Arithmetic		Algebra	
Shaw	100	1st.	100	1st.
Owen	66	2nd.	80	—
Paton	28!	—	100	—

Some more important ones on Monday!   Wilfred

---

[1] The maid with a sailor brother, described in *JO* I, p. 104.
[2] Mrs. or Miss Kemp, an old family friend, known as Aunt Kempie, lived in Wolverhampton.
[3] The name of the Gunstons' house, 3 Clement Road, Wimbledon.

19. To Susan Owen

19 April 1906   *3 Clement Rd, Wimbledon*

My Dear Mother,

Leslie is practising the violin now, so I have taken the opportunity to write to you. We had a good journey; our first fellow-traveller was a tall chap who came with us all the way from Chester. Presently another gentleman (?) got in, but he was enveloped in the *Sporting Chronicle*, so I saw little of him.

There was a map in the corridor but every time I got up to look at it the lady next to me put her parcel, satchel, fancy-purse, etc. on my seat. When I came back she had to replace them on her wrist. This happened about three times! & made her remark that there was a 'strong smell of apples somewhere' to her mother (ours of course.) Since she came in we or I had no peace.

It is now Friday and Leslie is p-p-practising again. We went on the Common yesterday arfternoon and again this morning.

I can read every word of Colin's letter quite easily. He can have the motor out most certainly.

Leslie has a good many chemicals, he has given me a good many little parcels of some of his stuff.

With best love to All   From Wilfred

20. To Alec Paton

Picture postcard, showing Insignia of the Order of the Thistle, addressed to Master Alec Paton, 57 Seymour Street, Higher Tranmere, Birkenhead

[*Postmark 11 July 1906*]   *Olive Villa, Carbis Bay, Lelant,*
                                                        Cornwall

Dear Alec,

We left Torquay on Wednesday. I like this little place much better than Torquay. We bathe here every day. We went to St. Ives yesterday, we can see it from our window. The people we are staying with have a donkey & I can ride it when I like. How I wish you were with us. I'm afraid there is not much composition on this card. Please write soon, don't take any care how you write to me.

                                                        Wilfred

N.B. There are plenty of 'we's' in this ! !

21. To Susan Owen

15 August 1906   *Colefryn, Waenfawr*[1]

Dear Mother,

Please excuse me for sending that awful post-card. I did not know

---

[1] Wilfred is spending the holidays with Mr. Smallpage and his son Eric at a cottage three miles SE of Caernarvon, N. Wales.

that the post-man came to the house & he was coming up the road before I started.

We went fishing all this morning (caught nothing), & this afternoon we went a walk up the hill. This evening we were playing in the fields & I quite missed the postman; but I am writing at last.

Eric has had two wasp-stings, I had one on the eye-brow. It is a tiny cottage, but we cannot see Snowdon from here. It is hidden by a nearer mountain, Moel Eilio. We are fairly near a mountain which looks just like an elephant at the top. We can see the see the sea & Anglesey quite well from the cottage. The Toy-Railway is a little larger than the Duke's,[1] but I think the gauge is the same. Mr Smallpage has just been for a horse-ride. (Postman has come now.)

Wilfred

22. To Susan Owen

Postcard addressed c/o C. Picton, Esq.,[2] 55 Bath Road, Wolverhampton

28 November 1906   [*Birkenhead*]

My dear Mother,

I have done my home work, & have come up to bed, but have time to spare to write you a post-card. You have missed Miss Taylor's[3] stories. Today she told us what vast sums of money her brother had lost by the soap Trust.[4] I am feeling quite all right now; you know I hope you are. I missed you most when I came to peel my apple at supper; there was no-one to say 'Here, I'll do it for you'. & it is the same with lots of other things. Of course you will thank Mrs. P. for the pencil. This isn't very grammatical, but I may(?) send you a formal letter in future(?)

W

23. To Susan Owen

Tues. Evening [*January 1907*]   [*Birkenhead*]

My darling Mother,

We have no homework to-night so I am able to write you a note to let you know that we are all well at home, [*four words illegible*] We have a new Mistress—Miss Jones—I have not had time to form an opinion yet—though I am sure I shall like her.

Everything is exactly the same in Shrewsbury again, & Wimbledon is only a distant recollection of past joys!

[1] The Owens had visited the miniature railway at Eaton Hall, the Duke of Westminster's seat near Chester.

[2] Family friends, Mrs. Picton being known as Aunt Peggie.

[3] Wilfred was now having piano lessons. Miss Taylor, his teacher, lived at Anfield, Liverpool. She continued to come to the house to give Wilfred free lessons after Tom Owen had said he could no longer afford the fees. See *JO* 1, p. 113.

[4] In 1906 twenty soap firms planned to combine to save the cost of advertising. A newspaper campaign, led by the *Daily Mail*, led to the abandonment of the scheme. Lever Bros. subsequently won a libel case (and £91,000 damages) against Lord Northcliffe.

Harold & Colin are going to buy railways, Father has written for them to L'pool; of course they could not get any in Shrewsbury. Please tell Leslie that I will write to him when you are home again, so he must not expect a letter before. And I have not found out who sent the Postcard. We all send best love to you & Mary, & to all at Alpina. I have got a cold somehow, & am rather tired to-night, so I will not write a long letter.

Your loving Wilfred

Mind you have a good rest & enjoy yourself, while you may.

24. To Susan Owen

April, Monday [*1907*]   *1 Cleveland Place, Underdale Rd,*
                                                                  Shrewsbury
My own dear Mother,

In the last letter I didn't tell you all I wanted to. We went to Grandpa's to tea on Saturday. They were talking about you, how you didn't take enough fresh air [*several words illegible*] & denouncing your habits of staying in! They don't know that its your self-sacrifice for us, I do though. I haven't asked you how you are, for three letters, I don't think, Mother dear, but you know I never forget to do something that is of more avail than 'wishing' and 'hoping' [*several words illegible*]

Father has suddenly decided to get me a new suit! He says I ought to have long trousers & a collar !! And when Grandpa said 'When shall I send [*two words illegible*]' I fairly choked with wrath !! The idea! of not asking you! Well father did say then 'Oh! We'll wait till Mother comes home'

You really must not think of coming home this week. We have managed quite well for more than a week now. I'm sure I can scrape along for another week or so. I've got a little cold & a cough, not much though, you musn't think of that. I've been going to bed rather late, the last few days and getting up early. Please excuse a short note to night I've got to write an essay yet, Hope you can read this somehow. Best love to all at Alpina, 'specially M.H. & C. And you actually asked me whether I wanted to see my old Mother, well, don't think I'm like Peter, please, or I shall answer like Peter. You know that I'm longing to see you.

Your loving boy Wilfred

25. To Susan Owen

Postcard addressed c/o J. Gunston, Esq., 3 Clement Road, Wimbledon, Surrey

April 1907 [*Postmark 19 April 1907*]   *Shrewsbury*
                                                                  7.53 o'clock
My dear Mother,

I am just sending you a card to let you know we are quite well. Father was at B'head all day Mrs Shields[1] asked me in to tea, I enjoyed myself

---

[1] Mr. and Mrs. Shields lived next door. He was a tailor (see Letter 252) who made a good many clothes for the Owen children. He and his wife bred King Charles spaniels, and had over twenty in their small house.

very much. She has offered us a white kitten; if you do not want us to have it, please tell me, as she is trying to find a home for it. Mr. S. is very clever at Phrenology, no room here to tell you what he says of me. I have begun letters to the others not finished.

W

26. To Susan Owen

[*April 1907*]   [*Shrewsbury*]

My own dear Mother,

I've got five lessons to do tonight, so please excuse a long letter, I would have sent a postcard only the scribble would be exposed, but I'm sending it in an unsealed envelope, to save expense! Hope the parcel arrived all right. Went to see about the kitten after tea, it hasn't learnt to lap milk yet so Mrs. S. is going to keep it for a few days more; it has a fine white coat of long hair.

We went to S. Giles' yesterday. Mr. Roberts[1] preached. 'Lo, I am with you alway, even unto the end of the world.' *Matt.* 28. XX.

H Y M N S 220, 281, 320.

No Scrip. Union card came, but it is all the better, I had already found my own in the drawer.

I thought you would rather have a little note to-night than I left it to write a long letter tomorrow, every moment is precious just now, so I must stop.

Wilfred

27. To Susan Owen

[*April 1907*]   *Shrewsbury*

My Dear Mother,

It is ten past 8, (post at 8.30. now) but I must send a note as there is something very special to tell you. I got the kitten this morning & in the afternoon I planted your ferns. I went in to Grandpa's for tea, & when I came home I thought Shah or Chat (French) (thats MY kitten's name) looked cold, so I asked B.[2] to light a fire in the dining room. You know it's her night out so she did it in all haste—result—it went out in 3 mins. Well I tried to light it & was drawing up the flame when the paper caught fire. I kept it from going up the chimney by the poker, but in spite of that the soot caught fire up the chimney. Just then B. was going out of the door came back to say the chimney was on fire. It made a fearful smoke, coming even through the tiles of the roof. We didn't know what to do by ourselves, Beat. was like a dummy! I sent her to tell the pol. constable round the corner, I thought the best thing to do in an emergency. I think we'll have to be summoned. I'll pay. Mr. Forrest who was in the garden & saw the smoke offered to come in & see. Then

[1] The Rev. Frederick Roberts, Vicar of St. Giles, Shrewsbury, 1894–1921.
[2] The maid Beatrice.

Mrs. Shields came in too. Well in about ½ an hour it went all right, but it gave us a fright!

Don't know what Father will say; he's coming home at 10 to-night. Is at Craven Arms.[1] Didn't go to Plimley's, because Father couldn't come, we are both to go together. Didn't buy a new tie when I want so many other things more important. The last entries on the 'Wants List' are Book on Geology & Geological Hammer![2] No time for more.

Hope you can read this mess.

B. has gone out, so I am alone.   Wilfred

28. To Susan Owen

[*April 1907*]   *Shrewsbury*

My dear Mother,

I am afraid that you did not get my letter this morning. It was Beatrice who told me the post was at 8.30. She says she saw it in the post-office. Now when I posted yours I saw the next collection was at 10.30, so I suspected something. I sent her up after tea, (she was pleased to go out, she said) to see if it was 8.30. in the morning, it <u>was</u>, she didn't know the difference between A.M. & P.M. I have left <u>it</u> rather late as usual. I have been bathing Shah all evening. I warmed a towel for <u>it & bathed</u> it in warm water. I have taken the liberty to use Mary's doll's towel to wash its dear little face. It lets me wash its nose & eyes without trying to get away at all, or squeaking. It's much more tolerant to being washed than children. I comb its hair with Mary's combs out of her set, I feel sure she won't mind. After its toilet I was warming it before the fire when it deliberately jumped into all the cinders in the grate. I hope you're not tired of hearing about it. I shall have to be careful that I don't get Father Vaughan on my track!

Well it's nearly five to eight now.

Father has been out all day again. He has [*several words illegible*] with an occasional salmon for a change [*three words illegible*] well I tell you all when I get back.. You say you think you'll soon be home now, do you, why we shan't open the door to you till <u>you</u>, anyhow, have stayed a month, & <u>then</u> . . ah, <u>then</u>
                                                                    W

Please thank H. for his letter, I'm sure I never wrote such a long letter at his age.

29. To Susan Owen

Sunday Evening [*April 1907*]   [*Shrewsbury*]

My own dear Mother,

Father has gone to St. Giles' this evening but I stayed at home to write to you, because I haven't written since Friday and you might be

---

[1] Near Ludlow.   [2] Both the book and the hammer were obtained, and survive.

wondering, I'm afraid I've spent too long writing to Colin, but it will please him to have a little letter & I know you don't mind the writing.

We went to Mrs. Simmons to tea. We had cakes & she made a trifle too, & all at 4 o'clock! I couldn't touch the trifle, I'd hardly got over the Sunday dinner. I sent the last letter for ½ because I hadn't got another stamp of any kind, I find now I haven't even got a halfpenny one, I don't know what to do.

I am quite alone again Beatrice is out until 9. Father went to a concert at the Music Hall[1] on Sat. night. I wouldn't go, with the excuse of not having done the homework. I didn't want to really either. However Father came out at half-time disgusted with it.[2] Father has got me a new tie, when he went out. I made him promise he'd only get me a 6d one. But sure enough he came home with a more expensive one he had to confess. It's a lovely one, & very good of him to give it me. Went to St. Giles this morning. Text 'Who walketh in the midst of the seven Golden Candlesticks.' *Rev.* II. 1. I think Mr. Roberts got it from 'Come ye apart'. It was just the same.

Nearly 8 now.

Hymns. 7, 266, 215,   Wilfred

30. To Susan Owen

[*April 1907*]   [*Shrewsbury*]

(PRIVATE)

My Dear Mother,

It is almost tea-time, but I must make time to scribble a note to you, to thank you for your loving letter. I do hope you are better, not only about the throat but altogether, you must remember that you have gone away for a rest & not to take the others for a holiday. We went to the Abbey, this morning. Mr. Dodd[3] preached, *John* (?) – –, 'Our reasonable service.' A sermon on the Holy Eucharist, as there was a celebration after. We came out a few minutes after twelve! (They are calling me to tea, 'Ugh!') . . . . (*After tea.*) When I wrote this I was under the impression, or rather delusion, that this could go in a parcel I am sending: Father tells me I can't send a parcel today, (Sunday) but I want you to have a note in the morning, so I am sending it on, alone. The 'parcel' is for Leslie. It is a piece (small) of my treasure, but still enough to show the fern-fronds.[4] I did want him to have it on Mon. morning & on account of my delusion, wrote him a hurried letter, but I will post it as soon as I can & the morning. I don't mind if you tell him what I am sending him, in fact I would like you to, then he will know that I have not forgotten his letter, & have written to him. We

---

[1] Shrewsbury Concert Hall.

[2] Tom Owen frequently walked out when dissatisfied.

[3] The Rev. H. J. Dodd was Curate at the Abbey Church, Shrewsbury, 1905–8, Vicar of Uffington, near Shrewsbury, 1908–13. Later he deprived HO of the sale of a painting (*JO* I, p. 211). See Letter 86.

[4] The cousins were both interested in geology, as appears later in the letters.

are going to St. Giles's this evening, I T͟h͟i͟n͟k͟, never know until five minutes before time. Father, as usual, i͞s͞ playing that beastly Welsh tune,[1] I've quite got it on the brain! Thank Mary & Colin for their letters, Mary's w͞a͞s well written, & Colin's composition was splendid. I don't think I h͞a͞v͞e thanked Harold for his beautifully neat letter yet, I have begun to write to him but left off to write to Leslie instead, & have no time to finish now. I am s͟o͟ glad he is able to go out now. We thank both you & Dorothy for th͞e toffee, it's delicious. Mrs Plimley called yesterday evening, I have got to go to tea on Thurs. much rather stop at home, but sometimes, I suppose, one must live under social obligations! Six o'clock, I must get ready.

Best love to all. Wilfred

31. To Susan Owen

17 April 1907   *Shrewsbury*

My own dear Mother,

Just a few lines to let you know Father is home again, he came in at about 7.30 [*several words illegible*] so I have a minute or two up in my room, to save carting all the paraphernalia downstairs.

Well, I do hope you have arrived safely, & have had a good journey. I was looking out for you at five to eleven, but at eleven we had to go back to class. I hope the journey has not tired you or made Harold any worse.

[*One line illegible*] went to tea with her. She tells me she has left her umbrella in the train with you, hopes you have noticed it!! We had a lovely morning, it went rather dark about 4 o'clock. I suppose the country looked very nice from the train. We have heard some more results of the Exams. I am dreadfully low in some subjects but I am top in French, the only one who passed first class!!

Well I am afraid there is not much news to scribble yet, so I can't write a long letter the first time.

Thank you for all I found & read on my dressing table.

Your own Wilfred

Greet ye one another with a kiss of charity. Peace be with you all that are in Christ Jesus.

Amen.

1 *Peter* V. 14.

32. To Susan Owen

Postcard addressed to 3 Clement Road, Wimbledon, Surrey

Tuesday [*Postmark 30 April 1907*]   [*Postmark Shrewsbury*]

My dear Mother,

I'm afraid I've got no time for a letter to-night, as I have 7 lessons to do, but I m͟u͟s͟t͟ send you a line. I s͟h͟a͟l͟l͟ be glad when you come home

---

[1] 'Men of Harlech', Tom Owen's favourite gramophone record.

again, not <u>only</u> because I want to see you, but I do miss your—er— 'supervision' over everything so much. I didn't put the ½ stamp on your letter, B. posted it, Father giving her 1d̄ for stamp. Thank you so much for your letter, Harold has written a lot to me & so have M. & C. Well I'm looking forward to Friday or Sat. if you really <u>can't</u> stay longer. Best love WILFRED

33. To Susan Owen

1 May 1907   *Shrewsbury*

My dearest Mother,

We had your letters this morning, tell Mary I'm sure there was nothing whatever to make fun of in her letter. She will excuse my writing to her again, as I suppose you tell her all the news, & I really haven't time to, I've got half-a-dozen lessons to-night again! I did laugh at your nocturnal rambles in search of the 'bird of night', Mary told me about it. Well, Father says you may be home again on Friday evening, I should like you to come at that time, I shouldn't have any homework, & I could meet you at the station, too. I shan't eat any tea that day! Mind you don't stay long at Wolverhampton, it won't do you any good there, I know, & when once you've left Wimbledon I shall really be quite impatient to see you. It is a pity though that you couldn't stay a bit longer to get <u>quite</u> well again. I think you know, by this time that I shall be quite allright if I know you're getting well again, & are enjoying, really <u>enjoying</u> yourself there.

It's growing dark now, I'm afraid this means another late night & early morning for me. My cold is no worse now; it goes fearfully cold here at nights now, it hailed until the ground was white yesterday

[*Five lines illegible*]

Best love to all the others, looking forward to Friday,   Wilfred

34. To Susan Owen

Thursday [*May 1907*]   *Shrewsbury*

My own dearest Mother,

I suppose this is the last letter now, I can't help thinking about tomorrow all the time. Father met your luggage, he says he wished he was meeting you instead. It's in your room now, so that's a sure sign that you're not far behind. I hope to meet you at the station, at 5.45 tomorrow. Father went to Frodsham, or somewhere, before 8 this morning [*several words illegible*]

There is some sad news to tell you too. A box fell on Pussey's head today, I don't think it is hurt very much, but its eyes are all swelled up, & it won't drink its milk. I do hope it's all right. If the others would like to, I should be pleased, if they would take notes on what they see in the train, so that when (?) I go I shall be able to look out for mines, hills etc.

It is fearfully windy again to-day.

Well, I've a lot of work again to-night.

Hoping you will have a good journey.

as ever your loving son Wilfred

P.S. You notice I put no number on the envelope. I don't <u>know</u> it to tell the truth.

35. To Leslie Gunston

15 November 1907   *Shrewsbury*

TO OBSERVE THE WORLD.

(To be read together if possible)

Dear Vera & Leslie,

At <u>last,</u> (by the way how often I begin my letters thus, I notice, too, that <u>you</u> have commenced so, no less than 4 times!) But I have no time for trifles now for I have much to say yet little time. I'm afraid that this scribble will have to be the last 'Soc. letter'[1] before I make my proposed visit, (to which I look forward with the keenest delight). For in less than 4 wks the exams will be upon us, & between that time who knows what I've got to do! Well I must get to the point. On thinking over the Rules, (for which I believe I have never yet thanked you) a new subject came into my head, that of Mountain Climbing. It is, as you will see, an almost essential branch of each of our studies, and mountaineering is also to the ambitious & strenuous outdoor naturalist, not only the noblest but the most insatiable of all <u>noble</u> sports. I propose that the aims of the movement shall be:

(1) The promotion of scientific study & exploration of certain glacial regions.

(2) *The cultivation of Art in relation to mt. scenery.

(3) The Christian education of the inhabitants to an appreciation of their mt. heritage.

(4) The encouragement of the mt. craft, & the opening of new regions as a national playground.

(5) The preservation of the natural beauties of the mt. places, & of the fauna & <u>flora</u> in their habitat (with special reference to V.)

* It is hoped that you, V. will become the Photographic Representative, for what is Astronomy without its sister-art Photography? & some pictures showing strata, etc. would be invaluable to me. Hence I

---

[1] The AGBS, or the Astronomical, Geological, and Botanical Society; the members were Vera and Leslie Gunston and Wilfred. See Letter 535.

earnestly hope you will accept this office, for none is better fitted for it than you, surrounded as you are by some of the foremost works in Alpine Photography.

As for You, Les: I don't know what you will think of me for not writing to tell you of the lecture on Nov. 7. (I certainly did get 'flurried' when I received a second letter from you!) The lecture was by A. R. HINKS. M.A.[1] chief asstnt. to Sir Robt. Ball,[2] Cambridge. It was entitled—'Our Place in the Universe' & the slides were as excellent as the Lecture was instructive. It really was, however, too boring to sit there in pleasure, knowing you were missing it all. I am glad you like long letters, (I do of course) but I really can't stay at it much longer, I will answer your last letter as soon as possible. And V. dear I will write to you but if my epistles are long you must expect them to be 'far between'. How are you progressing in your Bot: studies at the Tech:?

Amor ad omnes omnibus mittitur est! (as this flowery ending is wrong don't try it)

I remain, not doubting that you are equally faithful, A most zealous member of the A.G.B.S.
W.E.O.

P.S. I hope you will get this before Sunday, so I am going to the post myself tho' it's 10 P.M. It is a lovely night—a brilliant moon, & Orion looks superb in the Eastern sky. Have you seen it? It is nice, tho' we are separated by hundreds of miles to be able to gaze on the same objects! If possible would you tell me how to find Mars. I am rather vague as to its position at present, so I would be grateful for some directions.

W

36. To Susan Owen

26 December [*1907*]   [*Wimbledon*]

My dearest Mother,

I was so pleased to have your letters this morning. They all came together. I am surprised you did not get my card before—I sent it before 8, on Wed.

I had a letter from Alec this morng. too—he had quite forgotten the cap! We went to Grandpa's and had a very good dinner [*two lines illegible*] Then we prevailed upon Gordon to lend us his bike, so we had a lovely afternoon; for there was nothing else to do but to 'ass about' as Leslie would say. I have been a lovely ride over the common on Dorothy's bike this morning. There is a rather strong wind, but it was beautifully sunny & fresh. Went thro' the town,—passed motors, etc. all alone! & now my hands are as stiff as a poker.

[1] Arthur Robert Hinks, FRS (1873–1945), Secretary of the Royal Geographical Society 1915–45.
[2] Robert Stawell Ball, FRS (1840–1913), Professor of Astronomy at Dublin University and Royal Astronomer of Ireland 1874–92. He was Lowndean Professor of Astronomy at Cambridge from 1892 until his death.

There has been very little fog here—none while in the train—only a little misty on Thurs. morning. We are expecting the Cates [*two words illegible*] They may be here any minute—so I have taken this opportunity to write to you while there is nothing [*four lines illegible*]
Friday
Thank you for your letter this morning. I had no time to send this letter before, but I hope you will get it before you leave. We are all quite excited to think you are coming tomorrow. Hope you will have a good journey. Either Uncle or Dorothy will meet you at Pad. Thank Mary and Harold & Colin, for their letters I am sorry I have no time to write to them now.

Best love Wilfred

37. To Susan Owen

Sunday, 12 January [*1908*]   [*Shrewsbury*]

My dear Mother,

We have just come home from church and dinner is not ready yet so I am taking the opportunity to send you a line. I think you must certainly stay till Thurs. (or after) because we have managed all right so far & two days will make no difference to us, but I know it will to you. We shall be glad to have you back tho'. But you will find this house tiny after Alpina! Mr. Dodd gave a very nice sermon on 'home' this morning.

We were skating yesterday aftern'n on a pool near the Wenlock Rd. where we went once before with Aunty Emmy. I did wish Leslie & Dorothy were with us. Did they have any skating on the Common? Did I tell you that Mr. Timpany[1] sent us a pair of beautiful silver-plated skates. They were no use yesterday for a screw was missing. I am getting them repaired though.

I ought to write to Dorothy sometime today but I don't know when I shall.

Keep in mind the lines

> If the air is bracing & is helping you
> Don't be in a hurry, stay a week or two.
> Tho' of course we miss you, etc.

Best love to dear Mary, Auntie, etc., etc., & to you, Mother dear.

Ever your loving Wilfred

38. To Susan Owen

Wed. 15 [*January 1908*]   [*Shrewsbury*]

My own dear Mother,

It is nice to think that this time tomorrow, instead of writing I shall be able to see you yourself & dear Mary. I am glad you are coming on Thurs. because I shall be able to meet you, & get my work done before.

---

[1] Headmaster of the Shrewsbury Technical School.

I had a P.C. from Miss Carter[1] the day before yesterday about the party. I answered it at once. Mr. Dodd called while we were having tea yesterday to see you about the Confirmation Classes. I have not gone this evening (the first is tonight) because I wanted to see you about it first: I don't know what to do I'm sure.

Father is cleaning the bath this evening! with paraffin oil. The smell is permeating the whole house most abominably. (snorts) As I said yesterday the Mansell[2] game is beginning again (ferocious glares). We have lots more books to get (redoubled glares & snorts) but we have already got some e.g. *Kenilworth* & *Quentin Durward*. It is almost 8 so I must stop.

Fondest love W

39. To Harold Owen

[*10 April 1908*]   [*Wimbledon*]

My dear Harold,

I was so pleased with your letter this morning I did not expect one from you so soon.

Jimmy is grown into quite a big cat now but he is so lazy. The dove has gone; a cat got it Leslie says, so there is only one left of the family. I went a short walk on the common yesterday morning after going to school with Leslie, but it was very misty, so I soon came in. Leslie came home in a frightful bluster from the class. He was given homework! 'Why couldn't I have homework when Wilfred is gone. Why couldn't Wilfred come when I have no homework? Eh? Mother! Mother! What on earth's the good of me having homework when Wilfred's here?' When he began to do it, I heard nothing but 'Wilfred, Wilfred, do look here!' I tried to explain, but that was the way Mr. Latham[3] did it, which was wrong, quite wrong! I then did one of the sums for him, but he said 'Do you think I am going to copy that?' at which I left him to his own methods.

I should like to see the <u>peculiar</u> <u>skeletons</u> of flies you have found you must keep them till I come. I will write to Colin and Mary next time.

With best love from

Wilfred

I WILL WRITE TO COLIN SOON.

40. To Susan Owen

10 *April* 1908   *Alpina* [*Wimbledon*]

My dear Mother,

Leslie is at the holiday class this morning so I am taking the opportunity to write some letters.

[1] A Sunday-school teacher.
[2] Book buying at Mansell's bookshop, Wyle Cop, Shrewsbury.
[3] Leslie Gunston was having special holiday tuition under Mr. Latham, a master at King's College School, Wimbledon.

Thank you for the packet of manuscript I received this morning. I do hope your cold is no worse to-day.

Auntie has gone to Brixton this morning [*two lines illegible*]

Mr. Painter[1] called this morning with a pile of notices about the flower service, on the 26th. He wanted Vera to write on them: 'We hope that Mr. Schor (a Jew) of Jerusalem will give the address on Sunday afternoon the 12th.' I have done half of them, she was 'so busy'. Vera was at Kidmore End all yesterday with Uncle. The walls of the ground floor are built now, so it is getting on.[2]

I will not write a long letter as I must go to meet Leslie, & I hope Dorothy will be here soon

[*Three lines illegible*]

Mind you take care of yourself, Mother dear,

Your loving Wilfred

41. To Susan Owen

Easter Monday 1908   *Alpina*

My Dear Mother,

I must write another letter this evening I have got so much to tell you. First of all we went a bicycle ride on Sat. afternoon. Gordon punctured his tyre so he could not go in the morning. Harry Cates was to go with him in the afternoon, & somehow it was arranged that Leslie & I should hire bicycles and go with them. I had a fine machine that had been ridden once or twice & Leslie's was brand-new! It was a lovely ride to the pool—about 5 mls. We caught crowds of water-fleas which we examined under the microscope when we got home, but nothing else because Gordon broke his test-tube—it was a tube like this:

There were some very long hills coming home but I walked up them & Harry pushed my bicycle up and for a long way Harry & Gordon pulled me by a piece of string (see Colin's picture.)

Tues. Morning

Thank you for all the letters I had this morning. I am glad to hear that the family is generally better.

Leslie wanted to go to church on Easter morning, so we did not go to Mrs. Maynard's.[3] Mr. Moore's[4] text was 'I know that my Redeemer

---

[1] The Rev. Arthur Frederick Painter, Curate of Emmanuel Church, Wimbledon, 1905–14, formerly a missionary in India 1880–1901.

[2] John Gunston was having a house built at Kidmore End, five miles N of Reading, to be called *Alpenrose*.

[3] She ran a Sunday morning children's service in the Church Hall, Wimbledon.

[4] The Rev. E. W. Moore. For a description of his delivery in the pulpit see Letter 125.

liveth, etc.' It was an Egg-Service in the afternoon. In the evening Mr. Moore preached on II *Tim.* 2. 8.

Harry & Geoffrey Cates called yesterday morning to go a walk. We went over the common to Richmond Park. In the afternoon they came again with George, with bicycles wanting us to go a ride for an hour. I was not very sorry that the bicycle shops were shut, for it costs 9d. an hr. Instead of going a ride themselves Harry let Leslie & me have rides on his bicycle, while George and Geoff. practised riding backwards all the afternoon, until tea time. Did you know that Auntie, Uncle & Gordon went to 'Knickers' Bottom' as Uncle calls Kidmore End, yesterday. They started at 6.30 A.M. & are staying till this evening, but Gordon came home last night.

I must send this letter off soon or you won't get it tomorrow morning. I hope you will keep better. I do want to see you all.

Will write to the others soon.

Your loving Wilfred

P.S. Of course I shall want a ticket to Waterloo, for I gave mine up when I went to the Nat. Gallery.

42. To Susan Owen

18 April 1908   *Alpina*

My own dear Mother,

I must send you another little note while I have got the chance, as Leslie is now doing his homework. (that is I am doing one half of it, & Auntie the other.) Gordon did not get up at 6 to go bug-hunting, but he is going this morning. I think it is going to be fine although it began to rain this morning. Yesterday we had beautiful weather, the sun was out nearly all day. We went to the lantern service. I did enjoy it; the pictures were very beautiful, thirty-nine in all & all selected by Mr. Moore.

He explained all the slides, so that each was quite a little sermon. The Church Room was crowded, so that about 20 people were standing at the doors! After some of Mr. Moore's graphic descriptions there was a great deal of suspicious blowing of noses & one person fainted at the door.

I don't think I told you Mr. Moore's text yesterday morning. It was Pilate's sermon, as he called it: 'Behold the man' He told us a lot about Pontius Pilatus, & then about 'The Man'. In this he referred to Mr. Macdonald's[1] sermon on 'man' (*Gen.* 2. 7.) on Thurs. afternoon.— did I tell you we went to church on Thurs. with Dorothy? It was a very good address. He took the meaning of the word 'man' in Hebrew where it means 'a weak, feeble one'.

In Greek mng : 'one who prays'
In Latin mng : 'a strong one'

[1] Probably a visiting clergyman; there was no one of this name at Wimbledon in 1908.

& in Eng. mng: 'one who has the power of thought.'

Well I must stop this letter now, as I suppose Harold will like a note. Love to Father, hope your poor cold is gone.

Your loving boy Wilfred

43. To Susan Owen

25 April [*1908*]   *Alpina*

My own dear Mother,

We are just come home from the Tower—Uncle took us this afternoon; we did not go in the morning as there was a great football-match[1] at the Crystal Palace & most of the people came early to see the sights of London.

We got to Tower Hill about 3, & beheld crowds of people blocking up the gates. We took our place behind about half a mile of sightseers & moved inch by inch through the grounds till we reached the Armoury. We saw as much as we could but every yard the officials told us to 'move on'. We saw the Regalia I am glad to say, & also the Coronation Robes of the King & Queen—a 'recent acquisition.'

The Cornwalls[2] came yesterday for lunch & stayed till after tea.

Did I tell you we went with Uncle to Mrs. Maynard's Hooligan Entertainment? It was at her house, & while the 'Hooligans' were having coffee, etc, Mr. Maynard showed Leslie & me his curiosities & guns.

I will tell all other news when I see you. It will be nice to see all again.

I hope to get the 2.40 train from Euston, arriving Shrewsby 5.52. I hope there is a train at that time; Uncle got it from a rather old time-table but there is sure to be one about then.

I don't know when you will get this letter. I'm afraid it will be the second post on Monday.

Fondest love to all Wilfred

44. To Susan Owen

Postcard addressed to 264 Union Street, Torquay[3]

[*Postmark 14 June 1908*]   [*Postmark Brest*][4]

Dear Mother,

Arrived safely after rough passage. Everything is delightful—the hotel magnificent. Met a charming French young lady on the boat—talked to her all day. It is a pleasure to speak to the people here they are

---

[1] The 1908 Cup Final, when Wolverhampton Wanderers beat Newcastle United.

[2] Sir Edwin Cornwall (1863–1953), PC, MP, Chairman of the LCC 1906, Minister for National Health Insurance 1916–19, was a neighbour of the Gunstons. Bernice and Laura, the two younger daughters, were friends of the Gunston children. See Letter 73.

[3] The home of John Taylor, husband of Tom Owen's third sister, Anne.

[4] Tom Owen took Wilfred twice to France. This was the first occasion.

all so affable. I am easily understood, but can make nothing of what they say. I can't tell you everything in this post card, so I will leave all to when I see you.

Love to all,   Your enraptured Wilfred

45. To Susan Owen

Postcard addressed c/o J. Gunston, Esq., Fern Brae, Peppard, Near Reading[1]

Friday 8.40 [postmark 10 July 1908]   *[Postmark Shrewsbury]*

My dear Mother,

I must write you a line before I have no time. I am glad that you are not writing to me—write to the others & I shall hear all the news,—I am glad of it because you must divert your thoughts to Nature. I was also pleased to hear your person was diverted to 'the house' in a Bath-chair. I should like to see you in it.

We have had heavy rain the last few days, I suppose you have too. We have been on the river several times. Alice[2] & I went alone yesterday afternoon.

Tell Leslie I hope to write to him soon—only a week & I shall be free! It is certain now that Miss Douglas[3] is leaving. A subscription is being made for her present. I took 1s. How does Harold like the country down there? Has Uncle any hay? Needless to say we have not been down to the fields since you left. Have you heard a nightingale yet? We saw a huge owl over the river the other night.

I know how to make use of a P.Card, don't I! Only I hope you can read it! Love to Harold & all at Fern B. excluding your dear self—for it is best love to you. W

46. To Susan Owen

Monday Morning 20 July 1908   *Shrewsbury*

My dearest Mother,

What a surprise it was to hear that Vera is coming! and this week too—it will be lovely to have you home so soon. Make the most of your last week. I do hope you will have good weather. It is dull again today, but yesterday it was sunny all day. I was out all day (the day being from 11 to 9.30).—at the Abbey morning and evening, & I went a walk after the class till tea-time [*one line illegible*]

I wish we could get out today, it is sometimes dark and sometimes 'glaring', *comprenez-vous?*

By the way another post card from Annik[4] nearly turned my head, perhaps she is going to a school in London.

[1] The Gunstons lodged here while waiting to move into the new house.
[2] Alice Cannell, daughter of a sea-captain's widow living at Anfield, Liverpool.
[3] A teacher at the Shrewsbury Technical School.
[4] Unidentified.

Alice & I are talking about going to Church Stretton one day next week Wednesday probably. I think Mrs. C. is coming too.

I am to go to school on Tues. to help Miss Jones with the marks. Other boys are going so it doesn't matter if we go to Church Stretton[1] that day.

I didn't tell you that we go back on Sept. 8th. A rather long holiday, isn't it?

The *ménage* progresses satisfactorily under Mrs. Cannell's management—advantages are: I got up for breakfast this morning, and I fold up my serviette, disadvantages: (1) Have to wait an exasperating time for everybody to finish feeding. (2) Never glance at printed matter in any form while at table.

So that you must not talk of coming home, rather it will be home (personified) coming to us. Best love, and a 'multiplication sign' (x)

from your ever loving W

47. To Susan Owen

Postcard addressed to Fern Brae, Peppard, Oxfordshire

Tues. 21 July 1908, 9.15   [*Postmark Shrewsbury*]

Dearest Mother

We have just come in from a lovely row. We went as far as the oak tree where we picknicked, Alice & I rowing down, & Father & I up. (hence my shaky hand) I must send you a note, tho' to thank you for your dear letter. I went to school this morning but did hardly any work— it was all jokes & talk between Miss Jones & Miss Douglas. It became finer yesterday afternoon & turned out a lovely evening, so we went on the river & got to Uffington.[2] Mr. Dodd was in the lane, & tho' we didn't mean to go & see him, we went over the garden again.

No time for more now.

Only 3 days!   Fondest love W

48. To Susan Owen

Postcard addressed to Fern Brae, Peppard, Oxfordshire

Weds: 22 July [*1908*] *1.30*   [*Postmark Shrewsbury*]

We (Alice & I) are going to Church Strett. this afternoon by the 2.25 train return 7 something, so I am sending a card now or I shall have no time to-night.

Thank you for the P.Card.

I rejoice at your croquet victory. Went to school again this morning.

---

[1] The Owens often visited Long Mynd, the Shropshire hills near Church Stretton, south of Shrewsbury.

[2] Uffington was a village of particular significance for HO. See *JO* I, Ch. 7, and p. 170 for his first meeting with the vicar.

Only one other turned up. Dear Miss Jones gave us each a 3d packet of Peter's Chocolate.

It is a fine day but rather hot in the town, but we expect to enjoy ourselves on Caradoc![1]

Must get ready now.   Love to all Wilfred

You don't say whether you are feeling better but we conclude that since you have eaten cherries you must be. I Hope so, anyhow.

49. To Alec Paton
Picture postcard of Windermere

25 August [*1908*]   [*Postmark Shrewsbury*]

Dear Alec,

Am having a day in L'pool tomorrow. Shall be able to see you in the morning, some time after 10, if you are in. But don't stay in on my account if otherwise engaged.

Wilfred

50. To Harold Owen

Sat. September [*1908*]   *Meols*[2]

My dear Harold,

I am so sorry this letter won't reach you in time for your birthday. I meant to write yesterday evening but Cecil wanted me to go a walk, and this was the first evening he was at home so I had to go.

I hope you had a happy birthday I will give you my present when I get home.

I went to Anfield on Friday you know, but I did not go to the Park. I spent most of the afternoon looking for Miss Taylor's house but when at last we found it, she had moved so I didn't see her after all.

I liked Anfield very much but it is not like Meols. It is really lovely here. There are miles of fields in front of the house & it is not far from the sea. I went to see Miss Farrel[3] on Tues. or Wed., & she sent her love to you.

Tell Colin I shall be so glad to have him to come walks with me after Kenneth.

He always comes with me to the shore, but he doesn't seem to understand anything I tell him, & he says nothing but 'Is this water deep? Eh? Is it vewy deep in de miggle of de sea?' and whenever he sees a piece of rope or cord or chain he asks 'Could a steamer bweak this?' 'Eh?' But he is not so rude as he used to be.

---

[1] A hill to the east of Church Stretton.
[2] Wilfred is staying with the Quayles at Dorfold, Meols, Cheshire.
[3] Appears as 'Miss Foster' in *JO* I, pp. 33–5. The Headmistress of the Kindergarten of the Birkenhead Institute, H O's first school in Birkenhead.

Margaret began to howl when she first saw me, but now she is all right.

I must get ready now to go to Birkenhead.

Goodbye!

Love to Father and Colin,   from Wilfred

P.S. I forgot all about your cane at Anfield: so sorry.

51. To Susan Owen

31 December 1908   *Alpenrose, Kidmore End, Reading*

Dearest Mother,

So sorry to keep you waiting for a letter till next year but when you read the programme I have been filling up these days you will see I had not much time for writing.

The journey was <u>most</u> uncomfortable. In half an hour's time my feet were frozen & went on getting worse and worse, & my sufferings were increased by the prospect of three hours more with no means of relief. However a lady ordered a 'portah to bwing a foot warmah' which comforting article she invited us to share.

Vera met us at Reading; we drove up in a kind of trap, I in Leslie's Inverness & Mary in sundry cloaks of Auntie's.

Before tea the fowls etc. were inspected & Leslie took me (on bicycles) to the Smithie & Mrs. Baker's cottage.[1]

The snow was very thin down here then, but on Tuesday it snowed all day, and froze hard, with the result of a fine dry covering so deep that the snow-plough was used yesterday. We went to Kidmore Pond to see if there was skating but found ice broken & covered with snow.

On Wednesday morning Uncle had made a toboggan, the height of whose runners was 2 ins. so that it was useless in thick snow. Howbeit Dorothy, Vera, Leslie, Mary & I were going to try it on Peppard Common when we met the Cates with the news that Kidmore Pool would bear. Thither therefore proceeded Leslie, George, Geoff, & I to find we could skate around the sides, But the ice was frightfully hard being composed of wet snow frozen, & so presenting a surface like a species of nutmeg-grater. Dorothy was meanwhile tobogganing down Peppard Common, Mary & Vera not indulging in the dangerous pastime. I stayed in in the afternoon & imbibed *Cassell's Popular Science*.

In the evening Dorothy Leslie the Cates's & I took the toboggan to Peppard Common, & had a simply splendidrippinggrandmajestic-gloriousdelightfulscrumtiousexquisitelyexcruciating time. The moon was overclouded but there was light enough to see the dark forms against the snow.

When I went to bed last night I found blocks of ice floating about in

[1] Two adjoining cottages at Peppard, near Reading. Mrs. Baker's cottage was possibly 'Fern Brae'. See Letter 45.

my water-jug and this morning it was thicker still so you can imagine what a time we are having.

After breakfast Uncle spied tracks of a hare all about the garden. Uncle loaded his gun & we stealthily made our way to the Pit where it was supposed to be hiding. Approaching the stable the sound of many waters broke upon our wondering ears—thrusting the loaded gun into Leslie's hand he broke in to find a deluge of water spurting about over the bags of meal, etc, the tools, & the cows. The first thing to be done was to turn off the water at the main.

Now the main tap was in the road covered with quickly melting snow, & to find it was no easy thing. We frantically scraped, & kicked & shovelled & dug like searchers for hidden treasure until at last it was unearthed & the supply stopped. The tools & nails were conveyed to the house to dry, but the bags of meal were ruined. One sack worth £1. is utterly soaked, & unless used up at once will rot or turn sour, so I think Uncle will sell it for the pheasants.

It is fast thawing now but still horribly cold & a thick mist envelopes the land.

I am glad the boys had some tobogganning.

I had myself looked out that iron for sledge-runners!

Tea will soon be ready—the last day of the year is now closing.—so must this letter.

With best love from Wilfred

52. To Susan Owen
Postcard

4 January 1909   [*Postmark Reading*]

Dearest Mother

Thank you so much for your letter & card. The stockings came opportunely. I have been wearing three pairs per day lately! Leslie & I went to Reading today by Perrin,[1] arrived 12.15. Had my hair cut then went to Swiss café. After dinner saw Museum then Huntley & Palmer's Factories, description here impossible. Yesterday went to 'mattins & evensong' at Kidmore—don't know really what to think of the vicar. After evening service there was a Church Army Mission with lantern slides to which we went.

I did not want 'Yet not I' sent, & now I think it not worth sending Cousin May's. There are books here profoundly interesting but I can never hope to get through them—and then *Kenilworth*. I hope you don't think me negligent as regards letters, & don't you trouble to write. I understand your 'enforced silence' knowing too well you have 'burdensome duties.'

Love to Cousin May & best love to you Wilfred

[1] The Reading carrier.

53. To Susan Owen

April 1909, Sat.   *Clovelly*[1]

My Dear Mother

Your P.C. was not so welcome as it might have been without the injunctions concerning the straw hat! I had a most distressing dream last night: That I was buying one, & there were only 2 to choose between one was soft & flabby the other small & with a semi-spherical crown, thus I chose latter & thought I had done with the business & now I've got to go through it again!

Yesterday morning it rained so I had an opportunity to read *Tale of 2 cities* (now finished). Miss Eckford's brother was a friend of Dickens & Dickens' cousin taught Miss Montford music!!

At Meols I sat (& walked) still another morning & aft. in the sun & wind so that my jowl is like copper, brass, tan & vermilion at the same time—& especially the proboscis.

I went to L'pool yesterafternoon could not get everything wanted but saw a bit of museum

[*remainder missing*]

54. To Susan Owen
Postcard

[*Postmark 18 July 1909*]   [*Postmark Brest*][2]

Dearest Mother,

This is a summary of events:

Friday Night. Did not once lose consciousness in train.

Sat. Mng. Almost got carried on to Penzance, there being 'change' at North Road, Plym. Embarked *IBEX*. Slept in clothes in common saloon. Awoke (tired) at 8. Passed thro' various fogs, till about 5 o'clock engines suddenly stopped, & ship lay tossing frightfully (deck angle 35°.) Fog increased—so did anxiety. We were lost! Soundings were made but to no purpose, & we lay helplessly drifting. The log showed we were only a few miles off the most dangerous coast of the channel, & we could only see a few furlongs! However, the melancholy siren attracted a pilot. Such was the state of the sea, that the great bowsprit of his boat was smashed like a match! Pilot finally lost himself, until certain lighthouse loomed ahead. Again we proceeded but finally were forced to anchor. We slept on deck, & only reached B. at 7 this mng. Breakfasted at H. Continental. Then discovered Mme. Berthou's to be a dirty little house over a wine-shop! Wandered about—were told of an English 'Mees' who has directed us to an apartment. Are now at

---

[1] The name of Miss Montford's house in Birkenhead. Wilfred stayed with this family friend and her companion, Miss Eckford, during the Easter holidays.
[2] The second French holiday with Tom Owen.

Hotel de France, comfortable but cheaper than Continental. Had an excellent lunch, and am now about to rest being exceedingly tired (went to Church this morning). No more news now.

55. To Susan Owen

Picture postcard of Morgat: Aspect de la Plage au Départ pour les Grottes

Grand Hotel de la Plage

[*Postmark 21 July 1909*]   [*Postmark Morgat, Finistere*]

Morgat is the most delightful place we have ever come across here. This morning we had the most enjoyable bathe I think that I have ever had. The water is so warm and the sand perfect. We bathed among the rocks on the very left of this picture. Yesterday we bathed on the other side of the bay. We met a French family & got into conversation there, so I think I shall talk more here than at Brest. The weather today is perfect. Best love to all

W

56. To Colin Owen

July 1909   *Torquay*[1]

My Dear Colin,

It <u>was</u> stupid of me to forget your birthday. I'm sure I was more sorry when I found out, than you were on receiving not even a post card! However I hope you will like the paint box. We have got a <u>real</u> lizard, too,—dead of course and in a bottle of spirits.

There is something else in that bottle, something, long, green, and thin, . . . ugh!

One day as Father and I were going up over a cliff not far from the hotel, I suddenly saw what I thought was a great worm wriggling across the path. In an instant it flashed upon me that it was a snake!

'Look, look,' I cried, 'A snake'.

'What!! Where!' says Father.

'Ah, quick quick!' and he rushed upon it, just as it was escaping down the cliff, and nearly overbalanced himself over the precipice.

The first blow did not kill it, and it coiled up with its head in the air just like the pictures you have seen.

However the second hit finished it, and we cautiously took it up and carried it on the end of the stick. Since we were going right over the cliff & back we hid the serpent under some stones. We found it again coming back, and Father was putting it in his pocket when it moved, and wriggled its tail feebly! It was a pity to spoil it, by smashing its head, so I carried it home holding it securely round the neck, with its wicked little eyes still open.

---

[1] Wilfred and his father are staying with the Taylors.

However I think it was quite dead when we reached the hotel. They said it was a Viper! which very much surprised me, for I had thought it quite harmless & was not even disgusted by its wriggling. It is only a <u>small</u> one, you know, but still, if it is a viper it is very dangerous in<u>deed</u>, and I am glad we saw it in time. I hope Mother will not let this incident stand in the way of her visiting Brittany, for Morgat has one of the very finest shores I have seen and Mother need never venture on to the moors.

I have found no stones worth a place in your museum, but some very good shells, (if they are not broken)

It has rained all day. I am sorry for Father, but I am quite all right in the house with hundreds of books to choose from.

I hope someone will be able to read this letter, my good writing is taking a holiday.

Give my birthday wishes the cane for being so late. Their late arrival is due to a <u>fog</u> in the memory <u>channel</u>.

Your loving brother Wilfred

57. To Susan Owen

Mond. [*August 1909*]   *Torquay*

Dearest Mother,

This must not be a long letter: we have just returned from a Picnic, and my hand shakes with carrying heavy loads.

And it is getting late.

Your dear letters did not come till this morning.

I had time however to read them and the address today, and how helpful they both were.

I went to church on Sunday morning with Uncle & Edith.[1] In the evening I went again alone. Everybody else went to Babbacome by tram.

There was an Open Air Service by the Library at 8, held by the Plymouth Brethren, I think. Of course I went.

It was so like our own.

The same hymn book and the same Gospel messages.

The household did not arrive till after 9.30.

This morning Edith took me to Anstey's Cove.

We botanise. I consider myself proficient in that science now, being engrossed in Edith's botany Prize.

E. seems to know a good deal of Botany.

Our picnic this afternoon was near Kingskerswell[2] on what they call the Moors. We were supposed to see Dartmoor in the distance

[*remainder missing*]

[1] Edith Taylor, now Mrs. Brian Dymott.
[2] Between Torquay and Newton Abbot, four miles N W of Torquay.

58. To Susan Owen

11 August 1909   *Shrewsbury*

Dearest Mother,

Father had your P.C. this morning. I am afraid you had a very hot journey.

Today here is the same as or worse than yesterday (in temperature.) I set out for Haughmond[1] about half past nine, taking a few biscuits, plums & two pears. (The last comestibles were very palatable, despite the fact that they were obtained from Teece's[2] on the way.) I had a most enjoyable time. The flies were worse than the heat, especially when I sat down in the shade. Consequently I walked about nearly all day, & got as far as Upton Magna.[3]

I reached home at half past five—thoroughly exhausted.

*   *   *

After seeing you off I repaired to the Museum & found two priceless objects, of whose presence there I was formerly unaware.[4]

The museum & Haughmond are my only consolations.

> 'Without these two
> (Being parted from you)
> How should I long to flee
> From this vile Scrobbesbyree ! !'

In the afternoon I went to the Baths. Did not see Ivor,[5] but I made so bold as to speak to a stranger there. (N.B. I first heard the aspiration of the H.)

My news supply is scanty as yet, & have only a few minutes in which to write to Leslie.

∴ Conclusion.

Fondest love to all W

59. To Susan Owen

19 August 1909, 10.30 A.M.   *Shrewsbury*

PRIVATE

Dearest Mother,

A letter came from you this morning addressed to father. Father always goes to the office before post time now so I don't know what it contains.

---

[1] Haughmond Hill.
[2] The grocer in Cleveland Street, Shrewsbury.
[3] Four miles east of Shrewsbury.
[4] Part of a capital from one of the columns of the basilica at Uriconium (see next letter) and specimens of the mosaic floors are preserved in the Shrewsbury Museum.
[5] Ivor Williams, son of the Town Clerk. Later killed on active service.

This is the journal of our motions:

Tuesday. <u>Morng.</u>

Went to Museum & Library.

Aft.

Intended to go to Baths. Leslie suddenly fought shy of Baths, & wished to go to station.[1] So, at his suggestion, with mutual consent, we parted for the afternoon. He generously offered me the bicycle. Marvellous how soon I got there! I found, nevertheless, that Ladies occupied the 1st class.

I then watched the preparations in the Quarry,[2] & rode about till tea time.

Went fishing in the evening. Leslie caught a roach & another fish of the same size.

Wednesday.

Morng.

A dull, wet morning. Leslie was anxious to land a pike at least, so, perforce, we sat on the soaking grass, (protected by coats) all morning.

An otter jumped up a yard or two from us—and this was the only sign of life in the river.

Afternoon was much finer. Went to Show in due course. Everything as last year. Leslie is anxious to go again tonight.

Father has asked Mr. Shields for the bicycle, but only for <u>one day</u>. (Tomorrow if fine.) Uriconium[3] is to be the programme.

The wheels of the household run smoothly, being oiled with the oil of Sherlock Holmes in my case and a satisfactory domestic in Mrs. Cannell's case. Does this 'mixed metaphor' need explanation?

I offered *The Adventures of Sherlock Holmes* to Leslie. He is enchanted with it. Has read half of it already. This is a stroke of policy not counteracted even by Father's upsetting a glass of water over the volume—one of the most tastefully bound in my 'Library'—(Binding however unhurt by accident.)

I hear Alpenrose has a tennis lawn. Hope <u>you</u> play!

What is Colin's opinion of the district?

Love to everybody—

Wilfred

[1] The Gunston boys were keen train-spotters.

[2] Preparations for Shrewsbury Flower Show, held every August in the public park called The Quarry (red sandstone was formerly quarried there).

[3] The Roman city at Wroxeter, on the Severn, east of Shrewsbury. The city and its inhabitants were destroyed by fire and sword. HO still has several boxes of shards picked up there by Wilfred and himself. The first excavations were carried out 1859–61, and the more important finds placed in the Shrewsbury Museum. The site (and, later, that of Silchester near Reading) had great fascination for Wilfred, and a guide to the ruins survives among his books. A draft of *Uriconium: An Ode*, exists among the unpublished poems in the British Museum.

60. To Colin Owen

Postcard addressed to c/o J. Gunston, Esq., Alpenrose, Kidmore
End, Nr. Reading

[*Postmark 21 August 1909*]   *Shrewsbury*

Dear Colin,

Thank you for your letter. I was able to read your writing far more
easily than some in the Museum.

We went to Uriconium yesterday & found some bones & pottery in
the same mound that you & I dug in. It rained most of the day, so we
sheltered & had lunch in a barn opposite the field.

Today we have cycled to the Wrekin,[1] calling at Uriconium on the
way. Altogether we rode about 25 miles.

We often go fishing, but catch nothing.

Your garden is well watered by the rain. We did not go to the Show
again on Thursday, but had a good view of the fireworks from the railings
'down the lane'. Thank Mother for her card, which I received this
morning.

Wilfred

61. To Susan Owen

Mond. 23 August [*1909*]   *Shrewsbury*

Dearest Mother,

Your suspicions as to my acting as Sherlock Holmes are unfounded.
'Sherlock Holmes' was useful to me merely in the form of a book which
Leslie reads while I write to you.

He has already finished the Book (of one dozen adventures.)

My 'reading' has certainly been neglected this week, as you may
judge on hearing an account of our expeditions. Leave the books for
next term, however, I cannot, both being holiday tasks, & I have not
nearly finished one yet.

There is no need for you to see me off on Monday—am quite capable,
don'tcherknow!

Davies came round to see me one evening—(I forgot to tell you)—
before Leslie came—to arrange about the Thursday—a rightful holiday
for me since Centre Class does not open till follg. Thurs.

I took the opportunity to glean a few hints on the curriculum, way in,
kind of children, etc. I went to the Class last Sunday, as usual; Leslie
did not wish to go.

Last week, however, I <u>did</u> take a holiday, on account of the day being
so 'hotted up'. Today it seems quite cold after that terrible temperature
of yesterweek.

It has rained all morning, but is fine now. We are going, therefore,
to Quarry & possibly Baths.

[1] The hill ten miles east of Shrewsbury.

Must not delay, having promised to finish this letter in 'just a minute'.
Love to all. Thank H., please, for note.

62. To Susan Owen

24 December 1909   *Alpenrose*

Dear Mother,

A happy Christmas to you all!

I am writing on the veranda, with no coat on—in warm sunshine.
There is not a cloud in the sky. Can't imagine I was skating the day
before yesterday.

They have had hardly any snow here.

I did spend a delightful afternoon yesterday!

I am not sure of the exact time I arrived. The box being carried by an
outside porter, I reached the station yard & looked about for old
Mildenhall.[1]

I was not disconcerted to find him not there, since you had warned
me. I waited five minutes, ten minutes, quarter of an hour—then enquired of the person in charge of the 'Inquiry Office' whether he had
gone. Official didn't know. Thought he had.

Three quarters of an hour gone! How I anathemised that unlucky
carrier!

Imagine me with nothing whatever to do, couldn't even think—for
fear of losing sight of the box, or missing the cart—watching every
wretched carriage, trap, bus, van, cart, motor, etc. etc. that passed,
without a moment's rest. And one eye on the box at the same time.

Then darkness drew on with vast and rapid strides, and when neither
Perrin nor any other carrier appeared after two hours waiting, there
remained nothing but to leave the box at Station & walk. I was not at
all sure of the way and in the dark too! However, people had begun to
look at me askance. Was I a detective? A Spy? And perhaps they would
order me off the place for loafing. So I boldly set out, resolving to pass
the night in some one-roomed cottage if I got lost. By force of much
enquiry I reached the hill after Caversham[2] and there I overtook Perrin,
& got in.

I arrived safely without box & passed a good night after the nervous
prostration of the afternoon; the only discomforts being a dirty collar,
& muddy trousers after this morning's walk.

The poultry etc. are much the same. The calf is very pretty really.

As you prognosticated—fattened fowls for Christmas!

However I descried a hare, 2 pheasants, & a tongue in the larder as
well. Oh! I had a cup of tea on arriving, & a chop for supper at 8.

---

[1] The Kidmore End carrier.
[2] Caversham Hill, the area of Reading north of the Thames.

IIIc. Colin
(*see Letter 272, note 1*)

IIIb. Susan Owen and Harold

IIIa. Mary

IVa. The Vicarage, Dunsden

IVb. The Rev. Herbert Wigan

IVc. Wilfred at Dunsden, 1912

We are going out again this afternoon to gather decorating materials from the woods.

Best love and Christmas Wishes to all especially dear Mary,

from Wilfred

63. To Susan Owen

Postcard

31 December 1909   [*Postmark Reading*]

Private

Have just finished four 'thanking letters'. Splendid achievement, isn't it? Still there is Auntie Peggy![1]

Thank Mary for her 2 letters. Shall soon write to her, poor little dear.

I do not want any money sent, thank you. How lucky I am! This makes up for my apparant neglect on Christmas morning except for Auntie's 2s.

Walked into Rdg. yestermorn. Went to Museum, & (joy of joys) were shown all over Roman Remains from Silchester by Assist: Curator—[2] Explained everything what a morning! And what a Museum even to Shrewsbury's!!

Did not finish shopping in town—of course am going again. Have the boys got paintboxes? What do they want?

If you consider it worth sending my toothbrush in a letter, please do so. (It's in bathroom). If not, do not.

New's Year's love. W

64. To Mary Owen

1 January 1910   *Alpenrose*

Dear Sister,

Your beautiful card
has just come.
Uncle saw it, & said
it was 'very well done'
I think it is lovely,
& done in bed too!
How I wish you could
see Leslie & me
'fence-walking.'
We walk on the top of
the railing round the
haystack, on a bar
about 2½ inches
thick, & 4 feet high.

[1] Mrs. Picton. See Letter 22.
[2] Mr. T. W. Colyer, Assistant Curator, Reading Public Museum and Art Gallery, where the Silchester Collection is housed. At Silchester, ten miles SW of Reading, a Roman town began to be excavated in 1864.

At first we could only
manage a few steps.
Then we got quite around.
After that we had speed
trials. I did it first in
58 secs, then 55, 45,
38, & at last 34.
Leslie just did it in 34
too—so we are equal.
Once I fell off without
knowing it, & it felt as
if ten thousand plum-puddings
were sitting on my abdomen.
This morning we both did
it backwards.

There were some
poachers in the Hag Pits
Wood (just opposite the house
you know) the other night.
Uncle heard them shoot
with an air-gun.

Tomorrow afternoon Uncle
is going to sing a solo
in Church, at an Organ
Recital.

We have had no snow yet
& it seems as if we were
not going to have any
skating either.

Best love to the boys
& Mother.

                                   Your loving brother, Wilfred

P.S. I have printed for practice, not to make it hard to read.

65. To Susan Owen

Postcard addressed to Mahim, Monkmoor Rd, Shrewsbury[1]

10 April 1910   *Dorfold, Great Meols, Cheshire*

I managed all right with the bag, as Father has told you perhaps. We
all, except Margaret, went to Church yesterday morning. Cecil took

[1] The family moved to this larger house on the outskirts of Shrewsbury in the winter of 1909–
10. For a description of the house and its position see *JO* II, pp. 215–17. The name was
chosen by Tom Owen: 'but beyond saying that it was the name of a place in India that he
had known well and which held pleasant recollections for him he would offer no other
reason'.

me in the evening to the Parish Church at West Kirby. Do you know that I saw Miss Jones & Miss Wright[1] at the Shrewsbury station, just as I was moving off! Former said she w'd. call on you in the afternoon.

How is your throat? Do let me know. The remembrance of leaving you with that, is as the dark cloud which even now obscures the gay sunlight. Ah me!

W

66. To Susan Owen
Postcard addressed to Alpenrose, Kidmore End, Reading

4 May 1910   [*Postmark Shrewsbury*]

Dearest Mother,

I find time this Wednesday night for a short note. I must divide news into 3 classes.

A. P.T. Centric

F. Watson remains impregnable! For all my exam. successes, (e.g. French 91, History 94), her army of Term Marks she so diligently has mustered are superior to mine. I am still 2nd therefore, with I.P.W.[2] 3rd, & Walters 9th. We are all wasting a tremendous lot of time over Miss Strachan's 'We-convections'. I did one exercise no less than 5 times before it secured satisfaction! We (boys) are all working away in Recreation Time in the Gay Meadow,[3] mowing & rolling 2 Tennis Courts. I hope to play soon, may I? Already I have had some Cricket there. Hockey & Football go on at the same time! Isn't it a marvellous outburst! Chiefly, of course, owing to Miss Jones' energy. Moreover Miss Jones & Miss Wright wish to take the Cycling Boys for an excursion on Sat. My presumptive self esteem does not find any difficulty in seeking the reason of this innovation!

B. Wyle-Copic

'Hall the skule his 'aving er oliday, so Mist' Howin wunna ave is sums & stuff what 'e learns us wiv hon Fursdee same as hother times. Frot lt jugules meff rop rosh yremnmn srkrrrr.'[4]

C. Domestic

The virtues irradiated from you have not yet evaporated from the house but their influence grows weaker every day. Return soon therefore, 'ere the smooth-gliding & serene wheels of the household come to a standstill.

Please { Excuse nonsense intentional / or unconscious / Thank Les. for his letter.

[1] Botany teacher at the Technical School.
[2] Ivor Williams.
[3] Public recreation ground on the banks of the Severn.
[4] Perhaps an impression of the Shrewsbury dialect.

67. To Mary Owen

[*Postmark 7 May 1910*]   Signature completed in red ink   [*Shrewsbury*]

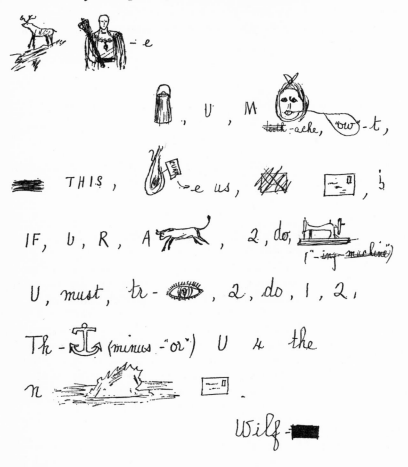

68. To Susan Owen
Postcard

Aug. 1910 [*Postmark 5 August 1910*]   *264 Union St. Torquay.*

Dearest Mother,

Thank you so much for your note & message. Went to Plymouth on Wednesday—met at Multey Sta. by Eliot & Miss T[1] after coffee at Castlehayes,[2] saw principal sights, e.g. Mayflower Stone, Guildhall, Hoe, etc. Then it came on to pour & continued all afternoon, so instead of visiting Dockyard (which has no shelters and has a floor of rusty

---

[1] Neither can be identified, unless Miss T is the music teacher from Anfield, holidaying in Plymouth.

[2] Presumably Eliot's home.

mud) we had to content ourselves with 'Buffalo Hunting in Indo-China'
in Animated Pictures, (1s. seats).

Eliot is a perfect marvel in constructing model engines, & electrical
machines.

Have quite lost a sort of contempt I once had for those who find
mechanics so exclusively engrossing. He has 2 Workshops, simply lined
with tools. Following must suffice as description of Castlehayes. No. of
reception Rooms = 4.

Quality of Wall Paper = 3/6 or 5s.

Depth of Stair Carpet = 1 in!

69. To Susan Owen

Aug. 1910   *Torquay*

Dearest Mother,

I daresay you will be as astonished as I was to find a Postal Order in
my letter!

The accompanying note will doubtless explain.

Leslie says he is delighted to hear of some <u>fixed</u> <u>arrangements</u>.

What are they please? And is it fixed that we leave Torquay on
Tuesday? Really, I am by no means 'fed up' with it!

The whole day to Harold & me centres round the <u>bathing</u>. The most
enjoyable we have ever had, <u>I</u> think.

It is one of those rare cases where the actuality exceeds, does not fall
short of, the expectation.

Since yesterday afternoon my senses have been considerably fluttered.
For I then discovered that a few furlongs away there lives a <u>descendant
of Coleridge</u>—Miss Christabel Coleridge.[1] I promptly discovered the
house by means of a directory, and a few minutes later my heart (liver
and cerebellum included)

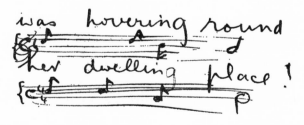

Would it savour too much of the tradesman's invitation to Lord
Roberts if I were to interview her?[2]

---

[1] The novelist Christabel Rose Coleridge (1843–1921), daughter of the Rev. Derwent
Coleridge, was Samuel Taylor Coleridge's granddaughter. She lived at Cheyne, Torquay,
and her brother, Ernest Hartley Coleridge, must have been visiting her at this time, for they
both inscribed their names with the date 10 August 1910 in Wilfred's copy of *The Golden
Book of Coleridge*.

[2] We cannot identify this anecdote.

But what relics must she possess, and what information with regard to the truth of the anecdotes about Coleridge.

Archaeological interest next consumes me. My American friend[1] tells me of a prehistoric Cavern near Meadfoot (Kent's Cavern).[2] I, however, have found out (from a Guide Book) about another and Prehistoricer cavern (as well as a Roman Camp)[3] near Brixham.

So we are together going to Brixham on Monday afternoon (if fine.) . . . [*one line missing*] nearly gone.

I hear scanty news of your throat!

Is it therefore quite better?

70. To Susan Owen

[*August 1910*]   *Torquay*

My dearest Mother,

Your letter, that is the sentence telling of Father's benevolent action, gave us the utmost joy, pleasure, satisfaction, gratification and delight. Indeed the exuberance we then displayed was most unseemly on the part of two sons who had not beheld their Mother's face for nine days and nine nights.

Not that we don't want to be once more . . . (the remaining part of the sentence may be filled in (a hundred times if you like) from reference to <u>your</u> letters when away).

One circumstance that would draw me to Shrewsbury I must not omit—namely to decide whether three handsome volumes of Macaulay's history shall lodge in the Book <u>Case</u> or on the new Book <u>Shelf</u>.

They are a present from <u>Uncle</u> (not <u>new</u> you understand but <u>not</u> embellished by finger marks.) [*remainder missing*]

71. To Susan Owen
Postcard

Aug. 1910, Wednesday   *Torquay*

Dear Mother,

Obedient to your message just received, I have written to Auntie[4] asking whether they have made unalterable arrangements for Sat. and what I am to do.

---

[1] Russell Tarr. For a detailed account of this boy, and the Torquay holiday, see *JO* I, pp. 186–99 (and see also Letter 80). His father, Ralph Stockman Tarr (1864–1912), was Professor of Geology, Cornell University, and organized the Cornell Greenland Expedition which went north on Peary's ship in 1896.

[2] One of the oldest identifiable human habitations in the British Isles.

[3] Berry Head, near Brixham, was probably a Roman encampment, and many Roman remains have been found there. Tradition is that Vespasian and Titus landed at this spot.

[4] Aunt Emma Gunston.

We have had another superb day, but I don't think fine weather can last much longer.

At all events we intend to see you before you go, hence will come at latest by Friday evening. But Auntie's reply will decide.

W

72. To Susan Owen

Postcard addressed to 12 Clifton Terrace, Melbourne Road,
New Brighton, Cheshire[1]

17 Aug. 1910   *Alpenrose*

Dearest Mother,

Am safely arrived here once more. We went to Silchester yesterday; found nothing much, for all the excavations are now filled in.

On Sunday-Monday night I hardly had any sleep, on account of a violent thunderstorm. Strange to say they quite escaped it here.

Dorothy came home yesterday.

Once again I am just too late to see a great personage, this time Sir Edwin Cornwall and Bernice, who motored over to take Laura home. The country here is very fine now, but how I miss my morning bathe. Love to Mary, & Miss Montford.

Wilfred

(Auntie will write soon.)

73. To Susan Owen

18 August 1910   *Alpenrose*

My dearest Mother,

Sorry I have not written before; I have been so actively occupied these last days.

So far I have thoroughly enjoyed myself. After all, open air coursing about is the only thing I can comfortably do here. For when I try to read, I <u>can not</u> lose sight of a figure sprawled across the table, kicking his slippers about the floor, tossing up a coin, a pencil, (or a pair of scissors if nothing else comes to hand), and whistling between his teeth some annoying tune.

Consequently I welcome the excursions he has planned out. I don't think I am getting overdone,—if I ever do I can counter-balance the effect by eating meat which is indisputably <u>underdone</u>!

To get to the point, on Tuesday we <u>went</u> to Silchester since Mr. Colyer was going away the next day. Rather disappointed since the mounds have been levelled down and the pits filled up, so that the city presents the same appearance as the ordinary country, except for the walls. We found nothing particular.

[1] Susan Owen and Mary are staying with another 'courtesy aunt': Aunt Clara, Mrs. Maddock-Jones.

Yesterday Leslie's friend Mr. Wilsher,[1] (who is a young married gentleman just beginning to collect fossils, etc.) took us (cycling) to see a great geologist and collector of prehistoric implements, who lives at Twyford, about 8 miles away. I never have seen in museum or house such a magnificent collection. Hardly less interesting was the mighty range of books on Geology, History, etc. And Mr. Treacher[2] himself, with his long grey hair, philosophical manner, and dirty old coat, was a character I would go a long way to see. Hearing I was interested in Roman remains, he took me round to a shed and fished out a small sack. 'You can have all this pottery from Silchester,' he said, 'No, don't open it, because if I should keep half, I should always be regretting that I gave the other half away.' If you, dear Mother, cannot picture to yourself, my feelings, and the semi-reluctance with which I took that sack,— then you don't know your own son.

For I knew that it contained treasures—whether I smelt or heard, or felt or tasted them I cannot say, but I knew!

Well, it turned out after Leslie carried them home on his carrier, that there were almost a hundred large pieces of various wares, (crowds of so-called Samian) including 2 with actual potter's names on (rare treasures)—and, above all, just half of a superb bowl.

We have divided the fragments between us, and tossed up for the bowl. Leslie won but I secured an equal amount of other stuff, and a bone pin. We both have several genuine Roman nails.

Today we cycled out about the same distance to another place, a chalk pit in search of fossils. Found several.

Mr. W. and Leslie helped me along at times, so I am not unduly tired.

Tomorrow we hope to see the last achievements of civilization instead of its earliest records, namely the aeroplanes (real, large ones) of a friend of Mr. Wilsher's.

And next day—the Exhibition![3]

We are debating whether I should go on early with one of the family to see the Brit. Museum in the morning, because the party do not get to the Exhibition till half past 3 ! !

If I pack my pottery, etc. in a suitable box, can I send it free and in safety—in advance?

Shall never get it into the porkmantle.

Excuse such quantity of matter, and such a quality of writing.

I do hope you see something of the sea, and not

[1] Managing Director of the Abstainers and General Insurance Company, Reading.
[2] Llewellyn Treacher (1859–1943), Fellow of the Geological Society, author of a paper on 'The Occurrence of Stone Implements in the Thames Valley between Reading and Maidenhead'. He presented his collection to the Geological Museum, Oxford.
[3] Probably the annual exhibition of the Royal Photographic Society. To Uncle John Gunston, a passionate amateur photographer, it would have been the exhibition of the year.

'the creeping tide come up along the sand
          And o'er and o'er the sand
          And round and round the sand
          As far as eye could see!'[1]

Fondest love Wilfred

74. To Susan Owen

23 August 1910[2]   *Alpenrose, Kidmore End, Reading*

My dearest Mother,

Many, many thanks for your long letter.

Do please call upon the Canon and ask him about the fees, etc. Certainly, if it is possible, it is my wish to get into such a College. As to whether I mean [to] be a clergyman is a different matter. You well know that I don't ask myself 'Is the life congenial to me' but 'am I fitted for, am I called to, the Ministry?' And it is my sure conviction that it is possible to serve Him, as you say, in any station just as well. Still, I say, as things stand, I see nothing I should rather do than enter—if possible—St. Aidan's.[3] For even if I have the brains I don't think I have the strength to read up for a degree in a situation in a school.

And really I have no desire to be chained to an elementary school for the best years of life by the King's scholarship. Of a secondary school is very different.

As for taking up French. I never thought of it seriously, but if the opportunity should occur, I confess I do not look upon it as the last thing in the world I should take up. Very disagreeably as experience is forcing upon me the fact that money must purchase even such pleasures as good books, still do I place first things first, and regard the life whose sole aim is money-making to be the most pitiable.

Perhaps you think me still hopelessly undecided, but I hope that the Canon's advice may clear things up a bit.

Auntie is going to Brixton on Friday, and returning on Tuesday. Hence we may stay till Wednesday (for Auntie must needs see Leslie off), or, if my inclinations so direct me, I may fly back on Friday or Saturday. I am hoping to see you much less tired-looking. Tho' I sometimes have sight of you in the night-season, the visits are short and unsatisfying and leave me full of anxiety about Mary (see Mary's letter)! Your verse was really clever, and in correct metre too!

Your loving son W

[1]   The Western tide crept up along the sand
          And o'er and o'er the sand . . .
Charles Kingsley, 'The Sands of Dee'.

[2] During the next five weeks he wrote 'Written in a Wood, September 1910', quoted in Edmund Blunden's Memoir to the 1931 edition of the poems, reprinted as Appendix I in *The Collected Poems of Wilfred Owen*, edited C. Day Lewis, Chatto and Windus, London, 1963.

[3] St. Aidan's Theological College, Birkenhead, founded 1846 and now affiliated to Liverpool University.

75. To Susan Owen
Postcard
27 December 1910   *Alpenrose*

Dear Mother,
Arrived safely after travelling with some 'swells'. Train very full. Leslie went to meet my train i.e. 10 o'clock, but did not stay till the 11 o'clock arrived—being told the latter was not running while the 10 o'clock was. Curiously enough a train did arrive at 1.32 (the time I told them)!
We have been playing games (e.g. Proverbs, Memory Tray, etc.) this evening.

W

76. To Susan Owen
29 December 1910   *Alpenrose*

Dearest Mother,
I am having a splendid open-air holiday. The weather has been perfect for the last few days with roads to correspond.
On Wed m'ng. Uncle, Dorothy, Leslie & I went a 'joy-ride' to Nettlebed in the m'ng, (Uncle on Leslie's old machine).
In the afternoon Leslie took me in to Reading to see West's wonderful Pictures[1] (animated.) Yesterday we also went into town, where I bought at a book-shop a one-and-fourpenny book of Scott's for 1d!

Uncle gave us a little shooting match in the chalk pit yesterday: I made one bull at 50 yds. (about this wide

←——————————————————————————→

Tomorrow we are all going to the Painters' to tea. This Mr. Painter was formerly a school-master and is now in a G.W.R. office. I have not yet been to the Museum. We have been prevented from going this morning by the first rain-shower of the week.
So instead of taking another trip to the town for which Dickens very nearly became M.P. (Reading), I shall get a chance of reading some Botanical articles in *Popular Science*.
How is Mary's poor eye? And are you getting any repose with a view to resuscitation after the Christmas activities? I do wish you were here to take woodland strolls with us, instead of wearing down the Shrewsbury pavements in obedience to the bidding of Cousin May.
'I must hear, deer Madam, start to begin to commence to draw to a close.'
                    Best love to all, including Cousin May, Wilfred

---

[1] West's Picture Palace, at 33 West Street, Reading, was one of the earliest cinemas in the town. There were regular advertisements in Reading for 'West's Pictures—travel, sport, drama, comedy, new spectacle, tragedy, and farce, 3d, 6d, and 1/-.'

77. To Colin Owen

1 January 1911   *Alpenrose*

My dearest Colin,
  How glad I was to have your little letter,
To know your throat is really, truly better.
(My words, you see, are falling into verse-gear,
I hope it will not make you any worse, dear!

About your new Bird's Egg Book worth six shillings
What <u>can</u> I say until myself I see it?
But <u>now</u> it's bought so dearly, so dearly
              so dearly
O carefully use it!
Oh brown–paper–bind it!
Or you'll certainly lose it,
Yes, and <u>I</u>'ll find it!
              (Oh really!
               Oh really!)
<u>Then</u> you'll see it never more
<u>So</u> don't you leave it on the floor!
              (D'you hear me,
               D'you hear me?)

Now let me tell you something of my doings—
We all went out to tea last night to Painter's
And played a game I know you'd like to play at:
We shot an air-gun at a target on their door
And even Vera did her level best to score.
Hence excepting Auntie (for such sports too aged)
We might have been all <u>Bis(i)ley</u> engaged.
That afternoon we also saw the 'Pictures'
The French boys always charm me, but the mixtures
Of Blood and Thunder Stories sometimes shock me.
How does Mary like her Book of Botany?
I wish I could find some Pheasant's Eggs or Partridges
To bring you; but I got you lots of empty cartridges.

———

<u>P.S.</u>
    'There was a boy so wondrous wise
    He tried to see his nose
    And turning inwards both his eyes
    He now in glasses goes:—'
        must now be changed to
    'There is a boy of Shrewsbury
    On whom all doctors dote,
    He lets them take hot iodine
    And burn out half his throat.'[1]

[1] The references are to Colin's new spectacles and H O's tonsillitis.

78. To Susan Owen

2 April 1911   [*Shrewsbury*]

Dear Mother,

Thank you so much for your letter, and for interviewing Mr. Robson.[1] I am very anxious to know 'what else' he has found or will find out.

I am not able to get much study done in school yet, but Mr. Edwards[2] is going to approach Mr. Lightbourne[3] on the subject (of allowing me to study when not actually teaching) as soon as I find out exactly what is done in other schools in the town where P.T.'s[4] are.

Leslie tells me you are often hearing the Nightingale. Is it indeed so enchanting? I crave to hear it, and yet I should almost be afraid lest it should not be as fine as I imagine it. At present my soul is in a ferment, and the 'leafy month of June' promises as many terrors as leaves.

> 'It is a flaw
> In happiness to see beyond our bourne,
> It forces us in summer skies to mourn,
> And spoils the singing of the nightingale.'
>   (Keats)[5]

You ought, if you feel so moved, dear Mother, to read the 'Ode to the Nightingale' by the same Poet, which you will find in his Poems, in the bookcase. Furthermore, if you [are] at a loss at any time for good literature, why not study the Introduction to this volume?

But let me warn you about believing what it says of Keats' 'attitude to knowledge, which cannot be justified, must not be copied, etc.' I know of something which proves the contrary to this view.

If you could find room for it in your trunk, I should be obliged by a present of some lumps of soft chalk. And might I ask for some complete specimens of Woodruff from the wood, of Mary (who seems to have dwindled into oblivion for ought I hear, of or from her, or her doings.)

                                      W

79. To Susan Owen

Apr. 1911   *Torquay*

My dearest Mother,

I was very glad to hear of your early exodus to Alpenrose, and I hope it means a longer holiday there for you. But since I shall not see you on Saturday to give a verbal account of myself here, I must write a longer letter now, which shall suffice for some days to come. I am really disappointed not to see you for those few days; our absence will now amount practically to a month. However I shall not 'rush home' on

---

[1] The Rev. Herbert Eric Robson (1877–1917), Vicar of Kidmore End 1909–16.
[2] A master at Shrewsbury Technical School.
[3] Headmaster of Wyle Cop School, Shrewsbury, where HO was a pupil for a short time. Wilfred was a pupil-teacher at the school for some months in the summer of 1911.
[4] Pupil-teachers.
[5] *Epistle to J. H. Reynolds*, ll. 82–85.

Friday as I have all too short a time to make my pilgrimage to Teign-mouth,[1] the passport[2] for which I expected in your letter. Will it arrive in time?

I have bought at last a Life of Keats[3] (in the same edition as that of Dickens) and began this morning 'with fear and trembling' to learn the details of his life. I sometimes feel in reading such books that I would give ten years of life to have been born a hundred years earlier (always providing that I have the same dear mother.)

Up to to-day I have been reading on the beach of course the French-books, bought as bargains from I. P. Williams, Esq. It was strange that after gazing for a long while upon the waves (which are now quite rough), I should come upon this passage which I will translate to you as giving a very true picture of how I am spending some of my time:

'. . . I used to go and put myself between two rocks almost on a level with the water, in the midst of the sea-gulls, blackbirds, and swallows, and I stayed there almost the whole day in that kind of stupor and delicious "overwhelmed-ness" which the contemplation of the sea gives. You know, don't you, this lovely intoxication of the soul? You are not thinking, you are not dreaming either. All your being escapes you, flies off, is scattered. You are the plunging wave, the dust of foam which floats in the sun between two waves, the white smoke of that receding steamer, . . . this bead of water, this flake of mist, everything except yourself.'

(Daudet: *Lettres de mon Moulin*)[4]

Well, I was reading the book at Meadfoot the other afternoon when who should I see but the boy—youth whom we met with Russell Tarr, and who played croquet with us on the hotel lawn, as Harold will

[remainder missing]

80. To Susan Owen

25 April 1911   *Shrewsbury*

Dearest Mother,

Father has arrived safely but has not written before being busy. Let me tell you of my holiday, now a thing very much of the past, for I have plunged deep into work again—(did not get out till 5.25 yesterday, took an object lesson requiring preparation today, and so on).

I went to Teignmouth on Friday. Perhaps it was a good thing that the soft buffeting sheets and misty drifts of Devonshire rain renewed themselves almost the whole day, since Keats's letters from here are full of objurgations against the climate.

---

[1] Keats lodged from March to May 1818 at 20 The Strand (now Northumberland Place), Teignmouth. See Letter 80.

[2] The railway ticket. Tom Owen always provided, or was called on to provide, tickets for railway journeys, free or at much reduced rates.

[3] *Keats*, by Sidney Colvin. An autographed copy, inscribed 'Torquay, Spring 1911', survives among Wilfred's books. A few days later he wrote a sonnet, 'At Teignmouth, on a Pil-grimage to Keats's House', mentioned by E B but now believed lost.

[4] From Chapter VI, *Le Phare des Sanguinaires*.

'You may say what you will of Devonshire' he writes, 'The truth is it is a splashy, rainy, misty, snowy, foggy, haily, floody, muddy, slip-shod county'[1] and so on.

I long to tell you of my good fortune in discovering the house (of Keats)—I will only say now that I saw it, and gaped at it (regardless of people in the window who finally became quite alarmed, I fancy)—to my heart's content. If I had only had a little more time, and a photograph or two, perhaps I might have made up a magazine article upon it —the district certainly lends itself to picturesque description.

Would you please ask Dorothy whether (1) she knows of Leigh Hunt's cottage[2] in the Vale of Health Hampstead? (2) Whether the house she has described to me (in what is known as Keats' Road) is, or was, in Well Walk? (3) Or is it a house (once semi-detached) now known as Lawn Bank, originally Wentworth Place,[3] near the bottom of John St. In this garden the 'Ode to a Nightingale' was written so that it is one of London's most holy spots.

I shall never be able to approach the metropolis without being drawn there. If therefore Dorothy would ascertain something about its position and accessibility, I should be deeply obliged to that dear cousin.

Mrs. Timpany called yesterday evening, her mission being to warn me against the Teaching Profession (Elementary). Her husband could not candidly do this, she said, but she thinks it 'wicked' that young people should enter it without a fair premonition of the hopelessness of their fate, and without knowing of the profound dissatisfaction among all who are now teachers.

Civil Service is her cry, and I am to see Mr. Timpany about it one of these evenings. I wish you were here to approve or condemn this good lady's counsel.

Have you ever asked Uncle John's opinion on these matters?

Really, indecision is rapidly turning into distraction. When I begin to eliminate from my list all those professions which are impossible (seemingly) from a financial point of view, and then those which I feel disinclined for—it leaves nothing. But is my inclination to matter after all? Yet what I do find so hard to distinguish between is aimlessly drifting, and waiting upon God.

If it must be done, I suppose I am not too young to destroy all my love of literature and such study, and turn to Office Routine, Customs, Revenues, Taxation, etc.—(I suppose this is what is meant by Civil Service, but as a matter of fact my ideas of this life are of the vaguest.)

---

[1] 13 March 1818, to Benjamin Bailey, from Teignmouth (*Letters of John Keats*, ed. Hyder Edward Rollins, Cambridge, 1958, Vol. I, p. 240).

[2] Still known by this name.

[3] The poet lodged with his brothers in Well Walk before moving to share with Charles Armitage Brown in one of the attached houses then known as Wentworth Place, later converted into one house and renamed Lawn Bank.

Dreams of the power of money, and the necessity of obtaining it in the easiest way, have run before me with special brightness at such times as a stay at Meols; yes and Alpenrose, too.

But of all those visions none is so powerful as one which I almost think has been cherished from my earliest remembrance, that of my sweet Mother, in a delightful garden, passing a bland old age among her greenhouses, and in a small carriage drawn by an ambling pad-pony . . . But till this comes, don't, oh don't, sign yourself, 'your old mother.'

There was no class on Sunday—we went to the Mission instead. I would not like to write down an opinion of Mr. Alexander: nor yet of Dr. Chapman; More than once my sense of reverence and 'decently—and—in orderness' was outraged by an attempt at wit on the part of a certain 'Sergeant' who spoke, and by the perfectly deafening shout which his voice passed into towards the end of his address. Nor did the words he spoke tend to disprove the words of Ruskin, which then came to my mind: 'Your converted children who teach their parents . . . your converted dunces, who, having lived in cretinous stupefaction half their lives, suddenly awaking to the fact of there being a God, fancy themselves therefore His peculiar people and messengers:—these are the true fog-children—clouds these without water; bodies these of putrescent vapour and skin,"swollen with wind and the rank mist they draw." '[1]

(Not that I quite hold with Ruskin either.)

However, I shall try and go again.

Please give my love to Mary, Auntie, etc. etc. etc. Small need for me to send it to One to whom it has been given for these last sixteen years.

81. To Susan Owen

7 May 1911   *Shrewsbury*

My dearest Mother,

At one o'clock on Saturday we, the 'Botany People', as well as the non-botanical members of the class, started by train for Condover,[2] for the expedition to Lyth Hill. Walters & Ashton were the only other boys. Miss Wright's sister was one of the party. She knows no Botany but has a passionate love of English literature, with the result that when we found each other out we spent the rest of the day comparing opinions, agreeing and disagreeing, quoting and counter-quoting, somewhat to the dismay of the other members of the party who (possibly) did not know what the subject of our rapt conversation was. As to the young lady's external recommendations you shall judge for yourself, I hope.

We had tea at 3.30 at a cottage on the hill, and very merry we all were over it too. For as we were coming through the wood, Miss Wright proposed that we should turn aside from the path for a short harangue upon the specimens we had found. We were hardly seated,

[1] John Ruskin, *Sesame and Lilies* I: 'Of Kings' Treasuries'.
[2] Five miles south of Shrewsbury.

when the whole wood began to resound with a shrill voice screaming abuses and threats at Miss Wright and us, whereat we all skipped like young rams on to the path again, and found a heated woman, frightfully excited, pouring forth a scorching denunciation upon us for not being duly impressed by the 'Trespassers will be etc.' Notice, at the gate, (which we never saw.)

We agreed later that it was none other than Mrs. MacStinger,[1] and indeed I found it beneficial to mutter 'stand by' to myself, after the manner of Ed'd Cuttle. I almost bugled forth the fact that she was addressing a B.Sc. but fearing I should have to explain that it meant bachelor, and seeing that Miss Wright looked most unscientific when told to stop her sniggering, I refrained.

We walked home of course and a tremendous way round we seemed to come, for though we walked steadily forward, it was after nine when I got in. Howbeit it is a long time since we so thoroughly enjoyed an outing.

I went to see Mr. Timpany again on Friday. He seriously advises me to get on a newspaper—as a reporter it would have to be at first. This is the best way to gain experience in journalism, with a view to 'writing'. Whatever have you got to say to that?

I have now got a half-holiday on Tuesdays. Some great person on the board calling upon Wright's parents asked whether Wright had Thursday afternoon 'off'. Finding he had not, this gentleman gave him authority to demand one both for himself, and the other P.T.,[2] even me. I suggested that Mr. Edwards would be inconvenienced if we both took Thursday, so I professed myself happy to take Tues. instead; with the option, I believe, of choosing any other afternoon when special reasons warrant it.

Father will give you instructions as to coming home. The verdict is unanimous. But don't stay longer than Thurs. or I shall become positively nervous of meeting you two strange ladies.

Let not Mary trouble about Woodruff. I found some at Lyth Hill yesterday.

Whatever more I have to tell you (and there is plenty of it) shall be kept till Thurs., when I expect an equal amount of news of various kinds from you.

Your loving son, Wilfred

82. To Harold Owen

[*June 1911*][3]   First sheet missing   [*Alpenrose*]

and I keep thinking

'Because red-lin'd accounts

[1] Captain Cuttle's termagant landlady in Charles Dickens', *Dombey and Son*.
[2] Wilfred had taken on the job of pupil-teacher at the Wyle Cop School for the summer term.
[3] There are BM drafts of an uncompleted poem, 'On a June Night (1911)'.

Were richer than the Songs of Grecian Years ?'[1]

Indeed, I sometimes think I have fooled myself that I have not 'gone in' for red-lin'd accounts altogether—when, for instance I visit the Penny Bank, and see that its Hours are 11 to 3, and realise that the idle, loungin' clerks must look in somewhere about 10, and be absolutely Free by 4!

What time does _my_ shop shut? Eleven! And then I merely as it were creep under the Counter to sleep, for I breathe still the same Atmosphere.

> 'I could lie down like a tir'd child,
> And weep away this life of care
> Which I have borne, and yet must bear.'[2]

I do not weep, but I snort and snuff, and quote.

I can never escape my thoughts or I would—'To France, to France . . . my boy'[3] with the £. Note I have in my pocket, and . . .

I know not what. Except that I must change my tune, if I want you to read this letter.

Saturday

Well, 'tis a fine day, to begin with.

The garden is very fine too, but the open lands are more so. I have to stop and look over the hedge every hundred yards or so of a walk.

I am trying to read Miss Mitford's _Our Village_, which village is situated just the other side of Reading.[4] Some of its descriptions are very pleasing, but I really find it difficult to read an airy-chatty collection of letters like this, when I am grappling as I never did before with the Problem of Evolution. I simply cannot form a Conclusion, by reading both sides of the Question, historically. The only thing to do is to make personal investigation, so it seems, into Botany, etc. But to return to the soothing side of Nature; I wished you could daub some representation of a Field which I saw, blazing with yellow charlock, backed by a Beech-woods, of a deep green so nearly black, that it puts one in mind of the colour of an ancient black coat assuming its green-old-age tints.

Leslie has been doing some remarkable bits of work with Pastels, on Art Papers [*several words illegible*] I shall never have philosophy enough to counteract the sensation that Time is increasing its velocity, in the Geometrical Progression, 1, 2, 4, 8, 16 . . .

---

[1] Keats, *Isabella; or, The Pot of Basil*, xvi.

[2]
> I could lie down like a tired child,
> And weep away the life of care
> Which I have borne and yet must bear,
> Till death like sleep might steal on me.
>
> Shelley, 'Stanzas Written in Dejection near Naples'.

[3] *Henry V*, II. iii. 57.

[4] Three Mile Cross, near Reading, was the original of *Our Village, sketches of rural life, character and scenery*, by Mary Russell Mitford (1787–1855).

Except the cold, nothing is really Autumnal here, yet. Alas, tho',

> 'In the mid-days of Autumn on their eves,
> The breath of Winter comes from far away,
> And the sick West, continually bereaves
> Of some gold tinge, and plays a roundelay
> Of death among the bushes and the leaves,
> To make all bare before he dares to stray
> From his north cavern.'[1]

In case you didn't take much notice of that [*word illegible*] it may raise your interest to know that that is the metre in which I have now written 30 stanzas of 'The Little Mermaid'[2]—and not half done yet. I should like to know what is the present [*word illegible*] of 'Little C. and Big C??'[3]

If you have any short spasm of extra good-nature to me when you see the Turner,[4] I pray you turn it to account thus :— (thanks denied in any other form)

Find the old copy of Keats I left (with Mother?); open it at the first page; begin to read. Get alone to do this; and read, as slowly as you like, say 300 lines. Then if you are not delighted thirty times at least, I will buy you all the Turners from the Tate Gallery for next birthday. This behest of mine must be conscientiously performed, before you write to me next. If you don't understand anything, write to me. I am sure you might ask many less capable of helping you in that way. Thus I hope this will be a 'red-letter'[5] on your Calendar; for I don't believe that a Painter (of anything above houses, cheeks or sore-throats) ever existed who had not only read much, but studied Poetry. And a more Pictorial or Artist-souled Poet than J.K. would be hard to find. Therefore hear my words, O brother, and in proof of your loving obedience, send me all the lines that strike you. I wonder whether you saw the *Graphic*, which contains photos of six or eight [*three lines illegible*] I think I must have seen the original; but that was in the old, happy, far-off days, when (to parody Wordsworth)

> 'Two dark eyes in a maiden's head
> Two simple eyeballs were to me
> And they were nothing more.'

(In case you don't know what W. wrote, it was

> 'A primrose by the river's brim
> A simple primrose was to him,
> And it was nothing more.')[6]

---

[1] Keats, *Isabella*, xxxii.
[2] *The Little Mermaid*, based on Hans Andersen's story, was completed during the course of the following year, in seventy-eight stanzas, and survives, unpublished, in HO's possession.
[3] *Little Claus and Big Claus*, another long poem based on Andersen, also survives. See Letter 138.
[4] *Turner's Liber Studiorum*, miniature edition, Gowans and Gray Ltd., London, 1911, containing 101 reproductions, was sent to HO, who still has it. Wilfred later bought another copy, for Susan Owen. See p. 161, note 1.
[5] This letter is written in red ink.
[6] Wordsworth, *Peter Bell*, prologue.

Again, anything more [*word illegible*] than the 'Samson' picture could scarcely be put on canvas. You sh'd try and see them.

Concerning these little Turners: I have of course glanced thro' them; but I have not seen any of Ruskin's writings on them. And I have not the cheek to criticise them, even if I had the Eye, or the Tongue. I will just enumerate which took my fancy during half an hour's inspection—5, 13, 14, 23, 38, 44, 49, 57, 78, 81, 82, 94, 97, and 101 (Page 126–7).

Now I must positively stop my ink-slinging. Keep, however, this Message, and it shall stand you in good stead when you don't know what to read, I warrant you.

Your most affectionate, Brother, Wilfred
My next shall be for Mary.

Kindly acknowledge a letter I had from Oliver,[1] begging my 2/6 sub.—if I continue an Associate.[2] I think it w'd be much more sensible for you to become the Associate, and pay for your benefits. At any rate, please instruct him at your earliest opportunity that I must be dissociated from Shrew. [*word illegible*] this year; for one reason I have not thirty pence to send him.

83. To Susan Owen

18 June 1911   *Alpenrose*

My dearest Mother,

I have been to see Mr. Robson this afternoon. He had prepared some notes to aid him in his discourse, which he gave me in his study, smoking meanwhile. . . . My pre-eminent plan is to borrow or become possessed of just £150, with which sum I can get a degree at College. If I have rich relations, I ought to try and get them to lend, repaying in the process of time at, say, 4%. Failing this, teaching in a secondary school might be tried, studying with a Corresp. College at the same time, but this is 'killing' work, he says.

Finally, he revealed what he had in his mind as being 'easier' than teaching.

It is:—to become the 'assistant' of some hardworked or studiously inclined parson, helping in parish work, correspondence etc. and being generally companionable to a lonely country-sequestered bachelor, such as himself. Not to himself actually, however, one reason being—that it would never do to have one with relations in the parish! He had heard, however, that 'Wiggan[3] of Dunsden' wanted help in the parish this winter, and suggested applying to him, especially as his views coincide with ours.

[1] Frederick James Oliver, brother of HO's childhood friend Herbert Oliver, of Shrewsbury.
[2] Of the YMCA.
[3] The Rev. Herbert Wigan (1862–1947), Chaplain of Bloxham School 1891–99, Curate of Sonning 1903–4, Vicar of Dunsden, near Reading, 1904–47. Wilfred was shortly to spend sixteen months in his charge. The Rev. Bernard Wigan, his nephew, writes: 'He was brought up in a tractarian rectory in Kent, and until middle age was an "advanced" exponent of that school of thought. As a young man, he had a bout of "Roman fever", of which he was

For we must be most careful as to the kind of parson I go to. Some would keep me trotting round the parish all day: some, (who have no servant perhaps) would require me to scrub floors. He knows of one priest, moreover, who celebrates Mass daily, and requires some one to say 'amen' in the consecration prayer since it is uncanonical to have <u>no</u> congregation.

On the other hand, however, it is a post not easily procured, and they are easily 'snapped up'. About £20. a year might be given, or less than that if <u>coaching</u> is required.

Mr. Robson would be pleased to frame an advertisement for me in the *Churchman*[1] or some such paper, if we like the proposal.

What do you think?

Parish work would not be by any means uncongenial to me, and as I suppose, far less worrying than teaching. And I could render myself 'companionable' to anyone if at all literary-inclined. But everything depends upon the kind of person the parson is.

Which risk shall I take then—(1) <u>borrowing money</u> (supposing such available—from E.Q.[2] Esq.—and why not?) and thus sail with a fair wind to B.A. or (2) put myself at the mercy of a reverend man, who may be exacting, eccentric, intolerant and all that?

I mentioned my scheme of getting a thorough knowledge of French in France, and he considered it a very good thing, but far better if a <u>degree</u> be obtained first. A year or two in France after that, and I should be worth <u>something</u>.

I am to go to see him again on Wednesday afternoon; and to play tennis with another priest who is staying at the Vicarage—a Mr. Thackrah,[3] who, in his purple socks, looks about as <u>secular</u> as the 'secularest' of laymen. I was asked to be prepared for tennis today, but it rained. One Allwright, however, was there, helping Rev. Mr. Thackrah to pass the afternoon at tennis. So we four bachelors had afternoon tea in the drawing room. The comfort afforded by the luxurious arm-chairs however, was somewhat impaired by the fact that we held our cups in our hands and had no plates. Nevertheless Mr. Robson, by his humorous stories, made us so much at home that I remained per-fectly placid and imperturbable when I dropped a large portion of cake into my unfortunate tea-cup. No liquid escaped the cup, and I am firmly

---

cured by a trip round the world. And, when he died, a biretta and signed portrait of Leo XIII were found buried beneath a mountain of evangelical divinity. He must have been a particular protégé of Edward King, for he went and stayed with him at Lincoln for his enthronement. One interest of the first half of my uncle's life was genealogy; and he printed a pedigree of the family in Crispe's *Visitations* series. But after he had been some years at Dunsden, he changed into a strong evangelical, and gave a family living to a protestant trust, although his sisters were still living in the parish. But in later life he mellowed considerably, and was always pleased to see me, although I was Curate at St. Barnabas, Oxford; and we discussed ecclesiastical affairs (and even his "unregenerate" past) amiably enough.'

[1] Founded 1879, and still published regularly.
[2] Edward Quayle.
[3] The Rev. M. W. Thackrah.

convinced that I succeeded in conveying (by degrees) the soppy blobs of dough into my mouth without my host suspecting it; and thinking me a bounder. That most or all elem- teachers are bounders is his unshaken faith. During our conversation in the study I had asked, 'Am I then to avoid elem^{ty}. teaching ?' He screwed up his visage, raised his hands, turned aside his head, and murmured 'AS PITCH!!' Now I have often touched pitch and not been defiled, but too much handling has always resulted in defilement. Hence in answer to the question 'Can a man touch pitch and not be defiled ?' I reply—'Certainly, for a certain length of time.'

Moral : If I don't want to be defiled I must drop the pitch with all speed.

Another power has sprung up to hold me in Shrewsbury.—'Uriconium is to be excavated in the near future.' according to Mr. Colyer.

Awaiting your reply to this budget before Wednesday (if you get it in time), including Father's opinion of course,

I am, Your own Wilfred

84. To Susan Owen
Postcard

23 June 1911   *Alpenrose*

I have chosen the 3 o'clock train on Sat. to carry me back to Scrobbesbyrig, where I expect to set foot on the nineteenth minute after seven.

The lights from 10 Bonfires could be seen from here last night.[1] I have written to Miss W. and Miss J.

Glad you are satisfied with the Result. Went to see Mr. Wigan this morning with Leslie as an introducer. I can only say here that he is a most delightful parson, and what he has said may or may not come to anything.

We stayed 'lunch', at which was another cleric, and Mr. Kemp,[2] who is the assistant of Mr. Wigan, and whom I choose to consider as my mortal enemy and rival, for reasons which you may guess.

W

85. To Susan Owen
Postcard

[*Postmark 9 September 1911*]   [*Wimbledon*]

Have arrived[3] in safety and good time, i.e. for meeting G.,[4] for he was at Paddie before me! My box came at tea-time. Unluckily the

---

[1] They celebrated the coronation of George V, 22 June 1911.

[2] The Rev. Alfred George Saxelby-Kemp was ordained in 1914 and went to Holy Trinity, Kilburn. For his recollections of Wilfred, see p. 91, note 3.

[3] Wilfred had arrived in London to take the London University Matriculation examination, for which he had been working while a pupil-teacher at the Wyle Cop School. The examinations were held in the Imperial Institute in Kensington. He stayed at 'Glenmore', 38 Worple Road, Wimbledon, a private school a short walk from the Gunstons' house in Clement Road.

[4] Gordon Gunston.

Goldsmith book, having much liberty in the box, has been doing a jig on the journey and got severely kicked by the boots which took the same liberty. Many of H's instruments[1] also lodged themselves in sundry corners, but my own preferred to lie still—thanks to your moving them.

Gordon is anxious to come with me to Cheshunt.[2]—on Sat. aft. next.

W

86. To Harold Owen

First sheet missing

[9 September 1911]   [Wimbledon]

Leslie sees a good deal of me just now. He brings me Novels and Poems and Sketches from his own pen quite often. They all have merit.

I wonder whether you ever try to draw a human face? I never remember seeing anything of yours above this stage

or at most this?

You must tell me what you do—and send me things when you can. I shall be interested to see how much improved is the '2nd Cottage' on the 1st; which I will not deny will bear improvement.

Has the 'Rev. Dodd' appropriated your Abbey Interior yet? Leslie has started work for the Senior under the Normal.

Just tell Mother, I don't want any money yet: but in my next will explain and will try to blow off a quantity of collecting gas to her, with which my bosom is already inflated.

Remember me to—anybody you think needs it.

Take my Blessing, and forget not all my promised benefits.

Your applauding Bro. Wilfred

[1] HO's set of compasses, dividers, etc., lent for the examinations. See Letter 92.
[2] Nellie, referred to in Letter 90 as living in Cheshunt, was to be visited. She was formerly a maid at Plas Wilmot, Oswestry, where Susan Owen and her sisters grew up, and may figure in the photograph reproduced as Plate Ib.

87. To Susan Owen
Postcard

Mond. [Postmark 11 September 1911]   *Glenmore, Worple Rd.*
                                                                    Wimbledon

Have just got home from the 'English'. Am fairly confident of a pass
in this; Wrote an essay, on 'The Ideal English King'.[1]

The Clerk at Waterloo B'kng Office told me the Ticket Order was
not signed—so I signed it on the spot, and, when I got here, all the
others too.

Thought <u>I</u> was the applicant, not Father! Have I left my comb at
home?

W

88. To Susan Owen

[12 or 13 September 1911]   *The Doldrums, Seven-times-heated—*
                                                —Furnace Road, Dumpshire

Ah me! What a time! The heat has been simply appalling during
every exam so far! And what with the excitement and the four hundred
roasting bodies jammed around me my brains have been spluttering in
my head. As a proof that it was not all <u>mental</u> heat, I may say that the
Vigilators kept on flapping their foreheads, and taking great breaths
and snatching whiffs of air at the open door as often as they could.

Not only did a morning like this melt the crystal sharpness of my
wits, but it gave me a strong revulsion to any [food], but I conquered
this rebellion of the lower man and went to the Imperial Restaurant.

Perhaps it is a good thing the weather has been so oppressive, it will
be a really good excuse in case of 'Found Wanting.'

Have I passed? I <u>do</u> think so! even in Arith. & Geometry. At least I
have done enough right to score pass marks. I might have left hours of
work untouched for the last few weeks for all the good it's done me in
<u>this paper</u>. But of course all that will come in for the <u>next attempt</u> (?)
. . .

As I was asking for the Institute at Kensington, a young gent. from
Cheltenham overheard me, and immediately asked me if our destinations
were the same. I saw him again & he says he has certainly failed, having
been sent to sleep (mentally) by the oppressive atmosphere; and so did
about 2 questions only.

Was asked by a gent. in Restaurant if I was a Matric. Candidate. He
said he had been in a few years ago & failed hopelessly first time, but
passed at the next. Showed him the papers & he pronounced them harder
than in his day. Did not see my Chelsea friend this morning but instead
—for I conceal nothing from you—I was spotted as a Candidate by a
young lady who was in mortal terror of being transported to the other

[1] See p. 80, note 3.

79

side of London by those wretched District trains, and accordingly I acted the part of Sydney Carton to the poor Seamstress.[1]

The entrance hall or cloak room is nothing but a horrid stuffy vault, where for half an hour the boys stand waiting packed like sardines. I could have thought myself in the Black Hole of Calcutta, especially as there was a fair sprinkling of black faces among us, and a pompous old Rajah of an Examiner—gorgeous in his silken hoods—came glaring at us from over a barred gate on the staircase. This gate was at last opened, and then followed a maddening rush up the stairs, which changed in a moment to a death-like stillness when we entered the vast Hall of Torture. For all its solemnity, I could not help being tickled by the sight of a learned-looking parson, past the middle age, sitting in his little desk and scratting away at his paper under the stern gaze of a fair young graduate very much like Miss Wright!

All of the men seem much older than I expected, many of them remind me of say Dr. Simpson.[2]

Many thanks for your letter.

I am, as you may guess, very lighthearted, and really am enjoying the high spirits which always connote low marks.

Slept very soundly, too, last night.

Love in abundance—like the rain which has just begun.   W[3]

89. To Susan Owen

14 September 1911   *Wimbledon*

Dearest Mother,

Just this moment had your letter—have been home from the last and grand Finale only half an hour.

Did a really excellent paper in French; and a most satisfactory in History—accomplished 25 foolscap pages!

According to today's work I ought to get a 1st. easily.[4] Alas I am not so sure of Botany! We had two apples each and a Gladiolus. Why didn't we grow Gladiolus instead of those stupid Monbretia's! Well, I made a very fine longitudinal section, and after much cogitation hit upon the natural order to which it belonged. But in the stress of having 5 more ques. to do forgot to write it down! Moreover the rest of the paper was not easy at all. Again, Gordon lazily forgot to bring my lenses which I ordered, and I had to take a miserable big reading-glass of Mrs. Lea's.[5] Not much good of course. AGAIN, dinner was so late,

---

[1] Charles Dickens, *A Tale of Two Cities*.

[2] The family doctor in Shrewsbury.

[3] These lines, struck out and EXCUSE written across them, follow: 'to set at liberty a prisoner who, in a drunken fit, had railed against the King's person. Scroop eagerly advised that the man should be punished, "Lest his example should breed more of such kind".' This may be an extract from Wilfred's essay (see previous letter) 'The Ideal English King'.

[4] But he did not do as well as he had hoped. See p. 254, note 1, and *JO* I, pp. 251–2, for an account of his reception of the news of his 'mere Pass'.

[5] Headmistress of the school in Worple Road at which Wilfred was lodging.

and I had to gobble down some cold meat wh. gave me indigestion for the rest of the afternoon.

The Answers to Maths. Ques. were given us all this morning by my Tutors. I have got quite enough right to pass! Wonderful, isn't it! On second thoughts am really doubtful of the English! in which I have done some unaccountable things I feel sure.

My Cheltenham College friend has not got a single one right in Arith. & Alg. Saw him for the last time today,—without saying good-bye or asking his name. Only saw one boy who took Botany. He is at Merchant Taylors' School.

How do you think I am spotted as a Candidate? Simply by the marks by which I spot other people—viz. I am bristling with rulers and pens and pencils, and not because my hair bristles with fright. I do feel so sad it's all over. That the noble Six Hundred can no more meet again, than did the Six Hundred after Balaclava—this is one of the trivial melancholies, in which I steep myself rather than brood overmuch on the awful possibility—which, to make things worse, you will not admit.

Many, many thanks for the Testament.

Miss Jones[1] will be at Finchley after Monday, she tells me on a cheering card, and asks me to go and see her.

A letter from Nellie[2] has come for Gordon with yours, settling our visit for Sat. afternoon. This is very nice: I really did not want to stay the night unless I went to Hoddesdon.

Goodbye—it's all over in a second—as Dr. Gray[3] said before he lanced me. I will tell you now, though I have spared to tell you before, that the abscess is not 'right' yet. No swelling in the cheek—but small lumps on both sides of the gum. This has caused me no pain but only apprehension lest the pain should suddenly come on and send me distraught.

Your loving Wilfred

90. To Susan Owen

17 September 1911   *Wimbledon*

My dearest Mother,

As Gordon is going to Kidmore on Sat., and as that day will just complete my fortnight here, I think I shall even stay on till then. For I have not half accomplished my sight-seeing and holy-ground-treading, as you will see from the following summary:

Friday—British Museum: spent some hours there in subdued ecstasy —reading two letters of J.K's and two books of manuscript poems (open at 'Eve of St. Mark' & 'Hyperion') which, of course, show all his corrections and crossings out.

These and the letters must form the subject of many a discourse to my dear willing Hearer, but I will note a few things—'before I forget'— I was going to say, but I can never do that.—At the side of the title

---

[1] Miss Jones had left the Shrewsbury Technical School, and was now teaching in Finchley.
[2] See p. 78, note 2.
[3] The Gunstons' doctor in Wimbledon.

to 'St. Mark's Eve' (unfinished) he has drawn an <u>ivy leaf</u> (not very like one, and it would shock Prof. Cavers)[1]—this of course while going round and round his subject and not knowing where or how to begin. Even then he made a false start, and struck out several lines. His writing is rather large and slopes like mine—<u>not at all</u> old fashioned and sloping as Shelley's is. He also has my <u>trick of not</u> joining letters in a word. Otherwise it is unlike anybodies' I know, and yet I seem to be strangely familiar with it. It is none too precisely formed—a proof that he is thinking of nothing but the matter and not of himself and his pen. The letters are to Fanny (i.e. the <u>sister</u>) but, poor fellow, he can't keep the name of Brawne out of it! I was <u>highly</u> jealous of other people seeing this at first, but was nevertheless gratified when various <u>French</u> visitors seemed familiar with his name!

Other manuscripts there are in abundance—Scott is absolutely illegible. George Eliot, Shelley, Milton, Byron, Tennyson, Browning, etc. are all represented. In the afternoon I drifted into the audience of the newly-appointed free lecturer, who conducted a party all round the Mummy- and Egyptian-Rooms.

On Sat. morning I went to Hampton Court by tram: more of this later. Got home in time to join Gordon [*several words illegible*]

Hence we made our way to L'pool St. and so to Cheshunt at about 4 p.m. Spent the time very pleasantly in recalling our reminiscences of the common fountain-head of our existences, known by all as the 'old Home'.[2] Nelly has also an album of very old photographs of the family in which Gordon was very interested.

Today, mng. and evening, have listened with delight to Mr. Moore. For tomorrow, I have luckily one more S. Kensington Ticket. I shall then be blocked, unless more arrive in time. I want Orders on District Rly: to the following stations:

(1) Wim[ldn] to Westminster
(1)   ,,   ,, Mark Lane.
(3)   ,,   ,, Charing Cross.
and on <u>Hampstead Rly</u>:
(1) <u>C</u>haring Cross to Hampstead

_____

(*Monday*) Am off to S. Kensington this morning. In the matter of *Macbeth*[3] I am again between two fires. On the very same afternoon, the Benson Co.[4] are giving in Wimbledon *Henry V*, which I have read, and learnt, and spouted these last two years. Depend upon it, whichever Fire indraws me, I shall but extract the brilliance and fervour of the flames, and shall come out unscathed. I think *Macbeth* will shall be the one, expecially as I have seen *Punch*'s Criticism on the same,[5] this week.

[1] Unidentified.   [2] Plas Wilmot.
[3] A production opened at His Majesty's on 5 September 1911 with Beerbohm Tree and Violet Vanbrugh.
[4] The company founded by Sir Frank Benson (1858–1939), actor-manager.
[5] A mixed review. The production seemed notable only for 'the extraordinary reality of the scenery'.

Am keeping well, except for the gum, and my nose, which is, like Bardolph's, 'all barbukles and whelks, and knobs and flames of fire!'[1]

Your own Wilfred

Love to Mary and me brethren twain. Had a card from Stanley.[2] No time for more now. I must apply to myself the nerve-lacerating speech of the pompous vigilator, when every exam was almost over—

Laydeezanjenulmun, You have abow-oot Five Minutes Maw!

91. To Susan Owen

20 September 1911   *Wimbledon*

Dearest Mother,

Have just returned from *Macbeth*. My pleasure has been completely marred by a most trying circumstance:—I had to stand the whole time. Though I was in the queue 1¼ hrs. before the time, every seat was taken when I got in, i.e. every seat under 5s. or 10/6 and these had to be booked. Hearing and seeing were therefore quite difficult at times; and, having promenaded the National Gallery all morning, I had much the same feeling as used to overtake me at the 'Cop'[3] of amiable memory, towards the end of the day. Hence I never 'lost consciousness' in the sense that I should have liked to have done; though two ladies close to me, also standing, lost consciousness in a very disagreeable way, and both dropped like logs simultaneously to earth.

The scenes in the witches' cave were simply marvellous, and quite took the breath out of the audience. At no time, however, was I so moved by the acting, as I was moved earlier in the day by a lifeless face-mask and a painted canvas. This was none other than a mould of Keats's face taken during life, so that of him as of no other writer, I and the world may gain a true idea of the countenance! Two paintings of his 'extraordinary beauty' are also there.—One of the whole figure, painted by Severn in Rome, after his Friend's death! Of this, of course, I have bought a copy, which you, as I hope, will be most anxious to see. It represents him in the Hampstead House. I have not yet been there, but have fixed Friday for this, the last of my 'sermons in stone'. On this day Miss Jones has asked me to Finchley, which I can easily reach from the Heath. For tomorrow, therefore, there is the Tower, or Westminster & St. Paul's, and maybe another peep into the National Gallery at some other Faces there, which have woven a spell over me. I must not begin to describe or to name even the pictures hanging there, and must stop not for 'lack of argument', but for sheer excess of matter.

Your own loving Wilfred

Thank you for this morning's parcel and letter: its newsiness and its assurance of Mary's good-health. Have you written to Mrs. Timpany?

[1] *Henry V*, III. vi. 110.
[2] Stanley Webb. The Webbs were a Shrewsbury family, whose children were friendly with the Owens. Stanley was killed in France in March 1918.
[3] Wyle Cop School.

92. To Harold Owen

20 September 1911   [*Wimbledon*]

Dear Harold,

Such was the effect of receiving so unexpected a card from you, and such the imperative force of the underlining, that I <u>immediately</u> sent off your compasses. I hope that you got them in time. I have thought much of you today, and during the week. I mean when I have been gladdening my eyes by the sights of works of Art,—of sculptures, and buildings, and portraits. So that now more than ever seems Art a noble profession, and to have a brother now fairly launched out upon its wide stream is enough to make me proud indeed. In my present state, I could wish for no better choice of profession for you than this; and then my only wishes for you will be Skill, Sense, and Success. Study the Fine, Strive for Finesse, and Strike the First, and you <u>will do</u>—you must . . .

So far I have seen no Galleries of <u>Design</u> (they are at S. Kensington, I think), but I wish you [could] have seen with me the loveliest of Designs,—the human face,[1] as drawn by the greatest artists. I was so rapt in gazing at one of these today, that I kenned not of a human Toe belonging to a lady behind me, and made a sudden retrograde motion which brought my heel upon it—much to the confusion of both parties.

To return to the serious, I wished you could have seen the marvellous <u>sketches</u> both in oil and pencils of people's heads. I wondered if <u>you</u> would <u>ever, ever</u> rise to the supreme height of—<u>mastery in Portraiture</u>.

Has Mr. Dane[2] supped with you yet? Thank you for your last letter and its very pointed birthday message. It has at least pricked my memory as to your <u>advancing age</u>, to which I begin to think I have been for some years <u>forgetful</u>. Soothly, I must now treat you—as I have begun to in this letter—as a responsible individual arrived at years of discretion, and as a schoolboy no longer. Indeed I must endeavour to cultivate your acquaintance [*one or two words missing, the corner of the sheet being torn away*]

Best wishes for a prosperous & happy Term,

Your loving brother, Wilfred

93. To Susan Owen]

25 September 1911   *Alpenrose*

My own dear Mother,

I joined Gordon at Padd. and came up in his train, <u>and compartment</u>, —tho' to precious little advantage, for he hardly addressed a word to me, being now engrossed in reading every scrap of news concerning <u>Ocean Liners</u> and—<u>the Queen</u>. He is quite enamoured with Her Majesty;

---

[1] Wilfred had visited the National Portrait Gallery earlier in the day.

[2] The assistant master at the Shrewsbury School of Art, where HO was a pupil. See *JO* I, pp. 204–5.

and the old Engine-Crank has not died out, but has re-developed as a Ship-Craze.

When we got outside Reading Sta. Gordon half-expected to find some Conveyance—but such not appearing, he imparted to me the necessity of pedestrianism; and like the returning animal, made a decided bolt for home. I, having flitted among the shades of the National Gallery all morning, and having been temperate in my lunch to a fault, soon began to feel as if I had to cross the very Andes—or perish in the attempt. I managed, indeed, by dint of constant reminders, to check the giant's strides, but after the second hill, had already begun to experience that 'chokey' feeling about the throat, which bodes ill to him who has long miles in front. But by a chance, which you and I know to be NO CHANCE, a young man, (whose name Gordon did not even know) overtook us with a trap, and drove us from Emmer Green,[1] as if by arrangement. What ills this has saved me from I know not, for Miss Jones tells me I do not look at all well. I merely say this to prevent you from being disappointed in me next week: I feel better than ever, for all that! Auntie's ankles are no better, but she will potter about, and was in the kitchen making mushroom pickle this morning. I am beginning to wonder how you are, not having heard news for some days.

We went to Kidmore Church on Sunday morning, and to Dunsden in the evening, but Mr. Wigan was away! Mr. Robson met us going into Church, and said to me 'You'll deserve tremendous credit if you do get through (Matric).' And in the evening he appointed Uncle & me to take lunch with him at the Vicarage, that I might show him my papers. We went. With—affected or sincere—modesty he confesses that he could not have passed in English—I don't think!

Leslie has a convenient return of the malady which attacked him in Shrewsbury, and, tho' he could yesterday walk twice to Church cannot ride to school to-day. I hope, for the sake of certain Reading which I have in view, that he will before long recover his cycling capabilities.

In view of my disappointment with *Macbeth*, I made so bold as to see my old favourites the Bensons in the *Tempest*. The performance, for divers reasons, was, and is, a pure delight. But my sins do follow me, and I'll be 'suspended' (to use a paraphrased version of my reverend host's expression this morning) if the Company hasn't tracked their sometime patron to Reading!

I spent a most delightful evening with Miss Jones, and was so wrapped up in the flow of eloquence that passed between us, that I only reached home a quarter before mid-night. We talked chiefly—Scandal. I have at last had my eyes opened to the despicable, nefarious, yea, detestable character of a certain Master of Science, known, but heretofore but half-known, to both. You must not ask me any questions on this subject, please! Nor must you repeat this.

[1] Half-way between Reading Station and Kidmore End.

We were so sorry not to have Father here, after all. Give my love to him, and thank him for the many 'Privileges' he has conferred upon me(!)

Your own loving Wilfred

Tues. Have just had your letters. I want (1) No underclothes. (2) No Telegram!

94. To Colin Owen

26 September 1911   *Alpenrose*

My dear Colin,

I was very pleased to have your letter, and have real pleasure in answering it. As for my head, you may be sure it is not busting with knowledge, for that was squeezed out of it upon certain sheets of paper, now enshrined in one of the grandest buildings of the greatest city on earth. Consequently, when a vacuum began to be formed, a 'cold' flooded in, for I never could be empty-headed. This, indeed, makes my brain-bag feel as if it would go bang if you hit it. But the fair breezes which are blowing up here should soon make me better—as I am glad to hear you are.

I have spent a good part of this morning picking mushrooms which abound in these fields. I said Father would like some, and a tin box has been filled with the best ones, and will soon find its way to Mahim. There are four fine turkeys now. They walk just about as awkwardly as I do on the polished floors here. This reminds me that at the Tate Gallery where the floors are just the same, a middle-aged lady came a cropper close to me. To add to her discomfort, an official came up with a note-book and pencil asking her name and address! 'Yes'm' I heard him say, 'We tikes the nimes of all lidies as slips dahn in the gelries.' Pore thing! You know I like London, but it worries me when I get into a 'bus or train where women are talking, because I could believe that it was full of nothing but Mrs. Raggs![1] I did not go to the wax-works. Nor did I find time for the Tower. But I spent a whole day at Kew, where every tree is ticketed; and all the plants have names attached. In the green-houses I saw pitcher-plants with wasps caught in them—some alive and buzzing, but trapped, and never to escape!

This morning I was awakened at quarter past seven by Uncle calling me to see the huntsmen, who were in the wood just opposite. Leslie and I stood on the window-sill of our bedroom in our pyjamas and wrapped the rosy curtains round our selves like woodland nymphs. But we saw no fox. This evening, we had a supper supposed to be of mushrooms, but the whole quantity was contained in a gravy tureen, and they were done in the daftest way imaginable, and tasted like boot-polish mixed with warm water.

[1] The Ragges and their two children, John and Mary, lived near the Owens, and were much liked. John was later killed in France. See *JO* III, pp. 106–7.

Since supper, and while I have been writing this, Leslie has had me out eight times in succession to see a new comet.

This is the second visible now[1]. The first may be seen with the naked eye; it has a faint tail. You will find it if you can understand this 'heavenly' map (!)

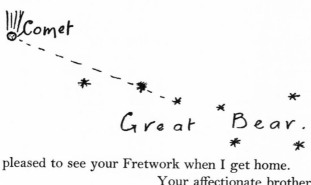

Shall be pleased to see your Fretwork when I get home.

Your affectionate brother, Wilfred

95. To Susan Owen

28 September 1911   *Alpenrose*

My dearest Mother,

I had your very welcome letter this morning. Leslie and I walked to Dunsden yesterday, only to find the Vicar in London for the day. He had gone by Auntie's train, and they saw him at Padd. and he appointed us to go to tea today. We played croquet most of the time, and once again put off finalities till 'another day'. This is to be as soon as I hear the Result. But I told him that my wants would be the same, whether I pass or fail. And he reminded me, that his offer still holds. Really, I am even more charmed with the Vicarage than ever, and nothing but the uncertainty as to the amount of Work—scholastic or parish that I should accomplish there, would prevent me from going—since it seems the time is ripe for me to wrench myself from Home.

Miss Jones urged me, if I pass, to state my case to the Registrar of L'pool or London University, and try for a three years' course, which under 'the Scholarship', will cost only £40 for the whole time. Living would be in a Hostel. Our old enemy, 'the Obligations', would certainly include such a school as Miss Jones is now at; i.e. Secondary. Further information would of course be supplied, if I wrote to the "Varsity". I shall at least do this, if . . . (?)

I think to stay on till the Intimation comes, then. 'Tis awfully near at hand—I feel its shadow upon me. But I am not a prey to doubts and fears on this matter: my mind is filled with cogitation and perplexities and despondencies which spring from deeper depths than that.

---

[1] Two new comets were seen in 1911. Quenisset's Comet, first sighted 29 September, and Brook's Comet, discovered 31 July and easily visible to the naked eye on 23 September.

May I quote you a sentence of a Poet—(need I name which?) that is marvellously expressive of what I want to say:

'The imagination of a boy is healthy, and the mature imagination of a man is healthy; but there is a space of life between in which the soul is in a ferment, the character undecided, the way of life uncertain, (yes!), and the ambition thick-sighted (yes indeed!)'[1]

Well, I am prosing instead of giving News—which seems to be the main intendment of the Letter in these days. Herbert Billing[2] is coming on Tues, to rest after his exam; but I need not turn out on that account.

Mrs. Lea charged the same as for Gordon: my accompt was therefore 30s. Thank you for the Convention Notice; Auntie knows Mr. Buchanan; he is a great friend of the Sharwoods'.[3]

I am already feeling a touch of Nostalgia (consult dictionary). What if it becomes chronic in the Future?

Your own Wilfred

96. To Mary Owen

3 October 1911   [Alpenrose]

Dear Mary,

Thank you for your note. What an achievement for a school[4] to double its numbers in one term! Shall be interested to see the new half of the establishment. (Is it called Monkmoor Academy or Monkmore Acadamy, though?)

I have been collecting seeds of various kinds from the garden and have got some hundreds of laburnums. My days are absolutely uneventful. I am reading *Our Mutual Friend* among other things.

Hardly any signs of Autumn are yet to be seen in the trees here. Hope you are making a last spurt with your Botany, before old winter grabs the materials from you.

Hope you are feeling better, dear.

Would you like me to bring you for your own lawful and undisputed possession a Book in Everyman's Library, called *Tales from Chaucer*?[5] There are now 600 and more volumes! Leslie has got an appetite for books—bound in this Edition—and I think its high time I got one. This book is just out, and recommends itself to me, (and therefore will to you) as being written by the son of the schoolmaster of a great hero of mine, who was also a great and valuable friend of the said hero.

Your affectionate brother, Wilfred

[1] From the Preface to *Endymion*.
[2] A Wimbledon solicitor, friend of the Gunston family. See Letter 353.
[3] Mr. Sharwood was Managing Director of J. A. Sharwood and Co., makers of Green Label Chutney. They were Wimbledon acquaintances of the Gunstons, and a Christmas hamper of Sharwood products arrived each year at Kidmore End.
[4] An infant school in Monkmoor Road, Shrewsbury, conducted by Miss Goodwin.
[5] No. 537 in the Everyman Library (J. M. Dent, 1911). The editor was Charles Cowden Clarke, son of Keats's close friend.

DUNSDEN AND AFTER

1911–1913

97. To Susan Owen
Postcard
20 October 1911   *Dunsden Vicarage*

Have arrived safely. Was met at Station by Mr. Wigan, who had been down to see Mr. Lewty[1] off just before. Met Uncle (riding)[2] on Caversham Bridge—but did not stop. My boxes will come up by 6 this evening. It is quite fine here now (i.e. the weather), but everything seems to be <u>fine</u> too!

                                                                    W

98. To Susan Owen
23 October 1911   *Dunsden Vicarage*

My dearest Mother,
    It is about time that I began to give you some account of my mode of life here. First as to the premises. The house is even larger than I ever thought—two staircases—and quite a labyrinth of passages upstairs. My bedroom is quite large, and handsomely furnished—containing a bureau and a wardrobe (which one might make a home of) as well as the usual appointments. The chamber is softly carpeted. Mysterious ministering spirits keep the room in order, for surprising things happen, though I have never seen a living wight therein. Thus—every night I find my pyjamas scrupulously laid out upon the coverlet in exactly that position in which it is easiest to put them on!
    At seven every morning a meek voice announces to the noble sir that his shaving water waits outside. Presently the noble sir deigns to rise—but 'uneasy is the head that lies on Down', for it has to wash in a silly pot of a basin, the bathroom being somehow connected with Mr. Wigan's room, and therefore unused. Having then moistened as it were his boiley neck in soap-solution, his lordship applies to it a towel like a white Turkish carpet, and then selects his suit. At the stroke of the awe-inspiring gong, he takes a large chair on one side of the fire, in the dining room, with Mr. Kemp[3] on the other, the Vicar at the table, and the domestics sitting in respectful admiration in a row at the end of the room. After prayers the said admiring domestics withdraw, and breakfast is

---

[1] The Rev. Walter Lewty (ordained 1903), Vicar of Rowston, Lincolnshire.

[2] Uncle John Gunston rode a tricycle.

[3] The Rev. Alfred Saxelby-Kemp remembers Wilfred: 'I liked him, and thought him pleasant and clever, a natural student (unlike me). Mr. Wigan had a soft spot for him. I had no idea that he was writing poetry, though I do remember that he wrote home a good deal. He had a room on the first floor; I had an attic room, but a study downstairs to myself as well. The house and garden were run smoothly and expensively; the servants were very good. Wigan was rather lordly, and I remember the village women curtseying to him; but he took little interest in the parish, and rarely seemed to go out. He was a silent, reserved, rather prosy man, always bringing out the same three standard jokes at dinner when anyone came to stay. I remember most the awful evening silences. I was homesick, watching the smoke of the London trains in the valley. It was all very quiet, and very dull.'

taken, when (as in all meals) his noble highness brandishes the bread-knife, and dispenses his cuttings as required.

Left alone, and with something of my gravity thrown off, I then set to work at a bureau-bookcase in the dining room till lunch. This afternoon the Vicar took me with him visiting, till afternoon tea. Then dinner at 7.30. of such things as jugged hare!

On Sat. we went to the Prayer Meeting in the Hall, where I read the Portion—to less than a dozen people only! On that afternoon I went to Alpenrose, but Auntie was out and I had tea alone with Leslie. There is a pony, but his only work is to pump the water from a deep well to the housetop, by a circular movement, just like the elephantine pigo-ox in the Chinese Scroll.[1] The garden is still very beautiful.

In fact every [thing] is on the scale of a fine country <u>manor</u>, and my
or
only sorrow is that you are not in a like man(ner) established!

Mr. Kemp is very pleasant indeed; thoroughly enjoying his parochial work, if not so much his studies; and, I believe, he is well liked about the parish. His exam.[2] is in December. He has already failed (twice I think), tho' he has no very advanced work, so far as I can see.

I will say nothing about dear Mr. Wigan. I never do sketch the characters of those on a higher plane than myself. But I was much enlightened concerning certain doubts in my mind when he talked of literary people at dinner today. He is a sixth cousin of the great William Morris! has heard Ruskin lecture!! was introduced to Holman Hunt!!!

Furthermore, is thoroughly at home in Dickens' country in Kent!! read Romola <u>in Florence</u> overlooking Ponte Vecchia!! was acquainted with the original of Sam Weller! and other Characters!

Other revelations may come out later! (Oh, also, he has dined with Marconi.) Do not think, however, that my admiration of him is vastly raised by all this, though it is somewhat, you may guess! I know, indeed, certain unlovely minds who would be shocked to hear him take any interest in these matters.

I have written to Torquay. I am anxiously looking forward to the time when I can present these new surroundings to you, and you to them, and when I can present to you my cheeks for the good-night kiss which I so much miss. Love to Father & all the stay-at-homes, with 'heaps and loads' for You.   W

99. To Susan Owen

31 October 1911   *Dunsden Vicarage*

My dearest Mother,

I find my weekly epistle is overdue, so I will forthwith set upon this pleasant task.

---

[1] The Chinese scroll on which this splendid creature appeared had been presented to the Owens by a missionary returned from China.

[2] The entrance examination for St. John's Hall, the London College of Divinity, then at Highbury and now at Northwood.

I took the address to Children on Thurs. in the Hall, did minor parts at the Prayer Meeting on Saturdays, and have been visiting several times. Other duties than these, I cannot find, except the very important one of talking at meals and in the evening. Dead silence sometimes prevails, which Mr. Kemp (Brother Kemp) is sometimes powerless to break; Brother Lewty used even to talk nonsense for the sake of saying something, Kemp tells me! However, I don't think this is the case now. After dinner we sit round the study fire till bed-time, (about 11 to 11.30); during which time poor Kemp is on pins and needles, I imagine, feeling he ought to be at his Greek. Generally the Vicar reads to us about the Irish Revival of 1859. Then, instead of family prayers as was formerly the custom, we have a private prayer meeting every evening. The Vicar has the hope of a Revival in the place much on his mind, during these times.

On Wednesday, the Vicar took me to a Bible Society Meeting at Henley. (For this, I gave up going to a lecture in French for which Leslie offered me a Ticket). Never was at a B.S. Meeting before. Most entertaining concerns I find. Vicar says he never was at a Bible Soc. meeting where there was so much humour! Dr. Dunn[1] gave a really fine address on its work. You must get him at Shrewsbury. My tyre went flat on the way, and we were somewhat late. But the Vicar was quite glad, for he didn't want to be elevated to the platform. Henley Town Hall is new, and (therefore) beautiful. The staircase is of pure marble every whit, and what with a statue of Hermes at the top, and strains of delicious music floating about, I could have imagined it a Greek Temple.[2] This was while we were waiting alone to enter the meeting hall. There was, as I have said, some musical concert at the same time, and, when Vicar asked the attendant the way to the meeting, the man looked first at him in his frowsy old habiliments, and then at me in my most unbiblical garb, and was fain to enquire—'Which meetin' may it be, sir?'

Last evening I went to a lecture on Charles Lamb, by Prof. Sir Walter Raleigh(!)[3]; in Univ. College Hall—with Leslie. Paid only 6d. for a splendid seat. The lecture was good, but the lecturer but so so. Next fortnight there's one on Radium. These will beat your Abbey Forgates[4] for abstruseness and refinement, if not for humour, too, for F. C. Gould[5] gives one on Caricature next week.

I have got U.C.C.[6] some books almost new, at second hand price (half price) in Reading! Will you please cause enquiries to be made for

[1] The Rev. J. W. Bradney Dunne, Deputation-Assistant of the Bible Society 1898–1913.
[2] The Town Hall was built 1900–1. The only statue is that of a coloured lady known locally as The Black Widow; the Town Clerk of Henley on Thames tells us that there has never been a statue of Hermes at the head of the main staircase.
[3] Sir Walter Raleigh (1861–1922) was Professor of English Literature at Oxford from 1904 and a Delegate of the Oxford University Press.
[4] A fashionable road within the precincts of the Abbey Church, Shrewsbury.
[5] Sir Francis Carruthers Gould (1844–1925), the cartoonist who edited his own paper *Picture Politics* from 1894–1914 and was knighted in 1906.
[6] The University Correspondence College, founded at Cambridge in 1887.

my *Modern Eng. Lit.* at Wilding's,[1] before you come? I am hardly expecting a Latin Bible from the Gleaning's People. Am not very satisfied with the hymn, which I sent just in time, yesterday. I prefer indeed original compositions to linguistical competitions.[2]

I spent yesterday evening at Alpenrose with Dorothy, etc. Saw Gordon at Church on Sunday, with Auntie [*three words illegible*] I have not yet got my parcel; but expect to today.

So glad you are coming so soon. The Vicar asked when next you were coming, before I had said anything, and of course said that you must come over. I will try and meet you, you may be sure. I must get my features into training for a Photograph![3] Love to Father, Mary, etc.

> Your loving, Wilfred

Thank Harold for his honest attempts to get my hair off. Luckily, some miles intervene between us, or I should have tweaked his nose for it, i.e. if I could get a grip of the thing.

100. To Mary Owen

7 November 1911   *Dunsden Vicarage*

My dear Sister,

Mother told me you would like me to write to you while she is here; and I am indeed pleased to cover a few sheets of this my Tablet for your benefit.

Mother has not been over here yet. Perhaps she is coming on Friday. But she came to church on Sunday Morning.

I addressed the Children's Service in the Parish Hall on Sunday Afternoon. I am also booked for the Scripture Union on Thurs. I enjoy speaking very much. I use no notes, and spend no great time in preparation; but I use no high falutin' words, but try to express myself in simple, straightforward English. I believe the children are impressed for the time being. I hope they will really benefit, for, of course, I give them the Messages, with one Purpose, and not with any idea of displaying my own bumptiousness.

Yesterday, the Vicar took me & Mr. Kemp to hear an address by Bishop Ingham,[4] at Earley Court,[5] the fine residence of some of the Suttons' Seeds people. I was introduced to the Bishop, and spoke a few words with him. I need hardly say that the Address more than justified

---

[1] This Shrewsbury bookshop and printing business still flourishes.

[2] *Bible Society Gleanings* in 1911 offered a prize Bible for the best verse translation of a French hymn by any reader not over 19. It can be assumed that a second competition in the same year involved the translating of a hymn from the Latin, but we have not been able to trace the relevant issue. It is known that the prize-winning poems were not printed. Wilfred's entry won second prize, a Latin New Testament, which survives. See Letter 103.

[3] A photograph was taken at the Arcade Studio, Reading, at about this time, and is reproduced as Plate 8b in *JO* I.

[4] The Rt. Rev. Ernest Graham Ingham (1851–1926), Bishop of Sierra Leone 1883–97, Home Secretary of the Church Missions Society 1904–12.

[5] Near Reading.

the great praise which I heard of him from you at Shrewsbury. He told the story of the Tiles of Budda's Shrine! In addition to his Lordship, I met about half a dozen clergy at the Meeting. This was at the afternoon tea which followed, (in the immense billiard room.)

From such mansions as these, I pass, next afternoon, to the wretched hovels of this Parish, and carry myself with equal ease in the crazy, evil-smelling huts of the poor, as in the wide, luxurious chambers of the rich.

Numbers of the old people cannot read; those who can seldom do so. Scores of them have passed their whole lives in the same stone box with a straw lid, which they call their cottage; and are numbed to all interests beyond it. Those who have within them the Hope of a Future World are content, and their old faces are bright with the white radiance of eternity. Those who, like the beasts, have no such Hope, pass their old age shrouded with an inward gloom, which the reverses of their history have stamped upon their worn-out memories, deadening them to all thoughts of delight.

There is one poor creature who cannot be said to live—she exists and no more: She can neither speak, hear, nor see; I suppose she can taste, smell, and feel. But alas, all her feeling must be that of pain, for she has a disease of the bone; all her smell must be the smell of a foul cottage; all her taste, the taste of bread and of tea. What a life! Why am I telling you these dreadful things? Simply to let them educate you, as they are educating me, in the Book of Life, and to make us rejoice in our own happy state.

I spend my afternoons in going round to these cottages. I am at my books in the morning; while there is nearly always some meeting to keep me busy in the evening. I have been so busy, indeed, that I have not been able to finish this letter till this morning (Friday). Let me hear from you when you have something to say—(I will not say when you have time—I know you have time to write me a note). Give my benedictions to the boys, and my love to Father, and take as much as you like for yourself.

Your loving brother, Wilfred

101. To Susan Owen

21 November 1911   *Dunsden Vicarage*

My dearest Mother,

I had half expected a line from you on Sat. and I was delighted to have the sweet little note:—to have an account of the barometric changes of your dear, warm temperament, instead of details concerning the temperature of the weather; the falling of a tear is more precious to me than the holding-up of any volume of atmospheric rain . . . I was not alone as you were, or I might have sought relief in a verse or two. As it was, I was mightily cheered, by finding several large volumes of the

Quarterly Review,[1] *c.* 1830–5, exposed for sale at Poynder's,[2] 1d the volume! I was astonied, for some of these must be quite valuable. Only a ten years earlier one would be priceless to me. (as, of course, you know, it was an article in this that helped to kill J.K.)[3] Strangely enough, a critic, in one of the vols. that I possess, apologises (half-mockingly, I believe) for the dastardly attack, and condescends, as it were, to pat Johnny Keats on the back, now he has been ten years dead. And warned by their mistake in his case, they hope to show more justice to young Mr. Tennyson, now making his second appearance in poetry! So far from this, they have not a good word to say for him, and make merciless fun of some of his best-beloved pieces!! Even I was, for the time, disenchanted, and roared with laughter with the *Quarterly* at his nonsense, and silly conceits.

The best pennyworth of humour I ever bought, albeit I would not let everybody enjoy it, lest Tennyson should come to shame. Thus, with all the guilty consciousness of infidelity to a professed hero, I spent a morning in naughty levity. But I am improved thereby, and look upon things now with a saner eye than formerly. Lamb, who died only a few years before, receives much attention in another vol. Byron, etc., etc. figure in others. So please don't tell [me] not to grind too much at regular study. I am rather in danger of falling into this desultory style of reading. I also at another shop picked up for 3d, a five shilling book of poetry by a modern aspirant, (unknown to me). The book is quite new (1911) and is also in a new condition (many leaves uncut) so I am idly-busy in trying to discover the talent of our own days, and the requirements of the public (if such requirements exist).

Thank you for the Book forwarded. I hope to glean much from this, too.

Brer Kemp and your servant are to take the choir boys to the C.M.S. Sale in Reading Town Hall this afternoon. We shall have to walk there and back, but as I am 'ever so' happy in the society of boys and youths of intelligence (even if unlettered) I trust I shall not find the way long. However, armed with your last injunctions, I flatly refused to go into Reading this morning for Tickets! Brer Kemp, therefore, had to bundle his lusty limbs there; he will be lucky indeed, if I don't make him carry me up the hills coming home, for we are not supposed to have tea there, and you know how restful a C.M.S. Sale of Work is.—I ought to say, that we are not going in order to patronise the stalls, but to witness the side-shows, and to enjoy the thrilling effects of puerile cantatas. 'Tis called a 'Trip to the East'. I ween the hungry choristers would trip more gaily if there were an 'F' somewhere in the title!

One of our cherubs (nomine Laurence Ambrose,[4] if you please!)

---

[1] Founded in 1809 as a Tory rival to the *Edinburgh Review.*

[2] The Reading bookshop and printing business, still flourishing.

[3] This was the notorious article on *Endymion* in 1818, thought to have hastened the poet's death in 1821. The reviewer was John Wilson Croker (1780–1857), secretary to the Admiralty and a regular contributor to the *Quarterly Review.*

[4] He became a gamekeeper and H O met him, years later.

cannot come, because engaged in the pressing duties of 'bird-starving', so he told me. This, of course, means scaring birds from newly-sown fields; but you notice how humanitarian these country folk are, (or birdy-manitarian, I should say) for they quite look at things from the bird's point of view.

The blue envelope, which I also thought to be the Matric. Tystisgriffe, proved to be a 'tystisgriffe' to the excellence of the borrowed-brain-stuff which I imbibed to help me through the Exam.—Sanatogen.

Therewith was appended a Chapter on Formamints. This reminds me of Miss Goshkins herms—I mean Miss Hoskins'[1] germs—and the thought thereof fills me with distress. If the fair Gipsy Smith[2] so much as thinks she's going to succumb, deny her entrance to the academical portals. Yea, an 'twere well to s'Macbeth, saying: 'Is this a Cadger that I see before me?—a cadger of microbes, With the (h)air all full of the signs of Scarlet death!'

But I am trifling with a serious matter, and I would pass on to you the excellence, hetsetterer, hetsetterer, of Formamint. For though it be expensive, it may be worth a guinea a suck, and may, indeed, form a mint of blessing in dis to you all. Tis time this foolish monologue was rung off,

So adieu, until your next 'call':   Your own Wilfred

102. To Colin Owen

[*Late November 1911*]   [*Dunsden Vicarage*]

Dear Colin,

I have by no means forgotten our young Prize-Winner, though to be candid, to tell the truth, I certainly did not remember him exactly, so to speak, as a matter of fact, in my last letters.

I am very anxious to know what your prize is like. [*Six lines illegible*]

Fritz is now out of favour with me—I mean I am out of his favour—because I have not taken him out for a long time.

I saw a Woodpecker the other day. I do a little Botany when travelling round the Parish. There are a great number of Elms, several Ashes & Oaks, but no sycamores!

How is my garden?

Roses are still blooming here.

Violets, of course, appear in places; but not in sufficient profusion for me to send you any.

I suppose you are having Terms Exams. soon. Leslie has begun. I can laugh at examinees now! But I am not altogether 'resting on my oars'—I ply them gently and slowly still, gliding over the peaceful

---

[1] Mistress, with Miss Goodwin, of the infant school, which now assembled at Mahim. See Letter 213.

[2] Beth Smith, nicknamed Gipsy, a friend of Mary. Her father farmed near Shrewsbury.

streams of history & philosophy—but I hear the thunder of the Examination Cataract away in the Distance, and I fear it!

You might somehow let Mary (dear innocent young lady, that she is)
know that that <u>Dorothy</u> is not spelt with an 'i'; that '<u>scene</u>' contains a
'c'; as also does '<u>Concert</u>'. Love to Harold; how goes my Book Cover?
Thank Mary, of course for her letter.

Your loving Wilfred

103. To Susan Owen

28 November 1911   *Dunsden Vicarage*

Dearest Mother,

The Tuesday Morning Packet (my only communication from the
outside world) was duly received today—with many thanks.

Mr. Kemp's exam. begins a week today (Tues.). Concerning the
<u>Bible</u>, I will make enquiries in Reading, and if I do not see one which
meets my taste, I will tell you, and you shall send me one according to
your own good pleasure, taste, and means. My first meed for Verse has
come: a <u>leather-bound</u> N. Test. <u>& Psalms</u> in Latin; excellent print; in
every way a most acceptable Second Prize.[1]

The Choir Outing was quite enjoyable. The walk, thanks to the talk,
was thoroughly pleasant, and, as we—Kemp & I—rested at the Fordhams for tea, one was not the least tired.

I took under my especial charge the bigger boys. Going, I tested
their Botanical knowledge—so far as was possible in November—and
found them really well-instructed in hedge-row plant-life. Returning, I
drifted into literature, and was considerably taken aback to hear the
name of Shelley on the lips of Willie Montague, stable-boy.

Of <u>dates</u>, however, they have no idea whatever, save only the eternal
'ten <u>sixty</u>-six'. When I asked Kemp what he had talked about to his
party, I was amused to find that History had also been his subject! They
will think it was a collusion! The entertainment was to my mind but
tepidly enjoyable. Costumes were perfect, but in most cases there was an
utter lack of dramatic power, and even distinctness of utterance, too.
Worst of all, there were hardly any who did not stumble through <u>forget-
ting their parts</u>! The accompanist was in her bed just at the time, so that
choruses were pitched with a supreme disregard to voice-compass!
Notwithstanding, Brer Kemp was enraptured at the Show: innocent old
heart; would I were susceptible of more emotion when I see an Indian
boy (with a white face, but no matter) supposed to be consigned to the
crocodiles of Ganges—in point of fact tipsily smirking at mamma
somewhere at the back of the audience.

I am pretty busy now. I put in 3 evenings per week at the club; I
spend all afternoon sitting on uncomfortable chairs talking to uncomfortable folk in uncomfortable cottages; I took the Chilluns last Thursday, I am going to take them <u>next</u> Thursday; I took a class of girls last

[1] See p. 94, note 2.

Sunday—(good girls most on 'em, but incapable of protracted attention); I am going to take the service next Sunday. (Also I took the
Sowers' Band in the Boudoir on Mon.) To crown all, I had to address the
Prayer Meeting last Friday, when I had the distressing experience of
forgetting every word that one meant to say . . . Furthermore, I
spend some part of the morning reading the classics at an agonizingly
slow pace to the distraught one. I must also say that one night since you
left it was midnight when we were at liberty to crawl up to bed. Latterly,
it has been, however, seldom later than 10.30.

Add to this such minor occupations as riding in to town to a Doctor's,
for medicine for a sick woman, and you may be surprised to know that I
have found time to read the whole of the book of Verse, and part of another and similar one, (not neglecting, meanwhile, Roman History
etc). The Poetry is not rubbish, but still it makes the position of the
dead and gone bards—safer than ever in mine heart.

I'm sure I should be enchanted to see my chubby brother in Pastoral
garniture: The news of added adipose tissue in his jowl convinces me
there must [be] a real bond of sympathy between us, because I am
certain I am getting fatter, too. I would fain lay his cheek to mine for
comparison and greetings.

Re the Chief Stenciller[1] of Mahim—I may say that I purpose to
devote a private and personal note of approbation to him in the near
future. Alack a day I am so long-winded when you are my audience,
that I have forgotten your request of me to be mercifully short next time.

Could any note of mine to Uncle John do what you think, or be what
you hope to him, I would be writing it now: but I have misgivings upon
that point; and think it would be better to wait till Christmas-time; Let
me know your revised orders.

I am now desired to take a message to the Fordhams[2] before dinner,
so I must 'Cease Writing, Please.'

Your own, Wilfred

104. To Harold Owen

2 December 1911   *Dunsden Vicarage*

My dear Harold,
    You will find enclosed an original design which shaped itself one
evening when I was in idle mood. I want a Cover for an Everyman,[3]
and in case your design might not please me, I venture to ask you to
adopt this, altering the size, etc. as you see fit.

I have no idea how you are going to execute it, for of course it is not
for a Stencil, but I trust to your ingenuity to produce some sort of cover.
I want the whole surface light green; the 'branches' dark green; the
'roses' (they are not cabbages) red; and the 'nameplate' yellow or

[1] HO.
[2] A Dunsden farmer and his family.
[3] This cover, and that for the *Atlas Antiquus* mentioned later, were duly executed by HO.

yellowish-green. I imagine that my Monogram and the other ovals would look well in Blue.

For I want a 'rich' effect; and not a rigidly pure scheme of colour. If the whole thing is not worth copying, don't be afraid to say so: and please make another and better design. (Leaving the Printing to me, please, unless you have mightily improved in that way of late.)

Supposing you have time for such a useful exercise, I am in need of a cover for a large 'Atlas Antiquus' (9½ ins. × 14½ ins. and ⅓ in. thick.) So should you like to design and make such an article, I should be much obliged. It might do for my Christmas Present?

The aspect of the Chiltern Downs is perfectly wintry now, but the land is by no means devoid of beauty or interest. The village of Sonning is one of the prettiest in the Thames Valley, and no wonder Holman Hunt chose to live there.[1] I have not yet seen his house.

I do not often venture out of the Parish; but yesterday I spent a morning in Reading. The shops are already beginning to wear their Christmas glories. When I view the triumphs of Fine Art to be seen in some of the most expensive Christmas Cards and books, I am overcome by an access of thriftlessness, and positively have to look the other way. Anyhow I shall be forced to spend a considerable amount on something because all the household staff expect something for Christmas. For that reason alone I should be glad to be at home for that season. But I hardly expect to, seeing no word has been said on that subject yet.

Brother Lewty is coming today, to spend Sunday. Brother Kemp departs in perfect peace to the City of Distraction on Monday.

If he stays over the next Sunday, I shall act Superintendent of the Sunday School, as well as Presiding on Thursday.

Fare thee well! I rejoice that you work hard, even as much as to hear that you are happy therein.

(I remember that I did not remember to remember Mary and her last letter, in my last letter. But I will respond anon.) Likewise to Mother's and Colin's last notes: to whom and to Father, Greeting!

From the faithful Wilfred

105. To Mary Owen

7 December 1911   *Dunsden Vicarage*

My dearest Sister,

It is more than a fortnight since I had your last letter, so you well deserve a 'full' one from me. I am pleased that you can exhibit some amount of spirit in your replies, and particularly because they are well expressed (!). I have no book called 'Notes' on L.L.[2] but a copy with Notes, which, of course, you will abstract from my shelves when required.

---

[1] William Holman-Hunt, OM (1827–1910), the painter, and one of the three founders of the Pre-Raphaelite Movement, lived at Sonning Acre.
[2] Sir Walter Scott, *The Lady of the Lake*. Wilfred had three copies, all of which survive.

I was altogether shocked by the News of Kathleen's[1] death, and, possibly because of the similarity of our ages, took it much more to heart than I imagine the 'other branch' of Cousins did. I even thought I had rheumatic fever one night—because I found my socks had been wet for hours.

Strangely enough, on that day, I went to the first funeral I have ever been to in my life; and I wore black and mourned there—for other cause than people thought.[2] Ah, at such times, like Lamb, 'I begin to count the probabilities of my duration, and grudge at the expenditure of moments like miser's farthings. In proportion as the years both lessen and shorten, I set more count upon their periods, and would fain lay my finger upon the spoke of the great wheel.'[3] For every circumstance of my present life reminds me that I am no more a Boy. Can a Boy speak at Meetings, as I speak; can a Boy superintend a Sunday School and six teachers as I shall do; Can a Boy carve a Pheasant at late dinner as I did? . . .

Well, even now, you see my moralising does not last long; and at the present moment my heart is filled with music. 'Tis thus: After the Scrip. Union Meeting which I took alone, and thoroughly enjoyed, I took upon myself (at Mrs. Lott's[4] desire,) to teach a Carol to the 'Sowers' and others; which they are to sing at the Sunday School Treat to my accompaniment. There were about a dozen, from ten to fourteen years old, and some have really exceptional voices, and all seem most intelligent; so it [is] with real pleasure that I 'doh-ray-me' before them; harp on first piano, then organ; insist on pauses, slurs and crescendo's, and beg the rosy mouths to ope a trifle widah!

Two choir boys came Carol singing here on Tues. and I enjoyed that, also. The skies have been warm and sunny here, and I enjoy that also[5]. The moon rose in full splendour last night, and I enjoyed that also. But alas! I do not enjoy the long hours spent doing absolutely nothing in the study nearly every night. Imagine me slobbering over my can of shaving-water and blinking over my candle these dark mornings—when I only get to sleep as near twelve as eleven! I tell you the honey-dew of warm sleep is not to be compensated by the honey (literal) on the breakfast-table . . . But I want something to complain of, don't I, when I hear of carters getting up at 4, and having no holiday from year to year—no not Sunday!

---

[1] Kathleen Loughrey, a cousin, fourth child of Susan Owen's sister May. See p. 17.

[2] A four-stanza poem on the funeral of a mother and child, 'Deep under turfy grass and heavy clay', is among the unpublished BM Mss. It almost certainly dates from this period. We quote four striking lines:

> So I rebelled, storming and mocking such
> As had the ignorant callousness to wed
> On altar-steps long frozen by the touch
> Of stretcher after stretcher of our dead.

[3] Charles Lamb, *The Essays of Elia*, 'New Year's Eve'.

[4] The vicarage housekeeper.

[5] A letter in verse, written 'one warm day in December 1911', was seen by E B, when writing his 1931 Memoir, but has not survived. See Appendix A.

Mr. Lewty spent Sunday here—for the last time. He is a splendid speaker, and an M.A. and is or was a reader of Modern Poetry; so it was a pleasure to be able to speak with him, and an honour to be called 'brother' by him. Harold is not to show my cabbage-patch[1] to Mr. Dane—where's his self-respect!

I have had no information about Christmas. The Vicarage is not decorated, I believe; but after all it accords better with my tastes to have a house well swept than garnished—and that it verily is. Mr. Kemp's exam is over, and he writes about it with confidence.

I think very often about you, on Sunday Evenings especially. You will, of course, thank dear Mother for her letter; (for whom this is half intended) Thanks be to Miss Rose[2] for her very kind and valued message—but 'tis not a fresh message to me, if Mother ever gave me a piece of advice.

Your affectionate brother, Wilfred

106. To Susan Owen

12 December 1911   *Dunsden Vicarage*

Dearest Mother,

Many thanks for the letters (& Syllabus) received this morning.

Do please nurse your throat and take something 'extry' (as Mrs. Lott would say) in the way of nourishment—if for no better reason than to be well when I come. . . For I quite think I shall be home for a few days—and very likely over Christmas Day itself.

Brother Kemp came back on Monday. I managed very well at Sunday School, and took a Class as well as Superintending. I also spoke for nearly quarter of an hour at the P.M. yesterday, I went with Uncle & Leslie to an Organ Recital in a Reading Church. It began at eight, & I got home at 10.30—so I snatched one evening from the Wasted Hours. Over and above this quiet source of satisfaction, the music was rapturous, and a violin—'yearning like a god in pain' (J.K.)[3]—gave such sensation as no prose can describe. I envied Father at the Orchestral—but— 'heard melodies are sweet, but those unheard are sweeter,'[4] and the last may be enjoyed by any who will read any master-poet.

On the whole, my 'Carolists' are not all that can be desired, but individual merit may save them yet. They can not sing 10 bars without going a semitone flat!

I have begun present-buying. What would mine own kin like for Christmas?

---

[1] The rose design for the Everyman cover.
[2] A missionary friend of Susan Owen. See Letter 171.
[3]   the music, yearning like a God in pain.
                                        Keats, *The Eve of St. Agnes.*
[4] Keats, *Ode on a Grecian Urn.*

I am reading G. Eliot's *Scenes from Clerical Life*,[1] which is very appropriate just now. I have heard about Dorothy.[2] This region will soon be over-stocked with 'unsettled-futurists'—for Brother Kemp will soon be in the same state—being in the dark 'about what to do after this exam.'

Longing to see you all soon,

Your loving Wilfred

107. To Susan Owen
Postcard

21 December 1911   [*Postmark Dunsden*]

'Expect me Saturday—early as possible—staying till Friday.' Such is the message which I have been longing to send, & which perchance will be acceptable to you all? I had already written to you yesterday when the Vicar asked whether I might like to spend Christmas Day at home. 'I should most certainly, but, of course not if . . ., etc.' Well, the 'buts', were all removed, for Kemp is going to have a 'service' on Sunday instead of School, (because 2 Teachers are absent, and I should have to attend School.) The Vicar has invitations to two dinners on the 25th, and Kemp has been asked to Mrs. Reading's[3] for the whole day. I don't know that either will accept, but in any case, I shall not mind being away from here, since the Vicar first proposed it.

I don't know the train yet, but must find out and tell you (if possible) tomorrow. W

108. To Susan Owen
Postcard

22 December 1911   [*Postmark Dunsden*]

I have chosen the train arriving Shrewsbury 2.4, which leaves Reading 10.43; this being the fastest and the earliest convenient. Moreover, should I miss this, there will be the 11.20. I shall walk in to the stn. I suppose, hence shall take as little luggage as possible. I have actually bought all my presents! I have not, however, got my Bible, since there is just a bare possibility of receiving one from elsewhere. I am writing to Grandma etc. tonight. We have had incessant rains, and shall have no doubt tomorrow.

Hence I shall not expect
    to be 'met'
    if 'tis wet.
    W

---

[1] *Scenes of Clerical Life* (1857) was the first of George Eliot's novels.
[2] Gunston. See Letter 125.
[3] Wife of a farmer at Caversham.

109. To Susan Owen
Postcard
29 December 1911   [*Postmark Reading*]

It seems very strange to be writing to you now, when only this morning I was talking—aye and grumbling, over my specimens but prithee put this down to an excess of zeal in the cause of Science.

I landed in full time for the Treat which began at 4. The Conjurer was just as might be expected—but sometimes above the comprehension of the infant multitude. His dummy in Ventriloquism, Mr. Marmalade, struck terror to the heart of one of these, while it gave the keenest pleasure to the rest. It was lucky I snatched my bowler hat this morning—for it was the only one in the hall, & was therefore used, and abused till we all had clear proof as to the truth of miracles. I wish your little party had been transferred here, tonight, and could stay here till I get used to the Silence, the State, and the Stiffness. W

110. To Susan Owen
2 January 1912   *Dunsden Vicarage*

Dearest Mother,

Such is the unseasonableness of the weather that I am writing in the Garden!

I forgot to say that I saw you and Mary from the bridge; and waved frantically, but chiefly behind a string of carriages. On Sunday night we went to bed at half-past eleven, so I listened for some signs of the death-wail of the Year. I had read 'Ring out, wild bells',[1] and had 'put my head into a pillowy cleft', and was 'thinking of rugged hours and fruitless toil'[2] when distant whistles began to shriek and groan, mighty bells began to knock their heads together in noisy desperation, rockets began to splutter up—until all the dogs were set a-barking and the cocks a-crowing for miles around.

So came in the New Year for me.

But being tired on account of the late hour, I was just too late for the horrid clanging of the Morning Gong—and so died my first Resolution. I must now wait till next year to make the next—which year will not be long in coming.

I am sending the Canon's letter, which I am proud to have, and which you will send back—to take its place among my 1912 'Received Correspondence' which I have resolved to keep, decently and in order.

I spent part of yesterday afternoon decorating the Hall for this afternoon—or rather I decorated a few inches of it—for Mrs. Lott, Miss Reading, Mrs. Bray,[3] and the two Hulcoop[4] (school-master's) boys were

---

[1] Tennyson, *In Memoriam*, cvi.

[2]
                    Thinking on rugged hours and fruitless toil,
                    We put our eyes into a pillowy cleft.

                                        Keats, *Isabella*, xli.

[3] Wife of the vicarage gardener.
[4] The village schoolmaster, Dunsden.

there. I however made suggestions, and gently but firmly altered one intended piece of decoration, which was about as much to my taste as Castor Oil fried in Gregory powder.

Mrs. Lott, Kemp, and Miss Reading, & I, then had an informal and very gritty tea on a Bagatelle Table; after which my Chorus Girls came for their Last Practice. It was all Mrs. Lott could do to get them away from the piano and the Manager, when he signified that he was quite satisfied, and they had done quite enough singing for that night.

Tell the Children that my portraits look lovely in my room. The Central figure, indeed, is quite adorable.

I was glad to have a note from Colin, and I would ergantly request him to use a certain little Book of Mary's.

I am so very glad you are coming soon—before any obstacle shall be interposed; and I shall be truly elated, on presenting 'my sister' to my new circle of friends.

Please excuse this writing—you must wait till next year for improvement in this respect.

Love and kisses,

from your own Wilfred

111. To Mary Owen

January 1912   *Dunsden Vicarage*

My dearest Mary,

I wonder how you are today. I am hoping to hear soon that you feel stronger, dear. The 'change' to this part of the country would not benefit you much at present, for today is the very worst day of the season. Rain is incessant; Temperature as near freezing as it can manage, Wind—East; Clouds—yellow and black, about 5 miles thick ! ! Anyhow it was so dark this morning as to send me to sleep at ten o'clock—over my book. Perhaps this was also due to the late hour of retiring—nearly twelve! We had been to Fritz and Arthur Wood's meetings.[1] Kemp & I went in to the 3 o'clock, with Mrs. & Miss Fordham, had tea at Mrs. E's expense, & then went to the 8 o'clock meeting. The 'Singer' Wood is simulating the Great Alexander in his spiral-staircase-windmill-arm-feats; he also has Alexander's trick of stamping, clapping, and grinning by turns, and what is more, complimenting individuals on their singing —(one of which individuals was the Vicar.)

Apart from all this preamble which led to nothing, I enjoyed the services. Brother Kemp has gone in this afternoon to hear their dicta on 'Questionable Amusements'. I had not the strength to wallow through and underneath the mud, and to treadmill back again, with twenty gallons of rain-water in one's clothing. Moreover I don't need to hear what I could say myself, and I don't want to hear what I don't think myself.

---

[1] Travelling brother evangelists. See Letter 512.

The social evening, considering the short notice given to performers, was distinctly successful. I simply couldn't sing my song with less than three mistakes in practice. I didn't the least know the tune, but read it. However, the actual thing went off splendidly and compliments upon the song, and the voice (when it matures(!)) were numerous. So I have made my début in one of the Fine Arts! Mr K's voice is very good indeed, I think; much better than the Woods' for instance.

I am thankful to say I was able to 'throw myself into' my recitations, and out of that stupefying nervousness which might have frozen me at your age. But I doubt whether the audience enjoyed the pieces as well as I did myself. I am sending you the programme that you may see what all the others did. The people numbered nearly 80 I should think.

My little patient, (not sufferer you will be glad to know) is on a fair way to recovery. I infuse life and mirth into him drop by drop, day by day; chiefly through the nasal channels of Mr. Punch's Voice. He has a Punch & Judy Book, and his little brother of about 3 will bring it open to a certain picture, gravely saying 'Laugh at this' whereat I laugh. 'Now laugh at this,' whereat we all laugh. He was asleep when I took Colin's crackers, and his pleasure on finding them by his bed on waking was, says his Mother, very, very real.

I find that Shelley lived at a cottage within easy cycling distance from here.[1] And I was very surprised (tho' really I don't know why) to find that he used to 'visit the sick in their beds; kept a regular list of the industrious poor whom he assisted to make up their accounts;' and for a time walked the hospitals in order to be more useful to the poor he visited![2] I knew the lives of men who produced such marvellous verse could not be otherwise than lovely, and I am being confirmed in this continually. I find my very slight medical knowledge of some use— not perhaps to the patients but rather to myself, in giving topics of confabulation, and in commanding respect to my advice, and, it may be, in winning a way into the homes.

Would I could give you some advice which would lead to better health. But myself am feeling at low vitality. No doubt this time of year is like the third hour of morning. For you know that at 3 a.m. our life ebbs at its lowest; that is 'the hour when sick men die.'[3]

*   *   *

I hope to take a trip to Town next week (or this), when I want to

[1] Albion House, Old Marlow.
[2] Wilfred had been reading *Shelley*, by John Addington Symonds (Macmillan, London, 1809); his marked copy survives. 'His charity, though liberal, was not weak. He . . . visited the sick in their beds . . . and kept a regular list of industrious poor, whom he assisted with small sums to make up their accounts.'
[3] Sir Lewis Morris (1833–1907), *The Epic of Hades*, 'Andromeda':
            . . . the dead dark hour before the dawn
            When sick men die . . .
Wilfred later returned to the theme in 'The Unreturning' (*Poems*, p. 90):
            Then peered the indefinite unshapen dawn
            With vacant gloaming, sad as half-lit minds,
            The weak-limned hour when sick men's sighs are drained.

buy my Bible. Would one of you send my Royal Autographs,[1] which you will find in my cash box? I may take it to the Brit: Museum.

Fondest love to all, Yrs. Wilfred

Canon B. Laurence[2] from London speaks tonight: I must get ready.

112. To Susan Owen

5 January 1912   *Dunsden Vicarage*

My dearest Mother,

Our Sunday School Treat went off with great success. I must not spend words describing it, but will just mention that the Carol was tolerably well sung, & that the games were most enjoyable. The boys were rough, but so were we, and no one was hurt. They derived great fun from my innovation of Earth, Air, etc., and also from Oranges and Lemons, when they passed under Miss Reading's and my hands joined. Had that young lady of (doubtful age) been anything but a farmer's daughter she must surely have gone home minus both arms and numerous locks of hair.

At this treat the Vicar announced a Bible Class in the Vicarage, starting next Sunday, held by Mr. Owen. (Mr. O. had only had definite knowledge that such a Class had been decided upon half an hour previously.) However, I have about 20 names eligible, and expect quite ten or a dozen. I shall enjoy it, and everything is as one could desire except the capacity of the Leader for such an undertaking.

I am very much interested in a sweet little boy of 5 who a day or two ago was at the point of death (from Peritonitis.) His whiteness was as the whiteness of snow. Now he seems past the crisis. I do want to give him some of my faithful veterans of Soldiers. Could you make a packet bulky enough to travel free per G.W.R.? I particularly want them soon, but rather than spend their worth on postage, would wait till you come.

—Not a moment to spare for more—Choir Supper tonight!

Your loving Wilfred

113. To Susan Owen
Postcard

6 January 1912   *Dunsden Parish Hall*

I am writing here while Brother Kemp is chanting the 'Lost Chord' to Miss Fordham's accompaniment. This is in preparation for the Mother's Social Evening on Monday next week. I am going to recite some of Tennyson's little 'bijoux'—and perhaps sing!

So if you have not already sent my soldiers would you enclose the folio containing the *Arrow & the Song*[3] (if Father does not want it)? And also my *Murdoch's School Songs*?

---

[1] We can throw no light on these.

[2] Arthur Evelyn Barnes-Lawrence (1852–1931), Hon. Canon of Southwark 1905–15, later Vicar of St. John the Evangelist, Boscombe, Bournemouth.

[3] An arrangement of Longfellow's poem beginning: I shot an arrow into the air.

Also when you come would you please bring my white(?) shoes, and my Box of Seeds. So sorry, darling Colin is 'flued'. Lots of people are down with it here. Many thanks for your letter—and do come very soon; I will mention Colin without asking at Alp-nr-s-. We had a fine time with the Choir last night—I did some 'Thought Reading'.

W

114. To Susan Owen

11 January 1912   *Dunsden Vicarage*

My dearest Mother,

Your news was a great disappointment. I had reserved all latest news of mine to tell you, and quite thought of meeting you at the station today. How long will you have to wait now?

There is one thing I am glad of—That I need have no fear of your appearing at the 'Concert'.

I am taking the Bass in three part songs, and may sing the *Arrow and the Song* (to another tune). But unless I improve wonderfully by Monday, I shall substitute for it a pianoforte solo or more recitations.

Last Monday we went to Mrs Reading's of Caversham to tea. The house is new and large—you pass it on Caversham Hill. We actually stayed till after nine—playing bagatelle and another competitive game, 'Carnations', which I will explain for our diversion someday. The Children made no appearance; but we had the pleasure of the company [of a] step-daughter of Mrs Reading's, who is a fashionable young lady from Town, and who, having travelled over Europe, and having, as I soon discovered, a tolerable leaning towards literature, made the evening most agreeable. Particularly as Mrs. R. is very nervous and jerky about the face. (But she was once a house-keeper to Mr R. and no doubt finds Self-possession and Placidity the most difficult of all lady-like qualities to assume.)

On Tuesday, the Sunday School Teachers assembled here for tea, and an hour's sitting on the Drawing Room sofas. A duller time I have seldom spent. We looked at albums of photographs and things—very nice in themselves, but when they run into thousands one begins to nauseate of 'A Street in Japan', Street in Winnipeg, Street in Norway, Street in Normandy, and a painful spirit of unrest begins to assert itself somewhere behind the eyes.

Miss Cheshire, missionary from India, is here now. She took Wednesday night, and will address Mothers, and Children today. We amassed some seventy people in the Hall for the occasion.—Alas! I am beginning to tire of all these meetings, and the goings and comings connected with them—not that they themselves are in any way disagreeable, but that I want to be reading. The time I am at Book and Pen seems to be growing smaller and smaller, and the worst of it all is that in the mornings, I am as dull as I used to be, say at eleven o'clock at night in the term-times. Given ten minutes quiet at any time of day, and a fire to sit before, I

could go into a sound sleep for hours. I am just now reading a Life of
Shelley, and I find that he exhibited these characteristics too. So I am
comforted. But even this does not relieve the tense nervous strain of
two to three hours solid idleness per night.

You will think I am all complaints—but believe me none hears them
but you—unless a mutual sigh with the 'other Brother' as we light our
candles—partakes of the nature of a complaint.

During the afternoons, I am mostly very happy, and the consciousness of bringing a stray gleam of pleasure into a sick room is in itself
ineffably pleasurable. It will be hard to part with the boys and others if
I stay much longer. Surprising how my opinions of ploughmen's sons
have changed now I know some. Thought they had round vacant eyes
and mouths and intellects to correspond—Find them possessed of (sometimes) fine features, and (somehow) nice manners . . . I wish I could
enlarge upon my experiences and the thoughts they engender. That
must be put off till anon, while I now distribute some invitations for the
Social.

Good-bye.

Thank dear Colin for his presents to my little patient. It seems that
nothing short of prayer answered has brought round this little fellow.
But even yet he must be in terrible danger—for years—I suppose. It
was contracted after measles. Consumption may take hold on him—
and then?

Consumption is all round us here. Scarlet Fever and Diphtheria are
at work near by. God grant that His mercies in keeping our dear family
together may be continued long, long years to come! And do you mind
and not get influenza. Some one has got Quinsy here—O what tremors
I have lest you should get it again.

Your devoted son, Wilfred

115. To Colin Owen

12 January 1912   *Dunsden Vicarage*

Darling Colin,

Hearing you are still very weak and poorly, I have overcome my
laziness enough to pen a few lines to you. (For I am sometimes lazy in
getting my mind to work independently: when a book leads my thoughts
all goes well, but take away that trodden road for thought and I begin to
wander.) The words of a living poet[1] might be applied to me:

> 'He meditates in silence all the day
> Reclining in an atmosphere of dreams,
> Meanwhile the bravest moments slip away
> And life is wasted in its crystal streams.')

This is not all true.

---

[1] We have failed to identify him—the lines may be Wilfred's own.

But <u>this</u> is not far wrong—

> 'Towards the hour of dinner, if you look
> You'll see him sitting placid as a rock;
> But round the left-hand corner of his book
> You'll catch his green eye fixed upon the clock.'

Some idea of the idiotic self-complacency he is assuming may be gathered from the proof I am sending of a recent portrait. Mind! this will fade if exposed a short time to Light. I should not have sent it, but that I thought it would interest <u>you</u> who are unable to get out and see anything better in the way of physogs. The mounted photograph will be several days yet in coming.

I am as disappointed [*one sheet missing*]

Now I oughtn't (selfishly speaking) to be writing to you when I have recitations and songs to learn for next Monday! And an hours discourse on Sunday to think of as well!

Therefore—Adieu!

And if your head allows it write to me.

At all events read!   Your loving, Wilfred

116. To Susan Owen
Postcard

20 January 1912   [*Postmark Reading*]

So sorry you were expecting a letter: I forgot to post—as you have seen. This is to ask you to send my Georgian Autographs by <u>Monday Morning</u>, as I hope to go to London on that day, and to show them at the British M. Anything you want in London? Am going to Alpenrose to tea today—first time for months. Vicar, Mr. K. & I went to Reading's of Playhatch[1] for tea & supper on Thursday.

So glad Mary is better. When are you likely to come? Love & apologies,
W

117. To Susan Owen

26 January 1912   *Dunsden Vicarage*

My own dear Mother,

It is hardly conceivable that I have been a month here since last seeing you; yet so it is; and I must remind myself that my U.C.C. Class should be started in March, if at all. Kemp seems pretty sure of going at Easter; and he tells me that the Vicar thinks of keeping me on in his place, and, I suppose, with his allowance. With a little obstinacy in the matter of evening work, I might at least find <u>time</u> for systematic study. But the isolation from any whose interests <u>are</u> the same as mine, the constant, inevitable mixing with persons whose influence will tend in the opposite direction—this is a serious drawback, and I shall have to

[1] Binfield Heath, near Reading.

fight against more things than a natural disinclination to hard work—if once I commit myself to the tender mercies of U.C.C.

Since Wednesday, Mr. Clark, who writes the daily portion on the Scrip: Union in *Life of Faith*,[1] has been here. I was astonished this morning to realise that he is the identical old gentleman who presided at Shrews. Convention two (and three) years ago. You remember—we thought him very slow. He is really quite different from what I had imagined that old chairman to be. I little thought at the Conven: that I should be on intimate terms with him. He wrote next week's 'portion' here at this desk, with this ink, and I saw him do it. This is the more interesting, because you know, at prayers every morning, the Vicar reads these commentaries; and I had often wondered what sort of man or men produced them.

Mr. Consterdine,[2] who was here a fortnight ago, is in the habit of reviewing books, and Canon Barnes Laurence, here a week ago, has written a good deal. So my surroundings are literary already.

This afternoon Kemp & I received an invitation to accompany our Vicar to a Clerical Confabulation of some sort—in his house. A Paper was read by one of the 15 clergy there, on 'Animism': All the company were then supposed to utter their thoughts upon the same. I had the good sense to decline to offer views on the subject, when it came to my turn; because the Vicar could not get anything out, and moreover if a circle of stodgy old canons had started to contravert me, I might have lost confidence, and the purple of my tie, already obnoxious enough compared to the stainless white all around, might have spread alarmingly upward . . . We have also an invitation to a drawing-room meeting somewhere, to be presented to Bishop Taylor-Smith.[3]

I spent a rapid day in London on Tuesday, (Monday being foggy.) The vicar travelled with me, (so I went 3rd). He went to get a 'Baby Organ', partly for my Class. We parted—and met—at Paddᵗⁿ.

I spent morning in Brit. Mus; afternoon at Nat. Gall. & shops. I saw an ideal (or nearly so) Bible, in Paternoster Row, for 8s. which I have ordered, it not being on sale at Frowde's.[4] I also went to B. & F. Bible Society House, & got a cheap R. Version. I see there is just a chance of another Prize. By French Hymn Translation, if only I can improve my riming capacities.

I herewith send a representation of my outward man; I[t] does not please me; nothing will, unless it were an oil by Sargent. And not knowing what to do with the second of the three, would Mary like it for her

[1] Originally *The Christian's Pathway of Power* (founded 1874 as a monthly), it became a weekly in 1896, and still continues with its weekly passage of scripture. We can find nothing of Mr. Clark.

[2] The Rev. James Consterdine, Perpetual Curate of St. Mary's Chapel, Reading, from 1895.

[3] The Rt. Rev. John Taylor Smith (1860–1938), Bishop of Sierra Leone 1897–1901, Chaplain-General to the Forces 1901–25.

[4] Henry Frowde (1841–1927) was from 1883 to 1913 the first London Publisher to the University of Oxford; the London offices of the Press at this time were at Amen Corner, Ave Maria Lane, E.C.4. Frowde's name appeared on the title-page of Oxford books originating at Amen Corner.

room? The absence of 'Spots' is not altogether due to the magic art of a Toucher; at this time I had none; lately a goodly number have put out an appearance. Does Mary continue to increase in strength? Truly, the news of a stronger heart is a thing to make this temporary weakness insignificant—I hope.

To Colin: Shelley, the brightest genius of his time, (yes, tho' I say it) received his education up to the age of 12, together with his sisters. But he worked, and was fit for Eton at that age. Therefore—Progress, and be thou a Good-Winner in very truth—a winner of Knowledge whose price is above rubies.

Mr. Clark took our Children yesterday but they behaved very badly—I am afraid he never once caught their attention, tho' it was a very nice address. My List of B. Class Members numbers 13 now!

Did not know Father had a cold—I do hope he is better. When is his holiday coming off? Longing expectancy to see you soon, after this horrid baulking;

W

118. To Susan Owen

31 January 1912   *Dunsden Vicarage*

Dearest Mother,

A thousand thanks for a 16-page letter! So glad you & Mary like the photos: I wish you would ascertain when Stanley Webb means to send me the snapshots he took of me, midst the crumbling battlements of Viriconium.

I am sorry you did not think of sending my skates: we have had 4 days of ice. I went yesterday mng. & had ¼ hr. on Kemp's skates in a flooded field in Reading—ice very poor. This was with Mrs. & Miss Fordham. This m'ng I went over to Alpenrose, to hire Leslie's skates and Dorothy's company. We went on some fields close to Caversham Br. where some two miles of really good ice awaited us—(not of course continuous, because of hedges). There was hardly anyone there: so we had a thoroughly good time.

Since writing this I have been unpacking a new portable organ, which has come for the joint use of my class and the Sowers. The bagatelle-table which the vicar ordered thro' the *Exchange & Mart* proved a swindle: nasty, cheap, thing, with 2d. hinges, which bust the first time we opened it—and with wooden balls! So it has been sent back without thanks.

Mr. Clark gave me a book upon his late wife (!)—of his own compilation—which Mary must read.

I am writing to Oliver.

The little Peritonite is marvellously better—I found him sitting up in bed last time. He likes very much bright picture-post-cards and old Christmas Cards—can you send some? And would you send me some of Christ-Church Magazines; the Canon's sermons will be of immense help to me in getting up subjects for Prayer Meetings, and so on. Just send as many as will post for 1d. at first, please. In return, I should be pleased to send our Mag. which has a special Paragraph about my Class and a short account of Christmas Treats.

The U.C.C. are beginning to bombard me again! I thought so! I find there are classes for my exam. at the Univ. Col: Reading—which I might join if the distance were not so great.

I am studiously looking into my present manner of life, to see if I can commit myself to it for two years. I wonder whether Foreign Meat is any drawback, for we certainly have it twice per day!

Thank Colin for his 'lettre': I must répondre as soon as je can. I hope Father is better. I don't hear how you are at present!

But trust for the best.

Your own, Wilfred

119. To Susan Owen

1 February 1912   *Dunsden Vicarage*

My dearest Mother,

I did get your letter on Monday, and I thank you for sending so soon, for I had arranged to go to the Cyclists this morning. I am very grateful to Father & you for the 30s. I shall on no account want more. For the machine is only £5. 19. 6! There are two at such a price, one Enfield, one Humber, both with 3-speed Gears. I simply could not choose this morning, so left it till my final call with the money. It will be a joy-ride when I am mounted on one of these! Today I have got a few more precious books, which I will enlarge upon on Thurs. or Friday, *viva voce*. Thus I am laying in a store of wordly goods, yet am I unhappy not knowing by what means to lay in a store of unwordly instruction.

I forgot to say my old machine 'will fetch' 20s. Considering Repairing Free Wheel would cost 7/6, and both tyres are like wafers, I am (secretly) pleased at this. Privately, I might dispose of it for 30s, says the Shopman—and so I might gain 10s. I suppose you don't remember anyone wanting it?

Your methodical table of Amounts & Sources is a marvel of Financial Genius. I had quite forgotten 'Bank'. Please do not send this money by P.O. but wait till Thurs. Shall I meet you? Can't, of course, in late Aft. or Evening.

Now I must hasten off to my Club (ah hem!)

The housemaid has been ill with sore throat, which Mrs. Lott imagined Diph . . . (that's enough!) But a charming Lady Doctor quite knocked that idea on the head. The Doctor's motor tyre exploded meanwhile, so I had the pleasure of showing her round the Garden, & of placing delicate snowdrops in hands which had been carving up gizzards a few hours before, ough!

Here follows a list of desiderata.

I must now really stop, and must unpack a Crate of China newly arrived. Fit occupation for me, who have far more knowledge of these matters than the kitchen-folk.

Your own Wilfred

120. To Susan Owen

My dearest Mother,

I was somewhat alarmed at the weight of the parcel I received this morning; you really must send me only pennyworths until you come! I have got no end of things for you to bring; but I will make a list of them at the last moment. I am very grateful for the benefits you send both for the outward & inward man; strange, that only yesterday I was attracted by a pile of Liquorice Sticks in a window—and nearly bought one—but not quite! Instead, I picked up two shilling books of real value to me at 1d. each! Reading is the place for 'Secondhands'. I am well known at 3 shops now, but I fancy my appearing is none too welcome; for they always lose by me.

My Bible is a gem. I knew there must exist one which would come up to my requirements. I have found it—after many months! That is, it is marvellous for the price, 8/6.

Thanks for the multitude of pictures etc. I would they were as many articles of food & clothing. We are very comfortably warm in this house —with a glowing coke-stove in the Hall, under the staircase; lamps burning in the lavatories, and fires continually replenished; one even in Kemp's bedroom. These luxuries would never be thought of if the pipes had not frozen. For lunch yesterday we could get not drinking water at all—so had Vichy! Leslie, Kemp & I went skating again on Sat. I on Dorothy's skates. My bicycle is quite disabled now—the free-wheel having worn out. It is all very well to consider getting a new one. I quite forgot I have not enough cash in hand even though I give the old in part payment.

Of course, I should want £10:10s.[1] or thereabouts [*half-sheet missing*] so it shan't trouble me. I mean to make things hum.

I am going to spend Wed. night at Alpenrose, owing to the visit of Miss Lingley, brother,[2] & friend, who are giving a Lantern Lecture on their tour among Korean Missions [*half-sheet missing*]

121. To Susan Owen

Postcard

Many thanks for the surprise P.C. received at Alpenrose. I was perfectly worn out on Wed. night. Spent morning in going to Alp. to ask

---

[1] The money for the new bicycle was eventually sent from Mahim. See Letter 123.
[2] See Letter 146.

for bed, and in messing about with the Acetylene Lantern, which was out of order, & on which Vicar & I spend hours of time & tons of strength in fixing up: let alone the anxiety lest it shouldn't work. Then in afternoon, I walked with Notices all down & up Playhatch Hill. Went down just after Tea to try lantern: came back & changed: back again to Hall to receive people early. Then I worked the slides and a horrid strain it was, when they are rapid. The vicar undertook to watch the gas-taps; and he was pretty nervous of it; and with good reason. But it worked splendidly; and the congregation was wonderful large. After a copious supper of hare I trundled over to Alp. by 11 p.m. Spent next mng. preparing to take Mothers Mtg. that afternoon. Then I controlled Children; then after tea wallowed into Reading to a Y.M.C.A. meeting with Kemp.

This will prove I have not got chicken pox tho' I have been in 3 houses where it rages: one is Mrs. Mayne's. I don't visit a case of rapid consumption, which is close to. List of 'Wants' to follow.

Love, W

122. To Susan Owen

Dunsden Vicarage

13 February 1912

Dearest Mother,

Your Sunday letter was again very welcome. If you are looking for my Ticket in this envelope, you will be disappointed; I can't find it, and am almost sure that, knowing I could not use it after Jan. 31st. I let it be collected at Reading. I will still keep an eye open for it when looking thro' drawers, but this is what I think must have happened. Anyhow it is not very likely I could get away for any time yet; and I will see to it that nothing removable shall stand in the way of your coming very shortly. Vicar has a great idea of the Gunstons taking a largish house close to the Hall, which will soon be vacant. He quite counts on Auntie for a Parish Prop. I don't think! Dorothy seems hard at work in Uncle's Growlery.[1]

The other day I sent to London for a lot of books at stupendous reductions: Surplus Copies of New Books. There is a 10s. Complete Keats for 3/6: Sad to see him on the Surplus List, but gladdening to my purse. Mind you go into mourning on Feb. 23rd![2]

I have finished off one translation of my French Hymn; but my metre is very unusual, and I may have to re-cast it altogether. I spent half an hour this evening composing a chorus on what may be my text next Thurs. 'Whatsoever, He saith unto you, do it.' We are so tired of our old Chorus Papers, and this may be a Change—Very simple tune at present, if any tune is discernible at all. The Vicar happens to be reading In the Hands of the Potter at present, at least I saw it open in the study.

[1] John Gunston's photographic studio at Alpenrose.
[2] Keats died on this day in 1821.

He is in London today, so will write his opinion as soon as possible. You should read *Broken Earthenware* first; I found it rather fascinating; But remember Begbie[1] is a clever journalist, and it is difficult to distinguish what in his writing is A R T, and what H E A R T.

I lately wrote to and received a letter from Miss Wright. D'you know I imagine Little Dorrit to have had exactly her features & proportions and, very often, her manner. Didn't that strike you? I am much enjoying that Book, tho' the Bathroom Scene made me quite ill. At no time do I now feel very well. Kemp too is for ever calling himself a wreck, feeling shattered, and so on. No doubt the weather?

I am very grateful to Father for his offered help for a Bicycle. Kemp tells me of a Bicycle Sale just [*starting*] in R'dg: Must go and [*two lines missing*] Mr. Fordham about a week ago also went to Torquay on business! Mr. Shields and many another Shrewsbury respectable, are rapidly passing out of my life. The 40–50 people I have seen today in a rapid trot round the parish—crowd out the old familiar faces—with exceptions. e.g. there is a lad of 13 who now seems ever so like Harold—in some respects. I shall pull his ears some day in mistake. Compliment W.H.O. [*final two lines missing*]

123. To Susan Owen
Postcard

16 February 1912   *Dunsden Vicarage*

Thanks for the Business Letter. I cannot yet reply to its Business Questions, except the Bicycle Matter. I went to a shop where there is a Sale just now on, & saw a New Enfield with 2 speed gear (which I specially want) reduced from £8 something to £6 something. There did not seem to be a 2nd hand one of my size or liking. They will of course take the old one and have eagerly offered to come up here to fetch it. I was rather frightened when I thought over what I had let them do, but it needs much repairing if I am to keep it, so it's all right.

I have only about £1½ until the end of the month, so heavy have been the cost of Boot Repairs, Washing, and recent extravagances over books—really necessaries after all.

I shall not (I speak foolishly) let my Raleigh go under 30s. Thought once of making it over to W.H.O. but even an artist's gentle touch couldn't guide those fragile tyres free from punctures. And it is too big? How much then Can you inveigle dear pater to contribute? You can

---

[1] *In the Hands of the Potter* (1911) and *Broken Earthenware* (1910) by Harold Begbie (1871–1929), author and journalist. Begbie wrote nearly fifty books, of which these two, on the inequalities of the existing social system, had an enormous popular impact. His most ambitious work was a two-volume *Life of William Booth* (1920); the one that made the greatest sensation was *The Mirrors of Downing Street*, by 'A Gentleman with a Duster', of which *The Times* wrote in its obituary: 'Begbie was much gratified by the praise lavished on the brilliance of the style, the insight and the power of irony of this man and unknown author by critics who did not think much of his work when published in his own name.'

guess & calculate without algebra the 'required unknown'.[1] Can you let me know as soon as possible? I do feel ashamed of begging thus when I live as if my income were £500, and sit on a chair worth £20! W.O.

124. To Susan Owen

5 March 1912. Good Friday   *Dunsden Vicarage*

Dearest Mother,

The slippers are in every way to my fancy, and I thank you for your promptitude in making them. The 'bars sinister', furrows, chasms and ridges, or whatever they may be, are indeed suggestive of Mme. Defarge,[2] or as you evasively write it " *the frauuuuu* ",

and I fear you must have been as constant a Knitter as she: (well since writing this I have been idly employed on the accompanying sketch, and as it somewhat realizes my 'Madame' I cannot resist sending it.) I'm bothered if I know how you adjust your digits when knitting, tho'.

My carbuncle is almost well now, thank you.

When you send a letter late on Monday Night, say, I do not get it till Wednes. mng!

(*Interval: Friday to Tues. Night!*)

I quite forgot whether I acknowledged 'the Parcel' or not. Anyhow the surprising amount of 'goodies' is worth a second time of thanking. I hardly can take a taste of the things, when I picture the delight of the Child when she hears the rustling of the paper-bags in my pocket! To quote Scott (for a marvel)

'All sunk and dim her eyes so bright
Her form decayed by pining,
Till through her wasted hand at night
You saw the taper shining.'[3]

How am I occupying myself? Well, 'but so so' on Monday; seeing the Spider invited me into his parlour, and there I was caught nicely, and had my patience sucked out of me, while bad blood took its place. During the whole afternoon we accomplished Nothing, save deciding that a whole batch of pictures, costing about 15s. each, were No good (i.e. for this house).

'Ha! Hum! Well! I'm puzzled. Very puzzled. Try this frame! Now that. Now this. Hum! well, I'm puzzled! Perfectly GHASTLY, isn't

[1] A pencilled calculation on this postcard indicates that Tom or Susan Owen sent £4. 10s. (£6 less 30s. for the old bicycle).
[2] The formidable leader of the knitting women of St. Antoine in *A Tale of Two Cities* by Charles Dickens.
[3]
Till through her wasted hands at night,
You saw the taper burning.
Sir Walter Scott, 'The Maid of Neidpath'.

117

it? Rather smitten with that, I must confess.' And so on, till it was time
to go to the Fordhams to tea. My boredom was completed there! Talked
of nothing worth rememb'ring; except I recollect, when the Vicar
repeated a snatch of 'To the Cuckoo', and finished up with, 'Well,
Wordsworth may have been a nice old man, and a lover of "Nacher",
but he was not a poet.' The Vicar's eyes caught mine, and the conversation speedily resumed a non-literary line. I shall remember that. And
oh! I remember how they all committed young Selwood to his grave;
shoved him in, one might say; locked the vault; trampled the earth
down tight.

Vicar: . . . thinks if he can only get away, he'll get better.

    Well, poor thing, we know better.

Mr. F.: I should just think so.

Vicar: Yes, humanly speaking, there is not a particle of hope.

Mr. F.: Absolutely; absolutely.

Mrs. F.: Well, vicar, as I was thinkin' jest now, when I 'eard you say
    'e thought 'e was gettin' better, well, I says, orfentimes, one 'as such
    delusions, an perchance its the doin' of Satan, and its jest a sign for us.

Miss F.: Yus. I only ope e may reelise it soon.'

What will you think of me, for this naughtiness! Perhaps you had
better burn my letter at once. Yet no! I would suggest what Junkets (so
he sometimes styled himself) said to his Sister,

'You will preserve all my Letters and I will secure yours—and thus in the
course of time we shall each of us have a good Bundle—which, hereafter, when
things may have strangely altered and God knows what happened, we may read
over together, and look with pleasure on times past that now are to come.'[1]

Ah! in my hours of 'ennui' as hinted above, what balm I find in saying
over and over to myself such lines as these;

> . . . 'The solitary breeze
> Blustered and slept, and its wild self did teaze
> With wayward melancholy, and I thought,
> Mark me, Peona!, that sometimes it brought
> Faint fare-thee-wells', and sigh-shrilled adieus.'
>   (*Endymion*)[2]

I left Fordham's early to be at the Club, for the boys could not spend
Bank Holiday Evening better than at the Hall and would not be put off.

On Sat. I secretly met with Vivian*[3] at a stile and went a delicious
ramble; lay in hawthorn glades, where antlered stags[4] would come
within a few yards of us. He read to me, and I told him tales. I took some
figs of Mary's for him, (for I . . . [*two words illegible*] and arriving

---

[1] Keats to his sister Fanny, 10 September 1817 (*Letters* I, p. 153).
[2] Book I, ll. 686–90.
[3] Vivian Rampton. See Letter 125 and p. 229, note 2.
[4] There was a herd of deer at Crowsley Park, near Dunsden. See Letter 142.

home at 6, I went without tea, willingly. The weather last week was glorious; and one afternoon I half spent in a daisy-meadow, with the 'Fairy Bray', with another and (to me) more enchanting elf, being older and well-spoken, and with various insignificant brothers and sisters. We sought the Biggest Daisy, and the Reddest† Daisy. My elf found them (oh yes, honestly!) and I found the Golden Age. Talk of Miss Moses!

What a black-slander about the brute black-hand, son of Bruce B——!¹ All the blacker‡ being true; but you don't circulate it do you?

I sang a solo on Good Friday—'O come and mourn'. I enjoyed it thoroughly and now quite wish you could hear me in the Hall. Such a lot of people turned up; (not to hear me, for I was only asked at lunch-time.)
Gordon stayed all day Sunday here; but I had to entertain Willie, who left our establishment today. A Dissenter is now installed here!
I don't expect to get any sort of Easter holiday. Vicar is going away next week for Spring Cleaning.
Really, I could go on all night with letter-writing To You: but now I drop pen, for I want to read over your last dear kind letter and wonder how you enjoyed today, before I tap-tap at the Study-door, and banish candid expression.

Á Dieu, Wilfred

Make up what loving messages you like to M, H, & C, and Father; you know my heart.

* —an' mind you, not the feminine termination '-en'.
† Little did I reck that the adjectives of colour have no comparative or superlative degree!
‡ There I am again!

125. To Susan Owen

March 1912   *Dunsden Parish Hall*

Dearest Mother,
    This letter is a few days late, in consideration of my rather frequent epistles lately. Once again, you see, I am writing at the Club while timing Red Lanterns (otherwise Boxers.) This is because after tea today the Vicar wanted us to go a ride with him; The evening was indeed very lovely; and I enjoyed seeing new country. You remember I half promised to give some music lessons to one of my favourite Boys (Vivian); well, he is very keen (at present speaking) and I have given him two on the Hall Piano after 'Thurs. Afternoon's'. I promised indeed to give him four lessons gratis, and after that to exact a slight fee.

¹ Unexplained. We have omitted the full name.

This has set his Mother all agog to get a piano. She saw an advertisement for one; and begged the favour of my going to examine and pronounce upon it. This I did; and again rode in today (to Reading) to meet the lady and help her to decide. All these negotiations are done unbeknown to the rest of the Parish (I hope): & the Vicarage in particular.

I could get no farther with my writing at the club, and so, having had my 9.15 o'clock repast in solitude and happiness, I now sit down before your distant presence and finish this communication.

Mr. Moore came in time for tea yesterday and stayed the night. We had a full enough Hall, made fuller by the Gunston Family complete, Mrs. Cates, & Mrs. Francis.[1]

The Text was: 'And the yoke . . (pause) . . shall be BROKEN . . . (pause & gasp) . . . becau-se of the anNOINTing!' (This extraordinary ciphering is meant to represent the manner of delivery.)

What the dear old man said, it is not the time to repeat here, but I must remark upon How he spoke.

Just precisely as if he had never slept, eaten, or stopped delivering since we saw him in Wimbledon—so unchanged is he. How I revel in his dramatism. With what absolute command he modulates his voice-tones. The shrill declamatory top-note (almost passing into a shriek) in an instant changed for a hollow, deep, sepulchral groan, that seems to feel its way beneath the very tables of the heart!

The subdued persuasive undersong quietly leads us through labyrinths of agreeable meditation . . . Then like a thunderbolt, flashes and roars a sentence, making one jump in his seat.

Gradually the storm subsides, until once more we are brought up with a jerk . . . and so on; until we fairly hang upon his words and it is impossible not to attend.

Then there is the hand-play—how he finishes off a thought with a trail of the fingers instead of words; clinches a statement with a clap, instead of an epigram; points to a long-dead figure, and we see it; sparing epithets.

Then there is the body-play: advancing, he forces an argument upon our brains; retreating he is horrified as if at the audience, bending forward he drives home his points as with a mallet; leaning backwards he pleads, as before a court.

Then there is the Foot-play, for he even drags heavily his boot upon the floor under the weight of some distressing thought.

Then there is the Face-play: the sharp grey eyes, shooting right and left at the close of every period; and never letting a single person out of sight for two minutes together. And how extraordinary sometimes is his resemblance to 'the Canon'. When he compresses his lips; droops the eyebrows, takes in a deep breath, and pats nervously with his hand upon the table—then the scene changes; I am in Christchurch!

---

[1] Her husband managed a game-rearing farm in the neighbourhood owned by a cousin of John Gunston.

What I like so is the sighs; and the 'tut-tut-tut's'; the apostrophes; the hand-on-chin asides; the confidential, confirmatory repetition of 'you do (click of tongue, shake of head) . . you do (click of tongue, shake of head) . . you do' in a whisper, after some telling affirmation . . .

Well, well; all this is beside the mark, perhaps you think, and to notice such is to defeat the purpose for which they were intended. And alas, the boys present could scarce keep from laughing. Ah! how could I have laughed ever!

For now he is among the chiefest prophets in my—what shall I call it?—Theogony. Yes—Theogony; for such aged benignity and saintliness on the one hand; and the youthful genius of poets on the other, press home to me the secret of much in Religion—at least false religions. I could (if I did not hear the 'See thou do it not!' within), fall down and worship either. And had I lived in the days of Buddha, Confucian, Zoroaster, or Mahomet, I should have been the first to start preaching their deification.

The dear man was seriously shocked to hear of Dorothy's apostasy;[1] quite unnecessary to tell him; for his quarter-hour expostulation with her before us all after the meeting was of none effect. I plied him with a few questions after supper; but gained nothing conclusive; where shall I?

The Vicar presides over the Plumber![2] Kemp is pretty sure of Highbury now.

I really mean you to send by rly. the 'Andersen'; and if needs, to eke it out with any 'school' Shakespere's you find; and my Arabian Nights; also the MS. book, I mentioned.

Do you know I have an idea of versifying such Fairy Tales as are suitable;[3] and of trying to publish them. They always had an immense attraction for me; and if I don't spoil them in trying 'to paint their roses, and throw perfume on their violets', they ought to do.

At any rate, some settled task, may kill my present lassitude. The very thought has made me sleepy, and so—a fair Good-night!

From your affectionate son, Wilfred

P.S. I hope you will be agreeably disappointed to hear that what you thought a 'Quotation' is perfectly original; 'a poor thing, but mine own'; & so far as I know not expressed before: it was 'printed' simply for the sake of emphasis. As you dwelt on 'When I survey', I might say what Canon Barnes Lawrence told me—Matthew Arnold was once in a Church in Liverpool, in 1888, when that was sung; and he was very moved, saying it was the finest piece of religious poetry in our tongue—or something like that. That day he fell down dead—from heart failure.[4]

[1] Later, however, Dorothy Gunston became a missionary.
[2] A reformed character, much in demand at public evangelical meetings. See pp. 126–7.
[3] See Letter 82.
[4] Matthew Arnold died in Liverpool, 15 April 1888, where he had gone to meet his daughter on her return from America.

Do you remember a girl at the Mothers' Meeting who looked ill, having had appendicitis. On Monday she thought herself dying; and was in a state of fearful terror. Mrs. Fordham dealt with her; and she has found peace now. She is better, too. You do not say how you are feeling; or whether a new maid has been found.

I am, of course, all right again; (and much enjoyed the Gingerbreads). How did Father enjoy Torquay?

126. To Susan Owen

11 March 1912   *Dunsden Parish Hall*

My dearest Mother,

I am taking out a few minutes from the Club Time to answer your letter. There are ten stalwart youths now under my eye, so pardon if I wander. The vicar & Mr. Fordham left early today, & a telegram tells us they are safe at a hotel.

Mrs. Fordham invited Kemp & me to tea, together with Miss Hendy; our music was cut short (as far as I am concerned) at seven. My photographs are not yet finished; but I am afraid they are all 'mucked up',—Kemp did not even expose one of the 3 plates, tho' he thinks he has! But I mean to try again.

You were right in guessing my occupation last Saturday at 6.45; I fancy I was thinking of you then—at least in my extensive mind-travels at that hour I touch usually upon Mahim, England. I indeed wished for your presence on Sunday. Most enjoyable service. I really shall never tolerate St. Julian's crashing organ-blasts and choking boys after our clear, stirring melodies and dim religious light. The sermons I could only bear interchanged once a month (say). The Concertina improves minute by minute. I was required to accompany the wheezy concert-screamer on the organ, and 'soothly one might imagine it a violin, so pleasant were some tones.

I had an Ambrose to tea on Sunday. With an easy glide, I entered upon Deep Waters, when we were alone, and the poor lad is in a fearful Fog. It thickens every day. I can get him to say little, but by talking what I knew was in his mind (for an hour) I have nearly apprehended his state. Marvellous how a farmhand should be inflicted with earnest self-questioning every time he is alone. Like many a famous philosopher, he leans to the opinion that the personality of man becomes utterly extinct upon Death, and he cannot profess a Christian's hope. How shall I answer?

If others knew the fog, fog fog which rolled in my mind, they would wonder that I should try to lighten another being. But I spend most of my time now in reading, analysing, collecting, sifting, and classifying Evidence, whereas he has neither time nor powers to probe the mysteries of Reason and Revelation. Of course I do not talk to him quite in this strain, but I try to uncover the grappling-hooks which are holding down his soul (supposing he has one.) His chief difficulty is <u>Language</u>. So is mine. In <u>his</u> case, <u>Bad</u> Language though one would never have thought it. He hates it, and he cannot escape it.

In <u>my</u> case, <u>Fine</u> Language, to yield wholly to the glamours of which would be accounted 'of this world' by those who aver they are not of this world.

I love it, and I cannot escape it.

More, I dare not say now. You will think I have been 'in the clouds'. Nay, I have been in my Cor Cordium, my heart of hearts.

I must return to externals again to say that I shall probably <u>not</u> go to a Doctor. This bright weather puts my mopes to shame. My body needs no physician. Then my eye got better without any pharmaceutical fumbling; for, feeling it slightly less painful, I went into the Library, and there, with a parting stab, the grit seemed suddenly to leave me [*final sheet missing*]

127. To Susan Owen

16 March 1912   *Dunsden Vicarage*

My own dear Mother,

I hope you will get this by your Birthday; though I know you must have given up hope of getting the Pen Case by the 17th. Anyhow I say Many and Happy be the Returns of the Day to thee! What would you like me to give you at the next 'return'?—so I may set about to think about beginning to start to choose something?

The Lantern worked splendidly under my manipulation on Wednesday; tho' I only brought up the Slides from the Station at the last moment. There was no solo-singing. Brother Kemp was rather amusing over his part of the duties; for not wanting to <u>stand up</u> to read; he had the <u>Study Reading Lamp</u> taken to the Hall, and <u>seated</u> himself at the table at my side, with the result that all behind were 'blinded with excess of light.' Of course this conduct was soon nipped in the bud.

I got (or rather allowed) a favourite boy (Vivian) to help me with the slides; and on Thurs. managed to smuggle the same urchin to tea with me, having conveniently drafted the 'Kemptitude' upon the Fordhams. Such a tête-à-tête tea, by the open window of the Den, with the odours of the Currant-Shrubs balmily wandering in and commingling with the essences in the solid-silver tea-pot—is a thing to enjoy.

On Friday afternoon, I was also in a pleasure-vein; spending an hour and a half in the School. I made a careful inspection of the drawings, dealt out the usual supplies of encouraging praise, and found the usual merriment in the dunces' work; tigers, for instance, which looked like your slavey's old boots thus:

Nevertheless, there were some very fine Drawings from some; and Lorrie Ambrose, now a 'bird-starver', showed unmistakable talent! His paintings should startle Harold, if he saw them. Then, I went out to see Mrs. Hulcoop drill the smaller boys and girls; begged permission to give them a few commands; was accorded the same with great pleasure; and so put them thro' the old familiar Hips—FIRM! Neck—RESST! Darlings some of them are! I could have hugged them, rather than put any in the corner. Such is the force of the reaction—from now living where the voice of children is not heard, because they are not! After this I went thro' a collection of fossils and flints brought by scholars, and found one genuine chipped implement.

From school, I rendered myself to Fordhams' tea with Kemp, and thence went a walk under lovely clear sky to Caversham Heights to visit an invalid lady; friend of Mrs. F.'s and also visited at her word, by the Vicar. This invalid lives with her old mistress, a lady, old-maid, accomplished, and having a rather nice house. Next door lives a boy (of 15) who has composed music to a Hymn, and the old lady would have hustled this prodigy in for us to behold, if he had not been out. Now this school-boy has an older brother who aspires to be a journalist; and when I heard this I pricked up my ears the more: apparently visibly, for I received an invitation to meet one or other next Friday. I wonder what I shall make of them! It was strange enough to find oneself 'at home' in a totally new household last Friday: It will be stranger still next week.

Is the Burden of your household shifted for a lighter one yet?

The Vicar has just returned: plus antiques as we had prophesied! Mrs. Lott wants me to teach her Niece Pianoforte Music, with some slight remuneration, of course! Her late teacher & Kemp will come no more. I shall not refuse, tho' I feel something of a Charlatan over it. What I receive may pay for one or two lessons for me.

Kisses & Love from

Your own Wilfred

128. To Susan Owen

19 March 1912   *Dunsden Vicarage*

My own dear Mother,

How shall I thank you for the letters, the counsel, the presents, the love, that have swamped me yesterday and today?—By a brief note, and by a few verses[1]—which you must not read before the letter. Alas, small comfort have I found in the food-gifts, as if to punish me for ever allowing such low, animal concerns to be sent to me. For on Sunday evening, after Church, I was stricken down, with genuine Indigestion, or some allied complaint; and when, for relief I prostrated my trunk on the Dining Room Floor, folks began to make much of me. After a

---

[1] The first indication that Wilfred was sending home poems for his mother's comments.

little supper of chicken and copious draughts of Ginger, I was ordered to bed by Mrs. Lott, who brought a 'Bottle'; and also placed a Brandy Bottle by me. I slept well. But on my birthday morning I was awakened by the unrelenting gnawings within, and took a bit of toast for breakfast. The couch from the passage was then brought down for me, and thereon I lay all day; finding relief however very soon after breakfast-time. To ease me, I employed my time upon the 'lines', which you have, with the ink, as it were, still wet upon them.

Today I am better still, insomuch that I <u>visited</u>, this afternoon. So prithee don't magnify my state; (tho' I <u>haven't yet</u> dared to open my tin-boxes.)

I had a card from Torquay on the 18th; and a note from Aunt Emma; which incidentally mentions that her Doctor has the 'Flue'. Hip! Hip!—unless I take a turn for the worse—when I shall change my tune.

I am delighted with the colour of the slippers; nothing could be better—(unless it were a rather less dark colour; for by gaslight this looks not quite bright enough.) But they are distinctly large, and I think I shall ask for a smaller pair if you would be so very good; tho' it is hard for me to wait, you know.

I will try and write to my dear kith and kin very soon. Let me have news of Father.

Kemp is in London today—seeing about 'hostels' and all that sort of thing; with a visit to Harris Jones,[1] to buck up the tardy money-mongers. How dare they be so slow in emptying their pockets; when so deserving a marvel holds out his hands?

I forgot to say—Mary may see my 'last production'—and then I want it back please. Don't be content with a first reading but if you fail to see any point at all, 'tis no fault of yours. Consider how quickly I wrote! I shall get the pen case at my earliest opportunity.

Your own Wilfred

129. To Susan Owen

23 March 1912 (Saturday)   *Dunsden Vicarage*

My dearest Mother,

I am enjoying my Saturday Night's solitude, and tho' tired (not to say, '*ennuyé*') after the P.M. I am sitting down to let you know that I am better:—Sitting at the new Chippendale Bureau designated for my use. (I say 'new', tho' its date is something like old Goldsmith's!) Naturally it is much more costly than the one parted-with, but its fittings are very crude, its drawers crazy, and its surface bears many an aged wound. The task of clearing out the old, dusting the new, and filling it has consumed far too much of my time! But all this is nothing to the blank disappointment I have suffered in being informed that the 'Roll Top' is sold, and is going next week.

[1] Unidentified.

My indignation knew its bounds and I refrained my tongue; but I shall be out when the moving-time comes.

Someone else may take a lesson in the taking down of window sashes. Kemp is furious within; tho' much cooler externally than I, and less gaudy, about the cheeks. For he spent hours in arranging his drawers to his liking. 3 chairs from the Den are also going; my bedroom chairs; table from the drawing-room, table from the hall, second table from ditto; candlesticks from den, fiddlesticks from everywhere! Mrs. Lott has 10½ fits daily. We are besieged by upholsterers.

As Miss Edgeworth says, parodying Shakespere's—'The Poet's Eye'—

> 'The upholsterer's eye, in a fine frenzy rolling
> Glances from ceiling to floor, from floor to ceiling;
> And, as imagination bodies forth
> The form of things unknown, the upholsterer's pencil
> Turns them to shape, and gives to airy nothing
> A local habitation and a name.'[1]

Concertina-practice fills up intervals not so occupied; Sundays not excepted. Shall I enjoy tomorrow's denunciation of things temporal; oh no doubt! 'Let us pray!'—'Certainly, by all means!'

Such is the current of my thoughts at the moment. 'Twill change with the wind, never fear.

I was so much better on Thurs. as to take my beloved children; and must be ready for my boys tomorrow.

I even ventured on the ginger-breads, and have almost finished the prunes. I am holding aloof from the short-breads; and I mean to give some to a gentle little girl of five, fast sinking under Consumption— contracted after chickenpox. Isn't it pitiable? She is going to a hospital (weeks hence of course), and may be beyond reach of doctors by that time. She can't take unappetising food, poor Violet;[2] but how is aught else to be provided her; when the Father is perennially out of work, and the Mother I fancy half-starving for the sake of four children. This, I suppose, is only a typical case; one of many Cases! O hard word! How it savours of rigid, frigid professionalism! How it suggests smooth and polished, formal, labelled, mechanical callousness! Even the gaunt Selwood is not yet provided for; and is not likely to be.

Have you read *Broken Earthenware* yet. I have got an Invitation from Rudolph Consterdine to hear 'The Plumber', at Henley Y.M.C.A. What a treat! It might almost be an invitation to hear Bill Sykes. Try and get up the Subject before Apr. 1st, the date fixed!

Do you think you could send my ponderous Andersen's Fairy Tales per G.W.R. I absolutely will not have it by post.

The garden is now gay with daffodils; but no break in the rain permits one to enjoy them. I spent one morning in the Conservatory, reading.

[1] From Maria Edgeworth, *The Absentee* (1812), ch. 2.
[2] Violet Franklin.

I could wish for no better colour than the Royal Purple for my slippers. The same shape too, please: but Length <u>under</u> 10 in. in sole; and could you make the ankle-gap an inch or two smaller?

These slippers are much too big for Kemp; and I should not think of offering them. Shall be anxious to get my own; but don't rush yourself with them.

I have not been able to get to Reading yet; nor even to Alpenrose. So your present may wait till next year!

<u>How are you all keeping</u>? Best love to all, from

Your own Wilfred

130. To Susan Owen

3 April 1912   *Dunsden Vicarage*

My own dear Mother,

I have just got a minute or two before we go down to 'the Lantern'. I spent the whole of the morning in the garden—O magnificent environment wherein to read Tennyson! And what a Summer it promises! But beware! For at breakfast his 'riverence' croaked something about Croquet, and putting up Hoops. I laughed, as if it were absurd at this time of year, but depend upon it, we shall soon start. Every hoop will be a gallows for my minutes; the tinkling bell will ring the death-knell of my time.

This afternoon I shot into Reading for the Parcel, but could find no trace of it at the Station yet.

Since I wrote last I have endured much at the hands of a 'boil breaking out with blains' after the fashion of last Sunday's Morning Lesson! Very Grievous. Situation—On neck between ear and chin! Mrs. Lott poulticed on Saturday & Sunday, sent in broth at 11 o'clock, and generally behaved in a Motherlike way. I just managed to take my Class; of course appearing before it and in Church with a neck-gear such as Wordsworth wore. I took care to be able to wear a Collar on Monday Night. Plumber much as you might have expected; wore the identical Belt which carried the lead, and thwacked his progeny. I feel too lazy now to pass remarks upon him, especially as the Vicar has secured him for a meeting here, some day!

A friend of Kemp's from Cambridge (Morley)[1] has been here today. He is going to take his first curacy in Reading at the end of the year.

(*Interval*)

Lantern Lecture is now over: but without ever showing the slides! The connecting tube cracked, so there was nothing for it but to turn the taps off and the lamps up.

So 'Dickey' is defunct.

---

[1] The Rev. Reginald Wragge Morley, Curate of St. John the Evangelist, Reading. In 1950 he became Prebendary of Inkberrow in Hereford Cathedral.

I do desire and demand of Mary to compose a short Elegy and send it me.

Many thanks for your longish letter, and for the unasked-for Contents of the Parcel (this in anticipation.)

Early service tomorrow, not Evening, so I mean to fight my way to bed!

Good Night! and Peace be with you,   from Wilfred

131. To Susan Owen

12 April 1912   *Dunsden Vicarage*

Lest you should fret, dear Mother, for some news, and in considera-tion of your full and increasingly interesting Budgets to me, here is a Note to go on with; tho' I am abominably tired, and could compose myself in my sheets of fine linen, better than compose my thoughts on sheets of paper; being indisposed to any effort at the moment, and ill-disposed to things in general. This is because, after my visiting, I joined the Vicar in an excursion to Reading. Had tea there; and spent the whole blessed evening, in looking through batches of pictures through someone else's eyes. The attempt to focus one's own vision with that other is rather a strain. All this has arisen out of the following position—Here are 4 frames; each is worth a picture; therefore buy pictures which will fit, and which also will be bearable!

Oh dear! had such a shock today: Vicar is talking of once more chang-ing my bureau; and made a show of consulting me about it with his desired-one before us (in Silver's Antique Shop). Then and there, I said I hoped and trusted that it would not matter to me for long; and mentioned the Den.—Perhaps I am not going to have the Den! was the drift of his evasive reply. In point of fact, I think I shall. But if not, I think I shall ask Mr. Robson to do a little framing for me, as he promised! You remember?

And yet I ought to be full of laudations of the Vicar, as indeed I was all yesterday. He has given me a 'Medici' Print of the Virgin's head which I admired for him (never thinking of a gift) but which he dislikes rather. Also a good frame to match! Price of picture alone, 10/6! How, then, should I be dissatisfied?

Kemp & I had tea at Cain's yesterday, & played Croquet afterwards.

I will answer your letter in more detail next week.

On Monday I go to see Leslie in M. of Venice.[1] About now my Histrionic (see dictionary) crave comes on; perhaps because 'my' Company[2] used to visit Shrews: in this month. Ever your

loving Wilfred

---

[1] LG, now a pupil at the Kendrick School, Reading, played the Duke in his school production
of *The Merchant of Venice* in the Town Hall.
[2] Sir Frank Benson's Company.

132. To Susan Owen

16 April 1912   *Dunsden Vicarage*

My dearest Mother,

What do you think of the latest work of Kemp's Camera?[1] I took Kemp, and I think it is splendid of him. I am not very struck with the 'Hatted' one of me, but the other appears to me very natural, almost animated. Would you like one to keep? Because you must please send all these three back, together with the 'unearthly' one.

This morning I went into Reading with the iron-clenched purpose of bearding the College Tutorial Secretary in his Den. After a long wait, I saw him, and settled to take only Botany Classes, this term:

> 2 hrs. on Tues!
> 3 hrs. on Wed!!
> 1 hour on Thurs. (afternoon).

This is grand. Now can you let me have £3? I may be able to return it in a few months' time. Classes start tomorrow. So please send off my Gown[2] at once per G.W.R.; and with it, if you find any, my Shakesperes (*Julius Caesar*; *As You Like It*; *Mid Night's Dream*.) (No Chamber's.) I don't think I need a Cap. I spoke to one of the Lecturers, Miss Rayner,[3] and she seems very nice indeed. Premises and all appurtenances are admirable. The lady, with her satellites was photographing the eclipse[4] when I interviewed her. I was riding home at 12.10; the sky was clear; and very weird the universe seemed; the atmosphere dulled as if charged with volcanic dust, especially on the horizon.

I am so glad you had a good time on your picnic. We go to tea at Fordhams' on Friday next.

Yes, the Vicar did speak thus contumeliously of Wordsworth; he sinned in ignorance. Did my tongue well in cleaving to the roof of my mouth?

Ah, Junkets, who? Why, Jun-kēts, John Keats; (so he signed a letter,[5] or I should not have dared . . .) Marvel ye, that I handle thus lightly his Name? Well, thro' reading his Letters, as I have just begun to do, I see him in a truer light; not one whit less to be reverenced, and fifty whits more lovable; having so many 'wits' unrevealed to me before. He didn't lack humour, narrabitavit, and his laugh lived in many ears, long after death 'had fed on his mute voice'.[6]

---

[1] Probably the photograph reproduced here as Plate IVb and as frontispiece in *JO* II.

[2] HO recalls a cap and gown at Mahim, presumably those worn by Wilfred when he took the Matriculation examination in London.

[3] Miss M. M. C. Rayner was Lecturer in Botany at University College, Reading, 1908–13, and was one of those to whom Wilfred later planned to give a copy of his collected poems after the war. See Letter 359, note 1, and p. 561, note 3.

[4] 16 April 1912. It began at 10.51 a.m. and reached its maximum at 12.11 (as Wilfred was riding home). It was the largest solar eclipse seen in the British Isles for fifty-four years.

[5] To Leigh Hunt from Margate, 10 May: 'Your sincere friend John Keats alias Junkets—' (*Letters* I, p. 136.)

[6]   Death feeds on his mute voice, and laughs at our despair.
                                                        Shelley, *Adonais*, 1.27.

Small time I now shall get for private reading; I am 'Correspondent of Dunsden School'; Yes, ma'am; hi! you there, on your knees, man; don't-cher-know who I am? Fancy Colin tweaking the conk of the Correspondent of Dunsden School! All manner of red-lined accounts, greasy vouchers, and type-written letters come under my lock and key. I pull the strings, and set five teachers and a hundred scholars chattering. You know how I detest 'ledgery'. Still, I suppose, it can do no harm to gain a working knowledge of moneys and usurances.

The Vicar is hiding his nose from the Spring Dust Storms among the rocks of Clevedon. Despite household-conditions which make Study or Composition impossible, Kemp & I are having a delightsome se'nnite; 'ho, ho, ho, ho; we make good sport,—with—ho! ho! ho!'

Kemp carols, from a full heart, indeed; his Course at Highbury is a fixed thing; £200 have been raised!

I am looking forward immensely to showing Father round about, and in and out; but they said something about being unable to have him sometime at the end of the month. I don't know!

A holiday in Scotland,[1] magnificent! I suppose I shall be taken to Keswick[2] in July.

Leslie looked a very ducal personage on Monday, spoke very distinctly too. Shylock gesticulated rather well; but spoke far too choppily; every other word seemed to have a full-stop after it.

Portia & Nerissa beautifully feminine; but P. must have had a cold; positively saying—'It droppeth as the ged-tle raid frob heaved upud the place bedeath.' Oh, it must have been the outcome, the issue of a bunged up nose; like something else of which the quotation is somewhat descriptive. Bassanio's (Hulcoop's) tights were all baggy!—No more of this Critique; my charge is ninepence, please.

Your own, Wilfred

133. To Susan Owen

23 April 1912   *Dunsden Vicarage*

Dearest Mother,

I had your Letter this morning, and your Parcel tonight! It got out of the Station before I could catch it on Sat; and Carriers have been bandying it about ever since. You must please, in future, label conspicuously—'To be left till called for—not per Carrier.' if it is small enough for my bicycle. Many are the thanks I owe you for so carefully detecting anything Shakesperean in my shelves. I suppose I must thank you for the eats too. But you must positively send no more. I am most distressed to hear about the Bills; and I do wish, for your sake, a scramble might be made to get, and keep 'Cr.' The College Sec. does not seem to

---

[1] With Mrs. Bulman and her family at Kelso. See Letter 147.
[2] The Keswick Convention, an Evangelical Summer convention run by Anglicans and Free Churchmen, has been held every summer since 1875 at Keswick in the Lake District. The Rev. E. W. Moore (see Letter 41, note 4) was one of the founder clergy.

want my fees yet; so I shall do nothing until Father brings me some 'spondoolick' (as Kemp calls it). Then, in a month or two, I shall be able to repay;—if I 'take Mr. Kemp's place' on the accounts, as I hope I shall do in space; having already more than done so in the spear of dooty.

One thing in your letter made me exceedingly ratty! the tent;[1] scandalous; I could not make out what you meant at first; and still can't make out why! Cussed be Canaan a servant of servants shall he be; for dwelling in the tents of ours. Had a letter from Stanley this morning too; I'll ha' none on't. They have enough 'putheriveleges', (as Canon Barnes-Laurence would say.) Here am I, my fee for one course of lectures, unpaid, with no-wherewithal to buy a College Cap, or a pair of Flannels. 'The Revolutionary Ideals, crossing the Channel into England, inspired the British School of revolt and reconstruction in Burns, Shelley, Byron, Wordsworth, Coleridge and Tennyson, till its fires have died down today.'[2] Have they! They may have in the bosoms of the muses, but not in my breast. I am increasingly liberalising and liberating my thought, spite of the Vicar's strong Conservatism. And when he paws his beard, and wonders whether £10. is too high a price for new curtains for the dining room, (in place of the faded ones you saw); then the fires smoulder; I could shake hands with Mrs. Dilber who stole Scrooge's Bed-Curtains; and was affronted that old Joe[3] was surprised, or questioned her right! From what I hear straight from the tight-pursed lips of wolfish ploughmen in their cottages, I might say there is material ready for another revolution. Perhaps men will strike, not with absence from work; but with arms at work. Am I for or against upheaval? I know not; I am not happy in these thoughts; yet they press upon me. I am happier when I go to 'distribute dole

To poor sick people, richer in His eyes,
Who ransomed us, and haler too than I'.[4]

These lines I quote, have haunted me incessantly. Perhaps because they are true. Anyhow, in obedience to you, and certain inward monitions, I have been to Dr. Gandy:[5] nominally to ask whether I can play tennis. No! No! No! and on no account to ride up hills! He sounded me most thoroughly, travelling round my trunk two or three times; and this was his conclusion at once. So I am eased; yes, I am glad I went.

This morning I had my first 'lecture' and also an hour's practical work with the microscope. I am sure I shall enjoy the Course.

If any more of my old set call, do tell them to write.

Here are some more photographs. The Best 'Smiler' is yours. The other (taken in eclipse, doncherknow) for Mary.

[1] A small tent, used in the garden at Mahim, had been lent to Stanley Webb.
[2] Unidentified.
[3] All from *A Christmas Carol*.
[4] Tennyson, *Idylls of the King: Guinevere*.
[5] The doctor at Peppard (whose wife wrote plays and poetry and published several books for children).

The one I like, and the boys, is Harold's—proviso—he takes care of it; for they are costly affairs. And we spent hours 'doing them' today; and Kemp's turned out no good; though he taught me with them. I mean to have one taken in gown. One of these for Colin. Now—no more.

Your own, Wilfred

I am really anxious to see Father again; despite the Tent affair.

Can't you get your camera to take you? At least you might do this; if you don't come with Father, to see your Mother-languishing son.

W

134. To Susan Owen

29 April 1912   *Alpenrose*

Dearest Mother,

Thanks for your last letter. I am sending this in advance of my usual hebdomadary journal, because Father desires it. He came to Dunsden on Sunday with Leslie [*two words illegible*] and stayed to Lunch. I took him a walk in the afternoon under strong sunshine. He stayed to tea & then Kemp took him to the Hall during my Class-time. But, no class appeared, except for two; and so I infer the altered time will never do. After church, to which Aunt etc. came, I walked half way home with Father.

Then, this morning I went to Dr. Gandy's again, with Kemp, who has something of a sore throat. The Dr. wanted to see me 'quieter', (because I had hurried in going the first time). And he said he found me so, i.e. 'quieter', today. But still it would be insane to 'crock myself up' for the sake of a game of Tennis. They have been playing today, and if I had taken Father's advice I should too; by the 'just-one-won't-hurt-you' fallacy, don't you know. Gandy didn't even tell me 'one or two wouldn't hurt me' as Dr. Livesy told Billy Bones in *Treasure Island* speaking of his glass of rum. But he as much as said a strenuous bout would be dangerous madness. I shall feel not being able to 'join in' considerably in summer evenings; but I thank my constellation, I have something better. And that I have never really whetted my appetite for any sport, game, play, recreation or diversion demanding muscular exertion under the sun. I wish, though, (especially as I am not working under pressure, and am under pressure not to play games) I could take up music again under a teacher,—well,—worthy of me.

During the last week or two I have been photography-mad. We have been sharp-shooting each other day after day; and murdering each other as often. Nevertheless I shall be able to send you some passable portraits very soon. On Friday we snapped 'the Children'; and spent the whole service-time in doing it!

I stayed to lunch here this afternoon, & it is now getting on for tea-time. Kemp has come for tennis & is staying tea [*two lines illegible*]

I cannot tell you how a Spring in the country is enchanting me. Not that it does not inspire me—but I am too inert to tell. <u>Alas that you</u> <u>were here!</u>

If '<u>Time</u>' is the Enemy,
  '<u>Space</u>' is his aide-de-camp.   Your own Wilfred

I really <u>will</u> write to one or other of the Family next time.

135. To Mary Owen

6 May 1912   *Dunsden Vicarage*

Dearest Mary,

I was very pleased to hear of your Prize, your Exam Results, & your little Holiday. Here are some more prizes for you, if you value them enough: two Portraits of me, made and marred by Mr. Kemp; and some we took of the 'Children'. Keep if you like, the Group of Boys & Girls Combined, but unless you particularly fancy them, send back the others. I am also sending two I took of Mr. Kemp; not to show you how much better I can snap than he, but to give you an idea of the braggadocio he looks in Cap & Gown. . . . I forgot! I promised Colin one of me; please let him choose between the (1) Bearded One, and the (2) Caesar's Aunt's Ghost. The beard is due to Mr. K's pen-knife, which for some unaccountable reason he tried to use as a razor on the negative & spoilt it.

The <u>hand holding the book</u> in (2) is a stray one of Mrs. Lott's. None of my <u>growing</u>.

Perhaps you will recognise some of the Children.

In 'Girls' Only' the Black Sheep, appropriately enough, wears a sombre coat; while my favourite (between meum and tuum, sister dear) wears a snowy pinafore, with her nut-brown hands disposed in front; (in the same row as the B.S.)

The boys make a very interesting study in expressions.

Mr. K. left this morning.

  'Toll for the Brave!
  Brave Kemp in felt is gone!'[1]

Yes, not with his eight hundred; but with his <u>two</u> <u>hundred</u>! For the Vicar made it up to that sum, this morning! The <u>Vicar</u> has an attack of Influenza, Sore Throat, Arthritis, etc, etc, and is still in bed. Vicar of Sonning took duty yesterday. Consequently I feel still more Kemp's departure. And if the pen was not in his hand when he went down (the

----

[1] Toll for the brave—
Brave Kempenfelt is gone. . . .
  His sword was in the sheath,
  His fingers held the pen,
    When Kempenfelt went down
  With twice four hundred men.
            William Cowper, *Loss of the Royal George.*

drive); it soon was in mine; even to write a sonnet on the good fellow's departure; But it came to nothing.

———————

I suppose Father must be better, as I hear nothing. Indeed I hope so. And how much extra toil does Mother find it needful to do, with the new abigail?

I shall be delighted with the Camera. Will Mother please send some Picture Frames with the Package: e.g. Post Card Frame; Tennyson, Virgin, (if not too big); (not the 'Flower One') and any others.

Please take great care of photos to be returned. They are expensive items.

Your loving, Wilfred

136. To Susan Owen
Postcard

[Postmark 8 May 1912]   *[Postmark Reading]*

I made up a Parcel of certain wearable tubes of cloth; intending to send by post—found it would drag too severely on what pockets I have left after sending these; and so am sending the thing by train tomorrow morning. A Letter is enclosed. Thanks for yours of this morning.

W

137. To Susan Owen

Sabbath Even, 12 May [1912]   *[Postmark Reading]*

Here is just a haypeth to give you dimensions. Dimentions did you say? Don't mention it!

I will only say I do want to carry the thing myself, so saving 3 to 6d. 'Use your judgment!' as an Examining Vigilator would say. There will be small need for Pictures; e'er a Wall, though. . . . I have many things to say to you pleasant & otherwise—but you cannot bear them yet.

Why? because it is 10.30 on my Day of Rest. And it's about time the Rest began to make itself felt. Let Wales enfold thee longer than you said! Two days forsooth! Yet May they keep

'A Bower quiet for thee,
and a sleep
Full of sweet dreams, and health,
and quiet breathing!'[1]

And so for us both tonight.
For such sleep hath not blessed me of late.
(So glad to hear of Father's recovery)   W

———

[1] From the opening lines of *Endymion*:

A thing of beauty is a joy for ever:
Its loveliness increases; it will never
Pass into nothingness; but still will keep
A bower quiet for us, and a sleep
Full of sweet dreams, and health, and quiet breathing.

138. To Susan Owen

15 May 1912   *Dunsden Vicarage*

My own Mother,

I will begin with acknowledgments—(1) of the P.O. which I had put in a drawer and entirely forgotten. And thanks for the extra neck-money. Dorothy has burnt my unimpeachable collar—the most insane thing I remember her ever to have done; but she was suborned, and destroyed in ignorance of the hidden virtues of the thing.

(2) Then I acknowledge your manifold letters & cards since last I committed any of my vain thoughts to you. I cannot say Begone to thy uneasy dreams; because, in all conscience, the last few days have been a time of unwonted depression: traceable to I know not what: certainly not to a conceited aping of Another, who wrote—'Truth is, I have a horrid Morbidity of temperament.'[1]

Perhaps to a Book—Borrow's *Lavengro*—entertaining enough in parts, but sometimes acting too strongly on the nervous faculties.

Bitter disappointments have not fail'd to well up at this time (but these are as a sip of brine after quarts of quinine).
Disappointment No. 1.

Den[2] is denied me—and with such evasive humming & ha-ing & childish surreptitiousness, that I have no heart to say another word about it. Ostensible Reason proffered—The General Principle that four sitting rooms is too much for two people!

Root-reason (?) Carpet of den required for Study; carpet of Study for part of Drawing Room. But then the Den Floor is polished, there are rugs and—Och—no more of this, by Apollo! Except this—that I am going to decamp—to my bedroom to work; and greater privacy than there is found could not be desired.
Disappointment No. 2.

Cheap Tickets denied me.[3] How's this? With my usual pig's perceptiveness I still feel, as in No. 1, that this needn't be! (And yet after reading Borrow I am something of a Necessitarian!—Oh where am I?)
Disappointment No. 3.

When I come home, I shall find you with a slut unmeet for you, instead of a responsible person, to be an help, meet for you. (Note the I's. I know no other way of appeal to you.)

But I weary you with disappointments and I now recount some of my recent pleasures.

First the College, day by day. Next an Excursion we went last Thursday, conducted by Miss Rayner; made up of about six young ladies and as many men.

---

[1] Keats to B. R. Haydon, 11 May 1817 (*Letters* I, p. 140).
[2] The downstairs study, vacated by Kemp.
[3] Tom Owen subsequently provided these for the forthcoming journey to Carlisle. See Letter 147.

Damosels nothing much to look at; and nothing more to talk to. With some of the men I am on more or less intimate terms. One is going to be an M.D. someday; some are common and undesirable. There is one extraordinarily like old Paton! What is more, he & I at once found some affinity attracting us. Maybe because he wears a tired expression sometimes, and the wags are fond of injecting water down his neck . . . And therefore I selected him as a safe person to ply with questions, etc. He used to be at Kendrick[1] of course knows Leslie. Well, after this trip, when Miss R. heard I had to get home to Dunsden to tea, she took me to her rooms, and gave me the privilege of a cup of tea and her private conversation. She must be over thirty; has bluntness of manner and great force of character, (I suppose,) and who knows what learning and cleverness. A great contrast to Miss Wright in many ways; but, like her, takes her recreation in literature, and foisted upon me a copy of Meredith's *Poems* when she heard I had not made the acquaintance of that gentleman. Poor stuff it is too! A jumbled barrel-organ after the soft Lydian airs I have heretofore heard from his predecessors.

Then, on Saturday, I went with the Geological Party to Wargrave,[2] and spent a strenuous afternoon thereabouts. Got home in time to take the P.M.

'Did jew notice Mister Owin?' says Mrs. Lott afterwards. 'Wern't 'e whoite!' But I was quite unaware of this phenomenon, and feel all the better after a tramp like this.

I am eating less meat.

I hear from the Station your Parcel has arrived. I mean to take it up Thurs. afternoon.

I have finished a story from Andersen in Blank Verse;[3] But I am dissatisfied with not only my attempt, but the story itself, which doesn't exactly inculcate peace and happiness, truth and justice, religion and piety. You shall see it anon.

It is Thurs. now; and I have received your P.C. from—a place whose name makes me think of a person with flatulence, nausea and hiccups all at once.

Adieu! Your loving Wilfred

139. To Susan Owen

20 May 1912   *Dunsden Vicarage*

O most sweet among Mothers,

Blessed is thy hand which writes to me so often! Blessed is thy heart which perceives the Sorrows of mine! O Blessed art thou among women!

[1] The Kendrick School, Reading.
[2] On the Thames between Maidenhead and Reading. There are indications of a Roman road running south, and coins have been found there. At Temple Combe close by is the 'Druid', a temple of forty-five granite megaliths brought from St. Helier, Jersey, in 1785.
[3] *Little Claus and Big Claus.*

Cheering was the testimony of a Bygone friend to thy youth and glad-someness of countenance! And cheering thy words of counsel to me. I did not know before that weak hearts went with craven spirits. I had hoped it were otherwise.

How can I tell what a Book is going to say next! *Lavengro* is one of the most agreeable autobiographies; but suddenly Borrow must needs describe one of his fits of the horrors. These are preceded by unmistakable physical sensations. He feels the sensations coming on again—and—Oh Horrors! . . .

Well, to return (if ever I started on them) to things more definite, you will be sorry to hear that Selwood is breathing, or trying to breathe, his last breath. He is nothing to me; but I cannot be indifferent, or dismiss him from my thoughts even in a letter. Perhaps because it puts me in mind (if ever I needed it) of another Consumptive—long ago—ah too long ago . . .

There I am on the old Junkets track once again, you say! And now I'm on, I'll not omit to tell you I lit on a picture of Isabella, in the Gunstons' Academy Pictures, the other day. There flourishes the Basil, tho' not so balmy as it should be, and fair Isabella kneels at a marble console-table (I leave the pun on this to you). Her features are almost those of Keats himself (feminised)—I suppose intentionally.

Now I do think you should have had yourself 'snapped' before you sent the camera. Oh how do I stand (yes and sit, lie, kneel & walk, too,) in need of some tangible caress from you.

Ink-slung ones are all very well in their way, and no one appreciates them more than I do; but my affections are physical as well as abstract—intensely so—and confound 'em for that, it shouldn't be so.

What if I feel 'strange' in your company after all this time apart; as I have done before after but a fortnight—surely that was the same I and the same you.

Then, when I recall the past, I often feel pretty sick at all the abominable rudenesses, ingratitudes, huffs, grumps, snaps, and sulks levelled at you. Oh my works do follow me!

How marvellously you have wrought upon my garments. And how well-packed was the parcel! What cannot you darn between Sun & Moon? I found something in a pocket! That was tangible and mangeable too. I must not write more—my head troubles me, which it has not done for months. And a weird kind of spiral

has been rolling round and round in front of my vision—what ever I look at; so to bed—and sleep it off.

Goodbye, which being interpreted, is God be with you.

                                                          Wilfred

140. To Mary Owen

29 May, 1912   *Dunsden Vicarage*

My very dear Sister,

I have forgotten—most things: 1) your age; 2) the thing you most would like for a present; 3) what I meant to say to you in this letter, and many things besides.

But I did not forget to fix in my mind that I must 'get some little thing'—now or never—when I set out this morning—and lo! when I left College at 1 p.m. every paltry shop had shut its door upon my unfortunate quest. I felt pretty sick at this, and roamed over the whole borough, and found about 23 shops open, namely,

Tobacconists'	Greengrocers'	Cyclists'
17	5	1
		Total—23.

Arriving home an hour ago, I made an attempt upon my bookcase; but in vain.

Have I now conducted my defence in a convincing manner?

I should at least have liked to send you a better-conducted letter for your Birthday, only Leslie has just dropped in to borrow a book for Dorothy's immediate consumption. It was Euclid's Book III. How I laugh within myself, yea even as heartily as Sarah in the tent, when I see Dorothy voraciously cramming away in her study! My own College hours pass pleasantly enough and are all too few.

The Vicar is in Folkestone since last Monday, & is staying at a Hotel—indefinitely.

Accordingly I invited Leslie to tea & dinner with me yesterday, and we held a most profitable discourse upon a subject for which his hunger is suddenly sharpening, viz. Books and their Makers.

Unfortunately—for this letter—he came again this evening—as I sez, and has only just gone. But so has my time, and I must wind up with the usual birthday wish—(raised to the Nth power if you like): a promise of another letter soon, (and one to Mother sooner); a kiss; and—something to follow (bother'd if I know what though)

Your own, Wilfred

My P.S. would never stop with messages & thanks to Mother, so I won't start it.

141. To Susan Owen

3 June 1912   *Dunsden Vicarage*

Dearest Mother,

You'll be thinking it's a woundily long time since you heard from me; more especially as you asked for newsiness and for answers to questions. But I have been in no cue for writing all week; and witness my occupation yesterday. Morning: Holy Communion, Morning Prayer with Baptisms; Bible Class. I was just leaving for Sunday School in the afternoon when the fact of a Children's Service and Sermon dawned like a thunderbolt on my slumbering soul. I rushed up and down stairs some half dozen times (for what purpose will never be known); marched unconcernedly down to the Hall and preached to scholars and teachers with more easily-onward-speeding tongue than a week's preparation could have ensured.

Then in the evening I went to a Cottage to administer consolation (such as I could) to a man very ill with pneumonia. Then heard another sermon. Then entertained my guest, the Preacher—A funny old man who is a free-lance (as he vaunts) and answered the Vicar's advertisement in the *Record*. He is Irish of Scotch extraction, and knows something of the Fleurys of Tramore![1] A bald, fusty-smelling, old codger, with fifty pits in his nose, each big enough to drown a fly. But much given to the interpretation of prophecy. He may come next week, if the Vicar is still away and is satisfied with my report of him!

In the week I have been three times pottering round Sonning Vicarage, arranging for the Vicar there to take a marriage here. If he had not come, Mr. Wigan said I must take it. Glad I didn't. The Bridegroom forgot or neglected to bring his Banns' Certificate and had to motor off for them for miles.

Last Monday there was a Conservative Fete at Crowsley Park (to whose Deer Park I took Father). Attractions: (to me) The Wild Gardens and F. E. Smith's[2] oratory. Smith is an old B'head school boy— older than people imagine—b. 1872. But if you want an account of the Flowers, whether of Gardens or Speech—I beg to say I cannot do it under a penny a line.

I don't think I have leisure enough to address a Birthday Memorial to Father, either.

I suppose you give him 'selected passages', more or less always.

But do you consider my Letters are strictly private? I hope you do. If not you violate a contract. And suppose I hear you don't—I will write in a weird—but real—strain never no more. . . .

Tues. 4 June

I had to leave off yesterday to write some letters to & for the vicar. But hardly had I started on this, than Mr. Gunston (senior) was announced. He had come specially to invite me over for supper, to see Laura Cornwall. She and Dorothy sang charming French songs after the manner of Dolly Varden; and played thundering duets. I did not cause a Lost Chord to vibrate once more by mentioning the name of B.[3] . . .

How deftly and satirically you touch upon Cecil's affairs. Ha! Ha! Ha! Ho! Ho! Ho! Ho! Vacancy!—Vacant—Engaged—Vacant—Engaged— Ho! Ho! Ho!

---

[1] A fisherman and his wife with whom the Owens lodged at the coastal village of Tramore, near Waterford, on the Irish holiday (*c.* 1901) described in *JO* I, pp. 68–84.

[2] Frederick Edwin Smith, 1st Earl of Birkenhead (1872–1930). At this time he was MP for the Walton Division of Liverpool; seven years later he was Lord Chancellor.

[3] Bernice Cornwall.

How about Mr. Morgan[1] (whose proper name should be Parsons, like the Jesuit in *Westward Ho!*)?

(In the middle of my second sit-down to this letter, the school-master is announced. Oh what a wind-bag is there! Inflated enough to carry me back to the palmy (I should remind you—Cane-Palms and Bamboozle-palms) Edwardian days; of blessed memory.)

Hulcoop says the School Doctor states there is no Consumption in Violet Franklin's frame—only debility due to malnutrition. I rejoice to see you check dear Mary's desire to send me food-stuffs. I trust you will never think even of such a thing again; when you hear of the fruit I am watching ripening round our walls; and on the strawberry-beds.

Now as to holidays, I am certainly to be one of the Keswick Party, and I have mentioned that you are flitting North for the first fortnight of July. I may therefore carry my project, but 'tis a ticklish matter. The Vicar is now on a recuperative trip only. He writes in a glozing tone; sending cheque for £7. 10. 0. for various purposes—'of which you will keep the £1. 6. 0. due to you.' 'Certainly, by all means! and thanks for Mr. Kemp's place indeed; but is it in the attic, or your boosum, or where?' Fancy that! And not long ago happening to speak of Mr. Robson, he observed—'I shall ever be grateful to him for having sent me you.'

Does the Railway Ticket Problem assume a different aspect now?

My time is up—I don't want to miss the Post—for your sake.

Goodbye! Wilfred

I had the [*two words illegible*] this morning. Many thanks. If I haven't answered all your interrogations I will anon.

142. To Susan Owen

12 June 1912   *Dunsden Vicarage*

Dearest Mother,

It was very good of you to be writing for my Tuesday pleasure at 10 p.m. on Sunday. As it happens it is just that time now, on Tuesday.

Public & Business Matters are very pressing just now, & I must deal with them first. I answered that U.C.C. Letter indecisively & not in the negative. I daren't do anything till the Vicar comes home. But as 3 months of the Course-Time have lapsed, and as you are or were wanting me to 'put off till yet another year'; and as opportunities for reading are not abundant here; and as my Latin is so tarnished; and as my machinery has a wonderful exhaust-system; perhaps I will wait till 1914! What a time, alas! Seemingly, too long! But a brilliant idea seizes me! I will take one or more Honours if I take that unconscionable time over the Business!

---

[1] The Rev. John Arthur Morgan, Curate of St. Patrick's, Bordesley, near Birmingham, in 1912. The reference to Kingsley's *Westward Ho!* suggests that plots were being hatched for Wilfred to leave Dunsden for Bordesley. Later (see Letter 171) he visited Mr. Morgan with this in mind.

What this means you will please learn from p. 30 and pp. 3–7 (Intro.) of the Guide, I am sending for your & Father's reference.

What you think after reading this (& as much other pertinent matter as you can e.g. Syllabuses) I shall be interested to know.

Just now I am in a fearful stew about it all. I know I could pass in 1913 with all day free,—other factors of course being propitious. But the last U.C.C. letter warns me I want 400 hours study in each subject. i.e. 400 hrs. × 5 = 2,000 hrs. Taking 1 day = 5 hours, nearly I require 400 days, or 18 mths. allowing for Sundays, Holidays, Illness (?) etc.

The Vicar 'said something' about teaching me Greek. I dread it; and Hebrew all Theological dustiness. But would substitute it for Latin willingly; and am going to attack the Vicar about it. I should love to read Greek; whose spirit giveth life to so much poetry: only the letter killeth.

One thing I may state, and that is—I definitely abandon the thought of Divinity Training till at least an Arts Degree is won. Such at present is my resolve. All Theological lore is growing distasteful to me. All my recent excursions into such fields proves it to be a shifting, hypothetical, doubt-fostering, dusty and unprofitable study. Such a conclusion at my time of life is not to be wondered at. It may change hereafter. All I can do now is to groan with Meredith:

> 'Ah what a dusty answer gets the soul
> When hot for certainties in this our life.'[1]

I need not this as a Wall-Text, though they are the verses of Meredith which have more than any others, appealed to me. I see them after 'Finis' in every book which takes upon itself to answer the soul with 'certainties.'

I am sorry this important letter is so badly written. It is not Private to the Addressed unless you choose to consider it so.

Do not haste to answer it, and be not at pains to concoct a sedative reply. I can come to no Fixation of Plans till I get closeted with the Vicar.

Meantime I may dissipate these clouds by a day at Shakespere's England. The Vicar wrote to ask me and the Fordhams to join him tomorrow in Town. I have not heard more. But I know the F.s' have backed out. I have every respect for Mr. F. as 'a fellow that hath had losses; and one that hath two gowns, and everything handsome about him',*[2] but I should choose him last of all people as a companion round Shakesperean realms.

Methinks, 'that unlettered, small-knowing soul†'[3] would worry me beyond bearing if he began to pat Wild Will on the back: an actor too! and dead against his principles!

[1] George Meredith, *Modern Love*, last stanza.
[2] *Much Ado About Nothing*, IV. ii. 92.
[3] *Love's Labour's Lost*, I. i. 251.

'He hath never fed of the dainties that are bred in a book ‡;'[1]
however admirable his appearance, diction and cosmogony may be.

Have you seen anything about a Keats-Shelley Matinée[2] in London?
I am nearly beside myself to know more; and I told the Vicar I was
fluttered! Leading exponents are going to recite and sing!

Here is a letter from Kemp. Really interesting, isn't it?

Adieu, sweet Mother. Give me particulars of your pulse, when next
you write. I think about it, oftener than mine own.

Your loving, Wilfred

* Shakespere.   † Shakespere.   ‡ Shakespere.

Can I get Cheap Tickets again?

143. To Mary Owen

23 June 1912   *Dunsden Vicarage*

My dear Mary,

I wonder how you are feeling today. I hope you are not now in such
a taedium vitae as I am; I, having already given two discourses to boys
of 14 and 4 respectively; as well as attending two Church Services myself. Evening Service is coming on apace; so I seize this hour for a
Letter to you; which I must write currente calamo. O sancta simplicitas!
I perceive I am in a Latin strain just now. Pray have your English
Dictionary to hand; open to 'Words & Phrases from Latin'; or else
this example of my cacoëthis scribendi will be a caput mortuum to you.

On the night preceding the morning when Mother told me you were
fallen into recrudescence, I dreamed of you. You were decked in fine
raiment, and methought I was treating you to a Show at a Picture
Palace! Absit omen! When inside, we found ourselves surrounded by
religio loci, in the form of the Sowers' Band. And so we made merry.

'Twas but one of my frequent aegri somnia—brought on by a magnificent romp with the Sowers, and the inevitable amabilis insania—must
I call it—that you may some day be imbued with like spirits and like
lissome limbs.

The firm Superintendent of their Sunday School, the silence-loving,
and the melancholy-voiced, on that day capered about the lawn among
them, a very Pan amid the nymphs. To Charades, 'Old Man from Botany
Bay',[3] and so on, I initiated them; and great was the delight. Oh! dulce
est desipere in loco! Amantes: Amentes!

Mrs. Lott's River Trip is to be next Tuesday. Most of the anile popu-

---

[1] Ibid., IV. ii. 25.
[2] Two special matinées took place on 25 and 28 June at the Haymarket Theatre to raise funds
for the Keats-Shelley Memorial House at Rome. Marie Lohr, Ellen Terry, and others
recited poems by Keats and Shelley and there were also songs and tableaux.
[3] A game invented by Tom Owen.

lation of this aldea compose the Party. Our destination is Dorchester.[1]

On Monday Week the Choir draws me with it to Bournemouth. I may possibly be taken to Shakespere's England. I am not very keen. Unless we see a representation in The Model of the Globe,[2] I doubt if there is much of interest. Not to see a play, and yet to go the the Place seems to be saying to Shakespere, (whatever that name may represent): 'Yes, you have done wondrous works, and we quite appreciate you'— but crying, as soon as he would open his mouth as it were, 'Hold your tongue—we wouldn't listen to you for worlds.'

. . . .

O tempora, O mores! The meanest seat at the Keats-Shelley Matinée is 7/6!

In one way this is very flattering. In what more forcible way can the man of the world be made to set value on a Poet, than by seeing the Price at his Matinée is 30s!

But that those two names should ever help to breed in me amor sceleratus habiendi! How long shall 'virtus post nummos' be detestable to me, when such spirits are under the foot of Mammon. I feel inclined to hang on my wall that striking picture in *Bibby's Annual*[3] (of Mammon) and buffet it daily.

When Mother asks whether I state my sum of ducats available for holiday-expenses, you must say 'zonam perdidit', for I shall only have about two gold pounds.

I thought at first, when Mother's letters came—'*adieu paniers, vendanges sont faites!*'[4] but tomorrow I go to make enquiries as Mother directs; and my reluctantly-closed volumes [*one sheet missing*]

My own countree likewise begins to feel romantic—if these lines are true—

> 'Where Severn flows she stands,—the encircled town.
> Two spires uplift the jewels of her crown,
> Two bridges are the portals to her feet.
> Through Wyle Cop to Dogpole climbs the street,
> And westward to the hills down Mardol goes,
> Where Severn flows.'[5]

These verses are not mine; I don't wish they were. I came across them in my deplorably desultory reading.

Basta! I must keep my [*one line missing, one line illegible*] loosen my tongue.

Do not get impatient with the formidable loci classici here given; and tear up the whole amphigouri.

---

[1] Dorchester on Thames, sixteen miles upriver from Reading. But the excursion got no farther than Wallingford. See Letter 144.
[2] A model of the Globe Theatre was a feature of this Earl's Court Exhibition. See Letter 156.
[3] See Letter 548, note 1.
[4] From 'À son ami, Chapelain', by Honorat de Bueil, Seigneur de Racan (1589–1670).
[5] We have failed to trace the source of these lines.

Aequam memento rebus in arduis servare mentem.

Forgive and forget!

Your most loving, Wilfred

Mrs. Ambrose's address
  1. Bishop's Lands,
       nr. Kidmore End,
           Reading   address for two weeks at least.
  or 2. Royal Berkshire Hospital,
       Reading

144. To Mary Owen

27 June 1912   *Dunsden Vicarage*

Dear Mary,

What an idiot I was to send you such a letter! And what a marvel you are better in spite of it! I think Mother's Card must have carried something of the Malady to me; for as I was reading Scott this morning an obstinate Black Spot foisted itself upon the Print; and danced in front of me, like a malicious goblin. Finally it took this shape

and appeared to be going round in opposite directions at the same time. This phenomenon so flabbergasted me that I lay down and dozed; but at lunch time woke up with a violent headache. After lunch I felt sick; but went out to do some business at the school, and tried to get into Reading. Finally I became so afraid of losing some of that refractory lunch upon the road that I made all speed home and slept again—until even now, when I am better already. There is going to be a meeting in the Hall to explain the Insurance Act,[1] tonight. I hope to be able to go.

Now, in order to prevent any germs of my latest complaint communicating themselves to you through this letter I will sprinkle it with that excellent disinfectant <u>mirth</u>—and tell you something of our river trip last Tuesday.

The clouds hung very heavily when we embarked; and at odd moments swelled so tremendously about the waist and cheeks that they had perforce to drop some of their fatness to earth—as the Psalmist hath it—as a balloonist might drop sand.

We started more than half an hour late—the last arrivals being the Fordhams. Annette by some extraordinary manoeuvring soon anchored herself by me; and as I looked so supremely happy, as the Vicar said,

---

[1] Lloyd George's 'Medical Panel'. The first form of National Insurance and the Introduction of the Panel Doctor system.

his riverence rallied me on the subject afterwards. Bless his soul—I was happy. For one thing the old <u>ladies</u> (as Mother would say) puffed <u>and</u> blinked so complacently in their snug quarters astern and in the bows, that it was a sight to be thankful for. Then, then . . . (see how candid I am—don't betray me) the cargo was not all anile, and behold, in blissful proximity, mine own favourite Milly![1] My favourite boys were not aboard; instead a regular rascal (as I had thought him) was there. Oft had I been down on him like a load of bricks at the Scrip. Union; and indeed he needed it. At school he goes by the universal name of 'Knowledge'—of course because that commodity has no part in his being. Well, on the boat, I 'noticed' him, so to speak; chatted with him, and joked; and was astonished to find what good points, what tender ones, are hidden under the somewhat spiky ones that fringe his shaggy head. The <u>comble</u> (there I am again—I mean the crowning-point) came when for about quarter of an hour, he fought Milly for the place next me. Sometimes the struggle was subdued, and carried on by craft; sometimes it was a matter of elbow-point and finger-nail. No interesting sights on the banks could make Knowledge forget to squeeze up to my side; no bribery could tempt him to go below for lemonade. Until at last he was caught napping and Beauty won. The adjacent good folk were immensely amused at all this; but they saw not the magnificent Allegory therein: <u>Knowledge</u> and <u>Beauty</u> wrestling for me! Heaven forfend that they should be antagonistic forces in my life; and that Beauty should win! . . .

Why! I had almost forgotten the most important thing of the day— incessant rain all morning. I preferred the dry but 'thick' air of the tiny cabin to the sodden deck, & the views of sodden fields seen from underneath a sodden overcoat; so I stayed below all the way there. Coming back, however, it cleared; and everything was delightful.

We had about two hours at Wallingford; where the Vicar took me (only) to a Hôtel. We had an excellent lunch of *'Poulet Fricassé'*, green peas, etc—and—veil not thy face, O Goddess Temperentia—a whopping beaker of Cider each!

Then the Vicar explored the Antique Shops. For tea, we moored up against a beech-wooded escarpment, miles long, on the left bank.

I and three élite, adventuresome children climbed to the top; and came down at a breathless rate; nursing the delicious fear that the boat had gone. Sailing home, Hymns were sung; but as different ones were crooning astern and 'fore, and I was just between, it was anything but pleasant.

We reached Caversham about 7.30; and I of course rode home; but I thought of two little feet that had to <u>walk</u>, even to beyond the Vicarage, and was troubled.

So ended that happy day; and I kept an aromatic weed, the Sweet Flag, (*Acorus*, N. Order *Orontiaceae*, don't you know) as a '<u>memory</u>', as the children called it. I didn't correct them. Memento is an <u>infinitely</u> less pretty word for such a thing than 'memory'.

[1] Milly Montague.

Childe Mary, I hope we are to have many such happy days, before long! Keep battling Unhealth; and I will do the same. And having won, watch dear, dear Mother that she overstrain not herself at this time.

I am expecting to hear very soon what Father has ascertained about my journey. The Vicar must be told. I am not particularly anxious to go to Meols; but 'shouldn't mind if I did.'

'God bless you, my dear Sister.'

Your loving Brother, Wilfred

145. To Susan Owen

Postcard addressed c/o Mrs. Bulman,[1] Pringle Bank, Kelso, N.B.

29 June 1912   *Dunsden Vicarage*

I've just had your fine News. Many thanks to Father, for his mighty labours on my behalf.[2] I was so unhinged by the news that I wrote off at once to Mahim, forgetting you go today; but remembered before posting. I shall almost certainly take the '2 days Course'—particularly as I want certain Books, and other things from Shrewsbury.

Am I right in imagining that there is none of the Wellington to Crewe Business if I stay at Shrewsbury? If that's the case I shall certainly do so. I hope you are having a pleasant journey. It is just 6.30 and I must make ready for the P.M.[3] Bro. Kemp is over here for the week end. On Monday I rise from bed at 3 a.m.[4] & shall not get back till the early hours of Tuesday. Mind you all 'get up' Scott while at K.[5]

Yours, W

146. To Susan Owen

2 July 1912   *Dunsden Vicarage*

Dearest Mother,

Your proposal to hustle me up in 1 day I readily accept, seeing it concerns pretty well all [*two words illegible*] Of course Mrs. Lott will find, (I sh'd say has found) no objection whatever to the time. What's 6 o'clock to me! who got up the other day at 3! Your dictum about my not wanting books from Shrewsbury, must be either ironical or abjectly unreasonable. Of course I want my Scotts'; and I wonder whether Mrs. Davies has the key of the house, & could open my Bookcase & send them; as well as Wordsworth. Fancy being among the Lakes

---

[1] An old Oswestry friend of Susan Owen's parents, and devoted to Susan. Known as Aunt Nellie. Her Scots husband had died by this time, and she was supported by two sons and a daughter. See *JO* I, ch. 2.

[2] Providing the tickets for the forthcoming journey to Scotland for a holiday with the Bulmans He was to travel via Shrewsbury.

[3] Prayer Meeting.

[4] For the Choir excursion described in the next letter.

[5] Kelso, Roxburghshire, on the River Tweed, five miles north of the Border.

without e'er a Wordsworth!—But perhaps you will be home before I need this last.

I am so glad you are enjoying the place and its enabitants; and that your constigution (as a man said to me this afternoon) is hundergoin' a 'ealthy chinge.

I am in a perfect daze as regards the past few days. I rose (bitterly regretting I had ever promised to join such a detestable Excursion) at three o'clock; had breakfast by semi-candlelight; and issued forth in old clothes into the raw air; was taken in a wagonette to the Station; with the Boys in a van in front; and entered the compartment labelled 'Dunsden'—which might as well have been ticketed Demonsden or my compartment in Purgatory itself.

Such a flesh-tortured three hours did I spend in it. The Vicar perhaps had the worst time of it going—pins stuck into all his limbs—paper missiles flicked at him from teeth-holden catapults—his hat snatched away—his paper bashed about—and so on. It is only fair to state, however, that now and again he would grasp an urchin, and thwack, lam, hide, beat, belabour, whack, smack, flog, flail, thump, lick, and kick the creature till the tears swam round its eyes. Coming home, I was the sufferer; for I kept slipping into Lethe, and being pulled out again by the frantic behaviour of one boy—who, being quick-witted and fond of leading, managed to make everybody laugh at him—and continued for some two hours in a state of what would be called advanced intoxication in a man. The Vicar sat like a log through it all; and seemed to see, feel, hear and think of—nothing. Not even did he show the least sign of perturbation when the Arch-imp shrieked 'Here comes Satan! Here's the Devil!' on seeing his own reflection on the Carriage-Window.

For my part, I quite believed it, and offered no contradiction.

As for Bournemouth itself it was just enjoyable—only just. Though I have not seen the sea for more than twelve months (isn't it) I have been so often at the Sea Side in Day-dreams of late, that its Sights, Sounds and Circumstance hadn't an atom of freshness about them. I took note of this fact with surprise and regret.

I shouldn't like to say it was altogether a Sign of a stronger imagination; because Bournemouth Cliffs, Pier, Steamers, & Sands and especially the Model-Boat-Canal were positively as familiar to me as Shrewsbury is now; simply through having gazed on them so long and longingly thro' Uncle John's Stereoscopic Views ! !

As on Tuesday last, the heavens were graciously disposed to be liberal of rain, and we had it fine at short intervals only! In the afternoon I conducted a party of 18 over to Swanage, the Vicar slinking away to Bro. Lingley's[1] home. Our home-coming in the carts through the midnight roads was most romantic. Only a *Feuilletonist*[2] could do justice

---

[1] The Rev. Trevor Hope Lingley, at this time living at Parkstone, Dorset. He had visited Dunsden. See Letter 120.

[2] A *feuilleton* in French newspapers was a ruled-off space devoted to fiction, criticism, or light essays.

to it—thus—'That night, a stranger might have marked, as the midnight moon rose dimly above the woods, a carriage slowly travelling through the sleeping countryside—a carriage in which six dark forms were discernible. One of these was a Clergyman of the Established Church, an Oxford man, of very decided and onesided religious beliefs, and one who held his pedigree very proudly indeed. By him, sat an Elementary School-master, of Elementary Education and elementary manners, reading, and powers of thought; a man of very orthodox religious beliefs and very ordinary income; a fellow of a sharp and quick-condemning tongue, with eyes to correspond; and one who carried his petty-grievances very proudly indeed. By him, sat a Ploughman; whose calling, however, could not be well made out (unless it were by a certain earthy, soddy, cloddy cast of face) for he now grinned from between the lobes of a wonderful collar, and bore upon his left chest half the floral production of his garden. Then there was a bushy-browed and horny-fisted blacksmith's assistant; who calls for no mention save that from his cavernous mouth rose vapours which had their origin in Burton-on-Trent.

Fifth of the company, (also suggestive, somehow, of the Roman Numeral XXX or the Clef 𝄢) was a taciturn, rusty-voiced man—a gardener and coachman both—now uttering his annual marvel of 10 words in succession.

Lastly, that carriage held a youth—a student and a philosopher by the thoughts that ran in his head; an invalid and a poet, by the pulse that coursed in his veins; and a fellow of fine palate by the victuals that slept in his stomach. Ah, and a Lover of sleep, too, by the lead that hung on his lids. A poor youth, look you, by his clothes; yet a rich one by his hands. A Poet, again, by his economy in Barber's Bills—and by his frequent glances at the rising moon . . .

What brought these strangely different beings together? What sentiment allows them to converse? O Clotho, Lachesis, Atropos! How have ye brought their threads of life within so small a ring as the circle of this vehicle? [*final sheet missing*]

147. To Susan Owen

Postcard addressed c/o Mrs. Bulman, Pringle Bank, Kelso. Scotland

5 July 1912   [*Postmark Reading*]

This Morning I received Passes to Shrewsb'y & Carlisle. The others have not yet come. Your letter came at dinner-time:—Just after my Box had left by Carrier. Starting on Monday & having to appear in Sabbath Days, non-Journey Clothes upon a Platform, is a Nuisance. I shall very likely leave my Bicycle, here. I don't know.

Last night I got home at 12.30 a.m. after an evening's dissipation with Miss Rayner & Mr. Jones.[1] She read Swinburne to us. I read—need I say. I did some good work for Bacon, (as Shakespere.) Fine, if I can infect the College, eh? Miss R. is very friendly w. Ruskin's Priv. Sec. & Biographer,[2] & is going to mention my sojourn in the Lakes to him; & I must go & see him! I have just heard Diphtheria has made its appearance in the Village: in the poor Idiot girl[3] of Bray's. Coward that I am I am glad I am off on Monday if that's about. I will ha' my wits about me on Mond. I am now in the thick of the School Correspondence, ∴ intensely practical.

W

148. To Susan Owen

21 July 1912   *Keswick*

Dearest Mother,

I am housed here at last. I left Keswick without any definite idea of my lodging but found my way, with difficulty, to this Camp, about a mile & a half from the Town. Arrangements had been made for me, & I was shown a tent with three beds, on this level

—No other furniture whatever except one blanket (of stuff like sackcloth)! We have meals in a large Marquee. The fare is very ordinary indeed; and the tea is horrid—just enough milk to make it muddy. Very different state of things from [*two words illegible*] Yetholm[4] too. Never mind, it will sharpen my appetite for Home.

My Camp-anion is perhaps the very one I sh'd have chosen among the arrivals so far—a divinity student from Durham.

Last night—our first—we hardly slept a wink—such was the force of the wind. Our tent thundered and creaked and shivered under the rain most frightfully; and at last we were positively nervous lest the pole sh'd come crashing down on one of our 'nuts'. All night the Captains or whatever they are called were going round; malleting & tightening or loosening cords: and on one of their rounds we heard the cry of 'tent down' next to us. We had heard not a sound of its fall; and wondered what it would be like to be struggling under a fallen canvas

[1] Lecturer in Botany at University College, Reading.
[2] William Gershom Collingwood (1854–1932), biographer of Ruskin, was Professor of Fine Art, University College, Reading. His home was in Coniston, Lancashire.
[3] 'The Imbecile' (*Poems*, p. 139) probably dates from this period, as CDL suggests; but a version in HO's possession, in French, with two additional verses, was written later in Bordeaux (the reverse side carries comments on his Bordeaux pupils).
[4] A village in the Cheviots, seven miles SE of Kelso, where the Bulmans had a cottage.

with no one to let us out—for the wretched bosses <u>would</u> sew—or somehow fasten—our tent door tight!

Since writing this ¶. we have had Tea; and some fifty men have now come. Some are absolute boors; downright 'dizguzders' over their meal; old blear-eyed horny-handers, some of them; but they are likely to be <u>sober</u> dogs; and men that fear Heaven, look you; which is not what I <u>could</u> say of my late companion, the wondrous-witty John;[1] whose sobriety, I find, is as noteworthy as that of most medical students.

I could say more on that point, but I see no use in it; unless it were to point out that a normal, manly, fellow like John or Bill,[2] might after all <u>not</u> be preferable as a son—to an eccentric being like me. I had my wits <u>about</u> me during the journey; and yet found that my luggage was not about me at Penrith. Some blighter of a porter put it in the wrong coach—for I saw it put in—; however it came on to Penrith by a later train. I have got Father's shoes and Cigar case; and I hope you will get the fishing rods all right. I spent 4 or 5 hours on Flodden Field; and saw the whole thing enacted to my great satisfaction—and to Blanche's[3] inward displeasure, it may be. I fancy an Englishwoman had something to do with James' weakness on the battlefield—anyhow I was not going to let a Scots girl spoil my contemplation there by dragging me to places I didn't want to see. As it was we cycled 28 miles, & walked several more! You will observe I have not a word to say about mountains or lakes or streams—Surely if Wordswth., Coleridge, Southey, Shelley, and Ruskin made it a matter of years to describe them, I cannot do so now, in this flapping, windy pavilion; with tongues, plates, piano, and such-like dinning around me.   Ever your loving Wilfred

P.S. [*one line missing*] as soon as you have my address.
P.P.S. I was much refreshed when seeking my luggage at the stn. to see Vera and Dorothy (and Miss F. this time) upon the platform—and created quite a sensation among the Conventionists by my <u>unconvention</u>-ally enthusiastic greeting of them. (Except for that moment, when I was in a <u>stew</u>, I have been too cold rather than too warm, & simply can't under<u>stand</u> your heat wave.)

149. To Susan Owen

Wednesday 24 July 1912   *Penrith Road Keswick*

My own dear Mother,

I found on reading Mr. Collingwood's *Ruskin* that Ruskin (my King <u>John</u> the Second) used to write elaborate (or at least full) letters to his <u>anxious</u> parents <u>every single day</u>, when he was once in one part of

---

[1] The elder of the two Bulman boys, a medical student. Later he had a general practice in Hereford, where he died in 1960.
[2] The younger Bulman. He was killed at Gallipoli in July 1915.
[3] Blanche is the Bulman daughter. Wilfred took a copy of Scott's *Marmion: A Tale of Flodden Field* with him on this expedition; facing the title-page he drew a pencil sketch of the scene inscribed 'Among the Cheviots, July 1912'. The copy survives.

Switzerland and they in another; and that a remissness in this respect—
say of three days would put Mama in a rare flutter.

Inspired by this ensample I sit me down on my tent floor, & leaning
on my fair green trunk, do pencil the following. I may say that I have
had to 'cut' family worship for the purpose, and that I can hear at this
moment every word that is being said there; and am forced by very
proximity of it, to hear another Prayer Meeting in my next-door tent;
groaning at the bottom of its voice.

This Camp is a magnificent thing in one respect; I am thrown into
the Society of just as many varieties of my species as I am capable of
taking stock of during a week. Irishmen, Scotchmen, Englishmen & a
German, from all parts—(including Birkenhead, Shrewsbury etc.) and
drawn from all ranks.

I have 3 others in my tent now—all from different colleges in Durham
University. Socially, I suppose they are the pick of the Camp, but they
are really not at all interesting . . . We are very merry together, and
agreed to have our photos taken before the tent. My suggestion (I
believe) of having it done in pyjamas (as the Photographer was coming
early in the morning) was highly acceptable to the rest, who proposed
the addition of turbans (of towels). I hope it will be a success.

Of course the whole Camp has been 'done' and this has indeed turned
out very well.

There is, in a tent remote from mine, a Northumberland lad who
works in the pits, whose soul-life and Christianity is altogether beyond
my understanding. He has absolute peace of mind; faith before which
mountains not only sink, but never become visible; and most other
virtues of which the Keswick Platform speaks. The watching of his
conduct, conversation, expression of countenance during meetings,
bids fair to speak louder to my soul than the thunderings of twenty
latter-day Prophets from their rostra upon these everlasting hills.

While your sleek Thomas, Hopkins, Dixon, Holden, Scroggie,[1] and
the rest of these double-barrelled guns, whose double-barrelled names
I refuse to write, while they, I say, preach that preaching is no witness
of a Christian Soul, your scar-backed mining-lad acts that acting is
efficient. Scar-backed, I say, through running along subterranean 'roads'
four feet high, and scraping against its jagged roof. And while my guide
to Edinburgh would calmly send people to the Devil for no greater
provocation than say having an ugly face, this youth lets no profane
word pass his lips, tho' pricked with piercing pain and surrounded by
the grossest human mud that ever sank to a pit's bottom.

Another interesting thing, a good antidote to student-superciliousness,
is that this pit-lad is wrestling with a Class-book of Physics—and taking
Correspondence Tuition in the Arts of Mining. He has no holiday and
during this week, his pay is stopped.

[1] Dr. W. H. Griffith Thomas, the Rev. Evan Hopkins, Dr. J. Stuart Holden, and Dr. W.
Graham Scroggie were eminent in Evangelical circles, and regular speakers at the Keswick
Convention.

Now I must return to myself—and chronicle that I have bathed in the lake; climbed Latrigg, seen the views from Castle Head, and Friar's Crag;[1] bought a pile of post-cards; had my hair cut (atrociously); and had my bicycle badly treated by an unauthorised borrower. It is right now; and I made the fellow pay (1s.)

I don't know what to say or think of dear Mary. I must bring her a present. Don't be anxious about me. I am feeling more energetic as the days pass. Great thanks for the parcel & letters.

Ever your loving Wilfred

150. To Susan Owen

August 1912 (Alack the day!)   *Dunsden Vicarage (Alas!)*

My own sweet Mother,

I didn't bring your pre-addressed envelope; so I mean to sport a penny letter already. I have had tea, and do not feel like laying my hand to anything except a letter to your dear self . . .

I don't know whether it be a sign of moral decadence,* or the unsurmountable force of circumstances, or what, but I never felt so near giving vent to emotion as this morning. I know not what you returned to the solitary house to do; but I know that I am glad I was the only occupant of my compartment. . . .

> 'Tears, idle tears, I know not what they mean,
> Tears from the depth of some divine despair,
> Rise in the heart, and gather to the eyes,
> In passing by the happy Autumn fields
> And thinking of the days that are no more.'[2]

These lines might have been written for me so true to my state are they —tho' I did not think of them at the time.

But when I got here, flabby and unstable as I felt, I tried to set down verses more entirely my own. You shall see them some day.

I am getting to like railway journeys less and less. Can't understand it, but they quite upset me. I was thankful to be across my bicycle again, and gathered strength as I passed, well-loaded, along 'the sweet security of our streets.'[3]

Now it is quarter past six; a thunderstorm has just broken overhead. The feeling of pent-up grief has not left me yet—not altogether an unpleasant feeling, but so strange and unusual—(I am thankful for .that)

Your provisions were over-ample; but I was glad to finish them when I arrived here at about 3.30. Only all these touching instances of your care add to my inward wretchedness of spirit just now.

I have sent a card to Mary.

Lightning & thunder and rain fill the air. (Fearfully near)

[1] Three peaks in the Keswick area of the Lake District.
[2] Tennyson, *The Princess*, iv, Introductory Song, 1.21.
[3] The source has eluded us.

>   'When shall we two meet again
>   In thunder, lightening, or in rain?'[1]

Ah when? Dunsden is already distressingly familiar; and all I love
proportionately remote. I never felt so sorry to leave as this time
(Uriconium has nothing to do with it) is the poor plaint

>   of your adoring Wilfred

* As Ch. Lamb, long 'alcoholised', would grieve to find himself
involuntarily weeping, often and often.

151. To Susan Owen

7.40 p.m., 14 August 1912   *From the extra-specially easy chair,*
                                                            In The Study
                                                      Of Dunsden Vicarage

My own dear Mother,
   I wonder what you will think of these my first (complete) productions
in photography?
   I am certainly proud of the profile one of you. For in spite of many
blemishes of background, and fogged top of plate, etc. I do think that
this represents in a wonderful way your side-appearance, and if nothing
else were satisfactory, the hand itself is a study.
   I wonder whether you are noticing anything unusual in my handwriting? Its only because I am writing without a supporting desk. The
fact is, however, my left knuckles are very considerably lacerated. Just
by the Well (in the P.C.'s I left out purposely for you,) I had the most
violent side-slip I have yet endured. (Miss Wigan[2] badly hurt her face
on this very spot from this very cause—only I didn't know till after my
fall.) I was hardly off the machine 10 seconds; for no bones were
broken; only the left knuckles, knee, and elbow grazed.
   I soon reached the Vicarage, losing only half a dozen drops of blood
from my hand, and felt remarkably unshaken. I purposed to whisk over
to Alpenrose, and have first aid from one of the experts there. Meanwhile I had summoned the Temporary Housekeeper[3] to bring bandages.
(The Lotts are away & Edith was out &, of course, the Vicar is away.)
I was washing some of the dirt out of the wound, & had applied some of
my Carbolic Ointment, when sudden twilight seemed to fall upon the
world, an horror of great darkness closed around me—strange noises
and a sensation of swimming under water overtooked me, and in fact
I fell into a regular syncope. I did not fall down however, nor yet lose
all conciousness; but the semi-blindness, and the chill were frightful.
   I murmured something about Brandy to Adelaide (who had little
idea of what to do, & who was as white as the proverbial sheet, (in
reflection no doubt from me.)

[1] After *Macbeth*, I.i.1.
[2] The vicar's sister. She did not visit her brother during Wilfred's stay.
[3] Adelaide. Mrs. Lott, Edith the maid, Bray the gardener, and the boy (Frank) constituted
   the permanent Vicarage staff.

When she brought up the whiskey, I had groped right away to another room! and found myself gasping at a window, without quite knowing how I got there. I must have implored for the doctor, for Adelaide sent off the Boy poste-haste into Caversham. He had hardly gone when my senses began to return—O it was a blissful moment when the lights were turned up again in my head! And the sensation of quickening circulation & warmth was like the Return of Spring for deliciousness. I found myself indeed in an icy sweat and of a really beautiful and romantic pallor. Half an hour later I had tea, & was keenly hungry. Since then, the doctor has been, & has sent up boracic things. I got Edith to call for Dorothy when she cycled in for the Lints, and dear old D. duly came and bandaged to my satisfaction. . . .

Now I have related everything most circumstantially, and there is nothing more to be said. You will not be able to make much of it—I had made the matter as big as it will be made. The grazes are trifling after all. And I am feeling now quite normal, and what is more, pleasantly sleepy. So I will off to bed.

––––––––

Nay I will stay to gossip—that you may see how lucid my mind is, and how calm my feelings.

I had a presentiment that <u>something</u> of note would happen shortly.

Further, I was riding away from an old man to whom I had been reading Spurgeon[1]—and the burden of the Sermon was the fact that our lives are 'leased by seconds—not by seventy years, thirty years, five years.' 'Not more frail are flowers, more fragile moths . . . or more fleeting meteors than Human Life.'

I was even moralising on this when I tried to put it into practice!—I remember hearing that a week or so ago Kemp had an accident—& damaged his machine!

These occasional minor mishaps do a great deal of good. They make one careful for many months to follow.

By the time this reaches you I must be getting into order for the dentist. I have an appointment on Friday.

Many, many thanks for your dear letter.

Hope I have made this <u>interesting</u>, at least.

Your (but for a sq. centimetre or two) whole, safe, sound, unsuffering, cheerful

Son, Wilfred

152. To Susan Owen

16 August 1912   *Dunsden Vicarage*

Dearest Mother,

My last letter missed one or two posts, so you have got it a day late. Still, I am sending another again to let you know I am no worse for

[1] Charles Haddon Spurgeon (1834–92), the Baptist preacher and writer who founded a pastors' college and an orphanage.

the accident. That is in system. My hand gave me a great deal of pain this morning, but that is only a sign that it is healing. I dreamt the night before last that a cat, a great fierce cat, had fixed upon my hand, and was driving tooth and claw deep into the very bone. I tried in vain to shake the brute off . . . I awoke to find myself waving my mangled fingers about.

The stiffness in my leg has quite gone now; and, with arm in sling, I did some miles 'on my travels' this afternoon.

The Vicar came home last Thursday. He is not going away to his Cousins next week: Captain Wigan has had a motor-bicycling accident!

I have had another rhymed letter from Leslie.

I forgot to tell you that when the Vicar asked after you as soon as I got back here, he added that he would have liked to have asked you over —only his pressing engagements were so many! His Brother's wedding is over.[1] The couple got some two hundred presents; and so much Silver that they had to put it in the bank for safety!

I have put off my Dentistry till Monday.

On Saturday I have to give some account of my Impressions of Keswick. It will be something of an ordeal: If they want, as I imagine they do, a relation of my personal feelings, I am not going to give them such. Some of my impressions were made with an instrument so sharp, so quick, that they should be called wounds rather than impressions.

These I have no intention of laying bare. On the other hand it will not do to give them an inkling of my unorthodox theology. So that I simply daren't be sincere; hence the preparation will cost a lot of thought.

I enclose more photographs. These are to be sent back, with the other batch excepting such as you really desire to keep. Of course you will want the Side View one: keep that. If Colin wants his, let him keep that. The one of myself is an experiment; done, of course, by myself; on a sudden impulse. The background is unfortunate.

No. 1 of the Views would be quite good with a little trimming. Which all want. They all bear marks of inexperience of course.

I am going to send Stanley round to see them. Rather would one of the boys intimate to him that some of my photos are worth presenting to him; but that they may be seen by him at Mahim? . . . Including the portraits. Also, I am anxious to see his.

The pleasing woe, the sweet melancholy, the not unpleasant grief, the sadly-pleasing tear, (or whatever your poet would call it) which at first possessed my thoughts, has, for good or for ill, vanished—unless I voluntarily put myself under its influence.

I made no outcry for you on my collapse; not that I did not dimly want you, but my faculties were altogether too obscured to think or utter anything at all.

Do not expect to hear again very soon. I shall soon cast off my bandages. Secretly, I am a bit pleased with my disablement—it excuses me from Croquet!

---

[1] Cuthbert Wigan, who later came to stay at the Vicarage with his new wife. See Letter 155.

Now farewell! Tell me in your next how your Rheumatism is. It strikes me that I never asked once about it after you got up—so admirably you did conceal it all!

Your inordinately affect^{nte.} son, Wilfred

153. To Susan Owen
Postcard

20 August 1912   *Dunsden Vicarage*

Great thanks for your letter, & H's. Hand continues to improve; but slowly, and the deepest cut is still very septic.

My parcel is 'to be left till called for'. I have left my little Bottle of Sanitas: perhaps you could safely stow that in the clothing? If you have any idea where my domino-goggles are, I should be glad to have them. The only other requisite is Mary & yourself, to be left at Alpenrose till absolutely called for to home. The Vicar's newly-married Brother & bride are coming to stay here next Thursday. Adieu.   W

I have left a thick leather razor-strop, somewhere. Want it most specially.   W

154. To Susan Owen

24 August 1912   *Dunsden Vicarage*

Dearest Mother,

I have been many times gladdened by a note from you since I last wrote. But what with attending to wounds, having teeth attended to, gingerly changing clothes two or three times per day, writing to other people, and so on, I have put off the pleasanter business of collecting things meet and proper to be transmitted to your sphere. There seem to be so many distinct worlds that I live in, now; and I have to play a corresponding number of rôles.

There is the Vicarage Life proper. Oh very proper indeed; which it is my object to get out of as soon as I shut myself up here in my room. So I will say not a word about that.

Then there is the Secondary Vicarage Life, consisting of my intercourse with the Servants. This has taken on new importance lately, for the most estimable Edith seems to prolong the bandaging operations as long as ever she can. I quote Shakespere to beguile the time, but seldom get beyond 'Was ever wound that healed not by degrees.' *Othello*, 2. iii. Moreover, there has been a startling *éclairissement* as the result of this conversation—viz. The Secret Correspondence of Rev. H. Wigan and Mrs. T. Owen, relative to the visit of the latter to Dunsden Vicarage, Reading; for the aim and purpose of the aforesaid lady's finding better health, and seeing her unsuspecting son's paws. The Vicar does not know that I know, so you must not let him know that Edith let me know.

At present, Mr. Cuthbert & Mrs. Wigan, his lawful wedded dame, are here. And I live the Super-Vicarage Life.

Jolly thankful I was for the black doublet and trews. For evening dress is *de rigeur* for this life. And actually if Cuthbert at the first dinner, didn't make some joke about a big Oxford savant appearing to a dinner with black coat but grey trousers!

I fancy I looked as smart as ever I did in my born days, however; and thought it a very good joke indeed. By the way that bungling Fowles[1] has made the Coat too tight; so that it would be almost impossible to wear a waistcoat.

Mrs. W. is very nice; nothing exceptional in looks or ideas or deportment generally: plays very well indeed, on the violin, tho'.

Cuthbert I rather like—not half so stiff as the Vicar; sings about the house; gets up in the middle of a meal; laughs spontaneously; speaks quickly and sometimes inaudibly—runs up and down stairs,—all things his stained-window-figure of a Brother couldn't possibly do. It is amusing to hear the Vicar call me 'Brother'; but Cuthbert never is addressed so!

To return to this 'warm scribe my hand'—I mean its left brother— you must know that the bandage is now left off, for seven of the torn places are now covered with beautiful salmon-pink silky skin! The eighth, and last, is still in the clotted-cream-mixed-with-birds-custard state; and I wear a finger-stall over that. All pain is at an end.

I find post time is at hand; so I must finish my 'Lives' another time. Also write to Harold another time.

So glad you saw the Show. I, too, went to a Horticultural Exhibition that very afternoon (Sutton's people's); 'old Bray' took me to see his fruit. He won two Firsts!

Of course you will let me know, now, if there is any chance of your coming.

W

155. To Susan Owen

31 August 1912   *Dunsden Vicarage*

Dearest Mother,

Now is the itching hour of Saturday evening before the P.M., and I am in duty bound to spend it thus. My fingers have so improved as to dispense with the last finger-stall; tho' they are still unsightly by reason of the fringes of dying epidermis upon them. May they soon be presentable for the admiring gaze of Mrs. Lott—for Edith made mention how Mrs. Lott once remarked upon the prettiness of Mr. Owen's hands!

[1] A Shrewsbury tailor, living on Pride Hill.

This I take as a crowning example of the good soul's utter barbarity in matters of taste.

_____

Leslie's failure is indeed deplorable. (Both the Hulcoops passed. I was glad to hear a bit of Kelso news.

_____

I did not write to Auntie Annie.[1] I could easier have written to Queen Anne on the death of G. of Denmark or to Martha of Bethany two millenniums ago, than to my aunt or Grandma on this melancholy occasion. What you said makes me glad indeed that I refrained from speaking.

The Visitors left on Thursday. On Wednesday afternoon I was asked to accompany them & Vicar on a motor-launch trip to Mapledurham. I scarcely remember having seen a finer company of noble trees, than populate the Thames Basin around here. Before this, I had made up my mind that if I had enjoyed nothing else round here this summer, I have seen more wonderful tree-forms to gladden me than ever before.

The weather has really been such as to make my ink flow copiously from my nib, much more imprecations from my tongue, and spirits from my heart. Since Thursday, however, the sashes in the windows of heaven must have snapped from over-work; anyhow the windows haven't been opened over these parts.

[*half sheet missing*] Sorry I have no leisure to say more now. I have no end of things to tell you in my head; but too many other things on my hands to allow it.

Therefore, Till four weeks be run, I am your (if possible) fonder-growing-through-absence,

Wilfred

[P.S.] [*half sheet missing*] news. If you see in this forgetfulness a truer touch of myself than any letter could communicate, <u>Be Consoled Thereby</u>.

156. To Susan Owen

Monday, 9 September 1912   *Dunsden Vicarage*

My most filial-neglected Mother,

Why have I been so long in writing again? Perhaps because of the very quantity of matter to tell you.

On Sunday before last I had a Children's Service.

On Monday following, Bro. Kemp came over, & stayed till Wednesday.

His friend Morley, B.A. of Camb. has been here Wed. to Saturday. Morley, if thro' Ordination Exam, is becoming a Curate in Reading. It was rather novel to see the ins and outs of this business; to hear him telling himself he must get a Frock Coat and Top Hat even if he goes to his Cure in debt. He plays the callow Deacon very creditably, and the clerical flavour will soon be part of himself. But—(I should say—

[1] Uncle John Taylor of Torquay had died a few days earlier.

Hence) he has a very solid opinion of himself, and thinks his energy, command, erudition and such like in public speaking are wonderful though a more stodgy, plodding, dough-faced candidate I have never met.

Good old Kemp was a delight to have here again. He says the like of being at Dunsden; but, poor fellow, a meal he had alone with the Lord Vicar of the Parish of Dunsden, was enough to remind him that all is not Elysian here.

On Wednesday, however, I had cause to feel all gratefulness to his reverence; for he remembered his promise of taking me to Town. Best of all, he gave me the leash all day.

My first move was to Watson's,[1] High Holborn. There I underwent the long-feared test; and was told the inevitable thing—'Your eyes badly need Glasses. You have pronounced Astigmatism, Hypermetropia, and all the rest.'—Was ever optician said otherwise to a client? Well, I had to submit, and have received spectacles to be worn reading, and walking, eating, and standing and sitting and laughing & crying, and coughing & sneezing . . . I presume I may behold Dream-Objects without them?

From Chancery Lane I looked in at the Brit. Mus. to see one or two things I wanted to;[2] thence to the New London Museum, but found it closed that day, and so straight to Earl's Court. I was highly pleased with the reconstruction of Shakespere's Globe Theatre. I was just in time to see the very play on my Exam. Syllabus—*The Tempest*. All was conducted on rigorously Elizabethan lines, and the effect was most instructive to a student; tho' the acting was in parts but so so. We took an early train home—fortunately, for driving over Caversham Bridge I spotted a Biplane, high in the Western Sky. My first sight of such craft was as impressive as I could have devised. Scarcely a breath of wind—the calm, yellow sunset sky, and the planes gliding smoother than wings, and so high that the engines are perfectly inaudible . . .

Och! Here comes Mrs. Lott, breathless, saying Frank waits for letters.

More <u>very</u> soon, W

157. To Susan Owen

17 September 1912   *Dunsden Vicarage*

My dearest Mother,

Your letter was one of five received this morning—quite an unusual bundle. Needless to say it was the one I opened first and shall try to keep longest. My letters are so accumulating that I am trying to systematize their storage.

---

[1] The scientific instrument makers and opticians (now in Barnet) where Gordon Gunston was now working.

[2] 'On Seeing a Lock of Keats's Hair' was written during the summer of 1912. E B prints an extract.

Leslie, the invaluable, has brought to my notice the *Bookman* Souvenir Number of Keats & Shelley.[1] It has proved the best shillings-worth I have bought for a long time. I could scarcely eat my tea for excitement when I first looked through it. It is teeming with fascinating Pictures. I have to tell the truth, scarcely looked at the articles yet. It is too oppressing to think how many great minds have exerted themselves for his sake, and for Shelley's.

Marie Corelli,[2] bless her, has done her best to effuse on 'Severn . . . lift . . . me . . . up.' But I cannot forbear quoting Lowell's[3] Sonnet 'To the Spirit of Keats'—Except for its merits of expression, I might have done it myself.

> 'Great soul, thou sittest with me in my room,
> Uplifting me with thy vast quiet eyes,
> On whose full orbs with kindly lustre, lies
> The twilight warmth of ruddy ember-gloom.
> Thy clear strong tones will oft bring sudden bloom
> Of hope secure to him who lonely cries,
> Wrestling with the young poet's agonies,
> Neglect and scorn, which seem a certain doom.'

I won't finish off this, in order to reserve your patience for a finer, By A. C. Benson.[4]

> 'Laughing, thou said'st, 'Twere hell for thee to fail
> In thy vast purpose, in thy brave design,
> Ere thy young cheek, with passion's venomed wine
> Flushed and grew pale, ah me! flushed and grew pale!
> Where is thy music now? In hearts that pine
> O'erburdened, for the clamorous world too frail,
> Yet love the charmèd dusk, the nightingale
> Not for her sweet sake only, but for thine.'
>
> etc.

The Sestette says almost what I did in Teignmouth about the 'writ in water'[5] (alas!); and I had already, too, got the last sentiment, about the nightingale, at least in mind, if not on paper.

Last week, being thus fired afresh, I got W. M. Rossetti's *Life of Keats*,[6] and, though he is horribly crabby over the early poems, throws more light on the Life & Character than I have obtained from Sidney Colvin. I cannot read either for long without getting wound up. I have more than once turned hot and cold and trembly over the first haemorrhage scene; and sobbed over Severn's 'He is gone . . .'

---

[1] *Keats-Shelley: The Bookman Memorial Souvenir*, June 1912, a miscellany of articles and poems, some reprinted and some written for the occasion.
[2] The popular novelist (1854–1924).
[3] James Russell Lowell (1819–91) succeeded Longfellow as Professor of Belles-lettres at Harvard in 1855, and was American Minister in England 1880–5.
[4] Arthur Christopher Benson (1862–1925) was Master of Magdalene College, Cambridge, and a prolific writer of poems, essays, and literary studies.
[5] See Biographical Table, 21 April 1911 (p. 9).
[6] London, 1887. Two copies survive among Wilfred's books.

But I never guessed till now the frightful travail of his soul towards Death; never came so near laying hold of the ghastly horror of his mind at this time. Rossetti guided my groping hand right into the wound, and I touched, for one moment the incandescent Heart of Keats.

I must not trust myself to say more on this subject now; but if you are so rash as to come near me soon, you will be in for hours of reading; both '*à bas*', and also '*à haute voix*' from me.

The other day I started afresh on *The Little Mermaid* and have done 19 stanzas. Would you like to hear one of the best?

IX.

O'er this,* she set a weeping willow-tree
To droop and mourn. Full dolefully it clung
About his form, and moved continually,
As if it sighed, as if it ever wrung
Convulsive fingers, in sad reverie;
And o'er the light blue sand it hung
A purple shade; which hour by hour the same,
Burned softly on like lambent sulphur-flame.

What has happened to *Little Claus and Big C.*? I meant to bring it back with me. Will you please bring it?

I will order *Liber Studiorum*[1] & forward it within a few days. I suffer slightly from toothache, but not acutely.

My hand shows little sign of its maltreatment, and gives (sensorarily) less.

I have not yet closed with U.C.C. but should be glad of £s when forthcoming.

Much love;   Your hopefully expectant Wilfred

* statue.

158. To Susan Owen

Sunday, 22 September 1912   *Dunsden Vicarage*

My own dear Mother,

I am in receipt of Letter, Bank Note, and Bill. The Note is, I hope, something in excess of what I required; the letter is,—with your pardon—something in defect of what I desired, as it does not answer one or two questions.

As for my silence upon such imp't things as Guests, I beg to say Mrs. Wigan[2] had no thought of coming since Rev. Herbert has been ill. Lingley has been however, since a week last Friday. I don't know when

---

[1] Presumably another copy of *Turner's Liber Studiorum*. See Letter 82.
[2] The Vicar's mother.

the venerable old lady will come; but the Vicar is already well enough to have preached this morning.

Sorry about 'the Herbert' interloper; I certainly see no reason why you sh'd not spend the 20th Oct. here.

Our Harvest Thanksgiving is not fixed yet.

Specs are quite nice for reading with. I will try & get someone to 'take' me, if you would like a photo [*three lines illegible*] I have had to get my black coat altered at a Tailor's; also the green one shortened in the sleeves at last.

On Sat. afternoon, I saw *Queen Bess* by Sarah Bernhardt[1] in Cinematograph, (with Leslie, Uncle, & Vera.) All very well; but it is positively painful to me not to hear speech; worse than the case of a deaf man at a proper Shakespere play; for all the finer play of mouth, eye, fingers, and so on, is utterly imperceptible, and so are the slower motions of the limbs spoiled, and their majesty lost, in the convulsed, rattling-hustle of the Cinema. Certainly, the old impression of driving through an electric hailstorm on a chinese-cracker is not now so easily got, as of old; but, still, I cannot enthuse over the things as Leslie does. His infatuation would speedily vanish if he knew 'the real thing'. Which, poor fellow, he hankers to do.

There is some talk at Alpenrose of putting together a Shakespere Circle; also a Glee-Singing Band, under the auspices of Miss Maitland.[2] I know not whether such dangerous snares will succeed in luring me. Uncle is to conduct the singing; and has made overtures to me to add my lorn voice to the choir. What they want most, however, is a Tenor.

How is dear Mary & Yourself? Did Father have anything to do with—I mean after, the Rly. Accident.[3] I tell enquirers NO.

I find it an exceeding pleasure to pass an hour or two at Alpenrose. You might even refer to this incidentally when you write thither.

I was as happy as at any moment in the week, when I was riding 'home' last time; and sang till I was breathless! The Sky was like one vast violet, and the moon as intensely yellow as the anther-scales therein, (whilk Botanist Mary will explain.)

        Ever as always your somewhat hasty-scribbling, Wilfred
Again, thanks for the moneys to the dear amasser of the same.

159. To Susan Owen

6 October, 1912   *Dunsden Vicarage*

Dearest Mother,

Harvest Thanksgiving is today: so you will miss the inestimable spectacle of the depraved Gothic of our shanty all belittered with fowsty

---

[1] The celebrated French actress (1844–1923). See Letter 325.
[2] Miss Crichton-Maitland of Rosehill House, Kidmore End.
[3] Fifteen were killed and fifty injured at Ditton junction, two miles from Widnes, on 17 September 1912, when the Chester-Liverpool express left the rails and crashed into a bridge spanning the line. HO recalls that Tom Owen was called out.

apples and fag-ends of the stubble-fields. Not to mention the choir and its thrills. One boy sings so flat as almost to reach two tones below his part, & sing alto. One good virtue this hath—it makes me sing imprecatory psalms with a right good will.

I can scarcely believe you will see me on Sat. I shall scarce see much of you unless you arrive early on account of the P̄.M. (Pious-Moments, 'Plainful mumblry, Pish-tush Muggery, or what-you-will.)

Sunday, too, if it's anything like this, will not permit me to come over.

I will mention your coming to the Vicar. You need not write to him.

Did I tell you I was prevented from going to London, by stress of work on the Coal & Clothing Accounts?

The Vicar went on Thurs.—speaking in the Caxton Hall for the 'Protestant Woman.' He brought me home an Etching of the Nuns House, 'Cloisterham',—quite framable—as a bit of sugar after my labour—(which was not hard, but so trivial—complicate.)

Excuse more of a letter—(and perhaps excuse further letters)—I must reply to Mary, tho' I am about at an end of original remarks, having taken a Bible Class before Church, and having prepared and deliver'd a Harvest Address at the Children's Service, in addition to the Church Service.

Ever your own, Wilfred

160. To Mary Owen

Monday, 7 October 1912   *Dunsden Vicarage*

My dear Mary,

I was glad to have your letter, with its news of pottery for me. You might bring over the best pieces for me to see, if you find room. Do you think of anything else I want from Home? All I can think of is (1) My little Sanitas-Bottle.

(2) *Little Claus & Big C.*

(3) As much of Harold's work as he would like me to see.

Then I want you to open my desk, and find in it a Green Portfolio Affair which Harold made me. If you see in it a sheet of note paper with some writing on it you are not to look another instant upon it, but fold it into an envelope which you will have ready, seal it up, and bring it to me. If you can accomplish this in secrecy, I shall be beholden to you.

_____

The Cold intensifies; it drives me as it does the grumbling Bears from the mountains down to the valleys, down from my private room into the warm dining room for the winter. Only I cannot sleep like the Bears, also! tho' I fain would drop off this moment—half-past eleven on a bright sunny morning, and hibernate till March 18th, say, or, soothly, for ever and a day, that I would . . .

I shall hope very soon to see you as well and cheerful as—(nay not as I) as Pæona,[1] and to have a gentle Pæona-kiss from you; and then it will be 'Goodbye' again; and 'Hope to see you at Christmas'; and then— 'Goodbye' again, and 'Hope to see you at Easter, perhaps', and then 'good-bye' again, and so on, till the last good-bye, and the dim wonder of our last Meeting in the Hereafter—and the Last Hope found 'not vain.'

Your most loving of Brothers, Wilfred

161. To Susan Owen
Postcard

26 October 1912   *Dunsden Vicarage*

A great stroke of ill-luck it was that sundered us so soon. I left the st'n quite bewildered; and with an unsatisfied hunger, which will not be appeased till Christmas Feast. I wended to Poynder's even as at the last Parting, and romantically let fall my choice nose-gay of jasmine into an area beneath the P.O. where it droopeth to this day, peradventure. Then I disbursed the sum of 1d. at the Bookshop, and entered into possession of my first 'First Edition', a Poem of Samuel Rodgers', 1819![2] I would not part with it under 3s. Leslie will be green. I went into R. again on Friday Night, and got drenched in a thunder shower. Today it has been raining most obstinately; most aggravatingly obstinately: not that I want to go out; but the clouds are like a horrid child that won't stop crying for love or money. I had much to say in that stolen ten minutes; but no more now, or this should have been a letter. Many thanks for yours. Vicar is returned. I have tomorrow to miss you in S.S.[3] of all places!

W

162. To Susan Owen

Monday 28 October 1912   *[Dunsden]*

My own dear Mother,

It is now a week to the very hour since I set forth to the Stella Carol[4] Concert. And here I may say that Stella's indisposition was all a humbug, if bodily indisposition was meant; the truth is (I get it from our organist) that Hickie[5] insisted on displaying one of his pianos at the concert: Stella likewise insisted on singing to one of her own; and wouldn't come! Or was prohibited by her manager. This was fixed some days before!

I have spent this afternoon, also, just as last Monday—at Edith Herridge's, for she is not yet in Hospital, nor is it certain she will be

---

[1] Endymion's sister in *Endymion*.
[2] Nothing by Samuel Rogers (1763–1855) has survived among Wilfred's books.
[3] Sunday School.
[4] The Soprano (b.1897), who made her début at the Queen's Hall, London, in 1911.
[5] Hickie & Hickie Ltd., 153 Friar Street, Reading, is still a notable music shop.

taken this week! The poor child has no more pain;[1] but as she has scarcely moved for a month now, 'twould be a marvel if she could be called gay. Yet is she wondrous bright, and enjoys <u>pictures</u>, be they never so mean.

—O despised and bemocked fashioners of florid Picture Post Cards (and by none more than I) how little ye wot of the appreciation of your art by childish eyes and souls! This six-inches of Yellow, Blue and Green representing Grimysands-on-Sea, may have its mission in the world no less than yards of speaking canvas, Botticelli's though it be. And, I say, (because I know my present audience is small and sympathetic)—Perhaps a <u>nobler</u> mission, too, by as many times as there are grains of sand in its <u>broad landscape</u>!

Therefore let me pray you to send me, as you did a year ago, a packet of P.C.'s and Christmas Cards (old of course), and that as soon as you may. This is why I have allowed myself to write <u>again</u> so soon;—even this boon.

I am in train, tonight, to declaim, as I have done too often before to you, against 'that most preposterous (disease) which from my snow-white pen, so often maketh the ebon ink to flow.' (Shakspere).[2] For, without doubt, here is another victim of Consumption.

I sometimes try to comfort people by saying that I have a sister who was once as near Consumption as may be, and that now she is hale and strong. My mind misgives me here; alas! Now <u>how is Mary?</u> [*four lines illegible*]

Methinks a course of jiu-jit-su, or a keel-hauling, or a drop from a balloon, or (Heaven forgive me) a lesson in the ballet-dance, would set her on her stumps.

I care not if you tell her so. And I write expressly that she send me a <u>letter</u> penned as she would speak, as long as she can make it, and as <u>badly</u> written as my own. Let there be no false starts, ruled lines, or ornate letters; let me have just a bit of Mary, and a bit of Shrewsbury, even though she find nothing to describe more dignified than the half-dozen leaves clinging to the lime-trees before the windows.

Next, pay my respects to Harold, for he well deserves them: and mention that I was never more serious than when I passed those ordinances of my last letter to him.

Finally, conserve your <u>own</u> <u>strength</u> to the utmost, for my sake, as I will do for your's: and, —<u>take not</u> offence at my wretched penmanship; I dare not make it beautiful, or I should earn more surely the title of

Your Conceited, Son

P.S. Now do detail in your next something more refreshing of dear Father, than that he is just shuffling off to bed!

---

[1] She recovered. See Letter 192.

[2] . . . most preposterous event,
that draweth from my snow-white pen
the ebon-colour'd ink.
            Love's Labour's Lost, I. i. 240–1.

163. To Mary Owen

[Early] November 1912   *Dunsden Vicarage*

My dear Sister,

How are you? I am jolly well—much better than this time last year—indeed much better than at our Holiday time to the North. Nothing could be falser than your idea that I am always having 'those giddy turns'—never had one before in my life. Quite likely, never shall again. No, I am in excellent trim just now.

Bro. Kemp has brought with him for the week-end a hog's head of good spirits. Our mirth seemingly ran too high for Black[1] and the Vicar, who are as solemn as sextons; and think us two pig-headed in-deed.

Your sacrificing gifts for Edith are very touching. I beg however to step in here—and withold your Musical Box. It's not right of you, to give this, when the Vicar won't lend his great big one! Too many associations are awakened by that twangling melody to allow it to go where it is sure to be broken in a day or two—for there is a little sister of the destructive age, who would not spare a toy such as this for all the sweets in the world.

Very kind of you to send chocolates. And the Game has passed away many a hour full happily.

I saw the surviving girl from 'the Accident' this afternoon [*one line illegible*]

Your devoted W

P.S. I have written to Harold; but the writing is so disgusting that I am not going to send it now; but copy it out; especially as what I have to say is interesting, and must not be obscured by indecipherability as well as a three-cornered-back-stair mode of expressing things.

Receive an holy kiss; and be thankful.

Long live our most irreligious and gwacious King!

164. To Susan Owen

7 November 1912   *Dunsden Vicarage*

Sweet my Mother,

I have got my letters sadly in arrears! No less than 4 unanswered ones of yours are now my happy possessions.

Dear Madam, in reply to yours of the 29th, I beg to state (who said I fall foul of business matters?) that I wrote immejit to Stanley, and began incontinent to revise, but owing to external high pressure, and internal low pressure, I have scarce given it an hour's consideration.

The Cards you looked up for E.H.[2] were just the thing! I thought

---

[1] Unidentified. He appears to have moved in to the Vicarage, and to have been in orders. A copy of Mrs. Browning's poems surviving among Wilfred's books is inscribed 'from his friend Clyde Black, Christmas 1912'.
[2] The invalid Edith Herridge.

you must have cleared the house of them by the numbers and variety, but lo! here are more and more arriving. Let 'em all come!

Then, your brief resumé of Mary's condition was a masterly touch! It was indeed no 'badly written letter.' Ah me! Nerves! Well, my philosophy teaches that those mortals who have nerves exquisitely responsive to painful sensation, have a perfect right to use them, when time serves, to respond equally keenly to enjoyment. I know I have a tingling capacity for pleasure on occasion, and if such be the operation of a tense nerve, then must I content me with nerves' foolish ado when things offend and lacerate them. Foh! how many things in this room, in this land, on this earth offend my senses! But I am willing to pay this price, to purchase the delight to the full, when delight is possible. Nerves in Heaven! There is a proposition indeed! If not nerves, why anything? Will limbs of the maimed be restored? Will toe-nails cease to grow; pimples to erupt?

> 'I look o'erhead,
> And there is sullen mist,—even so much
> Mankind can tell of Heaven.'[1]

Well, now, to turn to yours of the 1st. Nov. The vests fit very well; and are the very things I had been sorely wanting. Better a sore want than a sore skin, said I; and put off putting on the Merinos, luckily. Now, to reply to yours of the 3rd, I was much pleased to hear of Mary's wits polishing up. If it is her propensity to apportion her hours to cover several nights and days [*three words illegible*] It is now Saturday and [*word illegible*] in the same way, why not adopt the habit, and trouble [*one word illegible*]. I feel similarly disposed myself. Just lately, a sleeping bout has been the sign. I had a 4th Post from you after lunch. I feared to open it, feeling it must be replete with reproach. And lo! What is this? 'Lovely warm dressing Gown'; 'all wool' etc. What a surprise! I had banished the idea of such a luxury. I will not enlarge upon the colour, till I see it. By your pains in bolstering it, I should think it will prove not too superb a hue, an article which might carry Bile Beans in its pocket with good reason. However, trust me to thank the Giver every night and morning for this Boon.

I was so glad to hear your own eyewitnessing account of a Flight.

I was so $\begin{cases} \text{pleased} \\ \text{displeased} \end{cases}$ to know of Ethel's decampment. You will be surprised to hear that one of the eligibles I had in my eye, was 'taken worse', poor girl, on Monday after you left, and is now at Brighton, on the Vicar's (or Parish's) expense! Thoroughly weakened she is; and no wonder, for she was the only Philotis at Mrs. Reading's biggish place! The other, also decidedly in my eye, being a wench of religious convictions, look you, and lusty, and of good presence, withal, and wondrous pleasant to behold, is now in Reading.

I strongly protest at your mere notion of trying to do without!

---

[1] Keats, 'Sonnet written upon the top of Ben Nevis'.

If I hear not soon that one is not installed, even plus bunions, and divers excrescences, I will send a batch of young 'uns down upon you from this place at my own expense. Selah!

Mary's welcome shall receive attention before the week is much older.

Your own devoted Wilfred

165. To Susan Owen

Thursday, [*14?*] *November 1912*   *Dunsden Vicarage*

Dearest Mother,

I am writing in my bedroom, as I daren't sit up in the dining room lest the Vicar think I despise the new rule of retiring soon after ten, (one of the reforms of Black). This necessity for the invalid's health, I may say, has only been observed once yet; and midnight has been the nearest hour, on several occasions.

I flatly disobeyed your Return-Post command in order to have some conversation with B——[1] himself, who came this evening after first Post time.

Now, Mabel is situated with Mrs. Reading, so doubly out of consideration. Vera B— is 15+, ever clean in person, and Mrs. Lott vouches for her hair at any rate. Her Home has been a slovenly enough place, as you may imagine when the Mother has been out all day with the Lodger, and spending the evening at 'the public'. Oh I pity the man exceedingly, and the children; though I believe B— has winked at the affair for many a month. The Shelleyan Principles of Love being a Law unto itself loses its attractiveness when the Adonis is a loutish tallow-face with a blood-poisoned arm, and the Venus a bedraggled creature, with daughters at a critical age. B— is not poor; has regular work as Gardener [*two pages missing*] have opportunity to make first-hand observations, and Mrs. Lott will be able to say some profound things to you.

And a month here ought to give the girl such first-class notion of Housework, that if she slip back to second-rate ways, she ought to come up to scratch at Mahim. If you come across a suitable, don't hesitate to engage, all the same.

There! 8 pages in my own hand of registry office and police court chatter! Maybe I take a self-considering interest herein; for I feel that if my nature had but been more reckless, I had long packed up my traps and sunk exhausted in the recesses of thy bosom and my little room.

Think! I have not a single night free of meetings from Sunday to Sunday!

W

---

[1] A gardener in the village whose daughter Vera was under consideration as a maid for Susan Owen. We have suppressed his full name.

166. To Mary Owen

16 November 1912   *Dunsden Vicarage*

My dearest Mary,

Many thanks for your letter of the 4th. About time you sent me another. I hardly think Colin has sent me more than 3 lines in as many months. Now this is too bad. And as for Harold . . .! [*five lines illegible*]

I myself have been doing some graceful vol-planes and circuits lately. At quarter of an hour after lunch yesterday was I seized with a most dervishy vertigo. I was due to start with the Vicar to a Sutton-Drawing Room–Missionary–Reception; but I must have got 'run in' had I appeared on a public road, especially as I 'smelt' like any bacchanal, (after Edith's administration of a teaspoonful.)

So I lay down all the rest of the day, and had five hours gratis of a merry-go-round. Went to bed at 7.30. and find things slowed down this morning.

'Twas all due to (1) Cold mutton, overlayed by (2) greasy-soapy variety of Potato, overlayed by (3) Walnut Pickle, capped with (4) Stewed Apple. I will finish with an impression of the dining room at 2 o'clock yesterday.

For I won't trust myself to write more of other people and affairs, with so distorted a vision.

Your Brother, Wilfred

167. To Susan Owen

Tuesday, 10 December 1912   *Dunsden Vicarage*

My own dear Mother,

I am conscious of a glimmering sense of duty unfulfilled, after this three-weeks, is it? of silence: though why <u>duty</u> I cannot explain; when my half-hour of confidences and narrations to you is one I look forward to with gladness of heart, even as to a season when the righteous (dogmas) cease from troubling and the eerie (speculations) are at rest. If I must face the question, there may have been a moral reason for withholding my speech; just that I may not speak unadvisedly.

Now, For many months, in fact ever since I have been here, the Vicar has been praying, now hotly, now coldly, for <u>Revival</u>.

It has come.

At least, is coming.

Here is the Organist converted; the 'blower' and numbers of others 'under conviction'; here is Jack Dear writing to the Vicar of how he is completely healed of his backsliding, and has made a wholesale surrender of his will to God.

Here is a woman saying to our last Prayer Meeting: 'I should like help', and being 'prayed through'.

Here is a man, B— himself, accepting Christ last night at Black's Bible Class for men.

Here is Vera B—, the same evening at another mtg. being asked by Black whether she took Christ as her Saviour, answering Yes.

Here is a woman of the parish writing from Reading Hospital to say she has found Christ there.

Here is Willie Montague, being cornered by Black on Sunday afternoon, making his (second) profession of Christianity.

Here are women shedding tears in Church every Sunday night.

Here am I, halting between two, aye, more than two opinions, till sense deserts my mind, and strength my body.

Wednesday

Here I left off yesterday, and being in a different mood just now, it is a wonder I am letting that first Sheet pass a second reading—For already I have destroyed much more than that, earlier in the week.

Perhaps it is just as well I should send them; with the inference that I can no longer hope to do real study, amid the meetings, classes, spiritual excitements, and such like that prevail, and will prevail in this place.

With reference to my O. English, I mentioned to Mrs. Jones that I found great difficulty with Pronunciation, etc. and she very kindly referred me to Miss Morley,[1] Professor of Eng. at the College; whom I saw about two weeks ago.

She begged me to join the College, (for my sake, not the College's she was so urgent) and mentioned a scholarship[2] admitting one to the whole degree course, with residence at 'Wantage Hall'.[3] This is awarded to the person of <u>most promise</u> in the competitive exam., not necessarily the highest mark-scorer.

---

[1] Edith Julia Morley (1875–1963) was Professor of English Language, University of Reading, 1908–40, and editor of Henry Crabb Robinson's journals.

[2] Miss Morley's encouragement led Wilfred to sit for this (see Letter 188); unsuccessfully, as he had anticipated.

[3] Wantage Hall was built in 1908 for men students, the first residential building in the University.

As to when the next scholarship is open she was very dim; but spoke as if she would like me to get it. Then she <u>invited</u> me to her remaining classes in O.E., to which I have been.

In our interview, she asked me (what prompted her I know not) whether I 'wrote'. The kindly Minerva was favourably impressed by my genuine, (and well-founded, goodness knows) self-depreciations, said they were a good sign, and pressed me to go on with attempts; adding a few words of advice withal.

I wonder does Harold remember Seaward,[1] who was in his form, I think, at the B.I., and lived up Chestnut Grove (?) Well, Seaward's aunt is a <u>great</u> friend of Miss Morley's; Miss Morley reports that S. is now the mathematical genius of the school.

Now I am dry in the head; yet my mouth waters to lick up the envelope; but two items of your letter must not remain unnoticed: (1) The assurance of a good servant sharpens my desire for Home, more than by rights such a consideration should.

and (2) The idea of meeting *'une inconnue française'*, has the same effect on your ever-mother-faithful,

Wilfred

168. To Susan Owen

12/12/12   *Dunsden Vicarage*

Dearest Mother,

You ask for a Card, and I send you a letter: you beseech for a watered-down note, and I send you a drop of the milk of human kindness on cream-laid note-paper.

But it is well that I know I have but a short while to write it in.

I cannot put enough emphasis into my first petition: Do 'take it easy', right on till Christmas. You little know how my happiness hangs on the assurance of your health. Suppose you were the least bit strained in the ventricles where is my Christmas joy of Homecoming.

Never have I set greater store on a holiday to brace up my nerves. They are in a shocking state, and no mistake. My breast is continually 'too full'. Just as if one had been over-long in a putrid atmosphere, and had got to the advanced stage of being painfully conscious of it. A breath of another air <u>may</u> put things right.

Maybe only Fire will clear the Cobwebs.

But I had rather kill the Spider . . .

I have just heard that at the Mothers' Meeting this afternoon, Milly's Mother yielded herself to God, and was brought to the point by the visible happiness of her child. Is it cowardly to be influenced by the doings of others; I mean, being willing to follow if others will lead?

That is how it strikes me, if I at this juncture, were to make <u>my</u> sacrifice—of Reason.

---

[1] H O does not remember him.

My time for setting out for the Club is nearly here. I press on.

I dare not give an opinion about Harold's Future. Am I his Keeper?
[*two lines illegible*]

Curiously enough, both these cuttings were in *The Pall Mall* today.

169. To Susan Owen

Tuesday, 17 December 1912   *Dunsden Vicarage*

Dearest Mother,

Just as you wrote your letter (received this morning) so I write this.
There is

> 'a listening fear in my regard
> As if calamity had but begun;
> . . . and the sullen rear
> Is with its stored thunder labouring up.'[1]

Woe unto us all for the seals which are yet to be broken.

Meanwhile I bite my lips in silence; with quite enough provocations
to put up with, without theological distractions. Thus, tho' this morning
I put forth the modest request of Friday next to Friday, 27th, for
Holiday, I am granted Monday 23rd to Sat. 28th!

I would give a thousand week days for one Sunday out of these Courts
of the Lord; but no! I am indispensable for the Carrying-on of the
Sunday School. Utter drivel! Whether you feel as sorry about it as I do,
I can only suppose.

And hope.

Now, I feel I must talk things over, so were it only for as many hours
with you, I would take the journey. What about Fare? I devoutly
trust to the 'paternal roof'; or if not that, the paternal pockets. I am
wondrous empty; after my

> Spectacles Bill. ⎫
> Accident Bill. ⎬ etc.
> Dentist Bill.   ⎪
> Christmas Box Bills. ⎭

I cannot consent to giving Edith & Mrs. L. presents other than the
Slippers; unless you really promised them from yourself.

I shall leave behind me my bicycle, and boredoms. I am coming back
passably strong in the calf, heart, lung, etc. but weak as water about the
'nerves', whatever they may be. I catch them from Black, who said he
felt relapsing into his old condition today. And looked it too. Still I
hold together as your devoted son

                                                          Wilfred

---

[1] Keats, *Hyperion*, I. 37–41.

170. To Susan Owen[1]

Thursday, 19 December 1912   [*Dunsden*]

I have precisely 5 mins. before the letters go.

Was dismayed at sight of a P.O. to think no Pass was obtainable. But thank you for it as deeply as I hope to enjoy the issues of it.

You never frightened me so much before, as when you threw out dark hints of writing to the Vicar.

Do you want to 'do for' me completely?

You could not do more harm than by such an action.

Moreover [*two words illegible*] things follow in that week, and I positively could not miss them.

No! All you can do to help me now is to set my terror at rest, by writing at once to me, with a recantation of your maternal-instinctive menaces.

Also please say—Do I book Single or Return. I ask this because is there no possibility of a Pass for one launching out from Home upon the World?

Haven't the time of train fixed yet. Of course an early one.

Your own, Wilfred

171. To Susan Owen

29 December 1912   *Dunsden Vicarage*

Dearest Mother,

I have not long to give the required account of Yesterday. Black has a friend here, and talk has continued till it is quarter of an hour off Church time. So then:—

I found my way to the tram; rode for quite ½ hour through most depressing districts; walked on for 10 mins. as directed, and entered a more habitable region, the Ideal Village; which borders on what a Brummegemite would call the 'Country'.

Found the Parsonage, the Parson,[2] Miss Rose and Charlie, and a half-vanished lunch.

Mr. Morgan took me round the Parish in the afternoon, and gave me an idea of the nature of the work. The Church is a beautiful little structure, and the people are a pleasant folk; and I should quite like to dwell among them.

I can quite understand the zest Mr. Morgan finds in the Parish being absolutely new; and I felt an attraction for the work I should be called

---

[1] This letter shows signs of considerable agitation, not only in content but in the writer's normally vigorous and well-formed hand. As the following letters show, Wilfred was now near to a break with Mr. Wigan and was about to consult Mr. Morgan of Bordesley about another similar position.

[2] The Rev. John Morgan wanted a young man to assist him in his new parish (see p. 140, note). The meeting may have been planned through Miss Rose (see Letter 105), who is present at lunch.

upon to do—to start and organise meetings and unions, bands, and so on among 'the young'.

But I told Mr. Morgan plainly that I did not consider myself a fit person to dare to undertake such work, and revealed to him my state of mind.

As for my studies, I believe he would be a very good coach for Clerical exams, but doubt if he could help me in the very things I need help in, Science and O. English.

So matters are as they were. He tried to puff up Birmingham as a town, but though I have overcome old prejudices against its abominable skies, and outlying tracts of scrap-iron and coal mounds, I am sure there could be no possible benefit to health or spirits by living there. And it takes at the very least, 40 mins. to reach Bordesley from Snow Hill.

Moreover, Miss Rose told me that the house is very small even for the few that are already in it.

I am very grateful that you 'organized' my visit, however, because any idea of my being vastly better off there, will not remain to trouble me now.

The whole adventure is like a dream. Indeed the whole week at home is no more substantial in the memory than last night's dreams. To prove what a daze the rush through B'ham put me into, I actually enquired for the Shrewsbury train, and got on to that platform. The abstraction was partly due to the Palatial Architecture of the new Station. The entrance is a wonderful structure indeed.

I had a rather unpleasant walk up from Reading—so hot. If it hadn't been raining all the time, I should have ignited.

I find things here in every respect as they were; only more so.

Black's friend doesn't address a word to me; so there's one comfort.

I saw all the contents of Alpenrose on Sunday, except Dorothy.

If you haven't already sent the Parcel, kindly remember my tooth-brush, but not my old shaving-stick. With the Music please include that Mss. Chorus. Also, I lay it open to Mary's option to transcribe for me that seductive, dreamy air of Gurlitt's (?),[1] unless she could lend the Book for a while.

I was called away from my writing on Sunday Evening, so you will not get this till Tuesday, I fear.

                                        Adieu, dear Mother. W

172. To Susan Owen

[*4 January 1913*]   [*Dunsden Vicarage*]

                        First page missing

The furor [*several words missing*] now abated in the Vicarage, thank Mnemosyne; but I hope that I, who 'discovered' him something over

---

[1] Cornelius Gurlitt (1820–1901), German organist and composer, of whom Percy A. Scholes writes in *The Oxford Companion to Music*: 'one of the later 19th century's most liberal providers of well-graded and not uninteresting pianoforte music, often to be seen in the hands of the musical youth of all civilized nations'.

a year ago, may [*half page missing*] but the Vicar's presence (taciturn instead of wontedly gay) symbolic of my stern Destiny, sat heavy on my soul the night. I have already braced myself to one important interview; the upshot of which was that he begged me to spend the next morning upon Tracts! Others will follow.

Murder will out, and I have murdered my false creed. If a true one exists, I shall find it. If not, adieu to the still falser creeds that hold the hearts of nearly all my fellow men.

Escape from this hotbed of religion I now long for more than I could ever have conceived a year and three months ago. It reminds me of that old grange in *Westward Ho!* whither the priests would resort and hatch plots for the salvation of England.

To leave Dunsden will mean a terrible bust-up; but I have no intention of sneaking away by smuggling my reasons down the back-stairs. I will vanish in thunder and lightning, if I go at all.

It has just struck me that one of the occult Powers that Be may have overheard the ancient desire of my heart to be like the immortals, the immortals of earthly Fame, I mean, and is now on a fair way to granting it. This flight of mine from overbearing elders, if it comes off, will only be my version of running away from College (Shelley, Coleridge). Only where in me is the mighty Power of Verse that covered the multitude of their sins. It is true I still find great comfort in scribbling; but lately I am deadening to all poetic impulses, save those due to the pressure of Problems pushing me to seek relief in unstopping my mouth.

Here is a Sonnet that occurred to me this morning:—

On My Songs[1]

Although on many and many a sacred time	*a*
Poets have spok'n as if they knew my woe;	*b*
Though, as it seemed, they fashioned many a rime	*a*
To be my own soul's cry, easing the flow	*b*
Of my dumb tears with Language like deep sobs,	*c*
—Yet there are hours when richest[2] hoards of thought	*d*
Hold nothing for me. No heart throbs my throbs;	*c*
No brain yet knew the thing wherewith mine's fraught.	*d*
'Tis then I voice my own dim reveries.	*e*
Low croonings of a motherless child, in gloom,	*f*
Who fain must sing himself to sleep, are these.	*e*
Tonight, if Thou should'st lie in this same Room,	*f*
Dreading the Dark thou know'st not how to illume,	*f*
Listen; my songs may haply give thee ease.	*e*

I need scarcely explain the metaphors of the last lines. If however a conscientious '3rd Reading' fails to make it clear, I will cease talking in parables for ever.

---

[1] CDL prints the improved BM draft of this sonnet, *Poems*, p. 119.
[2] 'their rich' cancelled.

I gave dear old E.W.M's[1] pamphlet a conscientious reading. But you know such a course of study is now quite beside the mark for me. Discussions which <u>take it for granted the reader believes in Adam's getting outside some fruit or other</u>! and then going off into occult matters of retributive dogma, are not what I want. They are trivial, and annoying, like the tickings of the clock that so annoyed E.W., you know, that he shelved it deep in a cupboard. Perhaps there is enough here for you to digest.

Blessings attend you, dear Mother, and the dear kindred, whose message touched me to the heart.

Wilfred

173. To Susan Owen

8 January 1913   *Dunsden Vicarage*

Dearest Mother,

No reason appears to me why you should not come to Alpenrose next week. Rather, every reason that you should come.

I have had further talks to the Vicar; and our relations are taking more definite shape every day. The very crux to which events have been tending for months and months is now upon us. It is very meet and right that you should be near at hand.

I was at Alpenrose yesterday, and after supper had long debate with Dorothy, at which Leslie remained an interested listener.

Her position is extraordinary, and wholly illogical. She has no decided belief in the <u>first man Adam</u>; and cannot help regarding the talking-serpent interludes as not adapted to present-day needs, etc. How, then, can she attach any importance to the precise words of St. Paul (?):

> 'As in Adam all die,
> <u>So</u> in Christ shall all be made alive' ?

If all have <u>not</u> died in Adam, where is the possibility of all being 'made alive' (wha<u>te</u>ver that means) in Christ? More, where is the need? To me, if there be no <u>'As'</u> there is no 'So'; no Adam, no second Adam. Yet the more I read early Genesis, the more does it appear the work of a Hebrew sage (Moses, or somebody else of the same name !!) recording his own notions of the beginnings of things; so that 'the Fall' is a myth. This is only one difficulty, taken from the Science Instances; itself only <u>one</u> of the troublesome voices. On my other hand, but pulling the same <u>way</u>, is 'Literature', and all it means; and ways of life that will have to be changed, as well as habits of thought.

To descend to easier air: I was disappointed that Mary should find herself unable to cope with a piece of Musical Transcription. But I know

[1] The Rev. E. W. Moore.

the difficulty of such a task if one's tired, and wits and grit be slightly out of contact. Still, I have a fancy for that little tune, and <u>hope she may spare the page soon</u>.

I have written to Mrs. Dale.

Do you bring Colin to Alpenrose? I am obliged for his letter. Also Harold's. In conclusion, thank you for your wonderful sympathy and tolerance in the matters which would long ago have given a less sensible mother 'the hump'. Ever, or at least while Personality lasts,

Your Wilfred

174. To Susan Owen
Postcard

12 January 1913   [*Postmark Reading*]

So glad to hear of your decision to come on <u>Tues</u>. Unluckily there is a Manager's Meeting which can't get on with<u>out</u> me (from 6.30) and at 4.30 I am invited to Mrs. Lott's Tea for the Sowers' Band. I will however do my best to meet you at st'n., or else see you some time in the evening. It will be a real pleasure to have Tweak[1] over (Thanks for his letter). Only the Vicarage will be very full up; for another young protégé of B's is here for all next week; and Bro. Kemp also from Monday to Monday. Stuart Holden[2] was in Reading last Thurs., but as he could not spare me any time then, the Vicar is going to send me to see him in London on Thursday!

Please bring (1) your + New Test. (20th Cent.) if room is available. (2) *Little C. & Big C.* (How the poor thing is knocking about the world) (3) <u>Music</u>, as kindly promised. I don't think of anything else just now. How short a time since I had my last vision of you in the Potteries. I shall miss Mary this time.

W

175. To Susan Owen

24 January 1913   *Dunsden Vicarage*

Darling Mother,

Your First Letter of a 'new Series' came on Thursday. Its contents have been docketed in their proper place in my mind.

I watched the train bear you away, without any very deep sensations; either I have a premonition of no long tarrying away from you; or else passing sentiments are being destroyed in me by eternal themes. I steadfastly refuse to talk of these vast concerns tonight. My hands are

---

[1] Colin.

[2] The Rev. Dr. J. Stuart Holden (see Letter 149) was Vicar of St. Paul's, Portman Square, London, from 1905 till his death in 1934.

tired and restive; not my brain empty; oh not so! For the first time in life, I feel I could fill volumes; if I once started to write. It would turn out a Philosophical Work, of course. Oh the irony of my old title of Philosopher![1] I have become one without knowing it. It is a far, far different thing from what I imagined of yore.

You used to call me 'the Judge'; that is, alas, a long way from fulfilment! I can no more make pronouncements upon conflicting evidence than any moony-eyed dolt! My treatise on Philosophy would be a succession of interrogations from beginning to end. And that is not what the World wants:—though it is all it gets really—for the firm exclamation marks (!) symbolic of uncontrovertible asseverations, (with which such a book begins), generally curl up into Question-marks (?) before the end is reached.

Dear, dear, this is not what you want just now; you want news.

To begin with: the Vicar had an attack of Gout on Thurs. mng. and has just got up this (Friday) Evening. So I have not seen much of him.

The Vicar of Sonning buried Mrs. Hulcoop on Thursday. I called at Mrs. Ambrose's with the sweets; and found Lorrie and May ill with a (third) attack of measles.

Ha! Here is the bottom of the page approaching! I can't think why I have such a disinclination for scribing, tonight. Providence, perhaps, sees my further communications might not be salutary for you to receive.

Indicate to my Colin, Harold, and Mary, how my affection for them lives and grows; and bid them observe the laws of Health! (That's as far as my advice can go.) So also do ye, as I do.

Your own Wilfred

176. To Susan Owen

29 January 1913   *Dunsden Vicarage*

Dearest Mother,

Tuesday Mid-day brought your very welcome letter. Things are at a standstill again with me; because the Vicar has gone away for some days to Lingley's, at Parkstone Bournemouth. (N.B. Doesn't Mrs. Corbett live at 'Lingley', Parkstone?) I had infinite labour to find 'a clergy' to take the Evening Service on Sunday. Went to about nine people in Reading about it, walking from 2.15 till nearly 10 p.m. (Not unaccompanied, however.) Got Neatby[2] eventually, and for my pains had a jolly fiery sermon, which might have been framed for my own special edification—or demolition I should rather say.

I went to the Glee Practice last night. Leslie is troubled at the idea of my leaving soon. He had some more verses to show me—astonishing!

I have also been guilty of four Compositions since you left! I tell you,

---

[1] A family nickname for a short time.
[2] The Rev. George Wigram Neatby, Curate (1911–13) of Greyfriars, Reading.

I have no satisfaction so pleasant as the feeling of something attempted, something done, in this way. Yet it is very, very little that I have the heart to commit to writing.

I paid a visit to the School this morning. The children show no sign of missing Mrs. Hulcoop, but what signs would one expect to see?

And the other day I asked Milly if Mrs. H. were ever cross with them. 'Oh yes! I should think she was!' 'Did she ever punish you?' 'Made me "turn out" of my seat sometimes.'

'How often?' 'Oh, every day.'

'Dear me: what for?'

'Oh, I don't know.'

'Now, you must know.'

'Because, I read too quick, then.'

It is a mightily instructive, as well as pleasant thing to have the confidence of a child. In fact it is the only way to get at any notion of child-psychology.

Teachers in Colleges talk of studying a child. And they go about it with moral microscopes in their eyes, and forceps in their fingers. Not the way at all. All that is wanted in the hand is the child's own hand; the best lens for the eye is an earnest smile.

Children are not meant to be studied, but enjoyed. Only by studying to be pleased do we understand them. My opportunities of such observation are unique here. I can examine their home-influence, for I have the entrance of every house. I know their school-influence, for I know every one of their teachers. I know their spiritual influences, for I know every one of their spiritual task-masters. And I have a very good idea of their amusements.

Now is there after all some region of their natures which I shall never fathom? Is there a definite relation between them and the unseen, into which my curiosity, my jealousy may never pry? I think not.

I believe this sweet piety of theirs has reference to present environment only. Environment was the cause of it. Alter the environment and it will go. For already I grieve to say (though why I grieve is not very patent, considering) that 'impressions' are 'wearing off' in some cases, already. In fact I am convinced that I hold under my tongue, powers which would shake the foundations of many a spiritual life.

A week's conversation crumbles what promises to be an eternal structure.

This is speaking boldly, and terribly.

Think not I would use those Powers. Shelley scrupled not to play their whole force upon his young friends. But because the Religion he had met with was hollow, it does not follow that no religion is solid. He and all his thousand tribes may never have struck the real thing. It exists none the less, you say. Only I haven't met it—to know it—yet.

Nay, I should feel the (possibility of) the millstone tightening round my neck, and the bitter waters of the sea pouring in at my lips, if I essayed to recommend my persuasions on another. I look upon the child-lives with an eye too much like their Creator's, to play the part popularly ascribed to a malignant tempter.

By the way, when I survey a class of children in this paternal way, (for I can experience the happiness of paternity, fraternity, and amativeness all in one, sometimes) I find some excuse for the unswallowable bone of contention—the Doctrine of Election.

Nothing affords greater pleasure than singling out from a crowd. When I go through a picture-gallery I single out my favourites; when I stand in the company of the Poets, one has my enthusiasm ten-times-heated; when I live amongst a village of children, one claims seventy-times-seven-fold more affection than the others.

And this leads me—merely to the end of my letter. You won't suffer if you skip half this prosing till 'another day', and turn to the happy ending, after your manner with books: Where you will find—no expressions of devotion—but just the supplication Be strong (1) physi-cally—(Poor Kemp lost his Mother suddenly the other day) (2) spiritually (lest through loneliness and no support I quail before the Truth of Truths).

Your own, Wilfred

177. To Mary Owen

1 February 1913   *Dunsden Vicarage*

My dear Mary,

I cannot tell you, dear sister, how glad I was to hear of your experiences in spiritual matters—because my gladness is limited by hindrances of my own. I am intensely sorry therefore that I must bid you not look to me as in any way a responsible guide in your religious life.

But be thankful that, although you have abundant 'means of grace' around you, the finest Christian spirits are those who have direct communication with Powers Unseen, and who are consequently independent of what man can do unto them, either for evil or good.

I have made the discovery that no religion is worth the having, except the vital reality just indicated. At the same time I have to acknowledge that such a religion I do not know in my own experience. That is as much as I will say to you on these points,—I should say these vast spheres—now or henceforward: till I cannot but speak.

Now, concerning my outer man, I must observe that I now must really own up to that objectionable title—man!—I am boy no more; that is for the greater part of my time. I have enough grey hairs to whiten the ground if they were to drop out.

Ha! Zooks! Something necessitates my stopping short! I will explain 'tomorrow'.

Ever your loving Brother, Wilfred

178. To Susan Owen[1]

4 February 1913　　　　　　　　　　　　*Dunsden Vicarage*

Dearest Mother,

This morning I managed to broach the subject of my leaving, to the Vicar. He had only been waiting for me to be first in the matter. Unless I 'get right', I pack off this very week,—about Friday perhaps.

Tomorrow will be Ash Wednesday. How many just persons that need no repentance will sit in Ashes then! Scarcely a soul in the world will need repentance more than I.

Only is such a thing as repentance an actuality, or a delusion? There are left just a few hours or days for me to consider it. These days will be the intensest of my life. It amounts to finding out whether my sanest moments are really my maddest. If they are I am still—mad.

I ought to reply to Harold [*two lines illegible*] But in any case I must write again to you very speedily.—However much I wish to put aside immediate and circumstantial considerations, in my decision, the thought of leaving Dunsden weighs upon me terribly. Though Dunsden will contain little to attract me, if I become a religious devotee.

> '. . . All my pretty ones?
> Did you say all? . . . All?
> What all my pretty chickens
> At one fell swoop?'
>
> 　　　　　(*Macbeth.*)[2]

And my verse-making? O hard condition! The evidence of increasing powers of late (such as they are) is too tantalising.

I will say no more.

I don't want to communicate my calm frenzy to anybody—let alone you.

My allegiance to you and my Father is never to be shaken. For the rest, I have not the slightest feeling of humility for anything in existence, but the Eternal Being, the Principle of Beauty, and the Memory of Great Men.

Ever your Wilfred

179. To Susan Owen

Postcard

6 February 1913[3]　　　　　　　　　　　　*Dunsden*

Coming by train leaving R. 2.30 Friday. This was your train, wasn't it? Books are addressed to Father, to travel free, leaving vicarage by carrier tomorrow.

Yours, W

[1] In this letter, as in Letter 170, the writing shows that Wilfred is under nervous stress.
[2] *Macbeth*, IV. iii. 216.
[3] He left Dunsden the next day.

180. To Susan Owen[1]

9 April 1913   *Monkmoor Rd, Shrewsbury*

Dearest Mother,

If you have entertained any hope of a letter before the present date, I beg to suggest that your hopes were unjustified, because, unless I raked up matter from the past, or rummaged out a theme from some odd corner of the brain, I have had nothing to deliver myself of. Even now I am at a loss to fill a page with anything <u>solid</u>.

Here however is a *résumé* of the past few days, honestly put down for your relief, and diversion.

Saturday. Don't remember so far back as Saturday. Possibly slept all day. Although I certainly got up for breakfast.

Sunday. Went to St. Julian's in Mng. Psalms rendered in the original Hebrew—very exhilarating, but forbidding to the unlearned.

Thus:—My strethfaileth me cos miniquity'nbones acusume. I came proof-gall-anemonies; bushspeshly 'mongmnayb, 'n they've mine quaint-swere afrayme uncoveyselves frummy.

Monday. Morning—had tooth stopped, which gave me much more pain than I had bargained for.

Afternoon—looked in at Doctor's, and made repeated and various depositions to the effect that I eat well: <u>item</u>, I am taking food very well; item, have a very tolerable appetite.

'Sleep well?'—Yes, pretty well.

'Eating well?'—Very well.

'No cough?'—No cough.

'Taking your food?'—WELL!

These little preliminaries over, I mentioned that phlegm still collected in the throat. This was due to adenoid tissue, which he there and then proceeded to extirpate by touching with 'silver'. I touch them daily with an iodine paint.

I slunk into the Quarry from St. John's Hill, in order to expectorate in privacy, and enjoy the full flavour of silver at leisure.

Coming home by the Boulevard I was startled to see a magnificent swan flying down the River at a great rate. It clearly meant to attack four other swans; which then rose on their great wings and disappeared round the bend. The Aggressor settled down on the water at this, but the anger of his appearance was terrifying. It is my opinion that a swan can make as striking a display of dignity and displeasure as any living creature. But it was a most bathetic moment when the noble bird came sidling up to beg crumbs from me. I should have thought it an affront to offer them! But I picked up a crumb of philosophy from the episode.

---

[1] On his return from Dunsden, Wilfred fell ill with congestion of the lungs. Depressed, run-down, and unhappy, 'how dreadfully he was in need of peace of mind; but he could not find it. In this way, his bodily succumbing to the physical illness which seized him immediately after he had returned home acted as a safety-valve; it came just in time to prevent a nervous breakdown' (*JO* II, p. 263). The illness passed. Susan Owen always believed that it had been the onslaught of TB; the doctor categorically dismissed this.

I don't see much of Colin. I smell him a great deal. Whenever he goes to Fox Farm he persists in cleaning the stables, or scraping a cow or so. This is not the way to curry favour with me. Still I think we are mutually satisfied with each other, [at] least for eleven hours of the day. I had an external proof of my dual personality one night. Going into his room when he [was] three parts in slumber, I asked whether I should put the gas out for him, according to my custom.

'No! don't!'

'Why not, dear?'

'You're not to! I always like Wilfred to do it for me!'
I looked in the glass to reassure myself; then, 'Queer dog that Wilfred, eh?' etc.

I very much hope to hear that every inmate of *La Vallée*[1] is really in tolerable health.

I can definitely affirm that I have felt no undue weakness, unless it were on the evening of the day of the Dentistry, etc., when something of a 'sinking' feeling came over me; not sinking on to a bed of down, but up to the neck in quicksand. I have since kept my couch one or two mornings, with the result that I am better than I have been at any time of this year.

Now you must have had enough of dull thoughts and brilliant ink,

So *À dieu!* And may the vitality which thou hast spent for me, be restored to thee tenfold by my good brother, the rich sea-wind.

W

181. To Susan Owen
Picture postcard: on the Lyn, Devon

[*Postmark 18 April 1913*]   *La Vallée* [*Postmark Torquay*]

We had a good quarter-hour to spare at st'n! Read[2] saw us off. Raining here; but we walked up, not being tired, by the journey. Luggage has not yet arrived. If it does not come by 9 o'clock I must go down to Station and look it up. All are pretty well here.

W

182. To Harold Owen

[*April 1913*]   *48 Belle Vue Crescent, Chelston, Torquay*

Dear old boy,

You will not be disappointed with the brevity of this note I hope? I had made up my mind, so far as I ever do such an objectionable thing, to let you have a packet of my news at an Italian Port,[3] (which I will do) but Colin is writing now so I will just send this token, that I am alive as per usual, and very well as per unusual.

W

---

[1] 48 Belle Vue Crescent, Chelston, Torquay, the house to which the Taylors had moved on his retirement and in which John Taylor had died in August 1912.
[2] The senior clerk at Shrewsbury Station.
[3] HO had sailed for India on 13 March.

183. To Susan Owen

April 1913   *Torquay*

Dear Mother,

Finding by chanst as how my letters is mostly give to the flames, they will not in futur be wrote with the same pains as formerly in the past, or as the Swan of Avon so beautifully puts it 'in days of yaw,' I never was much of a scholard, nor I don't mean to try no more.

Now I must tell you of what we are engaged about in this glorious spot which I hope not to leave for quite a week yet if we are spared and I am rite in my reckning, for I never could rember dates.

Well dear and how is Mary?

The sea is verray blue and the sky and three battleships ankuered in the bay which is not often seen—so near the beech I mean.

I am very well and Colin is too.

Now dear I wonder how you are keeping. We had beautifull veal yesterdy it was the best I ever tasted as they all said so too.

Off your kind presant of eggs not many was smashed but the fowl was beautifuly perserved only so tought. The rain keeps off nicely and so it is nice and fine and we go to the sea quite once a day and I do enjoy it. Edith and Colin took one an other to the Pavillon last night and the lady next door but I didnt not being up to it like. Now I have no more news so I must draw to a close too much compoes gives me the beleak in my Chump but I hopes this little letter what I have erected in the gardain which is so nice will be a preciate.

I am, Best love to all, Wilfred

P.S. We do hop father will soon be well secur again from his panes.

184. To Susan Owen

Wednesday [23] *April 1913*   *Torquay*

Dearest Mother,

Your letter with the Order arrived 5 mins before we started for Plymouth; so we both went after all. We saw the Museum etc. in the morning and the Dockyards during the afternoon, and altogether had rather a strenuous time of it. So much so that I wrote a card to Alice Cannell[1] that night asking her to excuse me my appointment for a walk next morning. I lay in peace, therefore, until eleven o'clock when the poor slighted damsel came to beg me to lunch if I would not take a walk. Of course I went; and a very respectable luncheon it was; four courses with wines, followed by coffee. These old ladies know how to keep their state. I was perfectly at home though I hadn't the faintest notion of either of the Ladies' names. 'It would be delightful to see you again' quotha on my leaving, 'Come some evening.'

---

[1] Alice and her mother (see Letter 45) appear to have moved to Torquay.

Alice is very desirous for me to stay on here. The only thing is—no one has mentioned it. And I have a good fortnight's worth of Recuperation. I can solemnly and gleefully tell you that after the third day here (and ever since increasingly) I have felt better than at any time this year, better, I think, than any time last year. Life will be another thing if this persists. I have not tested for any improvement in the mental fibres yet, but with me these are the Pounds which will take care of themselves, if the physical Pence are taken care of. I scarcely think of anything but what I see before me, and not more than superficially about that.

While the rain kept us in, I prowled often enough across the windows, but my scowls were always tempered with a sort of angelic forbearance, simply due to a delicious sense of sunny health within. All the same, these five days of rain have swamped, so to speak, a 'tidy reach' of our fortnight. And a fine spell is prognosticated. So if I come away with Colin on Saturday, it will be with an effort.

It needs no Keats to say

> 'Here all the summer could I stay;'

but I can improve upon his reasons.
He continues

> 'For there's a Bishop's Teign (pr. Tin)
> And King's Teign
> And Coomb at the clear Teign's head;
>   Where close by the stream,
>   You may have your cream
> All spread upon Barley bread.'[1]

But

> Here all the Summer could I stay
> For there's better than tin,
>   Than kings' tin;
> There's Health for the heart and the head;
>   And I wake from my dream;
>   And I relish good cream,
> And fatten on barley bread.

I should enjoy treating at length of Plymouth and the Plyms, the charm of Devon, the many books I am not reading, the merry faces I am seeing, but a pen is a dangerous thing to hold too long, and I so easily lapse. Let my last Sentence be the most important—Has Father found me a job? I suppose he has mentioned how that I might do some Office work during the summer? I have scanned scholastic Ads. without finding anything. All my papers are sent in to Reading Coll:; I had a letter from H.M.T.[2] which I may as well enclose. What do you think! Love! and congratulations on the success of your feeding me up.

W

---

[1] 'Some doggrel' sent in a letter, 21 March 1818, to B. R. Haydon (*Letters* I, p. 248).
[2] Probably Mr. Timpany, Wilfred's former Headmaster, advising him on a teaching job. See Letter 185, note 1, last line.

185. To Susan Owen[1]

26 April 1913   *Torquay*

Dearest Mother,

Thanks for your letter with enclosures, and for your P.C. received yesterday. The non-arrival of news from us is only a sign of our health & much-going-out. I also have been spending all my indoor time (out of bed) on letters to other people. I have had a Post every day, & a big debt has therefore mounted up. And in the midst of this you plague me to write to the Vicar, whom I am quite sure does not expect further communication.

Leslie wrote me four pages of outraged excitement on his Grand Discovery of how it stood with dear old John![2]

I am not methodical enough to keep a Journal[3] for no one to read. Therefore I plunge into my Recollections and seize the nearest and uppermost objects, as doth the diver in the pearly seas; for a shark pursueth hungrily; and that Shark is Time.

For three or four days the weather was charming: only just enough soft-rainy intervals to remind one that this is Devon. On Sat. Torquay was a larger sort of fernery.

The uppermost Pearl in my mind is Teignmouth, from which I returned prematurely, yesterday. How melancholy-happy I was

'where the wide sea did weave
An untumultuous fringe of silver foam
Along the flat, brown sand',[4]

---

[1] The following rough draft of this letter, dated 21 April 1913, was found by H O among Wilfred's papers after the war:

21 April 1913   *Torquay*
Dearest Mother,

Thanks for your Letter & Enclosures, received this morning. I am not methodical enough to keep a Journal, for everybody to ask for, and nobody to read. Therefore I just take a plunge into letter-writing, and hastily seize the nearest & uppermost objects, as the pearl-diver doth; For a shark ever pursueth hungrily; and that shark is Time.

The weather has been charming; with just enough of the pleasant soft-rainy intervals to remind one that this is Devon.

The change in temp. was striking! On Sat. Torquay was a larger sort of Fernery, as Dickens might say.

The uppermost pearl is Teignmouth from wh. I returned prematurely. I will not relate how melancholy-happily I mooned about where the wide sea did weave an . . . sand. I fear domestic criticism when I am in love with a real live woman. What now I am in love with a youth, and a dead 'un! With the change of the tide the weather changed to rain (worthy of the Coniston road). I caught the 4.30 home, when comfortably installed in the carriage, saw the last drop of rain fall. The evening was serene!

The same thing occurred yesterday at Babba. It is just possible that the rise of such a vast surface of water compresses the air above to greater density, and so to condense out its moisture. Still I was completely happy in a shelter, for I amused five children, three ♂, two (♀). (These are the botanic symbols for flowers, quite permiss. here because the subjects were more nearly related to say—the Viola, the Lilium or the Primula, than to the adult species of Homo Sapiens.)

Now I have written to Mr. Timpany, Lightbourn, and others

[2] Keats? LG cannot explain this reference.
[3] H O confirms that Wilfred never kept a diary. See also Letter 330, postscript.
[4] *Epistle to John Hamilton Reynolds.*

I will not relate. To be in love with a youth and a dead 'un[1] is perhaps sillier than with a real, live maid.

With the turn of the tide came the Rain. Now whatever nasty thing I can find to say of Teignmouth Rain has probably been invented by Keats,[2] so I am paralysed even here. It was rain worthy of the Coniston Road,[3] and try how I would, I could see no poetry in its tears, this year. So I caught the 4.30 home; when at last safe-huddled in the carriage, I had the pleasure of seeing the Last Drop of the rain fall. The evening was serene!

The same afternoon-rain fell the day before at Babbacombe. It is just possible that the rise of such a vast surface of water as is occasioned by the tides, compresses the Air above to greater density, so that it is unable to hold its water-vapour, which then falls as rain.

We had to shelter for about two hours; but the Telescope I luckily gave to Colin acted as a talisman, potent as the Arabian Magician's Ivory Rod. For by feigning to see strange things through it (as indeed I did if mist and the blackness-of-darkness-for-ever are strange) I gathered five gentle children about me, three ♂, two ♀. (These are botanical symbols, but the specimens in question I classify as nearer related to Viola, Lilium, and Primula than to the adult species of Homo Sapiens.)

The Rain recommenced early this morning and is heavier than ever now, (tea-time.) The smudge on Page (1) was caused by one of its pestilent atoms; although I am yards from the window!

I heard from Miss Taylor[4] today, naming Tuesday, and asking Colin to come. Cannot Father get a Pass?—I suppose not. Sorry my Note-Paper has run out, and the writing is so filthy. But I have a faint recollection of what I said in a certain sane, and lucid interval,—it may have been days ago. Colin, though ignorant of that short recovery, seems to have imitated it; only, fortunately, his irresponsible fit is permanent. What am I saying ! ! Time for Goodbye!

186. To Susan Owen
Postcard

Friday [*Postmark 2 May 1913*]   [*Postmark Torquay*]

I hope you will get this in time. Expect us by the 7+? at Shrews. Starting at 11 something we shall have 2 hours in Bristol. We have been

---

[1] Keats.

[2] '. . . the abominable Devonshire weather—by the by you may say what you will of devonshire: the truth is, it is a splashy, rainy, misty, snowy, foggy, haily, floody, muddy, slipshod County—the hills are very beautiful, when you get a sight of 'em—the primroses are out, but then you are in—the Cliffs are of a fine deep Colour, but then the Clouds are continually vieing with them.' Keats to Benjamin Bailey from Teignmouth, 13 March 1818 (*Letters* I, p. 240).

[3] In Keswick, where it had rained throughout the Convention in 1912.

[4] Of Plymouth (see following letter and p. 60). Unidentified, unless the Birkenhead music teacher was now living there.

to Babbacombe this morning, Paignton this afternoon, and this evening I must call at Palanza[1] to say goodbye. The Plymouth Taylors gave no further invitation, (—why should they); nor have the Chelston T—s; so unless your letter (which I expect next post) gives definite instruction to the contrary, the forestated plans shall be fulfilled. Tremendous haste.

W

187. To Susan Owen
Postcard

[*Postmark 14 June 1913*]   *Alpenrose*

The Plot thickens. Miss Morley was not to be found in College, when I got there, tho' they had seen her a few mins. before. I went to her house, & she had just gone to 'Town'. She will be back on Monday Mng. I saw Mrs. Coates[2]—nice old body & nice house; she is willing to wait till Monday for engagement. All are well here. 'Tis very close; thunder not far off. Stood journey very well;—in two senses, for the people in carriage objected to my window open, so I withdrew to corridor. I hope Colin has found the Diamond. W
Give my love & apologies to old W.H.O.

188. To Susan Owen
Postcard

[*Postmark 16 June 1913*]   *67 South Street, Reading*[3]

Am persuaded to take Exam. including Latin. Miss Morley would not have me wait another year, rather I should come as Primary Student. I have nor hope nor chance of getting this Schol: now, but I am going in for much the same reason that Harold remained in the Heat:[4]— Doggedness. 'Twill change to Fox-edness soon—'After all it was a sour grape,— £40!'[5] Although I hear Harold's smile at this, I must say the heat is terrific down here. You see for instance, how limp is this P.C. I share a sitting-room with a young army captain, who is studying Horticulture. He is remarkably like Gordon Napier,[6] at all points.

W

189. To Susan Owen
Postcard

[*Postmark 18 June 1913*]   *67 South Street, Reading*

The whole party of Gunstons including Dor: & Gor: are going to the Academy on Sat. I am not very keen—never having seen a poorer 'year'

---

[1] Unidentified.
[2] The landlady of lodgings at 67 South Street, Reading (see following letter).
[3] Wilfred is lodging in Reading while sitting, at Miss Morley's insistence, for the Scholarship to University College, Reading. See Letter 167.
[4] A reference to HO's near-fatal heat apoplexy in Calcutta in the previous month. See *JO* II, pp. 131–59.
[5] The annual value of the scholarship.
[6] A friend of the Bulman boys. The Owens had met him at Kelso.

but if you cd give me a ¼ fare, I shd be pleased. I am doing very tolerable papers; but behaving very absurdly between times. You shall hear. One of my rivals has already published! Address Ticket if you can & will to Alp: Many thanks for yrs. The horrible thought that Father—will be away & unable to get Ticket just struck me. No matter: I repeat I am not keen; and the prospect of a party is not an incentive: quite the reverse. I finish exams w. Essay, tomorrow mng.

W

190. To Susan Owen
Postcard
Sat. Night [*Postmark 22 June 1913*]   *Alpenrose*

Just returned from Academy, to which Uncle treated me as I had not enough cash. Am not fatigued as you see. You were mistaken in fearing I had been at all unwell. I've come thro' the sleepless nights in a room like a brick-kiln very well; and did quite (self-) satisfactorily under the circumstances in the exam.
Tomorrow I must write a letter. This is just to assure you of my health and happiness.

W

191. To Susan Owen
Postcard
Thurs. Ev. [*Postmark 22 June 1913*]   [*Postmark Kidmore End*]

Am just come in from a walk with one Kingston, acquaintance of Leslie, & am like to miss the Post if I indulge in a letter. I will see old man Povey;[1] my cards etc. are in my desk, of which I have the key. Am feeling quite independent of Insurance Policies just now; & shall stay as long as I may. It will not be past Monday in any case; and very likely Saturday. Went over to D . . . n yesterday. Vicar out. No Result of E. known, but the Jones say Botany (the merits which alone could not gain the scholarship) is quite all right, & so far I am qualified.

Love to all. W

Gordon is not going to Switz'ld. but L'pool; and may look in at Mahim.

192. To Susan Owen
27 June 1913   *Alpenrose*

Dearest Mother,

I have been in open air all morning & afternoon; to Reading this evening & in the Vaudeville, so I am to be praised for writing now at all, not blamed for being heavy-witted.

Gordon is coming on Saturday & Miss Carr[2] on Monday, so I must clear out on Monday.

---

[1] A shopkeeper in Kidmore End.
[2] A Gunston family friend from Denmark Hill, London, who took charge of the Gunston children on occasions when their parents were away.

I have now 1d. with me. I still hope to have ½d. after Sunday, and see no definite cause for spending that for some weeks to come; but it might be safer to have some change on the journey. 11d. in stamps should be ample; Don't send an Order; they cost so much, & I might forget to cash it. How have I got through all the red gold? I can only remember I bought one pennyworth of celestial smiles from Harold Montague,[1] who was inclined to be tearful that day; that I paid for one pennyworth of Pride, in refusing to demand payment for a stamp which I gave to Captain Jennings, the easy-going; that I invested in 3d. of Policy in going to 'the Pictures' with Leslie, by whose will & for whose sake, I am staying so long. The rest went in Coates,[2] who observes the Jewish (i.e. inclusive) mode of reckoning time.

The Vicar being out, Mrs. Lott did the honours of a hostess, in the dining room; that is in conversation. I had a cup of tea at Mrs. Montague's (the last I had had was at Neilson-Jones, you remember). When I rode away soon after, Mrs. Rampton[3] lay in wait at her gate, and was mightily sorry I had not graced her table with my presence. There is nothing notable to remark about Milly except that she would eat and drink no tea; and had had no breakfast that day; that this is a common habit of hers; but that she looks well enough notwithstanding. A fact worthy of consideration about eleven o'clock every day, by a certain skinny academy of kittens. I saw scarcely any other children; but strangely enough met in the lane, a nut-brown face I thought I remembered, which was none other than Edith Herridge. Hospitals and fresh air are triumphing. Bravo!

I am here careful to introduce a statement to the effect that I have a good appetite, (and usually eat well.) If it would comfort you, I may tell you I am never likely to be poisoned, by my habits of tasting sundry strange substances. I have had a fright. I read that certain spurge-capsules, very like capers, are pickled to form a (dangerous) substitute for capers. If they are pickled wholesale, surely I may touch one with the tip of the tongue. I did so, & spat it out, swallowing nothing. No more. Ten minutes later I became conscious of a roughness in my throat; then on my tongue, then all round my mouth; which was all frothy with mucus. I swallowed pints of water; but held my peace, and waited for abdominal gripes. It is now 12 hours ago; and I regain confidence; but it will be long before I go meddling with a spurge again. Some species are so poisonous that a man is said to have died through carrying them in his hat. A few plants, bruised, and placed in a river are sufficient to kill the fish for miles below. These facts ought to be more widely known.

———————

Pop! Earwigs are dropping from the ceiling like rain from the eaves, after a storm!

[1] Younger brother of Willie.
[2] The Reading landlady.
[3] Vivian's mother.

I shall be glad to see you on Monday, O Mother mine. Objectionable men, and delusive, drive me back upon myself and Keats; unlovable women, and girls incapable of sympathy, drive me back to You.

My signature upon it, and my kiss.

Wilfred his mark X

Read yr. Card this mng., w. thanks.

My Train on Monday:

    3 p.m. Reading

    7.19 Shrewsbury.

       (if a Jan. Time-table err not)

193. To Susan Owen

6 July 1913   [*Shrewsbury*]

Dearest Mother,

  [*nine lines illegible*]

So things are as they were six weeks ago, unless a windfall of £80. saves me. I must therefore take Philosophy (in two senses) and Education, and wear out the seven-years sentence as best I may.

It will be a long, humiliating [*one word illegible*] with Hulcoop[1] [*two lines illegible*] But all this must be talked over when Father and you are back.

We are going to Church tonight, unless it pours with rain, which is not unlikely. I've not been to Uriconium again. Perhaps because of those two Oxford Blues, whose colours are to me as red to a bull.

Harold has not had a great deal to relate yet.

Still I have learnt a few pronunciations which shd. be useful in my Geography; e.g. Molta, Gibrolter, etc. [*four lines illegible*] had to ask 'what mean you?' at first.

I wonder whether Mary will come home wanting a Motaw.

I suppose you are not staying longer than Monday?—but for our part we are right enough for some days.

Love to all.

Your own, W

194. To Susan Owen

Postcard

[*Postmark 6 August 1913*]   *Dorfold, Great Meols, Cheshire*

Arrived safe, and fairly cool. Auntie has been in bed today w. a Chill, caught on Monday. But it is slight, and she is otherwise well. I have not yet seen the children. They are out at a picnic. Let me have news soon, not forgetting your Eye.

W

[1] Having failed the Reading scholarship, Wilfred was considering a return to Dunsden to assist the schoolmaster while continuing his efforts to get to a university.

195. To Susan Owen

[*circa 9 August 1913*]   *Dorfold, Great Meols, Cheshire*

Dearest Mother,

You will perhaps like to find a letter waiting for you in Torquay. At least I hope it will meet you there. I hope also you will like it: for I am not going to complain.

Not that there is nothing to complain of. There are the occasional outbreaks of ferocity in Kenneth, and of vulgarity in C.; but little else.

The air is perfect in temperature and humidity: and that for every single hour of the 24; The skies unclouded; the Rain waits till 11 o'clock, p.m. as it should do.

I make twice daily an oblation to You, in the form of a glass of good milk! I consume twice daily sacrifices of good red meat, to the god of Blood: sacrifices of long walks and exercises to the god of Health: ablutions, to the god of Baths; devotions hours long to the god of Children; and Eros is not wholly forgotten either.

Yes: I went w. Kenneth to bathe at 8 o'clock this mng. and it is always between 10.30. and 11 when we come in at night. I should not be so energetic if fresh air were obtainable in the house. But it is not. The drawing room now is as stuffy as a Severn Tunnel. Hence the hasty brevity of this letter. I have written to Agents.[1] Enquiries are made about your eye.

I have not been away from Meols; except on the Lake (W. Kirby.) The family are going on Friday to Connah's Head[2] so I am staying till Thursday.

Your own, W

Nothing for Harold.
Best love to All at Underdale.[3]

196. To Leslie Gunston

[*? mid-August 1913*]   [*Shrewsbury*]
First sheet missing

days; everything—Flowers, Music, Fireworks, Acrobats—were up to usual mark if not above the usual.

The Roses were so superb that I noted a few Names, with what purpose is not quite clear.

I here enclose a Sonnet,[4] rather in return for your trouble in writing out your things, than because I think it worth your reading.

---

[1] Scholastic agencies, in search of a teaching post.
[2] Two Cheshire coastal resorts.
[3] Grandfather Owen and his wife were now living in Torquay, having moved there from Shrewsbury in 1908 to be near their daughter Anne Taylor. They named their house Underdale, after Underdale Road, Shrewsbury.
[4] We date this letter by the visit to the Quayles and by the BM draft of this unpublished sonnet, with minor changes, which is dated by Wilfred July 1913.

When late I viewed the gardens of rich men,
Where throve my darling blossoms plenteously,
With others whose rare glories dazed my ken,
I was not teased with envious misery.
Enough for me to see and recognise;
Then bear away sweet names upon my tongue,
Scents in my breath, and colours in my eyes.
Their owners watch them die: I keep them young.

But when more spacious pleasances I trod,
And saw their thousand buds, but might not kiss
Though loving like a lover, sire, and God,
Sad was the yearning of my avarice.
The rich man gives his parting guest one bloom,
But God hath vouchsafed my meek longing-whom?

This was writ before Meols.

Can you tell me which was your longest day this year? With me it was the day I went to Dorfold. To begin with, I woke about 5 o'clock, because I had to have my bag packed by eight! I spent the morning at Uriconium, met new people there, and by 1 o'clock had done a good day's work & pleasure. Then I had $2\frac{1}{2}$ hours travelling, with incidents too many to note. Afternoon Tea in my Auntie's bedroom, where I met various friends of hers. Then went to a Tennis Party w. Cecil. Then dined. Then promenaded, and met the Set. So that by eleven o'clock, the Wroxeter Morning seemed about a week agone.

Mother has had a maid for some weeks: 'But I cannot tell. That is the rendezvous of it. There must be conclusions. Let it be so. For my part I say little, but when time shall serve . . .'[1]

Write longer next time!

W

[1] A string of phrases spoken by Nym, *King Henry V*, II. 1.

BORDEAUX AND THE PYRENEES

1913–1914

197. To Leslie Gunston[1]

Picture postcard: Bordeaux, Cours de l'Intendance, with letters
B.S. and arrow pointing to Berlitz School

[Postmark 21 September 1913]   *[Postmark Bordeaux]*

I think I can promise a monthly letter, but at present I have no paper,
& tis *Dimanche* evening. I am also v. pressed; for from 11 to 12 each
night I address an audience of many hundreds in French explaining the
working of a *Ballon dirigeable à distance* by Wireless. This is quite
apart from the Berlitz School tho' I was introduced to the Inventor[2] by
the Sub-Director.[3] The Inventor is so pleased w. my performance that
he has asked me to travel (America) etc. w. him! Shall I ? ? At the school
I teach pupils singly. They are ushered in to me by a *Chasseur*: & the
procedure is more like a doctor's consultation than a school. My screw
is <u>small</u>; but I am making something by the Lecturing. Congrats to
Dorothy. Please cram a P.C. soon.

198. To Tom Owen

Picture postcard: Bordeaux, Panorama et la Gironde

[Postmark 27 September 1913]   *[Postmark Bordeaux]*

Have just ascertained that neither of us English profs. is going to Nantes
till Oct. 15. So the St. Malo route is out of the question. But I shall be
hugely disappointed if you don't come.[4] I move into a cheaper & nicer
Room tomorrow:—*Chez* Mme. Dubo 95 Rue Porte Dijeaux B.
Am writing this in my dressing room; am 'going on' in about ½ an
hour. I hope the thing will reach you. Details of living if you have not
yet received, I will send tomorrow.

199. To Susan Owen

28 September 1913   *Chez Mme. Dubo, 95 Rue Porte Dijeaux*
                                                                Bordeaux

Dearest Mother,

It seems that you had not received my 2nd letter[5] when you wrote

---

[1] Six weeks later. Wilfred has accepted a post teaching English at the Berlitz School of
Languages, 46 Cours de l'Intendance, Bordeaux. 'The pay was pathetically small, and,
under the system, precarious, and after working it out it seemed almost impossible that he
could manage to live on it. But he was excited and keen to take it up; it was a chance to get
to France, and the very nature of his work would be the best possible way to fulfil a minor
ambition—to speak and think precisely as a French-born national.' (*JO* II, p. 265).

[2] Unidentified.

[3] M. Langholz.

[4] Tom Owen did visit Wilfred, in mid-October. The visit was a success. See *JO* III, pp.
49–56.

[5] Neither this, nor the first letter from Bordeaux, have survived.

your last card. I hope, if you have not yet got it, that you have at least had three postcards since you sent your last. I forgot exactly what I said in that letter; except that it requested you to send my Birth Certificate as soon as possible. It has just occurred to me that I forgot to write *Angleterre* on the envelope of that letter: but wrote England instead. If this has been the cause of its abortion, I renounce the French race for ever.

In reply to Father's questions I repeat that I shall be in Bordeaux till the 15th Oct. I also repeat the following points:

That my Room in Rue Castelmoron[1] cost 30 francs a month, i.e. 1 f. per day.[2]

That my present room costs only 20 francs a month.

That neither contained two beds; and the present room is very small.

But there is another room vacant on the second floor of this house, (I am on the first) which is much larger than mine; but at the same price. Hiring it by day, Father might easily get it for less than 1 franc a day.

I get very satisfactory *déjeuner* (12 o'clock) and dinner (7) for 1½ franc each: at a hotel not far removed from the Room and the School.

In any case it would be easy to find a cheap room near mine: and the full cost of *pension* at my Hotel is only 5 f. a day. I am lucky to have found a room which combines the qualities of cheapness, nearness to the school, tranquillity and a large window, overlooking a 'garden'!!

As I indicated on a P.C. I am earning about 4 francs a night by speechyfying in technical French on the subject of a Wireless Dirigible Balloon. I enjoy the business immensely, though it is often two o'clock in the morning when I get back to my Rooms. And sometimes I am teaching at 8 o'clock the same morning. Such is the influence of Climate and Environment! The demonstration is held in a Theatre (a fitter place, I take it, than the Cathedral); of course a highly respectable place; and the audience is composed of high class people almost entirely. On one occasion I had the honour of addressing the Mayor of Bordeaux—a great personage I assure you.

After all is over we usually sit drinking (syrops) in a Café till one or two o'clock. Syrops, mind, for my friend the Inventor neither drinks nor smokes and is in all respects a most amiable and estimable fellow (little older than myself, I should think.) Now, he is so pleased with the manner in which I show him off, and generally with my knowledge of French, command of English, and inklings of Wireless Telegraphy, that he has made me a proposition to the effect that if I should like to travel with him, he would give me 200 f. a month (£96. a year)—as well as travelling expenses paid. He speaks bad French and worse English, and consequently needs an interpreter and secretary while in Paris (November) and America—Mexico of all marvellous places! (next spring.)

---

[1] His first lodgings, in which he stayed no more than a fortnight.

[2] The franc was worth 9½d. in 1913; he paid £1. 4s. 6d. a month in his first lodgings, 16s. 2d. with Mme Dubo. His monthly salary from the Berlitz School was 130 francs, or £5. 2s. 11d. See Letter 204.

What do you think of the idea?

One clause of the contract is that we should teach each other our languages! I feel very tempted, especially as I can only just live on the Berlitz Salary.

My 'compatriot'[1] who smokes much and saves little, has to obtain Remittances from home. He was a student of Nottingham College, but failed to pass Inter-Arts, and now at 22, is spending his time in France, awaiting a Civil Service Exam. in Spring.

I don't particularly like him. He is tall, & something of a gawk, easily enraged; and of limp principles, (I should imagine). Neither have I yet discovered that he has any interest in life.

I am fond of all my pupils—nearly. One is a doctor, and yesterday I mustered all my medical ignorance into one vast conglomeration of terms.

Another, who is preparing for the French Equivalent of Matriculation has invited me to go motoring with him over the fair lands of Médoc; but I have not yet found time.

The Doctor has also given me an infallible prescription for a pomade which cures a cold in 48 hours. (I have a slight cold—or had rather. In 2 days I have smoked it out with some Eucalyptus Cigarettes. I don't blame the weather for the Cold, but must have caught it, either from the Inventor or Langholz the Sub-Director).

I don't know whether I told you: I saw the President[2] very well when he was here last week.

During the whole of October there is to be a Fair in Bordeaux whatever that may mean.

Hydroplanes are in the habit of planing over the Garonne, but I have not yet seen any.

I sometimes promenade along the docks, and see the ships of many lands.

It would be the time of your life if you would but come over with Father. Well, well! Anyhow, I hope to hear very soon that Father is really coming.

Excuse the scraggy air of these sheets: a bad pen and a good dinner are to blame. But our communication is not wholly dependent on the $2\frac{1}{2}$d post, as telegraphy is independent of wires, and I greet you night and morning as though no hundreds of miles or tens of years were between.

Ever your own Wilfred

200. To Susan Owen

5 October 1913   *Bordeaux*

My dearest Mother,

I am quite upset that Father has not started on Friday, and still more perturbed to think that there is a danger of his not coming at all.

[1] His name was Tofield. See Letter 256.
[2] Raymond Poincaré (1860–1934), President of France throughout the war.

On Saturday I took a walk on purpose to discover the G. St. Nav. Co.'s[1] Offices and Quay. But now it is no use sending directions from that quarter. I don't know at which of the half-dozen stations Father will arrive; so all the indications I can give are that everybody knows the Cours de l'Intendance, and once in that the Berlitz School cannot be missed. (N.B. The Entrance is round a Corner.) Once in that, he will find English spoken if he doesn't find me. And it is open between 7 a.m. and 10 p.m. The Rue Porte Dijeaux runs parallel to Intendance, and is easily known by the *Porte*, of which you have a P.C. My Front Door is on the left, a few yards through the 'Gate'.

My New Collars I should like in Size 15½. I have to have a large no. in consequence of the uncertainty of my movements, and the funniosities of Laundry Arrangements. And all clothes are disgracefully dear. I have not yet got my boots.

Matches are 5 times as scarce here as in Mahim, and vile sulphurous things when you've got 'em. So I advise Father to bring enough for his own use, at least.

If my Boots' Razor preserves its reputation, I should be glad of it. If not of a new one of the same kind. Also, if there is Room, my Shaving Soap. Also, if there is room my small thing of Oatine; but I don't suppose there will be room [*remainder missing*]

201. To Mary Owen

[*October 1913*]   [*Bordeaux*]

Dearest Mary,

I am at last sending a Correction of your Letter. I think it is most creditable. You use such idiomatic phrases. So much so, that I hesitated to correct it without consulting a Real French: the lodger who has the room next to mine & who was here when Father was over. He works for Pathé *Frères*, and has appeared himself in a film taken in Bordeaux. When this Film is showing he will give me a Ticket, to see his Cinemograph, (if that is English, or even so much as American).

Here then is the letter.

'Merci beaucoup pour votre lettre française. Notre plaisir fût grand, quand nous l'avons reçue.

'Je me porte très bien.

'Mercredi dernier je fus prendre un thé à la maison de nos voisins.' The rest is simple to understand.

Would Colin like to correspond w. a French Youth of 17.[2] Also would he be capable of benefiting (1) the *Français* (2) Himself?

I must bunk to the Post, if you are to see this on Tues.

Your loving Wilfred

[1] General Steamship Navigation Company.
[2] A pen-friend for Colin was found. See Letter 240.

202. To Susan Owen

Sunday, 19 October 1913   [*Bordeaux*]

My own dear Mother,

I scarcely allowed myself to think you were in train for anything so serious as Quinsy, but that you ever had the suspicion of it, gave me a shock. You were considerate not to have mentioned to father and me your fears: am immensely glad it is drawing off. If I could advise you a cure 'complete in two days'; it would be that you should set up as Suffragette, Dublin-Strike-Leader,[1] or Schoolmistress, so that you would be <u>obliged</u> to speak for seven hours a day.

That is my experience.

On Friday Morning I woke with a painful throat, but talked (loud) for 8 hours; yesterday I increased to <u>nine</u>, with the single variation of <u>shouting</u> in the evening.

Result: All soreness is now talked away.

The First 'Course' started on Saturday, and a racking thing it was: composed of a different class of people from my private pupils, and I just have to treat them as children, and shout them into sense.

I had the Countess also on Saturday, for the second time, with the same blouse and perhaps the same dirt. Her daughter however is married to one of the Dukes of France, and as there are only six dukes, she must be somebody. The English Professoress[2] arrives not till Tuesday, so I have still a few days more of pressure. But I shall be helped by a Russian, a German, and a Frenchman if necessary!

This afternoon I made tracks for the Church; and after much tracking, struck it. Service was announced at 3 o'clock, but as I waited till 3.15 it must be closed for the month of October (as <u>it statedly</u> is for Jul. Aug. Sept.)

So then I passed into the Public Gardens, which are quite near, and heard the band, and regretted Father. I had a Card from him this morning, giving the news of his *rétablissement*. He did not give me his <u>own</u> opinion of Nantes.

With your letter, I had the P.P.C. (when I came down at noon; but actually the card came at 8.)

I do not want any Views of Shrewsbury thank you, but if I <u>shall do</u>, I will say.

Two cards came for Father after his departure, of which I appropriated the news and the Love.

I miss Father considerably, and today even more than on Friday or Saturday!

Many thanks for 'the Syllabus'. It will be interesting to follow the Subjects week by week; I wonder whether you will go to many, and whether Colin will figure among Thomson's Boys?[3]

---

[1] In August 1913 a serious strike had begun on Dublin tramways. The industrial trouble spread, and 18,000 transport workers and others were on strike by October.

[2] She did not arrive, being taken ill. All the Berlitz teachers were called Professor.

[3] Colin attended a private school in Shrewsbury known, and still known, as Thomson's.

I need not dwell on my appreciation of your gingerbreads and toffee. But I must specially say how good the apples were.

This reminds me it is time to go for dinner: which, being out of stomach, was out of mind. In stomach, it is often in mind for several hours.

Sorry this letter has the appearance of hurry. Yours never betray that you are using time snatched from the Service of the Hearth.

Love, Hopes, and Kisses

from your own Wilfred

203. To Mary Owen

Dimanche, 19 October [*1913*]   *Bordeaux*

Ma chère Soeur,

Je vais t'écrire une petite lettre, exprimée assez simplement, de peur qu'elle ne t'ennuie plutôt qu'elle ne te plaise.

J'étais fort content d'apprendre que to es un peu rétablie.

Aujourd'hui il a fait de très beau temps, tout comme il a fait le dimanche passé. Tu as déjà appris comment je me suis promené en automobile avec un ami, et que nous sommes descendu à trois vignobles, et que j'ai mangé autant de raisins que je voulais. Ces raisins étaient aussi bons que ceux que tu as goutés, sinon mieux; et sans doute tu as trouvé cette grappe excellente?

Je suis curieux de savoir si Miss Goodwin connait le Methode Berlitz. Si elle la connait j'espère qu'elle te donnera des leçons (fran-çaises.) À mon avis, c'est une méthode très bonne,—pour les <u>élèves</u>, c'est à dire, mais pour les professeurs—poof!!

Adieu! et je te prie, d'écrire en français la prochaine fois!

Votre frère qui t'aime, Wilfred

204. To Susan Owen

Sunday, 26 October 1913   *Bordeaux*

My dearest Mother,

I should be writing to Father but that I am in greater letter-debt to you, who also have been ill, and waiting perhaps for news for some days. Still, I have not exceeded the Limit of 7 days! And I will surely send Father a line during next week.

Why have I been silent?

Because aweary.

Why aweary?

Because over-busy.

Why overbusy?

Because the English Miss is ill, and never started from England after all; nor ever will, but is sending another, who is to arrive <u>some</u> time next week.

Tomorrow I shall have 10 hours work; and <u>Courses</u> from 8 to 10 at that. I have now eight courses a week!

Even the <u>Spaniard</u> will give an English Lesson tomorrow!

I like this professor well enough. He is in reality a student of Law, but wishes to learn a few languages before settling down in Madrid. A Spaniard is also installed as lodger in this house; but he keeps himself very close; I have not seen more than his shadow on the window.

The French Student was dismissed in the course of a few days by Madame for moral misconduct. As he dines at the Hotel de Provence, this will be another motive for my changing to a nearer Hotel. Or getting a *Pension*. Alas! this I shall never do, it seems. I found (only yesterday) the House to which M. Canteloube (W. Star Ag.)[1] had recommended me, but it is not a *maison particulière*, but a boarding house where several parties are thrown together.

<u>Lowest</u> Price of *pension* per month	170 f
<u>N.B.</u> my doleful dole	130 f

A second *pension* where I was sent from the first, does it for 150 f. but it is a long way off, and I would not take it for 100!

So I shall engage for another fortnight my room, and pass from hotel to hotel as my fancy pleases. I don't do badly I assure you. Yesterday and today, I felt no inclination whatever for dinner, so bought a roll and cakes, and got some cocoa prepared, and had a rare feast in my garret, cutting my cake with a penknife, and having papers to serve for plates and table-cloth.

This meal I have in fact just finished.

I shall very likely do this quite often. It is the only hour of privacy I now have save when in bed.

Last night I forgot my keys, and entering at 10.30. found all shut and dead-dark. I rang 4 times in vain. Then I sat down on the pavement for an hour—Of course I mean on a <u>chair</u>, outside a café, in order to prove to myself that I could not keep awake for 7 hours, if I tried. (For the night being warm to the point of oppressiveness, I was much tempted to sit in a café till 6 o'clock in the morning.) However, I finally made up my mind to take a Hotel bedroom. As I passed the street door of the House, I noticed it still open, and through the passage shone a <u>Light</u>!

I was <u>saved</u>! (3 francs.) The people had been at the Cinema, and were <u>out</u>, not asleep.

It is now 9.30. and I am very heavy. Three wits are already dead asleep. I must keep two going while I thank you for the Card recvd. this mng. My throat is recovered, having transformed its relaxation into a sort of ulceration on the side-back of the tongue; which is a trifle.

For lunch I now drink <u>Vichy Water</u> which I can substitute for wine. If you are seeing Doctor <u>Matthews</u> you might inquire whether it could

[1] Unidentified.

be otherwise than beneficial in my case. I have reason to believe it will be good for me.

I was glad of the news of the Plants, and how you spent the Friday morning. Yes, take the Wallflowers indoors, please. Give My remembrances to the Merchant Prince,[1] & all the Family Royal on their return.

I will now summon up my powers and heave this to the post lest on Tuesday Morning you imagine things.

Always your devoted son, Wilfred x

P.S. I don't think I mentioned clearly that I had Father's letter, & was very interested to hear of his journey. He is come and gone like a spirit.

205. To Susan Owen

Sunday, 2 November 1913   *Bordeaux*

PRIVATE

My darling Mother,

Last Sunday you wrote the tenderest letter of all, as if you feared all the time I might be ill; so much so that you finally say, you think you must have a fit of the blues.

It was not a fit of the blues; it was an instance of the unconfinable sympathy that exists between us.

Last Sunday I had got somewhat low, through a week's double work. Then began another week worse than the first, and I only lost my headache (beginning last Friday week) this very morning. Everything was done that was possible (except sending away pupils) to assist me; but Aumont[2] was away in Nantes, and the Sub-director found himself so very Sub under the circumstances that he would not undertake to dismiss any lessons. So, being still able to walk to the school (unfortunately) I dragged on till Friday. I took my Courses sitting in an armchair with the thick overcoat; and looked and sounded, I suppose, like a nonagenarian bishop addressing a Confirmation.

Saturday was the Feast of All Saints; and caused a holiday at the school. I stayed in bed all day, and got, with some difficulty, enough cups of milk to keep me alive. I found to my dismay that Mme. Dubo was in no disposition to get or prepare things for me; and until I actually stayed in bed I had to crawl about myself—for firewood, for instance, with which I lighted me a blaze to dry the room; for it rained heavily. I had been having nothing but milk for the last 3 days, so for dinner, I ordered some Oxo, but alas! appeared a vile salty concoction, not like the bottled Oxo, but made from a cube. Small nutriment in that; nevertheless if I had not detained her by my requests, Madame would

---

[1] Edward Quayle.
[2] Maurice Aumont, Director of the Berlitz School, Bordeaux. He was also in charge of the Berlitz establishments at Angers and Nantes. See Letter 235.

have left me without anything to eat, (save a Siphon) and without anyone in the house (save the close Spaniard that I do not know)— and would have gone to the Fair. I was but <u>little</u> apologetic when she blustered 'it was now too late to go out!' etc.

I had long known one of my complaints, and at midnight I drank off a dose of Oil of Ricin,—French equivalent of Castor Oil. The effects are not yet entirely satisfactory. I was, however, able to eat an egg which I boiled for myself to tea today. Madame hied to the Cemetery for a large part of this day, to tend the Dead, and left the living to fend for itself. Fearing to contract more weakness, I therefore got up and dressed; and after a little promenade as far as 'the gardens' (for it was now sunny) I boiled water for my tea, and cooked egg and toast. With one knife, one plate, one spoon, and only half a stomach, imagine me taking this repast in the dismal evening gloom,—perhaps at the same time that you were round your cheerful table, and the twilight was pleasant over Haughmond, and Autumn spoke not of sadness; nor the evening bells of death. But, at this moment, are slowly tolling the most sepulchral-throated bells I ever heard. Tonight every family in France turns its thoughts to its dead.

But the melancholy of these bells! it is almost as distressing to me as the demonstration that threatened to dement me yesterday afternoon. It began with a hideous screech of 5 or ten bugles, all out of tune, and out of time. After a half-hour of this, commenced an infernal convulsion of drums—and all this seemed just below my window. Some hours of this, with intervals, (during which I doubted my senses), I abandoned the idea that it was devils, and rather adopted the theory of <u>French Soldiers</u>, practising, after dinner and wine. You know <u>just at this time</u> all men of 20 years are enlisted (for 3 years now, instead of two) Yet it did not seem like novices, either, but like old hands gone mad; & old drums gone bad.—It was in fact a concourse of some thirty miserables, who made offerings of music to the souls of the soldiers killed in 1870! And this was not all my disturbance, for in the morning I hear the people in the next room, separated only by a thin door, and in the evening a vile piano, played more vilely.

These things are not to grieve you, sweet mother, but out of the superfluity of my heart I speak;[1] How keenly I miss you I must not say; but you must not imagine that I now <u>need</u> you in an exigent sense, for I feel quite comfortable tonight, and need little but repose. You will be mad for me to see a doctor; but as a matter of fact I remonstrated with <u>Dr. Aumont</u>[2] on Friday, and he gave me Quinine. If one symptom continues, namely reddish-brown colour of urine, I shall consult Dr. Sauvaître[3] as soon as possible. I am due for a lesson at 8 a.m. tomorrow morning, but tho' I was out this afternoon, I shall probably not go. The School is the cause of my indisposition; it must bear a <u>little</u> of the consequences.

[1] 'I only mention *some*' struck out. [2] A Bordeaux doctor, apparently not related to the Director.
[3] A Bordeaux doctor. Later he conducted Wilfred round a military hospital. See Letter 288.

I now close the subject of my dolours with reassuring remarks. I have had no suspicion of my phantasies, a merciful provision, though it matters not whether you are here or there, for I should see you on the other side of the universe in any case;

Nor any approach to a Faint.

Nor any chest affection.

I am wise, wise, wise, in the matter of clothes. On Tuesday, when you read this terrible announcement, I shall probably be quite normal, and at normal work, but not abnormal work you may be sure. As soon as two English Teachers heard of the Courses they severally fell ill, and would not leave England. The last applicant is so beautiful (in photograph) that Aumont thinks he cannot engage her. There has already been a tragedy in this very school thro' such a cause.

Your letter of today, with Father's and Mary's, came bearing great solace; even as did the brief card of Friday, seen just after having posted my briefer note (on my last journey to the School.) I wonder how much suffering the dentist has caused and will cause you! Are you yet strong enough for it? Perhaps because you fear to smile you have vouchsafed me no photo of yourself. I am delighted with all four, (& should like several more of both kinds of self); But it was cruel to find no trace of YOU!

(*Later*) I have now prepared myself Liebig in Milk. The effect will be splendid; the only trouble is that these preparations have a strong psychological effect: and bring back a remembrance of your continual presence which is quite tantalising.

Still I have always the little portrait I took of you one September evening, last year.

I see the justly-proportioned face composed, yet with benignancy bright and active in the eyes; the mouth is set; and yet it ever smiles a gentle smile; With what firmness sits the head upon shoulder-throne! And lo! the arm, seemingly strong as a Titan's; and when used to succour and sustain, so strong in very truth! With the hand hanging in perfect grace, a lady's hand! And there are the four bracelets, each with its little tale and its significance not small.[1] And, on the ground behind, thrive the small plants She loveth so to grow; and the Tree is there, for she reverenceth trees as if she were their daughter; and not far away, not far away, the Kitchen-room, and the whole house She reigneth in as Queen.

So do I feel, and so badly do I write, in this State!

Now please note I have made out myself worse than I really am, rather than the contrary; therefore do not say to any friend or relation that I am ill. I am ashamed of myself; and what is more have not had an illness. God shield you, my sweet Mother, and bring us together both stronger than when we parted.

Your devoted Wilfred x

---

[1] Of Indian silver, one for each child, brought back from Bombay by Tom Owen before he married. H O has them now.

206. To Susan Owen
Postcard

Monday [*Postmark 4 November 1913*]   [*Postmark Bordeaux*]

I am something better today, & know you will like to hear it. Should be all right, only I took too cautious a dose of Ricin: I should have glutted the whole bottleful! Which I have now actually done. I put Thermogene on Chest last night. At 2 o'clock I woke up in perspiration and fright: my Chest ached. I thought there was nothing for it now but congestion, and a foreign grave. I imagined the broken, crushed, shattered spirits with which you met Father with the news. 'W. has Pneumonia!' LO! this morning my chest is clean as a bell, and a great deal clearer than the bells that keep moping in the towers of this City! So I went in the aft. to school, only to get lessons excused.

Yr. own W

207. To Susan Owen
Postcard

Tuesday [*Postmark 6 November 1913*]   [*Postmark Bordeaux*]

I supposed you wd. like to know that Dr. Aumont came and examined me this morning. He is extremely nice; does not speak English, but that is now no obstacle. He calls it a slight *grippe* (influenza); but temp. was under 100 this mng. & I have no spontaneous cough. I went out for 2 hrs. this aft. in the sun on his order. Tomorrow I shall almost certainly take classes and courses. Began to 'feed up' today, but the difficulty is tremendous; i.e. of getting foods. Took a raw egg last night. Dr. Aumont has sent me a bottle of old wine, for a tonic, but [it] is, fortunately or unfortunately, not nice. (Not old enough.) I am of course better today, & have nothing in the nature of pain; but how dismal I sometimes feel, I scarcely dare to confess, considering my seclusive habits at home. *Grippe* is very prevalent here. Hope you are all on the other side of the scale.

Yr. own W

208. To Susan Owen
7 November [*1913*]   Postcard   *Bordeaux*

These lines are to let you know I am all but well today. I drank milk so doggedly, (or cattishly) even with raw egg in it, that strength has returned all at once. Dr. Aumont has attended me most carefully and kindly. He still thinks my chest is untouched, tho' he makes persistent soundings all the time. I have his thermometer in mouth this moment. It is 38.3 tonight! Don't be alarmed: this is Centigrade. Thank you ever so much for the card & letter. One was handed to me in the midst of an access of nosebleeding, & helped to calm me. I am not fatigued after several lessons today. No sign of Chaplain! Letter soon! I now suspend my requests for your continual thoughts!

209 . To Leslie Gunston

Picture postcard: Bordeaux,
Place des Quinconces, Monument des Girondins

[Postmark 9 November 1913]   *[Postmark Bordeaux]*

I regret that a tremendous spell of work, and the result of it—some day's indisposition—prevent the Monthly Letter at present. Do let me have yours at once. This is one of the completest p.c's of the fine monument. I will send others. No pictures larger, but coloured p.c.'s obtainable for 5 sous; wd' you like one? Don't send stamps!! How is business w. Belle Sauvage. Tonight I read an interesting little story about the real B.S. Pocahontas by name.[1] Do you know of her adventures in London etc? Thanks for Cards. Love to all.

210. To Susan Owen

Postcard

[Postmark 10 November 1913]   *[Postmark Bordeaux]*

Sorry you did not get my card on Friday: no doubt you did on Sat. and another on Mond. I have no pressing news, so will excuse myself the inconvenience of Letter-writing. For today I am in bed. Dr. A. got another Dr. to see me when I was in School on Sat. who sent me to bed for Sund. & Mond. They do not mention any complaint but perhaps fear a *rechute* into the *Grippe* as the weather is horrid. Both doctors are coming to see me on Monday; Oh la !!—Just when I was doing my few hours work on Mond. Aft. the good Pastor[2] called. He will come again on Monday, I think: wishes me to send you a card, for he has no time at present to answer yours. I suppose he is an old gentleman: been in B. 36 years; so should know some *pensions*!

I was mightily cheered by the 3 letters this morning. I really feel nothing the matter w. me today, & am rather annoyed at having to stay in.

I like the new *Anglaise*.[3] She is no great shakes in appearance (the marvel finally refused to come) but seems ladylike; and has never taught in an Elementary School. I have not got *Notre Dame*[4] here. Hope you will find it. Your promise of stamps or money I must refuse. How is it to be done. But I will ask you to forward some letters for me.

Love and loving thanks for yours. W

[1] Cassells, the London publishers, to whom LG had submitted some translations from Victor Hugo, occupied the Ludgate Hill site of the fifteenth-century Belle Sauvage (or Bell Savage) Inn. The Cassells house design shows Pocahontas, the Indian princess who saved the life of Captain John Smith, a Virginian colonist, in 1607, married another colonist, and came to England in 1616—the *belle sauvage* after whom the inn may have been named.

[2] The Rev. J. W. Lurton-Burke, Chaplain of the English Church in Bordeaux 1882–1914.

[3] Miss Hewitt.

[4] A copy of Victor Hugo's *Notre Dame de Paris* survives among Wilfred's books.

211. To Susan Owen
Postcard

Monday [*Postmark 11 November 1913*]   [*Postmark Bordeaux*]

This mng. the Chaplain called, & found me, of course, in bed. A few minutes later Dr. Aumont came; but he stayed only a moment, and the Rev. J. W. Lurton-Burke remained till he had gone. The 'Pastor' is very nice. He is coming again. He knows of no *pension*; but will enquire. He has given me a recommendation to a *Maison de Santé*, in case anything should happen to me in future. There I should be skilfully tended —privately for 6 f a day; in a ward for 2½ only! In the afternoon the two doctors came—not a 'Consultation' but Mr. Aumont, going away, is leaving me in the charge of his friend. Tho' they listen like thieves to my chest (without stethoscope) and poke, probe, tap, and slap my abdomen, they are completely puzzled to account for my nightly temperature. I could enlighten them by reference to the month of Feb.[1] of this year, but I don't. But the truth is I am still obstinately c-nst-p-t-d; which accounts for all. In feelings I am now entirely well; and this is even stronger an indication of the truth than the Thermom: (with me). I highly enjoyed the *Punch*es. My laughs must have been heard all through the house. I didn't like the mute way you handed them to me. But that was your Postal Integrity perhaps. This corner is an example of mine.[2]

Your own W

212. To Susan Owen
Postcard

[*Postmark 12 November 1913*]   [*Postmark Bordeaux*]

I could scarcely get together a letterful of news if I tried, so monotonous are my days. But there is a special reason for a hurried card now—viz. the (Berlitz) Boy has just gone on some errands for me, & I will get him to post this on his return. It seems I cannot trust the people of this house to post conscientiously. I only hope you get all I send. Which seems to me considerable. I devour your news with never-failing appetite. At present I am physically hungry, (thankful to say) being on liquid diet. The temp. has gone down at last: only (equiv. to) 99 last night, and normal this morning. I shall not worry about being absent from my Classes: it will teach 'the Direction' a lesson. Let not Father write, I pray you. It wd. be useless now, & perhaps dangerous. The *Chasseur* waits!

Fondest love W

[1] The post-Dunsden illness.
[2] Susan Owen had kept to the GPO rule of not enclosing communications with newspapers or magazines sent open-ended. Wilfred writes the last lines of this postcard on the front, against the words *ce coté est exclusivement réservé a l'adresse.*

213. To Susan Owen

Thursday, 13 November 1913   *Bordeaux*

My own dear Mother,

Your dispatches have been received in such plenty that I am now in such a luxurious state that you must begin to diminish the supply, or I shall get too used to it. I do not fail to note that my notes are not frequent enough for you: thus—'had nothing since the card on Thurs. etc.' and: 'in case a letter came by the 7 post, but the time is past now' (Hum!) and: 'I had hoped to get a card today etc.' I am absolutely sure I wrote on Saturday, Sunday, Monday, Wednesday of this week, for I put it in my Diary.[1] I hope you will get all four.

It is good to hear all events connected with you.

I am highly annoyed with the Y.M.C.A. Secretary.[2] I shall probably confound the whole set by letting my beard grow: What?

When I said—don't tell Shrewsbury I am ill in bed, one of my intentions was: Don't speak it into the walking gramophones of the place, e.g. the one that houses in the Friars.[3]

How very distressing must the Building[4] be, standing like a rude man, between you and a fair picture. To my eyes, it will not be unbearable exactly, after the sight of a Wall, 2 feet away from the window, beyond which is nothing but roofs and chimneys, contemplated by me hourly for the last week. But, in any case, I need not concern myself on my own account: Mahim cannot be my abode for long.

Any hardships or apprehensions I may now be going thro' will be of wonderful value next year. The College Life, whereto I look forward more eagerly than ever, will seem luxurious; and so near home.[5] I shall fear nothing from men or women, dirt or diet; nor from noise nor from silence; nor from hunger, and, maybe, not from work.

I had an uncomfortable sensation when you conjured up before me the little school-day.[6] I don't know why. I wish someone would break that cord, or at least use it to hang the kittens. And they mewle still, do they? Do you know, I am sure it wears out the furniture, and pales the wallpaper; and as for the plants, poor things, can't you see how they suffer?

I don't know whether to admire the Piano, or to scorn it as a callous, insincere monster, for keeping its tone as it does. I shall not touch a note for many a month, it seems. I should be ashamed to now, if a family (?) ever did ask me to play. For my 21st Birthday, you might look out a small thing in Chester.[7] It will be useful in my College Room. No objection if PRESENT FROM E. DALE appears in 12 inch letters on the back.

---

[1] Used as a calendar, not as a journal.

[2] Mr. Robertson, a bearded figure, HO recalls, to whom Susan Owen had presumably spoken of Wilfred's illness. See Letter 271.

[3] Miss Kent, a garrulous family friend.

[4] A house had been built on the old Race Course, immediately facing Mahim.

[5] This reference is unexplained.

[6] Miss Goodwin's school at Mahim.

[7] A piano. See Letter 4.

You asked me what I thought of Colin's becoming a Scout. Well, I'm sure I couldn't do it. And I think I can count on one member of the 'family' who is bound to say the same, if you asked her. You have to remember what it costs to make a Scout. For instance:

B.P. Hat	2s. 6d.
2 Shirts (leather-lined extra)	5s. 0.
Shorts (colour of mountains in fog) . . .	7. 6.
2 pr. Socks (colours to resemble rabbits) . . .	3. 6.
Belt	2. 6.
Alpine Boots	10. 6.
Clasp-knife	2. 0.
Staff (Water-divining, extra)	2. 6.
Knapsack	4. 6.
1 Pot Eagle Ointment (should scout's sight fail) .	4. 6.
1 Invisible Ear-Trumpet (warranted to detect a German 'ACH!' within 20 yds.) . . .	15. 0.

To carry:	60s. 0.
car'd for'd. . .	60. 0.
1 Nose Protector. (useful when moving to leeward of French Soldiers.)	5. 0.
1 Copy of Scout's Almanac, containing portrait of B.P. executed by his own left-foot, while his right prepared sawdust-puddings, and both hands were writing dispatches to H.M. Gov. (Unique) . .	9. 6.
Sundries, (not including subscriptions.) . . .	10. 6.
	£4. 4. 0.

Four Guineas, eh? And, then, he must mind his face doesn't tweak too loud, or he'll be court-martialled, sure as Columbus discovered Gravitation. I wrote a long letter to the dear old boy some weeks ago, but it was such a sermon, and on exercise paper, too, that I didn't send it after all!

214. To Susan Owen

16 November 1913   *Bordeaux*

Dearest Mother,

Just a short letter to carry my tender thanks for your long ones: and for the *Punch*es; and for the L.F. received with the letter this morning.

I must not conceal from you my malady. It is Enteritis—Gastro-Enteritis. Caused by no other conceivable thing than the abominable food of the hotels. If there is any dish which really did the mischief, it must have been a certain Mucked Hare, which I remember to have been black as slugs. I ate little; but one has to remember that any dish refused, is so much food (?) lost.

The Enteritis is not likely to develop seriously, so I need not go to *Maison de Santé*; on the contrary I shall very likely go to work early in the week; carrying the gastro, like a young kangaroo, in the paunch. For it will be long in disappearing, they say. That also means I shall have to diet indefinitely. When at length I resume common aliments, it will not be in any of the Hotels I have formerly patronised. Sometimes, the meats seem splendid. But you never know when a bad i.e. putrid thing may be served to you.

The Spanish Prof. (who visits me sometimes) has decided before he knew of my experience, to continue at his first hotel, tho' the price of a meal is 2 f. 50 c. His father, who was over this week, insists on it.—He takes an *abonnement* for 100 f a month. I cannot pay 5 f a day, nor do I think it wise for me to take an *abonnement*. But I shall find a hotel, for 1½ f or even 2 f. unless a miraculous door opens into a *Pension*.

I do not need a remittance, tho' I thank you for offering so many times. I meant to say 'I must refuse'; for there is always the nightmare—fear that you might 'do without a servant'. To imagine you can do that, is to suppose we can do without you!

The Spaniard has monthly reinforcements of 50 f. from Home, but I think it is perfectly possible to live on 130. I must give up the hope of saving, however. At the beginning of the year I shall demand 1 f. for supplement: lessons, instead of ½ f.

You may depend upon it I shall give myself a good attention.

Signor Fernando Ruiz de Toledo (ahem!) finds it necessary to take a 3½ f. meal once a week! Excuse: 'They who work must eat.' I shall perhaps take a 2½ f. once a week, without needing to invent any excuse.

———————

I have not had any real pains until last night (Sat.) when they woke me up. I find they subside if I keep quite still. All day I have felt as if flatulent; but not as with ordinary wind; but rather as with some pungent gas. I look forward somewhat nervously to tonight's rest, which is really due to start now. I have little or no fever tho' the doctor now predicts that a temperature, (not over 101 I think) may occur nightly for a long time. I have no horrors whatever, but underwent a sad, sad dream the other night.

This aft. I went out; and was well able to walk about for 1½ [hours] without more fatigue than when starting: you understand. You must not be worried by this letter; but on the contrary relieved. The affection has now declared itself definitely; and is not overpowering. After all it is a babyish complaint, isn't it? Didn't a baby have it twenty years ago? It may not have survived, but it wasn't Enteritis that killed it. It was the Enter: I—tis I that killed it.

———————

You know what Gastritis is, don't you?

Ah but how I execrate the Restaurants! I feel much comfort in the fact that Father was upset by the deceptive stuff they produce. I feel assured of his sympathies (I sh'd be that in any case) but what I mean is—less ashamed of being bad again so soon.

Forgive me for pitying myself so loudly at you. It is simply to inveigle tendernesses from you and Home. It was kind of Mary to write to me today. This should give impetus for a few more. But mind the blue stamps[1]—or you'll receive a blue paper[2] one of these days.

I don't want people to know my complaint; but if, on your conscientiously confessing I am poorly, the said persons put on a knowing, contemptuous or doubting look, then you can shoot out: Gastro-Enteritis!, which, I hope, will shrivel 'em up.

Farewell, dear Mother, and know that if you make yourself uneasy (as distinct from moved, touched,) on my account, I shall be ten times uneasier. Madame is more attentive. Perhaps I remarked that the Doctor's visits seemed to have a good effect on her. There is always an animated parlance down at the door when he goes out. I succeeded today in getting some genuine gruel made. I do not find the Egg-in-Milk so horrid. I don't think I have much taste, really. Happily my tongue is *très bon, mais elle est blanche, blanche, blanche!*

Well, once more, good night! I hope you will get this on Tues. but no matter what time I write after tea the good folk are not inclined to carry my letters to the post. And usually I only get up for tea.

Your same old Baby (after all), Wulfie x

215. To Alec Paton

November 1913
Bordeaux

My dear Alec,

You will think me a weird bird for not answering your letter of 2 months ago. But it was natural to postpone writing till I was actually settled in France, and since I have been here I have been very, very busy. So much so that last week, just before relief came, I broke down, and had to take some days rest, which gives me leisure to remember my obligations to you.

I got a post as Professor of English in the Berlitz School of Languages, Bordeaux. For some weeks I have been the only English Professor; but at last a lady, one Miss Hewitt (of Liverpool or Birkenhead) has arrived to share my work. I like the work well enough, on the whole. It consists in giving individual lessons to well-educated adults; who may or may not speak English. In the case of the ignorants I am obliged to act on the Berlitz Method, and teach them English without one syllable of explanation in French. This is difficult enough, and I was some time

---

[1] The halfpenny stamp in 1913 was blue-green, the $2\frac{1}{2}d$. a deep, dull blue.
[2] A summons.

acquiring the method. At night there are Courses, and this is quite the most unpleasant part of the business.

I hire a room near the School for only 20 f. per month, but the innumerable extras and the cost of food, contrive to make living less cheap than it is imagined to be in these parts.

Bordeaux is a very fine town, and is of all French cities the one that most resembles Paris. The weather seems to be a regular alternation of powerful sunshine, and equally powerful rain. So far I have been rather lonely in this strange land; and it is my great regret that I scarcely speak any French; but on the contrary more English than ever in my life.

A little time ago my Father came over to see me, and spent a few days in the same house with me. It was very pleasant for both of us.

I hardly dare to ask for news of Mr. Paton. If he is capable of remembering me, I should be glad if you would convey to him my sincerest sympathies and regrets, and my thanks for the kindness that was shown to me, in the old days in Wales. And to Mrs. Paton let me offer sympathies no less earnest.

I was glad to hear that you thought well of your new post, and that the Authorities are well-inclined towards you. I must thank you very much for suggesting to speak to your Professors. There may yet be a time when I may avail myself of your services. Meanwhile, I am looking forward to spending at least the winter in these parts. I shall envy you at home, sometimes, especially at Christmas. I hope not without cause, and that the season may be a happy and prosperous one to you.

Always your sincere friend, Wilfred Owen

P.S. I was extremely sorry to miss seeing you, even for only a few minutes. Do write to me here: I am almost as lonely an individual as the well-known solitary, A.S.P.

216. To Susan Owen
Postcard

17 November[1] [*1913*]   *Bordeaux*

Mary did indeed tell me you were to be torn up into 10 parts on Saturday: but, reading it on Sunday, I did not gather it was Sat. of last week, but thought it was several days off. Do not think me stony, therefore, that I made no mention of it in the letter; (& I was as unsuspecting on Sat. as you could wish). But it seems marvellous that you can have gone through a ten-times-heated-horror; and worst of all, the Gas! What courage! It shames us all! May you be well cherished & in bed this week! The thought of you in 'the Chair' inspires me to despise my little annoyances. Last night, curiously enough after writing my letter, & getting into bed my legs ached as if they were on the racks.

[1] Postmarked 21 November. Wilfred subsequently discovered (see Letter 219) that his cards and letters were not being posted promptly.

But it was only a playful trick of the Humidity & cold; and did not prevent me from taking a class this aftern. of 5 Army Officers. This was quite interesting, & did me good. I feel confident of keeping on.

Your own, W

217. To Susan Owen

23 November 1913   [*Bordeaux*]

Dearest Mother,

   This is just to say that the Box arrived, but in a very loose state, and the jelly-pot had broken. The receiving of this Costly Casket put me into various states of mind, but I finally bring myself to thank you very heartily for the Presents. I ate the jelly at one bout, there being no other way of getting at the remaining objects. Horlicks is a welcome change, & Bovril too; not to mention Bourneville.

   Only this Package must absolutely preclude the sending of any eatable, drinkable, non-eatable or non-drinkable, at Christmas.

   I wonder when you got those belated P.C.'s. I got in quite a fume when [you] said you were already being disappointed on Thurs. and thought of wiring, but methinks the outside of a Telegram would do you more harm in 3 seconds than the inside wd. do you good in 3 days.

   I do not say I am well again to pacify you, any more than I said I was ill to perturb you.

   Voilà tout.

   If you don't hear within a month, it is a good sign,—I am well. I say this in case. Probably you will hear in 48 hours after having this mingy stuff. I hope you are really recovered after the operation, but also hope you do not consider yourself so.

Your own W x

218. To Tom Owen

23 November 1913   *Bordeaux*

My dear Father,

   I must expedite a hasty note on the Subject of the Translation.[1] I have rendered the circumlocutory French into as concise English as possible, just as I would have done it if it were a Task at the Berlitz School. There is no idea of Signatures (which have yet to be solicited) in the word *écritures*: it simply denotes the Clerical Work, Account Entries, etc. which the repayment will occasion. As for the Salutation, it can only be cooled down into the chilly 'yours truly, faithfully, etc.' or at best 'Assuring you of our careful attentions.'

   The English say 'Yours truly' and mean it. The French say 'Be so good as to accept, my dear Sir, the assurance of my most cordial salutations' and mean nothing. The Italians say 'I kiss your feet' and mean—I kick your head.

[1] Tom Owen had sent Wilfred a business letter for translation.

215

I do not get <u>enough</u> Translations to do, for I find it interesting. I wrote eight pages to a man in Lord St. L'pool, the other day, instructing him how to represent a Bordeaux Firm. I little thought I came here to learn Business Methods; but I have at least learnt the phraseology and abbreviations, (thro' having to translate). I have now got back into the usual swing of work, & find it going at a gallop at present: At least eight lessons tomorrow: 3 of which are Courses.

Today (Sunday), I thought it prudent not to get up till Lunch; especially as it is horribly raw and damp. In spite of this icy drizzle I stumped about the pavements during the afternoon hours for the sake of exercise. I took my dinner at the *Union Chrétienne* which is my latest discovery. It provides an ordinary table for 1 fr. 10 or 20 c. I was in hopes of getting French Conversation, but tonight I believe every fellow was a German! The one I was presented to, having taken his fill of English for tonight, went off congratulating himself on the prospect of meeting me tomorrow. He will probably await me in vain. There is a piano, but it was monopolised by a bullet-headed German; and presently the remaining bullet-heads conceived the idea of dancing to the music. They continued to step out, and after three movements to <u>step in again</u>, so long that I bade them a very good night, and so here I am in my cold room. Wood for fires is fearfully expensive, and there is no coal to be had. The cheapest *Pension* I have yet discovered is the best I have yet seen. The whole house, including bedrooms, is warmed by Radiators; there is a fine bathroom, and altogether it seems a very superior establishment. It is situated by one of the Entrances to the *Jardin Public*. I got the price down to 150 f. per month including washing. I said I would decide to come if it could be done for 140 f. but it couldn't.

The Rev. Lurton Burke knows of no *Pension* whatever. It is possible to get a room in the *Union Chrétienne*, but the one vacant at present does not please me as much as Mme. Dubo's. I thank you very sincerely for the £1. When I went to the P.O. they had not yet recv'd the Mandate from Shrews. Unless I go into *Pension*, (and nothing but dangerous cold weather will drive me in) I shall now be easily able to pay my way home, supposing I stay several months more.

I am practically righted again in Health, & have begun to eat ordinary food, and <u>plenty of it</u>. Hence I am visibly re-fattening day by day. I will not continue on to another page for I shall get benumbed, if I stay much longer out of bed.   Your affectionate, Wilfred

219. To Susan Owen
Postcard

Thursday [*20 November 1913*]   [*Postmark Bordeaux*]

I was astonished and dismayed to find the accompanying card unposted. I requested the proprietor to post <u>the same evening that I wrote</u> and this aft. I discovered it still in the house. It is evident that many of my letters have been likewise delayed. I write this on the 20th[1] you sh'd surely get it on 22nd.

On Mond. I took 1 Class; Tues. 4, Wed. 7. Today 7! I feel strong now, & the interior has ceased to be painful. I have begun to eat à la carte at a new Restaurant (1) (excellent) soup (2) fish, (3) omelette. So paying I find it cheaper than the old Restaurants! I spent all afternoon looking up *pensions*. The cheapest 150 f.—very poor. But one is magnificent—Radiator in Room, Bath, Select Society—160 f. (which may be beaten down) Your card came today, but no box yet. I do hope you are 'restablishing' yourself as quickly as I am. I trust you to be taking Horlick's etc. etc. as you me! I am giving way to a delightful hunger—for my hollow cheeks' sake!

W

220. To Susan Owen

27 November 1913   [*Postmark Bordeaux*]

The three letters came on Wednesday morning, bringing a threefold portion of pleasure. I have nothing definite to say about *pensions*, & all the news about my health may be put into one sentence: that I am quite restored. I have several *pensions* yet to visit, & must settle it before the end of the month. As for a family-residence, I have long given up the idea. My lessons have not been excessive this week; but every evening is now filled up, (8 to 10) and will be for months. The weather is miserably wet. I have had to get galoshes, according to the custom here. I was rejoiced to hear how satisfactorily you are getting over the Extractions. I had the *Westmins: Gazette*[2] with the letters; but as you say, I don't think it worth sending any more. Most of the English Magazines are sold here, but they are high-priced. I have made another attempt to get my French Lessons arranged; and really think it will come off this time. Fondest love, & promises of several letters incontinent,

W

221. To Susan Owen

Sunday, 30 November 1913   *Bordeaux*

Dearest Mother,

It is just half past six, and I can imagine you seated in the Pew, recovering from the exertions on the Cop. I am not having dinner today; I had tea, and shall take some Gruel later. For I am still in the old room; but it is no longer cold. Firstly, there has occurred a blessed change in the weather; secondly I have a good fire. It was chiefly the warmer weather which made me decide against the *Pension*, at least for

---

[1] But he forgot to add *Angleterre* to the address, and the envelope carries two postmarks, 21 and 24 November.
[2] Founded as a Liberal daily evening paper in 1893, it became a morning paper in 1923 and was incorporated with the *Daily News* in 1928.

this month. January is likely to be much colder; and I may 'go in' then. For the present, Fires are not only cheaper but much pleasanter. Also the *Pension* is 10 mins. walk from the School; a very serious disadvantage, now that I shall often have only 1 hour for meals. Again, it is risky to pay a big sum for food I may not eat: for the digestive tube may not be quite settled yet.

Lastly I have met a Swiss at the *Union Chrétienne* who is well disposed to talk French with me; and cannot speak English.

There is a piano at the *Union*; and I can enter there to warm myself, read, or play at any moment of the day. I forget whether I told you that it is situated as nearly opposite the School Entrance as the odious new house is opposite you. Under these circumstances, you will not think me unreasonable in resisting your kind persuasions.

The Italian Prof. recommended me a *Pension* (Table only) which I could obtain for 80 f. But the good Lady had the misfortune to inform me that there were German, Greek, Italian, and Spanish nationalities already represented. It was enough.

I do not see much of Miss Hewitt (Prof. *Anglais* II). We are both pretty busy. I usually take her home, after the 10 p.m. lessons; but she braves it alone on wet nights. She is in a Convent where she 'does it' very cheaply indeed. (I have begun enquiring whether there are any charitable Monks who would give me a cell.) Miss Hewitt writes stories and things for magazines; but I know no more than the mere fact that she does so.

Tomorrow her List of Lessons favours her with six hours without a moment's rest; followed by other stretches of several hours. I have therefore to help to reduce this, which will give me 10 Lessons!

I discovered in a Guide the address of a Reformed Church; and having asked the situation of the Street of M. Dubo, I went forth this afternoon in the full hope of attending a service at last. In vain I tramped over the district, till the hour of service arrived and past. On returning for an explanation to the House, Madame informs me that the street is in a totally different direction on the other side of the river, in fact! As well ask a beggar for gold as a frenchman for information.

Duly the Letter and Papers came this morning. I note all the items of news, but they evoke no comments; but only thanks.

I let Madame know that I was looking for a *pension*; and on the strength of that mentioned that I want an Armchair in my room. I think I shall have one this week! [*remainder missing*]

222. To Susan Owen
Postcard

Friday Night [*Postmark 5 December 1913*]   [*Postmark Bordeaux*]

As my pulses are reduced to the usual, now, so must my letters be; that is, I must not write till Sunday. This card if only you get it in time, should tranquillise your Sunday as far as I am concerned. I feel now better than I did this time last year in spite of a heavy List every day. Once I had 7 lessons in 8 hours. Such a fact explains why my P.C's get a little late. The weather is most disappointing: Rain has fallen every day for quite a month. I found your Card in the box this mng. So the letter is already written which I shall read on Sunday! On Sunday at 12 I go to a great breakfast (in honour of someone) at the Union. Affectionations (ees that Eenglish—no?) to all.

W

223. To Susan Owen
Postcard

Friday Night [*Postmark 12 December 1913*]   [*Postmark Bordeaux*]

I fervently hope this will reach you by Sunday: I shall post at the General. If you were expecting Letters instead of a card, I can only indicate that it is impossible for me to have written any. Today, with ten on my List, what time or inclination for sitting down to write? (Think it out) Nevertheless I am not overdone. It is the complete absence of worry that is so balmy to my spirits. Each moment that I am not Teaching or Eating, I spend out of doors; I could not live else. The *Punch*es came at midday, but I have not had time to read them. They are treasures. I repeat; I am going on splendidly in health, & refattening visibly! Your apprehensions about last Sunday were fortunately unfounded. It is long since I spent a more pleasant. Do not pity me on that day of all others. If you knew how I looked forward to it. But there is strong probability of a 3rd. Eng. Professor in a week or two. Then for a high time!

Affection to all, W

I did receive for the week of Absence: & of course the Doctoring was gratuitous.

224. To Susan Owen
Postcard

[*Postmark 15 December 1913*]   [*Postmark Bordeaux*]

9 Lessons today have scarcely permitted me to take my 3 meals & the hour of fresh air which is indispensable if I am to keep going. In the Interval between 4 & 5 o'clock I make me tea & drink it in the company of rare old *Punch*! On Sunday, (with maps & charts) I piloted myself to the Address of a Protestant 'Temple' which Address I obtained at the Union (Y.M.C.A). I found the Address but not the Temple. Finally I got directed to and into the *Maison de Santé*—the *Maison de Santé*!! It was swarming with People & Boy Scouts!!! It was the 50 Anniversary of the Estabmt. The 'Temple' was a shanty in the Garden of the *Maison*: crammed with a Congregation. I returned into the Hospital, visited the Wards, bought a cup of tea, & so the Afternoon was spent! It is v. cold again, esp. at 7.30 A.M.

225. To Susan Owen

16th [December 1913]   *Bordeaux*

My dearest Mother,

It is 10.20 P.M. But I must materialise a few of the innumerable communications which, every day, I reserve for you: Or you will cease to believe in them. I have made tonight a fire; but it is of the Alpenrose variety, both in the matter of Fuel and Intensity of Rays. One of my feet is therefore half up the chimney, & the other somewhere underneath the smouldering logs.

I was 'wistfully amused' that you should suspect the Sunday Swarry to be 'un-Sundaylike'. First, the *Union Chrétienne* is the Y.M.C.A.—or the French Equivalent of that Establishment. Last, the Swarry closed with Reading & Prayer. I did not play the Piano. It was a German who pressed me to; I agreed—not at once because one note is broken, & things might happen. Still it was arranged. In the course of the affair, the same German lumbered up to the Piano, sat somewhere around it, opened my *Blake's March*, & let fall his sausage-fingers, (possibly I am wrong here, & it was only the thumbs that were used). The Result was what a sack-race is to the March of the British Life Guards. At the moment, I should have welcomed a war with Germany. Such is the frailty of our Senses.

The same hulking fellow, (he has a neck like twenty bulls) nearly does for me every day—by the manner he eats his Soup. You know the Germans are said to be fond of saying Ach! Imagine this syllable extended over ten minutes, and you hear Herr — eating his soup.

In the morning, I take *Déjeuner* at a Restaurant where the Dishes are of wider choice, (and very good.) I have taken *cachets*, and, because I exclude wine, pay only 1 f. 10 c. per meal! This allows me afternoon tea, & a cake or so therewith. I have had to get a *service*, as Mme. not unnaturally objects to my monopolising her pot. I also object to the Coffee, which she usually leaves in it; for she uses it for Both. So, not wishing to buy heavy things, which I must leave behind, I have got a delightful Tea Pot, Sugar Basin, & Jug in Aluminium: unbreakable & portable, and elegant, & in lustre rivalling silver & surpassing all White Metals, and which I suppose, will accompany me in all my wanderings.—Such amiable concerns as tea-pots, you notice, check my wonted wanderings in letters.

This time last year—'pon my word I forget what I was going to say. Never mind! this year will do: You asked me a question? Ah yes!—I have no answer—ready:—have not the least idea how I shall spend Christmas Day, beyond that it will not be in B. School. Boxing Day may or not be in that Box (as the French call a 'Dirty Hole'.)

The '3rd English' was apparently a myth to keep us going strong. Fortunately I am going strong—but feel very troubled about one thing: I am thwarted in every serious attempt to improve my French. I cannot take lessons in the School:—Aumont says if I have too many lessons how can I take more? And now he has refused to make any facilities for me to follow the gratuitous Courses at the University. It appears that the Sub-Director has also asked to attend these Lectures: also to be refused! What is worse, with the continual drumming on English from morn to night, I have no linguistic hunger left in me and eschew 'Conversation'.

The student I met that Sunday at the Union says he himself was 'nearly a victim' of the Berlitz Schools; and is most anxious for me to find some employment where I should speak French. I shall seek for no such thing, unless I am told off the B.S. or find the work really excessive.

I do not suffer in the smallest degree from Heart.[1] I hope your inquiries were not suggested by any trouble of your own. I should forget I was not robust in that Muscle, were I not warned in a dream. For the other night (before you wrote) I was told by the people in next room that I groaned sorely many times; and I afterwards remembered having tried to impel you up the Cop, and of moving you about a yard an hour! Such dreams denote—Weak Heart. (Old Moore)

I have cashed the Order long ago, thanks, but have not broken into the Gold, even at my lowest moment! The Arm chair does not appear! I need absolutely nothing for Christmas & implore you to send nothing material, but a few drops of Ink, dried, after being suitably disposed over a few leaves of paper, by all your (plural) hands severally. My presents I think I must combine with Homing Gifts: but you may tell me if this is objected to. There is here no mention, no whisper of Christmas, nor ever will be. The Germans here will buy them Trees and look at them; the French will buy older wines, and gulp them, I shall buy a huge Yule Log—and feel it. And also, a few more Postage Stamps, and will lick them, all in good time.

For the Present, then, Goodbye! And fondest love   from W

226. To Susan Owen

Sunday, 21 December [*1913*]   *Bordeaux*

My own dear Mother,

I suddenly remembered today that if you are to hear from me 'on Christmas', I must post this very night. Today has whizzed by, and I am again sitting by my logs, and trying to render some account of myself. This afternoon I have once more been prevented from going to a 'Temple'; this time because of a Frenchman whom I have at last found to exchange lessons. I appointed him to call at two o'clock to arrange things.—He simply would not leave me. I hope to profit by this aquain-tance, (arranged for me by Miss Markowsky, Professor of Russian)—

---

[1] HO believes this to have been imagination (like the incipient TB—see Letter 180, note 1); but see Letters 133, 134. Wilfred was later passed fit for the Army.

for the party, M. Michellet,[1] (27) has been a French Master in an English Secondary School, & speaks very fluently English.

One of the <u>Young Men</u>, brought an elderly person to meet me one night, who had the reputation of having been a Berlitz Professor in Germany. He was willing to give lessons for 1 franc per hour, at any time, on any day. This is very convenient, & I <u>went</u> one day. I am doubtful of continuing, though I can't exactly say <u>Why</u>.—Perhaps it is the Franc!

Meanwhile the Hard Labour continues. Ten Lessons tomorrow. Christmas Day will certainly be free, tho' nothing has been said by 'the Direction'. I hardly expect any change to be made on the 24th or 26th.

I have not formed any plans for spending the 25th beyond that a portion shall be spent in Contemplation of what is going on at Mahim. May it be well and truly a day filled with peace and goodwill. As for the <u>good tidings</u>, the best I can give you are that I am well; and, if never gay, not often gloomy. Whatever grievances I have, I have no reason to repent having come to France. I eat (I repeat for your ease) generously and delicately, as I choose. There are many plum-puddings in the shop windows, if I needed 'em. There is even an English Grocery Shop, where if I shut my eyes to smell and listen the better, I might fancy myself in Teece's. Teece's Shed is hard and hideous, and the garden thereby, barren and dismal; yet it were well if I could alight on that Garden, and witness the simple festivities; and tell ghost stories— stories of the Ghost of Christmas Past. I have no Dickens-Book with me, but the Music of the Carol is remembered as if it were all a memory of my own life.

——————

I am, in a way, glad to miss <u>for once</u> the Association of Carols, Snow, Mincemeat, Presents, Holly, <u>Stockings</u>, Merry Christmas etc. They will have a huge interest next year.

In the same way I do not permit myself to think of Flowers, Trees, Grass, Hills, or Clouds, (No Adjectives even allowed) because I am preparing myself for a magnificent Revel one day in the Spring. Never, in all my born days, have I been so utterly towny as at this moment. Not even in Willmer Road,[2] in the old dark days; whereof, when I think, I come near tears, but not through pain. Ten years have matured those memories into Sweetness only. <u>You</u> are little changed since then; but, d'you know, Father seems more <u>so</u>. Mary & Harold—both little changed. Colin entirely. Alas, for Baby Colin!

If I should ever beget me a Child, he could not be more adored than was Colin in those days. . . . In those days when I taught him the colours, showing him the Wall, the Floor, & the Carpet, <u>exactly</u> as I do at this day—to a very different type of toddler! When I <u>begin</u> to think how changed is Myself, I just . . . stop thinking.

[1] See Letter 230 for more about him.
[2] The Owens lived in Willmer Road, Birkenhead (HO cannot recall the number) before moving to 51 Milton Road. In between there was a short time at another house in Elm Grove, Birkenhead.

'Tis just as well; at least in a Christmas Letter!

I have just remembered, as *à propos*, that the Spaniard is mightily anxious that I should dine with him on Christmas Day. The good Señor is very kind to desire it, but I don't relish giving Conversational Lessons without any Return. And his English is terribly jarring. However, I have to thank him for one piece of advice he gave me; 'If you work hardly, you must hardly eat.' Hardly eat! He is still wondering why I smiled so loud at the remark!

Now, I break off for a while . . . I can only reach out my arms Northward, yearn to you, and 'wish you a Happy Christmas', aye Two Happy Christmases, with the intermediate days, also happy, to be thrown in . . .

I continue to another page [*but it is missing*]

227. To Susan Owen

Saturday, 27 December 1913   *46 Cours de l'Intendance, Bordeaux*

Dearest Mother,

I am waiting for a Pupil who is not likely to come; so here is a good opportunity for the letter which is already overdue. I had the *Punches* yesterday, and with them a Postcard announcing the dispatch of the Box, which card was some day's late, and had a Red Ink Inscription: 'Found in Circular at Pentridges.' I wonder who is the Culprit and who the philanthropic Poster?

As for the Box: if you send another, unrequested, the kindness will kill me: for the incident puts me into a terrible state, not of Anger; but of Divided Personality. To treble my misfortune, it was a Commissionaire who handed the Package to me, fluttering with all the ribbons of French Formalities, and demanding from me a payment of nearly 2 f. imposed by the *Douane*! It is a mercy Scout-Colin, that canny Tweak, sealed up the *Briquet*[1] in an Envelope, or I might have been in Jail by this time. For it is illegal to carry any *Briquet* not bearing a Government Stamp. I judge of the consequences of trying to make such an object pass the Customs, by the penalty on introducing Matches, viz. one franc per match!

Next Page Please.

Never, therefore, think to send me any such things as matches (welcome as non-asphyxiating matches would be to one with tender throat.) However the *Briquet* is precisely the thing I want. They are very common in France, but their large, cumbrous nature & horrid Governmental Attachment saved me from buying one. Colin could not have found a handier thing for me than the beautiful little affair he has sent. The gloves I shall not soil for many a day, as I already have two pairs in working order. But the Hide-Nose (*Cache-Nez*) (as the French call a Muffler) has already done good service. I must confess to a Cold of

[1] Steel for striking light.

4–5 days standing, and certain looseness rather than tightness, under the upper ribs. On Christmas day, I had keen pains all through the Torso, and promptly buried my nose in as many wraps as I could carry; but I have No Cough . . . yet!

I found the Gingerbreads excellent; & the Chocolate a good change; tho' you must not imagine I never mouth a good morsel here. I do.

What a splendid surprise was the Photograph! It is certainly very well done. Such a privilege redeems the disadvantages of living in the 20th Century. I have now quite as good a reminder of your dear looks, quite as sure a warrant of your being in health, as if, say, I had seen you all, for one minute's space,—out of an aeroplane, which you all came to the gate to see!

As for the Pocket Lamp (I know not the kind donor)—the idea was a good one, but I already have one. I found it necessary to buy one, for seeing the time, in the dark mornings. The idea of lighting a match is in itself such a Nuisance that I doze off again without doing it. But a Pocket Lamp is quite tempting, & lies safely under one's pillow. Speaking of the Time, I don't believe I have told you, (extraordinary I am), that my old Armour-Plated Timepiece has gone on the shelf at last. It wanted a Repair which would cost 5 f. Tho' it would plod on still, it was too much. I fell under the attraction of a delightful silver Precision Watch, small (but not 'Ladies'), thin, and Anti-Magnetic, (in case I go Pole-hunting, like a gallant gentleman.)[1] It is of a good Make, & gives great satisfaction. Price: little more than 1 Guinea. N.B. I did not go to the Expensive Shop, where Father & I inspected the Windows.

I promise to have a small, cheap photograph done, but shall have to watch for my moment. Furthermore, at present I think that I feel that I look somewhat over-boiled-in-tomato-sauce owing to the Cold.

I have not said how I spent Christmas Day. Now, the 24th, is a *Réveillon*, or Watch Night, and as two members of the Union asked me to go to the Cathedral for the Midnight Mass, I agreed, always remembering that one of the fellows not only professesses-and-calls-himself Christian, but in fact delivered an Address on Prayer quite lately. Unfortunately, my impressions of my first real, Catholic Mass were marred (1) by the incessant sniggering of my companions, and (2) by a bleak wind, which blew freely about the vast nave. If Father had been there he would have had his head flying off several times: such was the draught.

↑   *95 Porte Dijeaux*

Since writing to the Line I have moved my camp beside another inkwell, & have had dinner & given a lesson. At dinner, at the *Union*, the identical youth whom I was beginning to slang for misbehaviour at Mass, has invited me to go with him to a place down nearer the mouth

---

[1] *Scott's Last Expedition*, Captain Robert Falcon Scott's journal of the second Antarctic expedition, 1910–12, had been published earlier in the year. The reference is to Captain Oates, 'a very gallant gentleman', who walked out into the blizzard to die when he realized that his failing strength was perilously slowing down the expedition's return.

of the River, there to spend the day with the Family of a Pastor. I am going. The fellow himself is one of the plain, open-hearted sort, and I have no doubt of being welcomed without Ceremony by his friends. As I have to be ready to leave my Room at 6.30 tomorrow I must discontinue my narrative (if ever there was one) and begin on my sleep as soon as may be.

I was going to conclude with personal tributes of gratitude for all the presents you have joyed me with, and all the beloved letters too. But you knew my feelings before you sent them, and I have nothing more to say: Except: Bother the Questions in the letter if you posed any at all. I can't find any just now. Will write again this Year. Oh depend upon it!

Your Mistletoe hangs on the gas-fixture in my Room.

I'm sorry Harold knows nothing definite of his departure. Leslie has sent me a present of a little leather Tennyson!

Adieu, Mother! Au Revoir, Father! Goodbye, Mary! Turn in, Harold! Tweek-tweek, Curlew-Colin!

Thanks all!! from,   Your Affectionate Wilfred

228. To Susan Owen
Postcard

1 January 1914   [*Postmark Bordeaux*]

Had yr. Letter on Wednesday & was much interested therein. There was no R. Bridges in my Box, and only one bed-sock. What sort of book was it? I am going to complain or else instruct you to. My cold is clearing off, and so has the cough. It only lasted one day. What happened to the lungs I don't know; but they are right again, so Cheer up!

I have not been to Photographer's yet. But when are the Photos coming, which you promised to get from Auntie Emmie. Please Keep my 5s. (from Mrs. D.)[1] I had to buy a waistcoat today, to complete the black suit: for the State Visit to Mr. Aumont which French Politeness imposes. The visit went off very well. It has snowed even here, and is perishing-cold tonight.

I hear from Leslie that Mr. Black is thinking of going to the South of France. Saw the New Year in at the *Union*. A swarry; but we got to prayers on the Hour of midnight.

                                              Wilfred

229. To Susan Owen
Postcard

[*Postmark 9 January 1914*]   [*Postmark Bordeaux*]

I am writing just before dinner at the *Union*. Perhaps a letter is due but is impossible yet. If by chance I have a spare hour I trot off to the

[1] Mrs. Dale.

University! I have suddenly had a batch of persons willing to exchange Conversation. I saw two, last Sunday and shall tell you more of what selections I make later. Also, there is rumour of M. Aumont giving lessons to the Professors, two by two!! I had H's outwardly-shocking but inwardly-interesting Card,[1] he says nothing thereon, but it was a sort of Olive Leaf, signifying that he yet roosteth on dry land. I can still report that I am well. So glad to hear Mary & you, etc. are likewise. Of course I enjoyed your letter of Sunday last & read the Almanac.

Au revoir x

I had a card from A. Paton (in answer to a letter) with news of Mr. Paton's death in September.

230. To Susan Owen

Sunday, 18 January [*1914*]   *Union Chrétienne, Rue du Temple*
Bordeaux

My own dear Mother,

I found this sheet of paper, and constructed a pen from various fragments. Then I begged an envelope from the Custodian of this place, and must next buy a stamp from the Tobacconist's. Where the Ideas for a letter are coming from I don't quite know. For I am getting positively stultified by the nature of my employment.

The Cold continues still. Nothing short of a conflagration would warm my room; and that is why I am here. Water in the Jugs etc. has been frozen for several days. There has been Skating since Friday, but not for me! Garros[2] did not come to Bordeaux today, as expected; I suppose because of the weather; but is advertised for a week hence.

For the second time in life, I have met a character out of a book.[3] The Russian Professor[4] (such a wizened, little piece of womankind you never saw) found a Frenchman[5] to exchange Conversation with me. I have been several times to his house; & find him very agreeable. He is about 27, has a pleasing & handsome young *Française* to wife; and a delightful progeny, of two years' growth. He had a position as French Master in a Secondary School in Derbyshire for some years; but left England, for his wife's sake. He talks with great gusto of his life in England; boasts of talks with G. K. Chesterton; arguments with Colonel Seely;[6] and so on. He appears (only slightly) in the Book of his friend, Raymond Guasco: *John Bull's Island*;[7] which consists of a

---

[1] From a South American port.
[2] Roland Garros (1888–1918), a sporting pilot who invented a way of firing a machine-gun forward from his Morane-Saulnier monoplane by fixing metal plates to the propeller to deflect the bullets. His name is commemorated by the Stade Garros in Paris.
[3] Mr. Treacher, the geologist (see Letter 73), was probably the first.
[4] Mlle Markowski. See Letters 260, 261.
[5] M. Michellet, first mentioned in Letter 226.
[6] John Edward Bernard Seely, 1st Baron Mottistone (1868–1947). Secretary of State for War 1912–14, he resigned office after intimating that troops would be used to enforce Home Rule in Ireland. He commanded a Canadian infantry brigade in France.
[7] J-Raymond Guasco, *John Bull's Island: Carnet d'un reporter*, Paris, 1912.

number of Sketches of English life, as it appeared to a philosophical Frenchman. Michellet (my friend) is 'the Professor', and into his mouth are put the reflective remarks, whether he actually made them or not. I enjoyed reading this book extremely; and shall buy a copy to translate to you—someday. The Author is in Paris now, making much money by his pen.

Michellet has also an Artist-friend, who has a studio in Paris. Himself has bought the Rights of Translation of Kipling's Works (some of them). Hence he is an interesting acquaintance; but, I am afraid, has an incorrigible tendency to potter. Now I must shun Potterers like the Plague. One day, he busies himself with a microscope; another day with a telescope;—and, today, it was an electric battery. Pictures, and Antiquities also interest him. In this he is so much like myself, so little more learned than myself, as to be annoying. But at least, he can help my French, if he will.

No Lessons have yet been started (in French) for us Profs. Meanwhile we have anything between 7 and 10 hours per day. One must take the good with the bad; one says; the good, so it seems, is to be enjoyed only in Summer. This is hard lines for me; and tempts me to abandon the idea of returning for a horrible exam! It would be easy to have lessons in German or other languages in the Summer, and this appeals to me likewise. If only I could dispense with the competitive Exam. and return in September, at the beginning of the term! By the way, the Sub-Director yesterday broached a 'marvellous thing' to me. Would I like to become Director of a small B. School in the N. of France? There would be plenty of work in winter; hardly any in summer; and clear profits of 4,000 francs a year. He will be pleased to tell me more when I have thought it over, and told my parents! 'But it's a marvellous thing' says he! Only I doubt my business capabilities.

I wonder how you have spent today. I have not been to Temple; in the week I sometimes get the opportunity of attending a Bible Class at the *Union*. I have not now space or time to make observations on the Religious Life in this Town, except to say that there is extraordinarily little of it. The Bible is unknown; especially to the Christians. I have met non-Christians who read it, however. It is indeed a sweet and precious thing to hear it read once more,—though in another tongue, yet, with the same earnest intonation as of old.

I am 'writing' just nothing; but I prosecute my Enquiries in Human Nature, and learn Philosophy, as I teach Speech, by the Direct Method. The B. School is a wonderful place for testing intellects. There are some pupils who, 3 months ago, knew not a word; and who now speak quite tolerably; others do not advance one bit. The younger and busier they are, the quicker they learn.

Don't forget your Portraits, if Uncle is so good. I shall be glad also to have the ones in which Leslie is so good. I have discovered a cheap place for my own, but the difficulty is to find the moment; as it is a long way from my usual haunts. There is a great racket going on in this room, which acts on my pen as on a Phonograph needle taking Records. Remember your Prime Object in being at Alp. is rest. Receive my fondest salutations.

x Wilfred

231. To Susan Owen

Postcard addressed to Alpenrose, Kidmore End, Reading

Wednesday 21 January [*1914*]   [*Postmark Bordeaux*]

I was 'ever so' glad to have your letter this morning. I have no news worth spinning out. What occupies the tongues of Bordeaux at present is the extraordinary Cold. They are skating on the lakes of the Parks. Of course skates are scarce here & therefore too dear for me to buy. And I have not the time either. Today I was able to spend an hour at the University. Shall probably write letters (including Reply to Leslie) for Sunday.
You will of course convey my 'feelings' to Torquay.[1] I am glad, however, you are not there. Affectionate wishes to all, thanks to Mary, Embraces to you,

W

232. To Susan Owen

23 January 1914   *Bordeaux*

My dearest Mother,
    It is Friday afternoon, and I have an hour (3–4) for your extra special letter. It is likely that a pupil will excuse herself—from 5 to 6— dear nice, thing! And they make such profuse apologies when they excuse themselves or come late. In this case I will enclose something for Leslie. If nothing comes he will know Madame has turned up after all. This dame merits a word of description[2]—she comes with rings on every finger of both hands save one; i.e. wears nine or ten rings. She has the reputation of being beautiful; and is certainly very nice; but a greater boggler at languages I never met. If it were not that I laugh-over her howlers with Miss Hewitt I should howl for misery or else box her powdered cheeks!
    There is an almost entirely new set of pupils from that when I first came. As soon as they begin to progress, they leave. The M.P.'s wife, who used to arrive in a magnificent automobile, has left for Paris, where she continues her lessons. I have one pupil over sixty—rather difficult because of her incessant lamentations. 'Oh la! la! My poor memory! eet ees not as eet was!' At New Year she said: 'I thought my Professor would like some cigars' (I groaned) Then: 'But perhaps my Professor not wish the cigars; would he accept so leetle a thing . . .?' (a five

---

[1] Unexplained.
[2] Possibly the first mention of Mme Léger, with whose family Wilfred was to spend the late summer of 1914 at Bagnères-de-Bigorre.

franc piece). Except for some confection which made me sick in the night, that completes the list of Presents!

Next to the few who are able to take Literature, the Officers are the most interesting. Sometimes they appear in gorgeous costumes, with swords, etc. They have to be treated like babes none the less. After the doctors, lawyers, and business men of the day, the evening comes very disagreeably with the young artisans and shop-girls!

I have ascertained that nothing can be done about 'the book'. You see I did not know what the parcel originally contained, and had to sign for it on receiving it. Thus, having signed, nothing more can be done save to take warning. It seems sinister, does it not, that your defiance of my wishes should so turn out. (I am not annoyed.) There are however several of my books which I really need. If I have to send for them you will please make an inventory for me beforehand; and if you must include fresh eggs, cabbages, half a pair of old socks, pack them in hermetically-sealed lead coffins, because of the smell.

For my 21st Birthday, the traditional Watch can happily be waived; but I have quite a hankering for a Waverley Fountain Pen. There are various styles, I think; and should you be disposed to subscribe for such a treasure, I would pray you to obtain the catalogue and let me consult it. My spectacles[1] remain intact, but I still feel nervous about breaking them; and also fancy the less-grandmotherly pince-nez. Hence if Gordon comes to Alpenrose, as indeed if he does not, would you please inquire

(1) The Prices of Watson's Rimless or Rimmed in various metals F.O.B. Bordeaux.

(2) Whether I could get lenses similar to the present in Bordeaux. There are plenty of shops where pince-nez are quite cheap, but I must be sure of the lenses.

I have quite a mania, sometimes, to take you about Bordeaux, O Mother! If I won't come home, perhaps you might be induced to visit me!

The slight sketch of Dunsden folk you gave me brings it all back most vividly. You will I hope tell me even more in your next. I sent cards to both my protégés in the village, (M.M. & V.R.)[2] but had nothing from them at Christmas.

I smile and shake my head like an octogenarian over the mention of Bernice Cornwall.

Yea, I almost laugh. But see the early chapters of *David Copperfield*. So glad you keep resting.

The cold persists: but my cold has gone.

I should like to enclose a note for Mary, but had better hurry off to post before my lesson, in case of delays in post.

Of course, if Mr. Wigan is at Dunsden, & you speak to him, you will give my cordial wishes for his health and happiness.

---

[1] He seems to have worn them very little. HO never saw them, and there is no indication in later letters or photographs that he wore them in the Army.

[2] Milly Montague and Vivian Rampton.

Has Black gone <u>already</u>!
And where?
Also, if so, why?
Give, too, my blessing to all the good villagers whom you meet, and in return collect all their news!
About this time, was it not, that I began to be ill? When I think thereof I have no blessings left but only for <u>you</u>!
Receive the devoted benison of your own

Wilfred

233. To Susan Owen
Postcard

Saturday Night [*Postmark 31 January 1914*]   [*Postmark Bordeaux*]

Have had such a frightful bout of teaching this week—9 per day—that the letters must wait. Hope you are safe home. I have been given a 5 f. Ticket for the Students' Ball (University) & shall probably look in tonight—with a domino! The gentleman who gave the Ticket to me is a prof. of the Univ. & an Author! Am keeping very well, considering the work.

Yours ever, W

234. To Susan Owen
Postcard

[*Postmark 2 February 1914*]   [*Postmark Bordeaux*]

This will serve as well as a letter to assure you of my health and happiness; and to enquire after yours. On Sunday we had delightful weather & I went a refreshing walk of many miles (with a new friend), to see more flying: it was more and more astounding! After, I had dinner with this youth. His people are very homely but quite 'simple'. I have a letter to father which shall follow close on the heels of this.

Affectionate wishes to all, W

10.30 Monday. Had your Card on Sunday. Thanks

235. To Tom Owen

Monday, 2 February 1914   *Bordeaux*

My dear Father,
    I have now got more information about the 'school in the North of France'. It is none other than our Branch at Angers, of which the present director is M. Aumont. It is the Sub-Director, Herr Langholz, only, who has spoken to me about it, and he does not wish me to speak to Mr. Aumont until I am certain about bidding for it.
    Why does Mr. Aumont wish to part with the business?—Because, says Langholz, he is already too much occupied with Bordeaux and Nantes; and the Lady who at present manages it, is inefficient. The

230

profits have certainly gone down in the last year; but this, I am told, is entirely due to the Lady, who speaks bad French and has no notion of how to deal with the Clients.

Langholz himself directed this school for some years;—so is worth listening to on the subject. The profits then reached 9000 f. per year. Out of this, he thinks at least 4000 f (£160) would be net gain.

I learn, however, that Aumont is asking 4,500 f as the price of its sale!

Unless, therefore, some Rich Uncle is prepared to advance some 5000 f, the thing will be impossible. Langholz says I might possibly obtain such an arrangement as this: to take the school on trial for 1 year. with a deposit of 1000 f, and pay the remainder if I found it worth continuing.

Angers is within easy reach of St. Malo; so I should not be hopelessly cut off from Home. Moreover the Summer Months are so slack, that one might well manage a month's absence! In Winter there is plenty to do, as the Director is his own English Professor under ordinary circumstances. The German Professor does the Secretary's work. Spanish & other Teachers are to be found in the town and summoned as required.

Langholz speaks in enchanting terms of the premises! There are three rooms for classes, an apartment for the Director's growlery and night-lair, and a Kitchen, as well as the Office. Cleaning and Personal Attention is done by Boys or Women.

I am certainly very young to take on me the Direction of a School! And unless the emoluments were really considerable, it would not be worth the Responsibility. But I should do better first to take posts as Professor in other countries, Italy for instance, in order to be capable of teaching several languages.

This is always supposing I cannot first finish my English studies, at College.

You were right in judging that I am not hungering for the Examination; None the less, I pine to devote two or three years to uninterrupted, unencumbered Study. If this Desire, now ten years old, be not realized, I must carry a heavy load of disappointment to my life's end! . . . Thus, if, considering the Angers-Box a marvellous chance, you obtained the £200 necessary for its purchase, I would still rather see the money invested in College Fees!

The more so, as an English Degree admits one to a French University, where one does a little English Instruction, while following Courses for French Degrees. Last Friday I met an English fellow (the first since I came) who is doing this. With a Double Degree, one has no mean Educational Chances. I must enquire whether the little English Teaching this man does is sufficient to maintain him.

The fact that Langholz thinks me capable of managing a school, and in a foreign element too, proves that I do not wholly live in dreams.

I have no false ideas of Business. 'Anything we do to make money is

Business.' If I have shirked the idea of Shop, or Office, or Elementary
School, it is only because I am more clear-sighted than another; and see
that once fixed in a low-level Rut one is ever-after straightened there;—
straightened intellectually and socially as surely as financially.

Neither am I under any delusions as to Literature as a means of
livelihood.

But I must not wander from the purpose of this letter, which is: to
ask your opinion of the Berlitz Affair; and, secondly, to state that if you
find it beyond your power to supplement either of the Reading Scholar-
ships, I willingly resign this Scheme, rather than be the least cause of
adding to your worries or perplexities.

I am wondering very much what will come of all this.

I don't feel inclined to stay in Bordeaux all the summer; especially
as I hear the heat is terrific (save the mark, O Harold) in July! But if
the lessons are few it will be more supportable. At present they allow
me little leisure: (I have been munching my afternoon refreshments
while writing this letter.)

I hope you, dear Father, are fairly free of worry, and in your usual
spirits.

Your most affectionate Son, Wilfred

236. To Mary Owen

Tuesday, 3 February [*1914*]   [*Bordeaux*]

Dearest Mary,

It was good to have some Violets in my Room that the Oxford Clays
and Alpenrose Airs had nourished! I like these tangible specimens of
my Motherland's sweetness, and of my Sister's Love. Many thanks for
the Post Card also.

I wonder whether you are doing anything at French? My serious
advice to you is not—to work hard; but to leave it entirely! Time spent
on Grammars and Translations under the direction of an English
Teacher is wasted. Such is the conclusion I have come to! I now realise
that I must have had an abominable accent; for tho' I have made radical
alterations in my pronunciation since being here, I am still a long way
from perfection. The majority of English Teachers have an execrable
Accent, and what is worse, no notion of the Direct Method. If only I
could give you a few lessons à la Berlitz! But I will, too, before long!
We will form a French Course in the dining-room every night. I
guarantee I would have you all talking good French in 3 months! At
least, there are dozens of pupils who have learnt English in that time.

You must tell me if you take to my idea of your giving all your
attention to English for a while! Except as a mental exercise, your
laborious Translations are useless; in fact harmful! The Bertenshaw
Grammar has my everlasting anathema. Forgive my ardour: I yearn
over your welfare.

W

237. To Susan Owen

Picture postcard: Bordeaux, La Porte Dijeaux

[Postmark 9 February 1914]   *[Postmark Bordeaux]*

On Sunday I got your and Father's letters & also a Catalogue of Waverleys. I am swamped in work for the moment! I like your photos very much, & will say more later. I spent a very pleasant Sunday, of which the reading of yr. letters formed part. The weather is now fine & warm. Had the *Punch*es Today (Monday). Now I will trot through The *Porte* & post this.

Adieu.

238. To Susan Owen

Saturday, 14 February [1914]   *Bordeaux*

My own Mother,

I fear you will have already have got restive for the receipt of these pages tho' they are not yet written. For I haven't the faintest idea when I wrote last. It is quite by a heroic fortitude that I resist my couch this night. The week has been a whirl of lessons. However they never tire me to the point of doing me harm. There was a time when I went on till I trembled, and talked nonsense, (and finally of course lost ¾ of Life for a week) but I won't do that now. Yesterday six lessons following were set down for me [*three words illegible*] and then 2 more!

I took the list to Aumont and told him what I thought.

Strange to say, it seems to have some effect; for today I have had two lessons less than Miss Hewitt, (who goes on turning, turning, turning out lessons as a Mangler mangles hour by hour) and it is she (and not I) who is confronted with the enormity of Eleven Hours of it on Monday!!

I believe the Angers Box is already sold; so that is off one's mind. As it would have required much working up, and would on no account have been worth taking for less than five years or so, I am glad I am not tethered to it.

I shall write to Reading very presently, and I thank you very heartily for telling me to! This Bordeaux business is all very well for now, but it must not be for long. I am at last beginning to sport something like an accent. At least those who stared when I spoke French, or answered off the point, now compliment me on my pronunciation. I consider it a scandal that such teachers as taught me French should be allowed in Schools. Dear Mary must no longer muddle her head with rules & exceptions, or corrupt her tongue with what Miss G. will teach her.

Let her study English Rules, & cultivate fluency in one language, before she undertakes to be halting, in two—for I never yet heard her compound three consecutive sentences within two hours. Moreover I shall need a little assistance in English when I get back, because only today I told a pupil that the preterite of 'bring' was 'brang'!! And, again, read 'Artchangel' for 'Arkangel' and only the Blessed Ghosts of Nuttall or Webster know what spelling errors appear on these sleepy pages.

I rejoice over the photographs and their tale. You are certainly plumper; but I shall soon have to dispute the statements you make concerning your age, and consider them as a hoax, invented to hinder us from marrying young as you must have done. Keep up the game for a few more years, for I shall be young for many years yet. There is no immediate reason for Mary (or any of you) to learn French, for the countess has not yet crossed my path. In fact I was never so absolutely free of 'heart trouble' within these ten years past. This will no doubt give you immense satisfaction. But it should not . . .

You ought not to discourage too hard.

If you knew what hands have been laid on my arm, in the night, along the Bordeaux streets, or what eyes play upon me in the restaurant where I daily eat, methinks you would wish that the star and adoration of my life had risen; or would quickly rise.

But never fear: thank Home, and Poetry, and the FORCE behind both. And rejoice with me that a calmer time has come for me; and that fifty blandishments cannot move me like ten notes of a violin or a line of Keats.

All women, without exception, annoy me, and the mercenaries (which the innocent old pastor thought might allure) I utterly detest; more indeed than as a charitable being, I ought.

But I should not like to have seen myself in this town, two years earlier [*five lines illegible*] Still, if you never had any [*one word illegible*] to make to me, at [*one word illegible*] I shall have no confession now [*two words illegible*] At least, none such as must make me blush and weep and [*two words illegible*]

But I shall perhaps continue my Reminiscences next time, according to the spirit in which you receive these present. Mistake not my spirit; if I seem joking I am really grave; (even as when my writing is most worthless my thoughts are most worthy). We say strange things in our sleep. I have been partially so for half an hour.

The enclosed is for Mary. Her photo is lovely; they are all precious, yours: though not such works of art as is Leslie's; which is quite a masterpiece, don't you think?

I have met more desirable aquaintances, (Univ. Students.) Tomorrow I am again dining with the violin boy.

I must not now depict scenes, pickle juicy bits or pick tricky characters to pieces to tickle you (witness if my wits are going)—goodnight! call me at 7 in the morning, no Sunday—*demain c'est dimanche n'est-ce pas: à 9 heures alors; oui, madame*, language—*mixé* . . . ah! put out the light there—ah! warm, comfortable; pillow—soft, all identity lost —save am

Mother's Son

239. To Susan Owen

Postcard

Wednesday [*Postmark 25 February 1914*]   [*Postmark Bordeaux*]

I don't think I asked about your headaches in my last; but I think about you most constantly—just now of all times, today a YEAR ago the pneumonia definitely appeared. It was 'to-night' I had the first phantasms.—and how have I been spending the anniversary?—Revelling! in the Carnival! I had huge success with my Costume: Nothing more elaborate than my Gown on my back a laurel wreath on my head, & a palm branch in the hand. These 3, (with of course a Mask—my own home-made domino) made an imposing combination! I was with a student (whom I like very much), & his friends. The crowds were enormous, & I was twice choked with confetti. Weather magnificent. But the purpose of this card is really only to thank you for your interesting & valuable letter, & Colin's also; to carry any poor comfort it can to your neuralgia, to say my throat is now tickled by nothing worse than confetti-particles; & to beg for a Standard Waverley Nib; & to ask is there any thing in the realm of France you wd. specially like for the 17th of March? Dearest Love to All,

Wilfred

Sorry I forgot a stamp the other day—or night.

240. To Colin Owen

[*? late February 1914*]   [*Bordeaux*]

My dear Colin,

I hear you have lately been in bed; nothing 'strordinary in that, of course; I go there myself, but not much now. Fancy, when you are scarcely at breakfast at 8 o'clock, I am already engaged in mental & physical work, pumping phrases in, and pumping them out again, and certainly very wide awake!!

I don't know whether you have heard from your Correspondent[1] here; I heard he had heard from you. Now, I know of another boy whom I would prefer as your correspondent; the first is a limp, gawkish fellow of seventeen!

I will give you the address of the second one next time. You can easily slip out of the first one's reach if you will. The name of the Second, who is a real schoolboy like yoursel' is Jean Thouverez.

———————

Here follows something important: Will you please give me the address of Pitman's, the Shorthand Publisher, with such particulars of his works as you can.

[1] Possibly Raoul Lem, who later stayed at Shrewsbury. See Letter 242.

It is for a lady, in fact the sister of Jean, who wishes to master the English system. Kindly answer <u>at once</u>.

Forgive more scribble this time.

Your affectionate Brother, Wilfred

Do hope you're well.

241. To Susan Owen
Postcard

Monday [*Postmark 2 March 1914*]   [*Bordeaux*]

Had a pleasant Sunday again, but lo! Monday is here with 9 lessons & I have not accomplished my letter! The weather here is not cold; & there is sun every day! I do hope your pains have vanished. Thanks for the Catalogue of Pothook-books.[1] Here is the address of

> <u>Jean Thouverez.</u>
> <u>58 Cours de Tourny</u>
> B.

I hope Colin will write <u>as soon as he can</u> (expatiating on his football if he likes, as Jean is not a <u>student, but heroic at football</u>). Only supervise Colin's spelling, eh?

Fondest Love. W

242. To Susan Owen

6 March 1914   *Bordeaux*

Dearest Mother,

There is still no break in the work, so I can only scratch you a letter, in the hour between 'Dessert' & the 2 o'clock Lesson. On Wednesday I had a grand bust-up with M. Aumont and told him there was enough work for <u>3</u> profs. He agreed, but is unwilling to engage another, because ther<u>e</u> is certain to be a slackening at Easter, i.e. in a month's time. However if <u>one</u> more pupil engages this week, another 'speaking-apparatus' sha<u>ll</u> be ordered from England.

But I should not use the term <u>speaking-apparatus</u>: we are very much more than mechanical tongue-waggers, & the early Method Lessons are a severe tax on one's ingenuity.

Nevertheless, tho' the work is such & so much, it is not <u>wearing</u> me. I only complain because I have no time to write English, or to speak French, nor yet to <u>think</u> in any language whatever.

Such a state of <u>things</u> must not be allowed to continue, and this very week I shall write to Nice & other Berlitz Schools enquiring for vacancies. M. Aumont himself suggested this, for, he says, the work is certainly less in smaller school.

You see, it doesn't pay me at all, at all to give supplementary lessons. I am ashamed of myself for doing it. And I find Extra Work necessi-

---

[1] The Pitmans catalogue asked for in Letter 240.

tates extra eating—I consume no end of Chocolate. I make money for this by doing a few translations (for a member of the *Union*) of business letters, Advertisements, etc., which are to find their way all over the world. I do them at a tariff more profitable than the lessons:—and I get an insight into Business Matters & Manners without having the stigma of *Employé de Commerce*.

If only I could get to Nice for the Spring!—(where I could bathe betimes, and smell cool winds in June.)

I would fain make my 'Return to Nature' at such a place: I should do well to creep out of my present burrow on the Côte d'Azur, or at Sorrento and Amalfi, by the blue Italian Seas.

Tho', the city of Bordeaux, as such, is very far from disagreeable! I am better six months here without one 'Saturday Afternoon', than six weeks in Birmingham, Liverpool, or any such Conglomeration (save London) of Humankind.

On Sundays I am (usually) wondrous happy. As with you the air was very clear last Sunday, at about 5 or 6 o'clock, and here everything bore the full 'April Gleam.' It was for me a time of elevation, in all respects equivalent to Divine-Service-at-half-past six.

I went again to Lem's.[1] (Pronounce Raoul as Rowl.) He would be a perfectly suitable companion for Colin. They are Protestants; the Mother is a pious little woman; the father is a worthy man, but very 'bourgeois', if so much as [*one word illegible*]. I am not sure whether their French is very distinguished, but later I shall be better able to judge whether Raoul's is a fit accent for Colin & Mary to learn. I told them you could take him *en pension* for 20s. a week,[2] and they thought that quite moderate. I could not hear of your doing it for less, and he must give one or two hrs. of French to us at that.

I am still scratching with an ordinary pen, but have begun to give anxious looks into the Post Box every time I pass it. I thank you very heartily for the Waverley, the more so as I know it has received your Blessing!

There is a book which I specially want at the present moment: It is Shelley's Collected Poems, the Oxford Edition.[3] If the three Kindred would like to contribute to it I should be enchanted. In any case I must have it, &, considering Postage etc. I don't think India Paper, Leather-Covered Form (about 3s.) would come much more expensive than the ordinary, rather bulky volume. If the price is too high for my brethren you must deduct from my Christmas money. But let me have it immediately, as my Pupil who wishes to read it with me has already her book.

The Oxford Poets is sufficient indication to the bookseller's. It is just a year since I was on the verge of buying this very volume, but I remember I decided on something else!

[1] M. Lem lived at 12 rue St. Louis, Bordeaux.
[2] When Raoul stayed at Mahim, he was treated as a guest. Tom Owen would accept no payment. See *JO* III, ch. 4.
[3] *The Complete Poetical Works of Percy Bysshe Shelley*, ed. Thomas Hutchinson, Oxford University Press, London, 1905.

I have another Commission to trouble you with, and for this you must again draw on my Christmas Moneys. Order, if you please, six (6) copies of *How to speak Esperanto*.[1] 1d. each.

The Farringdon Press,
180 Fleet St. E.C.

They are for a pupil; who will pay me. Please tell me total expenses!

I do hope Colin has written to Jean Thouverez. No reason why he should not write to both boys; he can say the same thing to each. In future, letters to Jean may be posted as enclosures to your letters. I will deliver them.

I marvel Harold has not 'made a move', neither by acceptance by the (*one word illegible*] nor by rejection by Papa. It makes me mad. Your accounts of his occupations[2] made me furious; (it was quite like being at home.)

I suppose Father was not long in Torquay? How is he? [*three words illegible*] When is Father coming to Bordeaux? and When are You? . . . How are You? Who is Mary? . . . (Herself I hope.) What is Harold? . . .

I am that Being that for 21 years has lived as your dear-loving,

Child

243. To Susan Owen
Postcard

Thursday [Postmark 13 March 1914]   [*Postmark Bordeaux*]

It must seem horrid of me not to have answered your Sunday's letter till now. But in fact I half wrote a letter on Monday; but to finish was a physical impossible: On Wednesday I did Eleven Hours of Lessons!!! with no worse effect than a slight 'scrape' of throat. What better testimonial could you desire to my present health & ultimate soundness of constitution. I haven't the least headache, tho' I would willingly relieve you of yours if I could—the idea of your suffering is my one source of discomfort. But I have had yr. letter of Monday & deeply hope you are better.

Yr. own W

Am charmed with the Pen,[3] 1000 thanks!

244. To Susan Owen
15 March 1914   *Bordeaux*

My darling Mother,

I thought and searched in vain for any object (encloseable in a letter) which might act the part of a Present:[4] but the delicacy of these scissors

---

[1] A copy of *Esperanto for the Million* (Penny Series) survives among Wilfred's books.
[2] HO was still at sea. His adventures in and around South American ports in 1914 are recorded in *JO* I I I.
[3] Wilfred's twenty-first birthday was not until 18 March.
[4] Susan Owen's birthday was 17 March, St. Patrick's Day.

pleased me, & may please you. Though Nail Scissors are not peculiarly delicate Birthday Presents . . . Nevertheless are they not symbolic of those dread Scissors of the Fate, which more than once have forborne to cut our thin thread of life?

For the first time, I am writing to you with my Fountain Pen. It is a most elegant shape, and of course does not leak or blob. I have not systematised my writing yet, as you well see, simply for lack of time; but if I spent too long in the pursuit of a model style, I should end in changing the present European Characters entirely.

Dear Mother, your headaches seem interminable. I cannot find any definite expressions to account for it, but I know the significance of your last-but-one Letter made my spirit mourn all Sunday. I yearn to know that, compared with last year, your health is really more satisfactory. Am I to understand the contrary? On Monday I started to write some advice to you, which was something like this: (1) to come and stay a while in Bordeaux and experience an absolute change in everybody you see, hear or communicate with: (N.B. except me) & an absolute change in everything you see, hear, breathe, eat or drink. Or, failing this (2) To pillow yourself in bed; close down the blinds of your room, surround yourself with perfumes and flowers, feed on fish, milk, honey and wine; forbid any sound to reach you—whether alleged as musical or not, and depute the least and greatest household matters to Mary.

And, if you must have any excuse for such idleness, (and genuine idleness it must be) let the memory of your deeds of a year ago[1] speak, and make music in your soul.

But what on earth do I hear in your next letter? [*three lines illegible*] I must not make a single comment, but you may know my state of mind on hearing this. I ramped about all day, and gave my pupils the dickens of a time. I should not have done eleven lessons but for that; but I did eleven lessons; and would do anything now to preserve your strength [*one word illegible*] Let not such a birthday message discourage you! I am mightily bucked up. I begin to realise.

Forgive a longer letter; I am only sustained by the blessed air of this place, and woe is me if I do not take it when I can.

And I am not yet twenty-one and the good resolutions are not made. 'Never do anything today if it can possibly be done tomorrow' is still my motto. I pass into my twenty-first year very far from serene; but yet I would not forget so many things as I would fain remember and experience once more. There are not many individuals with whom I would change Personality if I could. And I know I have lived more than my twenty-one years, many more; and so have a start of most lives.

I have yet to open the supreme present you made me on the day of my birth. I must not thank my Parents for any precious thing in my composition until I know it is there. I certainly[2] have Hopes; the value

---

[1] Nursing Wilfred through his illness.
[2] 'Still' struck out.

of which is that of the cotton-wool enveloping the gold; but as my hopes are heavy on my soul, it is a good portent; there may be worth therein. For the rest, I have no long confessional to make [*seven lines illegible*]

Was so glad to have good news of Mary.

Thank for all the birthday wishes I know they will be sending.

I shall expect a letter from Father on Wednesday?

Do thank them at Torquay: but I can't think of anything: would rather wait.

245. To Susan Owen
Postcard

Thursday 19th [*Postmark 19 March 1914*]   [*Postmark Bordeaux*]

If I started letters at this time o'night (10.30) I should be like a log tomorrow morning! I don't know what's in store for tomorrow but I do hope to get some time for thanking you all at length for all the dear letters I have received. The 18th was much like other days, except that I had the Evening Lessons taken off, and went to dine with my latest friend,[1] a new pupil, boy of 14, who has an extraordinary aptitude for languages. His father is a Primary School Teacher, & his mother also. I had a most enjoyable evening, & will not forget to tell you more. Shelley is a magnificent present. It arrived in perfect condition. Leslie also sent me a little Tennyson; & I had letters from Torquay. Convey my thanks for Seaton's[2] card please. Au revoir Till morrow.

W

Had your card this mng: thanks so much for Esperanto Business. Rejoiced to hear Headaches are at least relieved.

246. To Susan Owen
Postcard

Saturday [*Postmark 28 March 1914*]   [*Postmark Bordeaux*]

I am writing between the courses at my lunch. Have had another week of incessant travail. Hope you have carried my thanks to Torquay & Alpenrose. I shall try & write tomorrow; but don't know what to say about the present they would send me. I had your last card, & shall be expecting your letter tomorrow. I have of course delivered Colin's letter to Jean; but hope he will soon write again at some length. We

---

[1] Pierre Berthaud (see Letter 292) was in correspondence with Susan Owen after the war. He wrote to her from Bordeaux on 14 February 1925: 'Yes, Wilfred came very frequently home; he was coming every two or three days, to teach me English, and I remember that he spent his 20th [21st] birthday with us. My mother loved him. He was such a fine, a charming, a perfect fellow. . . . I had been in acquaintance with him in 1913, or 1912, at the Berlitz School. He lived then at No. 95, rue Porte-Dijeaux. My family invited him home, and he took several times dinner with us.' Earlier, on 27 December 1920, he had written of '. . . the unhappy death of my dearest friend'.

[2] The Seatons lived next door to Mahim.

had 4 weeks of daily rain, but not cold. Today is magnificent. The Moss Steamers[1] were 8 days in getting here last week!

What Easter Holidays are you having? I shan't get more than one day, but expect an easier time thereabout. If not . . .!! My pen keeps very well; but I wish I could give it more to do!

Always your own Wilfred

247. To Susan Owen
Postcard

Wednesday [*Postmark 8 April 1914*]   [*Postmark Bordeaux*]

On receiving your Card I was not desolated, for I wd. as well have an extra week-end after Easter, and just on Saturday there wd. surely be a pandemonium travelling. But now I have your letter and there is no more likelihood of a *recontre* at La Rochelle I am indeed undone, even as H, as he saith, is <u>done</u>. I feel for your vicissitudes and my Hopes go thro' the same gymnastic movements as your own, according to the instructions you send. I wonder indeed whether there will be a break-up of the Home[2] at Show Time. Whether I shall be among the scattered remnants which return I know not; but this must be considered. I hear such accounts of the July Heats of Bordeaux that in any case I must shift somewhere. Up to today has been no abatement of work but (1) Thurs. aft. (2) Sat. Aft. (3) All Monday are to be free. Shall then get together some letters. I may go into country with the good family Lem for Sunday & Monday!

Fondest Love to all. W

248. To Tom and Susan Owen

Saturday, 11 April 1914   *Bordeaux*

My dear Father & Mother,

[*opening lines missing*] Full many times in your recent letters, you incline to dissuade me this year. 'Your <u>reason</u> does not say <u>come</u>.' yet etc.

It will depend, of course, on what <u>you think</u> of my <u>entering</u> R.[3] as an Educational Student in October—but suppose I decide not to—when am <u>I going to see you again</u>? When, in [*line missing*] your letter consenting to my speedy return could not reach me till April 15th. Allowing 15 days for finishing [*one line missing*] anything but a [*several words missing*] on your Fortunes. In 1915 the £70 award is definitely announced. Either I wait for that (Examination) or I qualify (by passing Matric in Geography) as a Primary Student. I was certainly wise to shy at attempting the Double Course last October as in 1915 [*one line missing*]

---

[1] Steamers run by James Moss & Co., Liverpool. They plied throughout the war.
[2] Accommodation in Shrewsbury during the annual Show was at a premium. Tom Owen had been offered up to £30 a night for a room (Mahim overlooked the Race Course where the Show was held). On all but one occasion (see p. 263, note 2) he refused.
[3] Reading.

Tomorrow I go with the Lems to a country place, Castelnau,[1] not very distant, but in the heart of the Médoc. How much rather would I be watching the port of La Rochelle, for the merry midshipman! [*one or two lines missing*] I cross the Alps it will be harder to get back again.

I had no replies from the schools on the Riviera, and judge this sufficient indication that there are no vacancies. However as I have since discovered that the addresses I used (following a list not up-to-date) are in each case incorrect, I shall write once more: and also, with your consent, to Italian ones. Naples, says the Italian Professor, is [*several lines missing*]

I hope old Colin writes to Jean. I shall invite Jean to dine with me, one day this week [*several lines missing*]

Good Friday is not observed here (contrary to the ideas of the innocent Anglican-pro-Catholics) and we had no holiday. If English people had an inkling of what this people's religion consists of . . . but Father Duncan[2] knows . . .

I do hope I shall get your letter before I start in the morning, and that you are not impatient [over] this.

Your own W

249. To Leslie Gunston

Picture postcard: Castelnau-de-Médoc, La Gare

[*Postmark 13 April 1914*]   [*Postmark Castelnau-de-Médoc*]

Beloved L,

I breathe at last—and have escaped among the Médoc Pines to enjoy my short liberty to the full. Am sending a card to warn you of a following letter, lest the shock of receiving a letter from you might be injurious. Have had an intoxicatingly happy day—the cause was not the Vintage —guess what?

Au Revoir W

250. To Mary Owen

15 April 1914   *Bordeaux*

My own dear Sister,

Exceeding joyful was I to see your handwriting in my letter-box on Tuesday Morning; and the more so when I read of how you spent your Easter; how you thought of holy things; how you remembered me; and how you walked out, seeking the new flowers. To you then, shall I deliver such account of my own doing as is meet and right I should; hoping it will 'amuse your heart and instruct your mind'—(nay: I prefer to change the old formula, and to say 'amuse your mind, and instruct your heart.')

A soon as Rochelle scheme was impossiblised (is this English, I

[1] Castelnau-de-Médoc, ten miles NE of Bordeaux. There is a lyrical description of this Easter week-end in Letter 250.

[2] The Rev. F. N. Duncan, Vicar of St. Julian's, Shrewsbury, 1904–16.

forget?) I told the Lems I should be glad to accept their offer. I had twice met the eldest daughter of 'the Inviter's'[1] at Lem's house, and as she spoke good French, had pleasant manners, and was only good looking in a large and vague sense, I said—now here's an opportunity for two days' real peace.

I joined the Lems at 7.30 on Easter Morning, inside my old green suit,[2] old boots, old tie, sans cuffs, gloves or hair-parting; prepared for a rare escapade in the country; so was a little abashed to find Raoul in his very best, cuffs protruding shirt-front bulging; all prognosticating that either we were going to a fine family or that some member of it had fine eyes. The first member we saw at Castelnau put me at ease an ancient man, in wooden boots, corkscrew trousers, and a coat twice as ancient as himself. But lo! waiting for us at the station-gates, stood the young lady I already knew in costume as modern as her grandfather's were antique; and with her a superb specimen of human beauty, the younger sister of sixteen!

I walked behind them to the House feeling mighty queer. There, I was presented to the Mother, a pleasant dame of conical figure that continually put me in mind of a broody hen; and to the grandmother, who began weeping forthwith; and made me thrice welcome, as she said, for the sake of her darling grandson, who has been in Algeria six months; then, entered the father, with his dog & gun, a brown and handsome figure, with dark and terrible eyes, in rustic clothes & sabots, as scorning to appear anything but what he was, plain proprietor of vineyards. So we sat around the best room; looking at the inevitable album of post-cards, while various children of the family's dependents were exhibited before us, and the grandmother, all heart and kindliness, moved round and round the room in tears, sure that the grandson must be deadly ill in that far land.

Then all but *Mère* & *Grandmère*, (who had dinner to see to) went into the woods. I took the side of the eighty-year grandfather, and we spoke of France, and of her Past. There were multitudes on multitudes of primroses & violets, gigantic marsh-marigolds, of which a little peasant boy who followed us, gathered bunches for me; which bunches Mme. Lem contrived to make me present to the right fair lady. Her name I soon learnt was Henriette—(abominable, while her sister's is so pleasing—Armande!) Knowing her beauty was of the stimulating, & quickly-effective kind, I was watching Raoul, and at dinner his restiveness began. For my part I could only sit like an Egyptian piece of Statuary, hands on knees, staring apparently into space; but seeing well enough to count how often the marvellous eyes looked in my direction, which was exactly four times per minute. Finally, Raoul made a complete ass of himself, and H. fled from the table, and locked herself up for half an hour.

---

[1] M. Poitou. All we know of his family is in this letter, 252, and 258, where the elder daughter's engagement is reported.
[2] This appears again in 1917. See Letter 538.

In the afternoon all went to the oakwoods. Old man Lem is a merry old elephant, and in the woods ran here and there, capering and singing for pure delight. Raoul retired behind a tree and mildly sulked. I, strung up, paced along, stiff as a frightened cat. Then the blessed quiet of the woods, the subdued sunshine, the cuckoos and the nightingales worked on us all. Old man L. quieted down, I grew more at ease, Raoul returned. We reached an opening in the trees, where the oaks gave place to blossom-trees, a dance was proposed. Father L. set the time with voice and hands; but I spoilt the fun by not having the faintest notion of how to step!

In France the afternoons are long, and there was time for a second walk before the *Collation du Soir*. For this occasion, Henriette fished up a plump friend from the village, clearly to be a buffer between herself and Raoul. This time we walked arm in arm. I could scarcely have been happier. Raoul might clearly have been happier than he was; but it was hardly my fault. And the memory of those moments will remain sweet to me, chiefly, my dear Sister, chiefly because I took no advantage of that young and ardent nature, neither even said what I thought of her 'appas', but left the compliments, with the vows, to Raoul. Perhaps I listened with too much sympathy to her plaints of captivity: how she is watched and warded everywhere: not even allowed to visit people in Bordeaux; but has no gayer, nobler, or learned companions but the grandmother, everlastingly regretting her grandson; the little villagers; the father forever lauding his wines; and a professor who prepares her for an examination.

At dinner, Papa enjoyed himself hugely with astonishing the company by the ancient bottles of Médoc which he brought forth from time to time. The corks were opened with alarms and flourishes; and a little lecture on the harvests of the various years. Finally we got back to 1870!! It is needless to say that not one of the convivial guests overdid his proper number of glasses!

Before the dessert, Madame Poitou insisted on reading publicly the last letter from her son, (which was six times as long and circumstantial as my own) describing his adventures with some English girls in the mountains of Algeria: including such minute & numerous remarks on the character and appearance of one of them, as led to sage comments by the old people, and gave me an opportunity to exhort his sisters to learn English without delay. Afterwards they all begged me to write a message in English to the boy; which, when I translated it, delighted them beyond measure.

I shared a bedroom with Raoul. Perhaps it was the air of the pine forests (forests not woods) that made each breath a thing of joy—or perhaps it was the agitated calling of the nightingales; but I did not sleep well.

On Monday Morning, Raoul, his Father, & M. Poitou, instructed me upon the vineyards, and we spent the morning viewing the country, and picking snails from the new-budding plants.

Lunch took an immense time—and there was only time for a game of *cache-cache* about the farm before the four o'clock train. Raoul, at the last moment, got leave to stay till Wednesday; when he will come back with Armande, who will stay at Lem's for a fortnight.

Twenty minutes we waited at the window of the train, and the adieus were many. Rich masses of lilac encumbered the carriage, and the odour was carried by the inblowing breeze into my brain, to be an everlasting memory. Then those faces and those places fell away from me.

The city, at 6 o'clock, was strangely hot and empty, save of dust and glare; and back in my room, I underwent a sad reaction. But I recovered; and soon demonstrated how much I was benefited by the excursion, by writing 50 lines of poetry in as many minutes! (thing not attempted for 'years'); and by getting better results out of a piano than much practice could give; and by generally soaking my specs. in that rosey liquid young blood; so that all people, all plants, all tasks, all books, appear to me far fairer than they did.

Sunday

I have kept back these pages just a little too long: but I can now acknowledge the Thursday Letter of dear Mother; and felicitate Harold on his eventually getting on *La Esmeraldas*[1]—prettier name, for one thing, than 'Carcoodoodledo'. I wonder whether Harold will have the opportunity to learn Spanish. Let him not take a S. American Spaniard; their pronunciation is bad.

Poof! here I am on 'Languages' again: a subject which gives me pain; for I am learning a hundredth part of what I teach which isn't fair!

I certainly never undertook to inculcate Slang upon my brethren; but don't thank me because you are a purist; for I have tried to make you pedants, and thank Minerva, you are not that yet.

Miss Hewitt had a day or so's notice to bundle off to—(Ha! Slang! be cheesed, vile slang!) that is to transfer herself to Angers. Another Miss has taken her place for this week but is going next week to Germany. 'The One remains; the many change and pass.'[2]

M. Aumont mentioned that he hoped I should now remain till August; but if I am given so much and so little as I have been given, I shall do no such thing. I already know several persons who would like private lessons with me. . . .

I commend you to God who surely fends you; and to our sweet Mother who no less tends you; I, who am your devoted and very-much-elder

Brother

251. To Susan Owen

Picture postcard: Paris. Monument de Gambetta, Place du Carrousel

[*Postmark 27 April 1914*]   [*Postmark Bordeaux*]

I haven't an instant to spare today as the one sole hour unoccupied by

[1] HO's ship.   [2] Shelley, *Adonais*, LII.

school has been spent at Dentists! I have 6 or 8 cavities to be filled!!
Fortunately the dentists here are not dear only 3 f. per tooth. I had a
joyous time yesterday, & learnt 5 dances! But will tell you more when
can. Tomorrow Dentist again! Do hope you are righting yourself again.

252. To Susan Owen

Wednesday, 29 April 1914   *Bordeaux*

My dearest Mother,

Respecting your long letter of the 24th, I am extremely sorry about
the Bills, of Shields[1] in particular; and still more so that it is not in my
power to remit anything towards their payment. Remember that my
smaller expenses are innumerable: various parts of clothing have to be
renewed from time to time: boots to be repaired, lamp-oil, alcohol for
lamp, matches, (50 a penny) soap, baths, hair-cut, socks, razor, paper
& papers, washing, all these consume my 'Supplements'; and now that
eight teeth of mine have to be stopped, my small margin of gains will
vanish entirely.

So soon, however, as I find a residue of 40 f. in my purse I shall
certainly let you have it, always keeping enough for the home journey.

You must not be troubled with the idea of my wasting my substance
in smoke! I cannot be said to smoke. It is only true that I have smoked.

In your relation of a certain dream which visited your slumber, you
conveyed a certain element of warning to me, and also, methought, of
anxiety about me.

The warning I willingly accept, but the anxiety I can utterly explode.
I am not subject to the least temptations to excess, either from within
or without.

Only in an aesthetical and ideal, or else in a 10 f-per-bottle and
Chateau-Yquem way, has Wine any seduction for me.

Alack, you will have been shocked at my dancing!

First, it was *Dimanche*; and though *Dimanche* is quite another thing
than Sunday, still you have not lived (happily) in this country, and do
not realise how irresistibly Convention, French Convention, operates
on the conscience, and, without deteriorating character, dissolves away
the traces of what I may call 'Keswick Convention'. When, therefore, the
Lems invited me to a *Sauterie* I was not likely to refuse, and to choose to
spend the afternoon mooching, ruminating, or mooing languages. If
you were Aunt Emma, I should fall back on Theory and Casuistry, and
show how much more preferable a thing it is to take exercise by a
rhythmical movement of the feet, treading so to speak on Music, instead
of an ambling perambulation on pavement-dust. But it is enough to tell
you that I had a rare time, and among delightful young people.

Mlle. Poitou was indeed there, but we did not dance together because

[1] The tailor.

246

both of us needed a strong partner. On the whole I was less pleased with her than at first. Extraordinary to relate every one of the score of demoiselles there was handsome, with two or three exceptions. One of the exceptions was the gay and kindly lass who undertook my training. A blind man's piano was our only orchestra!

Of course everybody wore afternoon dress, and danced in walking-boots, and the dust raised by the Gigs was stifling! However my dry throat next morning was useful at the Dentists; as it dispensed with the sucking-apparatus.

Friday

I have been put off finishing this, chiefly by the Dentist. I have now had eight holes filled up. The decay was only just beginning, so I had no great sufferings to undergo. Strange enough, one of the wisdom-teeth, which has scarcely emerged from the gums has been attacked: and the dentist had to burn away the gum with an infernal red-hot iron. Afterwards my mouth tasted like an overdone beefsteak.

These operations have tired me for today, and now at 11 p.m. I have only time to trudge away to the G.P.O. before sleep assails me.

I think specially often of you just now, and only hope you are not any worse than you give me to understand. A few weeks in Bordeaux, I do seriously think, would do you mighty good; but, there you are, and there you will be.

I heard from Miss Hewitt for the first time yesterday; likes the Box very well; only has some 20 lessons a week, & is thankful to have seen the last of the Bordeaux Pupils!

There are now other Boxes for sale: among them, I believe, Nantes, which prospers exceedingly! If I could buy it, I should be assured of a turn-over of 20,000 f, i.e. £800. a year! How do uncles lack in perspicacity, (benevolence out of the question!)

Always your tenderly-loving Wilfred

253. To Mary Owen

Sunday, 10 May 1914   *Bordeaux*

My dear Sister,

Here is six o'clock on Sunday Afternoon, and unless I seize the moment and my pen and paper, you will be kept waiting for an answer to your letter indefinitely. I read your letter about 9 o'clock, and then fell back on my pillow and snored for another two hours. Then feeling I had cleared off any debts I owed to Morpheus, I made my first toilet, and collected my towels & soaps and 'clean things' and walked to my bath-room, (which is quarter of a mile away!) & paid 6d. for a few gallons of water!

Returned I made my Second Toilet, and prepared a dinner: for it is my custom on Sundays to eat in my room. On all other days I am at a

Restaurant. Then I went out to read with my friend Bizardel,[1] and had a pleasant time under the chestnut-trees of his garden. This young man was until lately in the Banque de France, and now he is studying Law at home. His father is a judge.

On my way home, I noticed an imposing Funeral Service was being held in an old Church, and I went in. The gloom, the incense, the draperies, the shine of many candles, the images and ornaments, were what may be got anywhere in England; but the solemn voices of the priests was what I had never heard before. The melancholy of a bass voice, mourning, now alone, now in company with other voices or with music, was altogether fine; as fine as the Nightingale—(bird or poem). And although the chanting was Latin, yet was it more intelligible to the human soul than could be statements distinctly enunciated in the vernacular. (I hope you will at least try to understand me) So that I fell, only for a few minutes, it is true, under the spell of the Catholic Religion, and re-entered a phase of my Experience which had been buried under three or four successive and different phases of thought. The illusion soon passed and I spent the rest of the time considering this form of religion, from aloof.

There was only one fault in the Funeral Ceremony, which if it were intentional would be chiefest beauty of all. It was the Undertakers' Men. They wore imitation top-hats and kept them on in the church. What these articles were made of I cannot imagine, but their hideous shininess was most fascinating. Also, the men were noisy of foot, clumsy of hand, brutal of face. Now if these creatures had functioned in the disguise of skeletons or demons, they could not have been more abominable, and as their duties cannot be anything but abominable to the mourners, perhaps it is a stroke of real art to let them be as horrible as possible!

I suppose Grandpa is already buried.[2] I wonder where.

I was glad to have some account of your confirmation. I know who is the Bishop of Lichf'd. I remember studying his work as Rector of Liverpool, recounted in 'the Treasury' many years ago. His face also is quite familiar. I almost remember his name: something like Kempenfelt,[3] I think?

I never hear from you as to what you are reading. Circumstances considered, I am of course more pleased to hear of your industry in the house than of your much reading, and busying yourself with imaginary circumstances in which you will never be called upon to act.

But circumstances re-considered, nothing would be more painful to me than that you, most serious of sisters, were not more read and more instructed than the fast type of schoolgirl which you despise.

[1] On the outbreak of war in August he was working in the offices of the Prefect of Bordeaux. See Letter 284, note 1.
[2] Grandfather Owen died in Torquay at the beginning of May. His wife survived him by several years.
[3] The Rt. Rev. John Augustine Kempthorne (1862–1946), formerly Bishop of Hull, Bishop of Lichfield 1913–37.

Vb. Wilfred at Castel Lorenzo with Laurent Tailhade,
September 1914

Va. Castel Lorenzo, about 1914
The figure on the left may be Madame Léger

VI. The audience at the Casino, Bagnères-de-Bigorre, 17 August 1914

Front row, l. to r.: Mme Cazalas, Wilfred, Mme Léger, Nénette Léger

(see Letter 285)

Therefore I hope you are serious in reading at least one genuine book per fortnight; and if the Book is Jeremiah or Jude, so much the better.

I wonder who are now your friends. Have you any bosom friend, or are they all of the arm's length variety? I have read more than once in your letters of some Miss H— who, you confess, is 'shoppy'.[1] Now that is distressing. The fact of being employed in a shop does not matter; but shoppiness does matter.

Do you ever write to Dorothy, or she to you?

You may ask me what friend I ever made among the living of this world; [*eight lines illegible*]

I have half a dozen students of Bordeaux University with whom I might become intimate, but the sad pity of it is that I am as much a prisoner from social life as any wretch in the jail. Yes, and the galling part of it is that Leisure here would be so much more precious than in Shrewsbury.

Heaven knows I appreciate such leisure as I ever had, and used it, I hope, not ill; but here I could amuse myself so admirably. Thus I could any morning see the Surgical Operations of the Hospitals under the protection of a student who has invited me; or any afternoon attend the Sessions of the Law Courts, under the protection of an eminent advocate who is my pupil.

I shall have to spend here at least a fortnight living on my capital after my Engagement is done with.

(*Mond.*) Here follows a message to Mother: I have now received my Back-Supplements, and cashed the cheque this afternoon. I find I have more than £5. I am therefore able to pay my passage.

Now my green suit which, it will be remembered was bought, a ready-made article, about midsummer 1911, is still going strong, but I foresee a sudden collapse not far off. Thus I have only one suit left, whether for the exercise of my profession, or (as I remind myself) for garden-parties, or Royal Functions. Just when I perceive this, I find myself in a position to save 20s. by buying a suit immediately; for Monsieur Dubo through the intervention of some friend, can get stuffs at Tailor's Prices from Paris, and in fact a fine selection of Spring-Summer Patterns is in my room at present. The total costs would be between 50 and 60 francs. Ought I to take this opportunity? . . .

I once more address myself to you, dear Sister, to beg you to understand how hastily I am writing, which makes it impossible to revise any weird things I may have said. May it be not long before I see you all again.

Adieu!

Need I add: my warmest Love for Dear Mother, Father and Childe Colin.

---

[1] Common. Miss H—, whose name we omit, was a dispenser in Boots, Shrewsbury.

254. To Susan Owen
Postcard

Wednes.[1] [*Postmark 13 May 1914*]   [*Postmark Bordeaux*]

Your card reached me this morning & I was glad to have assurance of your healths, and am glad to be able to give you the same assurance of myself. Weather is not too hot, but summerish all the same. I do between 8 and 9 lessons now, and any time between is seized by my student-friends, who want help with translations of Kipling! Shall enclose Harold's letter in a few days. I don't suppose you'll see any real aerobatics at Robertsford?[2] Let Colin give me an account.

Your loving W

255. To Leslie Gunston

[? *late May 1914*]   First sheets missing   [*Bordeaux*]

spent many years in Italy, & they cannot praise it enough. We call them the Milano Brothers. Florence is crammed with English, I hear. An impossible place. I should like a job at an Italian University, say Milan, which is very Italian.

Now, O.A.J's[3] FATE is a very beautiful poem, very lovely. I do not find that the riming of the same word [is] at all upsetting: and, believe me, a wrong rime is often the right thing to do. Ah! you sea-green incorruptible! Aristocrrrat! *À bas les tyrans!*

As for Sunrise, no glimmer of light has yet begun to break through its obscurity. A better title would be 'Eternal Midnight', or 'The Retreat of the Dubious Doors, to the tune of Hail, smiling morn'

Don't repeat this: but praise Fate for all you are worth.

I thought I would try a Roundel. I find it exceedingly easy to write one without having either emotion or ideas.

Thus: Roundel on the Statue of Hercules reposing from his Labours in the Quarry, Shrewsbury:

Roundel[4]

In Shrewsbury Town e'en Hercules wox tired,
   Tired of the streets that end not up nor down;
   Tired of the Quarry, though seats may be hired
          Of Shrewsbury Town.

Tired of the tongues that knew not his renown;
   Tired of the Quarry Bye-Laws, so admired
   By the Salopian, the somnambulant clown.

---

[1] Wilfred wrote Tuesday. The pencil correction is in Susan Owen's hand.

[2] This seems a slip for Robertsbridge, Sussex.

[3] Olwen Joergens, daughter of an artist friend and neighbour of the Gunstons at Kidmore End. She, LG, and Wilfred exchanged poems on set subjects. See Letter 484. *The Woman and the Sage* (The Little Books of Georgian Verse, Erskine Macdonald, London, 1916), a collection of her poems, survives among Wilfred's books.

[4] Not in *Poems*.

> Weak as a babe, and in likewise attired,
> He leaned upon his club; frowned a last frown,
> And of ineffable boredom, so expired
> > In Shrewsbury Town.

Thanks for sending Parcel, which I never hope to have. Please don't send *P. Review*.[1] I have May–June from home. Rather Footy, as you say! I think I have had all your letters. The last to arrive (yesterday) was of may 5th! Very best wishes for your Exam. I hope it will soon be over for my sake and the Epistles'.

Love to all   Your most affectionate W.E.O.

I will send 'How do I love thee'[2] in my next.

256. To Susan Owen
Postcard

Sunday Night [*Postmark 17 May 1914*]   [*Postmark Bordeaux*]

I rejoice to acknowledge your cards of the 13th & 15th for it seems that you are really better, & that Mary & Colin keep well to say nothing of Father.

Instead of your cold, dull weather the last fortnight has been here a *temps splendide*. Small difference they make to me—these brilliant mornings; and of the balmy evenings I reck no whit;—but I verily think a number of pupils will 'drop off' during the next 15 days. Meanwhile I hang on. It is always something to eat and sleep like a beast; which I do; even if my days profit me no more than if I worked a treadmill. At least I have taken my rest today. I have refused to give Sunday-Lessons, which lately a certain dummy of a pupil has demanded. But Tofield[3] gives it,—for the money!

Fondest Love. W

257. To Susan Owen
Postcard

Friday [*Postmark 22 May 1914*]   [*Postmark Bordeaux*]

Your letter reached me on Wednes. On Thursday I went into the Country with the Y.M.C.A. & Y.W.C.A. & Boy Scouts, & had Jean Thouverez to dinner with me, so that the early reply to your ?? will not reach you till Sunday, alas. But I do not recommend Arcachon[4] for Father's holiday. It is an expensive place, the resort of Parisians even. I should have not time unless I resigned, & immediately. If you would come over too, we might all three have a rare time hereabouts: but you

---

[1] *The Poetry Review*, founded in 1912 by Harold Monro (1879–1932). Wilfred met Monro in 1915. See Letters 386 *et seq*.
[2] This poem cannot be traced.
[3] See Letter 199.
[4] Coastal resort twenty miles S W of Bordeaux.

will treat the idea as absurd, I know. Yesterday, a real heat-wave swept down on us. There is no refuge from the temperature, out of doors or indoors, night or day. Expect me presently: Lessons do not abate at all, still less is it likely the temperature will. I am sorely concerned about your digestion. Is it any comfort to know I am really body-whole.

258. To Susan Owen

24 May 1914   *Bordeaux*

My dearest Mother,

I wonder what Father will have arranged about his holidays. I hope you have not been waiting since Friday to hear from me. On Thursday, as I said, I was out of Bordeaux all day; and on Wednesday all I could do between the lessons was to sprawl on my armchair, and watch through half-shut eyelids my little fingers tremblingly dropping dew on the floor.

It is a blessing that lessons can be given sitting down. And I am always cooler than my pupils, who (haven't I seen 'em from the balcony!) scorch through the streets and scramble upstairs like a mad motor-car in a Cinema, lest they should miss two minutes of their sixty. Yesterday, one pupil fell faint and couldn't go on, but needless to say, this happened exactly 4 mins. before the end of the lesson.

Today it is much cooler, after a night-thunderstorm.

I suppose now I must talk about myself or you will not consider this as a letter. Such self-expatiation makes letter-writing not only an unwholesome habit, but a distasteful task. Wouldn't it be better to invent things about acquaintances, till they seemed interesting to you; or relate weird things of pupils (no need of invention here) or even translate from local journals? Or, if I were dear . . . I might note how glorious was that last Lobster-Mayonnaise; or if I were . . . might specify what boats were in the docks, and how many tons each displaced; or if I were . . . I might babble of Victor Hugo, and why he is the greatest possible of all the grandest, and also the highest, deepest, and thickest, and toughest.

But it happens I am full of thoughts about myself which it will be relief to expel.

It was curious you asked about my grey hairs, for just last week I noticed they were cropping up again. In winter they died down, with the grass. My face is certainly satisfactory, as regards skin & muscle, free from whelks and knobs and mud-volcanoes; but whether 'of lovely colour' as your dreams reveal, depends on the light. But I wish Dr. Carrel[1] (who startled the world by exchanging people's hearts, putting

---

[1] Alexis Carrel (1873–1944), French-American by birth, had been awarded the Nobel Prize in 1912. Among his publications was a paper in the *Journal of the American Medical Association*, 14 November 1908, 'Results of the transplantation of blood vessels, organs, and limbs'. With a medical colleague he later became widely known for work in the treatment of war wounds (the 'Carrel-Dakin Method').

in monkey's gizzards for rhino's giblets, sausage-skins for wind-pipes, pig's tails for ladies fingers (the last operations are confined to America, I notice))—I wish the man would put-me-in a new skull,—nothing less will help my profile. When that little job had been satisfactorily arranged, I would give in exchange my brain and heart (for they are but snares to me), for various other parts; e.g.

Pair of Eyes, which I would seek in France,

Mouth & Fittings, which I would pick up cheap in Italy;

Head of Hair, fine samples plentiful in Greece;

Chest—from Sweden;

Legs, (badly needed)—France again;

Shoulder—America, of course.

The foregoing rhapsody is only an abortive expression of a solemn enough verity: which is, that, supposing I have progeny, they must be given the maximum chance of being fair of face and limb; and that that Chance, so to speak, must be classically and romantically, generally and particularly, in sunlight and in starlight, in sickness and in health, skin, bone—; and — muscularly Beautiful. By this, must be understood that she satisfy my sense of beauty: not entirely, of course, I have gone too far in aesthetics, seen too many persons, pictures and statues, lived too long for that—but she must exhibit say 75 out of the hundred essential characters. Not every man need have even his own sense of beauty realised in order to be happy, limited and distorted as his ideal already is; but that was settled for me time and time ago. In thus laying down such exigencies I risk making myself ridiculous later on; but at least you will admit that my present mind is a safe and useful one, considering my prospects.

I was much astonished the other day to find that Tofield, *Professeur d'Anglais* II, is married, and trails a French wife about with him, from Berlitz School to Berlitz School. The young lady naturally has to be half-supported by her parents. Anyhow, though obviously happy, they are certainly not comfortable; for Tofield came borrowing 25 f of me the other day.

I am reminded by this of another episode which I ought to have told you a time ago to give you the full effect of its suddeness. The elder Mlle. Poitou of Castelnau, the large and statuesque of bulk, during her fortnight's stay in Bordeaux, snapped up a fiancé and is to be married about August. This however is quite a usual mode of procedure in France. Another convenient French institution is the *Dot* which is never missing except among the really indigent. Also the suitor invariably sends a representative to the lady's papa, which I think the only effective time-saving device, invented by the French.

You asked me whether I should really like to direct a Berlitz School, if Uncle Ted would raise the capital. (Perhaps the personal allusion was not your's) Certainly. I could be happy enough for a time in France, Switzerland, or Italy. And these Schools can always be sold. Compared

with the ordinary teaching-post, whether private proprietor of Boys'
School, or on a government staff, Berlitz Direction is incomparably more
agreeable. And compared as a business with other businesses of like
capital, such a School is much more profitable.

But I must cultivate more grey hairs before that.

I must study—It is among students that I feel at present the most
unhappy.

Such as I teach at School respect me as a man of mature learning, and
wide experience of letters & science. While by such students as meet me
casually I am supposed to be a young fellow employed in a Commercial
House, and am often asked which wine-business I serve!

But I am neither of these. When I ask myself what I am I finish my
interrogations in a *crise de nerfs*. You see these self-examinations, after
a year's rest, begin again. At such times the sensation of the passing
of Time sharpens into agony. How much have I advanced in study since
the Matriculation 1911? Enormously in some fields, but not along the
marked-out high-roads, and through those absurd old toll-gates called
examinations.

I sometimes wonder whether my mere Pass in Matriculation[1] disenchanted everybody. But no one has any idea of the crushing disadvantages that I suffered through the Wyle Cop work. It was a thrice-evil
system: I did what should on no account ought to be attempted by
anyone under 25; I did it precisely at the moment when every precious
instant should have been devoted to undivided study, and the care of
my frame. And I tried to do Both under the most unfavourable of particular circumstances.

Before that time I fought with my hands free and the result was a
first place on the List of my first public examination.[2] Such a result will
now never be possible more; or if possible less and less probable; more
and more cruelly difficult . . . Nothing gave me the creeps more
surely than the sight of old Kemp, trying to learn his Latin Conjuga-
tions at 24! Is any scene in George Eliot more piercing-sorrowful than
Baldassarre the Scholar failing to read a paragraph?[3]

But think not it is examination results which attract me, and constrain
me to a manner of life much less easy than my present. It is more like
the call of an Art, which, morning and evening, makes me unhappy in
my unfruitful labour. What Art? ——— Any! Where lies my happiness, there lies my usefulness! I know when I am happy. We may not
know what is good for us; but we know what is good to us. (Alas for
the man who deceives himself in that.) I am happy with Art. I believe
in Science more wholeheartedly than in Art; but what good could I do
in that way?

I am only conscious of any satisfaction in Scientific Reading or Thinking when it rounds off into a poetical generality and vagueness. I find

[1] See Letter 89.
[2] Taken at the Shrewsbury Technical School.
[3] In George Eliot's *Romola*.

purer philosophy in a Poem than in a Conclusion of Geometry, a chemical analysis, or a physical law.

But all the time, you are asking: 'What Art is the fellow driving at?'

Music? If only I dare say Yes! I certainly believe I could make a better musician than many who profess to be, and are accepted as such. Mark, I do not for a moment call myself a musician, nor do I suspect I ever shall be; but there! I love Music, Violin first, Piano next, with such strength that I have to conceal the passion, for fear it be thought weakness. Strange to say, I met last Thursday in the woods of the Chateau Olivier, one of my pupils, who is a student of the Conservatoire here, and has the intention of being a soloist on the piano, and of giving concerts, and takes care to remark that he has no idea of being a Professor of Music. But what is chiefly strange is that, though he has had the energy and endurance to vanquish a Father and wit to escape from a commercial post, I doubt if he understands Music apart from Crotchets, Rests, and appoggiaturas. When I asked whether he thought of Composition, it was clear that he considered it entirely a matter of Counterpoint Rules.

But if I were a pupil of the Conservatoire . . . I should not complain of overwork. What a blessed tyranny would be the tyranny of a genius of a Master! If I failed . . . but even the despised 'Professors of Piano', (if anything above kettledrummers), command six and ten francs per lesson in Bordeaux; which compares well with the Profession of Tongues! But it is as extravagant of me to think of Music now as it would be for, say, Father to think of training as a sea-captain. And then a little incident has stuck in my mind like a thorn. It was quite seven years ago; I had just played one of my juvenile pieces before a 'Company' and Grandpa was so well pleased that he said quite gleefully 'He! He! But you'll make your livin' at it yet:' which remark was instantly crushed with a storm of Pooh-Pooh's! Grandma, though admitting she couldn't have done the thing herself, snubbed dear Grandpa as a mere matter of principle and habit. But everybody else was sincerely indignant. That indignation I have felt and redoubted ever since.

Failing Music, is it Pictures that I hanker to do? I am not abashed to admit it, when I realize I was never really taught even to draw: for it was evident that Miss Martin[1] who sat in our Room during Drawing Lessons, could not draw as well as the majority of the class.

But Heigh ho! If there were anything in me I should, following Legend, have covered with spirited fresco say Teece's Shed; or carved the Staircase Knob into a serene Apollo!

Yet wait, wait, O impatient world, give me two years, give me two free months, before it be said that I have Nothing to Show for my temperament. Let me now, seriously and shamelessly, work out a Poem. Then shall be seen whether the Executive Power needful for at least one Fine Art, be present in me, or be missing.

[1] The art mistress at the Birkenhead Institute.

My Temperament I have now no right to doubt. That I believe in-fallible; though it remains to know which, if any, Music, Painting, Sculpture, or Verse, is the most possible.

Witness, to confirm what I believe of my composition, on one side the Tragedy of Uncle Edward Shaw,[1] torn up by the roots by a perverted appetite; and on my other side, the Comedy of Aunt Emily Owen,[2] who literally palpitates with excess of physical sensation.

These are the natures which, labouring for self-expression, produce Art; and which rolling in retrogression produce Nothing or Crime.

Are you saddened by these declarations of mine? Anyhow, you know that as Parents You have, of all the world, the least title to find fault with what I am.

You must not take for granted Bernard Shaw, when he says:

> The true artist will let his wife starve, . . . his mother drudge for his living at seventy sooner than work at anything than his art.[3]

Nor will I for my part put any faith in this statement, which I read in the same play;

> When a man who is born a poet, refuses a stool in a stockbroker's office, and lives in a garret, spunging on a poor landlady, or on his friends and relatives sooner than work against his grain . . . we make large allowances for him.[4]

The large allowance may in Wordsworthian Years have amounted to as much as £200. Today it takes the form of a large allowance of space between the poet and his father's door.

Here I must take breath. I may find more to say another day. Mean-while I am not in a garret, and have been working for money, since I was sixteen, disguised as the fact is!

Now it is Wednes. and I have had with delight your news. I shall hope to have an important piece of your mind on Sunday.

Your dearly-loving Son

259. To Mary Owen

Monday, 1 June 1914   [*Bordeaux*]

Dearest Mary,

Your last letter gave me very much pleasure. Mother did not remind me of your Birthday; none the less I suddenly thought of it in writing the date on Saturday. A tremendous downpour of rain prevented me from making a tour of the shops; I just dived into a Bookseller's; but found nothing fit for you except a cheap copy, (of Gowan's production) of a

---

[1] Susan Owen's only brother was an alcoholic. He left home, emigrated, and was last heard of in Colorado.

[2] Edward Quayle's second wife.

[3] 'The true artist will let his wife starve, his children go barefoot, his mother drudge for his living at seventy, sooner than work at anything but his art' (*Major Barbara*, Act I).

[4] *Ibid.*

French Poetess. And, as yet, you are not yet fit for Marceline Desbordes-Valmores![1] But I have a design in sending you this, viz. to keep you hungry to learn French and I hope it won't be long before you read such works 'without tears'; at least without tears due to grammatical difficulties. Don't be disconcerted by the portrait on the cover! Remember you also have had ocular attacks; and have been seen to give fifty-seven double-winks at the ceiling every three minutes. You, also, have exhibited a nose, shiny enough to read by at night. You also have worn unfortunate bodice-yokes of ancient-british design. Hence say nothing horrid of poor Marceline's picture. But regard the book as a mere rubbishy brown-paper packet, and wait for me to untie the string—gently I promise you—and then you shall find in it many 'unvalued gems, inestimable stones'.[2]

Today has been Holiday.[3] The Lems earnestly invited me to go up the river with them in the afternoon: they went to visit some friends who lived in a riverside village. This family inhabits the *Mairie* or Town-Hall, the *Patron* i.e. Papa, being 'Secretary to the Mayor' = 'Town Clerk', I suppose. One of the curly-haired daughters I had seen at my famous first dance. Unfortunately there were no boys. I do really regret it, because with French girls it is quite impossible to talk soberly and intellectually, since they have the brains of linnets; and it is equally impossible to speak amorously and poetically for fear of being compromised.

It is their own fault that they are watched and warded, as is proved by this incident. The *Jeunesse* consisting of two boys and four damosels were for a short time separated from the elders. And it was not I, who was just then engaged in a Botanical Investigation; nor yet Raoul; but one of the young ladies who suggested that now was the moment *pour s'embrasser*. I was so taken off my guard that I kissed the curly-head without so much as looking round; but I finished off the rest only with much pressure and bad grace! Clearly, it was a solemn and established custom, not a merry improvised lark!

After this I several times fell asleep conversationally, and had to be roused up by Raoul.

I now learn that Raoul is proposed for the English Scholarship, but not elected yet. I am a little bothered about him; not simply because his English sets my teeth on edge; but because he eats half his words in speaking French, and such expressions as do drivel out are in the intonation of the Bordeaux Commercial Students. I am now able to recognize four or five species of French. First the ugly accent of working-class (not peasant) *Bordelais*: which includes the Dubo Family, certain of my night-pupils, and certain of my Boy-Scout acquaintance. Next, the manner of speech of the Higher Grade Schools and School of Commerce: characterized by great rapidity and fusion of words. Next the

[1] *Les Chefs-d'Œuvre Lyriques de Marceline Desbordes-Valmores* (Paris, 1913), with an unflattering portrait of the author on the cover. The copy survives.
[2] Inestimable stones, unvalu'd jewels. *King Richard III*, I. iv. 27.
[3] Whit Monday.

Bordeaux University Students' French, which certainly differs from the French of Parisians, which likewise is not the Best. Such is only to be got in the neighbourhood of Tours. Hence I shut down my imitative faculties when speaking with the majority of people I have to speak with: and very regrettable it is.

I say Raoul gabbles; but I know I also once spoke as untidily and indistinctly as I write now. Father did what he could to misunderstand me, and Mother to excuse me; but now a sterner Mother, whose child is Invention, has obliged me to mend my speech; and with such effect that both pupils and director thank & praise me for fine articulation!

I don't know whether you will remark any difference in my vowel-values when you hear me again. It will be joyful to hearken to you all. How fluent you will all seem, even thyself, O Sparse of Speech! I sometimes dream of being back in England, and am always sorry! It seems to my dreaming mind too soon, that my purpose has not been accomplished; and that it is so hard to get back to France! But when I wake I think differently!

Please set about finding some pupils for French, from which I might pocket 2s. per hour! . . . I mean it!

And now lay to your gentle heart my gentlest Wishes for your 'Future' (as there was anything but Future for us!) Be Strong. Cherish the Cherishers of our younger lives; and lead my darling Baby Colin along gentle ways!

Wilfred

260. To Susan Owen

Picture postcard: painting of a country scene, with
poppies and haystack

Saturday [*Postmark 6 June 1914*]   [*Postmark Bordeaux*]

My horizon is as doubtful as that of this picture, for a mass of new pupils has loomed up & Markowski is already doing five or six English lessons per day! It is most disheartening. Aumont has promised me lessons in French & Spanish but I can't find a moment for either!

Note how the effect of this picture lies in the Low Eye-Level. What a moral! Fondest love: looking for your news tomorrow. W.

261. To Susan Owen

Picture postcard: Bordeaux, Les Allées de Tourny

[*Postmark 11 June 1914*]   [*Postmark Bordeaux*]

I had your letters this mng. & hear with glee that you are less *souffrante* & even got to and through the Sale. I have got through 10 lessons today; but in one I was the pupil! It is now 11 p.m. and in view of the 8 a.m. Lesson tomorrow I must not begin to write now. I come now from this

Square, where I saw the poor little Russian Prof. into her tram. She does as many as 6 English lessons a day!

I shall post to Harold. Don't expect me for the Show. There's nothing for me in it. Why doesn't Colin write?

Yours ever, W

262. To Leslie Gunston

Picture postcard: Bordeaux, Colonnes Rostrales

[*Postmark 12 June 1914*]   [*Postmark Bordeaux*]

I don't seem to get an instant large enough to hold the debt of writing I owe you. But don't withhold your letter. Remember I am in want of news of what is happening in Kidmore Dunsden The College, etc. while in Bordeaux is nothing to excite your interest in a newsy way, and anything of a musy, kind can wait. So do you would be, etc. Shall not be home for Royal Show in Shrewsbury. When is yr. Holiday?

263. To Susan Owen

15 June 1914   *Bordeaux*

My dearest Mother,

I had your loving letter on Sunday and I think I quite well understand by now your attitude towards my Home-Coming!

But now I want to know your attitude towards my passing-of-next-winter.

Certainly I shall not be at the Agricultural Show. For though there may be even four more weeks of maximum work, I don't doubt that July and August will be much slacker and so worth waiting for.

Now in September and October are held special Courses of French for foreigners, at the University,[1] at a very low fee. At the end of these courses, one takes an Exam. which qualifies for a Diploma, stating the holder is 'Capable of Teaching the French Language'. Such a Diploma has, I know, some sort of value in England. Anyhow I should benefit immensely by the Courses. If, then, I could maintain myself for those two months, and I think I could, ought I not to hold out against the seduction of Home yet a little longer?

What is important to note is that persons registered for these French Courses are entitled to a Reduction of 50% on French Railways! This would make it even cheaper for me to go back thro' Paris. I might even engage myself for a month or so in the Paris B. School. It would be quite a safe undertaking for in Paris, Professors are not allowed to do more than seven hours per day. I should then arrive home for Christmas, and have plenty of time for reading for the Reading Scholarship, or even for Inter. Arts itself 1915. In fact I feel the time would be too long to

[1] Of Bordeaux.

259

remain at home, unless it were certain I could get some pupils for French, (or anything else).

The Alternative would be to come home immediately I am 'told off'; and at once to pack off to some other part of the world. For I am less sanguine than ever of 'Junior Posts in Boys' School'. Both as regards amount of leisure, difficulty of work, and style of living, I should be better in France or Germany as Berlitz Prof.

But better than all would be a few hours private independent lessons a day in Shrewsbury, by which I might profit twice as much as engaged by a school whatsoever.

And with the title *Diplomé de l'Université de Bordeaux* this should be quite possible.

Raoul's people are highly anxious for me to accompany him to Eng. He should be ready in about six weeks. But I really cannot let this consideration interfere with my plans.

10.30 p.m.

Let me know what you think of these plans; and if my alternatives are not clear to you, or if you have still another alternative tell it me. I am too sleepy to make a longer letter of this.

It might seem curious that I never write to Father or hear from him: [*one line illegible*] There is no sense in my writing out again for him what I say to you; and I have no time to write more. Father has no more to say than you tell me. And [*two words illegible*] suspect he reads a good part of my letters. I always make my salutations to you alone because some things I say are not meet for an audience. I had a fearful attack of mosquitoes 2 nights ago, and haven't made up the six hours of sleep then lost. I only hope I shall reach the P.O. to drop this in the Foreign Box without napping on the way. Good Courage at the Dentist's! My pat-on-the-back for Mary: nasal-tweak for Tweak for not writing to me.

Your devoted Son, Wilfred x

I have sent a card to Harold.

264. To Susan Owen

Picture postcard: painting of two sailing vessels, stormy sea

[*? 17 June 1914*]   [*Bordeaux*]

Best thanks for your Card. I had also a letter from Leslie this day, with the newly-discovered Sonnets of Keats.[1] It was meet that L. should inform me but I wonder you haven't heard anything of the noise made

---

[1] *The Times Literary Supplement* of 16 April 1914 (pp. 181–2) carried an article by Sir Sidney Colvin, 'Keats and His Friends. Unpublished Poems and Letters', in which two lyrics were published for the first time, 'Which of the fairest three' and 'You say you love'. On 21 May (pp. 241–2) the same journal printed an article by E. de Selincourt, 'John Keats. Recent Additions to our Knowledge'. This included comment on Colvin's article and the text of the two 'laurel crown' sonnets, here first printed.

by all the papers. I can scarcely bear to think of Keats at present; so long forborn to live in his spirit. Yesterday, in the middle of the day, Tofield was suddenly dismissed. The causes are dark & sinister to me; but the effects on me are like to be darker and more sinister, unless he is speedily replaced. I made a haul of penny pictures the other day; rather remarkable thing, because I dreamed of choosing postcards (!) and next day saw a collection in a shop which I enter once in two months! This is by no means the best of the Lot.

Fondest Love to All. W.

265. To Susan Owen

Picture postcard: painting of two mountaineers

[*? 18 June 1914*]   [*Bordeaux*]

I have urgent news! This m'ng a pupil, Parisian lady, *distinguée*, asked me whether I would like to spend a month in the Pyrenees with her as she must speak English before October. Her husband is a 'man of letters' & professor of elocution.[1] They travel a great deal. They have a villa in the mountains, marvellous spot! Various friends from Paris will visit them. Madame has a daughter of 11: will take 2 maids.
Monsier Léger came yesterday to see Aumont, not wanting me to lose my post permanently. Aumont refused to say definitely *Je verrai, je verrai*. It makes no difference whether he agrees or not!
I am in great excitement. Will tell you immediately I know more. Such as I know was communicated in an undertone during my lesson, for Aumont promised Madame to speak to me, & hasn't yet. The Tofield Affair is quite a mystery still.

266. To Susan Owen

Picture postcard: painting of sea and rocks

[*Postmark 21 June 1914*]   [*Postmark Bordeaux*]

Letter came by 2nd Sunday post. As you hadn't had my 2nd Card (so sorry about stamps—had made inquiries too) I am expecting a revision of your draughted schemes. Nothing more is settled, but if tomorrow I find that Aumont does not intend to get a second prof. I shall threaten resignation! Raoul doesn't intend to go to school in S. Whoever said so?? Stays 4 or 5 weeks. Hope to settle something between Mr. A. & Mme. L. tomorrow.

Dearest Wishes. W

[1] M. Alfred Léger and his wife. He was an actor-manager running an experimental theatre in Bordeaux and teaching elocution. His wife, now 31, managed his family interior-design business. They had one daughter, Nénette. A clear picture of all three emerges in Letters 277–92.

267. To Leslie Gunston

Picture postcard: painting of a sailing ship under stormy skies,
blue sky breaking through

[Postmark 21 June 1914]   *[Postmark Bordeaux]*

Thousand Thanks for Letter & Enclosures. I am still having a rough
time as the other prof. was dismissed one day this week, so I am like to
be drowned in work. But a fair Promise is seen on my Horizon (P.T.O.)
—A pupil has invited me to spend a month in the Pyrenees—her husband
is Dramatic Author & Professor, sending pupils to Odeon-villa[1] on
mountain-side, 1 hour from Bagnères de Bigorre. 2 servants—1
daughter (11 yrs) visitors from Paris to make house-party! What ho!
Shall write when I know more. W

268. To Susan Owen
Postcard

Wednesday Night [Postmark 24 June 1914]   *[Bordeaux]*

I don't doubt you will be glad to have a card on Friday, although I shall
not be able to give more precise facts about my Holiday (for such it will
be) till tomorrow, when I am going to talk over matters with Mons.
Léger. But of course the thing is already settled as fast as is humanly
possible: and I reck not of 'terms' as I shall certainly be the gainer if
they are 'mutual': M. Léger will talk French with me, and he has a
reputation for his classic accent: he sends pupils to the Odéon, Paris.
The friend[2] of Madame is a marvellous Violinist, apparently professional; and Madame regales me with descriptions of her daughter. I
shall give you the descriptions of all in my letter. Raoul came round this
evening to tell me he has got the scholarship: evidently likes the idea
of sea-side. Tis hot here & lessons cease not; but in the Pyrenees there
is snow: and Balm in Bagnères de Bigorre!

269. To Susan Owen
Postcard

Friday [26 June 1914]   *[Postmark Bordeaux]*

I had a five minutes interview with Mons. Léger at 1.30 yesterday, but
I couldn't get together a letter and shan't today, as again I have 10
hours. It is now quite definite that I go for 1 month, fare paid, terms
(so-called) mutual. They go July 15 till Sept. 15. As I may choose my
dates, it will be I think before the 1st of August, say the 27th July, in
order to be in time for opening of classes supposing it comes off that I

---

[1] The villa was rented by the Légers from Doctor Cazalas of Bagnères-de-Bigorre. See
Letter 278.
[2] Mlle Levallois. See Letter 278.

take the Course.—Depends on whether I find pupils enough. Raoul's affair I'll settle on Sunday. (Went there at 10. the other night & found all abed.) My health is marvellous! Shall I last out till Christmas without seeing you all? Do hope you'll get to Aberdovey.

Your own Wilfred

270. To Susan Owen

Picture postcard: painting of sea and rocks

[*Postmark 28 June 1914*]   [*Postmark Bordeaux*]

It seems I shall have some Questions to answer soon, so this is an excuse for retarding a letter. In any case I haven't so much as ½ hour writing today: all aft. has been spent at a school *Kermesse*[1] and all evening I shall be at Lem's. How I hope you'll get to the sea,—no less than I hope my own project will come off. There is nothing fresh to tell you, and I hope there won't arrive anything fresh in that way! Salutations all round! W

271. To Susan Owen

Friday, 815. p.m. [*?3 July 1914*]   [*Bordeaux*]

My own dear Mother,

I have no lesson at 8 tonight so I think I shall make it worth while spending 2½d on a letter! I feel comparatively energetic at this moment, having just got over a miserable stomach-ache: (the first for months), one of the effects of the renewed Heat Wave;—and I always feel in a benign and docile mood on such an occasion.

Your letter & news of Harold were very welcome on Wednesday. I naturally am glad about your bit of commerce on Show Visitors,[2] that is if you didn't over-exert. I guess Raoul's dates will just suit you. He may stay six or eight weeks, if you have him. Of course he will be glad to go to the sea. Don't you worry about his English. I do not hold myself responsible in any way for what he half-knows. I repeat he has not shown linguistic talent. But that makes no difference to you. Let him peck up what he can. As for amusing him you mustn't think of it. Turn him out to grass with Colin once a day; and when in the house tell him to study! Get Doris over by all means; at least she is a study in the cold & colourless 'English Type'.[3]

And now, I on my part, have some Questions wanting Replies: What trains leave Paddington at decent times for R's journey: and what is the fare Padd–Shrewsbury, 3rd Class?[4]

[1] Garden fête.
[2] Letting a room at Mahim during the Agricultural Show.
[3] Doris Wharmby, daughter of a chocolate manufacturer in Mansfield. She spent a good deal of time during the holidays with the Owen children, and was particularly liked by Wilfred, HO recalls, despite his comment here.
[4] '12/9d' is pencilled here by Susan Owen.

I am really sorry you don't think of going to Hereford for a while. You don't mention any reasons, and I don't wonder.

Give my particular remembrances to Grandma, etc.

I heard from Father Kemp this morning. In how short a time has he got through his Brothership. He seems cheery as usual, and talks of having preached three sermons now. His Vicar is one Tiarks; now, upon my word, I believe Mr. Robertson told me he knew a cleric of that name in Reading.[1] And Kemp tells me his Tiarks was in Reading long ago; and mentions it as curious. Ask Mr. R! How are Mr. Robertson & The Young Men, etc? The frequenters of the 'Y.M.' here are a very different set. The Shrewsbury fellowship never spoke against Morality ('far be it from us, etc.') but they treated 'mere morality' as a hopeless plea; a filthy rag. Here, the students, discard Morality entirely, and go without a rag. It may be an 'outsider' who has done it, but practically all my Music Sheets which I had left at the *Union* have been stolen! I am annoyed, although there was not much value in it, because there is a piano at the villa, & leisure also. Now could you find in Shrewsbury the Tuppenny Series in which I had the *Marche Funèbre* (in five sharps) and send it me, together with any others you may select. I should be glad to have at the same time the sixpenny book containing Chapel in Mountains, etc.; and also cheap copies of Largo, Blake's March, Melody in F. and what more you will. The postage will be trifling. My copies were already in shreds, but I shall obtain some compensation for this theft from the Secretary. In any case you will draw upon my Christmas Moneys in doing this little commission. I specially should like to have what I have named, and if Mary finds any more, so much the better. I have, yesterday, bought a book for Mary which will help her French famously. It is the French equivalent of a Reader in English which has great success with my pupils.

The only news I have relating to Bagnères is that the Légers cannot go into the villa before the 20th (they wanted to go next week) because it is flooded! Owing to a great melting of the snows under the late heat; a stream which divides the house from the road, has burst the bridge, so that one can't get at the house. Water has entered the downstairs rooms, and other catastrophes have happened. But it will make no difference to me I hope.

I trust you'll get this on Sunday. If not I shall be sorry, but the weather & work together are terrible enemies to writing.

Dearest Love from your own,

                                                              Wilfred

272. To Mary Owen

Le Quatorze Juillet 1914   *Bordeaux*

My dear Mary,

The first important thing I have to say is: Send me, regardless of Risks, Costs, or Pains the 'Adorable Portrait' of Colin. I imagined I

[1] The Rev. Hope Charles Tiarks, Vicar of Holy Trinity, Kilburn, 1914–47, was at Greyfriars, Reading, 1906–8.

had it with me, and being seized the other day with a mania to see it I plunged into my archives, but didn't find it. I was sick at heart. So you'll send me both photographs, won't you: i.e. the one with the gun and the serene, the immaculate-innocent, the noble face;[1] and other with the semi-coy, slant-smiling . . . face. The gap is to be filled up when the English Language shall have evolved appropriate adjectives for that Expression. As a matter of fact I can see that picture at this moment as well as I can see, (and better than I can see) the words I am scratching on this paper: and the truth is I only want the pictures to show my friends what our family can do when it tries.

P.S. Need I explain that July 14th is the National Fête, day on which Bastille was stormed. Grand military Reviews all over the country, & general holiday.

15 July

I had only got so far when I heard the fireworks beginning in the vast public square; so I dribbled round in that direction; and fell in with the most tremendous assembly of human creatures I ever saw in a public place. In Shrewsbury we like to think there is a great multitude in the Quarry at the Show, but I suppose ten quarriesful would not amount to the mass standing in the Place de Quinconces last night. The fireworks were not so pretty as 'ours' but more striking and comprehensive, they fell over the heads of the people, and embraced the whole sky. What made it the most remarkable was the lightning which sometimes blazed out at the same instant as the bursting rockets, and kept up a continual flicker in the pauses of the *feux d'artifices*. The people had hardly turned away when a ferocious storm broke. The noise of hundreds of thousands of feet and voices surging back into the town was a noise not to be forgotten. It re-awoke all the mysterious terrors which one feels for the first time in reading the *Tale of Two Cities*. And then such a pandemonium of thunder claps to finish—or rather never to finish! For they lasted till six this morning and awoke me half a dozen times in the night. Result was I fell asleep in my room after lunch, and didn't wake up till after the time for my Lesson! I had such a shock that I scuttled round to the school without waiting to awake more than half of myself; and afterwards I couldn't get more than half awake; so I sat out that lesson in a very queer mentality, very queer indeed. But I 'feel better' after a right good dinner, and no wine!

I feel quite self-conscious, the centre of observation, if, as I sometimes do, I drink nothing but water. Strange is the change.—The first time I uncorked a Claret I was in a great funk. I am glad I was; but I'm not less glad that just at the moment of my third bodily-renewing, I have been able to fortify my tissue with real Bordeaux Red & White. I am conscious of at least an appearance of robustness in my face: for when shaving I have a tight round skin to deal with now. And there are no black shadows in the corners of my eyes. Ask Raoul, though!

[1] The photograph reproduced as Plate IIIc.

I am enclosing his photograph. He has just given me a larger one, but I am sending this, equally good, for lack of a big envelope.

The boy states he will arrive at Shrewsbury at <u>9.5 p.m. on Tuesday, July 21.</u>

Mother was very thoughtful to ask whether I preferred him not to have my sanctum. I should certainly rather my own Colin were there if anyone.* But I don't understand whether it is a choice of one or other.

I rather suppose from recent accounts that Tweeks is at present in a state of fishy degeneration, reverting to our original aquatic habits; and, now completely amphibian, sleeps in the bathroom under water. He had better emerge and write me a letter, if he wants me to remember that he is near fourteen: How I wish the Pater would send him back with Raoul: to share my room for two months, and learn French enough to last him terms and terms without opening his Grammar. What bliss for him, eh?

I have another project for the Autumn. Herr Langholz is leaving Berlitz Schools for ever this term. After many years therein, both in Europe and America, he has got a 'name' but it brings no money. He is going to do commerce in fruit, oil and wine between Russia & Spain. But this winter he is going to Nice where he gets from 5 to 10 francs for a lesson. Now it is possible that I might go and work with him;[1] if, as he says, I should have 3 f. per lesson for myself, I should be glad to do it. Langholz is now in Paris, but we shall talk over this when he comes back.

No change in Bagnères plans. Thanks be! You will find my first visiting–card, necessitated by present circumstances, and costing 1½ franc per 100!

Give me a hint what Colin wants for 24th.

Thank dear Mother for her loving letter.

Overlook the haste-marks of these pages, but always look well into any signs you may see of my impatience to be among you.

Your fond Wilfred

* I don't mind of course Raoul having 'my room'. Certainly not. Only keep locked the Book Case, eh?

273. To Susan Owen

Sunday [19 July 1914]   *12 Rue St. Louis, Bordeaux*

Dearest Mother,

I am writing from Raoul's domicile. I hope things will work out all right: and that unless a telegram tells you otherwise he will arrive at 9.5 p.m. Tuesday. I shall <u>not</u> send this by Raoul but shall post it tonight in the hope that you'll get <u>it</u> before Tuesday Evening. Perhaps you'll be piqued not to have a word on Tuesday Morning. Ah me! But I have been 'on the go' ever since 6.30. this morning. At that early hour I got

[1] This project seems to have been seriously considered. See Letter 274.

up and went to the Park where one of my pupils[1] had offered to take me horseriding with him. I was almost as eager as Colin might be to get once again into the saddle [*four words illegible*] But no chance! Every horse but one had already been taken out from the stables. So it will be for next week.

The inviting gentleman is a new acquaintance: perfume inventor & *commerçant*: don't know if I have spoken of him before. Went to his house the other day; he has a large & lovely garden: where the smell of flowers is eked out by puissant odours from his laboratory.

It was he who gave me the 'Otto'[2] Flask which I am handing over to you. On no account must you open the bottle. I was desperately put to to find anything for Colin; fell back upon the commodious handkerchief & necktie!

Hope Father won't find the cigarettes a species of poisonous straw: it's what we get here.

Mind you give me your first impressions of R.

In gt. haste,

Always your own, Wilfred

Later: in my Room

I was obliged to write the accompanying sheet at Lem's, and under the eyes of R. who audaciously overlooked me—on the pretext that he didn't understand, but found it interesting. Consequently, I flicked out a few messages as illegibly as possibly; but couldn't say the important thing: concerning the bicycle. Now, he knows I have a bicycle; and knowing, hinted at using it, to which I returned no definite permission. Six weeks is too long to put my new machine—so hard-earned—at the disposition of another. If that other were one of the boys I loved it would be different. I therefore beg you to persist in your scheme of hiding it away. Can't the Seatons accommodate it for me?

If R. looks about for my bicycle you must make out it is the one the boys use. Invent what casuistry you can! . . .[3] I can't have my tyres tired, brakes broken, saddlebag bagged, and pinchers pinched by him. There is one other mystification:—I sent you a small photo for convenience. Now Lems fancy you are in receipt of a larger one. You must also fancy so.

I think I may understand from your letter this morning—so welcome an event—that my bookcase is well-locked, and that you will impress him with the sanctity of my room. Of course I have no objection to his being there: fifty Frenchmen are preferable to half Harold—(lower or upper half an indifferent matter) in respect of preservation of furniture.

So you are at last getting the Curtains, about which we fidaddled so long a year & more agone! I can trust you to please me with the Design!!

---

[1] M. Peyronnet, a scent manufacturer, for whom Wilfred carried out an unspecified commission at the British Industries Fair in London in May 1915. See Letters 345–54.

[2] Originally *attar* flask: containing the fragrant essence of roses.

[3] We have omitted nine words.

Do pack off R. to Y.M.C.A.; yes!

Fancy Harold home again. Soon! Until when?

In an extravagant burst, (such as I love and value so much) you speak of licking Raoul since he has touched me. Now, I understood the word in the slang sense at first: and I hope you won't ever come to revise the original import of the word!

It is certainly interesting to have a real, live sort of letter to send you; tho' scarcely more intelligible than my dead 'uns. x Another kiss!

Wilfred

274. To Susan Owen
Postcard

Wednesday [*Postmarked 22 July 1914*]   [*Postmarked Bordeaux*]

A poor return—is a P.C. for your two letters, Colin's, a photograph and a pack of music, especially as I have had only 3 lessons today! But this evening I found there was a Bible Reading at the *Union* and went. So you'll excuse me? So glad you found the pieces of ♪ named. I hope Edith won't choose Rustle of Spring (Sinding):[1] I've got it here. I go to Bagnères on the 30th: Légers only go on the 27th. Shall send my address in good time. £.s.d. not lacking yet, but I foresee difficulties in October! 'Nice'[2] would be after Oct. if at all. Weather delightfully cool at present. Do rest! Don't expect the seaside to work miracles in a fortnight. T'aint as if you were going to Lourdes, hem! Give my salutations to Raoul. Sorry I can't pity Colin's throat; happened so opportunely! Eh! W.E.O.

275. To Susan Owen
Postcard

Sunday [*Postmark 26 July 1914*]   [*Postmark Bordeaux*]

On Saturday evening I was a free man—after 11 months without vacation. This mng. I rested: cleaned myself & also appurtenances, e.g. boots: this afternoon I visited 'my *Patron*' and received minute (and hour) instructions for Thursday's journey. This evg. I had dinner w. M. Lem & had good news of Raoul. I am so pleased with your accounts. Tomorrow I go as pupil to Berlitz School (for Spanish!) Delightfully cool weather we are having! Hence I 'go well', but I feel vaguely Baulked by having finished with Berlitz & not finding you at the End. x x x x x x x and *poignée de main* where appropriate.

Your own W

---

[1] Christian Sinding (1856–1941), the Norwegian composer. 'The Rustle of Spring' is his best-known work.

[2] If he were to join Langholz there. See Letter 272, note 1. But war was to intervene.

276. To Susan Owen
Postcard

Wednesday Evng. [*Postmark 29 July 1914*]   [*Postmark Bordeaux*]

I have had, as you may imagine, a day of fearful doings,—which is not over yet. Mr. Lem has been so kind as to offer the services of one of his men for the transportation of my trunks. One of the boxes I am leaving at his house, by kind permission. I am wondering if is a good thing, or whether it is a pity that I am not in Austria,[1] as I very nearly was-to-be-to-go. I start by 7.30 train tomorrow. I shall be near the safest spot in Europe—Spain at present. Had yr. letters this morning! You have my Address? Best wishes to Raoul.

Your own W

277. To Susan Owen

Friday, 31 July[2] [*1914*]   *Villa Lorenzo La Gayeste*
                                          Bagnères-de-Bigorre[3]

Dearest Mother,

Getting up at half-past five on Thursday, I caught my train without any scramble. I met at the Station a pupil, young commercial student, with whom I was on good terms (Raoul knows him: Dufau); with his sister and small cousin; and I travelled with them three quarters of the way. The weather was on the change, after three weeks rain, and the country was very fair. I saw something of the vast pine forests of the Landes. The first sight of the mountains was highly exciting. They rise up with scarce any preamble in the way of spurs, hillocks, or terraces. But there was no snow. At Bagnères I found Monsieur, and outside the station Nénette holding the Donkey's head, for they have a donkey-*charrette*, and my green trunk was carried up therewith. The Villa is snugly placed on a hillside, not very far from the Town, but out of sight. It is very pretty, tho' not in the English style. It is not conspicuously comfortable; but the very box for an open air treatment. My room, on the ground floor, has three windows, one of which is a door. (Hem!) I have a *Cabinet de Toilet* (ask Raoul) where there is running-water, very-running-water: the tap doesn't act, and the water runs on for ever. 'Men may come' to repair it, but I don't expect them. I have to deaden the noise at night by a system of rags. A few yards from my door a brook keeps up the 'noise of a hidden stream, that to the sleeping woods all night, singeth a gentle song'.[4] The garden is wildish but rich in

---

[1] He may have planned to holiday with Langholz in Austria before going to Nice.
[2] 'From My Diary, July 1914' (*Poems*, p. 117) expresses his first lyrical reaction to the Pyrenees.
[3] Ten miles east of Lourdes in the High Pyrenees.
[4] A noise like of a hidden brook
In the leafy month of June,
That to the sleeping woods all night
Singeth a quiet tune.
Coleridge, *The Ancient Mariner*, Part V.

leafage. Bamboos grow prosperously. Enormous hydrangeas (hortensia) with purple inflorescences are all about . . . This instant I am informed that Madame is going into Bagnères, & I must go to buy my *espadrilles*. So shall go on with my accounts later. On arriving I went out with Mr. Léger to see the country, & did not even send a card as there is no post from here. All letters have to be taken to Bagnères. I am very content here. What Luck!

Your very own Wilfred x

278. To Susan Owen

Saturday, 1 August 1914   *Chez Monsieur Léger, Villa Lorenzo,*
La Gayeste, Bagnères-de-Bigorre, Htes. Pyrénées

My own dear Mother,

I was cut very short in my letter of Friday. I resume. The Villa is not ideal in plan, but pretty and practical. Only it is in a bad, bad state of repair. One ought to live here three months, says M. Léger, before it is 'anything like.' It is not, you understand, the property of the Légers but of a doctor[1] of Bagnères, who is aged and invalid, hence it is shamefully neglected. There is a largish 'property' around about, consisting of copse, meadows and a farm. There is in the garden the beginning of a *Vivier*, which I think is called in English 'stew' or 'kettle of fish' or something like that. But although two charming rivulets leap across the garden, the work is not finished. Here is a rough plan of the house:

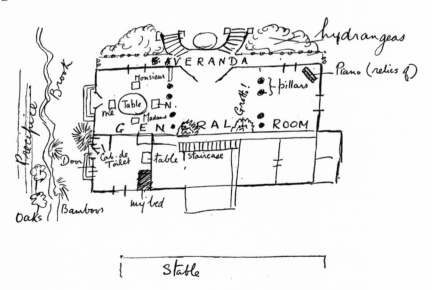

The whole front consists of one piece—dining-room, hall, & drawing-room without separating-walls. The piano is wicked: absolutely un-

---

[1] Dr. Cazalas. Mme Cazalas can be seen in Plate VI.

touchable. O la! la! Mademoiselle Levallois[1] hasn't arrived yet; comes next week.

There is a second-story to the villa, which only half-covers the flat roof.

The view is not vast, being obstructed by a near hill, very like one of the Stretton brotherhood[2]—in fact exactly like. However, we see beyond and above this, the great Pic-du-Midi, and the Mont Aigu, on which there is yet snow. I shall not attempt any arduous climbs, and none at all the first week.

Now let me speak of my excellent friends. Monsieur Léger, was educated in a Paris Engineering School, but 'abandoned the Sciences for Dramatic Art' (so saith a short notice I have read on him.) He played Comedies, I think; and the mere stamp of his countenance is enough to confirm it. He is quite small, but his bearing is notable, and his head typically dramatic: no hair on top to speak of, deep, dark eyes under prominent and moustache-like eyebrows, broad mobile mouth, clean shaven. Head beautifully poised, a little leaning-back. Voice agreeable— (but I have not yet heard him recite.) There is nothing stagey about him, absolutely nothing in manner of speech, gesture, or idea; and that is remarkable considering. But the most mysterious thing is his age. In some lights, whether regarded, entire or in part, behind, before, or aside, he looks just thirty. At other times he is an old man, a grandfather. As a matter of fact, he is over fifty.

Madame is much younger. She is elegant rather than *belle*; has shapely features luxuriant coiffure, but is much too thin to be pretty. Probably she has been very pretty indeed. She is obviously of the same opinion herself. Her toilette, even for driving in donkey cart, is unimpeachable.

Yesterday she pointedly told me she could not stand plain people. *Je les déteste* were her words. I felt uncomfortable. You, who may take the inference in a sense more complimentary to myself, may be uncomfortable in another way. She has even confided to me that she doesn't love her husband excessively. This is all very amusing for me—and nothing else.

But I am immensely happy to be in the company of Nénette. I am enclosing a picture, with the warning that it is not very like, is not complimentary, and must be seen through a lens. Nénette, (not a nice name, *tant pis*) is perfectly a child, and, with that, is almost a perfect child. Papa prefers that she should not be educated in a town school, where they learn a great deal, but not of studies. So she goes to school with the peasants, and makes great progress. This is at the sacrifice of her accent, which is an important thing to a father like Mons. Léger. But that can be cured. The result of living out here is that Nénette's physique is magnificent. As far as I can judge, she has also more than her share of intellect. Anyhow she began to compose dramas at nine years of age. Some of her writings are astonishing. I said that our piano

[1] See Letter 268, note.
[2] The hills round Church Stretton, near Shrewsbury.

was atrocious: hence I don't know whether she can play with sense or not; but she goes through her exercises admirably. I made the mistake the other day, of striking the opening bars of *Marche Funèbre*; since when she pesters me daily for more. It is a torture to me, but I do it for the sake of her expression. We walk into Bagnères together sometimes, when we talk chiefly of armaments and what help England is giving to France!

The news of War made great stir in Bagnères. Women were weeping all about; work was suspended. Nearly all the men have already departed. Our household is one in a thousand. Mr. Leger, who doesn't look his age, and I, who look French, are objects of mark at present. I had to declare myself, and get a permit to remain here; where I must stay still under penalty of arrest and sentence as a spy—unless I get a special visa for emigrating. I don't know how this state of things will affect my Courses in Bordeaux. Our food is already much dearer, and we are all getting ready to live on bread and maize-soup. If need be, Monsieur & I will undertake the harvest between us. Nobody is very gay.

I don't know whether you will ever receive this letter. I only know everything is horribly upset, in the Post, on the Railway—everywhere. I have got your last letter & Raoul's and feel upset that Father may not get his holiday. I hope you don't feel the least anxiety about me. I escaped from Bordeaux in the nick of time. Here I am in the hands of most amiable friends, away from danger to life, and sure enough of food. I shouldn't like to be in Germany. Nor yet in Aumont's shoes. Fancy, he is now at the front,[1] and I airing my fancies in a charming *villégiature*. I finish in haste. Shall send cards often. If I find I am a burden to the Légers, I may have to sneak home. So be prepared.

Ever your devoted Wilfred

279. To Susan Owen

Saturday, 8 August 1914   *Bagnères-de-Bigorre*

My dearest Mother,

How miserable it is not to get your letters, and not to know whether you are getting mine. I have so far had yours of July 31st: and it's a wonder I got that considering the scanty address. Fortunately Monsieur Léger is well known in Bagnères, (having at one time directed the Casino there.) I last wrote (letter) a week ago (to Aberdovey), posting the next day. Since I have sent cards. I shall with this letter forward a Card to Mahim, in case, in consequence of the mobilization you have been obliged to stay in town.

Practically all the men have now gone to join their corps. The last time we sent to Market it was empty. In villages around there is no more bread. The women pass their time knitting in the streets. Monsieur

[1] Not so. See Letter 297, note.

Léger spends his day tramping to and from the town, though, as a matter of fact, news only arrives once a day. All sorts of absurd stories are circulated about spies and lurking Germans. I saw a man who had the foolhardiness to call himself German (I don't think he was actually) all but killed by a mob. I never wear my spectacles now, as the Légers say they look foreign. I have received glances from knitting women which not Madame Defarge could make more menacing! It is because they think me an idle French youth, who has got himself excused! On the other hand, when Monsieur L. introduces me to his friends as English I am cordially and respectfully saluted. No one is permitted to pass out of his *Commune* (a very restricted area) after six o'clock in the evening!

Madame Léger has definitely offered to keep me with them as long as they remain up here, that is until the 15th of September. It is no use even discussing what I shall do then; it is yet much too soon.

I continue meanwhile to be immensely happy and famously well.[1]

I dropped into a Photographer's the day before leaving Bx.; and here is the result. Three points need to be mentioned. (1) The lop-eared-ness of the left hairs is accidental. (2) The shadow quite spoils the chic effect of the moustache. (3) I look pale, while, at present at any rate, my rich colour is a marvel to behold. The difference that has taken place in my physiognomy since the moment I was liberated from the Bordeaux Box is incredible. Bagnères is specially noted for Throat Cures, and indeed I breathe this air with as much gusto as I eat my meals.

We live very quietly. I get up about eight, and pass through the glass (!) door of my bedroom to my *déjeuner* of coffee with milk & cream, toast and butter. About nine or ten I give my lesson: not always easy, but never boring. It is often in the garden; and is usually interrupted by Nénette, who doesn't at all like this hour; and has to come for kisses and hugs at intervals.

---

[1] About this time Wilfred scribbled out the following draft letter (see Plate XI a), which was found with his papers after his death. It carries later corrections, in a different ink (as does Letter 319, also a draft with later corrections). All the words first set down and then struck out are shown here in italics.

'In these days my present life is a lived-out book. If I have loved books it is not because they are an alternative to life, or an artificialized life, as Parson Wigan said, but because they are the *Best* Prime of life. If I seek the company *of such as write books* of *lettered* men of letters it is not because they write *books chapters thoughts* lines, but because they read things; *not because* they *alone* who compose *chapter verses* chapter and verse are they who dis-compose characters and events. So little had I *lived* been in contact with people of a mind either abundantly creative or poignantly analytic (*which I am devoutly thankful are not to be found in my family*) & devoutly thankful am I that such are not to be found in my family—so much have I lived with children, *trees, a* brothers boys and nothing more—a sister, a girl and sometimes something less, a mother who is *an* more angel than woman of the world, with *men*, such *who* as, if they read in books reaped not therefrom; and therefore had not *where*withal to sow, that I had begun to believe all romance contained between the two covers of a ballad-book; In the same way as I supposed all philosophy in the [*blank*], all culture at Oxford, all religion in Christ, all Poetry in J. Keats: and all love in *Miss Elsie wouldn't you like to know? little* what's her name?

Here is a typical day: last Wednesday, I think. I got up when I like: breakfast alone with Nénette, began with a *furious* tiff: and indeed with the recital of her dreams, which were *of a so* as shocking *that I couldn't listen.* as could be! Evidently there is no Censor'.

We lunch at 12.30: have *gouter* consisting of a cup of milk at 4: and dinner at 7.30. Meals are not by any means sumptuous; for the time is a time of war. This afternoon Madame and the servant have gone with the donkey, for victuals. Mlle. Levallois, violinist, hasn't yet come: and I wish she wasn't coming: otherwise a Poet, a real live Poet, with a wife of famous beauty would have come. But in any case, the Poet has now cut his hair, and gone to war! In a few days an old lady, very distinguished, will arrive; her son is an important M.P. I shall finish my news for Mary & Colin.

Your own, happy, safe, fortunate, and devoted Son

280. To Leslie Gunston

Picture postcard: Bagnères-de-Bigorre, Route de Bagnères à Lourdes

Thursday, 6 August [*1914*]   [*Postmark Bagnères-de-Bigorre*]

I don't feel inclined to send a letter until I know that there is communication between us. I have no news from England and even telegrams take 5 days to cross France. I got out of Bordeaux in the nick of time. I am pretty safe in this corner, but naturally everybody is much upset. Excursions are impossible: I may have to do harvesting and shepherding! Do send a card by return to Villa Lorenzo, La Gailleste, Bagnères-de-Bigorre. Htes. Pyrénées.

281. To Colin Owen

Monday, 10 August 1914   [*Bagnères-de-Bigorre*]

Darling Lad,—Colin,

I thought your last letter to me a very nice one. I hope at this moment you are in Camp; but I am desolated not to have had any news from Aberdovey,[1] (or from Shrewsbury either since Mother's letter of the 31st July.)

I suppose you are studying the War, with all your Patrol. Are the Scouts doing anything really useful at this time? I feel shamefully 'out of it' up here, passing my time reading the Newspapers in an armchair in a shady garden. Numbers of Bordeaux ladies are going to the Armies as Nurses. The only thing I could do, so Madame Léger says, would be to serve as stretcher-bearer, on the battlefield. After all my years of playing soldiers, and then of reading History, I have almost a mania to be in the East, to see fighting, and to serve. For I like to think this is the last War of the World! I have only a faint idea of what is going on, and what is felt, in England, as perhaps you have only a faint notion of the family affliction, the public enthusiasm, the standstill of business there is here.

---

[1] Colin was camping with his Scout troop at Aberdovey, on the west coast of Wales, at the outbreak of war.

Please send me a newspaper whenever an important issue appears; and <u>keep</u> some historical numbers, for my archives. Yes, I should honestly and solemnly like to be in Alsace at this moment! But I know your opinion at home as to such an idea; so I won't even ask for permission to engage myself as nurse, etc. What a time for the Journalists!

Meanwhile I could hardly ask for a more perfect (holiday-) existence. I have found a spot to bathe; and my daily bath is a matter of much wonderment in the family. When I proposed it, I met with all manner of opposition: stream too cold; not deep enough; people may pass: better go to the *Piscine* (Plunge Bath) (which is quite warm, ugh! and costs 1 franc.) Now I am, as you very well know, acutely uncomfortable in hot weather without a tub. So one fine morning I went forth, pretending I was going to herborise; and finding, as I knew I should, an enchanting stretch of water in an alder-glade, I was not long in 'getting in.' So now I go down every day, and I know, when I vaunt my coolness and freshness, the others would be green with envy, if they were not so infernally red with heat.

Oh! certainly it is hot here at mid-day! I daren't think of what it is in Bordeaux!—or on the Continental Plains in Uniform!!!!!! But after four o'clock, just when in cities, the air begins to be intolerably *étouffant* down from the mountains comes trickling a delicious current of oxygen and we are saved. And that is why I can find Nothing the matter with me: and why I eat anything and sleep anyhow: and that is why (for a double reason) the stars are twice as brilliant than I have ever seen them before. Now, do write something for me: and say that you continue to feel my affection and respect my influence.

x Wilfred x

P.S. Down with the Germans!

282. To Susan Owen

Tuesday, 11 August 1914   *Bagnères-de-Bigorre*

Darling Mother,

I am miserably disappointed to know, by this morning's post, that Father is kept from his holiday, and that you are not going to Wales at all. I sent a letter yesterday to Aberdovey, (with the Home Address as alternative) so you may get it at the same time or even after this—if you ever lay hands on it at all. It contained notes for Raoul and Mary, and photographs of Nénette, and of me. Your two mails of Aug. 2 and 5 I captured together this morning. I was going down to my bathe when I met the Postman on the road. Having an iron-pointed alpenstock in my hand, I made him stand and deliver. I rather suspect that my letters for England are quarantined for several days in this beastly town: if indeed they are not opened and condemned. I have sent

A Card on my arrival.
Letter on Sunday. 2nd.

Two Cards in the Week.

Letter on Monday 10.

and Cards to Torquay, Alpenrose, and various people in Bordeaux.

In case people act the goat with my Envelope at Aberdovey I here repeat that I am admirably comfortable; with people who just suit my momentary taste; and completely out of reach of the war.

I don't think I have ever enlightened you on the occupation of Madame Léger. She has an important business in Bordeaux & Paris designing and selling House Decorations, Embroideries, and so on. She goes to Canada once a year, and there makes piles of money. In six years she says her fortune will be made; and she shall sell the Business, and return to her original state of perfect lady! In two years they will remove to her dear Paris. She was not educated to be a business woman; but as Monsieur Léger had no turn for business she managed the House since the time of her marriage. She is only 31; while 'Charles' is 52. One would take her for Nénette's sister. She is a most amiable hostess, and I am as neither a guest nor a 'teacher' but as an old friend. She was once vaunting how that she could do whatever she liked with her men friends. Never did she meet with resistance. I told her that if she found me compliant to her wishes she must remember my position in her household. On which she declared that I owed her no obligations whatever. I was entirely free: in my goings-out and comings in and in the language I speak: and how I behave. So, considering the charming country and everything else, I am one of the most enviable young persons in France.

I am going to write about Nénette to Mary. This is only a supplementary Note: writ in a hurry, for in 3 mins. I must trot into Bagnères.

It makes marvellous hot in the middle of the day, i.e. at present.

I find I have no answers to attend to in your letters: but I would like to answer your anxiety on my part and grievous disappointment on your own by a Declaration of my personal Liberty, Health, Happiness, with no prospect of any immediate change.

Signed, Your Wilfred

283. To Mary Owen

20 August 1914   *Bagnères-de-Bigorre*

My dearest Mary,

Although I have very nearly written several long epistles to you, I never quite wrote one!

You understand that one or two hours of my day are taken by my 'professional duties'; that one or two more are not less strictly taken up by Nénette, for whom I draw, play the piano, make boats, act comedy, invent stories, play hide-and-seek, bury dolls, etc. that, nearly every day I go to Bagnères for some reason or other; that when it is fine, I scramble up the hills to see 'the Chain' of the Pyrenees; and that when it is hot (remember we are more south than the N. Coast of Spain) it is a sore temptation to prostrate myself on the Verandah in the contemplation of the Peaks; the near valleys; . . . the silver-birches and the hortensias of the garden; . . . Nénette . . . and the end of a cigarette . . .

You, especially You, would be enchanted with our Villa. The name, following the inscription at the end of the Drive is Castel Lorenzo, but you might as well call Mahim a manor, as this a $\overline{Castel}$. It is a bijou-residence: too much like a toy in appearance to please M. Léger; and indeed is a long way from being my own ideal of a country villa. This reminds me that I spent an afternoon of last summer working out my ideal of a practical English country house. I made some rough plans[1] which I think I put in one of my stained boxes, among the pottery-collection. I should be glad if you could find those sheets (note-paper size) and send them me <u>quietly</u>; because Madame Léger would be interested to talk over the subject. You know her business is to set in order the houses of rich people; chiefly in Canada, where all her clients are millionaires. She sells her articles at an extremely high price; and will have made her fortune in six years hence. She works like this: inspects the house; tells the people what they want (for they never know); takes measurements, makes her designs; has these designs executed by her 30 or 40 *employées*; and makes a fabulous profit.

But you will be more interested to hear about Nénette (full name Albine)—both which names I have told her Mother are not at all pretty; and she agrees. However they belong to a very pretty Body. Her head is not without fault: there is too much recession in the line of the chin. Her hair is not at all in the manner of the photograph; but in two *macarons* on the temples, like Queen Victoria's in 1837. This gives her an air of a Russian Ballet Dancer, which she resembles in other respects also. Her dancing is said to be exquisite. I haven't seen her dance. Her voice is a continual music. But her chief feature is her eyes, which are like Margaret Quayle's in colour, and richly fringed with lashes. Upon occasions they become extraordinarily alive; so that we say—she has the devil in her eyes tonight.

Her character has been a stiff problem for me. At first she was a model of obedience, meekness, and politeness; but when I ceased to be a stranger, the rebukes of *petit-papa* and *petit-maman* were differently received. Towards me she varies a good deal. We have only one subject of quarrel; and that is the superiority of the English nation over the French, or vice versa. She is coquette in matters of dress and is sensitive to my least remark in this respect. Everything I say to her that amuses or pricks her she repeats to her mother, when she 'sees her into bed', who duly re-repeats these tales to me. I consider I have an important rôle to play, for Madame has announced to her daughter that she desires her to marry (at 19) an Englishman, ten years older than herself, who is to be intelligent and *beau*. So I am a sort of sample. But it is difficult to know what Mademoiselle really thinks of me. *Dis donc, petit-maman* she said one night *Mais Monsieur Owen est très-joli garçon, n'est-ce pas?*— Oh! said Madame—Nothing special—'for I didn't want to put any

---

[1] HO recalls these detailed designs, but they have not survived.

ideas into her head; and I don't want her to suffer any chagrin when you leave!' It is only in the last few days that Nénette has been free with me: to the extent of her pulling my hair and letting me stroke hers!

And it was only this very morning that I received her confidence of confidences; namely that she is beloved of a certain boy of her school, and loves him exceedingly; and that they have the firmest intention to get married as soon as convenient. She got this out immediately that [we] were alone after breakfast, and finding I did not laugh, but was extremely grave—having my own reasons,—ah! the days when I was eleven—she continued to relate how they contrive to exchange notes, sweets, and— even kisses; and how that her schoolmistress knows of the affair; but not her Mother or Father; and how Pierre is dressed; and that he is twelve years old. It has taken me three weeks work to win that confidence. But it is more than I ever won from You! Such an affair is not a proof of genius in Albine; but it is an indication; and I shall watch her future with keen interest. Very probably I shall spirit her over to Mahim for you to influence and know—if you will. Anyhow, her father said to her mother, before ever I thought of it myself, that he would like to send Nénette to my home. And her Mother asked me what would be the costs of *pension* in my family. Afterwards, I have shown them Mother's photograph. 'Oh, but she must be good, your Mother,' said Madame! Said Monsieur, with genuine enthusiasm: 'Why this is the face of goodness itself! This woman is goodness itself.'—So your theatrical man is the one who knows faces and character after all.

Please tell Mother she has jumped to erroneous conclusions about Madame's past: she never had any connection with the stage. The suspicions about her attitude to me, and her *Coquetterie* are more or less correct. But I don't care two pins, so let her be tranquillised, I prithee.

If it gives you all any pleasure to know that I am happy, I can tell you from the bottom of my heart that these weeks are passing like Elysian time.

Great thanks for the poems which Mother sent me and for her dear and dearly-treasured messages.

I am going to meet a great French Poet[1] in a day or two! Neither the Violinist, nor the old lady authoress are coming here it seems. Salute Scout Colin with a martial *geste*! Give my hearty condolence to Father on the suppression of his holiday. Can't be bothered to correct Raoul's letter now. In fact I don't begin another page because Nénette is at my window, stamping with impatience. Embrace sweet Mother as you would yourself—for your fondest

Brother

It is evident my letters have been detained 4 days or more in Bagnères. In fact I now know there have been no trains for Bordeaux.

---

[1] Laurent Tailhade (1854–1919), French poet and man of letters. Wilfred saw much of him in the four weeks that followed. For a discussion of the older man's possible influence on Wilfred's writing, see D. S. R. Welland, *Wilfred Owen: A Critical Study* (Chatto and Windus, London, 1960), pp. 89–92. See also Introduction, p. 2.

284. To Susan Owen

Monday, 24 August 1914   *Bagnères-de-Bigorre*

My own dear Mother,

I had yours of Sunday, Aug. 16th, on Sat. last. Tell me if you have got my budget addressed to Aberdovey, containing Photographs; and a following letter to Raoul; and lastly, a letter to Mary. I see there is a question in one of yours:—would I like a *Christian*? I should be strongly interested to read a Keswick Number; and also to know what is said by prophetic students about the Armageddon. On Sunday, if possible I go to Church with Nénette; but yesterday, having quite lost count of the days, I was not aware it was Sunday until late in the afternoon! It is not that one behaved in an unsundaylike fashion; but that every day is a Sunday here. Nearly a month have I been; and perhaps have as much as a fortnight more. We do not, however, stay till the 15th, as had been arranged, but till the 7th or 10th. But I am to live with the Légers in Bordeaux for another month, on the same understanding; on Oct. 10. Madame starts for Canada, if not held up by the War. This is capital for me. I am to have Nénette's charming room, and shall be virtually a guest. Their house is in the very best residential part, between the vast Place de Quinconces and the Jardin Public. (rent £320.) I shall hope to meet some interesting people, and if not too early for the season, I suppose I shall have the run of M. Léger's Theatre. It is the only Theatre in Bordeaux where classical, literary, or decent plays are put on. Consequently it has failed four years running. Nevertheless Léger perseveres heroically.

You were quite wrong in supposing Madame Léger to have been an actress; though curiously enough, most people who see her for the first time suppose it. Most women of Paris powder and rouge; and Madame is no exception: I have never seen her without either; but it is mild for every-day. Only once have I seen her fully made up (one night last week for the Casino) and then, with blue-shaded eyes, I can tell you she looked a surpassingly fair and dangerous woman. As for her history, I only know that she was educated at one of the tip-top boarding-schools of Paris, which she entered at the age of $3\frac{1}{2}$! . . .; that she was asked in marriage at 14; and was married, at $17\frac{1}{2}$ to Charles Léger, who is 20 years older than herself; that she undertook at the time of her marriage the affairs which were previously in the family of her husband; that she is at present 31 years of age, and is driving a commerce of enormous success.

I am conscious that she has a considerable liking for me, both in a physical and intellectual sense. She is now equally conscious that the former liking is not reciprocated—not one little bit—and continues to like me for my mind's nature. If it were not so,—I should hop it, immejit. The first week was sufficient to enrol me a friend of the family: a talk with Monsieur in which I gave him my views,—another with Madame when I dared to argue with her, and matched her on her own ground (linguistic);—an inspiration to amuse Nénette by translating various people on the piano—and my position in their estimation and in their household was assured. That translation into music—or discord— of the characters we liked or disliked, e.g. The proprietor of the villa (discord), Monsieur Aumont; Nénette; a little peasant, friend of Nénette; etc. was the result of a pitch of sensation which is alas! so rare in me that I should not dream of repeating it. I translated Nénette by the marvellous 'Rustle of Spring' of Sinding: and I maintain the likeness to be perfect. The grace of the whole, the absence of any melancholy, the pretty rippling triviality of the greater portion; and the sometime sinking into a rich, rich abundance of life and earnestness—that is Nénette.

As in my letters, this child naturally occupies a good deal of room in my thoughts; but I am—alas or happily, who shall say?—too old to be in love, as you predicted. And then I see her too often . . . With her it is different, and my continual presence has caused a commotion and an alteration which her mother perceives with alarm. It is true that she talks incessantly about me in my absence, and that she won't put on this or that dress for fear Monsieur Owen will not be pleased (!); and that she worries me to shave my moustache!!—But I knew the real state of affairs; and, as in self-defence, had to throw some light on the school-boy side. If *petit-papa* knew he would take it much more seriously, and remove her instantly from her school, and send her to goodness-knows where—England probably. Poor Pierre!—so sorry, old boy: and she had a fortune too!

On two days last week, Laurent Tailhade, the distinguished French poet, gave lectures in the Casino, for the benefit of charity. Monsieur Léger gave recitations. I was of course presented to Tailhade; and Madame invited him to lunch next Thursday, for my benefit. It is possible that Mons. Léger will be in Bordeaux all this week; but in any case I shall get at the poet alone, as I have engaged to 'fetch' him. It was interesting to see how he enjoyed being rallied in his capacity of poet, for being incapable of remembering the date or the way.

My friend Bizardel, whom I used to meet on Sunday afternoons writes to me today saying that the Prefect of Bordeaux has taken him into his Cabinet.[1] So I am more sure of information and protection!

I also had a card from Leslie in Llandudno. I keenly regret that you didn't manage to spend a week or so with them.   *Tuesday*

I was writing yesterday in the nearest Thunderstorm I have ever experienced. We were right in the midst of the lightning, which I positively felt warm on my cheek.

The news of war today is decidedly bad. We understand that the Germans are over the frontier in N. Belgium,[2] and French and English losses are heavy. We are very unquiet.

But I have a piece of personal news which makes my heart bound. Madame Léger has asked me to go to Canada with her. Alas! for this

[1] See Letter 253, note 1.

[2] The Mons battle began on 23 August; British troops fell back on the 24th.

VIIa. The Châlet, Mérignac, winter 1914–15

VIIb. Family group at Mérignac, 5 July 1915

Back row, l. to r.: the Castéjas girl, Charles, Johnny, Bobbie, Wilfred, David
Front row: Mlle Puységur, ? Miss Hall, Miss de la Touche, unidentified, the Castéjas boy

VIII. Hut 6a, C Company, Artist's Rifles at Hare Hall Camp, Gidea Park, Essex, November 1915. Wilfred is second from the left, back row

(*see Letter 395*)

voyage (Oct. to January) she says it is too late to arrange; and she would prefer the next (March–May about), which would interfere with my Exam.[1] Perhaps Nénette will go then, which I should prefer. Nothing has been agreed about fares and expenses, but, while I don't expect to gain a cent I cannot of course be responsible for any costs whatever. The entire conversation on this subject only lasted five minutes, so I have no more to tell you. But what a go!

Always your own Wilfred

285. To Susan Owen

Friday, 28 August 1914   [*Bagnères-de-Bigorre*]

Sweet my Mother,

I wonder if you'll have any difficulty in picking out your son, among the audience at the Casino, on the afternoon of Laurent Tailhade's Lecture.[2] I need scarcely tell you that on my left is Madame Léger. Nénette is a mere nebulosity. To right of me is the owner of our villa, Madame Cazalas, a weird bird, who seems to have tried to attach her left leg to me. We didn't know we were being taken; but I don't dislike my head. The radiant polish of my cheek is due, partly to happiness, partly to sunshine. I was evidently amused at the moment, and about to make a remark to Madame: possibly Monsieur Léger was reciting just then.

The Group[3] represents the poet Tailhade, on the same afternoon, posing (and proposing to the young lady who sang (infamously badly)). Monsieur Léger, behind Tailhade's left, is not at all 'like'. His mouth is never to be seen in such a pugnacious 'mug'. As a matter of fact he was furious about something when the photo was taken. The remaining people, are (obviously enough,) local johnnies who helped with the music. With these groups, I enclose two very fine views; both of which are visible—modified—from the estate. They are worthy to be framed, even for their own sake.

Tell me if you like them, and also your opinion of me & the Légers. Tailhade came to lunch yesterday; but I had very little real conversation with him. In the first place, he was suffering from his heart, precisely after your deplorable miss-fire fashion, my dear mother, and only with difficulty and opening of all windows did he sit out the meal. However—he is coming to live up here with us. At least, chiefly for my sake, Madame asked him, and he accepted. It is not yet a fact, but I don't allow myself to doubt it, although Madame says she suspects he sees some difficulty—about the distance from Bagnères, and so on. He lives generally in Paris, whence he has not yet retired into private life. The donkey-cart doesn't frighten him, because he is too Parisian to care about the amused public. A <u>Bordeaux</u> celebrity, so say the Légers,

[1] But hopes of a university were now dwindling.
[2] This photograph survives. See Plate VI.
[3] This has not survived.

would never consent to go a-riding in a donkey-shandy. They beg him to attack the Bordeaux public, which they hold in merited contempt. For Tailhade is one of the wickedest satirists, and cruellest enemies that have ever used the French language as a lash. For all that he is a charming old gentleman to meet. I called at his Hotel this morning to know his mind about the day of his removal. I saw him up at his window in shirt-sleeves, mooning. He received me like a lover. To use an expression of the Rev. H. Wigan's, he quite slobbered over me. I know not how many times he squeezed my hand; and, sitting me down on a sofa, pressed my head against his shoulder. [*two lines illegible*] It was not intellectual; but I felt the living verve of the poet . . . who has fought seventeen duels (so it is said).

Quite apart from the prospect of this Friendship, I am, for quite an appreciable length of time, imbued with sensations of happiness. The war affects me less than it ought. But I can do no service to anybody by agitating for news or making dole over the slaughter. On the contrary I adopt the perfect English custom of dealing with an offender: a Frenchman duels with him: an Englishman ignores him. I feel my own life all the more precious and more dear in the presence of this deflowering of Europe. While it is true that the guns will effect a little useful weeding, I am furious with chagrin to think that the Minds which were to have excelled the civilization of ten thousand years, are being annihilated[1]— and bodies, the product of aeons of Natural Selection, melted down to pay for political statues. I regret the mortality of the English regulars less than that of the French, Belgian, or even Russian or German armies: because the former are all Tommy Atkins, poor fellows, while the continental armies are inclusive of the finest brains and temperaments of the land. There is no exception made but for the diseased, the imbecile, and the criminal. The world is madder than—

Your own bundle of eccentricity Wilfred

286. To Susan Owen
Postcard

4 September [*1914*]   *Bagnères P.O.*

Dearest Mother,

It seems quite a long time since I last heard from home—a P.C. from you—and longer since I wrote. I have been waiting for definite news to give you. Mme. L. is obliged to leave here before the 15th and Bordeaux early in Oct. She is taking a boat from Bordeaux to Havre, & thence to Montreal & would like me to go on the same boat to Havre. But if Raoul stays at Home I would rather remain at his house. The Government is at Bordeaux,[2] and as many of Parisians as can get there. Laurent Tailhade has got installed in the Villa several times and as many times

---

[1] He first wrote 'snuffed out'.
[2] The French Government moved to Bordeaux on the outbreak of war.

retreated because of neulralgic abcess. No end of a fuss. I am dining at his hotel tonight. All serene with me. I have seen many 'Wounded' arrive here.

Fondest love. Wilfred

287. To Susan Owen

Picture postcard: Bagnères-de-Bigorre, Place Ramond,
Marché Convent

[Postmark 18 September 1914]   *Bordeaux P.O.*

I choose this view to persuade myself what a beastly place is Bagnères de Bigorre. For it cost dear to leave. Starting on Thursday at 12 noon we arrived at midnight! We passed many 'cages' of German wounded. I found a letter & card at Lem's, but neither referred to the momentous affair treated in my last letter. I will write tonight nevertheless. 'Madam' takes a boat to Havre about Oct. 7. What if I return that way? Berlitz S. is closed. Am marvellous well but worried of course. W x
Write: 12 Rue Blanc-Dutrouilh.[1]

288. To Harold Owen

Wednesday, 23 September [1914]   *[12 rue Blanc Dutrouilh, Bordeaux]*

My dear Harold,

Just a word to say how glad I am that you are safe at home: and to send you a few belated birthday wishes. One of them is that I shall see you before you start again: though this is not really my expectation. I hope anyhow that the next voyage won't be a long one. I was sorry and annoyed that you didn't send any pictures by Raoul. You might have done so without fear of damage or of criticism. Both M. and Madame Léger are artists. Monsieur had done some oil-painting, and Madame of course has a genius for Design. She employs three designers for her business, two men and a young lady. Do you know anything about styles yet? I mean the way of recognizing and imitating the Louis XV, XVI, Empire, etc? Methinks the less you know the better, for I infinitely prefer the modern manner, and, at any period of history, the English to the French.

The house where I am is spacious, rather than very large. It is not furnished as it might be. There are in the drawing-room two fine oil-paintings representing M. Léger; which have been hung in the Paris Salon. Also there is a very pretty statuette of Madame L. about six inches high, in sitting pose. Above all, they have an original bust, by a greatish sculptor, Escoula,[2] of Mr. Léger in his youth. I have seen a fair number of busts and statues in my time, but I only know of one

---

[1] The Bordeaux address of the Légers.
[2] Jean Escoula (1851–1911), the French sculptor. 'Angéliques', 'La Douleur', and 'Jeunes Baigneuses' are his best-known works.

which expresses so much energy, and manliness, and feeling, as this; while at the same time it is a marvellously faithful portrait.

The photographs of Nénette are innumerable: Some of them absolute artistic perfections; not a whit below the best work Uncle John ever did. There are also plaster-casts and wood-carvings of this fair child.

The business-work of Madame L. is carried on in comparative secrecy: she won't allow me to go into the work-rooms until the articles are completed. Whether it is for fear of my cribbing the <u>patterns</u> or whether the <u>work-girls</u> I haven't well decided. Anyhow I can't inform you about either yet.

I have been living in an admirable fashion, as well in Bordeaux as at Bagnères. My friend Bizardel, who is in the Cabinet of the Prefect of Bordeaux, has two automobiles at his disposition, (all the cars are now monopolised by Government.) One day he had to make a call on all the French ministers, and he took me in his motor. I didn't see many Ministers, and nor did he; all he did was to leave the Card of the Prefect. But of course we were dressed in *grand chic*: and wore an air of tremendous diplomats. The Minister for War[1] is in the University where I ought to be having my Courses; Minister of Finance,[2] in a school; Minister of Justice[3] in the Law-Courts; Minister of Fine Arts[4] (a friend of Tailhade) in the Theatre; and so on. Poincaré is installed a few steps from my old room. Most Paris newspapers are fixed up around about this street; even money is being coined in Bordeaux. The aspect of the streets has changed a good deal. Fifty thousand extra people are here! It is easy to recognize Parisians. In certain streets pass a dream of fair women. The populace grumbles that *chic* toilets should still be worn; but if not for such gentle ladies, what on earth is the Fighting about? It is the old story of the Lists: the Princess sits in flowers, while the warriors scuffle about in the ring. As a matter of fact, there are already <u>too many</u> ladies offering to help with red cross work. This afternoon two friends of Madame Léger, Mlle. Levallois, (a violinist who has toured all over England, Scotland & Ireland) and another Mlle. (once a great singer) have gone out hawking copies of a new patriotic song, to get money for the hospitals.

I went with my friend the Doctor Sauvaître to one of the large hospitals one day last week, where he is operating on the wounded. The hospital is in the buildings of the Boys' *Lycée* and appliances are altogether crude. First I saw a bullet, like this ▷ cut out of a Zouave's[5] leg. Then we did the round of the wards; and saw some fifty German wretches: all more seriously wounded than the French. The Doctor picked out those needing surgical attention; and these were brought on stretchers to the Operating Room; formerly a Class room,

[1] M. Millerand.
[2] M. Ribot.
[3] M. Briand.
[4] Unidentified.
[5] Member of French light-infantry corps, originally formed of Algerians and retaining their uniform.

with the familiar ink-stains on floor, walls, and ceiling; now a chamber of horrors with blood where the ink was. Think of it: there were eight men in the room at once, Germans being treated without the slightest distinction from the French: one scarcely knew which was which. Considering the lack of appliances—there was only one water-tap in the room—and the crowding—and the fact that the doctors were working for nothing—and on Germans too—really good work was done. Only there were no anaesthetics—no time—no money—no staff for that. So after that scene I need not fear to see the creepiest operations. One poor

devil had his shin-bone crushed by a gun-carriage-wheel, and the doctor had to twist it about and push it like a piston to get out the pus. Another had a hole right through the knee; and the doctor passed a bandage thus:

Another had a head into which a ball had entered and come out again.

 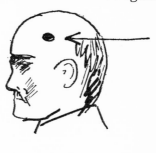

This is how the bullet lay in the Zouave. Sometimes the feet were covered with a brown, scaly, crust—dried blood.

I deliberately tell you all this to educate you to the actualities of the war.[1]

There were two Englishmen here wounded, last week; but when Bizardel & I motored out to the Hospital, they had just moved somewhere else: one having developed scarletina.

[1] HO was sailing in submarine waters at this time.

I was not much upset by the morning at the hospital; and this is a striking proof of my health. I understand that you are likewise 'strapping' and I felicitate you. It will be to me enormously interesting to hear of your voyages. If you return from Canada after a month I may just catch you at home. Of course give my dearest love to everybody: I remain here until the 12th Oct., I think!

Your affectionate, Wilfred

289. To Susan Owen

Postcard

Wednesday [*Postmark 30 September 1914*]   [*Postmark Bordeaux*]

Your Card—both sides of which gave me a special delight—came yesterday. What a fine sensation was produced by the 'hope to hear what day to expect you'. Nevertheless I have seldom passed such agreeable days as these present. Dozens of interesting people defile before me. I spend my time 'looking up' friends in the town and studying French Literature. If Harold has left, I suppose you will have opened his letter and learnt that I am fixed here until Oct. 7. as Madame leaves Havre by the *Chicago* on the 12th. I have only one pupil at present. I have answered advertisements in *Schoolmaster*. French Master wanted temporarily in Birkenhead. I wonder if Father could call at Town Hall, & see Sec. R. T. Jones? Also in Chester, apply to Lovell, Educ. Off., Town Hall. I won't think of coming by Havre then. Do you know Gen. St. Nav. Co. to London is cheaper than Moss Line to L'pool. and I should prefer to land in London.

Do begin a course of Rest Cure to prepare yourself for my examination of your Health! Don't worry. The Affair Léger[1] is 'settled'. Your own W

I've received the balance from Raoul.

290. To Susan Owen

Postcard

Monday [*Postmark 12 October 1914*]   *Post Office* [*Postmark Bordeaux*]

Not wanting to write contradictory plans I have left my news for Raoul to send.[2] I am still fuddling round after pupils, but with so little result that I think seriously of embarking next Saturday for London, in order to see Harold. If more pupils present themselves I shall stay on. To-morrow I shall know. We still have superb weather. Many thanks for your 2 letters and Harold's. W

Mme. Léger left yesterday for Havre.

[1] In addition to worrying Susan Owen, the 'affair Léger' had also disturbed Wilfred. See Letter 292.
[2] Wilfred had now left the Légers, to stay with the Lems at 12 Rue St. Louis.

291. To Susan Owen
Postcard

Wednesday [*Postmark 14 October 1914*]   [*Postmark Bordeaux*]

The whole days of yesterday & before-yesterday have been spent in looking up people likely to take lessons. I have found just enough, I think, to justify my staying on a while in Bordeaux. I have nothing and <u>nobody</u> tending to attach me to the place; but having already determined to resist home till Christmas, I feel I ought not to refuse work when it presents itself. Some lessons are at 3 francs, which is really not bad: the only difficulty is to find <u>enough</u>. I am ever so sorry not to see Harold this time. Give him Good Speed! I shall write him a letter before he leaves. Tonight I am positively fatigued after my heroic efforts, notwithstanding I keep up a blissful good state of health. Don't be disappointed: it is but a matter of weeks before Christmas! If pupils fall off I shall be obliged to pack off sooner! Your own W
Raoul sends best tanks for your letter.

292. To Susan Owen

Address your next letters till further notice :

Wednesday, 14 October 1914   *12 Cours St. Louis, Bordeaux*

My own Mother,

The reading of your letter this morning was quite emotioning for me. You speak so cheerfully of yourself, you say such nice things about Harold; you tell me that dear Father approves of me yet, and will be glad—I hope gladdened—to see me; and you show me Colin, pale, and crumpled-up under Homework! I was so near booking my passage at the beginning of the week! But, all at once, three or four pupils turned up, and after all my exertions in turning 'em up, I thought it a pity to turn 'em down again.

One is a boy who began with me at Berlitz, and who interested me by his intelligence. We grew friendly, and it was at his home that I spent the evening of my 21st birthday. His parents are both schoolteachers. His mother is one of the most genuine good-natured Frenchwomen existing. It was through her that I got three more pupils—girls who have done five years English already; but I haven't seen them yet. While I am still unsettled, this good lady, Madame Berthaud,[1] has offered me a room; but as it is for the moment occupied by a wounded soldier, I may not be able to take advantage of it. For, you know, I must leave the Lems' next Saturday. They have a young lad coming to lodge with them for a matter of some years. He is entering Raoul's school; & the matter had been fixed up long ago with his wealthy parents. This youth, whom I have seen and liked, is going to receive English instruction from me, twice a week. I am glad of the excuse to

[1] See Letter 245, note 1.

leave here; for, though wondrous neat and clean, my room has no writing-table, no wardrobe, no drawers, and no armchair. The window looks on the streets, giving me advantages and annoyances. From six o'clock in the morning begins a thundering and a racketing of lorry-wheels on the stone causeway; and a growl of barrels rolling, and a clank of iron-rods flopping: above all of which, like a clarion on a battlefield, resounds the braying of Sieur Lem's ass! But the day is quieter, and at 4 o'clock I can look down on the children coming from a school close by, which never fails to make me tender and poetical. Poor children, these; for the quarter is poor but not low. Indeed I never see in France any scabby-haired, mud-stockinged arabs, hoarse of voice and hard of eye, such as breed in Liverpool muds, Birmingham cinders, and London fog-smoke.

In the *Jardin Public*, in the afternoon, gathers another type of youngsters: a great part of them are Parisians, and very *chic*. It has sometimes happened that when I have been reading there, a boy has stopped his hoop and come up to me, hat in hand, just in order to talk to me. These incidents give me hope that the Léger episodes have not taken the bloom off my innocency. I don't think I told you I have an interesting 'protégé' who would cost me dear if I had any help to give him. Before I left for Bagnères I encountered at the *Union Chrétienne* a youth of 15.[1] The first thing he said to me was that he loved Song and Music above all things; and straightway began to sing! Now his eyes, and indeed his whole countenance were the most romantically beautiful I had ever beheld. So remembered him, and having his card, looked him up on my return. I found his house in a shabby quarter. And I found his household in tears and sighing. His father was dying. Some weeks before his employer had reduced his little pittance owing to the war. The good man was so upset, that he contracted jaundice and such complications as a result of his contrariety of spirit. Now he is dead. The mother is a good soul, all heart, and, as I have seen her, never out of tears. Arriving at the moment I did, she vows I was sent by the good God. I was indeed able to do some small services; and have now won her affection, even as her son has mine. She begs and implores me to be a Counsellor to her sons. 'Oh, my dear young Sir! Give them your Advice: look after them: warn them: be their friend . . . Oh the poor, dears, left like this fatherless, oh! oh! oh! . . .'

And that was the moment when I began to realize better the seamy side of Madame Léger's cap: if you understand me. Indeed, I hope you understand the rest of this incoherent effusion: for on reading it over I scarcely make much sense of it myself. But so long as I am as wise in policy as I have proved I can be, you will let me dream and scribble as idiotically as I like!

There was no mention of Mary in your last. I hope she is mentally alive: and should like some sign of it. Let her write soon!

Ever your loving Wilfred

---

[1] André Martin. See Letter 375.

293. To Susan Owen
Postcard

18 October [*1914*]   *12 Rue St. Louis*

I am still here, as a room I wanted was not vacant on Saturday. As it happens I am glad I have not taken that room—Today I had a card from the Consul (whom I had been to some days ago) telling me to 'call around' at a certain address, where 'they would give me a job'. The job is to 'accompany' a young fellow for some hours of the day, three times a week. I have not seen the young fellow, nor his mother, the Viscountess of Maud'huy, but I am going to see her and settle things tomorrow. On the strength of this I must take a respectable room; and have in fact chosen a delightful apartment,

31 rue Desfourniels, which I will describe when I get installed, Monday I hope. The young lodger of the Lems' comes in today.—The summer has finished—miserable rains begin. There has been no Autumn for me!

Dearest love to All—W

294. To Susan Owen
Postcard

Monday, 19 October 1914   *Gen. P.O.* [*Bordeaux*]

I moved in at 9 o'clock this morning—Papa Lem carrying my 3 trunks; for my worldly goods have so increased that I have been obliged to get another box. At 10 o'clock I flurried round to see the Viscountess: Instead of the whole day arrangement mentioned before, we shall do 2 hours lesson twice a week. I believe the young man is a son of the General governing Bordeaux at present. I like my rooms ever so much but nothing is yet in order—I have been out all day. I have nothing new to signal in points personal except the approach of a Cold. Vicious Weather! Remember address 31 rue Desfourniels.

295. To Susan Owen

[*Late*] *October 1914*   *Chez Veuve Martin, 31 rue Desfourniels, Bordeaux*

Dearest of Mothers,

Your loving letters never end without a prayer for my happiness. Let mine begin with the assurance that they are answered: (I mean the prayers, not the letters.) If not greatly happier than I was this time last year, I am infinitely more comfortable. And the feeling that I am under obligations to no man, is as sweet as it is new. For the moment I have neither schoolmaster nor taskmaster, neither patron nor boss. I have slain—so far as I am concerned four tyrants: first, Timpany, who taxed his subjects with grievous work; next Lightbourn, a bullying boss; next Wigan, who essayed to dominate one's entire being; next Aumont, unmercifully grinding, being goaded by avarice.

These men are not my enemies (except perhaps the last); but they are not the masters I feel called to serve. Indeed, though I look up and down the world, I see no man whom I could serve without a suffocated feeling of captivity. This may turn out fortunate after all. . . .

For the moment, my decision to throw myself on the world and live by my wits, has proved happy. I confess that, when I wrote putting off my return, I knew only two certain pupils, who would have brought me in a revenue of eight francs a week! But the pain I had to put off seeing you yet a little while pricked me so that I did a rare thing, I made an effort. And now I have every expectation of prospering—in the manner of our old friend in the *Tale of Two Cities*, the husband of Lucie Manette, (forget his name)[1] who gave lessons in Soho: and was offered the backward urchins of his friends to instruct. All my pupils are children, (thanks be); except the Viscount, who is nineteen. He is not the son of the General, but his nephew. I like him quite well; and shall finish by a friendship, I foresee. The Consul, who sent me round to these people, spoke of a sort of supervision of the young spark on my part: Guide,—Philosopher, and—Friend sort of thing. His lordship is notably flighty, according to his aunt whom I interviewed first. Probably I showed too young for this business. Indeed I hinted I couldn't be bothered with his morals unless well paid. So twice a week I resort to his room—on a fourth story—and give a two hour lesson which just covers my total expenses for that day (5f.) In virtue of this, I have taken a handsome room: twice the rent of the last. But as all rents have risen lately, the difference is less real. I spent a good part of three days, hunting for a den. I nearly put up in a garret, at 15 francs. The Lems found the hole: near them: in a poky lane, behind the docks: view of thousands of roofs. Attracted by the romance of a real garret with white-washed walls and a prospect of chimney-stacks I actually went to engage it: but the proprietor being out, the Lems made up a bed for one night more; and next day I found it would be necessary for me to have a room to receive people. For that purpose my choice is well fitted:— fine old house—looking on a little square—out of reach of tram-noises, but two minutes from trams—my rooms form a corner—a great window each way—room well carpeted—four armchairs—Louis XV (genuine) bureau—Louis XV Wardrobe—second wardrobe with mirrors modern, Louis XVI,—bed and night-table to match—fine marble fireplace— thirty (supportable) pictures—and—a piano, out of tune, but with-out tone. A Dressing Room leads out of the Chamber: no lack of mirrors and shelves & cupboards—and even a gas-jet is fixed up for my hot-water. This window faces east as every dressing room should, and is blessed with a delightful morning sun. Suppose I help your imagination with a few lines—

[1] Charles Darnay, whose place on the scaffold was taken by Sydney Carton.

The rest of the story is occupied by my widow-landlady, whose son is at the war. She takes care of me in a manner that would gratify you. The good soul, for what reason I know not, often asks if my mother and father won't come and stay with me: and as much as sends you the message that she would be glad to put you up. If only you had the <u>energy</u> to come over . . .!

I must run out now to a Lecture. Courses (free) are now started every evening in Raoul's College. I get up early and couch me late; but between the arrangement of my room; my lessons; my visits on & by friends; my interesting books, I don't seem to be able to succeed in Correspondence! But as for losing any modicum of desire to get home . . . what possessed you (to speak plainly) to pen that imagination???

Your very own, Wilfred

I had Harold's telegram: 'Not Calling Rochelle' <u>before</u> your P.C. I really think I should have started off to see him, and <u>feel so</u> disappointed.

296. To Mary Owen

Friday, 29 October 1914   *Bordeaux*

My dear Mary,

I am upset about this malignant cold of Mother's, and hope you will keep telling me precisely how things are. For my part I have shaken off my cold in eight days.

This Nursing Training is capital for you.[1] When I saw so many French ladies busying themselves so, I meant to ask you what you were doing, and whether you couldn't join classes. I therefore am ever so <u>glad</u> to know you are take Gardener's lectures. I confess I <u>look for the</u> benefit to produce itself in yourself more than for the Soldiers: and I myself shall feel a security and a comfort to know that you are able to deal with accidents and make war on microbes! I only hope you will attack the subject seriously, and get something like an orderly notion of Anatomy: and, later on, to understand the functions of the different organs. About this I am still much in the dark myself; but I used to know the names of the bones and muscles, so look out for some quizzing. If you pass your examination I shall be radiant.

I spent Wednesday morning at the oral examination of the French B.A. which is reputed to be as easy as London Matric. and is passed at seventeen years. One of my pupils for English was sitting, and I was at his elbow all the while, as well for English, as other things. I used to have a horror of the mere idea of an oral examination in anything; but having seen, I don't think the system bad. Half a dozen professors instal themselves behind tables, in odd corners of a large room: with a label above their learned noddles, telling what was in them. The candidates saunter in about eight o'clock in the morning, and if one sees an examiner

---

[1] Mary became a VAD when war broke out.

unoccupied one sits down on the chair before him, and he straightway begins to ply you with questions. Anybody may gape around, even the succeeding candidates; but 'the public' was restricted to myself and one or two anxious mothers. Five minutes after the last student has been examined the results are known! Five minutes! and in England we wait six weeks! I recognised the professor of Latin and Ancient History, he having accompanied his daughter to my lessons at Berlitz. (This young lady was the greatest dunce imaginable, and many a time have I thumped the table, glaring at the papa, but little thought he was so erudite a pot). In the exam, I heard this Prof. telling the daughters of others what hopeless flounderers they were in Latin. To my friend, he growled— 'My lad, you know nothing at all of Latin, nothing at all.' Nevertheless my friend passed.

Thus I spent all a morning; and the afternoon with my lessons, and the evening with my Free Classes finishes the day, and so finishes every day; but I don't find time to write to Mother as I should like to, or even to Colin. I have told you about his double who is a cousin of the pupil just mentioned. At times, I only just fail to punch the fellow's head for daring to resemble my incomparable brother and yet baulking me of the reality. Only let my incomparable brother see to it that he resembles himself, in my idea of him!

As much as I long to feel the soft caress of My Mother's hand, and to behold the hearty countenance of my Father, and as much as I long to hear the rare voice of my gentle Sister, I long to slap the shoulders of that Colin, and stroke his little chin. As for Harold I shall regard him with great astonishment for having rounded the vast mass of South America, and with ten times more admiration for having rounded off his own address.

Father's letter this afternoon, which followed Mother's of this morning, gave great pleasure. I cannot justly say that the matter of Mother's was pleasing—what with the complication of her Cold, and the miserable sketch of Dunsden—Oh my! But when I hear that Mother is on the ascending scale again, I shall be your 'most content'

Wilfred

297. To Susan Owen

1 November 1914   *Bordeaux*

Dearest Mother,

There is nothing really fresh to tell you. November is not a month of freshnesses. But the date will remind you how that just a year has passed since I fell ill here. I was reminded in the most august of fashions, namely by that sinister big bell, that sounded so gloomily to me, in my bare room, and with no company but the fear of a serious illness. It was not till the seventh that I was really 'taken worse'. That I have never seen or heard you since seems quite inexplicable. It will take Fate a mighty deal of labour, if he (or she) has the unfortunate idea to prevent me from getting home for Christmas. However I continue to be of a satisfied mind for having stayed now. I don't feel the least bit tied-and-bound by my work: I don't realise that I am working these days. That is the beauty of it. Some days I have nothing at all fixed to be done. Yet I 'touch' a revenue just about equal to the Berlitz Screw.

The other day I escaped a danger by a mere instinct. You know the English Professors were sometimes sent to a School in the town to give courses. I was never given this business, but the German did it instead.

Now, I 'called around' at this school some time ago, and found they wanted to continue these lessons; but that the Director was away, & would be back on a certain date.

On that date I sallied out to see him, but on the way, felt a disinclination to bother about the business: and so went the next day—to find that at the very time I had proposed to call, M. Aumont[1] had been, and offered to take these classes himself. Otherwise I should have been certainly accepted. But what luck that I wasn't. For if Aumont had found I had baulked him in that way, he would have been on me like a pile of bricks;—and certainly he would have discovered it. As if he knows at all of my remaining in Bordeaux, I am not snatching the bread out of his mouth, as the poor wretch would have regarded it, if he had found me installed in that school. So I leave him with a good grace to his dufferly school children, and for myself I content myself with the following pupils—

(1) Raoul's boarder. As Raoul acts the goat during all the lesson, it is at least not somnolent for me.
(2) Berthaud—already referred to often.
(3) Two demoiselles, preparing exams.—advanced pupils—agreeable lesson.
(4) Demoiselle—fair creature, not agreeable lesson.
(5) Two kids of 11 or 12—dear little fellows—on whom 'the Method' succeeds, happily.
(6) The Viscount de Maudhuy.
(7) M. Peyronnet—manufacturer of perfumes: (not yet started)
(8) A Russian—prof. of mathematics.

I could do with twice as many, but—Time of War my dear! The Evening Classes for my French are disappointing. The fellows speak with a shockingly bad accent—and the Professors scarcely a whit better. But for M. Léger I might have learnt to speak a French like a Lancashire mill-boy's English! I called on M. Léger yesterday. A telegram from Madame announces her arrival at Montreal. When I went into her house I seemed to have travelled a long, long distance since I left my room here. The two places are in my mind's estimate, as if very remote. How remote is Home! Since I left my bed on the floor at seven o'clock that Sept. morning, I have couched in exactly twelve different rooms!

---

[1] Wilfred had imagined him at the front. See Letter 278.

I think more & more of my little room—and 'moster' and 'mostest' of my little Mother! The same nostalgia that I had November last is recrudescent now: But Christmas is Coming.

Hearty thanks for Father's letter: Your fondest Wilfred x

298. To Susan Owen

Friday, 6 November 1914   *Bordeaux*

My dearest Mother,

Many things of interest were to be found in your last envelopeful; but what most impressed me was the confession to perpetual headache. It gives to me as much uneasiness as it gives you unease. Such a state of things should be given its right name Disease, and should be treated as such. I know not what druggeries you are given, nor what semblances of rests you take, but if one thing more than another seems to me probable to clear your dear head of these distempers and infesting dreams, it would be a radical displacement of yourself, a voyage into France, bag-and-baggage into a new atmosphere, and a fresh mentality. Suppose I returned here after Chistmas, would you come? Raoul has hinted something about your having certain intentions of staying with him! What is this, pray?

I have written a card to Oliver.[1] But I don't think I could bear to live in Cambridge except in one capacity alone . . . yet. However, let us hear all possible about it.

And so you say Talking fatigues you to the point of irritation. I suspect it is the Talk and the Talkers that are to blame. For me, I never took such pleasure in Conversation as at this present time. The French put such an astonishing intelligence and elegance into their *Causeries*, that these equal, and supplant even, Novel-Reading. I speak now of the French represented by Tailhade, and the friends of Monsieur Léger. While, more's the pity, I think of such English representatives of Conversation as old Mrs. Williams, waddling round to waste your afternoons; or else of that loud-protesting Protestant Miss Kent: or else of that meek handmaiden of the Lord, Mrs. Fordham, whispering prophecies, scandal, visions, prayers and shop-prices world-without-end. If this gives you a headache I feel a wicked satisfaction to know it. It ought to. To think that you are in ear-shot of Mrs. . . .[2] What commerce hast thou with these folk? I think with sorrow of your isolation in the human world. For upon my word, if you secretly deem that your sister-in-law is living an animal life, I secretly suspect your sister of vegetating. Who shall blame 'em? The mineral state is perhaps the most preferable, after all.

But, like a Poet, thou hast thy own Creations to comfort thee, and

[1] Frederick Oliver, a Shrewsbury friend, had gone up to Cambridge. He was ordained in 1919, and was Rector of Swithland 1925–30.
[2] We have omitted the name.

may we, thy Works, follow thee with more consolations than the creations of art.

In any case you are less isolate than I.

I begin to suffer a hunger for Intimity. At bottom, it is that I ought to be in love and am not. Though I have abundance of acquaintance, and a thousand times more friends here than in England, (since out of the Family, I have not one in England) I lack any touch of tenderness. I ache in soul, as my bones might ache after a night spent on a cold, stone floor.

You ask about my pulsations. Now, only today I had a severe attack of palpitation: this way: in a populous street suddenly I saw bearing down on me a hard, hunting-cruel Face: Aumont! His expression alone was enough to terrify, but when that expression was worn by the very eyes one wanted to avoid . . . For it was the face of Sherlock Holmes gone to the bad. There is one of my 'neighbours' whom I hate as myself. There are not two: and that one is Maurice Aumont. One thing I may thank him for, and that is for providing me with a visual impression of the avaricious brothers in *Isabella*.[1] But he didn't recognize me, and no wonder, I am so much changed since the day of my emancipation. And my nerves were soon after caressed by the meeting with no less than six other faces, which were all fair in their way, and kindling with smiles. One was Master Pierre Berthaud, who bore the aspect of 'snatching a fearful joy' (as Gray put it)[2] in being out of bounds. He just had time to caution me not to remember having seen him in town, and vanished on his mysterious errand. Another was Thouverez, Colin's non-correspondent; whom I have not seen for months.

I have to signal the loss of two pupils. The Viscount de Maud'huy is going to England this week. I had a note this morning telling me of this new plan, & in which he hopes to meet me over there. In reply I opened the bars of Mahim's gates to him! For he is a fellow of some fellowship for me. My land-lady cut out the enclosed ¶. and begged me to send it to de Maud'huy 'with felicitations'. Good soul. So I send it to you in case she find it in my waste-paper basket. Och! I forgot you may not make head or tail of it. How droll! I lose also the Russian Pupil, gone to Pau, travelling in the same carriage as my landlady who went down that day to see her soldier-son, ill in hospital.

I heard that Tailhade, together with Anatole France,[3] is shouldering a rifle! Now I may be led into enlisting when I get home: so familiarise yourself with the idea! It is a sad sign if I do: for it means that I shall

---

[1] Keats, *Isabella, or the Pot of Basil*, in which Isabella's two brothers murder her lover.

[2] Still as they run they look behind,
They hear a voice in every wind,
    And snatch a fearful joy.

    Thomas Gray, 'Ode on a Distant Prospect of Eton College'.

[3] He was 70 (1844–1924). Novelist and man of letters, his real name was François Anatole Thibault.

consider the continuation of my life of no use to England. And if once
my fears are roused for the perpetuity and supremacy of my mother-
tongue, in the world—I would not hesitate, as I hesitate now—to enlist.

———

To have the Photographs, so real and fresh, and naïf as they are, is
a high pleasure for me. I think you look never so sweet. I like the
attitude of Colin, and feel a special admiration for his Right Hand and
there end my compliments. Mary is so stiff, though the self-effacement
of the left-arm is characteristic enough [*remainder missing*]

299. To Susan Owen

Postcard

Tuesday [*Postmark 11 November 1914*]   [*Postmark Bordeaux*]

I hope you have had my last letter which I left in the hands of a friend
who came to see me on Sunday Morning. If it costs $2\frac{1}{2}$ to send a *Christian*
I don't think you'd better send any more. I am anxious to have your
Dunsden Accounts which haven't yet reached me. A cold spell has now
begun. I shall have to start my fires. I have just secured other pupils to
fill the gaps left by de Maud'huy. I made some experiments with my
Camera for (the first time) the other day. The prints will be some days
in obtaining. Beware the Cold!

Yours W.E.O.

300. To Colin Owen

Evening of Friday, 13 November 1914   *Bordeaux*

Dearest Colin,

Here are the Prints. I had no idea that you didn't mean me to keep
them! I am waiting for some Photos to be finished that I took in my
room, with a French lad, who is doing the developing himself. If they
are not available tomorrow, or if quite freakish, I shan't send them after
all. From your letter I had hints upon all I wanted to know:—First,
that you look forward to my coming-back; secondly, that you have
plenty of homework; thirdly, that you are very strong, five feet, and
pugnacious; fourthly that you still mess-about with animals. So that's
all right! I think your pictures are marvellous well; I shall never see
such a result with my old Box. Is yours a 'Bellows'—Concertina Type?

You haven't ventured to write me anything in French yet! And you
don't tell me much about your school, except what goes without
saying:—that you have homework! But you couldn't have more than
the French boys have at the *Lycées*. Yesterday I got poor Pierre Berthaud into a beastly scrape. You know I give him lessons. When I was
there on Wednesday he handed me a secret missive which he had

intended to post to me. It requested me to signify if I would be 'at home' from 3 to 6 o'clock on Friday, as he would like to come & see me then; but that I might say nothing to any living soul about it, for reasons to be explained later. I said: By all means. But, like the old boggler I am, I left this letter on his dining-room table, where it was discovered by papa soon after. So out came the secret of the secrecy: namely that Pierre was to be let out of school at three o'clock, and planned to enjoy this liberty in swaggering about the world in general, and calling on me in particular. I was in my Grocer's shop ordering a good stock of Spanish Liquorice, and a syphon of soda-water for the Reception, when I discovered that I had left the Letter behind me! Poor lad! He has neither brother nor sister; and both his parents are school-teachers; every moment that he is at home, his nose is kept on his books. Just imagine how you would like that. As well as English he works at German, Latin, and Greek! And all this without neglecting other 'sides'. In Algebra he is nearing where I left off. True, he is a year or two older than you. But Buck up!

I have just come into contact with a fellow who belongs equally to the two countries which interest me most. Egypt and Italy. Antonio is his name. Antonio! He is really Italian, but has lived all his life in Cairo, and received an 'English' education there. So when he speaks, with hands on heart and eyes upturned of 'his Country' it is Egypt he means. The language he talks most naturally is Arab: but he speaks French very well indeed; Italian is what he uses with his parents; and he knows also English indifferently. He is in Bordeaux to study Medicine. At the same table (at the Restaurant) with us are other young sawbones—one French, and two Peruvians, who talk Spanish (of a kind). So between us, when we five are gay, we make a babel almost as uncouth as makes one German when he is ratty.

Sunday

I now have the Photos and my best complement to yours is to send these miserable blotches.

This afternoon, Bizardel, Secretary to the Prefect of Bordeaux passed some time in my Room. He has told me not a few interesting affairs. Among others, the Government is thinking of leaving Bx. in about a fortnight.[1]

But as Bizardel has the right to open this letter—mum.—You know one of his occupations is to read suspected letters! Another is to accompany the Prefect of an afternoon into Antiquarys' Shops, which is the daily form of recreation that this Dignitary takes!

Hearty Wishes to All,

Your own Wilfred

I've had a letter from the Rev. H. Wigan, and card from Oliver, Cambridge.

---

[1] The Government left Bordeaux for Paris 10 December 1914.

301. To Susan Owen
Postcard

Tuesday, 30 November [*1914*]   [*Postmark Bordeaux*]

This morning I had the very serious news that two more merchant vessels (Eng.) have been sent to the bottom by Germ. submarines in the Channel, off Havre. Yesterday a Marine Insurer told me the Bay of Biscay & Channel were safe enough, but the Irish Sea was certainly mined. So now what am I to do? I don't want to lay the responsibility of the decision on You, I must decide for myself before the end of the week. I shall be utterly desolate if I have to pass a solitary Xmas here; but you may be more desolate if on Xmas Eve you read of 'Gen. St. Nav. Co. vessel sunk off Cherbourg, by the Enemies' submarines!'

Your rather—perplexed Wilfred

302. To Susan Owen

Wednesday, 2 December [*1914*]   *Bordeaux*

My own dear Mother,

You must now know all about the sinking of the English coal-boat *Prima* off Cape Cantifer, and how the crew were given ten minutes to get off into a 'whaleboat'; from which they were picked up by another collier. I believe this is the third boat sunk in the Channel by German submarines. And I don't know how many in the Atlantic. No wonder you disquiet yourself about Harold. I should look for nothing in the papers but Atlantic shipping news; if I wasn't watching the Channel, and practising swimming exercises. Madame Léger, who meant to start back just at present, is not venturing yet.

Now what am I to do?

I have upset my digestion by imagining to myself that after all . . . after all and after so long, so very long, I shan't, shan't be with you for Christmas!

On Saturday I consulted my Insurance-Agent-pupil who was quite settled that the Irish Sea is mined; but that the Channel ought to be safe. So I passed a happy Sunday, saying to myself: 'Three Weeks Today . . . etc.' Then I got that fright; and everybody's saying—'Of course, you won't start now.'

I may.

I haven't bought my ticket; but I have given notice to leave my Room. It isn't, however, let, and I have asked for a few days grace.

I was considering going round to the Consul one afternoon (Monday) when I was handed a card from a Miss Patterson, sister of the Vice-Consul, asking if I was 'still at this address as a lady wishes someone to coach her nephews nr. Bordeaux.'[1] I trotted round to the Vice-Consul's

---

[1] The lady was Miss Anne de la Touche; Miss Patterson had been acting as part-time governess to the two younger of her four nephews. Miss de la Touche, now 51, was a member of the old French-Irish family of which Rose de la Touche, Ruskin's pupil, was a

rooms yesterday. Found them 'having tea' brother and sister together: as English as English could be. She a lengthy, young lady, neck as long as a lamp-post, blond-hair, blond as dead palm-leaves. (I am sorry to say it but Miss Patterson is ridiculously English). She gives lessons of some sort to these kids, of which there are four. They were born in China where their father remains. The aunt who takes charge of them said by the Pattersons to be a 'charming Irish woman, of old family' is not satisfied with the education of the two elder boys who are at some Bx. School, and very much wants an Englishman to take them in hand. That was all Patterson could tell me. So this afternoon I took the tram that carries one to Mérignac in some twenty minutes. I arrived at nightfall at 'the Chalet'. I found Miss de la Touche (the Aunt) out. Two boys of ten or nine were there, English thoroughbreds. We debated a bit as to when I should come again: till finally I was led by the Bonne to 'Mademoiselle'[1] whoever she may be. 'Mademoiselle' was lying in bed, being infirm and after a few apologetic words in French, addressed me in un-English English. I am no wiser about the nature of the lessons, or the number, or the terms; but, although, the people are not apparently rich, they will have to make it jolly advantageous for me, if I stay for 'em. And Miss Patterson says the boys are thick as all English boys: (for she never knew a French lad who could be so dull as the average English dummy.)

I shall go again tomorrow morning and shall let you know result immediately.

The afternoon was not lost; for the weather was Aprilic, and I had not been into the country for months. The shock was so great that I lost my memory a little while (a rare thing to lose one's sense of memory.) Indeed I am too continually revising the Past, and trying to peep over the Wall of days that separates us and which is daily higher and higher. If you give me permission to start, I shall start home. But if Father thinks it imprudent, I stay. And if you will be more flurried during the two or three days I am on the sea, than you will be regretful during the two months more that I lie low here—I stay. For me, I shall suffer more from 'ennui' in missing Christmas at Home than from nervousness on board ship.

I talked to the Vice-Consul about it. But he just hummed—and ha-'d as only a genuine well-bred Englishman can.

---

member (see Letter 304, note 3). From 1900 to 1909 she had been in the household of one of the Belgian Princesses, the Duchesse de Vendôme, as governess to the young princesses. She came to Mérignac, on the western outskirts of Bordeaux, in 1910. Her sister, the Baronne de Bock, lived in Bordeaux. A brother, father of the four nephews mentioned, was in the Chinese Maritime Customs Service, and had left Charles and David, twins, with their aunt at Mérignac. The elder boys, Johnny and Bobbie, were at Downside School in Somerset; the outbreak of war found them on holiday at Mérignac, unable to get back to England. Miss de la Touche felt the need of a tutor, having tried a Bordeaux school (École Ste. Marie) for the older boys and found it unsatisfactory.

[1] Mlle Marthe de Puységur, invalid daughter of a neighbour, stayed with Miss de la Touche during her parents' frequent absences from home.

It is, as you say, 'a good thing Herbert Oliver has his skin.'[1] It was, as I remember, a first-quality skin; and Herbert is about the best specimen of the 'English type' I could find if asked to produce one. Where is he? Convey my personal felicitations. Wrecked survivor, is he? And here am I imagining I have some adventures while these sparks of midshipmen are hopping off sinking vessels in mid-ocean, or dodging German Cruisers! Nay, but the tables are turned for me and my English friends since last year. Now I have leisure, health, a snug retreat, many friends. And they have Military Drill, fatigue, stone floors, desperate Enemies. Now, let me talk seriously. The *Daily Mail* speaks very movingly about the 'duties shirked' by English young men. I suffer a good deal of shame. But while those ten thousand lusty louts go on playing football I shall go on playing with my little axiom:—that my life is worth more than my death to Englishmen.

Do you know what would hold me together on a battlefield?: The sense that I was perpetuating the language in which Keats and the rest of them wrote! I do not know in what else England is greatly superior, or dearer to me, than another land and people.

Write immediately what I am to do.

I should take the boat for London on Sat. Dec. 19. My greetings are almost tearful: but take good heart. Are we not still much happier than the majority of families: and safer?

Your devoted Wilfred

Friday

I went over to Mérignac yesterday morning as I said, and found the Aunt—grey-haired lady, of quiet ways, and very nice ways with the four boys. The two elder boys,[2] my affairs, arrived on bicycles from Bx. about 12.30 with a half-holiday. I am well-impressed. The eldest is thin; but it is his features rather than his health which are delicate. He is pretty rather than handsome. The second is neither; but equally intelligent, and more sensible. The third is David, who gives the appearance of fatness without being so; and bears a really close resemblance to Harold at his age—10 or so. The youngest[3] is temporarily crippled. One brother threw him down in play, fracturing the pelvis:— $2\frac{1}{2}$ hours operation! Justifies the fragile appearance of the lads. In spite of their speaking French at will, they are all from top to toe, English schoolboys. The jargon they kept up was delicious for me to hear. The good Aunt questioned me about these weird words and their meaning, not having the faintest notion of what means 'clout', topping, etc. etc. When I got back to Bx. I seemed to be returned from a brief visit to England. We had lunch in the (Here my landlady brought in your letter: glad to know Harold's safe, and that you're expecting me don't be too

---

[1] Frederick Oliver's younger brother. He had gone to sea shortly after HO, his closest friend. His ship had been torpedoed in the early days of the war and he had sailed 600 miles to safety in an open boat after being marooned in the Galapagos Islands. He survived the experience, and the war.

[2] Johnny and Bobbie.

[3] Charles.

benevolent to perfect strangers—shall be destitute mysel' on arriving in England.) so as I was saying—we had lunch in the garden: We boys at least—and it rained 3 times, soaking the table-cloth and our hair, and diluting the soup, and we all swore the wine tasted weaker—and Auntie let us stay out in the wet to our inexpressible delight. (I had a cold the day before—but haven't felt it since!) At lunch I put the lads through testing questions on their studies. They don't seem much advanced: but seem capable: and then the English is sound, and not only sound but elegant: (lahst, get off the grahss, silly ahss! etc.) The Aunt wants me then to go to their school, and take the two aside for a special Grammar & Literature Lesson. In the Holidays she wants a Tutor to help her with them generally. The Chalet is not large—and she would take rooms in the village for the Tutor and his wards. I didn't jump at this, preferring my present mode of life: and then—I mean to start for London on Saturday, the nineteenth day of this present, towards nine in the Evening! Till—would I could state it—Till Then—

Au Revoir.

Your own Wilfred

P.S. Can you give me an address of a <u>Rubber</u> Rain-Coat Business House. A Frenchman wants to buy direct from England.

—What a mixture of things your Reply will be: But be clear on <u>one</u> point.

303. To Susan Owen

4 December 1914   *Le Châlet, Mérignac, Gironde*[1]

Dearest Mother,

My occupations are at an end for today. It is striking ten by the village clock. I managed to get a letter off to Leslie yesterday. I forget when last I wrote. Always, when new places occupy my attention I muddle my sense of time. And here is a totally different environment to get used to from that of Bx. city. We went on Saturday to the finest Chateau[2] I ever beheld. There were the traditional 'extinguisher-topped towers'; and all the rest: a vast affair. The people are comparatively simple. The heir is a seraphic-faced, gentle little boy of eight, so I don't grudge him the possessions. There is an English governess of the conventional type, to look after this boy and his sister. The Lady of the place was one of the 'full-length portraits' in the Paris Salon. But as she was one of the miserables who this morning waited twenty minutes in pouring rain for the tram, that dignity seemed to unstiffen somewhat. I am invited to go and play tennis at the Chateau on the first fine day!! However as it will probably continue to rain until June, that proposal is not really so odd as it seems.

We also have the run of the grounds of two other rather nice estates[3] close to; and alternately invite and are invited by the boys to tea.

[1] Wilfred writes from Mérignac, but is not yet living there.
[2] The Château du Parc, Mérignac, home of Admiral Castéjas. The boys were frequent visitors.
[3] Owned by the De L'Estapis and Piganeau families.

All the photographs are admirable, as much in execution as in pose. Father is the only one in whom I spy no change whatsoever. I am sure there is an alteration in your mouth, tho' it is not the work of Time's fangs, but of Rice-Oxley's[1] complete set. Mary is more truly youthful than she was. There is still something Ancient-British about the statuesque arms-folded one. These also are capable of caricature; (but I'm not). Father, rising discreetly into view from amid the mystical flowers, his nether parts yet confused with the background of luxuriant verdure, is most captivating. I suppose I may keep the prints with me. I am ever so pleased to have them. The Masked Lady is a joy to see; you look so well and happy. I hope Father is having a real holiday in Devon.

How decent of Fred. Oliver to blow my trumpet in Cambridge and Bournemouth. Keep him at it. One piece of news was really startling for its novelty: namely that a degree is necessary for teaching in England.

After ten years of hammering, that nail is beginning to give me a headache.

No doubt you know about the sinking of the *Formidable*.[2] It caused a sinking of spirits and hopes here: and Mlle. de la Touche, who for days has been hinting at keeping the boys, definitely said tonight that they should not go if only I would stay. The Principal of Downside,[3] (a Public school), her solicitor, the boys' father, their other Aunt, insist that all is safe for going over; nevertheless, and especially as the boys beg for it, Miss de la Touche would prefer to keep them here with me. I feel flattered to compete with Downside, but would rather throw it up than risk not seeing you for another batch of months. I promised her to tell you how she wishes me to stay; and you will say what you like. I can't enumerate all the pros and cons tonight. I have to get through four lessons tomorrow morning; which will make a scoop of 12 francs, not so bad seeing there are no expenses. This, however, is not a typical day, and I must beware being lured by this state of things. For tho' I am not needy, I am poor. Better to be poor than needy, but woe unto him that is both . . .

So in the meantime I am documenting myself with shipping news: and, in fault of another bust-up in the Channel, hold to my intention of starting, with courage and with love.

Yours ever, Wilfred

Don't mention Bordeaux on address!

304. To Susan Owen

Wednesday, 8 December 1914   *Bordeaux*

My dearest Mother,

After a day of tormenting indecision I have at last made up my mind, and have arrived at a sense of sanctified peace: I have made up my

[1] The Owens' dentist.
[2] British pre-dreadnought battleship torpedoed in the English Channel 1 January 1915, with the loss of thirty-five officers and 512 men.
[3] The Roman Catholic school at Stratton-on-Fosse, near Bath.

mind—Hold Tight!—to put off my voyage for 4 weeks. In those four weeks I ought to make a haul of nearly £8. When I realised the Alternative of costing you £8. or of earning them myself: my better nature left no choice. But it was hard to refuse my poor old childish soul, the 'Christmas at Home', (though I know very well that the expression 'Merry Christmas' will not be heard in the land, or ought not to be.)

Moreover I shall be in an English family, very differently situated from a year ago: so you can be quite happy about me.

Indeed, if you want to give me a Blessing and a Christmas Wish, you can only do so by clearly saying that you completely approve, of, and acquiesce in my resolution, and admire me for it. But if, instead of saying nice things to keep up my heart, you should hint any disappoint-ment on your part, or lack of it on mine: I shall not be able to bear the thing: but shall throw up my promises, and take the next train for Calais. I mean it. You have only to telegraph . . . if your self-control or your confidence in me are not strong enough to support 30 days delay —and I can yet book a bunk on the *Fauvette*.

I went yesterday to see a man, caretaker of the 'Sailors' Reading Room' (who is in touch with the crews of all English boats in here) in order to find out whether any Collier or Cargo-thing whatever would be able to take me cheap. He knew of none such: and said that Captains nowadays weren't 'tickalarly gone on that game, bein' responsible for whatever 'appened to the passenger. If the passenger 'signed on' that's another story. There certainly was a scare on in Bordeaux, by reason of the submarines: but if that Marine Insurance Agent Pupil is no more sharp-witted in his Marine Affairs than in his English lessons I ought never to have hearkened to him. So I think there is not more risk than just enough to make the trip exciting.

Two days after this scare, cropped up this other obstacle: Poverty. At present I am worth the dazzling sum of £90. a year while my expenditure merely amounts to £89.19.11¾. If my board & lodging were paid for this expenditure would be reduced. Such is my prospect for the next month. I have been twice to talk things over with Miss de la Touche and have come away without settling anything. Today she stated explicitly what she wanted: Me to live out there, and look after the boys in the afternoons; terms mutual; and I to keep up as many Bordeaux lessons as I wish, tramming or bicycling in every morning. We should work about two hours a day; and amuse ourselves the rest. I took good care that, in lesson-time the boys seemed likely to work, and that in play-time, I seemed likely to amuse myself. It is of course only the two elder that are to work, though in our excursions we shall be half a dozen with the French comrades. Since my writing last, we went a shooting expedition, all the more enhanced for that shooting is forbidden. There were two cartridge- and one air-gun, and it might have made you creepy to see the loaded pieces in such reckless hands, but we came home (save the mark!), but left the game equally so. All the afternoon great guns were booming from the manoeuvring grounds, and a hovering aeroplane kept buzzing overhead. (And I thought of the thousand redeemers by whose blood my life is being redeemed. To read the Casualty List is like the twenty-first chapter of St. Luke;[1] or the last passages of Severn's *Journal*;[2] neither readable without tears.)

I think the country-month ought to repair what Bordeaux has undone of Bagnères' work on my constitution. Mérignac seems a well-wooded part; it is about half-an-hour on foot from the boulevards surrounding the city.

Miss de la Touche is of mysterious age: nearly white hair; but fresh Cousin Mayish complexion, and the evidence of very fine features. She is a cousin of the Rose de la Touche[3] whom Ruskin didn't quite marry; and who died in youth; but seems to have lived in the age of the Prophet. Will you please take down Mr. Collingwood's *Ruskin* and refer to 'de la Touche Rose' if she is mentioned therein; as I think and trust she be. If someone would copy what is said I sh'd be grateful. Miss de la Touche is in touch with the Belgian Royal Family, having in some manner fostered one of the Princesses,[4] sister, I suppose, of the valiant King Albert, so much 'at the front' today.

The father of the boys has a Customs Post in China, where the mother still stays. Three years ago, the boys began school at the Roman Catholic College, at Downside, Somerset. The fees are extremely high, and when, in France, the operation on Charly[5] cost a formidable sum, and war reigned, the Aunt thought it best to keep them here. But papa doesn't like that; and now the Abbot of Downside writes saying that if it is only the fees that now keep them away from school, he will facilitate, etc. So, tho', last week, the Aunt thought of keeping them in Bx. next term, she now means to send them home next January. Till, then, she is frightened at the prospect of having to manage them during the holidays. and also wants someone to take them home about the middle of January. So the Consul spoke to the Vice Consul, who sent his sister to me, who have just arranged it. Now, have I done well? Yea, when I do enter my little room it will be ten times more snug, and my bed under the paternal roof ten times more comfortable; and when I do hear your voice it will be ten times more sweet. Thus only 5 or 6 more Sundays must you write! At last I tell you! Neither Love, Fear, nor Money shall prolong that:

Witness my hand Wilfred x

(If the fatted calf be already killed this letter may serve as a refrigerator.)

---

[1] Christ's prophecy of the destruction of Jerusalem.

[2] Joseph Severn (1793–1879), painter and friend of Keats, went with the poet to Italy in 1820, attended him at his death, and recorded it all in his journal.

[3] A second cousin. Rose died in 1874 aged 27, out of her mind. She had been Ruskin's pupil at the age of 10, and his love for the child—she was thirty years his junior—led her parents to refuse to let them meet.

[4] See Letter 302, note 1.

[5] A fall while playing had led to the hip operation three months earlier, mentioned in Letter 302.

305. To Susan Owen
Postcard

Sunday [*Postmark 14 December 1914*]   [*Postmark Bordeaux*]

Your 'last' letter came yesterday night. I was glad to find that you attached small importance to 'sentiment about Christmas'. About this date next month I ought to be starting. As you love me, send no material Christmas presents; and expect none. We shall keep the feast on the 25th of January, about!
I don't know anything about the return of Mme. L. and don't care. Yes, I am waiting to talk over my Future, first with You; and then either with a Professor or a Recruiting Sergeant! I move to Mérignac on the 19th I think.[1] How about Mary's Exam? Fondest Love to Everybody

W.E.O

Don't write more to Raoul. He is out of my books!

306. To Susan Owen
Postcard

Thursday, 17 December [*1914*]   [*Postmark Bordeaux*]

I have been expecting your answer to my Postponing-Letter for some days, & am anxious to know what you have to say to me. I move out on Sat. next. The Lems' Boarder has asked me to spend Christmas Day (& Night) at his place in the country. Raoul is passing his holidays there. I may go. As for news I have none and scarcely can fill a P.C. let alone a letter. Nothing happens. How keeps your throat? I have neither Cold, nor any manner of meegrums: tho' the weather is filthy. Bordeaux is the more dismal, now that the Paris gentry have drawn off. The Country will be a change, but I shall be thankful to get away. Remember me to all Folk to whom you write Christmas letters, with appropriate messages.

Yours ever W.E.O.

write Chez Mlle. de la Touche Le Châlet Mérignac Bx.
I have had your letter (Friday). How perfect of you to write so!

---

[1] Miss de la Touche wrote to the Headmaster of Downside on 15 December 1914: 'I have taken a young tutor for them for the Christmas holidays, he is giving lessons in Bordeaux preparing for Oxford. The boys will work with him at English, History, Geometry and Algebra and do some literature as well. . . . He goes home about the 19th of January, and the boys can travel with him.' On 23 December she wrote: 'J. and B. are quite well and have begun their work with Mr. Owen. He teaches them in a most interesting way. . . .'

MÉRIGNAC AND THE ARTISTS' RIFLES

1914–1915

307. To Susan Owen

21 December 1914   *Chez Mlle de la Touche, Le Châlet,*
                                            Mérignac, Gironde
Dearest of Mothers,

So here I am; I racketed about all Saturday making luggage out of lumber; and at four o'clock, rolled away in a four-wheeler, with one box, leaving the rest with the old dame. The Châlet is not very spacious: Just a well-built bungalow, with one upstairs-room, which is mine.[1] There are four servants, one a man, who all dwell in an out-building. So all the good traditions of an English country-house are fully observed. I am more comfortable than at Dunsden, for example. I get up at 7.30, have a double-egg breakfast, with the boys and their Aunt, who have been already to Mass. Then I catch the tram and reach Bx. to start lessons about 9. Sometimes I shall not get through all my lessons in the morning, & must have lunch in town. Although two or three pupils are taking holidays, I have just been written to by two new people. The first is a doctor, mental specialist, with a Sanatorium for treating morphio-maniacs. This gentleman is, all round, an 'interesting' pupil, and what the French call 'a Brain'. Moreover his wife wants lessons too. But I just can't give them as many as they want!

The other applicant is a railway official; but as he only felt inclined to take one a week, I had to tell him to wait.

Until five o'clock in the afternoon we go out, or the boys amuse themselves as best they can. From five to seven the two eldest work with me. Today we spent the whole time on the Roman Occupation of Britain; and it was I who benefited by the lesson; for to have an attentive audience for two hours, comprehending what I said about early history was an unmixed pleasure. At other times, these fellows make a frantic noise, with lungs, feet, and every object at hand. At table they behave well, but not well enough for 'Auntie',—who having lived in a Palace and 'shaped' a Princess is naturally a stickler for correctness. She is ever so kind to me, and clearly is as fond of her nephews as Aunt could be.

I am sorry you could find nothing about Rose de la T. in Mr. Collingwood's *Ruskin*. I must make a pilgrimage to the Lakes and ask Mr.

---

[1] The Chalet, though small, was pleasant (it was demolished in 1964). It was set in a spacious garden, with plums, greengages, peaches, and figs, running back to a small wood. David La Touche recalls the scent of lime-trees and roses; the limes provided lime tea for his aunt's frequent migraines. Accommodation was difficult. The four boys crowded into one of the four rooms, the others being drawing-room, dining-room, and the aunt's room. The one 'pill-box of a room' in the roof was allotted to Wilfred. Somehow, with a bed in the drawing-room, the invalid Mlle de Puységur was fitted in. A succession of English, French, or Irish governesses came to look after the two younger boys; they did not live in. Of Wilfred, Charles La Touche writes: 'The only setting in which I can remember him clearly is at night prayers, when he used to stand respectfully in the background.'

Collingwood. I must certainly make a sojourn at Alpenrose, and at Meols, and anywhere else not excepting even Scarborough.

We had three reports of that 'business':[1] the first said 'no real damage'; the second said 'a few persons killed' a third said 'more than 80 killed, 115 wounded.' When I read that a shell fell into a group of sixteen schoolboys and killed fifteen, I raved. Talk about rumours of wars and earthquakes in divers places: all that's historic now. The beginning of the End must be ended, and the beginning of the middle of the end is now.

I must be beginning to end my Christmas letter. You understand that I have every minute jammed-full of some occupation; and it is eleven o'clock when I write. The word Christmas hath lost his savour. In vain I stare at a sprig of holly and languish at a mistletoe-berry. They mean nothing. I repeat like a poor idiot 'Merry Christmas to you', 'While Shepherds watched their flocks by night'—Father Christmas—Dickens —Charles Dickens—Scrooge—Bob Cratchit—Plum Pudding—Tiny Tim—Mince Pie—Christmas Tree—Once in Bethlehem of Judah— Haunted Grange—Yule Log—no use. I can't get the atmosphere. Best to leave it, then; this year the 25th of December is the day that comes after the 24th and before the 26th: merely so. Nevertheless, all the mottoes of a million Christmas Cards could not express my Affection for You who most care for me; or tell my Wishes for You.

Know, also, that I shall be in something very like an English Home for Christmas; for I am not going with Lem, etc. where I shall be far from unhappy; but the greatest happiness of the Day and of the Season will be the Reading of your letters, and hoping for the Meeting in January.

Mother's and Father's
Mary's
Harold's
Colin's

} Wilfred

308. To Susan Owen

First sheet missing, the remainder stained by damp and occasionally illegible

27 December 1914   *Mérignac*

The man-servant brings me hot water for my bath every morning. I breakfast on two eggs (instead of [one] as formerly); at 12.30 I come in hungry to find a 'smashin' dinner [*two words illegible*]; at five I have tea and toast and at seven another dinner. The maids wait at meals; and the cook knows her trade. Magnificent coal-fires warm the cockles of my heart. Moreover a gold box of finest Turkish cigarettes are at my disposal; and also four 'hoards' of chocolates: for the boys

[1] German battle-cruisers shelled Scarborough, Hartlepool, and Whitby on 16 December 1914, killing 122 people and wounding 443.

had 'No Christmas present'; that is to say nothing but sweets, of which there were no lack.

I of course had a Box for me from my kindest of hostesses [*one word illegible*] is not the word. We all went to Midnight Mass on the 24th–25th: cripples included. For you know there is a lady-friend of Miss de la T. who lies on her back all her days. We made two journeys to church with the bath chair, and installed both the boys and ourselves in the very sanctuary. An interesting position for me, all mixed up with candles, incense, acolytes, chasuble and such like. If I didn't bow, I certainly scraped, for there was an unholy draught. How scandalized would certain of my acquaintance and kin have been to see me. But it would take a power of candlegrease and embroidery to romanize me. The question is to un-Greekize me.

It was three o'clock when we went to bed. I think the efforts of the dear, darling little acolytes to keep awake was what took most of my attention there. Johnny and Dédé both dropped asleep. 'On Christmas' then I got up somewhere about lunchtime. We spent the afternoon mostly on trams on the way to a Hospital where I accompanied three of the boys to see the Soldiers' Christmas Tree. Anyhow we spent 3 f. 80 c. on trams to get there. Then after enduring the fetid-stinking [*one word illegible*] place for 1½ hours, we went to the boys' old school, for them to get their things, and I met their Superior. After dinner we had a few games and a lottery-thing in which everybody won [*two words illegible*]! The chief incident of the day from the boy's point of view was the smoking of a long-promised Cigarette each; and from my point of view was the turning of my thoughts to you-wards. I have not yet been able to [*one word illegible*] your Christmas Letters, but shall certainly tomorrow.

Your one mentioning my present, and containing Harold's things I read on bicycle, riding over to lunch.

You must be relieved about Harold.

Commend me to Cousin May.

I used to have the *Daily Mail* (Continental) given me; so I [*one word illegible*] English opinion.

Yes, please, keep the papers: such for example as, Annexation of [*one word illegible*] the Scarboro' affair, and, when you get it, the Fall of Berlin. Raoul merely gave me much annoyance in the Lessons I gave in the meanwhile. Not having any notions of [*one word illegible*] 'English properness' he gave me offence with his protracted drivelling, sniggering 'pleasantries'. I found I should be of service here on [*one word illegible*] so telegraphed an excuse to [*one word illegible*]. I guess my Present is a down [*one word illegible*]—how 'topping'! The desire of my ten toes, for as many winters past: and having had one in my last Rooms, it will be the one thing needed.

One thinks of the 'trenches' with guilty feelings, in the midst of my surroundings; but my conscience is easily cleared by the recollection of certain happenings in my past.

I had a letter from Dunsden, expressing such a [*two words illegible*] of the Pope of Dunsden's [*one word illegible*] that I have just lain low and said nuffin.

Well done, Mary. I shall have some creepy things to tell her to 'steady her nerve, like', such creepy things that creep around and live on living men's flesh!

Now my 'mental' Doctor has sent me to yet another, whom I am obliged to refuse lessons to at present not having time. Isn't it annoying! No wonder I show signs of hurry tonight and yet all afternoon I have been sauntering, and spying sparrows in the greenwood!

My Wishes to dear Kin, and to you

Myself!

309. To Susan Owen

Friday, 8 January 1915   [*Mérignac*]

Dearest Mother,

I am replying to yours of 3rd. and 4th. and am 'sitting up' to do so. I may make you 'sit up' likewise. Two days ago Miss de la Touche asked me to stay for 3 months more. I promised to, if you were agreeable, since work with these boys (in Latin especially) would do no harm to myself. Moreover, keeping on my Bordeaux lessons, my total earnings would be equivalent to £200. a year. Next day comes a telegram from China, saying 'send boys Downside', and this was a bolt from the Celestial Land which knocked us all on the head. The Aunt is more afraid of going against her brother's will than she is afraid of mines and bombs. Still people here all counsel her to continue the present arrangement, and exaggerate the dangers of crossing. On the other hand 'the Head' of Downside writes persuasively and even has the undisguised cunning to write to each of the boys personally. The boys of course have no sort of wish to go back, but are beginning to lose their appetites at the thought of it.

When I first made the necessary output of strength to carry back the date of my homecoming over three more rocky months, I was not a little jolted by the new turn of affairs.

We are not really settled yet.

I am able to preserve a strictly neutral attitude, so that should simplify the decision-problem.

It would be profitable for me to stay, and not unpleasant; whereas to start, tho' what you might call 'mighty 'greeble' would be little profitable.

The very latest report that I am able to give you is that Miss de la T. has written to Downside tonight[1] saying she means to send the boys <u>by train</u>, judging that 2½ hours on the water entails less danger than 3 days.

---

[1] She wrote to the Headmaster: 'I have decided to send them by rail via Boulogne–Folkestone accompanied by Mr. Owen. . . . If any sea-trouble arises before the 17th, I have made arrangements with Mr. Owen who will remain here and teach the boys.'

(You know a boat that left Bordeaux early in the year went down in the Bay, the sea was so frightful.)

This is much more expensive, but the excess of the train—over the boat-fare in my case is undertaken by the de la T's. Considering how much safer it would be, I feel equal to the ennui of a land journey. We may pass a day in Paris, so that will brighten the whole business. I think you will be easier knowing I am not exposed to chances of mine or torpedo. In case I am wanted to stay, I know I have your willing consent. After all, these bogus starts bring us nearer, than a long imperturbably, settled period of sojourn.

Now follows something important.

I have long been talking to and talked at by a very 'businessy' business man, who deplores that I do not consecrate myself to Business, even as Miss Rayner did of Science, and Mr. Wigan of Religion.

Not to ramble about this good Merchant, and his impossible tenets, I want to propose that Uncle Ted, that is Ed. Quayle, Esq. be approached about the possibility of doing great things with the French Government. Recently, the Minister for War has asked for Tin Articles, since an enormous number of pots and pans are needed for the new recruits. I understand that it is the manufactured article that is required; but if the prospect of relations with the French Army interests in any way Uncle Ted I can tackle the Minister for War. What my friend advised me to do is to get price-lists and samples from England immediately. Unfortunately the *Ministère de la Guerre* left Bordeaux yesterday (the last to depart), but I still have access to the responsible officials. Mark, it is not an enterprise of my cute friend (Peyronnet), for I myself, supposing I am here, would represent the Canning Tin Plate Co., if permitted. Poor Peyronnet is a Manufacturer of Perfumes, and is mad that Eau de Cologne is not strictly necessary in the trenches. His friends, the Boot-maker, the Bicycle-Maker, etc. having Gov. Contracts, are making piles. Why not his friend the nephew of the English Metal Merchant. Let Father act immediately: repeating my words to Uncle. (On no account show these scrawled pages.)

Multitudinous thanks for your voluminous last letter. I keep well, very. Am seeing Dentist—paying with English Conversation! Clever Dentist, I believe.

Fondest Wishes to all, Yours ever, W.E.O.

310. To Susan Owen

Postcard

Monday, 11 January 1915   [*Postmark Bordeaux*]

I have [been] expecting to hear from you in answer to my 'notice' of possible staying on. It is still unsettled. The Balance swings up and down on each succeeding day. Shall have to telegraph at the end, if coming. Much safer, anyhow, to come by rail. You must be relieved to

313

know that. This indecision would be a nuisance if I were responsible for the choice, or if my own interests were not equally balanced. As it is I let well alone; and only hope for the same treatment in return. I hope you are not now in communication with Uncle Ted about that business.

Yours, Wilfred

311. To Susan Owen
Postcard

[?*Early January 1915*]   [*Postmark Bordeaux*]

All serene: bitter cold weather: pleasant: good fire: went in Prefect's motor to Antique Shop yesterday: another trip tomorrow to see Russian encampment hereabout: no 'Sunday letter':—dinner with Raoul—'Mrs. Owen not write more since one month': month hence quit France: Alas! Hip-Hip-HOORAY! Much health—many friends—no worry—much hope—no money—How's Yourself? God save the King—an' You-an'-Me.

312. To Susan Owen
Postcard

Wednesday, 15 [14] January [1915]   [*Postmark Bordeaux*]

Have just had your letter: & am sending this to acknowledge it. Will write to Alpenrose for Sunday. Father may well inquire about the weather here. It is phenomenal; it has snowed on three occasions—(the first snow for some years.) One of my pupils says he does not remember such a cold for thirty years. At this moment it is snowing hard, & the snow has every sign of 'sticking' for days. I am perfectly warm, thanks, both night and days; thanks to Extra Vest & Two Mufflers by day, Dressing & Academic Gowns by night, and extra Internal Fuel, in the shape of Swiss Milk! There are excellent stoves in the *Union*—I have already said it is situated almost immediately opposite the door of the B. School: i.e. Rue du Temple. Best love,

W

313. To Susan Owen

Postcard addressed to Alpenrose, Kidmore, Nr. Reading

Thursday, 15 January [1915]   [*Postmark Bordeaux*]

I am sorry to say that the hour I had counted on for my Letters has just been filled up by a Trial Lesson; so shall not be able to post in time for Sunday.
The Cold continues; the frost on my window-panes has not thawed for three days! I do hope you will have enjoyable weather at Alp:—perhaps you will have skating or tobogganning, eh? I wonder what it is like in Meran.'[1] Please give a good report of me to 'Dunsden' if you go there.

[1] Unexplained.

What news I hear!! And much love to all at A. Garross is going to engage in *Aerobatics (ah-hem!) on Sunday: over Bordeaux. Shall probably see something of it. *Adieu* x W

* See any good Dictionary, Webster Nuttall, etc.

To Leslie—Great thanks.

314. To Susan Owen

Thursday, 14 [*15*] *January* [*1915*]   [*Mérignac*]

Dearest Mother,

In consequence of the appearance of Zeppelins in the Channel, our departure is put off for a fortnight at least. That we shall stay on for three more months is by no means fixed. If I wanted I could so work it, and I think I could also bring about an early departure, if I so desired.

It was my pupil the Marine Insurance Agent who told me on Tuesday that twelve Zeppelins were careering over the Channel, while sixteen Aviatiks were about to spring across the Straits. And the announcement of this at once decided Miss de la Touche. I went to the Consul about it, at Miss T's request, and had the advice I expected: 'Really can't say; but Go if you have any reason to go.'[1]

I was gladder to know that you, considering the matter from a purely business-like standpoint, are inclined to my coming, than I should have been if you had wholly advised long-tarrying. The only thing that might make my three months tutoring expedient is that I should be obliged to work at Exam. Subjects, especially Latin, which work would be quite useful.

I wonder when and what I shall hear about my great Business Project with Fr. Gov. The good man who pointed out the affair to me is Peyronnet, the Manufacturer of Perfumes. Without offering anything definite, he interests himself in my future, mightily, and, (as I think I said) tries to convert me to 'Business'. In particular he lauds the position of commercial traveller and apparently nothing would please him better than to see me fairly launched in that line. Now, I have a most praiseworthy desire to get at the root of all evil; but it seems to me that the digging would be too long and laborious. I have every confidence that if I wholly gave myself up to fortune building, and were content to work, and working, wait, I should 'arrive' within ten or twenty years. I consider, however, that that would be a literal losing of my soul; for that those things which my heart would put forth would then come out no more; and those things which my mind would take in, would then enter no more.

All I ask is to be held above the barren waters of want, and moving

[1] Miss de la Touche wrote to Downside on 14 January: 'Mr. Owen went to see the Consul . . . who would not give him any advice about the journey. . . . The boys are working steadily with Mr. Owen. They have taken up English, History, Arithmetic, Geography, and Latin with him. . . . Greek is the difficulty, it is not taught in the same way by French teachers, and Mr. Owen says he cannot teach it.'

over the darkness of those waters to brood and to create. Woe is me, should I take to battling with the stream, and wet my wings of imagination!

I could never conscientiously work hard and wholeheartedly at a business. Truly, if I found myself in a fair way to becoming a London surgeon I should not, as Keats did, throw it up, and trust to the voices and visions. . . .

And if I could devote myself to training in Music or Painting, I would take the plunge, were I never to read a book more. I halt between Professions, not between Business or Profession.

Last night I read a sentence that came as gall to me:

'It is very fortunate that Morris[1] did not lack money, or he would never have been able to afford these changes of opinion as to his career; and English Literature, and the beauty of English homes would have lost one of their most important factors.'

When I was with the Consul he suddenly interested himself in me; and, tho' I dreamed not of such a thing, said he 'wondered I didn't go in for this sort of thing' meaning a Consulship. And he straightway gave me books to read up particulars. He says it would mean a coach, and a sojourn in Spain (for another language), but that the appointments really depended on a 'Tea-Party Examination' with the Foreign Secretary or one such. Mr. Rowley[2] himself has £600. a year. This must be considered, as the age limits are something like 23–28. What must no longer be considered is the Assistant Elementary Certificated or Un-Certificated Schoolmaster. One of the wisest steps in my life was the one I didn't take (I am with Irish people) in 1911, namely hanging back from what the P.T.'s called 'College'. 'What you want' said John Bulman to me, 'Is a course in the University of Life'. I have taken that Course, and my diplomas are sealed with many secret seals. . . .

Be more definite in your counsels to me to Come and I will come; or vice versa.

Your very own Wilfred

315. To Susan Owen
Postcard

[*Postmark 20 January, 1915*]   *Bd. P.O.*

Yesterday aft. I learnt of your new sore throat; I dreamed thereof all night. For I really think I shall not see you for another spell. The state of Paris—in darkness, expecting 10 Zeppelins makes even a Rly. Journey seem full of terrors. Do tell me just how you are. If you got a real weakening sore-throat, I sh'd start off! No news from Uncle Ted. Fondest love,

Wilfred

[1] William Morris (1834–96), poet, artist, decorator, printer, and Socialist. We have not identified the source of this passage.
[2] Sir Arthur Langford Sholto Rowley (1870–53), British Consul, Bordeaux, 1912–19, subsequently Consul-General at Barcelona and Antwerp. Knighted 1932, succeeded as 8th Baron Langford 1952.

316. To Colin Owen

[*22 January 1915*]   [*Mérignac*]

Dear Colin,

Thank you for putting in a message. It was a scrap of paper, but your message was not without its weight. You would like to be here, and try your gun against Johnnie's and Bobbie's.

This morning I was looking over Lloyd's Index of Ships, and turned up the *Esmeraldas*. I find it is noted down with very best marks as being a tip-top cockle. It has ✠ A1. The Cross alone means in very good condition. A Red Cross means of doubtful seaworthiness; and no mark at all means most insecure : . . . cork jackets, prayers, sharks and shrimps, so to speak!

When I was at the Consul's the other day, a half-breed hindoo came pestering him; and suddenly the Consul skipped round his counter (like a Grocer who sees a dog run off with his ham), and positively butted the wretch outside. This morning I met the Consul in the tram, and laughing over the incident, he told me that that is not uncommon, and that his methods of dealing with coloured men have been raised as a Question in the House!

I am so glad that Uncle John has been photographing Father, and I think it's high time you were given that honour.

I wonder how we shall get on together? I have obedience on the part of these youngsters, and if there is any trouble, give them lines or send them to bed.[1]

I have developed a mechanical way of correcting bad English, useful enough in tedious lessons, but likely to prove incommodious in certain company. I haven't heard what is settled about your school?

Adieu, my dear lad. May thy tasks be heavy, but thy heart light.

Brer Fox[2]

(this is what I am called in our games, by the boys, who are variously Brer Rabbit, Tarrypin, Bar, etc. There is also a Miss Cow!)

---

[1] Wilfred is recalled by Charles and David La Touche with respect, as a disciplinarian. He was liked, especially out of doors botanizing and butterfly-hunting in the Mérignac woods, but did not arouse the affection given to his more easy-going successor Bonsall. See Letter 342. The boy's father wrote to Miss de la Touche on 19 April 1915: 'J'ai reçu il y a quelques temps le rapport de Mr. Owen, rapport montrant que c'est un garçon qui voit juste et clairement. Avec cela, étant un garçon encore très jeune, il manque d'indulgence dans son appréciation. C'est une qualité qui vient avec l'âge. Les jeunes gens jugent sévèrement parce qu'ils manquent d'expérience. En somme son rapport et fort juste. . . . Mr. Owen blame Johnny de préférer de guetter un moineau sur un arbre que de s'appliquer à sa leçon.' On 27 April he wrote: 'La lettre de Mr. Owen quoique très sensée était fort dure et il faut que tu voie qu'il fasse la part des choses et que sa discipline soit paternelle en même temps que ferme. Il ne faut pas que ni les uns ou les autres grandissent en se croyant *incompris* et s'il y a chez les uns ou les autres des goûts ou tendences qui a première vue paraissent puerilles, il y a à examiner si ces tendences n'indiquent pas quelque chose de peutêtre plus sérieux que Mr. Owen, un tout jeune homme sans expérience, ne soupçonne pas.'

[2] Charles La Touche still has the Mérignac copy of *Uncle Remus* by Joel Chandler Harris (1848–1908).

317. To Susan Owen
Postcard

Wednesday [*Postmark 27 January 1915*]   *Mérignac*

I don't know <u>when</u> I last wrote: not, I devoutly hope, as long as a week ago! Your several P.C.'s reached me, all giving happier news of your throat. We are now settled down to the prospect of passing Spring here. I must certainly bridge at Easter. Must compose a letter one of these days. Meanwhile am busy and well-working and working well. Time Tweak wrote! Dearest wishes to all.

W.E.O.

318. To Susan Owen[1]

31 January 1915   *Mérignac*

Dearest Mother,

Both your last letters were full of charm for me, and I feel you must find it abominable of me to throw back a few stray cards, instead of meet answers to questions and your sentiments. As it is with me in these days I am never alone, and therefore neither reflect nor practise ink-slinging. Every morning I still fly in to Bordeaux and out again for lunch; ramble about the country with my family till 3 or four; hold lessons till seven, then the last boy is tucked in about half-past nine; a somnolent smoke till about ten with Miss de la Touche, and after that I reach out for the nearest book, and ruminate over a few ideas, until my mental saliva dries up.

At the present moment, my family of four are all writing to their papa; and as they have the not-uncommon habit of composing aloud, I cannot wander far from the sound of their voices. That is to say, this must be a small-focus letter.

Having had more trouble with my teeth I am again under the dentist. My dentist is a first-class fellow, with Chicago degrees, and does work on me for nothing! or for the mere pleasure-and-profit of hearing me talk English to him. You remember I have had a permanent abscess for four or five years. He is going to set that right.

The wife of that mental doctor I think I once spoke about has English relations I find, her husband's uncle, her uncle-in-law, very-much-in-law, I might say, is Lord Reading, Lord Chief Justice of England.[2] She was in Reading recently. She is Russian herself; and her brother was one of those fifty students of Moscow, who were slaughtered by Cas.[3] In the Univ. during the Revol. I asked her once why the R's are doing so

---

[1] This letter, uncharacteristically scribbled with pen and pencil, was not sent, but discovered by HO among Wilfred's papers after the war. The first paragraph is adapted to open Letter 319, itself a draft for a later letter, 330. One phrase 'this must be a small-focus letter'—turns up again in Letter 332.
[2] Rufus Daniel Isaacs, 1st Marquess of Reading (1860–1935), Lord Chief Justice 1913–21, later Secretary of State for Foreign Affairs.
[3] Cossacks.

little positive work and she says the Gen. & off.'s are all incapables, or rendered so by Vodka.

I am sorry that my Tin Scheme won't go. I so suspected. Your pun on Tin[1] was very sharp, but the edge was rather sharp and cut me   there is mettle in your wit but the joke had a sharp edge and cut my heart.

Monday. Fearing that after all my Friday's might have been a dream I resolved to pinch myself, and the pinchers I used were Dr. & Cr.

I made sure that money for my travel the first part will be advanced by Peyronnet. At Alex. & Cairo I should have already a good Comm. to my Credit and this will be forwarded as needed.[2] One other cooperating firm will probably

W

319. To Susan Owen[3]

Saturday, 6 February [*1915*]   *Mérignac*

Dearest of Mothers,

Your three last letters were full of charm for me, and the very last did even charm me to a tear. Which is more noble than being 'cheated to a sigh' as many things do at present, notably the 'debosched' Bosches, (By the way are They called that in England?) and my Boys. Today I first used the stick on them! Generally there is no trouble with them, but this afternoon Johnny (the-eldest-and-ought-to-know-better) got up a tree and wouldn't come down. So instead of taking a hatchet and felling the tree, I promised a caning and gave it last thing at night. A little later we go into the Orangery of the Chateau[4] (not shown in the Picture Postcard) and I give the order 'Now, don't touch the fruits.' Straightway Master Dédé begins to caress the most fattest[5] of the oranges. So I caressed his fattest parts with a great flat ruler. Only I was in an agony of laughter all the time, and all but shattered the foundations of our Government with my roars. If the poor boy had guessed what my sort of addled smile meant . . . but he mistook it for a sardonic frown.

The Schoolboys are to spend the Easter Holidays in England with some friends; so I quite hope to make a start at the beginning of April. Have you seen the latest declaration from the Germans, that the English waters are considered after the 18th of Feb. as being the seat of war, and no more consideration will be given to passengers and crews! God speed Harold!

I am sorry I have no photograph to bring true your recent dreams! I

---

[1] Money. Susan Owen did not discourage Wilfred's resentment of their straitened circumstances compared with those of Edward Quayle.

[2] One of the many schemes he was considering at this time. It is not mentioned again.

[3] Apart from the first three paragraphs, this is a draft for Letter 330. It seems to have been received by Susan Owen, however, and was presumably enclosed by Wilfred with Letter 330 in error. It is in Wilfred's usual hand, but carries a few small corrections by him in a different ink. It seems that on this and other occasions (see also Letters 185 and 279) Wilfred worked out very carefully what he wanted to say. 'I like to think you'll keep this Letter', he writes in Letter 330.

[4] The Château du Parc.

[5] 'Anaemic' struck out.

did take to myself a cloak at the beginning of the winter; and cold is the last thing I suffer from. And then there is the excellent breakfast before I start out every morning: and a great lunch, followed by coffee, at twelve-thirty, and a toast-and-tea at five, and a savoury dinner at seven-thirty! (Our Cook[1] was late in the service of the Minister for War; and you may know the reputation of the French Magnates) I could not bear to draw comparisons with the life of the trenches and mine; unless I felt in a manner to have suffered my share of life. And I feel I have.

I have not abandoned all idea of enlisting, but it need be discussed before I get home. My present life does not, as Father points out, lead to anywhere in particular; but, situated where I was, say in 1911, I don't think I could have done wiselier than I did. I have not struck out in any direction yet. I have made soundings in deep waters, and I have looked out from many observation-towers: and I found the deep waters terrible, and nearly lost my breath there.

Of the many prospects of the world that I have spied upon, there is only one field in which I could work willingly, and would work without wage. Only, I must wait for the water[2] of many seasons before I hope to produce one acceptable flower.

If I study, I shall do so not 'to make a comfortable future for myself.' I should go about things another way for that. But suppose I missed the purpose of my life?

I talk randomly; but I think discreetly. My faith is like a weather-cock; but my hope is like a Tower, a strong and haughty Spire. And my love is as wide as the wide world. I seem without a footing on life; but I have one. It is as bold as any, and I have kept it for years. For years now. I was a boy when I first realised that the fullest life liveable was a Poets. And my later experiences ratify it.

320. To Mary Owen
Postcard

[? *Early February 1915*]   [*Postmark Bordeaux*]

Would you please send me over the following books,[3] which I need for my lessons. Postage shall be covered by T's.

(1) *Eng. Gram. & Composition*: a Univ. Tutorial Book—dark green, I think.

(2) My leather Pass Port Case—in my pigeonholes?

(3) *Richard II* Two Copies, I think you will find.

(4) Buy in *Era Shakespere* 2 copies *Hamlet*. 8d. each.

(5) Penny Poets. *Hiawatha*. 3 copies.

---

[1] The gardener's wife.
[2] 'Wealth' struck out.
[3] They all survive.

Nos. 1 & 3 are most important. Don't wait for (4), but send these. I hope Mother & Father are getter righter. Am splendid, me. Mother's letter came today. Too dreadfully busy to palaver in a letter. Your own

W.E.O.

321. To Susan Owen
Postcard

Saturday [*Postmark 13 February 1915*]   *Mérignac P.O.*

I am turning into the P.O. in the middle of a walk to acknowledge your last letter received at noon. I don't deserve such dear long letters. All is serene. I had a two-days' cold only. Glad to hear the Chicken Pox was a false alarm. I dreamt I was at home last night, and it was a right sweet dream. When are those photos of Father going to arrive? When are you going to Alpenrose next?

Yours W.E.O.

I wait anxiously for the Books!

322. To Leslie Gunston
Picture postcard: Prince Leopold of Belgium

[*Postmark 15 January 1915*]   [*Postmark Bordeaux*]

Take this to apprise you that I contemplate writing to you one of these days. Yea, I shall write incontinent. Would I were off the Continent: and could parley. Pray hard I may get over at Easter! Have you these photos in England? You know, Mlle. de la Touche knows the Belgian Princes. I haven't been introduced. Do you consider the seas safe!

W.E.O.

323. To Susan Owen

Thursday, 18 February 1915   [*Mérignac*]

My own dearest Mother,

I sent off a P.C. this morning as soon as I heard of your *Grippe*, but I couldn't say all I should like to. I wish, now, that I had got over to England at Christmas, since the plots thicken all the time, and if Easter passes and I am still stranded, I shall be downright unhappy. At present Homesickness is not a declared malady with me; and only makes me troubled when I read your letters or definitely let my thoughts run on home. Your last news has not caused me to worry but only to spend all my spare thoughts upon you. I hope Mary has stopped her Hospital Business, and devotes her professional experience to your profit. You must indeed be wondering about Harold. (His P.C. was not in my letter). For my part, I have not—like him—touched smoking. I leave it involuntarily for days together. With me, I never produce a cigarette at fixed hours of the day. With me, smoking is not a habit. It is rather a mild mania. And be sure I prize my heart-beats more than tobacco-puffs.

There is much talk of English soldiers arriving in this region, but until they come I shall not expect them (so to say) I saw among the wounded in the Ambulances which pass along the streets every day, a wounded Hindoo.

What does R.A.M.C. mean?

What name is that along with Eric Smallpage?

Is Harry Green in the Navy?

Have you any news of Miles Robson's brother?[1]

What are you reading at present? I am conscious of having lost my omnivorous appetite for books. Novels, Magazines, Newspapers, Essays, bore me exceedingly. I read men now; instead of about them. Apart from pure strong Poetry; which, tho' much remains, is hard to find, I cannot savour any [*one sheet missing*] It is well. All that novelists have to tell has been told me, and by the best of them. I have even found out more. And that more which I had not been told I feel I ought to tell.

As for Poetry, I have let the cares of this life, Indolence, Time, and 'No-Time' do their worst. All winter, all last year and longer I have read no poetry, nor thought poetically (at least not by act of will). Neither have I reasoned seriously, or felt deeply on 'matters of faith'. Thus have I sown my wild oats, that my harvest of poppies may be the more abundant, poppies wherewith many dreams may be fed, and many sores be medicined. . . .

I pine spiritually for need of talk with you, my dear Mother, I like no audience but either the whole world or You. There is no other, with enough sympathy or understanding. I have small affection for the people around me. I have had many affections, and shall have great ones, according to my Mood; but the only affection without Mood and without Tense is that for 'My People'.

It must be getting near the date of my pneumonia-time. I have only to think of you as you were then to me, and I immediately get into a kind of sweet anguish, an ecstasy, (very difficult to describe, but something like the effect of a great music). I hope you will think of those times, and let that memory bring its sheaves with it. The older I grow the better I understand your devotion to me, to Mary, to Harold, to Colin, to us all.

The next and nearest thing you can do for us now is to hoard, economise, bolster up, eke out, husband, spare, reserve, your own strength. Promise it to your

wholeheartedly-loving son, Wilfred

I was indeed glad to have the Hymn Words which you so lovingly copied out for me.

I shouldn't have known H. Green. Thought it one of the Cates brood.

When are Father's Photos coming?

---

[1] HO recalls Miles Robson as a clergyman in Birkenhead, whose brother entered the Navy at the outbreak of war.

324. To Susan Owen
Postcard

[*Postmark 18 February 1915*]   [*Postmark Bordeaux*]
Thursday

I couldn't help being upset by the news of your influenza, however
glozingly and lovingly it may have been told. It seems you have never
been free from sore throat for about six weeks! And all the time I have
been chucking desultory postcards over, and never answering your dear
letters. Today we are all on the point of starting on an excursion on the
River.[1] Perhaps where Father & I went. The new books arrived yesterday, but not the other packet. So I am both annoyed & anxious, if I
have any anxiety to spare from You.

Your very own Wilfred

325. To Leslie Gunston
Picture postcard: Bordeaux, Le Grand Théâtre

23 February [*1915*]   [*Postmark Mérignac*]

I hope you wore a black tie![2] You may be interested to know that Sarah
Bernhardt has gone through the operation all right.[3] The doctor
(Denucé) was the same who 'miraculised' upon one of my boys here.
I pass by where Sarah lies, daily. Have this m'ng. had Father's photo-
graph.[4] Very fine, indeed! Yours W.E.O.

326. To Susan Owen
Picture postcard: Entrée du Chateau Foucastel, Mérignac.
On it is written: We were here today shooting!

[*Postmark 24 February 1915*]   [*Postmark Bordeaux*]

Photo. came today, together with yr. card and a card from Margaret
Quayle! Infinitely happy to find you are able to go out. The likeness is
parfit. Just as Father looked when I saw him last on Bx. station. Mary
has boggled a *Richard III* for *Richard II*, otherwise everything was in
place. Mind Mary adds 1s. to my account!
Precautionise!   W.E.O.

327. To Susan Owen
Picture postcard: Mérignac, Place de Capeyron

[*Postmark 1 March 1915*]   [*Postmark Mérignac*]

Very many thanks for a very dear letter. My only news is that a case of

[1] The Gironde.
[2] On the anniversary of the death of Keats, 23 February 1821.
[3] Her leg was amputated after an accident. Though now 71, her activity was not diminished,
and she acted at the front later in the war.
[4] Taken by John Gunston.

Cerebro-Meningitis has appeared in Capeyron (P.T.O.) close to us. Miss de la T. thinks of sending boys to England. On Mond. she is going to consult Dr. Denucé (who operated Sarah Bernhardt—and Charlie). Nothing will come of it. However, at a pinch, I have information that a lane of armed boats guards the way: Calais–Dover.[1] Between which this very card will have passed! Now, 'ware of your influenza. And keep clear of hospitals! Am hoping every day to hear of Harold's safe arrival. Three cheers for Mrs. Wigan![2] Tell me more.

W.E.O.

328. To Susan Owen

Picture postcard: Mérignac, Entrée du Bourg.
On it is written: We are on the other side of the Church,
a little way up to the left

[*Postmark 3 March 1915*]   [*Postmark Cauderat*]

A delightful Spring day has been To- } day.
                                Tues }

The Cer. Sp. Men. scare is over, now that Dr. Denucé says don't trouble. The average of one or two ships sunk per day keeps up. Shall I hear tomorrow of Harold's arrival. Am dried up in the matter of letter writing, having just covered nine great sheets to Mr. de la Touche in China![3] Horrors! Kenneth Q. wrote me this week. (I sent cards some while ago) Till Soon! x

W.E.O.

329. To Susan Owen

Picture postcard: Bordeaux, Le Lycée National

[*Postmark 5 March 1915*]   [*Postmark Mérignac*]

Dearest thanks for the letter & card which came to my hands simultaneously. I was at a Concert for the wounded in this (temporary) Hospital this afternoon. The great Bréval,[4] who just came over to see Sarah Bernhardt, was seized by my friends last evening, and promised to sing. She sang, perhaps six minutes in all; but she did sing! Well, its great to be certified that Harold was safe a few days ago. Nothing doing among the C.S.M. microbes. I had a bottle of *Eau Oxygenée* in my pocket at the *Lycée National* and thought hard about it! Your own

W

[1] This information was exaggerated.
[2] The Vicar had married.
[3] This must have been his second report to Mr. de la Touche, who wrote to Wilfred from Chinwangtao, China, on 6 March:
Dear Mr. Owen,
    I received today only your long and very kind letter regarding our boys. Thank you very much indeed for the great care you have taken about this report.
[4] Lucienne Bréval (1869–1935) was one of the greatest French singers of her day. A soprano, she sang at Covent Garden in 1899.

330. To Susan Owen[1]

5 March 1915   *Mérignac*

Dearest of Mothers,

My late letters have been writ for the <u>object</u> thereof; for <u>subjects</u> I lacked. But today I have subject enough [*nine lines missing*]

Supposing I underwent the rigours, boredom, disgust, danger of Barracks or Camp, or saw Action on the Field, I might have better claim to a Subsidy from my Rich Uncle, which Common Sense, Common Decency, Common Charity are not quite common enough to realize. I say, it is a matter of Common Sense. Consider; I ask not for a Defence from Life-Troubles or an Excuse for not labouring, but I ask for a Weapon. I <u>will</u> fight through Life; (have I not fought?) but no headway is to be made without an Arm, whether the Sword that is called Science, or the Munition, Capital. To struggle vulgarly with fist and brick-end, I do refuse. I had rather fall back among the Camp Followers of Life and mend potsherds.[2] My present life, as Father points out, is not leading to anywhere in particular; but situated where I was in 1911, I don't think I could have done wiselier than take the steps I did. True, I have not yet struck out in any direction. Since taking Soundings in Deep Waters, finding them fathomless and terrible, and all but losing my breath there, I have looked out from many observation-towers; and I have lifted the curtains from many a human secrecy.

Of the various prospects of the world which I have viewed, I found only one Field in which I could work willingly, and toil without wage. Alas, but we must wait for the waterings of many seasons before hoping to produce therefrom a single acceptable flower!

If I study, it will not be, as writes Father, 'to make a comfortable future'. A comfortable future for myself is to be provided for by other means than study. To some, I seem a fellow without a footing in life. But I have my foothold, bold as any, kept for years. A boy, I guessed that the fullest, largest liveable life was that of a Poet. I <u>know</u> it now; but have still to know whether it is the highest and <u>richest</u>: though I begin to think so. Was I born for it? Well, so far, I find myself in possession of a goodly number of birth-certificates to that effect; while I can find only two or three flimsy arguments for the B.A. Craze, and half a dozen sadly unworthy ones for the 'Reverend' pretension. (In measure as I am in darkness, I keep open my ears for the Voice, should it speak. Think not I have stopped my ears to a Call, dear Mother!) But know that my prime object is not to boss a staff of schoolmasters, any more than it is to boom a monster business. There is <u>one</u> title I prize, one clear call audible, one Sphere where I may <u>influence</u> for Truth, one workshop whence I may send forth Beauty, one mode of living entirely congenial to me. In proof, I swear I cannot appreciate

---

[1] See Letter 319, note 3.
[2] He continued, but struck out 'My meaning is (though you see it) Equipment for the front rank of a professional career, or—such a business as'.

any other dignity: Headmaster of Eton; Archbishop of Canterbury; King of the English Race. My ambitions are lesser than Macbeth's and greater, not so happy, but much happier.

I said 'in proof'. I should have said 'for evidence'. The real verification is what can I write within say, a year's time? And the Crux is this—that to be able to write as I know how to, study is necessary: a period of study, then of intercourse with kindred spirits, then of isolation. My heart is ready, but my brain unprepared, and my hand untrained. And all,—untested. I quite envisage possibility of non-success.

My hopes rose on a tide of enthusiasm common enough in youths whose Spring is open to the Sun of Sense and Moon of Melancholy. That tide may now be about to ebb. Should it be the Tide that leads to Fortune, miserable me if I take it not at the flood! Shall Poverty leave me unlaunched? Shall my Timidity bar me? Shall my Indolence moor me to the mud?[1]

Pray, dear Mother, that I may be loosed in time. The last two shackles are my own task; and now perhaps I shall forge levers for the First.

One more word: A Captive begs to be set free. Is his Begging contemptible? Is his supplication comparable to the whine of him who begs to eat? Better to beg boldly once, than to beg meanly all the rest of one's days.

So saying, I kiss you my own Mother, and confess I long to see you just as much as I long to see myself as you would have me.

Wilfred

P.S. I like to think you'll keep this letter; as indeed all, not, of course, megalomaniac's reason; but just because I keep no Diary; and the landmarks of one's Thoughts fade away still quicker than Events. You will impart my messages to Father. I never begin 'Dear Mother and Father' because I have the feeling of addressing an audience.

P.P.S. I keep unquiet about Harold.

331. To Mary Owen
Postcard
[*Postmark 9 March 1915*]   [*Postmark Bordeaux*]

Would you be so good as to send by return of (Book) Post:—

(1) A Green Bound Elementary Algebra. If there are two very similar, send the one with Answers at the back. If neither have answers, choose the one with the limp cover.

(2) *Euclid* Book(s) I (+II)—A brown volume—If not visible a backless Geometry by Godfrey & Siddons will do.

(3) *Gradatim*, a latin reader (Important)

(4) *De Bello Gallico*. by Julius Caesar.

---

[1] See p. 521, note 1.

Many thanks. Debit my Account! I have a piece of good news to impart. Wait a sec! Now, how's Mother?

Yours W.E.O.

Don't worry about *Richard II*!

332. To Susan Owen

Saturday [*13 March 1915*]   *Mérignac*

My dearest Mother,
Even while licking-up the envelope of the last Missive, on Wednesday, I noticed that my saliva-glands were a trifle addled, so to speak, and sure enough on Thursday morning I was down with a sore throat (sore neck, rather than throat) and a head sore all over:—Influenza—a dry, grim, sardonic form, born of the devilish winds that prevailed in the early part of the week, glacial, stabbing, filing the eyeballs, as a dentist's scraper files the teeth. The headache left off this morning, leaving an ordinary sore throat. All this must be exactly what you have been having, not for three days, but it seems for weeks and months. I used to hold a superstition that, by wishing one could draw off somebody else's pains to oneself. If it were so, how willingly would I stay on up here in this little pill-box of a room incapable of reading, talking, or swallowing. As it is, I shall no doubt get up tomorrow or Sunday. Miss de la Touche has nursed me with the utmost pains: up and down stairs with gargles, inhalations, paintings, poultices, pastilles, hot drinks, and cold drinks, eau-de-Cologne, Bandage, Thermometer, and such like, not forgetting the country doctor. I think you might write a nice little letter of thanks to her.
What a relief to know that Harold is landed [*one page missing*]
I have numbers of letters of apology to pupils to clear off.
This must be a small-compass and a small-focus letter; but let the substance of it be that being now quite unused to pain, I had a nasty week-end; but am not ill (temp. not over 100.5!) and a good part of my pains are caused by my suddenly realizing what your off-hand tales of rheumatic pains in head and eyes, really meant.
Ah me! (and Ah You!)

Yours ever, Wilfred x

(I beseech you make no observance of Mar. 18.)

333. To Susan Owen

Postcard

Monday [*Postmark 15 March 1915*]   [*Postmark Mérignac*]

I had the books today. Great thanks! All correct. The *Richard II* was superfluous; tho' it was also superfluous to say so! I came downstairs

today at five o'clock, but have now had enough (7 p.m.). What a chagrin for Harold[1] and for Father! What hope remains? I forgot to tell
you that I wrote a card to Grandma when you said. Fortunately we are
having the mildest of weather now. Am expecting something from you,
if not from Father, very soon. A poor Birthday Card, this, but here I'm
stuck these 5 days! Exceeding many joyful Returns! Your own

W.E.O.

334. To Susan Owen

The 17th [*Postmark 19 March 1915*]   [*Postmark Mérignac*]

I had your letter in bed this mng. for I got up late. Many thanks for the
kerchief, and many more for the dear messages. I can call myself quite
better now. It seems I had a 'Diphtheric Throat'; tho' they didn't tell
me. Tomorrow I shall have a birthday treat—Miss de la T. is sending
me & 2 boys to a Concert got up by Miss Patterson for Profit of
Refugees. What a swizz about Harold! Fondest love to all,

W.E.O.

335. To Leslie Gunston

Picture postcard: Mérignac, Vue générale du Domaine Beau-Désert

[*Postmark 25 March 1915*]   [*Postmark Mérignac*]

Was highly pleased with your letter. A prompt answer turneth away
grief. I will try and learn to do as well; but shall have to store up a
little more news yet. I thank you for samples of Noyes;[2] shall consider
a large order shortly (Mark how my Business has got hold of me.)
Bye the way don't spread the news of my Travel. I beg you. This is a
glimpse of our country. I like this Tree, sort you always see in left
corners of pictures of Bay of Naples.
    J. Richepin[3] is lecturing in Bx. on Ap. 4! *Vale o Carissimus.*

W.E.O.

336. To Susan Owen

le 4 avril. Dimanche de Pâques. [*1915*]   *Mérignac*

My own dear Mother,
    It is Easter Sunday morning, and we have just come back from High
Mass: real, genuine Mass, with candle, with book, and with bell, and
all like abominations of desolation: none of your anglican simulacrums.

---

[1] HO, on board one of the ships about to sail with the Dardanelles Expeditionary Force, had
  been taken off before sailing because of an Admiralty ruling that no officers under 21 were
  to take part. HO was 17.
[2] Alfred Noyes (1880–1958), the poet.
[3] Jean Richepin (1849–1926), playwright and poet. A copy of his *La Mer* servives among
  Wilfred's books.

On Good Friday I went also. Always I come out from these performances an hour and a half older: otherwise unchanged. I was going to the English Church in Bordeaux, but was snared into staying with the others. They were given Easter Eggs this morning: and I found on my Breakfast plate a Box of Egyptian Cigarettes, (which I dote on), and a leather cigarette-case, (which I don't like.)

My chief Easter Joy was your postcard: the handwriting alone, comforting and reassuring—and what a pack of matter in the mention of Harold—Dardanelles, less Danger—Submarines, Larks—swallows, your Charities—Meols. My next-best treat was a charming letter from the Poet Tailhade,[1] who is now in Paris, lecturing this week at the Odéon, on *Britannicus*, and next week on the Art of Belgium, and his personal souvenirs of that country. He, of course, advises me to travel via Paris, and talks of arranging to see me there.

On Monday afternoon (tomorrow) I'm going to a lecture by the famous novelist and poet Richepin: going with the young (?) lady[2] who undertakes the French side of the de la Touche's education. About three weeks ago I met, through Miss de la T., a rather remarkable Parisian lady—'between the two ages'—whom I should like to know more. She has a Salon in Paris where many literary notables congregate. Her husband is a Ministre Plenipotentiare of some sort; but doesn't function at present. In earlier days this lady stayed in London at the French Embassy, her step-father (I think) being Ambassador before Queen Victoria, and a man whose influence is largely responsible for the *Entente Cordiale*.[3] He and King Edward seem to have fixed it up between 'em. But of all the mighty ones this lady remembers in England the chief was Burne-Jones,[4] whom she saw at work in his studio. Miss de la Touche, I suddenly found, has great talent in Life-Drawings and Oil Portraits; studied in Paris, under some great Unknown-to-me, naturally of pious memory with her. When the money gave out she had to give it up. She is, as a matter of fact, and contrary to my first ideas, badly off; and though spending irishly, spends every penny. That crippled young lady, not often referred to in my letters, being no concern of mine [*three lines missing*]

I wonder what sort of domestic you keep at present: I do hope a competent person! I will do without being considered a 'Doctor' if the creature herself needeth no physician. I feel glad you didn't pay 2 Guineas for a hum-hum-ha! [*three lines missing*]

I don't remember speaking of anything I had in mind for Harold. Well you know, and he knows, what I have at heart. That he paint, paint, paint, until his signature be known to the Rank of England, and the Bank of England. You seemed afraid [*one word missing*] Harold [*one word missing*] didn't go to church alone for Father Duncan's

---

[1] This letter survives.
[2] Mlle Duval or her successor Mlle Ducarpe.
[3] The French Ambassador in London 1898–1920 was Paul Cambon (1843–1924).
[4] Sir Edward Coley Burne Burne-Jones (1833–98), the Pre-Raphaelite painter.

sake; but rather lured by the vain deceits which do lead astray etc.
But can't you make as if not to see! (*two lines missing*] can't you
'deny yourselves' the fun of 'badgering' him! Badger me and I'll
snap my own head off!! Do learn the importance of not being earnest.

Now, we can't have Dame Cannell at home when I land. I am indeed
sorry to miss Harold again. I don't think I ever congratulated him on
selling those sketches. I hope he has left plenty at home for me to see.

What Report has Colin this term? My word, I'll coach him in French.
Is his body strong? How does he talk English? Does he seem to think,
from what he says nowadays? What new aptitudes is he showing?
Will he be 13 or 14 next birthday? Is he darker of hair now? Are his
rabbit-teeth humanising? Is he 'polished' yet? And is he still tender and
affectionate? Can he want to see me as much as I him? Does he give you
any sort of annoyance, or provocation, or uneasiness for any cause
whatever? What modifications are to be noted in Harold and Mary
also? [*one line missing*] Is Father as well as usual? Is the Gardening beginning again? What Questions! One I need not ask of you, nor
you of me, for I am the Unchanging,

Your very Childe Wilfred

337. To Susan Owen

Picture postcard: Mérignac, Hôtel de Ville

[Postmark 8 April 1915]   *[Postmark Mérignac]*

I can't yet be positive about my starting. I said all I knew in my letter,
viz. Nothing. Since, Peyronnet has said I must go this month. So Miss
de la T. wrote to her solicitor intending to send Boys. Then comes at
aft. tea advice from the Castejas' (Monsieur is an Admiral) not to
think of crossing Channel. Never was such danger as now. So Miss de
la T. won't send her letter: and there is a deadlock. Help me out, with
peremptory letters, which I can read to her!

We're going a picnic with friends on Sat. Party of 16! We're too
safe in this Region; and would forget the War; but for the Travel
inconvenience. Best thanks for your letter of this mng. Richepin never
gave that lecture—indisposed.

338. To Susan Owen

Wednesday [Early April 1915]   *Mérignac*

Dearest Mother,

I have little time, and am only writing a closed letter on account of
reference to Mrs. Cannell [*several words missing*]

Now about Mrs. Cannell. I shall be altogether constrained, uncomfortable, annoyed, unnatural if the old lady is there. More especially as

she is a critical old lady. You must pack her off. I shall only start on
Monday. Does that give you time? Say I am bringing some French
people and you haven't Room, (for, indeed, I am an Englishman of 20
yrs. plus a Frenchman of 20–22 years, which makes two) Or, say you
expect Leslie; which is true. You do expect him. I remember Mrs.
Cannell's physionomy always had a Medusa-like effect on me. She is in
a continual state of offering criticisms without any right to be critical.
I don't regard her criticisms; but certainly I shall have my own critical
spirit at work; which I don't want to be so. It would be a pity after all
not to meet you really. But before the old lady I shall either be taciturn,
and tell you nothing, or else be malicious, and go about giving the old
dame a thorough shocking. She must go.

She is the Hat that obstructs your view at a performance, she is the
fourth person when Love is the Third; she is salt in good coffee; and
will have the effect of the salt that the cook forgot to put in the soup.

Receive her again afterwards, but dispose of her for 7 days. I shall be
with you not more than 10 days. Keep in the pink of health, as I am in the
crimson of it.

Your very own, W.E.O.

339. To Mary Owen

Wednesday, early April 1915   *Mérignac*

> Caution: To be read
> at Arm's Length!

Dearest Mary,

No doubt you had not expected that I should be writing to you before
I saw you, and may guess that it bodes no good. And indeed you may
not see me quite so soon as expected, because I've got Measles! It's
Measles that Bobby, Johnny and I have got! Two days ago after being
in the sun for an hour in the afternoon I felt rather hot in the face, and
consulting the looking-glass got quite a turn (I think that's the English
expression?). One would think I had been drinking: drinking for a
ten-year Eau de Cologne and Methylated Spirits! Wicked lines in forehead—pouchy, overlapping cheeks, watery and bloody eyes—toad-
spotted, raw-meat-coloured skin. Then I went deaf in one ear. Thought
it was a sunstroke! Next morning went in to Bx. as usual, because I
was to see a Doctor that day, whose wife is my pupil. Now this Dr. is
the Director of the *Service de Santé* of the whole region, Chief Medical
Officer for Health, or something of the sort, and he thought it was Sunstroke, and gave me a prescription for an ointment. I just managed to
get through my Lessons with the boys in the evening, tho' my breath
and Bobby's perspicacity were quite unusually short. So was the Sunstroke. I was awakened this morning by three excited boys bursting into
my room (unheard-of proceeding!) and thrusting forward poor Bobby:

with 'Oh Mr. Owen, you've given your spots to Bobby! Look!' Then Bobby bares his breast like a soldier exhibiting grievous wounds, and there was the rash! I got up. At breakfast I noticed Johnny's eyes getting out of order, and in half an hour he too was spotted. The two juniors show no signs. Then came the Doctor and pronounced *La Rougeole*. There is an epidemic, so it seems. But he didn't send us to bed, and here am I, large as life, and a little larger about the face, sitting up, at my uncomfortable writing table, on an uncomfortable chair. I even spent the morning with the boys who behaved like fiends. Poor Miss de la Touche had arranged to send us all out on a whole-day picnic today, because certain relations of the sick young lady she looks after, were coming. So she felt near the termination of her wits [*two lines missing*]

This measles will certainly alter my dates a little, tho' not greatly. I shan't book by the *Oronsa*, anyway.—Mother's letter came this morning. I still prefer the Paris Route: and think it safer! When is Mrs. C. moving on? Mother writes these words: 'Mrs. Cannell will be pleased to see you I know—' Kind of her! Perhaps she'll even let me open the front door without ringing! And not object if I spend a few nights! Dear old soul! So indulgent! But if she were not pleased, by chance, I think you said the 'Raven' had the best name in the town. . . .

Now, really, I know measly people are specially touchy; but I wish you brats wouldn't make such a racket when Mother's writing to me. I have long waited for some photographs of the Place and 'Ourselves' but none are yet ready, except the enclosed which shows the dining-room and a bedroom-window. The youngster is not of course a de la Touche, but a neighbour, (grandson of the ship-owner).[1] He is the sturdiest piece of boy's flesh going on legs: but not a favourite of mine. My favourite is the Admiral's boy, of the great Chateau du Parc; who plays with me rather than with the boys. Into his woods we go in the hot afternoons; into the woods we go; and the floor of the coppice surges with verdure; the meadows heave with new grass as the sea with a great tide; the violets are not shy as in England but push openly and thickly; the anemones are dense like weeds, and the primroses like the yellow sands of the sea. And there the nightingale ever sings; but I had rather she did not, for she sings a minor key. And the idyll becomes an ode-elegiac.

Adieu, good sister, you wouldn't think I had *Rougeole*! But don't put your nose on these pages!

Ante-Script: (*Thursday*)

It can't be 'the Measles' as you understand it: it must be a false variety hence known as German Measles: since we have no temperature: and today the rash has disappeared, and my face has already begun to peel!

W.E.O.

[1] M. Grasset, a wealthy neighbour.

340. To Susan Owen

Saturday, 10 April [*1915*]   *Mérignac*

Dearest Mother,

Supported by a French Admiral, her brother, her sister, her solicitor, all her Friends, and the whole population of Mérignac, Miss de la Touche is now quite firm: she will not send the boys. She leaves me free to do what I like, always letting me understand that she would be thankful if I would stay. She can't have them unmanaged and uneducated and knows of no one to take my place [*one line illegible*] So I am the Rope in a tug-of-war between Home and Business on one side and Courtesy on the other. I think I have found a compromise: to come over for, say, three weeks, and return here for the summer term and the summer holidays [*ten lines missing*]

The people in the 'Place' neighbouring ours have a ship of theirs going to London shortly. We know these people rather well, and I have asked Miss de la Touche to try and get me a passage, if the date is convenient.

Miss de la T. is frightened at the idea of having the 4 Ruffians alone even for 3 weeks and is going to try and find someone to replace me. If there could be found an Englishman who would take on the job permanently I would be glad to leave for good. It is scarcely worth my paying the fare, and I have not yet extorted a promise that Miss de la Touche will. I had cherished the hope of staying at Home until the moment of my great expedition, and devoting myself to certain writings, which I would fain accomplish. For this a month or so of seclusion is indispensable. Gardening, sketching, photography, writing for magazines may very well thrive on spare effort in odd times; but a Poem does not grow by jerks. If it is to be worth a place in Human Time, it must be worth more than fag-ends of the Poet's time. A patch-work counterpane or a ship full-rigged—in a bottle, may be perfectly fabricated off-an'-on, between-whiles, casual, like. But Poetry, 'coming naturally as leaves to a tree',[1] grows as incessantly and as delicately. And as trees in Spring produce a new ring of tissue, so does every poet put forth a fresh, and lasting outlay of stuff at the same season.

Well, well, I have not now the time to continue on paper this trend of thinking.

Let me know what your comments [*two words illegible*] you first read of my Proposition of coming back here after three weeks. I like it little, after all. I had rather coach Colin! I have no doubt his English no less than French needs it! I gather that Miss de la T. considers the boys have made immense strides in these few months. If so it is their own intelligence, not mine, that provided the seven-league-boots. I can do nothing at all with even middling pupils. The 'teaching body' should regard me as an offending mote, happily withdrawn from its longsuffering corpus.

[1] 'If poetry comes not naturally as leaves to a tree it had better not come at all.' Keats to John Taylor, 27 February 1818 (*Letters* I, p. 238).

I promise not to show shock at any of Colin's crudities of speech. (Slang, by the way, I like to hear) (And these boys swear like troopers). I will stand even dialect. Better a twang in the tongue than a twist in the eyes. By the way, does Colin's sight improve. And by the by-way, let him leave off his odious goggles when he 'comes to meet me' or I shan't know him.

[*several lines missing*] I also am sore bruised, but I am challenging many another Blow yet. Ambition may be defined as the willingness to receive any number of hits on the nose. 'There is no fiercer hell than the failure in a great ambition.'[1] (The words are sacred to me; hence you know who said them.) Ah, others also were knocked as hard as Aunt Sally . . . Yes, it needs a hard kick to get sent up to the stars. Perseus was a sailor lad;[2] and never, I take it, bore epaulets on his brown shoulders or gold-braid on his bare chest; but his name is written in stars, because he trusted in the armour of the Immortals [*several lines missing*] I go [*several words missing*] in the early morning to buy provisions.

So Goodnight, my own dear Mother! From your very own Wilfred x

341. To Susan Owen
Postcard

Thursday [*Postmark 15 April 1915*]   [*Postmark Bordeaux*]

Your letter of the 11th was posted before you had mine telling of my latest scheme. I am most anxious to know what you will say to my returning here! I think I have found a substitute for myself. Am going to interview him this aft.—public school man[3]—giving Eng. lessons in Bx. Met him on Tues. at a lecture by an English lady on 'England before the War.' Thus I think to start within the next 15 days.

On Tues. Night I heard Richepin. His *Conférence* makes a glorious close for my sojourn in this land.

Your letter came with power and great store of strength—not to help me to 'push off' that was already determined, but certainly to start without Fear and without Reproach.

Yours ever, W.E.O.

Mourn not for Harold, nor fear: Think that every French family is ten times more exposed & threatened than we.

342. To Susan Owen
Postcard

Monday [*Postmark 20 April 1915*]   [*Postmark Mérignac*]

It has just been arranged that Mr. Bonsall,[4] public school man, shall look after boys in my absence—(3 times a week—not living up here.)

---

[1] 'There is not a fiercer hell than the failure in a great object.' From the Preface to *Endymion*.
[2] See p. 408.   [3] See next Letter.
[4] Charles La Touche recalls him as a Welshman, about 40, who had been left money while a law student and had spent it in travelling about the world. He was now tutoring in Bordeaux.

I had a word with him about taking the job permanently, and asked a little while to think it over; but he rather seemed to like the idea. If I start, I don't at all fancy the trebled risk of Rochelle–L'pool, nor yet the journey Bx.–Rochelle. Know no more of our neighbour's Boat, as Miss de la T. hasn't asked. So we'll leave that idea. This only I have made sure: To leave in a week or so, and for a week or so, but perhaps for always. That's something! Your own W.E.O.

343. To Susan Owen
Postcard

Saturday [*Postmark 24 April 1915*]   [*Postmark Mérignac*]

Your card this mng. It can't have been Measles proper—so sorry I gave a false alarm, tho' we all thought we were in for a fortnight of it. I am all but right again—nothing left but swollen glands. So still hope to get away next week—say Thursday. Land-route, I really think. Shall be glad of Forms for passes or ¼ fares. Sorry to trouble Father a third time. Probably I shall return here. So it is arranged at present. Yours ever,
W.E.O.

344. To Leslie Gunston
Picture postcard: Mérignac, L'Église

[*Postmark 25 April 1915*]   [*Postmark Mérignac*]

My very best thanks for your abundant supply of Catalogues.—They were for a Frenchman: I shall want some more for myself when I come! Am really trying to get away next week. Had a sort of measles a few days ago, which soon passed. I shan't see as much of you as could be wished: staying in Eng. only 3 weeks.

Yours W.E.O.

345. To Susan Owen
Postcard

Monday [*Postmark 26 April 1915*]   [*Postmark Mérignac*]

Peyronnet is not yet ready with his chattels, so in any case I can't start before Friday. Having well weighed both arguments, I find it best to return here after a few weeks. 'Twill be but a tabloid dose of home-life. I am wondering where to stay in London. And not particularly anxious to put up at Worple Rd. Wimbledon. Have you other addresses of Hotels, Boardings, or Rooms? I am now re-established in health. What we had was Roseola, or Scarlet Rash!

Yours, W.E.O.

A raconteur and bon-vivant, a fine cricketer, with a genial, easy-going temperament, he was a great contrast to Wilfred and made a more direct appeal to the boys. He taught them Latin and Greek; Wilfred continued to take the other subjects.

346. To Susan Owen

Saturday [*Postmark 30 April 1915*]   [*Postmark Mérignac*]

I have no reason to change news of last card: and can add that my train
leaves Bx. at 10.30 on Mond. night, arr. Paris 8 next morning. From
here I can't book further than Paris, & as officials don't know which
Route is practicable after, I must wait till my arrival at the Capital. I
may stay there the day, or even night. Don't expect telegram till I
get to London, as I shan't know trains at Dover. I had Order to B.
Clerk at Dover, & hope for others in case. Have insured my luggage.
Certainly, as I must have said, I mean to have a week at home, & do
business[1] afterwards. I firmly trust my last letter was not in vain. I
should be excited, if not a little harassed.
Shall write once again.

347. To Susan Owen

Saturday [*Postmark 1 May 1915*]   [*Postmark Mérignac*]

Nothing fresh except this: that Miss de la T. finds this m'ng. that relations of her invalid charge want to stay here, so my room will be wanted.
I shall not be sorry to be free and easy in my own Chambers; & tho'
don't want to pass Summer in Bx. If compensation is not made, there
may be a Rupture with Mlle. This matter I can only discuss tonight, &
am now only able to say—'don't be too sure of me till you have the
Telegram, which don't expect too soon.' Sorry for you and myself.
Shall be pretty shattered on arriving, as well as preoccupied a little with
the Business!

348. To Susan Owen
Postcard
[*Postmark 19 May 1915*]   *Cranston's Waverley Hotel,*
                                London: Southampton Row, W.C.

Here I am; and a very suitable place it is. Had a room without difficulty,
the same no. as my room in Paris!

Yours, W.E.O.

349. To Susan Owen
Postcard
Wednesday [*Postmark 20 May 1915*]   *Cranston's Waverley Hotel,*
                                          London

Did the first stroke this mng. by getting the Attaché to look up information, which will be ready tomorrow. Exhibition is open Thurs. and

---

[1] For Peyronnet, at the British Industries Fair.

Frid. Hence I just got my Ticket (a matter of much bus-riding and lift-climbing) then went to the great meeting in Guildhall,[1] of which you already read in papers. To hear Mr. Asquith[2] on a day like this was a unique thing! Bonar-Law[3] spoke too, and the Earl of Crewe.[4] The Archbishop hearkened, but spake not. I think I saw Rudyard Kipling! The public was not admitted but I got my ticket without trouble. I feel intensely happy in dear London!

Your W.E.O.

350. To Susan Owen
Postcard
Night of Thursday [*Postmark 21 May 1915*]
Cranston's Waverley Hotel, London

Have spent greater part of day at Exhibition, working hard, and not I think without avail. But am no more advanced towards my prime object —and it may keep me in Town over the Week End. I forgot to mention that my suit came on Wed. morning. It is satisfactory. My cough has disappeared. That's London!

W.E.O.

351. To Susan Owen
Picture postcard: colour reproduction of an oil painting 'When I Meditate on Thee in the Night Watches', showing King Saul sunk in thought, at the side of his throne the sleeping boy David with a lyre

[*Late May 1915*]   [*London*]

Was prevented by a new turn of affairs from leaving Town today as expected. (happy turn of affairs.) Passed a joyful time at R.A. This picture is not one of the Exposed—I send it because it represents or suggests all of the dozen things I hold dear in the Universe. (but one—Home). What these are, I will enumerate when I get Home: let us say Monday. Many thanks for your letter. It came with a nice note from Peyronnet. I found a gold purse in Brompton Rd. on my first hour in London.
An Omen? Amen! So be it.   W.E.O.

[1] 19 May 1915, organized by the Central Committee for National Patriotic Organizations. The Lord Mayor presided; the meeting was to pay homage to the self-governing Dominions, Colonies, Protectorates, and the Indian Empire.
[2] Prime Minister 1908–16. Herbert Henry Asquith (1852–1928) was created 1st Earl of Oxford and Asquith 1925.
[3] Andrew Bonar Law (1858–1923) was at this time Leader of the Opposition in the House of Commons. He was Prime Minister 1922–3.
[4] Robert Offley Ashburton Crewe-Milnes, 2nd Baron Houghton and Marquess of Crewe (1858–1945), was Colonial Secretary 1908–10, Secretary of State for India 1910–15.

352. To Susan Owen

Picture postcard: Imperial Hotel, Russell Square, London

[Postmark 11 June 1915]   *[Postmark London]*

There wasn't room in Regent Palace Hotel; so I came here prices as at Waverley, situate a few doors higher up Southampton Row. My room is in front, but I can't spot it. I have now entered into parley with another agent, in case first ones have to be abandoned. There is a Cook's Office in the Hotel. Your

W.E.O.

I lunched w. Leslie, which was refreshing. I <u>may</u> be kept waiting for Passport.

353. To Susan Owen
Postcard

Saturday [Postmark 12 June 1915]   *General P.O., London*

I have spent all morning waiting my turn at the Foreign Office, and all afternoon at the French Consulate. At last I have Passport and Ticket, & am ready to start by 8.30 from Victoria tomorrow morning. I have come to a conclusion with my Agent—though he won't become a buying agent. I passed by accident the spot where a Zep. Bomb fell in a cross-roads. The paving-stones had all been re-laid. Called on Herbert Billing yesterday to get the signature of a barrister that I am a fit and proper person to hold a passport. To find Billing's address I had to see Gordon & so had eyes tested. They have improved. Billing as special constable arrested a German spy this week! Goodbye!

W.E.O.

Shall try to drop you a line from Paris; but shall also try to catch a train to Bx. on Sund. Mond. night.

354. To Susan Owen
Postcard

Sun. Night [13 June 1915]   *Quai d'Orsay Station, Paris*

Here am I; and though this morning I saw five hours of Day in London, I feel already very far from Home. I have had time for an evening promenade in Paris, and somehow found that the place palled on me. After writing the card in G.P.O. last night, I sallied down Whitechapel, and spent a delightful evening with the Israelites. That was my Sabbath-keeping for this week; but I could not do otherwise than travel today— my funds <u>just</u> lasted out. Now for 9 hrs. more train Phew! *Adieu!*

W.E.O.

355. To Susan Owen
Postcard

Monday [*Postmark 14 June 1915*]   *Post Office, Bordeaux*

Arriving at 7 this morning, I had plenty of time to go around hunting a Room.[1] I am now installed in a spacious, high-ceilinged apartment, with a balcony overlooking the Cathedral. very satisfactory—only 30 f. a month. The journey was not pleasant from Paris. I got filthy and spent a good part of this afternoon in a bath. I could not sleep, but had no lack of dreams in the train—for the Dawn coming over the rich lands round Poitiers was the most faerie spectacle in Europe. I went & saw Raoul this evening. Shall get together a letter soon.

W.E.O.

Address: 18 rue Beaubadat (*1er étage*) Bx.

356. To Susan Owen

Tuesday [*16 June 1915*]   *18 rue Beaubadat* [*Bordeaux*]

My very own Mother,

I'm fairly settled down to Exile, work, heat, and the rest of it; and my *bagages* both of fine apparel and of learning are well unpacked. Having given my lessons up at the Châlet, and looked up old pupils in town, I have already sealed up remembrance of this last happy month. But the first few hours in France were troubled with real nostalgia; and I had a lively longing for the idle, protected, loving, wholesome, hidden, intimate, sequestered Home Life of mine; I felt responsible for coming out here again, into a far different atmosphere and my first breath of Bordeaux air was a gasp, and my first step on its soil was a spiteful kick. Extraordinary how foreign everything flavoured again. But in three hours all that wore off.

I have found, not by luck, but by three hours' search, a most suitable chamber; let by most superior people. I have already said it is large & lofty, up two flights of stairs; situated in the most convenient quarter; and with high-class houses round about. There are two large windows opening on a balcony, over which the whole front of the beloved Cathedral towers tho' just before my windows is an office of some sort. The corner is haunted by a continual draught of cool air which ought really to raise the rent by 20 francs a month. My bed is all that could be desired; there is a wardrobe, marble mantelpiece, & handsome mirror, hanging-curtain-wardrobe, a vast writing-desk, beautiful old round table, marble washstand, two armchairs, desk-chair, etc. wall-paper an unfortunate colour; & in design like ten thousand cabbages, over-boiled, and partly digested:—clean, however. And the ornaments are all

---

[1] New lodgings in Bordeaux, for his room at Mérignac was wanted. But he continued his tutoring at the Châlet; he and Bonsall went out there on different days.

supportable, and one or two acceptable. These are not the usual lodging-house keepers; and my room is looked after by their servant. The lady is a *modiste* (milliner). There are two children, boy of 9, girl of 12, but these are not likely to disturb my peace in any manner whatever.

I found it impossible to stay less than 3 days in London; first I had to obtain an Application Form for Passport, return it next day, & wait for the Passport itself; then have the thing visa'd by the French authorities in London. The voyage was delightful: marvellous clear. France was plainly visible from the train at Folkestone! The Dawn among the lovely lands of central France was an experience for me: the only experience of the journey.

—But I have not yet made up my back-accounts with Morpheus, and must rise early again tomorrow for seeing Peyronnet, who was out this morning. I forgot to say how gladly everybody welcomed me at Mérignac; and how undeniably pleasant it was to have to do with the dear, clever lads Johnny and Bobby. (Tell Colin). Yes, I do seem a long way off; but I also feel a short time off.

Your own W

By delaying to return I was saved the annoyance of a frightful storm over Mérignac on Sund. night. The Châlet was struck[1] and a poor unfortunate in the village struck fatally. I saw the flashing from hundreds of miles away, & felt the horror of it in Paris.

357. To Susan Owen

[c. 20] June 1915   *18 rue Beaubadat. Bx. 1ᵉʳ· étage*

Dearest Mother,

Notice my address. I have not gone down a floor, but find that an intermediate story between the ground & mine is not counted as a story: so, I am for postal purposes on the first floor. A week's stay has now proved that I couldn't have done better than choose this place. I have now 'touched', as they say, the reimbursement of my stay in London, from Peyronnet, amounting to 165 francs, or £6. I was all but penniless after paying my rooms on the first day, and during the day enjoyed the romantic sensation of being absolutely and literally *sans le sou*. Now if you would like me to post back some part of what I have borrowed from you, I can do so. Peyronnet received me very well, and considered I had managed the affair very properly. So he renews his proposition of an Eastern Voyage; to begin in Sept. if possible; but not until the Campaign of the Dardanelles be finished. I told him therefore that if the way were still blocked when I return home in Sept. I should try to join the Army. For I noticed in the Hotel in London an announcement that any gentleman (fit, etc.) returning to England from abroad will be given a Commission—in the 'Artists' Rifles'.[2] Such

---

[1] David La Touche remembers the storm. A tree was struck by lightning.
[2] He joined up in the Artists' Rifles four months later.

officers will be sent to the front in 3 months. Thus we shall watch the
Dardanelles with a little more interest than before. And, in very sooth,
I rather hope things there will last out as long as the war, which will be
through the winter. Still more Frenchmen have been mobilised since I
left France; and the outlook is not one shade brighter. I don't want the
bore of training, I don't want to wear khaki; nor yet to save my honour
before inquisitive grand-children fifty years hence. But I now do most
intensely want to fight. In redoubting the exercises during these months
of July & August I have perfectly sufficient reason for not 'joining' yet.
But when I learnt that Peyronnet prefers me to wait until the East is
more settled I felt full of peace—and of war. So the most patriotic thing
I can do is to hope for non-success in the Dardanelles! In a month or so
from now, forces will be as certainly lacking as munitions are now. So
let us hope Lloyd George will have my shooter ready by then. Meanwhile, I lead a really enviable existence. I am adapted to the climate,
and re-adapted to the mode of life. I shall play Tennis religiously.

When you were writing last Sunday I had just got in the train at the
Quai d'Orsay. I shortened the Boulogne–Paris stage, by having dinner
on the train; it took 1 hour and a quarter! On the Friday Night before
leaving Town I was seized with a desire to see the Mile End Road, in
which I had not set foot since I wore strap-slippers, at five years old.
Although it was dark, I remembered the old spot perfectly; and Dr.
Loughrey's[1] name is still up on red-lit glass above the door. On Sat.
being now tired of the West End, I thought a little ugliness would be
refreshing; and striking east from the P.O. walked down Fenchurch St.
and so into the Whitechapel High Street, & the Whitechapel Road.
Ugliness! I never saw so much beauty, in two hours, before that
Saturday Night. The Jews are a delightful people, at home, & that
night I re-read some Old Testament with a marvellous great sympathy &
cordiality!

Stay long at Kidmore!   Your own W

Convey every good wish to all good people at Alp. & thereabouts &
try and convey some photographs to me.

Bother Mr. Seaton's demand.[2] Refer him to the Opinion. Perhaps I'd
better send him samples.

358. To Susan Owen
Postcard

Tuesday [*Postmark 22 June 1915*]   *Mérignac*

Am waiting for my Tram 5.30 p.m. & cannot fill my time better than by
commending me to you. & wishing you a good journey tomorrow.
There is an even heat, which is no longer inconvenient.—I hear my
tram grinding along. So *au revoir!* W.E.O.

[1] His uncle, Dr. Richard Loughrey.
[2] Unexplained.

359. To Susan Owen

Picture postcard: drawing of war orphans knocking at a door

[Postmark 29 June 1915]   *[Postmark Bordeaux]*

These works of art are thrust upon one by charitable persons, for all France is collecting for its War Orphans. I have no news to detail, the most noted events of my days are the arrivals of your letters. The letter you forwarded was a piece of literature by L. Tailhade. Miss Morley said precisely what I expected, & therefore I could not have been better pleased.[1] Would you kindly send in next letter, 1 doz. Gillette Razor Blades. I shall soon be run out of them.

                                              Fondest Love W.E.O.

360. To Susan Owen

Wednesday, 30 June [1915]   *[Bordeaux]*

My dearest Mother,

Your letters are very dear to me; but these are days when my side of correspondence languisheth like a leaf in fiery June. I cannot exaggerate the painful feelings I experienced in the first days of my change of air; but at the same time I repeat I have nothing to grumble about here, and am therefore of an untumultuous spirit; whatever I may have of England to regret. But as the School Term seems to start about Sept. 21st, there is really a mere wisp of time to be consumed before the Return to England. Tell Leslie that the weather was astonishingly clear in the Narrow Seas that day, and I thought much of H. Belloc;[2] and have added much to my appreciation of Travel, since reading *Hills & the Sea*. Another thing: was it not Belloc's great forefinger which pointed out to me this passage of De Vigny: If any man despairs of becoming a Poet, let him carry his pack and march in the ranks.[3]

Now I don't despair of becoming a Poet: 'Before Abraham was, I am' so to speak [*one line illegible*]

Will you set about finding the address of the 'Artists' Rifles', as this is the Corps which offers commissions to 'gentlemen returning from abroad.'

I certainly went a promenade with Raoul one Sunday afternoon in a 'Garden' in the Town, where choral songs were rendered by schools. I

---

[1] He had sent her *The Little Mermaid* for criticism. See Letter 361. Edith Morley almost certainly read and commented on other poems, as probably did Miss Rayner (see Letters 132 and 138). An unpublished poem in the BM about a young sailor in a train (possibly inspired by HO's return from his first voyage) carries this comment in the margin, in a firm, feminine hand: 'There is as little imagination in the second couplet as there is much in the first.' See Biographical Table, 20 October 1911.

[2] Joseph Hilaire Pierre Belloc (1870–1953), essayist, novelist, poet, historian, biographer, traveller, and critic. *Hills and the Sea* (1906) does not survive among Wilfred's books; *Esto Perpetua* (1906) does.

[3] From *Servitude et Grandeur Militaires* (1835), the best-known work of Alfred Victor, Comte de Vigny (1797–1863), poet, dramatist, and novelist.

got so heartily bored that I took leave of him before the quarter of the programme was over; this was facilitated by having paid his admission [*several words illegible*] With him, Philippe, his Boarder.[1]

We have had delightful weather: gay, boisterous Rains, spasmodic, don't-care-a-hang weather; free Turkish Baths, hot, with a sensation of continually cooling, in a word delicious and sensational. Only the vines will be spoilt and a good part of the hay. Tennis has been out of the question; round the garden walks, ducklings swim. Reports come of drought, and agricultural calamity[2] in England. Is this so?

Yes, 'it pays' to be able to talk learnedly of the war; as indeed I do over the coffee, regularly every day. At home I retailed neither news, ideas, nor hopes. But here I have so many sources of information. I often see the Viscount de Maud'huy; and a Norwegian gives me items from German papers. The admiral's wife told me yesterday that his fleet bombarded a Ger: Consulate in Asia Minor,—because the Germans had dug up the ashes of Napoleon's soldiers, & scattered them to the winds!

I have just walked back from Mérignac all the way, with the boys around and upon me arriving at the Boulevard at 7. o'clock. I then hastily dined & must more hastily run to the post; for the last delivery is near; and—horror of horrors—my boots are wet! Yes, I do get Thursday-posted-letters on Sunday, so fortunate and so gratitudinous am I [*one line illegible*]

Yours ever and ever—Wilfred

Call to mind what pleasant impressions I gave you of Dunsden, & repeat them there. Every manner of salutation to my Cousin of Cousins and Cousine of Cousines, D.

361. To Leslie Gunston

First sheets missing

[*? Early July 1915*]   [*Bordeaux*]

> Now, let me feel the feeling of thy hand—
> For it is softer than the breasts of girls,
> And warmer than the pillows of their cheeks,
> And richer than the fulness of their eyes,
> And stronger than the ardour of their hearts.
>
> Its shape is subtler than a dancer's limbs;
> Its skin is coloured like the twilight Alp;
> And odoured like the pale,[3] night-scented flowers,
> And fresh with early love, as earth with dawn.

[1] Philippe was the current lodger at the Lems, and one of Wilfred's pupils.
[2] 1915 was not a bad year for farmers. The summer was fair. But the weather was dry in late August and September, with no rain in some areas for sixteen or seventeen days, which constituted a drought.
[3] 'large' struck out.

Yield me thy hand a little while, fair love;
That I may feel it; and so feel thy life,
And kiss across it, as the sea the sand,
And love it, with the love of Sun for[1] Earth.[2]

I was interested as you in these 'L. Books of G. Verse',[3] and beseech you to inform me more. Would it be too much to ask you to send me one? I must post-pone the luxury of a Book-plate. I am at a low-water mark of funds, and I spend some of my substance—at last—on French Lessons! I seem to be falling, naturally enough, into the Bordelais pronunciation of certain vowels; which is wrong, wrong, wrong! e.g. I don't properly distinguish my è, é, and ê. Moreover I want to read Old French. I have looked into the *Chanson de Roland*[4] & find it quite as delightful as, say, Chaucer.

I am glad you read to Mother. It is almost as worthy an occupation as writing to me! Press Mother to begin again to paint! Did you see Miss Morley's critique of 'L.M.'[5] I think not. This is the gist: 'On several occasions you slip into Poetry.' I am already looking forward to your letter(s?) from Oxford.

Your ever (and ever) W.E.O.

362. To Susan Owen

5 July [1915]   *Bordeaux*

Dearest Mother,
I found yours of July 1st waiting for me at my entrance, at eight o'clock. The boys had their photographs taken by a professional this afternoon; there were also some groups[6] in which I count.

I hoped you would get to the Academy, and I knew the Garden of Peace[7] would have your attention. Now, the tree-trunks are all I like about it!! I am glad you reminded me of the syringas at home. There

---

[1] 'and' struck out.
[2] Not in *Poems*.
[3] The Little Books of Georgian Verse: 'A series of original volumes, each devised by a single author', selected by S. Gertrude Ford and published by Erskine Macdonald, London. They were in paper covers at 1s. each. Macdonald also published the XXth Century Poetry series and *The Poetry Review*.
[4] The oldest and best-known of the *chansons de geste*, French historical romances, many connected with Charlemagne. The story of Roland and Oliver, and the destruction of the rearguard of Charlemagne's army at the Battle of Roncevaux in 778, was translated into English by C. K. Scott Moncrieff (*The Song of Roland, done into English, in the original measure*, with an Introduction by G. K. Chesterton, Chapman and Hall, London, 1919); HO has a copy inscribed for Susan Owen 'From Charles Scott Moncrieff in endless memory of Wilfred, February 1921'. The book is dedicated to Philip Bainbrigge (see Letter 590, note 1), Wilfred Owen, and Ian Mackenzie. An early draft dedication survives in Scott Moncrieff's hand, beginning: 'To Mr. W. O. To you, my master in asssonance, I dedicate my part in this assonant poem: that you may cover the faults in my handiwork with the protection of your name.' For Wilfred's first meeting with him see Letter 585, note 1.
[5] *The Little Mermaid*.
[6] One is reproduced as Plate VII b.   [7] By Tom Mostyn R.O.I., R.W.A. (1864–1930).

344

should be a hedge of them at Alpenrose; but if that were the case I should like that garden more than I ought! So, you find that painting, as represented at Burlington House, is 'going down'! I was taken with a great and monstrous gladness to read of your resolution to 'take up' your painting; and it will be henceforward a continual disappointment if, after all, nothing happens. I have a discreet expectation that you will neither copy picture-postcards; nor yet study onions, cabbage, and beetroot; but that you will fill a space of canvas with all you love of copious-coloured gardens; or the rising of a moon, the bend of an old road; the smile of a fair child. It was, I suppose, natural for you to dislike the movement, roar, and odour of London; but I find all that, the very best strengthener of nerves. Where does Dorothy meet Miss Morley? Does D. also agitate for Mixed Clubbing? Kindly keep me well informed of all these movements, and give the source of all your news. For instance, what practices of Wigan's does Mrs. F. allege Romish? Do not fail to call at the Vicarage! I hope very much that Dorothy keeps well. I was aware of an unwonted inertia on her part; and as my own inertia (at Alpenrose) is chronic I saw less of Dorothy than I would have; that we should by time or place become estranged alarms me.

Colin sent me a letter—about fishing, my bicycle, pigeons, rabbits—neat and correct. (remember). The end was a pretty sample of his way ('I have got to do my work, so if you don't mind, I will finish off.

(This cross-bone is probably only a disguised blot!)

How long do you stay at Alp? I must get up at quarter to six to-morrow, to meet Raoul at Stn. for Preignac. I don't think we shall stay the night. Many thanks for seeing about my half-dozen[1] razor-blades. What is this about all Englishmen between 15 and 60 being enrolled, 'or something?' Don't forget about Artists' Rifles. I had the rare plea-sure of a letter from Father two days ago. He learnt my last news with-out your intervention, interpretation, or amelioration, I see! But you had better not send on this, most unliteratic of letters.

I called at Mons. Léger's the other day; but the house was shut up and the brass-plate tarnished; so he must be already at Bagnères again.

I feel an increasing indisposition for any of the things that most should engage me; and thought once the cause was in myself. But it is the War after all. I don't see how it can end, I don't see. I only feel traitorously idle: if not to England then to France.

Yours ever, Wilfred x

This handwriting looks 'groggy', not to say 'red-winey'. Be not disconcerted! The heat makes the air so tremble, as over a furnace! Moreover, I got up at four this morning!

[1] He had asked for a dozen. See Letter 359.

363. To Susan Owen

8 July 1915   *Bordeaux*

My dearest Mother,

[*two lines illegible*] but tho' I mean to cover the expenses, if <u>permitted</u>, I am in no hurry. Father indeed agreed that I should send back some portion of my borrowings, but now that I know not how soon I shall start home, I have changed my mind. Moreover I make no profit here these days. Mlle. de la Touche begins to despair of having money for sending the boys to the sea. Their French Lessons finish next week, and of course, they ought to have a complete rest from English work too. Mr. Bonsall goes up on certain mornings for their Latin & Greek; he is a weird, mild bird; and hath much love of Classics, and great power of Music. It is amusing to think we are rivals in Bordeaux— though not up at Mérignac; for Miss de la Touche declared once that Mr. B. 'had no manners.' He is rather lax with their discipline; and generally works under the plum-trees of the garden. Hence once or twice I have used the stick I took for Miss de la Touche, correctionally. The other day I roared: 'Dédé, I shall give you five strokes!' A few minutes later, I felt a hand smoothing my hair most caressingly. This is not an unusual procedure, but it was done with such a merry gusto that I asked what it meant.—'Oh! I'm giving <u>you</u> the <u>strokes</u> instead.'

The photographs taken the other day are not good; but the general group (in which I am) is very good: but it is not yet ready.

I went with Raoul to Preignac, & came back well pleased with the day. It cannot have been so hot here as with you. Why, at three o'clock we were dancing on the terrace, with the country maids that turned up on purpose. Then we went cycling about the country—(finest country of the Gironde)—except Raoul, who had discreet rendez-vous' in the woods. Later we tried table-turning, for the good lady, Philippe's aunt, was a great believer in the thing. We had, it seemed, marvellous results: the table tapped out right answers for hours. But I worked hard and cunningly to <u>prove it</u>; found certain questions wrongly answered; and suspected everybody in turn. Finally I had proof of Raoul's trickery, and made him confess it on the way home.

What is Harold's next address? How long do you think to stay? I shall try, then to find in Bx. my Razor-blades. What does 'are having' a motor mean. Is it bought?

In the French papers today I read that Mr. Asquith in reply to a member's question said that the government had 'no intention whatever' of establishing either obligatory service or work. Yesterday, papers made allusion to fresh arrivals of Zeppelins on London [*four lines illegible*]

Am I supposed to know? (I had even forgotten H's ship.) [*two lines illegible*] What is the principle of the magic waistcoat?

Is the Quayles' new shanty[1] boxed-in, or an open tub? Who pedals? What colour is his livery? I hope you get plenty of driving at Kidmore.

Adieu, sweet Mother, from your Wilfred

[1] Motor-car.

IRONY—pretty wooden too.

364. To Susan Owen
Postcard
Saturday [*Postmark 10 July 1915*]   [*18 Rue Beaubadat, Bordeaux*]

I have nothing to report to you; if I have many things to hope for you. I have written to Artists' Rifles without address. If I don't get an English commission I should like to join the Italian Army. In any case I shall probably be out of work here in August, as the boys want an absolute holiday. So much the better! God save the King! and bless us all, said Tiny Tim.

Your W.E.O.

365. To Susan Owen
Postcard
Friday [*mid-July 1915*]   *P.O. Bx.*

Had your Card this mng. and what you say of Artists' Rifles is so; the Camp is at Epping. The Commission might be very long in coming. I seriously should like to join the Italian Cavalry; for reasons both aesthetic and practical. If you are too terribly opposed I will think no more of it. Certainly, I shan't join French Army. Miss de la T. now suggests I should take a room in Mérignac, to be with them during August. Can't Uncle be more precise about 'good job in War Office?'

Yours ever W.E.O.

Lord Leighton,[1] Millais,[2] Forbes Robertson[3] were in Artists' Rifles!!

366. To Susan Owen
23 July [*1915*]   *Bordeaux*

My dearest Mother,

I am sorry to be niggardly of letters. It escapes my memory, the date of my last; but I hope you got my last postcard. Unless your letter of this morning had put in a claim for more of my news, I scarcely think I should be writing <u>now</u>! I have <u>no news</u> and shall have none, as I hope, before the end of next week, by which time I ought to know the manner of my departure. So far, I only am sure that I am <u>not</u> going to move up to Mérignac, again, but mean to remain here till about the middle of August, going up to M. for lunch and the afternoon, as now, although <u>lessons</u> stop on Aug. 1st. If a ship sails about Aug. 15 you may expect me by it. I went to Sailors' Reading Room last night, and had parley with the donkey-man of a 'Moss' Boat,—non-passenger. It would not be possible to make a cheap passage by private treaty with the Captain. In a delightful Liverpool brogue (delightful <u>Now</u> and <u>here</u>) which made me think of Cecil when he was Cicil, and of Tranmere, the Pier Head,

[1] Frederic, Baron Leighton (1830–96), President of the Royal Academy 1878–1896.
[2] Sir John Everett Millais (1829–96). Originator in 1848, with Holman Hunt, of the Pre-Raphaelite Movement; President of the Royal Academy in the year of his death.
[3] Sir Johnston Forbes-Robertson (1853–1937), actor and theatrical manager.

Sefton Park,[1] and such like, the lad told me of the dangers of the passage! and how they carry a cannon, and were once chased by a submarine off Hormes' Ed![2] I may land at London on account of Peyronnet,—whom I shall next see on Monday. The 'eastern voyage' is out of the question. It will be pleasant to round off the 'Mérignac Period' of my time with a week or so of nothing but 'Ragging'. We shall go some excursions. For one, I want to visit the battlefield of Castillon, where, in 1453 Talbot Earl of Shrewsbury suffered the defeat which lost Guienne and Bordeaux to the English for ever.[3] I can't understand it, but this battlefield will interest me as much as the field of the Marne;—and I am reading a tale of the Punic Wars with more interest than the Communiqués. There is only one cure for me! I am already quaking at the idea of Parade; and yawning with the boredom of it. Now if I could make it a real, live adventure, a real, old adventure, by flinging myself into Italy . . .?

It will be painful now to quit Bordeaux!! I shall part with the four boys with regret,—with three of them regretfully, with two of them sorrowfully, and with one of them very sorrowfully indeed. It is an advantage of old age that meetings are joyful, as separations are sad; but in youth meetings are indifferent; youth is the time of partings, not old age [one line illegible] But don't expect to before the day on which I assume the role of National Hero, number million, grade Private, allowance one bob.

However I mean to run up to Meols for a day or so. When is Colin going to Torquay, and how long Holiday will Father take? (I can't help feeling the anomaly of Parliament's cajoling the Miners to work on Bank Holiday, & themselves taking six weeks holiday!) I am always annoyed to hear of your headaches; supposing them preventable, rather than curable. Miss de la T. has had 'migraines' continually. On such days she sits and hides in a corner of the garden, and I carve the joint! She has all the 'rough work' with the boys now! It takes a lot to give me a headache;—let's hope it won't need a bullet! I rejoice exceedingly in the power of the midday sun,& am strengthened by its strength:—a sure sign of being Right with Nature.

Your devoted Wilfred

Ante-Script [*at head of letter*]: I can't re-read these lines, but under-line plentifully instead. 'Cute idea!

367. To Susan Owen
Postcard

Sunday [*Postmark 23 July 1915*]   [*Postmark Bordeaux*]

There is not much sense in writing again so soon, but since yesterday's

[1] All Birkenhead.
[2] Ormes Head, the North Wales headland on which Llandudno stands.
[3] The English army under John Talbot, 1st Earl of Shrewsbury (*c.* 1388–1453), heavily out-numbered, was defeated and its commander killed at Castillon, thirty miles east of Bordeaux. This was the last campaign of the Hundred Years War.

letter was a trifle contradictory, I had better repeat that I have reason
to hope for a free passage at least to Havre; perhaps to Newhaven. On
Tuesday I leave these rooms, but haven't looked up the new one yet.
Hence write to Mérignac until further notice. Life jogs on easily enough
over here. Of course plenty of new people now want English lessons of
me! Many thanks for your card, which was kept company by one from
Leslie. Is he going to stay on the way back?

368. To Leslie Gunston

25 July 1915   *Bordeaux*

My dear Leslie,
    I had waited in double-daily expectation of your lines, and it was a
'high luxury' to read them in my bed, this *dimanche* morning. The only
way of excusing yourself for having jilted me for my beloved friend
Icarus, last Sunday, is to send me the 90 lines of sixty-lines-an-hour
verse, non-stop-till-we-frizzle-up-in-the-solar-terminus. Couldn't you
divine why 'Oxford'[1] is a banned word with me. Because it is one of my
most terrible regrets. I ought to be there, not fuddling among the Vines.
I ought to have been there, rather. Surely, you knew the cause of my
'flare'. Now I am going to get flary again. You say you 'hear of wars and
rumours of wars'. *Vous en êtes là seulement?* You hear Rumours? The
rumours, over here, make the ears of the gunners bleed. . . . It doesn't
matter 'for my purpose' that the Dardanelles are closed; but it matters
to my sentiment that Belgium is; now I don't imagine that the German
War will be affected by my joining in, but I know my own future Peace
will be. I wonder that you don't ply me with this argument: that Keats
remained absolutely indifferent to Waterloo and all that commotion.
Well, I have passed a year of fine-contemptuous nonchalance: but having
now some increase of physical strength I feel proportionately useful and
proportionately lacking in sense if I don't use it in the best way—The
Only Way.
    I was not aware that nothing remained of Cumnor, and imagined the
moon still 'silvered the walls of Cumnor Hall'.[2] I believe the Black
Bear still is?
    Your demand for my ideal wife is too frightfully the non-limit. I
have a fairly good bodily notion; but the other qualities I can only
specify by negatives. However, I will make notes! I fairly roared with
joy that you were taken, and taken in, by the pseudo-translation. I

[1] LG was in Oxford doing measured drawings for the Intermediate R.I.B.A. examination.
[2] The Hall was demolished in 1810. Traces of the gardens can still be seen south of the
churchyard.

> The dews of summer night did fall,
>   The moon, sweet regent of the sky,
> Silver'd the walls of Cumnor Hall,
>   And many an oak that grew thereby.
>   William Julius Mickle (1735–88), 'Cumnor Hall'.

merely translated from some lines I had begun in French. For Gautier[1]
. . . Zut! I never read him. No, I won't forget to give you information
regarding the Author!! Kindly preserve the copy. I made no other. I
can't now roll off the *Chanson de R*. It is of spenserian length, and
chaucerian charm. I hope you don't consider shaking hands with H.B.[2]
knowing him. I meant make him a factor of your life and yourself of his.
I thank God for the intercourse you and I have set up between us. I
should be a sadder soul if you 'were not', or were other than you are.

'Shall you' say ever-loving, etc. I should hope so. There is no mere
entente-cordiale between us. There is a blood-alliance. If you object to
anything in me you will shout at me like a brother. I for example object
to your speaking of getting 'my money's worth' of a letter! Shocking!
Though I congratulate you upon trafficking in books! I still hold the
violin capable of 'better' i.e. more essential, music than the organ, and
shall do. while I hold Keats a more poetical poet than Milton.

I have read *The Prisoner of Zenda*:[3] mediocre! At present I am
deciphering a monument of French literature Flaubert's *Salammbo*:[4] not
that it is difficult reading, but every syllable deserves attention. Flaubert
has my vote for novel-writing!

Farewell, fare-very-well-indeed,   Your affectionate Wilfred

I 'started' at the idea of Llandudno; I mean, joining you there. I scarcely
dare envisage such luck. I could get in time; but the material considerations . . .! Moreover, is it not an exclusive family holiday!

369. To Susan Owen
Postcard
Thursday [*Postmark 1 August 1915*]   [*Postmark Bordeaux*]

has been a picnic day. The Castéjas (Admiral's people) got it up; I was
invited by special request at the last moment; we had a jolly time, from
10 a.m. to 6 p.m. I now think of travelling by land. The reason is that a
new, brand-new acquaintance[5] of mine has invited me to spend a day or
two in Rouen. There is no French town I want to see more than this
and as we shall spend 1 day in Paris, & my friend is Parisian, I can't
resist; since the said friend, having no baggage, will lighten my excess-
luggage-charge. And there will be no risks. The fellow is a Radio-
Telegraphist on a French-American Liner, is only 18, recommends
himself to me by reason of his perfect French. He comes & jaws to me
until about one in the morning every evening and I'm blowed if he isn't
here now! I try to understand Wireless but don't really.

                                                Your W.E.O.

---

1 Théophile Gautier (1811–72), French poet and novelist of the Romantic movement.
2 Hilaire-Belloc. LG had been introduced to him after a lecture.
3 The best-known novel (1894) of Anthony Hope Hawkins (1863–1933), who wrote plays
  and novels under the name of Anthony Hope.
4 Gustave Flaubert (1821–80), the author of *Madame Bovary* (1856), published *Salammbô*, a
  Carthaginian story, in 1862.
5 His name was Thuret. See Letter 370.

370. To Susan Owen

Monday Night, 2 August 1915   [*Bordeaux*]

My most dear Mother,

It's only by false pretences that I am able to write to you tonight; because I am continually besieged by that Wireless Telegraphist. Every single night of this week he has been inseparable from me, from the moment of my arriving in town at 7 o'clock. So this evening, to avoid a bombardment of my locked door, I have invented 'an invitation out for the evening'. So poor Thuret can swot up his lecture on Wireless, which is to be on Wednesday. I mentioned this at the Châlet, and Miss de la T. wants to send the boys to hear it. Thuret has written to his people about my staying in Rouen. He starts on the 20th; so you may take that as my definite date of leaving.

I think Colin ought to turn to thinking about such a post as Wireless Operator.

I just got your card on coming in tonight, and am indeed pleased to know Bill is supposed only taken prisoner;[1] and not less happy to think of Harold as an Officer![2] In the Artists', one is paid the usual 1s a day!

Did I tell you a Norwegian acquaintance of mine went over to Swansea, a fortnight ago, to marry an English girl. They have just got back. *Madame* was rather upset the first few hours after arriving (at the *Union Chrétienne*) but felt less lost in a strange land on meeting me. But, if uncommonly comely, she is common of speech, and I cannot introduce her into English society here. Traëmber, the hubby, is a rather *distingué* person, of 28 yrs. Miss Hall[3] is going to befriend the girl. Miss Hall leaves about a month later than I; so that will just accommodate the boys, or rather, their Aunt; for they would infinitely rather travel alone; for obvious reasons. It was Miss Hall's pupil's people who gave the Thursday picnic.

On Sunday morning I had got magnificently attired with the intention of going to the English church. Now I had refused to go in the river with Thuret for this reason, and hence Thuret must needs promise to come to my church. I agreed. But lo! instead of appearing in officer's clothes, as he ought, he lounges up in a disgraceful *déshabillé*! But, in the afternoon your good wishes for Sunday, were well realized. We had four hours of music. You have heard me speak of Richepin: one of his pieces *The Tramp*, an opera, was being played in the Open Air. The Music was by Xavier LeRoux,[4] and the Composer himself conducted the Orchestra. It was a daring opera in more ways than one; for instance, the whole thing passes between tramps and rustics, in cornfields, roads,

---

[1] Bill Bulman had, in fact, been killed in action, at Gallipoli.

[2] HO, formerly apprentice cadet and Fourth Officer in the Merchant Service, was now made Third Officer. In October 1916 he transferred to the Royal Naval Air Service; and to the RNR, as midshipman, in spring 1917.

[3] Apparently English governess to the Castéjas children at Mérignac.

[4] French composer (1863–1919), Professor of Harmony at the Paris Conservatoire.

and kitchens. The total cost of costume might be three bob, off a wholesale and retail rag-picker. The music was not particularly original;
very pleasant to listen to; but there were no airs that one remembered
ever after. There was very pretty work done by the drums, so much so
that one listened to them rather than to the violins, sometimes. The
voices, of course, were best Paris choice. Certain of the songs were
marvellous touching. Anyhow I was proud to have shaken hands with
the Composer—(in Paris). If anybody enjoyed himself that afternoon,
it was he himself!

I think next Sunday will be spent at Lacanau,[1] that sea-side place,
where the Boys are not going. But the Boy Scouts of the *Union* are
going; and Thuret is 'in with' them. As, curiously enough, I have had
no dealings yet with this group of kids, I think of going too. We start
on Sunday night.

This afternoon although work is now over, I spent at Mérignac
roaming the woods. The heather is extraordinarily abundant and purple.
I look at it, and think of Broxton,[2] as it were, weeping; and again I
examine it, and think of Doctor Rayner, and smile.

Miss de la T. gave me a pot of her plum-jam on Saturday, for my
small-breakfast!

This evening I called on a Bordeaux specialist who wanted English
lessons; but the time is too short. There are, in promise, a good number
of pupils, for next term. Moreover, Miss de la T. would be glad to have
me for Dédé & Charlie. But all this is no temptation: for it is not a
Career. This aft. I ran, with the boys, almost a mile—significant!

We will drop the subject of Italy, though your arguments are distinctly feeble in comparison with the real objection. You fear I might
never get into the army. Absurd! They take what they can get, even
wrecks like me. The whole difficulty is getting out. Probably the end
of the war would not liberate the volunteer as in England. He would
have to perform the term of service required by the nation in question;
in France it is three years! Many people are surprised that I don't
join the French forces, and that I take the fag to go back to England.

It is time to look after details of travelling. I suppose I cannot use
the old ticket I have kept, to 'return' from Padd? Did I mention to you
that Leslie 'wants me' to go to Llandudno with them? I don't of course
hold myself invited. Depends on them.

---

[1] On the coast N E of Bordeaux.
[2] A village in Cheshire. Susan Owen took Wilfred there for a few happy weeks before the
family left Birkenhead for Shrewsbury in 1907. 'It was in Broxton among the ferns and
bracken and the little hills, secure in the safety and understanding love that my mother
wrapped about him . . . that the poetry in Wilfred, with gentle pushings, without hurt,
began to bud,and not on the battlefields of France' (*JO* I, 101–4). See also Letter 593. HO
has the only fragmentary draft of an unfinished poem containing these lines (also quoted
by E B):

> Even the weeks at Broxton, by the Hill
> Where first I felt my boyhood fill
> With uncontainable movements; there was born
> My poethood.

Betimes I have a horrible great craving to behold the Sea. But for the time, the Wind is very wild and fresh upon these moors; and not a day passes but I receive a nature-shock, such as some spend six weeks seeking and find not . . .

The fruit is softening in the vineyards; the muscle of France keeps resisted,—while her heart scarcely beats faster—The Emperor yet frowns imperially; and our ministers yet wear a ministerial smile.[1] And lo! the end is not by any manner of means at hand.

At least, let me end this piece of literature,

and with my lovingest x, Wilfred

What a luxury it seems to think of 'going home' again so soon!

371. To Susan Owen

Saturday, 5 August 1915   *Bordeaux*

Dearest Mother,

A little later on this afternoon I shall be starting for Lacanau, with the Boy Scouts. I haven't the faintest idea where I shall sleep, or what eat, or when return, or who meet, and that's why I am going. Thuret passed a 'Final' exam. today, proving he can send (and receive) 30 words a minute. His brother whom he went to meet at the station at midnight has got appendicitis; but this in no way alters Thuret's plans of taking me to Rouen. Appendicitis is a family complaint; Thuret was operated years ago. The brother's operation is on Sunday. It may make this oddish character 'sound all right' to you that he wanted to sing hymns for his brother last night; and I made the music.

I think I told you 'the Boys' are going to Downside, by edict from China. Mr. de la Touche has Scarletina over there! Miss de la T. has been occupied in finding a Governess for the girls[2] (eldest 8 yrs.) She has I think met an English lady here, speaking Eng. Fr. & German, willing to go out.

Delighted to have Harold's letter, tho' you had already quoted it. Dare I hope that your project of a week in Wales and the Welsh waters, will come off? It seems a rare opportunity! Now that I have published my intentions of enlisting there is a general disapprobation among my friends. I hear through a Swiss that many of the Germans I knew here are still alive, fighting in the Vosges.

The Anglo-Norwegian couple quarrel childishly most of their time, at least at meals, where I see them. One of the girl's former adorers is called Clymo, and works in the N.W.[3] offices in Shrewsbury! I know the name. I had a voluminous letter from Leslie by the same post as your last. He hopes (speaking as it were to himself) that this will be the last 2½d worth to be torn from his pocket! Incidentally, I may point out

---

[1] These sentences turn up again in an early version of 'The Dead-Beat' (*Poems*, pp. 72–73). See Letter 541.
[2] There were three, all with their parents in China.
[3] The North-Western Railway.

an evidence of poor old Dorothy's psychological condition: Leslie objects to my five half-penny stamps on my envelopes, and D. says I am robbing the Government of some paper by using them!—The remark was meant to be humorous; but the idea, the initial idea!—Phew!

I have just read a charming piece of fiction lent by Miss de la T.— *The Incomparable Bellairs* by Agnes & Egerton Castle.[1]

I pity you your bad weather. Here bad weather is impossible, for if it rains the nights are deliciously cool, and if the sun opens out like the mouth of a seven times heated furnace I am not incommoded. This kind of blazing heat stuns one pleasantly, like strong music.

I can't yet say the date of my arrival, and you'll be kind if you'll take me, literally, as I come, and when I come! I haven't been able to see Peyronnet, as he is on holidays.

I like to think you have been keeping pretty well these last weeks. Keep on! It has just occurred to me to ask whether you prefer to avoid an inter-family party by choosing Llandudno for the holiday. I think it preferable not to join, but have you considered it?

Always your dearly-loving Wilfred

372. To Susan Owen
Postcard

Saturday. 6 p.m. [Postmark 7 August 1915]   *[Postmark Bordeaux]*

I don't like to leave my letter with statements now falsified by events. The brother of Thuret has just died under the operation. Thuret wants to go up to Havre for the funeral but hasn't a sou. I try to persuade him not to go, but he may be able to borrow from a Member of the *Union*—the Norwegian, in fact. Thus, where I should have written Deus Volens is now writ Deus Nolens. All this may change my journey completely.

Yours W.E.O.

373. To Susan Owen
Postcard

Thursday [Postmark 12 August 1915]   *[Postmark Bordeaux]*

I had the *Times* Poems[2] at 9 this mng. and your letter coming at 11 was an unexpected pleasure. You will now be further enlightened, or rather obscured, as to my movements. I can't really give you dates. There are too many contingencies. For one thing I may have to wait for my moneys from Miss de la T. It is therefore possible that I may wait for the Boys, esp. if I can't go to Rouen. I went to Lem's last evening. I do hope I shall see Coz May.

---

[1] Egerton Castle (1858–1920) and his wife Agnes (d. 1922) wrote a large number of novels and plays in collaboration. *The Incomparable Bellairs* was published in 1904.
[2] See Letter 374.

374. To Leslie Gunston

Picture postcard: painting of Arras Cathedral in flames

[Postmark 12 August 1915]   *[Postmark Bordeaux]*

Best thanks for your card of New College. I fear you will be in Wales
before this reaches Alpenrose. I am not forgetting the Casts, but today
am too hopelessly *à sec* to enter the shop! *Vrai!!* Hast seen the *Times*
War Poems.[1] Newbolt's & Clark's splendid! Watson, Binyon all right!
Tagore interesting. But who on earth are Maitland, de la Mare etc?
Simpson's cartoons (Britannias very much excepted) are marvels.

W.E.O.

My turn for letter.
Look thou stand behind the ARRAS!—*King John.*

375. To Susan Owen

Wednesday, 18 August [*1915*]   *Bordeaux*

My most dear Mother,

I knew it would be so, however hard I believed it would be otherwise
—I do not start next Friday. Miss de la T. wants me to wait for the
Boys, who go to be at school on the 15th Sept. Miss Hall is not sure
when she can start, and is certain not to start in time for them; moreover
the fellows don't want to travel with her. Anyhow Miss de la Touche
offers me 50 f. to cover the expense of staying on in Bordeaux three
more weeks. Is this a surprise? I have a bigger one over the page!

(Post Script *Friday*: Don't believe the following)

The Telegraphist is going to Havre & Rouen by boat on Saturday
next, & has just offered me a free passage with him there and back. I
cannot but accept. Otherwise I should not see Rouen. And what fun—
shiver-me-timbers! Bay of BiscayO! By the time you read this, as I
positively believe, I'll be rounding Ouessant![2] A thousand pities, you'll
be saying, that I don't cross over home from le Havre. I may be
tempted—must consider that tomorrow—(or later on today: it is
quarter to one on Thursday mng.) After all I may have the chance of a
second voyage to Havre & even to Newhaven but whether I shall take
it depends rather on Miss de la Touche.

---

[1] A supplement was published by *The Times* on 9 August 1915: *War Poems from The Times,
August 1914–15.* It contained: 'Wake up, England' by Robert Bridges, Poet Laureate;
'Song of the Soldiers' by Thomas Hardy; 'For all we Have and Are' by Rudyard Kipling;
'For the Fallen' by Laurence Binyon; 'The Battle of the Bight' by William Watson; 'Called
Up' by Dudley Clark; 'Gods of War' by A.E.; 'Into Battle' by Julian Grenfell; 'The
Trumpet' by Rabindranath Tagore; 'Resolve' by F. E. Maitland; 'The Search-Lights' by
Alfred Noyes; 'The King's Highway' by Henry Newbolt; 'Invocation' by Robert Nichols;
'Happy England' by Walter de la Mare; 'Expeditional' by C. W. Brodribb; and 'August,
1914' 'by the author of *Charitessi*'. Each poem is framed by a drawing by Joseph Simpson
(1879–1939), the artist and illustrator who contributed to a large number of British and
American magazines and was made CBE in 1920.

[2] Cape Ushant.

A nasty nuisance is involved by having given notice for my Room. Behold it already let to a pest who has a violent fancy for it. What a vile discord and confusing this will bring into the flourish of my Grand Finale to Bordeaux. I have to clear out on 30th Aug. Truly I should dearly love to make a scramble for it on Saturday Night—and sort o' call roun' Mahim on Wensdy Mornin! Only it might look shady to take French leave of the French. And then my Papers! Papers of Identification to prove I'm born, curl-papers—ode-and-sonnet papers, Pink Papers, (which I haven't got). I should never pack by Saturday. But to make a false start—delightful flutter! Hating decisive measures as I do, I shall taste all the sweet melancholy of leaving my endearèd Gascony, by sea—without the bitterness of the Irrevocable Finality about it. And I shall feel all the poetry of the thing, without needing to feel in my pocket if my ticket is quite safe.

I had a most memorable dinner last night with the well known Professor Devaux,[1] Botanist, who sat down to table with me at the Restaurant. Fortunately I knew him slightly before. I cleared up a lot of 'points'. The professor was very funny about his visit to England & his staying with Lubbock,[2] Darwins, etc.

On Sunday I had a pleasant two hours with a poor apprentice-tailor, formerly door-keeper of the Berlitz School. We had many a laugh over the old days, and he said many quaint things, and we rescued the boats of the little boys around the pond in the *Jardin Public*, and I earned a momentary place in the garden of boyhood, whence I am now so long banished, and that afternoon was generally very happy. Likewise also on Monday morning, strolling round the town with Bonsall who has fine— if few—wits; and an antique-flavoured—though second-hand—wit. (I think I told you such of his history as I know?)

This afternoon 10 wounded & convalescent soldiers of the Mérignac Ambulance were invited to the Chalet garden. I sort of played the host and tennis with 'em. But the wounds played the devil with my patriotism. One or two nights ago I looked up one André Martin,[3] whom I once succoured when his father died. The whole family did their level best, the Mother by producing tears, and the lads by producing bits of shrapnel horribly sharp—to dissuade me from leaving their peaceful city. Worthy souls! I threw out from the Monkmoor P. Office a card to this lad—and lo! the thing preciously preserved among the *billets-doux* and secret photographs of his pocket-book!

I think of dining with Raoul one of these evenings.

Friday
I kept back these extraordinary announcements under a presentiment that my Voyage would not come off—and, indeed, at six o'clock this evening I learnt that it <u>can't be done</u>. Principal reason stated—my

[1] Unidentified.
[2] Sir John Lubbock (1834–1913), banker, author, and scientist.
[3] See Letter 292.

English Nationality. The Voyage to Havre might be managed but not a Return. But, a fortnight next Saturday, I shall most undoubtedly be able to sail to Havre, & perhaps cross to Newhaven, free of charge, for I shall be returning to join the Army. Apparently, this aimless cruise makes the Cap'n suspicious. Anyhow I still believe in the 11th Sept. trip. Boys be bothered!

Your W.E.O.

376. To Susan Owen
Postcard

Sunday [*Postmark 19 August 1915*]   [*Postmark Bordeaux*]

There is no excuse for a letter: all my news is in the future. These are the possible courses: (1) to remain in Bordeaux or France, (2) to get a 'post' in England both of which I do solemnly abjure. (2) is mean. Thus I shall either
I Join Artists' Rifles
II Work in Gov. Offices
III Join French Cavalry (?)
IV   ,,   Italian Cavalry (?)
For Your sake & yours only, III & IV must be queried, much to my own loss & disappointment. Answer this saying just what you think. I may get away early in Aug.[1] & shall take 'the boat' (don't know which). A. Rifles training begins in London, continues at Epping, & finishes in France.
Yours ever W.E.O.
Very many thanks for so many letters & cards.

377. To Susan Owen
Postcard

Sat. [*Late August 1915*]   *Bordeaux*

Very many thanks for your letter read at Mérignac, & card at my address. I am writing in the *Tabac* where these cards are bought. Have had a long but pleasant afternoon at Mérignac, finishing up with Tennis. Am so glad you're going to Alp, & shall send a letter to meet you. Am puzzled to know just what Seaton wants. Shall make enquiries.
Yours ever, W.E.O.

378. To Susan Owen
Postcard

Tuesday [*Postmark 1 September 1915*]   *1 Place Saint Christoly, Bx.*

This is my latest address, tho' my present position is on the square itself—which is a triangle, about 20 yards from my old door. The moving was the most jolly affair imaginable. I got three little boys aged 12 to

---

[1] A slip for September.

carry my books, and then the trunk was easily carried between us, divided into trays, and this in broad daylight. Thus I didn't go to Mérignac today & don't know what letters await me there. But I had the *Christian* on Monday. Haven't seen the Telegraphist. I don't feel very canny about the free trip!

Yours ever W.E.O.

379. To Susan Owen

Postcard, re-addressed from Shrewsbury C/o Miss Jones,
10 South Marine Terrace, Aberystwyth

Monday [*7 September 1915*]   [*Postmark Bordeaux*]

I perceive, with something like fright, that nearly a week must have gone since my last card or letter, whatever it was. Today I think I can assert that I start, with the boys, on Friday Night. I saw Peyronnet today. The Gov. just now grabs every drop of alcohol in the Republic; so Peyronnet is paralysed for the time. What a blessing the Boys are starting! How else should I be got to move. Yet I look forward to seeing you as much as last time, and more by reason of Harold!!!¹ Expect me about the middle of next week.

380. To Susan Owen

Postcard, re-addressed from Shrewsbury to
10 South Marine Terrace, Aberystwyth, N. Wales

Thursday [*Postmark 10 September 1915*]   [*Postmark Bordeaux*]

Miss de la T. finds Sunday Night more convenient for the Start, to avoid a Sunday in London or Paris. But you can still expect me about the 'middle of next week'. I don't know how to manage about the Ticket London–Shrewsbury. I have been afraid to part with the old Ticket, seeing the shortness of the time. I hope this will find you in Wales with Harold. Best of Love.

W.E.O.

381. To Susan Owen

Postcard

Tuesday 11.30 p.m. [*Postmark 15 September 1915*]
Regent Palace Hotel! Piccadilly Circus, London W

We arrived here last night, after a not-too-troublesome journey, considering the <u>nine</u> *bagages*. The Boys² thought to leave for Downside tonight, & we went to Padd. but there was no train connection from

¹ HO was expected home on leave.
² Johnny and Bobbie. Charles and David stayed with their aunt.

Bath. I shall do my Enquiry Business tomorrow, & may not arrive
Shrewsbury till Midnight, Wednes. Perhaps you are not yet home? we
have come in from a walk round Whitehall & Westminster looking
out for Zeps. but saw nothing in the sky & little more on earth. Behind
the Admiralty there is Pitch Darkness. The Channel Crossing was
uneventful. Till Tomorrow!!

W.E.O.

382. To Susan Owen
Postcard

Saturday [Postmark 16 October 1915]   Mr. Cummings[1] Office
[Postmark Reading]

I have been preoccupied by my trunk which yet remains in the Cloak
Rm! They forgot to put up the P. in the Window! All are well. & Vera
leaves today. I saw Miss M.[2] for an instant this mng.—am going to
tea this aft. Dr. Rayner says I should become a Munitions Worker at
Birmingham, earning £5 a week. Mr. Jones is there in the Fitting
Shops, but as a Voluntary unpaid hand. What do you say to this? I have
just written to Mr. Jones for facts & advice. No news of Leslie's business. The Joergens came to tea yesterday. Shall have something to write
about in another day or so.

Yours ever Wilfred

383. To Susan Owen

Thursday Mng. [21 October 1915]   Les Lilas, 54 Tavistock Square, W.C.

Dearest of Mothers,

I [*several words illegible*] attacked the day by going straight to
Headquarters.[3] It was found that the Doctor had not given his signature
to my papers so I was examined again—and passed. Three others at the
same time were refused. One was mad about it and insisted on knowing
why. 'I don't think you look a strong man' was the first reply. (But he
did!) More expostulation.

Dr. 'I shouldn't like to risk you—with those teeth in your head.'
Recruit. 'They can come out.'
Dr. 'Well, if you must know, your heart murmurs sometimes.'
And so on with other apparently robust fellows!

I still did not 'swear in'; but spent the afternoon hunting for Rooms.
Four hours I passed on this job; and finally I chose on a French Boarding
House, where Guests, Conversation, Cooking and everything else is
French.

This should be quite valuable to me; but I don't know whether the

---

[1] The Reading architect who designed Alpenrose for John Gunston, and to whom LG was
now articled.
[2] Miss Morley.
[3] Of the Artists' Rifles, whose headquarters were in Duke's Road, Euston Road.

price is too high—35s. a week. Bed & Breakfast at other places is 17/6 a week. I scarcely think it would come cheaper, if I took (proper) meals at A.B.C. Moreover there are no A.B.C's near at hand. I am two minutes for the Headquarters. Only 3 minutes from Imperial Hotel, and 5 from Waverley, so I am at home in the region. Tavistock Square is a replica of every other Bloomsbury Square; wadded with fog; skeletons of dismal trees behind the palings; but the usual west-end pervasion of ghostly aristocracy. In London I cannot be unhappy in any surroundings, for what in Manchester would be dismally forlorn, is here Mysterious; What in Liverpool would be detestably sordid, is here romantically free and easy; what elsewhere seems old dinginess is here suggestive Antiquity. (I have a notion that Dickens lived in Tavistock Sq.)[1]

In the middle of this letter I was called to lunch; and then went to 'swear in'. This time it is done: I am the British Army![2] Three of us had to read the Oath together; the others were horribly nervous! and read the wrong Paragraph until the Captain stopped them! 'Kiss the Book!' says Captain. One gives it a tender little kiss; the other a loud smacking one!!

After that we had to be inoculated for Typhoid. And that is why I am in bed since four o'clock! The delightfully kind, confidence-inspiring doctor gave us full instructions. There were scores of Tommies taking the ordeal before me, and believe me some were as nervous as only fine, healthy animals can be before doctors. One fainted before his turn came, merely as a result of the Doctor's description of possible symptoms!

You will be glad to hear, that though it is three hours ago, I have no constitutional symptoms whatever! Merely a local soreness! Some will have fever & 'influenza-pains' all night! (My ink is giving out.) I quite expected such myself; but I feel so physically happy that it might have been Morphine injected! We have sick leave until Monday morning. The hours are 9.30 to 5! Jolly reasonable!

The Poetry Bookshop is about 7 mins. walk![3] There is a Reading this very night!

A Crowd of Belgian Ladies fleeing from Brussels through Holland are staying here today on their way to Paris.

There are just one or two hitches in this pleasant time in bed. First, I have broken the bridge of my specs. and can't read without risk of headache; second, I daren't smoke (Doctor's Orders); third—empty pockets!

You will like me to write again tomorrow mng. This I promise. If only you lived near London!

Fondest Love to Father, Mary and the Dearest of Boys,

From your lovingest of Boys Wilfred

[1] Charles Dickens lived in Tavistock House, Tavistock Square, from 1850–6, and there wrote *Bleak House* and *Hard Times*.   [2] The omission of 'in' is possibly intentional.
[3] 35 Devonshire Street (now Boswell Street), Theobalds Road, W.C. It had been opened by Harold Monro in January 1913. The building no longer exists.

384. To Susan Owen
Postcard

Sat. Morn. [*Postmark 22 October 1915*]   *Tavistock Sq.*

In the night the arm got pretty bad. I still feel as if a horse had got my arm between its teeth. But so long as it keeps out of the other members, I don't mind it. Those who are not right by Monday mng. will be put on Light Duty, which I believe consists of standing still and staring. The men are really 'picked men most on 'em', anything but boisterous. I am thankful I <u>did</u> put up in a Boarding House, not in a poor Bedroom without meals <u>or</u> attention! Looking forward to your letter tomorrow,

Yours ever W.E.O.

What is Harold's next posting address? Is your headache now quite over? I have heard that the Camp is going to move to Harrow. Pip-ip! Recruits are very numerous now—17 on Monday last! . . . .[1]

385. To Susan Owen

Monday [*Postmark 25 October 1915*]   *Post Office* [*Postmark London*]

I had the first drill this mng. but got off this aft. because my arm is not really well. I went to Watson's, & shall have my specs. by tomorrow. I got full marks for Eyesight test at exam. On Sunday afternoon I went to Westminster Abbey: scholarly sermon on sociology and a dazzling fine Anthem. I am not yet in Khaki. The boarding house still pleases me, but I don't know if I shall like the servitude of conforming to its menu and hours of meals! The conversation at my table was all against England. I made no objections. Tomorrow I shall surprise them. Many thanks for all the kind letters received. I am quite all right again, now you know. Another injection in ten days.

Yours ever W.E.O.

386. To Susan Owen

Tuesday [*Postmark 27 October 1915*]   [*Tavistock Square*]

I fear I should have written my last card sooner than I did: but you can't expect to hear <u>every</u> day! I did a full day's parade today, the arm being only ticklish now. The drill is a curious compound of monotony and *qui vive*. Fortunately our Sergeant is a gentleman, and, what is more, considers us as such. As a Sergeant I admire & respect him devotedly. Harold Monro himself read at the P. Bookshop this evening, and I had a talk with him afterwards. Dorothy was impressed by his Poems which I left at Alpenrose. Please send me Tailhade: *Poèmes Aristophanesques,*[2] which is on the top shelf of the Book <u>Case</u>. Don't send the Pyjamas till

---

[1] We have omitted twelve words.
[2] Paris, 1904.

I say if we are given any. It <u>was</u> so nice of Colin & Mary to give such cheery letters. The enlisting <u>was</u> a <u>plunge</u>, and it <u>has</u> put my wits a little out of breath.

Your own W.E.O.

387. To Susan Owen

Friday Night [*30 October 1915*]   *Tavistock Sq.*

Dearest Mother,

I am dog-tired: N.B. I don't say exhausted—but stupidly, muscularly tired. I got my outfit some days ago. I have not the patience to give you a list of the contents of my Kit, but it contains numbers of footling things— tooth-brush & razor-brush for example, whereas I had to buy a belt (3/6) and shall have to buy a swagger-cane. These are regulations special to our regiment, because the discipline is frightfully minute. I spent all last evening polishing my buttons. We are cautioned against appearing in the street with a single over-coat button undone: belt must be worn over the overcoat, collar never turned up (except in very incle- ment weather when permission is granted to do so) etc. etc. etc. There is no doubt we are as smart as anything except the Guards, whom we ape. Yesterday morning we went a Route March through Kentish Town to Highgate. I had just got my Brogues repaired in time, but those wretches who wore new service boots had to go home by tram! This morning we had 'Physical Drill' under a special Gymnastic In- structor and it is that which had so bewearied my bones. We do all this in shirt sleeves in Cartwright Gardens, a 'crescent-garden' bounded by the usual boarding houses. I have scarcely seen an officer. All our instruction is done by sergeants, who are as chummy between times as they are smart on parade. Impossible to get them out of temper. One is a rare wag, and gives plenty of exercise to the Risible Muscles. I never felt devotion, and not much respect, for any authority or individual in this world since I left the 3rd form of the Institute; but I am beginning again under these fellows. Astonishing what a changed meaning has a Captain or a Colonel for me. If a Major-General approached me I think I should fall down dead. We had to practise Salutes (on Trees) this very morning. You would be surprised how long it takes to do the thing properly.

This aft. was pay-day. Now we waited drawn up in ranks from 3 this evening, till just on 6!! And those at the rear, as I was, never got it after all. Then was the moment when you had best wad up the ears if swearing upsets them.

I spent the heavy time pleasantly enough in conversation with one who I believe will be one of my best friends. Everyone is willing to make friends, and everyone is eligible; so there is really no guide as to which one shall go for beyond the expression of his phiz. There are now five on special terms with me, one very young, another quite forty, but none artists in any sense, no enthusiasts in my line. So I am still on the look- out. I believe

Sat. morning. Here I was suddenly cut short by my bath being ready. and the arrival of a large packet of literatures from Leslie.

Today is our Second Inoculation. I must run!

Yours with dearest love, Wilfred

388. To Susan Owen

Sunday [*2 November 1915*]   *Tavistock Square*

Dearest Mother,

I have no post-cards, hence another letter, simply to say that the Second Inoculation has taken mildly enough. It was done at midday yesterday : there was enough pain to justify a morning in bed! This time one of my 'friends' did a faint. It must be pure nerves : the 'poison' can't invade the system in half-a-minute. I stayed in by the fire in the afternoon, enduring a Singing Lesson which our Proprietor gives to a Marseillais youth betimes. It seems mine host is an ancient public singer. There is generally music of a sort in the evenings which drives me up to my room. I spend a good part of my leisure polishing my buttons and badges. It is a frightful bore. Can this explain the military oath—'Dash my buttons!' ? This morning I have massaged my new boots with Castor Oil. We were told to <u>pour</u> it inside the boot! The stench resulting is perhaps the very first inconvenience I have yet endured. I have bought my swagger cane, and now feel perfectly normal in Khaki. Apart from the treasonable unlawfulness of appearing in mufti, I should feel positively ill at ease in it. No collar & tie means an economy of dressing-time ; but it is paid for by the puttees, which, not being Foxes',[1] are difficult to arrange neatly. I wear the trousers bagged below the knee ; but such as care to buy breeches may dress in cavalry style. In the Inns of Court no one wears the khaki provided but buys officer's stuffs, (without stripes of course.) There is a pretty general feeling of contempt for the Inns of Court among our men, that may be founded on envy. <u>We</u> are forbidden to wear waterproofs or Burberrys or mufflers or brown boots—by a special Battalion Order! So far, then, our chiefest cares have been frivolous details of this sort, but there is a stern time coming—in Camp. There is a story that three men deserted from Camp. They were not shot at dawn, but simply excluded from Commissions.

I got my Pay by going early on Sat. morning. Did I ever acknowledge the £1. you sent? It does annoy me to have to take it. Now that the Inoculations are over I am looking for a Room. If only this Life went on indefinitely I should be well pleased. It is really no great strain to strut round the gardens of a West-end square for six or seven hours a day. Walking abroad, one is the admiration of all little boys, and meets an approving glance from every eye of eld. I sometimes amuse myself by sternly contemplating the civilian dress of apparent Slackers. They return a shifty enough expression. When I clamp-clump-clamp-clumped

---

[1] Fox the theatrical outfitter.

into the Poetry Bookshop on Thursday, the poetic ladies were not a
little surprised. The Readings were from Rabindranath Tagore,[1] read
by a Lady without much insight into the Hindu spirit. I could not speak
to Monro, but he smiled sadly at my khaki. He has a poem in his last
book, which goes

> Happy boy, happy boy,
> David the immortal-willed,
> Youth, a thousand thousand times
> Slain, but not once killed,
> Swaggering again today
> In the old contemptuous way;
>
> Leaning backward from your thigh
> Up against the tinselled bar—
> Dust and ashes! is it you?
> Laughing, boasting, there you are!
> First we hardly recognised you
> In your modern avatar.
>
> Greybeards plotted. They were sad.
> Death was in their wrinkled eyes.
> At their tables, with their maps,
> Plans and calculations wise
> They all seemed; for well they knew
> How ungrudgingly Youth dies.[2]
>
>   etc.

Leslie talks of coming up at the end of the week. Did I tell you I got
in half-price at 'the Strand' to see the *Scarlet Pimpernel*.[3] Fred Terry[4]
was indisposed, but I could hardly imagine a better impersonation than
was done by the Understudy. I have just read *El Dorado*, the last tale
of the S. Pimpernel—not very readable. Thank Father so much for a
special letter for me: It gave me good reassurance, which you must all
try and do. What breed is the Dog? Ah! if Colin could share my bedroom (double bedded) for a few days one week-end! I am free from Sat.
1 o'clock to Monday mng. Just enough time to meet you at Alpenrose,
one day next month, eh?

Monday. The Parcel came this morning. The handkerchiefs were just in
time, and the chocs I seized with schoolboyish relish! Our drill consisted of standing-at-ease and standing-easy alternately in the Drill
Hall, because it has rained all day! 'Our' Sergeant has not appeared for

[1] Sir Rabindranath Tagore (1861–1941), the Indian poet. He wrote mainly in Bengali
(much of his work was translated into English), but also in English; one of his poems was
included in *War Poems from The Times* (see Letter 374, note). See also Letter 482, note 1.
[2] 'Youth in Arms' (*The Collected Poems of Harold Monro*, edited by Alida Monro, Cobden-
Sanderson, London, 1933). Wilfred omits the third and fifth of the verses that constitute
Part I.
[3] By the Baroness Orczy (Mrs. Montague Barstow, d. 1947), playwright and novelist. *The
Scarlet Pimpernel* was published in 1905, as both novel and play, and was followed by many
further books and plays about her hero, Sir Percy Blakeney.
[4] Actor (1863–1933), youngest of the famous theatrical family, brother of Ellen Terry.

some time. Sgt. Knight has charge of us now—the county cricketer:[1] do Father or Colin know of his renown? There is a legend that our Doctor attended the King. Certainly he belongs to a noble Order, K.C.B. or something. There seem no Artists whatever among us!! This morning I was talking to a recruit of a Henry-Irving countenance, who persists in wearing long strands of hair visible in front of the Cap. He has been 'ticked-off' four or five times for it; but is not yet shot at dawn. I am fairly close cropped.

From an Adv. in 'The Y.M.' I found a room[2] at 5/6 per week, right opposite the Poetry Bookshop!!

A plain enough affair—candlelight—no bath—and so on; but there is a coffee-shop underneath; so I have theoretically decided to go there, and shall move as soon as practicable. Indeed I gave notice this evening at this Boarding House.

There is no symptom of patri-avuncularism from Meols!

I think, if it be possible, I must beg £2 for the next remittance, on account of the Advance Payments I may have to make. This should be quite the last Allowance. If anything should turn up from Meols later be reimbursed therewith, of course. I used to think Uncle Ted's readings of Scrooge funny. I don't now. I shall move from here as soon as I have paid up.

Rumour has it that we shall be billeted for the Winter!!

Fare thee well, thou dear, dear Mother, prayeth   her Wilfred

389. To Susan Owen
Postcard

Frid. Ev. [*Postmark 2 November 1915*]   *Post Office* [*Postmark London*]

This is posted at 7.30, you should get it in time. We go to Camp on Monday Mng. Tomorrow we may get off early, so that there is just a chance of arriving before you. But in any case I sh'd take a bicycle, for I must leave on Sunday Night.   W.E.O.

The P.O. was providential we had to pay the Corps subscription this mng!

390. To Susan Owen
Postcard

Monday [*Postmark 8 November 1915*]   *a Post Office* [*Postmark London*]

Am rejoiced to know that Father's operation[3] is well over. Surprised not to have news of him this mng. but perhaps you are saying as much of me. All my time is being given to an Author—Prof. of Lit. at Brussels, who, after 22 yrs of research has found the true Shakspere. Not Bacon

---

[1] R. F. Knight (1879–1955), who played as a professional for Northamptonshire.
[2] 21 Devonshire Street. See Letter 436. This building no longer exists.
[3] A minor nasal operation.

but the Earl of Rutland.[1] His proofs are overwhelming. There is going to be a sensation. When I am convinced, I may start the propaganda in the papers. I had the registered letter. Great thanks! But I am not out of Tavistock Sq. 54, for reasons which I will explain later. I quite hope to be able to get to Alp. on Sat. What a delight!

Your W.E.O.

391. To Susan Owen

Postcard addressed to Alpenrose, Kidmore Reading
From: Pte W. E. S. Owen,
2nd *Batt.* 28th London *Reg't.* C *Coy.*
Address reply to Hare Hall Camp Gidea Park Essex
No 9 Platoon Hut 6 a

1 p.m. [*Postmark 15 November 1915*]   *Y.M.C.A.*

I did everything in good time and order. We arrived by train at midday. Just settled in our huts. All very nicely set out here, Y.M.C.A. in full swing. I have a nice bed-side fellow. who knows of Bulman & Forrest!

W.E.O.

392. To Susan Owen

Postcard

Friday Aft. [*Postmark 19 November 1915*]
Y.M.C.A. [*Postmark Watford*]

Had your letter & the socks at mid-day. We have had a rough time today—up at 6 again. 3 men out of the 700 took cold Shower baths. I was one of the 3. But holding rifles frozen over with snow all day was ghastly. Sorry not to have had even the bad prints of my photos. We have an extra blanket now i.e. 1 blanket & 3 rugs. Food has been so-so today.

Love to all W.E.O.

393. To Susan Owen

Postcard

Friday Aft. [*Postmark 19 November 1915*]
Railway Train [*Postmark Watford*]

20 men were suddenly called up to do some cleaning up at High Beech. Of these am I and my two best friends. We just had time to snatch a lunch, & I managed to rip open the Parcel, & get out the socks. We may stay till Monday, but write to Gidea Park. We are carrying a sack of meat and a sack of bread. This is 'Fatigue Duty' but I am glad of the Change.
Many thanks for sending so promptly the pyjamas etc. Don't know how we shall sleep tonight. Am quite well.

Your W.E.O.

---

[1] Célestin Demblon, *Lord Rutland est Shakespeare: le plus grand des mystères dévoilé*, Paris, 1912.

394. To Susan Owen
Postcard

[*Postmark 21 November 1915*]   *Y.M.C.A.* [*Postmark Romford*]

Just returned (by train) from High Beech. Worked like slaves at Transport Waggon Loading from 7.30 to 2. Thoroughly enjoyed the change, & benefited by the exercise.

Your W.E.O.

395. To Leslie Gunston
Picture Postcard reproduced as Plate VIII

[*Postmark 23 November 1915*]   [*Postmark Romford*]

Here's a part of our Hut of 30. I slaved for them, all Sunday as Orderly—never thought myself capable of such strenuosities as to do skivvy's drudgery from 6.30 a.m. to 6.30 p.m.! Note the bareheaded man on my right. Shall tell you about him and men when I can. Great thanks for Book. I read one page when lights went out!

396. To Susan Owen
Postcard

[*Postmark 26 November 1915*]   *Y.M.C.A.* [*Postmark Romford*]

Too downright tired to get off a decent letter to anybody. But I wrote a Picture Card of my Hut to Harold. Please add to address Hut 6 a, and call me Cadet. (new Order) splendidly well! and happy (after 4.30 p.m.)

Your own W.E.O.

Socks fit perfectly. Am getting away to Town this week end.

397. To Susan Owen
Postcard

Thursday [*? 28 November 1915*]   *From Cadet W. E. S. Owen, 4756*
Hut 6a, Artists' Reg't. C. Coy.
Hare Hall Camp Romford Essex

I was put on Guard Duty from 9 a.m. yesterday to 9 a.m. today. Miserable time: not allowed to take off packs or boots during 24 hrs. I was Sentry from 11 to 1 and 5 to 7, etc. a. and p.m. I was with fellows that I don't like—chumps all of them. We got enough to eat; and I made toast on my Bayonet. There was not much Challenging to do. I am one of the orderlies again tomorrow. Now that the novelty is wearing off, this Camping is beginning to get troublesome. I had a card from Stanley Webb today. I am not off this week end. How is everybody?

Your W.E.O.

398. To Susan Owen
Postcard

[Postmark 29 November 1915]   *Υ.M.C.A.* *[Postmark Romford]*

Many and great thanks for the Parcel which I found on getting back from London on Sunday night. I enjoyed the Leave;—took a shilling seat at the Opera on Sat. Night. We are getting on fast with our Drill: have already started the Attack. I haven't yet seen my Photographs. I had posted my Card to Harold. Have no idea about Leave for Christmas. Hope Father is quite all right now. Your Pills kept off another cold. How we suffer in this weather!

Yours ever W.E.O.

399. To Susan Owen
Postcard

Sunday [Postmark 6 December 1915]   *Υ.M.C.A.* *[Postmark Romford]*

The Card I had this morning, but the promised parcel has not yet got to my hut. What can it contain? How good of you! I don't want more socks, nor any underclothing. But my funds have got very low! There is a rumour of our leaving these huts to make room for new recruits, and being put into empty houses. I have had sore throat for some days which has now gone. Had a good deal of cleaning up to do today, but went to Church this morning at Romford. When does M. leave Alpenrose?

W.E.O.

400. To Susan Owen
Postcard

Friday [Postmark 18 December 1915]   *[Postmark Romford]*

The latest about Christmas Leave is that only those who joined the Corps before Oct. 25 will have any Leave at all, whether at Christmas or New Year. I joined on the 21st. Anyhow my Number is on the safe side! The Majority in our hut are too late in their dates!
We expect 6 or 7 days.
We were digging trenches yesterday. Today I had my first chance of acting as Company Commander. We lost in the Match with Eton. (This for Colin). Highest of expectations

Your W.E.O.

401. To Susan Owen

Tuesday [21 December 1915]   *Υ.M.C.A.* *[Romford]*

Dearest Mother,
    Your two letters came together yesterday! Up to an hour ago I still hoped for Leave over Xmas Day, but no longer think it likely. Yesterday I couldn't write for the same reason that I can't say much today. Thus.

On Sat. I noticed three Boy Scouts, about camp, and out of the bounty of my affections gave them tea & biscuits at the Y.M.C.A. This is my reward: two of them asked me to come to their houses. I went yesterday to the first; but can't tell you all about them. In a word they are an excellent family: (Girl 18, Boy 13, Boy 11, Girl 8.) who take pleasure in inviting and feasting soldiers. They are Welsh in origin, and the circumambience of their home is as nearly akin to Mahim as possible!

Tonight I am going to a fairly large house, and the kid is waiting for me this moment, to catch the horse bus which is to take us there.

I am to eat the Christmas Dinner with the first family (Williams) if I don't get Leave.

But one of the Boys has already asked me to a kind of House Party with him, in the sad event of my not getting home. Am pretty sure to know for certain tomorrow, & shall write in any case.

Your own Wilfred

Leslie wants me to go to Bath for a day or two in my Holiday. So do I if I can get a glimpse of Johnny & Bobby there.

402. To Susan Owen
Postcard

Wednes. Night [*Postmark 23 December 1915*]   [*Postmark Romford*]

No news of Christmas Leave which is bad news. Yet sorrow not. We shall have a merry time even in the Hut, and I am sure you will like to know I am in the bosom of a family at dinner-time! I must take a present with me for Raymond.[1] Could you send me the brand-new Pocket Book secreted in my Pigeon-Holes? I had a good time yesterday: Pa & Ma ordinary, but darlin' little chilluns. Can Father get me a Pass to Shrews. via Bath, if I travel in Mufti. If not, I shall need Ressurees. Do you consent to a day or so in Bath? I have written to Johnny on the strength of it! Men have gone out tonight to buy decorations for the Shanty. Thank Seatons for Xmas Card. Don't make up my bed. I will bide with Colin: Keep the Feast on the 25th. I am pretty sure to be with you for New Year's Day. Dearest love to all.

W.E.O.

403. To Susan Owen

Thursday [*23 December 1915*]   *Y.M.C.A.* [*Romford*]

Dearest of Mothers,

I have had no letters today. I believe there is a muddle in the P.O. this year, but I hope you will get this by Christmas Day. The certainty is absolute: I shall be here over the 25, with the majority of my Hut, and, indeed, of my Company. The latest rumour is that we shall not be

---

[1] Raymond Williams.

allowed to get out of Camp till we have fairly eaten our Christmas Dinner under its auspices. Anyhow we shall feast rarely. Donaldson is giving us two birds, (geese or turkeys) and there will be any number of plum-puddings. We are allowed 1/6 per head extra pay for the Day, which is funded and spent on delicacies and drinks. You will be pleased to hear that no spirits will be allowed at table. The best of it is we are all pleased.

I may go to the Williams later in the day, or on Boxing Day. Both Scouts have their lunch in my Hut now, instead of the Q.M. stores, where they are alone or with alien men. It is remarkable how their presence kills bad language, for the time. The Restraint is beautiful, but if the novelty wears off and usual conditions are gone back to I shall turn out the kids.

We had a lecture this afternoon on bombs, from an expert. We shall begin firing after New Year.

I am being waited for now to go into Romford and buy special provisions. One has gone to London for the Turkeys. I wonder what you will be having. It is galling to be kept away from Home for no useful reason, but it is not as if I were far away or long away. I really think to start on Tuesday or Wednesday.

Goodwill let there be; but Peace is a word that jars today and word for hushed breath. I shall write continually, but this poor sheet may be the one to carry you my dear Christmas Wishes the most ardent and solemn of any year yet.

Wilfred x

404. To Susan Owen

Sunday after Christmas [*26 December 1915*]   *Y.M.C.A.* [*Romford*]

Dearest Mother,

Your dear, lovely letter reached me this morning. It was the one thing lacking yesterday to make my Christmas the happiest possible, away from Home. I had no letter, parcel or card whatsoever yesterday; but I had my consolations. The Plenty that overpoured in our Hut of good things was noised all over the Camp. In our Hut 'it snowed of meats and drinks.' One Wiggins, a noted gourmand made all manner of custards & jellies; and Donaldson's turkeys were *à point*. Healths were drunk; but none among us were. I had scarcely accomplished my last nut, at 3 o'clock (we sat down at 1.30!) when my Boy Scout came for me. And not long after I got to the house, we began my second Christmas Dinner, rarely good. So I made up for the Lost One in 1913! Afterwards we played Charades, exactly as we played at Home. But I shall have to tell you all about these excellent people with the live voice. There was no extension of time, last night we were all in at 9.15: but the uproar in camp could be heard afar off.

We went to Church Parade this morning as well as yesterday. The Major read the Lessons.

I have some fine Caricatures of the Colonel[1] etc. to show you which appeared in *The Tatler*.

I am sorry you don't countenance my little stay in Bath with a fair regard. Yet it is no great *détour* from London, and I am sure I could get a Permission, via Bath. But I haven't heard again from Leslie. I hope you got all my letters: a succession of 4, Dec. 21, 22, 23, 24; The pocket-book-parcel hasn't been delivered to me yet. Thanks for sending it: I hope it is safe. There seems no possibility of getting off before Wed. or Thursday.

There has been a new desertion from Camp. The boy was captured at Norwich. Two lusty ones from my hut were told off to exercise the Prisoner on Christmas Day. I have not too much spare time today, being Orderly. My Batmanship finished yesterday.

I read your dear letter many times, and <u>shall</u> read it. I quite well know how busy Colin must be.

It is fine to feel that now that Christmas is over, there is a greater treat in store. May my plans be sooner fulfilled than they were this time last year!

Ever your loving Wilfred.   x

405. To Susan Owen

Postcard

Monday [*Postmark 28 December 1915*]   *Y.M.C.A.* [*Postmark Romford*]

I have just been told that I take my Leave on Wednesday next. But a man in B11 whose Leave dates from Thurs. wants to change with me. This will rather advantage than hinder my arrangements, as I am not quite persuaded about Bath one way or the other. I don't know the day of Return to Duty. I have still not had your Parcel. Don't be stunned if I arrive at an unholy hour; or if I happen upon you before or after my time: and don't make up a bed—or a feast! For we are fairly sated today!

Your W.E.O.

[1] Colonel W. C. Horsley (1855–1934).

TRAINING

1916

406. To Susan Owen
Postcard

Thurs. [*Postmark 6 January 1916*]   [*Postmark Romford*]

I stayed with Leslie till 5, and caught a train from Liverpool St. by chance, not knowing the times. You may be surprised to know that I had a Commission offered to me today. Are you yet more surprised to know that I refused it: Lancashire Fusiliers, just going into Fighting Line. And I haven't fired my Musketry Course. I can tell you no more. A list of names was read out, and we said Yes or No according to our feelings!
So glad the Dog turned up. We had an all-day march (of course) so I haven't seen my Narks. The Gingerbreads made a warm pudding for lunch. We parade at 8.30 now!!

                                                    Yours W.E.O.

407. To Colin Owen

Sunday Evening [*10 January 1916*]   *Y.M.C.A.* [*Romford*]

My dear Colin,
    Last Wednesday seems very long ago. I suffered on Thursday from the fresh shock of discipline, cold, rough blankets and vile-tasting food; but I am habituated once more.
    I had a good journey, travelling with the A.S.C. men you saw, merry dogs. I got into camp half an hour before the Time, but many arrived late. There are stricter Rules than ever about Boundaries, and Leave, etc. However, We find ourselves, that is, my Platoon, among the veterans of the corps, and we drill and go to Lectures with the Officers' School.
    Two men of my Hut offered themselves (I think that's the way to put it) for the Lancs. Fusiliers Commissions. When my name was read out I said NO! with a loud voice. We have not even started Miniature Range Firing yet.
    We had Church Parade this morning. One Major read the Lesson and another played the organ. This afternoon I have been reading a book which I just received from Leslie.
    Ray came for me yesterday and we had some parlour games: like Smiling Snap, which was new to them. Mr. Williams was hopelessly unsmileable.
    I left my keys in the lock of my bookcase (or inside). Find them for me, dear boy, and send them at once. (3 or 4 keys on a small ring.) The cake was well praised by the whole hut, and the gingerbreads by such fortunates as got any. I had no letter since Mother's first card. Love to everyone.

                                                    Your W.E.O.

408. To Susan Owen

[*Postmark 14 January 1916*]   *Y.M.C.A.* [*Postmark Romford*]

Quite impossible to write more than a card. Our Training is becoming intensive. We now finish at 6.30, and we have maps & Reports to do all evening. The Colonel gave a brilliant lecture on the causes of the War this aft. He is an expert after the style of Belloc. I had all the things you sent. Thanks, tho' only the Keys were desired: By all means let the Diary be Mary's. I must now get straight away to my Mapping. We spend the day with Note Books & Compasses in the district. I had a Card from Coz. May. I will tell you tomorrow about my coming week end.

Your W.E.O.

409. To Susan Owen

Postcard, addressed to 'Underdale', Studley Road, Torquay

Thurs. [*Postmark 21 January 1916*]   *Y.M.C.A.* [*Postmark Romford*]

I hope you will have a happy time with Grandma & Auntie and that all are well. There is only this news: I have twice held back from Chances of being accepted Commission since the time I was offered one. Both were Lancs. Regiments. No thanks! We still work from 6.30 a.m. to 6 p.m. We ran across an R.A.M.C. party the other day, by Brentwood, but I did not spot Stanley. I had your long letter the day after posting my last.

Always your own W.E.O.

410. To Susan Owen

[*26 January 1916*]   *Y.M.C.A.* [*Romford*]

Dearest of Mothers,

I send a letter out of sheer lovingkindness, seeing there is no fact, complaint, desire, fear, regret or fancy to be addressed unto you, but only the fact of my sonship, and my greetings to the most gentlest of mothers.

I had a letter from Leslie under this same Y.M.C.A. Heading, for he was washing coffee-cups during his week-end;[1] Mars and Minerva help his soul, fingers and all the cockles of his heart.

They have now put up a chapel in the camp; 4 or 5 days ago the place where it stands knew it not; and the Bishop is coming down to dedicate (sanctify as he would say) tomorrow.

We are now—at last—on our Musketry Course. Many are falling sick about me, by reason of January, and the dead season, but I have not so much as a cold. The hours are still early and late. Still I am never tired, and often walk to Romford in the evening. An occasional Ray

---

[1] War work. LG had a mitral murmur and after several medicals was not called up.

from the outer world visits me. I may be going in for the 5th Manchester Regiment.[1]

Did you know that no officers can be sent to the Firing Line without 5 months waiting in England.

                                        Your lovingest of Boys Wilfred

Post Scriptum.

Give my distinguished salutations to your hosts[2] at Weston. You know Miss Ingram is at her Brother's school there. Is a school of that Name known?

411. To Susan Owen

Tuesday [*1 February 1916*]   *Isolation Hut B11* [*Romford*]

Dearest Mother,

How frantically I wish I had complained a little louder, or been a little worse, or that you had been more touched by my groans—so that I might never have returned to this hot-bed of disease, this Quarantine, this Prison, this Charnel House. When I opened the door of the Hut in the deep midnight, and smelt the smell of Disinfectant, used wholesale,—I knew what Trap I had run into and I knew why my bones ached. But, it is nothing worse than Measles, and what is more, I don't think I've got it. But there is no doubt my system has been fighting a ferocious battle with the Germ. As usual, the Good Microbes got the best of it in me. All the same, my eyes run continually, and my brain is like a hot coal within my head. Of course I 'paraded sick', but having no rash, I just have to crouch in my Hut, now half-empty of its men, and the centre of the measles outbreak. Moreover we are refused admission to the Y.M. or Canteen, and shall not be able to leave the Camp for 16 days.

When I was going up the subway at Liverpool St. from the Underground to the Gt. Eastern Platform, I noticed the passages unduly encumbered, and found the outlet just closed, and Liverpool St. in complete darkness. We were corked down in those subways for close on 3 hours. This should appeal to <u>your</u> susceptibilities especially. There was just room to move from one Exit to another seeking an escape. After all the Zeppelins never got over the City, though we heard the guns. The result of this piece of providential by-play was that I reached Camp in the early hours of this morning. My bed had disappeared, all my belongings were hidden all over the hut, for the whole place had been emptied

---

[1] He was commissioned into the 5th Battalion the Manchester Regiment on 4 June 1916. This was the 5th (Reserve) Battalion, formed in May 1915 as a draft-finding unit for the 1st/5th and 2nd/5th (the latter, originally formed to provide drafts for the 1st/5th, having also become an active unit). It began to send out drafts towards the end of 1915. At Codford on Salisbury Plain until summer 1916, the battalion then moved to Witley, near Guildford, where Wilfred joined it as a newly commissioned officer. See Letter 438. All officers gazetted to the 5th Battalion reported to the 3rd/5th, or Reserve, Battalion to await posting.

[2] The Rev. William Davies, Rector of Norton Fitzwarren, Somerset. Susan Owen's first cousin.

for disinfecting, and the things thrown back anyhow. It was the bitterest moment of many years. I found some blankets, but all night I was per-suaded I should [not] warm my limbs again in this world.

The doctor won't sign my commission papers for 3 days; supposing I may contract measles yet.

I don't think so.

What a prospect to be imprisoned in this hut for several weeks.

I hope Colin won't get it.

Nobody of my Friends knew my address, or perhaps they might have warned me.

A horrid sensation to be imprisoned with Germs. Far worse than the shutting-down under London last night.

Do not worry about my condition.

What frets me is that I ever let myself away from Home.

Do not send any things to eat. I cannot taste: and I can get by deputy something from the Y.M. if necessary.

No more of this now—at least for your ears. For me: 'Buried alive for 16 days!' I cannot bear to think of Sat. & Sunday.

Farewell, Wilfred x

412. To Susan Owen
Postcard

Wednesday [*Postmark 3 February 1916*]   [*Postmark Romford*]

I have not given way to Measles, and am not going to. My cold is much less severe than yesterday: a genuine change sets in. The apparent recovery on Monday was an artificial one, brought about by deceitful drugs. Would I had taken 'Bromo-Tablets', and never revived at all! About 5 men remain well in this hut; and more measley ones are carried off every day.

I was affrayed when I saw this morning that Zeppelins got into Staffs.[1] You are not so snug in Shrews. as we imagined. What local news is there of the Raid? I shall go on parade tomorrow.

Always your W.E.O.

Hope my letter was posted in London yesterday?

413. To Susan Owen

7 February [*1916*]   [*Romford*]

Dearest of Mothers,

I have 5 minutes 0 seconds to do this Note—for I must catch the early post—or you won't get it tomorrow.

I have no news of myself since all my thoughts are to you. I was dis-

---

[1] Nine Zeppelins were raiding over the Midlands on the night of 31 January–1 February 1916, making for but not reaching Liverpool. Fifty-nine people were killed in Staffordshire, and 101 injured. One raider came close to Shrewsbury.

turbed all morning through having no news, but Father's most welcome letter came at mid-day. I try to read into it some intimation that you are better, but I find it very hard. How joyful I shall be tomorrow if you are able to say so.

We had the General's Inspection today, and the whole business went wrong: chiefly through a strange Captain who gave wrong commands at the critical moment.

I am now quite normal.

Congratulations to dear old Colin for doing so well at Footer!

Every Praise to Mary for the splendid nursing I know she is doing.

Know that I think of you not continually but continuously.

> Your very own Wilfred

414. To Susan Owen

Wednesday [*10 February 1916*]   *Hut B 11* [*Romford*]

Sweete my Mother,

How great peace of heart did your own beloved handwriting give me this morning! Mary's card came (to the Hut, at least) simultaneously. Thus I was all yesterday without a word. Very unhappy was I; nor did I find courage to write, even had I time, for I was Hut Orderly and drudged for 13 hours without a break.

This morning was a delightful morning. At the bottom this was owing to the news; but in addition we worked at visual training—in lovely weather—trying to locate 6 men only 500 yds. away, who could see us and were themselves exposed enough to fire blank-cartridges upon us. It was all but impossible to see them!

This afternoon we all had a Throat Inspection by the Doctor. He passed everybody's in the Hut but mine: says I have a granulated pharynx. (2 or 3 lumps on the back wall) You remember Dr. Mathews[1] attacked these with Silver Nitrate in 1913. The Medical Officer says I should get them removed—I asked if he would do it—but he can't. I may be able to go to some hospital, but he advised me to see 'my own specialist'—in as he said a Turkey Carpet place & full attention. I am going tomorrow morning to see the M.O. privately—to find out whether the army will pay expenses. If possible, I shall come to Russ Wood![2] But I can tell you no more until tomorrow. If I am sent home (unthinkable good fortune) I hope it will not be just while Harold is in London, as I do hope to show him the Camp and the glories thereof.

I had a note from the Williams asking me there next Saturday, in spite of measles. I shall take a Pauline departure thro' the hedge, probably, because the Restrictions will not be taken off for another week or more.

The Photograph was done on the Tuesday after my Weekend. I did

---

[1] The Shrewsbury doctor who attended Wilfred during his post-Dunsden illness in 1913.
[2] Dr. Mathews's house.

not know your news then. The Corporal, of course, has the stripe. Brown has riding-breeks: and a card.

Thursday

I have one day's leave (today) to go down to Bart's Hospital and have the blobs cauterised. They won't cut the things away, as I should like! Quite a pleasant day-off.

I must get away at once. Shall post in Town.

Yours ever, Wilfred

P.T.O.

Do take extreme care of your self just now. I hope you have the fine, keen, sunny weather that is here.

415. To Susan Owen

Friday [*Postmark 12 February 1916*]   [*Postmark Romford*]

Went to Bart's as letter indicates, but the required Dr. was not there. I am to go again on Tuesday. So I had a pleasant afternoon. There is a great likelihood of going to H.Q. next week. Ever so glad to have your letter this morning. We had a written exam. today. Fresh cases of measles in other huts! No more in ours. I quite mean to make an escape to Williams' tomorrow afternoon. Hoping to have bulletins 'each one better than the last, as it should be' (as your governess said of your maps!)

Your own W.E.O.

416. To Susan Owen

Monday [*15 February 1916*]   Hut B 11 [*Romford*]

Dearest Mother,

And was it really Congestion of Lungs! I did indeed suspect it, tho' you only spoke of Bronchitis. I should have been miserable unspeakably if I had known. I am thankful it is over—critically—but I am not keen to hear of you going about yet. There is plenty of time for that [*two lines illegible*] allowed to bustle your Convalescence.

When I went to Williams' on Sat., I made no secret of my Infected State. Consequently I only saw the Children in the garden! As I was going 'home', earlier than usual, I was arrested by a string tied across the road. I said to myself Boys! and took breath for a chase. When I had stood still for some minutes, I heard whisperings behind shrubs, as I knew I should. I made a charge for the shrubbery, and 'started' two figures that scampered like bunnies. The chase was too funny to describe. The kids were terrified by the swift, relentless soldier. When I came up with them I found one to be the Scout Harper the 'other' scout, who had taken me home. The chase so jogged his memory of me, that on Sunday morning he came to Camp to ask me there for the afternoon & evening.

I was Orderly that day, & so was late, and kept the little brother, a Colinesque, adorable little creature of 10, waiting in the rain. He had come all the way (some miles) to meet me.

I had a very excellent good time indeed. Mr. and Mrs. Harper played piano duets, not badly, and Bertie performs on the violin. There was also a distinguished old lady—some great-aunt—who spoke noble English, and so raised the social tone of the house in my imagination for ever. The Children call me Uncle. Their affection—which has come up swiftly as the February flowers—seems without bounds and without restraint.

In the woods around the place, we found 1 crocus,
1 lesser celandine,
10,000 leaves of hyacinth.
And we ate the Vernal Eucharist of Hawthorn leaf-buds.

These are the days when men's hearts (some men's) become tender as the new green. I have also the reminder of your cares for me in these days three years ago; and all this makes me beyond measure—tho' the measure were sighs and tears—sad to think that you should be stricken, harassed, and undermined by those same pestiferous germs!

I had your prized letter this morning; together with characteristic epistles from Leslie, & Bobby at Downside.

I must now-at-once see about my Pass for tomorrow.

Your lovingest Wilfred

417. To Susan Owen
Postcard

Wed. [*Postmark 16 February 1916*]   *Romford*

The specialist made a thorough examination of Throat & nose yesterday. The cauterising was nothing did not even tickle. So glad to read your letter this aft. I have nothing from Harold. Please give me his address. I may go to Barts. again on Friday to have a tooth out. Hope Colin is now back at School! Our Isolation—in this Hut—should end next Sat.

Yours ever, W.E.O.

418. To Susan Owen
Saturday [*February 1916*]   *Hut B 11* [*Romford*]

My own dear Mother,

I am in more trouble than I had better say about your Complications. I am glad you didn't write under the circumstances, but it is altogether uncomfortable, disconcerting, and disquieting to hear about you. I am much more affected, if that be possible. I most uneasily look for better news tomorrow.

Do you think you aggravated your cold on Monday? Alas! the day! Woe worth the hour! That I might be at your side now.

I have nothing left of my attack (whatever it was) save the lingering rear-guard of a cold.

A General is coming to inspect us on Monday, so we are slaving away at our Huts to get them immaculate: as well as our Packs, etc. etc.

Many thanks for sending the *Punch* & *Chronicle*. I shall write again tomorrow. Best thanks to Mary for writing so faithfully and lovingly of her patient.

Your loving, & sorrowing Wilfred

At least it is good to have such news from Harold.

419. To Susan Owen
Postcard

Saturday [*Postmark 28 February 1916*]   *Guard Room H.Q.*
[Postmark London W.C.]

It did not occur to me, writing from so renowned (?) a place as the P. Bookshop to give you the address:

35 Devonshire St.

W.[1]

Don't put Poetry Bookshop. Tonight I am on Guard, so that my week-end is quite spoiled. But I saw Harold last night. He sailed at 1 a.m. (?)[2] We got paid today: so there is no immediate need confronting me. I stand in need of your news, but for this I have to blame myself. It goes on snowing. Shall try and write tomorrow. Tell me if you wrote to H.Q. or elsewhere.

Your W.E.O.

420. To Susan Owen
Postcard

Monday [*Postmark 29 February 1916*]   [*Postmark London*]

Just a card to forestall Harold with <u>my</u> Greetings: (although after all I don't think I shall go forth to post tonight, the snow is still jiggering about.) We finished work at quarter to 7 today! Lectures nearly all day, on Gas, Horses, Bombs, and such subjects. I have seen nothing of Monro, as I am out all day & he all evening. But the young house-keeper,[3] who is French, has reeled off as much information as I can desire. I had the Letter & Enclosure yesterday and thank you heartily & sadly.

---

[1] On a ten days' course in London, Wilfred was allowed to find private lodgings, and stayed at the Poetry Bookshop. 'Above the shop, he [Monro] had bed-sitting rooms for poets; Wilfrid Wilson Gibson, T. E. Hulme and Wilfrid [*sic*] Owen lived there for some time . . .' (F. S. Flint's biographical Introduction to *The Collected Poems of Harold Monro*). In fact, this was Wilfred's only stay, and it lasted for a few days only.
[2] H O's ship had just berthed at the East India Dock after an eventful spell at sea; he recalls spending the evening at 35 Devonshire Street, and meeting Monro. On the next day, 28 February, he sailed to Liverpool, from which port he proceeded on leave.
[3] Alida Klemantaski, later Monro's second wife. See Letter 558.

Fondest love to Mary. All praise to Colin for 'washing up'. It is the most soldierly thing he can possibly do. Do keep warm. Are you at all stronger now?

Your W.E.O.

421. To Susan Owen
Postcard

Wed. Night [*Postmark 2 March 1916*]   [*Postmark London*]

Depressing news was announced today. All who left Camp last Wed. must return to camp in a day or two. We are too sick at heart to discuss it, even. Still it has its advantages financially. In view of leaving before Pay Day, I must beg another 10s. We are to have another month or more of 'Officers' School' Training, i.e. Lectures & Exams. Even here we work till 7 p.m. instead of 4.30! Has Harold arrived. Write here till further notice; we may extort leave to stay over Sunday. You may have noticed that the Gazettes have ceased in the Papers since some considerable time. Is the end of the war in view? There is only one consolation from this Delay, and that is a Coward's.
This aft. in the lecture-room I am sure I saw Ernie Hulcoop of Dunsden & Kendrick, among the Recruits! Ardently hoping you are getting well—

Your W.E.O.

422. To Susan Owen

Saturday [*5 March 1916*]   *Y.M.C.A.* [*Romford*]

My darling Mother,
    Here we are again! The reason of the Remove is that all men with 'Papers in' must go through a six weeks Training in a School of Instruction before they can be gazetted. The War Office, indeed, has stated that none can have Commissions within 4 months from now. But that is sure to be changed. At the end of the 6 weeks there will be an exam. This is tiresome beyond words (tho' we *have* among ourselves certain words to fit the case.)
    Our 10 days in Town were so annoying that the departure was made less galling than it might have been. Every day we 'worked', *doing nothing*, well into the evening. On Thursday the Draft left Waterloo for Southampton, and we marched with them thro' London, with several Bands, to say Goodbye. Thus we came in for a deal of cheering and staring from the windows & pavements. All day we marched about, and were recalled in the evening for Night Operations on Hampstead Heath, up to which we marched, over which we marched, and back from which we marched. I got in at 9.30!
    I thought I should never see Monro; but last night at eleven o'clock, when I had strewn about my goods preparatory to sorting and packing, up comes Monro to my room, with my MSS! So we sit down, and

383

I have the time of my life. For he was 'very struck' with these sonnets. He went over the things in detail and he told me what was fresh and clever, and what was second-hand and banal; and what Keatsian, and what 'modern'.

He summed up their value as far above that of the Little Books of Georgian Verse. The curious part is that he applauded precisely those phrases which Prof. Morley condemned!

So then, I have gained his esteem and a (first) handshake! I need not say that he is a peculiar being; and I doubt whether ever we shall become 'Friends'. For my own part I should prefer a Business Relation, and I believe it possible—when he re-starts his Journal *Poetry & Drama*,[1] now checked by the War.

I have quite won the heart of the Swiss Housekeeper, and on two evenings she brought me up Hot Soup etc. out of human kindness. I left this morning without settling my Account, since, luckily, no Bill had been presented to me, and when I left in the early morning nobody was stirring. I have not had your letter. This is my Address now:

> Cadet W. E. S. Owen, 4756.
> W. Co.—Officers' School—
> Balgores House,
> Gidea Park,
> Nr. Romford, Essex.

We are crowded into large empty houses, sleeping on the floor, far less comfortable than the Hut. But we have Batmen to wash up, and a Mess Room with table-cloths, properly set out. We expect the work to be strenuous.

I am so anxious to hear when Harold arrived, and whether you have nearly reached your normal <u>health</u> (?), and withal how Mary improves.

> Loving wishes for Everyone, Your Wilfred

423. To Susan Owen

Postcard

[Postmark 7 March 1916]   *Y.M.C.A.* *[Postmark Romford]*

We have just been given our proper Address:

> W.E.S.O. 4756
> Cadet School,
> Gidea Hall,
> at 'Balgores' Romford, Essex.

I have had no communications since your letter rec'vd on Friday last. I don't even know if Harold arrived. We are to have a snowball fight this afternoon. We now have excellent meals (4 a day) but our quarters are most uncomfortable.

> Best of love, W.E.O.

---

[1] Monro started this quarterly in 1913, and had published eight numbers when the war came. He did not revive it after the war.

424. To Susan Owen

Monday Evening [*14 March 1916*]   *Y.M.C.A.* [*Romford*]

My own dear Mother,

I found your Letter on the Table where our Post is displayed this afternoon. I was twice blest to find the stray letter refound, as I was no less annoyed to think the 5s. was lost, than I was needy of it. We have been obliged to buy all manner of Note-Books for our work, and shall soon have Maps and such materials to find. I shall consider my running clothes as my Birthday Present. There is no book that I hanker after, because I can borrow anything that there is time to read; but there are some half-dozen Military Books which I ought to get, but which I can also borrow until my Gazetting.

There are probably another 8 weeks of this schooling.

We now have started in earnest; we have a lecture at 6.30 a.m. drill and field operations all day—another lecture 5 to 6 p.m., Dinner 6.30 to 7.30 and from 7.30 to 9.30 time for cleaning—preparations for next day, study, and writing up of notes. I have exactly 30 mins. of my own today, and 15 of those are being consecrated to these pages. How I wish I had more, and could tell you what a merry time I had yesterday, how I ran, the moment I was free, to find my 'Nephews', and how we wandered in the Wood, and how I did the Arithmetic Homework; and what a Bath I had. (For there is no bath-room in Balgores, and no time to go over into the Camp!) So I asked for a Hot Bath, and had it! My younger nephew—of 10 years—comes to pay me visits during the day, but I am always out!

I have not seen Ray, because on Saturdays I am no longer free, and even on Sunday Mornings we do the same old, insupportable drill. This last week has been enough to send crazy any thinking being—eternal inspections, parades, inspections, punishment parades, & more inspections. Every morning we alternately (1) stand and freeze, and (2) hustle around till we are blown as race horses. Meanwhile, the Colonel himself, cursing us from the top of a Golf Mound, drills us, foaming at the mouth. Sometimes he follows at our heels, barking like a collie after straggling sheep. After this, we are at the mercy of a Coldstream Guard Sergeant, who abuses us in bad English and worse Language. I know—at last—what all this Rumpus means. Somebody very great—probably Lord French[1]—is coming down this week to overhaul us!

We had a first Exam. this evening.

There is still room for anxiety both about Mary and You. Perhaps it is as well I am so occupied, for I could easily grieve myself ill about You, if left alone to do it. I do hope Father won't get a bad cold.

What about Colin? And Harold?

Leslie is at Chelsea.

Unbounded love, Your Wilfred x x x

---

[1] Field-Marshal Lord French (1852–1925), 1st Earl of Ypres, C-in-C British Expeditionary Force August 1914–December 1915, was now C-in-C Home Forces.

425. To Susan Owen

Saturday 18 March [*1916*]   *Y.M.C.A.* [*Romford*]

My most darling Mother,
    The Day of St. Patrick and of Saint Mother is passed and you had
no note or any word from me. The thing is abominable. Excuse? Not
the right word! Cause and Reason enough! You know our 'Evenings'
consist of 1½ hour. On the 16th, I am obliged to rush into Romford for
Running Clothes for a Run announced for the 17th. Next evening a
Compulsory Lantern Lecture until after 10, so that on that day we had
not so much as 3 mins. off duty, though in our Room we got up at
quarter past five. We are not forced to get up till 6, for Physical Drill
at 6.30, but we are punished so severely for impeachable dress that we
rise in our sleep almost and begin to do our scraping, cleaning, washing,
shaving, polishing, scrubbing, rubbing, brushing, oiling, sandpapering,
folding, tying, tidying, cleaning up & clearing down, cleansing, ablutions, bucklings, foldings, etc. &c. Etc, and caetera. So we toil and moil.
    Your Note arriving on the 17th gave me the comfort and renewing
of a sacrament. Thereby I had communion with those things which are
now passed behind a cloud out of sight, but which shall come to us in
like manner again. Now is the winter of the world. But my life has come
already to its month of March . . .
    Yes, I take and read these your words with thanksgiving.
    Thanks, also, and more than thanks, I owe you for the Present of
Moneys.
    Previous sums having been necessities absolute for the physical fact
of living in the Artists, I take them from the letter with a wince, loving
not to handle them.
    But a Present I can look at without fear and without reproach.
    It was my Week-end, and Leave was announced for all Balgores. I
promised my sore bones rest from drilling, and my sore chin rest from
shaving, and my sore spirit from chafing. In my Poet's Room I might
have lain me. There would I have lighted an incense of ten cigarettes,
your own burnt offering. There would I—Thunder and the bolts of
heaven confound their knavish tricks, Authorities have cancelled all
Leave! Some say it is a General Order for the Eastern Command, in
event of a naval Raid on the coast. I had arranged to meet Leslie, too!
I have quite 'won' the Housekeeper of Monro's, for with my Washing
she sent a box full of Soup Tablets, biscuits, buns, not forgetting the salt,
so that I make myself suppers! I know how to value acts of this sort,
though the soup is useless to me now; and I mean, one day, to promulgate my feelings in no uncertain tones, so terrible that the uttermost
confines of the wirral[1] shall be shaken.
    I look forward to meeting Harold again either here or in Town. Leave
is cancelled 'until further notice'.

---

[1] The Cheshire peninsula on which Birkenhead stands.

The winter is steadily drawing off; but no large trees have yet ventured to show the green flag of safety.

The Almond-trees which recall Wimbledon, are in the pink of perfection among the quaint houses of the garden city.

I am hoping that this sudden great warmth will play the angel of healing to your chest and throat.

I am quite all right, tho' a man had Influenza in our room. All those who go on sick leave are 'washed out' of the School. We are learning far more in a week here than a month of camp. The only nuisance is the Sergeant Major, Coldstream Guard, a consummate bully, amusing enough in *Punch*, but not viewed from the ranks.

The Army as a life is a curious anomaly; here we are prepared—or preparing—to lay down our lives for another, the highest moral act possible, according to the Highest Judge, and nothing of this is apparent between the jostle of discipline and jest. Again, we turn from the meanest of jobs scrubbing floors, to do delicate mapping, and while staying in for being naughty, we study the abstractions of Military Law.

On the whole, I am fortunate to be where I am, and happy sometimes, as when I think it is a life pleasing to you & Father and the Fatherland.

All the love of the whole heart of your

Wilfred

426. To Susan Owen

Saturday Aft., 2 April [1916]   *Y.M.C.A.* [*Romford*]

My own dear Mother,

You have indeed written long & frequent letters, and I am not worthy to receive them. I was agitated when you mentioned visiting new Houses, but your next letter says you have not given notice. What manner of houses are these which you have seen?

It is very disappointing to know that Colin is not even trying for the Exam. I get on well enough in our Exams. having high and very high marks in Musketry, Reconnaissance, and Drill—full marks for Drill—But in Military Law I came pretty low!

I am sending you a sketch done by Muff-Ford[1] in the Canteen the other day, struck off in 10 mins. while we had our coffee. I think the resemblance to Father in youth is traced with something like divination. I find my nose growing alarmingly amorphous with my advancing years. Anyhow it is not exactly a weak face: and that is all I am concerned to know. (Note I wear my hair ½ in. long now.)

Muff-Ford has studied Art in many branches at the Polytechnic for 3 years. He is of German birth, and has altered his name. I like him well. As you see he has a clever eye and a cunning hand, but he is by far the slowest-mover at drill in all the Platoon. And he is punctiliously unpunctual.

---

[1] Lieutenant J. W. D. Muff-Ford.

Last night I saw the Zeppelin! <u>Lights out</u> was ordered while we were undressing. Then soon after, our room being over the Guard Room, we heard the sentry cry 'There she is! Guard—turn out!' It was larger than I thought they appeared, and just then was heading straight for us! Half a dozen Searchlights concentrated on it, & kept it lighted up, tho' it was moving fast. Suddenly a furious cannonade set up from below, and the shells burst in scores around it, but none seemed to touch the Gasbag. Some burst about 3 miles behind!! The beast looked frightened somehow; nosed about as if lost, turned eastward, inclined steeply upward, and vanished behind a 'cloud'. Now, the sky seemed cloudless & all stars of ordinary size were clear. I <u>quite think the vapour was of its own producing</u>. Anyhow the searchlights lost it, the firing ceased, and it was all over. I can't say I saw any bombs fall tho' we thought we heard the peculiar noise of them. We 'turned out' on the Parade Ground, but were sent back to bed by the Major. About midnight I heard four more gun-shots, but nothing was to be seen. London was not touched by bombs but our brute got very near. In fact <u>we actually saw its turning-back</u>. Altogether a highly entertaining 15 minutes.

Bugles are now sounded at the proper times. We have also our Drum & Fife Band as well as the Regimental. A thrilling affair. The sound, together with the gallant bearing of the twenty fifers, has finally dazzled me with Military Glory.

The fifers are worthy to rank with the demented violins that make Queen's Hall to spin round as a top, and with the Cathedral Choir that pierces thro' the heights of heaven. Sweetly sing the fifes as it were great charmed birds in Arabian forests. And the drums pulse fearfully-voluptuously, as great hearts in death.[1]

I have hopes that you are now as well as when I was Home. Is it even so? Is Harold better than when in London? In truth, I am perfectly well, tho' during last week the cold clawed up my throat effectively, every night & morning!

Everlasting Love from your own Wilfred
No individual importance to be given to Hieroglyphics in last Letter! Shall spend week-end on Notes.

427. To Susan Owen
Postcard
Wed. [*Postmark 6 April 1916*]   *Y.M.C.A.* [*Postmark Romford*]

Just 5 lines to say that I can't write 50 yet! We had 'Night Ops.' yesterday till 9.30! Today a terrible being from the W.O. came down upon us. I was not one of the unfortunates picked out by him to drill, etc. He has quite upset our nerves, for he was quite nasty to one of our Lieutenants. Very many thanks for your loving letter. No more Zepps.

---

[1] This paragraph seems to foreshadow images in 'Anthem for Doomed Youth' and 'Greater Love'.

have been seen here. On Sunday I resolved, not to go to Harpers', but to work all day. But they came for me, & fetched me out.

Your own W.E.O.

428. To Colin Owen

Sunday Night [*Early April 1916*]   *Romford*

My dear Colin,

[*six lines missing*] last I wrote: but I may mention that neither on Sat. did I go to Williams', nor today to Harper's because I had such a Mass of Notes to write up. We were made to dig trenches on Sunday Morning . . .!!✝✝§?? !!!

When a barrel is full of nuts there is yet room to pour much oil therein, say the Arabians. It is only by combining systematic physical [*six lines missing*]

I hear you are applying yourself to some solid study for the J. Oxford.[1] I am bucked to hear it. I am sure that 3 months of this kind of work will get you through.

Let it be a time of worry—only don't worry yourself but your subjects.

It is the only way, not only for average brains like you & me, but for the best of them.

Now approach the days when the evening light draws out seductively: tempting all such as have movable hearts and movable bodies to stray forth and behold clouds, games, lamps, stars, riversides, swallows, and the daughters of men.

But the Student longeth after none of these things.

I have discovered two young men of letters in this House.

1. King, who seems well versed & well-connected, in modern literature. For instance his sister knows Bernard Shaw, and Yeats.
2. Denny who is an old Reading student, still under the wing of Prof. Morley!

Do write me a rough note with plenty of wild talk about your intentions, and some accurate information upon dear Mother & dear Mary.

Be full of thanks nightly for a Fire, a Chamber, and a Bed, not to mention a loving Father Mother & Sister about you.

Not to mention 2 Brothers.

The Lord loveth not the speed of an horse, nor delighteth He in any man's legs.   *Prov.* Ch. — V. —

Your devoted Brother Wilfred

429. To Susan Owen

Sunday [*10 April 1916*]   *Romford*

Dearest Mother,

I am reduced, by lack of both time and experience, to saying simply

---

[1] The Oxford Junior Examination.

that I am very well, and that my thoughts turn to you-ward some three or four times a day with lovingness.

I am desolated that you will not have so much as this news (? ?) before Monday Night. We had Night Operations again. I was isolated scouting—felt like scooting.

That war office Major (who snubbed our officer) was really 'very pleased with what he saw here'—Semi-official.

We had a Church Parade open air this morning. This afternoon I got up a few notes—and at last got off a decent reply to the enclosed—note date!

Visiting I eschewed.

The afternoon was again sunny. There is a long greenhouse in the Garden, where I peacefully spent 10 minutes of the sabbath afternoon swotting the details for the Assault with Fixed Bayonets. But I was turned out of the greenhouse.

One or two have been 'washed out' of the School already, but I survive yet. These wash-outs are sent to the 60th Division in France: where in fact they will be safer than with Platoons to command.

Our Course may last 3 weeks more.

Many and true thanks for asking about my funds. I really am trying to last out this week: but may have to ask for 10 bob in the course of it. I don't as yet.

I don't care for any of the fellows in my room, and shall be glad to remove even to 'Somewhere'.

Unless Colin writes I shall be a sorry brother.

You cannot imagine how the regularity of your letters supports and tranquillizes me.

God shield us all; and bring Harold home from the Sea, and Colin from Horseflesh.

Your most-cherishing Wilfred

430. To Susan Owen

Wed. [*14 April 1916*]   *Y.M.C.A.* [*Romford*]

Dearest Mother,

I have a few minutes. They shall be Yours.

Yesterday we had an Oral Exam. in the form of an Interview with a no. of Officers. Apparently I made a satisfactory impression. I answered successfully the 3 Questions put to me. We also had another Written Exam. in which I have done pretty well, being above the average, and top of my Room. I can never beat a young blood of 17, but as he is going into the Scots Guards, and the Army is his family profession I am not annoyed. I have frequent tiffs with this Johnny, and call him the Scarlet Cockatoo, and the Crimson Toucan variously.

I was suddenly struck the other day to realize that my Section, thrown together by pure chance, contains some desirable fellows. First Muff-

Ford, Artist: then a Journalist & Reporter, then an Actor, now well established, tho' quite young, and taking no end of money. He has promised me a job after the War, at £5. to £6. a week! He is a gentleman, and loves his profession. I wonder?'

Then Briggs,[2] of the 5th Manchester, chemical student at Leeds. He is quite my closest chum: a boy of admirable industry in work, inquiring mind, a hater of swank, malice, and all uncharitableness, and very Provincial.

This spark King, poetical aspirant, Public School Exhibitioner in Classics, sportsman, gamester, wag, has something of a 'Set' about him. I am partly of them, but my variable moods, and relapses into solemnity, won't do for them.

There are rumours of Week-end Leave.

I am anxious to know Harold's movements. Are you going to take Mary to Manchester? Now, have you quite got over the Chest Troubles, and is the weakness nearly gone? Nothing could possibly have put me into so fit a state as this Army Trade. You must be duly glad; Father should indeed crow. Is he quite well? Would Mary write?

All my love. Wilfred x

431. To Susan Owen

Sunday, 16 April 1916   *Romford*

My Dearest Mother,

Very many thanks for the Letter received on Friday, which duly— or unduly—enclosed 10s. This I have not yet cashed but during next week hope to do away with it at one blow, and more than that, because there is a promise of 4 days Leave to 50% of the School. Preference is given to married men, and such as live at a distance. I am almost certain to get it, starting on Wed., Thurs. or Frid. next. Shall I come home? The time is wretchedly short. Yet the 'Week's Interim' for getting Outfit may be no longer than 4 or 5 days, and would be better spent near the Tailor's after all. I think I may, shall, and must come home for Easter.

There is no change in our position, and no foreknowledge of events when we 'leave School'. Still there is every reason to think that the Gazette will follow immediately after it.

Depend upon it I shall bestir myself to obtain this Leave, and heavily exaggerate the distance from here to Shrewsbury. Ah! The long time it seems since I saw you I cannot exaggerate. We said 'Till Easter' and till Easter it shall be; though I lie knavishly to the Orderly Room, and under the seat of a carriage all the way.

The early days of the week are to be spent on grand manoeuvres, and

---

[1] Later, at Craiglockhart Military Hospital, Wilfred interested himself in theatricals. See Letter 538, note 3.

[2] Lieutenant H. B. Briggs, Manchester Regiment, was wounded on 17 September 1918.

we shall not return till quite late. This may upset my Postings, but in any case I shall not be sure of getting away till my Pass is snug in my pocket, and, cheek by jowl with it, my Ticket.

Let me find you in rising Healths and Spirits, as you shall me, I promise you; for the War has but grazed us yet: and the slight wound which Soldiering has inflicted on my susceptibilities is being repaired into a Pearl, a very goodly pearl, as befits

your solitary old Oyster

432. To Susan Owen
Postcard

[Postmark 19 April 1916]   *Y.M.C.A.* *[Postmark Romford]*

Expect me not before Friday Morning.
Leave is granted till Monday night.   W.E.O.

433. To Susan Owen

Sunday Evening [*8 May 1916*]   *Canteen—Romford*

My own dear Mother,

I safely received, first the Letter containing 10/– then the Parcel with Key, Frankincense of Araby and the Mexic Nutriment. Hearty & true thanks for all.

We had our Final Exam. on Friday, and I am sending the Papers together with the Syllabus, which Father will be interested to read— and which Colin may be, may not. I am confident enough of a Pass: and although the Time was too short (2 hrs) for so very extensive questions, I 'got in' something for every one of the 10 Questions, which is more than certain men did.

When you have seen them, please drop the Papers in my Desk or thereabouts.

I didn't know the Seatons were moving, emigrating, Simple-Life-Campaigning, absconding, or whatever is it?

Very distressing about the Lawrences.[1]

What of new about Childe Colin? I fear the needle of his Ambition, having no Pole, must be sought in a Haystack.

We have to go back to Camp on Monday! There are a number of Tents now standing: perhaps for us! I have not been to Hornchurch this Afternoon, but finding a well-furnished Room over a Tea Shop here vacant (of all but sleeping Artists), there remained; and, on the strength of Coffee, read, the whole afternoon. Yesterday aft. Briggs took me to the Romford Baths. There I proved two things: first that there is no ill effect of cold water within 20 minutes of a big meal;

---

[1] Shrewsbury friends. The father had a stroke about this time; the son, Keith, was delicate and in declining health.

second that one touch of Nature's garb makes the whole world kin:—
Since, the Entrance being twopence, the place was beswarmed with
swart pestiferous brats: at the same time there were two Guards
Officers (potential) and one gilt youth with £2000 a year of his own:
from which I deduce that there are two things, and no more, which
cause distinctions to disappear from between men: they are Animal
Sports and Mortal Danger. And neither Religion, nor Love, nor
Charity, nor Community of Interests, nor Socialism, nor Conviviality
can do it at all.

Knowing well how well you are remembering me tonight, I say
Goodnight, with all my love, and many prayers.

Your Wilfred x

434. To Susan Owen
Postcard

[Postmark 11 May 1916][1]   *Y.M.C.A. [Postmark Romford]*

How welcome and consoling was your Letter which I found at Balgores
by calling there tonight on the way from the station. I have only 5 mins
now. but had I an hour I must have waited till my memories of these two
days dwindled: Academy yesterday! *Hamlet*[2] today!! And every minute,
the luxury of breathing LONDON. I am glad at heart for Childe
Colin. How could you imagine I should fail to write to Him? Neither
shall I fail to make a letter for you Tomorrow.

W.E.O.

435. To Susan Owen
Picture postcard of Venice

Thursday [Postmark 19 May 1916]   *[Postmark Romford]*

Had 2 extractions without Gas at Dental Hospital: painful, but the
worst trouble has supervened yesterday night & today. Was Grub
Orderly yesterday, & have been toiling in Trenches through the heat
of today. There is likelihood of L.P.G. (Leave pending Gazette) beginning as from Tomorrow!!! Dearest thanks for your Letter.

W.E.O.

436. To Susan Owen
Postcard

[Postmark 19 May 1916]   *The Croft Emerson Park, Hornchurch,*
Essex[3]

The old School were sent off with Leave pending Gazette this morning.
I came up here to say goodbye, and am staying the night! I have a

---

[1] The MS of 'To—' (*Poems*, p. 137) is dated London, May 10, 1916.
[2] Sir John Martin-Harvey (1863–1944), actor-manager, presented his production of *Hamlet* at His Majesty's Theatre on 8 May 1916.
[3] Home of the Harper family.

dental appointment on Monday mng. & in any case can't leave town till you send Rly. Fare. Can you advance 15s. to 21 Devonshire St. W.C. c/o Mr. Middleton.[1]

We shall be allowed 3s. per day. Isn't the thing delicious! I had better bring my trunk. I expect to arrive on Monday Evening. And when depart???

Your own W.E.O.

437. To Susan Owen
Postcard

7 June [*1916*]   [*Postmark Finsbury Park*]

Although they got my Postcard on Tues. morning, Pope & B.[2] can't get my suit ready till Friday, & this will keep the men working all night! I have got my things together now, but had some difficulty at Cox's,[3] since I am not gazetted (unless it appeared today.) Met several fellows in same predicament.

Your W.E.O.

438. To Tom Owen

Monday 10 p.m. [*18 June 1916*]   *Manchester Regiment*
5th Battalion[4]

My dear Father,

I got everything done in London in good time. I even got the strap changed at Gamages.

Got a car from Milford to the Camp 2 or 3 miles off: a vast affair on the top of a hill with Pines interspersed among the Huts. The Officers' Huts form a big settlement apart. I was introduced by Briggs to the Adjutant, who shook hands and left me to my own devices.

Supper was an informal meal today. I was helped to an enormous portion of pies and things. The Band meanwhile played outside. I need Camp Tackle, but have been provided for tonight.

I know nothing of the officers, other than our Set of 'Artists', and nothing of my duties. The men seem a fairly superior crowd.

The site is delightful for a Camp; but we are all confined in it.

My fellow-traveller the Sculptor saw me in the Train at Wolverhampton and moved to my Compartment for the rest of the journey.

I shall have more time and more impressions in a few days. Tonight I feel as if I had left Home about 7 days ago!

Fondest love to all,   Your W.E.O.

---

[1] Wilfred kept a furnished room here (at *5s. 6d.* a week) for some months: probably until he went to France in December 1917. See Letter 388.

[2] Pope and Bradley, military tailors, of Bond Street, W.1 (now of 35 Dover Street).

[3] Cox and Kings, military bankers.

[4] The battalion was stationed at Milford Camp, near Witley, five miles SW of Guildford, Surrey.

439. To Susan Owen

Saturday [*19 June 1916*]   *Manchester Regiment*
                                               5th Battalion
                                               My Room

My own dear Mother,

I quite hope for your letter tomorrow morning. I am an exile here, suddenly cut off both from the present day world, and from my own past life. I feel more in a strange land than when arriving at Bordeaux! It is due to the complete newness of the country, the people, my dress, my duties, the dialect, the air, food, everything.

I am marooned on a Crag of Superiority in an ocean of Soldiers.

I have had chiefly General Duties so far, such as Supernumerary Officer to the Battalion, Company Orderly Officer (today) etc.

The generality of men are hard-handed, hard-headed miners, dogged, loutish, ugly. (But I would trust them to advance under fire and to hold their trench;) blond, coarse, ungainly, strong, 'unfatigueable', unlovely, Lancashire soldiers, Saxons to the bone.

But I don't know the individuals of my platoon.

Some are overseas men who have seen fighting.

Had to assist inspection of kit, this morning.

I see a toothbrush and a box of polish missing. I demand in a terrible voice 'Where's your TOOTH-BRUSH?' and learn that the fellow has just returned from 'overseas'! 'Somewhere in France' is never heard here. All our draughts go to Egypt; thence to Mesopotamia. I am glad.

One of our officers at Mess has been wounded.

There is none of that Levity amongst us which prevailed in the Artists'.

The Sub. has a stiffish day's work: has to do the 'Third' Physical Training (i.e. most strenuous) at 6.15, carries pack on parade & march, and has a good deal of responsibility, writing, and ceremonial to fetter him. I had the misfortune to walk down the road to some Camp Shops when the men were 'at large': and had to take millions of salutes.

I have nearly got together my Camp effects, Bed, chair, wash-stand, etc. all necessary here.

Shall be glad of socks as soon as you can send them. Would you include my enamel mug, left on my dressing table.

My servant has nothing else to do but serve, so that is satisfactory.

If I am not pleased, say with my bed, I send him to change it at the shops. He is indispensable for taking my messages & reports to the Orderly Room.

Frankly, I don't like the C.O.[1] nor does anybody, except one major, his sole friend. But never fear, we shan't 'go out' under him.

I like my Company Commander, a Lieut., and nearly all the rest.

The doctor cured my deafness, by syringing, yesterday.

Five of us, how chosen I don't know, took the Army Exam. to

---

[1] Lieut-Colonel W. H. Ridge. See Plate IX.

qualify for Service, yesterday. There is more on Monday. Briggs did not take it.

I am staying in this week-end, in my new chair, having no pocket money whatever.

Cox's were 6 weeks in opening their account with the fellows in my room!

My most irksome duty is acting Taskmaster while the tired fellows dig: the most pleasant is marching home over the wild country at the head of my platoon, with a flourish of trumpets, and an everlasting roll of drums.

Your own boy Wilfred x

How I miss the delightful time you gave me at home is not for me to think of now.

440. To Susan Owen

Sunday Evening [*20 June 1916*]   *Manchester Regiment*
                                                     5th Battalion
Dearest Mother,

Your Thursday Parcel arrived only this morning. Many loving thanks for the Chocs. But you really mustn't send any more. I fare sumptuously every day.

This afternoon I borrowed a (very groggy) bicycle and rode through Godalming to Guildford, in perfect weather. I accomplished being alone, and conversed with no creature all the five hours. Guildford is an old town of great charm, with suggestions of Shrewsbury. I had tea in an old casement overlooking the High Street: a real old lattice Bay, no shams: I remained there an hour longer so pleasant was the place.

One of the dear old Houses took fire yesterday, and the ruins were still smoking.

I thought of you at tea in the Garden, scarcely able to believe I was with you seven days ago.

Alas! I feel, as well as appear, a different being, here & in uniform, from the lounger on divans, the reader of verse, the runner of dogs on racecourses, the midday riser . . .

Guildford seems to exist in another age than Buildwas[1] & Much Wenlock.

It is a rather peculiar type of country, neither mountain nor plain. There were some lovely bits of road, field, cottage, and street. As I was coming back the footpaths undulated with saluting arms.

I am Orderly Officer tomorrow, and intend to make a rumpus about untidy huts. 'My' Sergeant-Major is a young fellow, of capacity. He marches at my side, & very priceless he is.

I am perfectly well, not a bit worried or overworked: though I trod on knife-edges at the first.

Your very own W.E.O.

I don't yet want Pyjamas, but shall I think. There are rumours of moving Camp to Formby Lancs!

[1] Buildwas Abbey, Shropshire, whose ruins Wilfred had visited on leave.

441. To Colin Owen

19 June 1916   *Manchester Regiment, 5th Battalion, Ante Room*

My dear Colin,

Perhaps Mother has told you as much as I have told her of my Camp and my Work, how huge it is (the Camp), how my men are rather rough Lancashire Lads, some of them from overseas, how I like my brother-officers, but not the C.O.—and so on.

I have had an exam. today: a written one yesterday, and an oral one held in the open air this morning. I don't greatly care if I fail: it means I stay in England longer. If I pass I shall quite likely be moving to Egypt soon.

I had permission to leave Camp on Sunday afternoon and cycled to Guildford by myself, and had a pleasant jaunt in solitariness.

I share a room with 3 others. I have bought a fine Bed, Chair, & Washstand all of which fold up into bags.

We have to get up at 5.45. for strenuous physical drill. Our Sergeant-Major gives it us. But he is none the less deferential on and off parade.

I gave 'Eyes Front' when I meant 'Eyes Left' in passing a guard this afternoon!! The Sergeant Major never even smiled. Nor did I! As soon as we got back I gave the Company a Lecture on Marches.

Generally our duties end about 4.30 p.m. but we can't leave Camp without C.O's permission.

The Mess at 8 o'clock is a fairly dignified performance. We get food 'à la Grand Hotel' always.

I have a servant who has no other duties but to serve.

I scrawl this to encourage you to scrawl me something.
Goodbye dear boy.   W.E.O.

How is Tony[1] getting on.

442. To Susan Owen

Sunday [3 July 1916]   *Manchester Regiment, 5th Battalion*

Dearest of Mothers,

I could have gone to London from Sat. Evening to Monday Morning, but having nothing in particular to go for, didn't. I made my usual sally into Guildford, however, and had a happy enough ramble around Thorpe's Bookshelves,[2] and the Town and the little River, where there are Punts and Canoes. It is hardly wide enough for sculls.

I think I told you about my Course at Aldershot, beginning on the 11th. It may be postponed, for another course which a party of officers & men have to go to somewhere else. I have had both parcels. No hurry about the Music. I shan't be able to play till next Sunday now! (I may get a long week-end, starting next Friday.)

I am sending the Cheque to what's-is-name, in Coventry.

[1] Colin's new dog.   [2] T. Thorpe, Bookseller, still in Guildford High Street.

I am glad you are able to realize my signature in Shrewsbury. I shall try to send one weekly.

I have now enough Socks till Winter thanks! They fit very parfitly. [*Six lines omitted*]

(The way they have in the Army is not My way, saith the Lord of Hosts.)

I am 'commanding' numbers of wounded men, now restored. It gives me a great deal of pain to speak severely to them, as now and again need is.

I am beginning to pick out the Intelligent, and the Smart 'laads' from amongst the uncouth and ungainly. But I have no individual dealings. My Servant is a Grandfather, with medals of old wars, and sons fighting. I had the Leave Party to conduct to the Station the other day. Poor old man, my servant, had to fall out of the march! Waiting for the train I had more individual dealings, & was wondering whether it would be unwise to give my men some cigarettes, but deciding not to, when one of the 'Underage' came to me with an offering of apples!! Poor penniless school boy! But you must not think there was anything but ingenuousness. These Lancashires are extraordinarily open, honest, and incapable of strategy. I often have a Platoon completely to myself on the Moors.[1] Red-Hats gallop up to us at startling speed, or sometimes whizz up in Motors, but they never stay long, or criticise. We have been expecting the King to visit our trenches, and have worked overtime every day this week. Our anxiety begins again tomorrow! I give an extra ten minutes to shaving every morning in consequence. It is most annoying.

It seems to me many months since I left Shrewsbury. I am tempted to run up for a week-end, but don't really think of it next week. I was so happy to learn that your motor-smash[2] came to no harm, and the imagination of what might have taken place was so intolerable that I dismissed it from my mind effectively. I am now given to think that I shan't go out for several months.

Your very own Wilfred

443. To Susan Owen

[*7 July 1916*]   *2nd. Lieut. W. E. S. Owen attached to 25 Middlesex Regt., Talavera Barracks, Aldershot*

Dearest Mother,

I have just arrived. It is an old style Barracks, about as old as the Battle of T! And the regiment is a Regular. This with the mere name of Aldershot makes it quite like my old ideas of ARMY. It is the finishing touch in my transformation into a Soldier.

I share a room with a Lt. from Witley who travelled with me, but is not from the Manchesters.

I returned from London [*remainder missing*]

[1] The Surrey Downs.
[2] H O recalls nothing of this.

444. To Colin Owen

11 July 1916   *Aldershot*

My dearest Colin,

Just a page to show you where I am living, and that I am living, still. I am here for a Course of Musketry.

It is the first time I have set foot in an English Barracks! It is an old place, used by the Regulars in the old days. But we are not so comfortable or so well messed as in our Witley Huts.

Residentially, Aldershot is a hateful little place. As a soldier I am glad to be here.

I have bought a miniature rifle and some cartridges. It won't shoot sporting shot, but is very accurate with its lead bullet at close range. Is it any use to you?

I wish we could meet at Alpenrose or something.

Write always to Mother, and some time to me.

Among so many fellows that I must know and 'care for', I don't forget the only chap I really care for: the Shropshire Lad.

The man sharing my room now, a stranger, is a budding High Church Parson and the most insupportable bore I have ever been quartered with!

My What-yer-call 'ums to the Jones'.[1] (don't say that).

Your own Wilfred

445. To Susan Owen

Wed. [13 July 1916]   *Aldershot*

Dearest Mother,

Brief Note (wish my Musketry Notes were as brief) with

(1) My Love.

(2) Request that you will rout out my Musketry Note Book from the Cupboard of the Bookcase. It is a shiny black book with purple edges.

Include a letter to save your stamps and my disappointment.

I am anxious to be told 'truthly' that your rheumatism is once again gone from you.

We are having horrible cold wet times.

I was so annoyed with the High Church Divinity Student who shared my Room, not because of his Divinity, but by reason of his dogmatic, pig-headed, preachifying, self-sufficient manners and domineering tone, that I gave instructions to my servant this morning to move all my furniture into another Room, which I discovered in the Barracks.

I am now alone and in peace.

I could tell by the shape of the man's head that he was a dogged dogmatic dog.

A Parson is a Lamb in a drawing room, but a Lion in the Vestry, said

---

[1] Colin was spending the summer working for a farmer, Mr. Jones, of Oaken Gates, near Shrewsbury.

Keats.[1] In a Bedroom and arrayed as an Officer, he is an Ass in Lion's Clothing.

(The origin of our Quarrel was his insistence on singing Rag-Times, and my commanding him to shut his mouth.)

Always your Wilfred

446. To Susan Owen

19 July 1916   *Aldershot*

My own dear Mother,

I have been unfortunate in Letter writing (as you will readily admit.) On Tues. last I wrote to Colin, but it was returned, from Liverpool, as unknown in Shropshire. None the less the full address was on it, as may still be seen.

Then when I went to Reading I left two stamped letters on my Table, one to Mary, and found them still here on Monday Mng! I never could abide the sight of my own misfired letters. So I threw them at my servant.

I had as enjoyable [a] time at Alpenrose as you no doubt suspected. But many and loud were the pities that You couldn't be there. I may get Leave next Sat. week. Can you?

I went to Dunsden, and the Vicar was as horrifyingly dismal in Church as ever—and as merry at the Porch! 'The war will be over very soon' he proclaimed, just in the Pulpit manner. 'Bray has been called up. Couldn't do without him after all, you see.'

Meanwhile I perceive Vivian hovering behind the yew trees. He is at the Reading School now, where even Leslie could not go! He looks well with his gay hatband, and melancholy brown eyes; but his H's are a trifle uncertain still.

I have not seen Vera since last June! There is now more of her to be seen than ever. Uncle took 5 or 6 portraits of me, one very good, which he spoilt within 10 seconds of taking. Don't mention this!

I have more Exams. tomorrow & Sat. to play the Bogey with my Leisure. In the Divisional Exam. at Witley Camp I missed Distinction by 1 mark; tho' I took more than any from the 5th, but one, who is an old stager.

This 25th Middlesex is the Navvys' Battalion with John Ward, the labour M.P. for Colonel.[2] It is a most unsatisfactory, meagre Mess.

Owing to the filthy water in which I shave, I have developed septic places on my chin!

The best indication of my health, and probity, which I can give you is that I got 3 out of 10 shots on the Bull itself at our first and only Test.

Best of thanks for your infallible Letter, coming today.

---

[1] Keats to George and Georgiana Keats, 19 February 1819 (*Letters* II, p. 63).

[2] Lieut-Colonel John Ward (1866–1934), Independent MP for Stoke-on-Trent 1906–29, raised five battalions of the Middlesex Regiment and commanded the 25th. He founded the Navvies' Union in 1889.

Haven't the dimmest idea whose Wedding you went to the other day.
I'll be off to London this week-end; but as the Course ends on the
28, may not get free on the following Sat. (as I said).
Will Colin be 16 or 17??[1]
What lacks he?

Have you any initial-tapes W.O. for me?

Dearest Love to all, Your W.E.O.

447. To Susan Owen

[? 23 July 1916]   Manchester Regiment, 5th Battalion

My dearest Mother,

Monday evening, so this should get to you by Wed. I had a shock
on arriving. Three of 'the Artists' are now in France!!! But Briggs is
left in Aldershot, and my happening to be there was the reason, I
suppose, that I was not sent. I think it is necessary to tell you this, in
case you should be too surprised if I went next week. Mind, I haven't
the slightest intimation, but this disappearance of Foster,[2] Jubb[3] and
Crampton[4] is a warning.

At present I parade as Company Commander of B Company, a
Captain's job! I am also in tonight's orders as Fire Officer of the
Battalion. Fortunately two fires which raged in the scrub last night
were just too soon to bother me. I am also detailed for some Lectures
on Gas, in which certain officers are initiated into many secrets. I <u>may</u>,
thus, become Gas Officer.

I can't promise anything about next week-end.

In the train from Aldershot, (I did <u>not</u> taxi) I met W . . .[5] the man
from my Room who has just married. His wife insisted that I should
go to supper with them in their cottage, near the Camp. The mad thing
doted over me all evening. I shall never go there again. Poor W . . .!

I might have taken a later train from Reading, for no one looked
for me till Sunday Morning, when I led my Company to Church
Parade [remainder missing]

448. To Susan Owen

Wednesday [late July 1916]   [Manchester Regiment, 5th Battalion]

Dearest Mother,

I am most frightfully hard-worked. It is one of the worst weeks I
ever had in the army. <u>Work</u> begins at 6.30. and never finishes all day.

[1] 16.
[2] Lieutenant W. A. Foster, Manchester Regiment.
[3] Lieutenant Norris Jubb, Manchester Regiment.
[4] Second-Lieutenant Hubert Crampton, M.C., Manchester Regiment.
[5] We have omitted the name.

I am deaf with the 7 hours continual shooting, and stomach-achy with the fasting from food.

Even Colin would not change work with me, if he knew.

My gray hairs are valuable now, when I have to reprimand a whole unit, including N.C.O's at my Orderly Room.

Shall be glad to have the Bike: tho' so far have not had half-an-hour for going out.

I have granted one of my men 4½ days leave, but myself I cannot award.

Yours as ever Wilfred

Many, many thanks for the most welcome letter today.

449. To Susan Owen

[*Early August 1916*]   *Manchester Regiment, 5th Battalion*

Dearest Mother,

Most desperating! No help! Must go and fire a Course near Aldershot! There are a number of men, N.C.O's and two Officers, of whom I am the Senior. We have to march there, a performance which I grow weak to think of. But it will be some solace to know that the Halts and Halting Places are of my own sweet choice.

166 men are going on Draft tomorrow, but the two conducting officers are coming back. There will be scarcely any men left to us!

I am now as well up in Gas Warfare as can be. It is some satisfaction to feel knowing in these matters, because I am sure it will be used more and more.

Gregg[1] and I have devised a slight improvement in the P.H. Helmet,[2] but it is not worth noising abroad since the Helmet is really out of date now, displaced by—But, here I am beginning to 'Leak information', (when I have to read daily a solemn W.O. Letter, saying that no talk of the War is ever to be indulged in, even in private letters and so on!)

I had command of a Party firing on the Range with Gas Helmets on. One old blitherer let his bullet off by accident, but as it hit no one, I was not interested to follow its course.

We had a Concert for the men yesterday, and the gay ladies could not be got out of our Mess Room till 12.30 a.m! And we set out on our march every morning at 7.

We had a fearful field-day yesterday, too. Luckily we 'attacked' a Lake, where there was bathing afterwards.

I found a sandy cove for myself, inhabited only by a solitary, mysterious

---

[1] Second-Lieutenant R. A. Gregg, Manchester Regiment, whose death in action Wilfred reports in Letter 667. See Plate IX, front row, extreme left.

[2] Anti-gas helmet, taking its initials from the Phosgene and Hexamine with which it was impregnated. When goggles were later incorporated, it was known as the PHG helmet.

kind of boy. It turned out he was Portuguese, a noble, whose father is in the suite of the exiled King.[1]

There was something in our Orders about a bicycle stolen from a P.O. I did not heed it, but perhaps it was Leslie's!

I search your envelopes in vain for $\boxed{\text{W.O.}}$ s![2]

I have long ceased to look for Colin's letter, tho' certain smudges on the envelope aroused my suspicions of his handwriting.

Do be careful to 'avoid unnecessary movement' as the military phrase goes.

The adjutant encourages me to believe in Long Leave next Fortnight.

I don't know my address, but it won't be Talavera.

Your lovingest Wilfred

450. To Susan Owen

Sat. Eveng. [*Early August 1916*]   *Manchester Regiment, 5th Battalion*

Dearest my Mother,

I am sitting on my bed, which has just been rigged up. It was cruel to see it pulled to pieces at 4 a.m. this morning; but it meant a cool march, at least.

There were a dozen other Regiments going as well as the 5th Manchesters, but by a lucky chance I got the head of the column, and marched beside the O.C. of the whole Body of Regiments.

The dust in the rear was something abominable.

I am in for a busy fortnight, being in command of the 5th Man. unit, 45 men, and two officers junior to me, already!

The afternoon I have been [here] has been spent in arranging the men's quarters. I had no time to see to my own bed, 'as it should be', and my nap on the floor of my hut was quite spoilt by Sergeants and Corporals and Telephone Calls. As well as ruling this little family I shall have to shoot myself, (I don't mean in desperation.)

It is perhaps better than turning Hay, tho'.

I had a quaint letter from my Colin, perfect in its way. It did not mention the Gloves.[3] I thought that most original. I must bring (?) him the Miniature Rifle, if he could use it.

I very badly want my Bike here. Would you send it to Aldershot Station: bearing the address also:

W.E.S.O. etc.

MYTCHETT MUSKETRY CAMP

ALDERSHOT.

Always your lovingest Boy   W.E.O.

---

[1] Manoel II (1889–1932), ex-King of Portugal, succeeded to the throne 1908, fled his country at the Revolution (1910), and took refuge in England, settling at Twickenham.
[2] The initial-tapes requested in Letter 446.
[3] Wilfred's birthday present to Colin.

451. To Colin Owen

12 August 1916   *3rd East Lancashire Division*
                        Mytchett Musketry Camp, Farnborough, Hants

Dearest my Colin,

I got my bicycle tonight. It came to my own door almost.

I am sorry if it is a deprivation to you, but I most needfully want it.

I slept out in the open last night, but was so pestered with Gnats and all the flies of Beelzebub that shall in future prefer the snores of my brother officers. (Brother is too good a word for 'em, though, dear boy.)

These snores indeed saw through my dreams, but the insects make me as it were a mangy dog, with a hot nose.—itching to the roots of my teeth.

I love not one of my subalterns. He is a pert, bad young thing. And has a face like a still-born spaniel preserved in vinegar. The other junior officer is a married man, most settled, a strong, silent man, and one who has travelled in the Far East at his will. But now he travels over the Parade Ground at mine.

Let me know if you got my last.   Your own W.E.O.

What fine news of Harold![1]

452. To Susan Owen

Sat. Night [*13 August 1916*]   *Mytchett Musketry Camp*

Dearest of Mothers,

Just had your Letter which came, as you designed, tonight. It came refreshingly, comparable to the cool rain that broke over this desert this evening.

I have just been to Aldershot for my bicycle only to find it was waiting up here, 200 yds. from Camp.

For having displeased the Brigade Musketry Officer, all officers were confined to Camp till 6 this evening. Chief cause of our Strafing: bad Marking behind the Butts. But I am not concerned with marking.

I am well punished, because I gave my men 2 hours extra drill this morning; not in punishment, but because they have been detailed for Guard tonight, and most have never fixed Bayonets in their life.

My own shooting, alas, is the least of my cares. But it is a bit of a worry, because, in duty bound, one strafes the men for bad shooting, and is never sure of not doing worse than the worst of them. They keep a relentless watch on my Target. I have so far got a Pass every day, but I only do well in Rapid! I can get off 5 rounds in 30 secs. scoring 3 bulls and 2 inners, 17 marks out of 20. If allowed more time I do less well. It is an interesting point of my psychological 'erraticness'.

There is no chance of next week-end. Excellent news of dear old W.H.O. No more now but this x.

                                                    W.E.O.

[1] The news that HO was to train as a pilot. See Letter 488.

453. To Susan Owen

Tuesday [*16 August 1916*]   [*Mytchett Musketry Camp*]

Dearest My Mother,

Just a scrap to thank for your letter just arrived tonight. I was so busy that I scrawled notes over the envelope before ever I opened it! This Napoleonic Work will stop on Sat. Meanwhile I have just scraped enough points to be a 1st Class Shot.

Most of the men are 2nd Class and more are 3rd.

But then 9 of them have defective eyesight.

We were caught in Monsoonal Rains this afternoon, and my poor troops were wet to the bone. (But I had my Trench Coat.) It was the first time I had seen these men really cheerful. British troops are beyond my understanding. On a bright warm day they are as dull and dogged as November.

There is a Rumour[1] that all the Manchesters move to Newhaven on the 28th.

Yours ever W.E.O. x

454. To Susan Owen

Monday Evening 9 p.m [*22 August 1916*]   [*Manchester Regiment,*
5th Battalion]

My own sweet Mother,

What an age since we were at supper yesterday!

At Tamworth there was an hour to wait on the miserable little Station, so I wandered into the old Town to try and look up my old friend Lord Marmion.[2] There was a low, glamorous Moon and to see any strange place by a vague moon, for an hour, is better than a week's stay there; and I was already tuned up to an emotion not pitched in keys of moon or castles. . . .

Sure enough I found Tamworth Castle, and was informed by the policeman that Lord Marmion had lorded it there. I was an event of much perplexity to the Bobby, and he shadowed my rubber heels all the way back to the station.

I was conscious during all this venture of a very peculiar odour following me and was so sure I had never smelled it before that I began to seek about for some local phenomena.

But it was only that Quinine uncorking itself in my pocket!

We were an hour late at Euston, so I was a bitter mixture of sleep, quinine, and panic.

There were no taxis.

---

[1] Without substance.
[2] They hailed him Lord of Fontenaye,
   Of Lutterward and Scrivelbaye,
     Of Tamworth tower and town.
        Sir Walter Scott, *Marmion*, Canto I, 157–9.

At last I held up a Growler and pushed on for Waterloo.

The dawn broke as I crossed the Bridge, and the Dome, and the East End showed so purply against the orange infinite EAST that in my worship there was no more care of trains, adjutants, or wars.

Thus I caught that train by 1½ mins. From Milford, I pushed on to the Camp by motor miraculously waiting at the station; and had plenty of time for a second breakfast and shave.

I was on Bomb Throwing with real live Mills Grenades.

I went to sleep in a safe spot when I had thrown my own; but the noise was too frightful to go on. After lunch I fell asleep; and remained so long after the rest had fallen in! But none noticed me! Arriving back in Camp I was called upon suddenly to lecture on Discipline. I was now feeling 'rotten'; but I thought obedience in this case would make a good opening verse for the Lecture; and so it did.

I am Orderly Officer tomorrow, which means work up to midnight.

Father please excuse. I had plenty to breakfast on in the train, and am sorry I panicked about the drinks.

As you may know, there was a General Mobilization on Sunday, and a longer leave would have been cut short in any case! Their Sunday was spoilt here: they were in perfect readiness to march off: officers snatched rifles for themselves, and packed their pockets with Rations. All for the N. Sea Bubble.[1]

No more now!   Your Wilfred

455. To Colin Owen

23 August 1916   *Manchester Regiment, 5th Battalion*

Dearest Colin,

I was frightfully disappointed to miss you: and I spent all the time scheming to get you over. Somehow my plans found no favour with Father or Mother.

There is none else can thwart me.

I noted all you said in your last letter and remember those words before the best things I have read.

There are changes happening daily, but I remain. Briggs went this morning to be attached to another Regiment; no choice of his.

One or two are trying for the R. Flying Corps. Shall I? I think so.

Of the last Draught that went out, men I had helped to train, some are already fallen. Your tender age is a thing to be valued and gloried in, more than many wounds.

Not only because it puts you among the Elders and the gods, high witnesses of the general slaughter, being one of those for whom every

---

[1] On Saturday, 9 August, the Grand Fleet, concentrated near 'Long Forties' with the Battle Cruiser Fleet thirty miles ahead, was attacked by U-Boats. Zeppelins were sighted, as well as the German High Seas Fleet. HMS *Nottingham* and HMS *Falmouth* were sunk by torpedoes.

soldier fights, if he knew it; your Youth is to be prized not because your blood will not be drained, but because it is blood; and Time dare not yet mix into it his abominable physic.

Only, all bright mettle rusts in the open air.

Don't rust rustically.

Love Nature more than the Country, and know that to be natural is not to be countrified.

False men grow in the country more commonly than in the Town, for they are often turnips in disguise.

Your farmering is not without its dangers.

For me, Germans, Turks, and mysterious spiritual devils, For Harold, Torpedoes and dark deeds in evil ports, For You, the hob-nobbing with cattle and carrots, and the deep sleep after over-labour.

Meanwhile, however, get the highest profit of happiness out of your present job.

Let your hands be gloved with the dust of earth, and your neck scarved with the brown scarf of sunshine.[1]

This is not poetry which I write, but the Sun is, and the earth may be. Write very soon.

Look to me for counsel in all affairs of thought and learning; but look to your early self for a prototype of sweetness and good living.

This is no sermon, but a substitute.

If you should straitway go and be baptised in your Bethel or Ebeneezer Place,[2] I would never wash my beard more.

Cheery-ho!

Your own, Wilfred

456. To Susan Owen

Sunday 27 August [*1916*]   *Manchester Regiment, 5th Battalion*

My dearest Mother,

Your letter came on Sat. Night. We do have a Sunday Post.

You need not be anxious about Final Leave coming yet.

The C.O. himself told me on Thursday that he was putting me down for the New Battalion, so that I am not being kicked out of the Manchesters, whatever happens. The C.O. appears to have found my work— or my person—not too offensive to him.

There is only one other of the Artist Batch now left, and he has not been told he is to remain on the New Staff. Briggs awoke one morning

---

[1] The earlier of two BM drafts of 'Disabled' gives a stanza, later cancelled, between the present stanzas two and three:

> Ah! He was handsome when he used to stand
> Each evening on the curb or by the quays.
> His old soft cap slung half-way down his ear;
> Proud of his neck, scarfed with a sunburn band,
> And of his curl, and all his reckless gear,
> Down to the gloves of sun-brown on his hand.   *Poems,* p. 68.

[2] Jones the farmer was a strict Baptist.

and found himself gone. He is attached to some Lancashire Regt. and 'goes out' in a month's time.

I was on the point of sending in an application for the R. Flying Corps, when, at tea, the C.O. spoke to me about being kept on.

I said 'I thank you, sir', being an Englishman.

But I still have a big idea of turning to Flight.

It is not quite a determination, or I might say it would certainly come about.

There are ways and means, and I will work them, if I decide to.

On Tuesday I am going up to London, on Dental Leave, in order to see a high official at the War Office. Nothing succeeds in Aerial Matters without some boldness. So I am starting well.

I have not sent in my application for Transfer, as, once I did so, I should commit myself to the C.O's eternal displeasure.

Now what do you think about it?

Flying is the only active profession I could ever continue with enthusiasm after the War.

Once a certified pilot, the pay is £350. The Training lasts three months.

By Hermes, I will fly. Though I have sat alone, twittering, like even as it were a sparrow upon the housetop, I will yet swoop over Wrekin with the strength of a thousand Eagles, and all you shall see me light upon the Racecourse, and marvelling behold the pinion of Hermes, who is called Mercury, upon my cap.

Then I will publish my ode on the Swift.[1]

If I fall, I shall fall mightily. I shall be with Perseus[2] and Icarus, whom I loved; and not with Fritz, whom I did not hate. To battle with the Super-Zeppelin, when he comes, this would be chivalry more than Arthur dreamed of.

Zeppelin, the giant dragon, the child-slayer, I would happily die in any adventure against him. . . .

But I am terrified of Fritz, the hideous, whom I do not hate.

Fondest wishes for a fine old Aberystwithian Holiday.

Your own Wilfred x

The 5th. won most points of all the Regiments; and so gains the Cup, in Saturday's Sports.

457. To Susan Owen

Friday [*Early September 1916*]   *Witley*

Dearest Mother,

I feel myself to be in a Passage when to think much about you in your merry days at the mouth of Ystwith would be more than I could cope with. I am harassed with events.

I went to London on Tues. saw the Authorities and had my name put

[1] HO has the only draft of this unfinished and unpublished early poem.
[2] A full-scale poem on Perseus was projected. See p. 551, note 1.

down with certain particulars. I was told by the Major that I had every chance, but the regular Transfer Papers (almost as exciting as those sold at 4 a penny) must go through my Division. My C.O's signature is necessary. The Adjutant said he would sign it on Thursday. At tea the C.O. severely refused, on the ground that I could not be spared from the Regiment. And indeed he had put me down on the Posted Staff, a favour shared by none of the Artists and only half of the old officers. I am on the Musketry Company, so my 'D' did it, and your earnest behests are now fulfilled. I am even as your 'Type', Fred Oliver.

On the strength of my good success at the R.F.C. H.Q. I had that old vicious tooth drawn by my kind dentist; saving half a guinea.

At tea today I was alone with the C.O. and succeeded in making him promise to sign my application for Transfer, and that without losing his favour!! He was frightfully decent about it. I was tickled at the idea that you & Father required time to consider: that it came as too great a surprise to be grasped. But the whole thing in modern public (I won't say Business) life is <u>instant</u> adaptation to the Fittest Environment. I have not gone about <u>this</u> affair without a great deal of strain of mind, & the more so that everything in the Battalion is upside down. The 6 & 7 Manch: are amalgamated with us today. You can't imagine what a panic it causes. But for one thing let us be proud. The old Fifth keeps its name, & is the nucleus of the whole new Battalion. Alas some of my men, whom I know, and who know me are sent to another Regt. to be drafted to France immediately. It is most disheartening. The Rumpus will soon settle down. Leave should then be more frequent.

G. Thomas sent me this tonight.[1]

Leslie is likely to get a Sedentary Flying Commission.

Goodbye, Darling Mother. Have a good time.

Your very own Wilfred x

458. To Susan Owen

Sunday [*12 September 1916*]   *Witley Camp*

Dearest of Mothers,

Best thanks for your two letters, and for sending on the Artists' Journal.

Meeting the Edjutant's sister is a curious chance. He was a great nut, you know. Tell me more about 'em, and get to know them better! I hear from Leslie that he is finally rejected. He will go back to Winchester, and wants me to go for a week-end. I shall get one sure enough next week; it is a month since the last, and I am independent of the Company Commander. I have only 'Muskets One' to consult. I am known as 'Muskets Two'.

---

[1] Probably the copy of *The Voice of Peace: Poems* by Gilbert Thomas, Chapman and Hall, London, 1914, that survives among Wilfred's books. It is inscribed 'W. E. S. Owen, with all good wishes from Gilbert Thomas'. It is not known how Wilfred knew him.

If Harold is at home I should come home. But if not may I not go to Winchester, seeing my life is cheap again, and last leave not imminent.

I am not particularly happy this Sunday: Merely the clouds, which hang like dirty lace curtains in Birkenhead windows.

I am not overworked!

If you have any cares for Colin's survival socially you will not allow him to be overworked by those meagre mangel-mongers. They shall not work his body as their team-horses, and if they cramp his immortal soul, I will go and drown them in their Baptistry.

I hope you will not go boating in wild weather. Noyes swam 3 miles to shore at Aberystwyth from a sunk boat. The remainder of the party drowned.[1]

I have no news from Harold, and no more of myself.

Dearest Love to all,

Your Wilfred

459. To Susan Owen

Wednesday [*15 September 1916*]   *Witley*

Dearest Mother,

News! The Battalion moves North next week:—the Advance Party on the 19th, the Main Body on the 20th. It is supposed that the place is near Conway N.Wales. What luck for us.

Harold came over yesterday afternoon in response to my telegram. He came out with me on my Afternoon Work, and we had a little supper in Guildford. He stayed the night in my Hut, where I am now writing at present. He looked many tints and pounds healthier & stronger than last Winter: and we had a jolly time.[2] If he were sure to be in London this week I would go to him on Friday, but expect Leslie and Winchester will have it! Why, from Conway I can come over on Sunday Afternoons!

I find that by today's orders I am detailed for a Sniper Course at Aldershot on the 19th. I shall probably have to go, and move North independently of all the Rumpus.

This will be quite decent and in order, especially if I travel via Shrewsbury!

I hope my last Note was forwarded from Wales.

I believe there lies in my Drawers a medium-thickness vest. Could you send it at once here?

Of course I tell you all I know as it leaks out. I only heard this bit of news quarter of an hour ago.

Your own Wilfred

Please include in Parcel Keats's *Letters*. (Vol. IV & V) (in Bookcase)

---

[1] Henry Noyes, brother of the poet. The yacht, *The Band of Hope*, foundered offshore in a storm.

[2] Their meeting is described in *JO* III, 151–8.

410

460. To Susan Owen

[*16 September 1916*]   *Manchester Regiment, 5th Battalion*
<u>OSWESTRY</u>!!!¹

This is a good war today: just heard that we go to the Oswestry Camp next week, Thursday I think, <u>for a while</u>. It has a reputation of being a wretched Camp, and all the <u>officers are</u> in a bad way about it. But I wink at the ceiling.

My Leave is cancelled of course. So is my Course at Aldershot. I shall be in the thick of the migration.

But I go on winking at the ceiling. Was just opening your letter when the name of Oswestry fell on my ears!

Your W.E.O. x

461. To Susan Owen
Postcard

Monday [*20 September 1916*]   [*Postmark Witley Camp*]

Just had your Letter. While reading it I heard the times of our trains announced 1, 2, & 4 <u>a.m.</u> on Friday mng. I should have loved you to come to Station, but <u>it is</u> not likely we should stop, even by day. I am not looking forward to the Friday. We are to be under Canvas which will probably not be pitched when we arrive. You must come over, staying at the Parrys'.² Thus I can see you every evening. Many thanks for the Right Clothes & Books etc. in the Parcel.

And Colin must come to Oswestry.   Your W.E.O.

462. To Susan Owen³
Picture postcard: Southport, Kings Gardens

[*Postmark 20 October 1916*⁴]   [*Postmark Southport*]

<u>My Address is 168a Lord St.</u>

Where I have a room to myself: The Mess is not yet instituted. I have to go out to meals. The same old Musketry carries on: but in a pleasanter place. I arrived here at about 3 p.m.

Nothing was said about my Halt at Shrews.   Yours ever W.E.

463. To Susan Owen
Postcard

Sat. [*Postmark 21 October 1916*]   *Park Stn. P.O.* [*Postmark Birkenhead*]

Am on my way to Meols, enjoying the usual 40 mins. at Birkenhead.

---

¹ His birthplace.
² Oswestry friends from the Plas Wilmot days.
³ Susan Owen pencilled on the card the name and address of an old Oswestry friend now living in Southport: Mrs. Avery, 143 Southbank Road, Southport. Wilfred duly called on them. See Letter 465.
⁴ 'Storm' (*Poems*, p. 105) is dated October 1916; and during this month he began 'Music' (*Poems*, p. 104).

Can't think how We ever survived the place. Southport is the most unsatisfactory sea-side place in Europe. But I have a cosy digs. I had your Letter all right. My landlady still refuses to provide food. But the good soul dried my gas-helmet bone dry, as it felt damp to her!!

W.E.O.

464. To Susan Owen
Postcard

Friday [*Postmark 27 October 1916*]   *Post Office by my Parade Grd.*
[*Postmark Southport*]

Am waiting for contingents to turn up. Best thanks for your Letter this morning & for that to Capt. Davies.[1] I shall certainly go & see Avery. No notice to move house yet.

Your W.E.O.

465. To Susan Owen

[*2 November 1916*]   *Queen's Hotel, Southport*

Dearest of Mothers,

Everyday I have kept putting off my letter for fear of giving you wrong news. But now I think it is quite sure that I can't get off this next Saturday. I am most likely going to Fleetwood in command of our next Firing Party, which should start on Sat. This means a fortnight's stay. It will be best to save up 8 weeks and get a Long Leave, early in December.

I had a really pleasant time with the Averys. They have a nice little house (which is saying a great deal) and a pianola, (which isn't saying much for them) I am very glad you recommended them to me!

I went last Sunday. Avery called for me on Sat. but I had started out to Preston to see the Famous Art Gall.[2] I arrived at closing time, but I got an Illus: Catalogue to keep me going till next Sat. or the following.

I shall have no end of work if I go to Fleetwood. Still I want to see as much of Eng. as poss.

I have got a largish room, with a quiet (wounded) officer, Ciceri[3] by name (half Italian.)

Most of them are wounded in our Mess now.

I am trying for a draft to Egypt, going shortly. Shouldn't mind the Flying School in Cairo, what?

Now I am much wondering about the Edjutant's reply.

But, still more, I wonder if your headaches are clearing?

Dearest Love, Your W.E.O. x

[1] Captain H. B. F. Davies, 7th Manchesters.
[2] The Art Gallery is in the Harris Library and Museum.
[3] Second-Lieutenant J. C. Ciceri, 5th Manchesters.

466. To Susan Owen

[Early November 1916]   *Queen's Hotel, Southport*

Dearest Mother,

I shall be going to Fleetwood, on Sunday at 10 o'clock as O.C. Firing Party. I am glad to see a bit more England. I am still trying to understand the English. We shall be in easy reach of Blackpool, but I don't expect to find much time for that.

Now I most urgently want good Field Glasses—part of my Equipment. Do let me have the Zeiss[1] (for this fortnight only.) I shall first need it on Monday, but don't think you had better send it here—but you could quite safely as a Registered Parcel to Fleetwood Post Office. Please do!

Or could Father come over to Fleetwood with it?

I am, compared with my 'situation' this time last year very comfortable here. I think I was inoculated about now? [*three lines illegible*]

Your lovingest W.E.O.

467. To Susan Owen

Sunday [6 November 1916]   *111 Bold Street, Fleetwood*

Dearest my Mother,

My good comrade is using my pen, so I profit by the moment of silence to pencil my Address, and my self-congratulations on being in so snug a Lodging. We are two in these 'Apartments' as the vulgar call them. I should have chosen Rickard[2] before all the Battalion as it now is. But, then, I am in a Position to choose. I am O-in-C. of the Brigade Firing Point!! Long ago, I left the Platoon for the Company, then the Company for the Battalion, and now if you please the Battalion for the Brigade!!! I shall at the Firing Point be responsible for the discipline of the 5th Manchesters, 8th Man: and all the various Lancashire Fusiliers and their officers. I have handed over the command of our own party of 120 to Rickard. I'm far too important for these petty administrations!!

But it was interesting to see to their billeting when we arrived. We made the journey without worse mishap than the loss of our oil, which was certainly pinched by another Regiment.

I must have Field Glasses, (was told so by the Staff Officer at our Meeting this afternoon.) So I hope I shall find von Zeiss at the P.O. tomorrow. Anyhow I have done my best to persuade you on what dazzling an eminence they shall be worn.

---

[1] A pair of Zeiss field-glasses was lying unclaimed in the Lost Property Office at Shrewsbury Station. Against his better judgement, Tom Owen agreed to lend them to Wilfred for use on the firing range at Fleetwood, arranging to telegraph for their return if the owner turned up. The owner did appear, and Wilfred returned the glasses (see Letter 469); but Tom Owen had to extricate himself from what might have been a serious predicament. The case was damaged in transit (see Letter 473) and Tom Owen had to pay for repairs.

[2] Second-Lieutenant A. R. Rickard, 5th Manchesters.

Our own Major Eaton[1] (whom you saw) is in supreme command. He is an imposing warrior, and things will go well under him. He has promised £5. (from our Funds) to be distributed to Marksmen.

Has the chair arrived? Are you any better?

I like this Digs far better than the Queen's Hotel life.

It is the first time I ever shared rooms, in the Keats–Brown manner.[2] I confess Rickard is not kin spiritually or literarily, but actually and personally and militarily we agree famously. He has more than once been mistaken for me.

I like Fleetwood.

Have finished tonight a fine novel by Wells:[3] which I must shake off before tomorrow. I shall go and inspect the men's billets to see if they are comfortable now.

Goodnight, dearest Mother! W.E.O. x

468. To Susan Owen

Picture postcard: Fleetwood, St. Peter's Church

[*Postmark 13 November 1916*]   [*Postmark Fleetwood*]

To this Church I took my little Family today. Lofty service, elevated singing &, the complement, a flat sermon. Have stayed in all day. H. G. Wells has a book (which you shall soon read) with an Oliver twist[4] about it, but which for me knocks *Oliver Twist* back to workhouse readers. None of the best news from you. But it is good news of Alpenrose! Decidedly!

W.E.O.

Yes, tell Meols.

469. To Susan Owen

Picture postcard of Fleetwood, the Promenade and ferry

[*Postmark 14 November 1916*]   [*Postmark Fleetwood*]

I return the Parcel[5] as it came. Certain, is it? What a blow! I had the telegram on the Range this afternoon. The only consolations are the good scoring of the men, and this sentence which Major Eaton showed me from a letter from the General: 'Owen should be of great assistance to you.' Didn't know he suspected my existence!

W.E.O.

[1] Major T. R. Eaton, 7th Manchesters, later joined the 2nd/5th in France.
[2] Charles Brown, friend of Keats. 'With Dilke and Brown I am quite thick—with Brown indeed I am going to domesticate—that is, we shall keep house together—I shall have the front parlour and he the back one . . .' Keats to George and Georgiana Keats, 16 December 1818 (*Letters* I I, pp. 4–5).
[3] Herbert George Wells (1866–1946). Wilfred met him on several occasions in 1917 and 1918. See Letters 559 and 565.
[4] Probably *The Passionate Friends*, London, 1913. See Letter 512, note 2.
[5] The Zeiss glasses.

470. To Susan Owen

Picture postcard: Fleetwood, Pharos Street, the lighthouse in the background,
A child is posed in the foreground to give the impression that she carries the
lighthouse on her shoulders. The photograph is superscribed: Pharoh's Street.
No doubt the curate will know his address. (Pharos is Greek for lighthouse.)
Clever little girl to carry it on her shoulder. Doesn't mother look pleased!
Have just come from a free show at local Theatre. It was free and easy. Some
of my men performed. They are having a good time. Dance last night! I think
we 5th Man. are winning, but the weather's putrid.

Tues. [*Postmark 15 November 1916*]   [*Postmark Fleetwood*]

Please do send your Glasses[1] if you will. Thanks for Letter this morning.
Is it an Officer at Kinmel Park, who claims. Are you quite sure it is
genuine, & that no one has got wind of the thing? Do not send parcel
later than Thurs. Tho' I may have to stay another Fortnight.

Your W.E.O.

471. To Susan Owen

Wednesday [*23 November 1916*]   *111 Bold Street, Fleetwood*
Page 1 (evidently enough)

My own dear Mother,

It must be more than the limit of a week since I wrote. The time
begins to speed now that I am used to the Place, and engrossed in my
work. I have a good deal of writing in the evenings. Only twice I have
been to Blackpool. The first, I was utterly bored, having nothing to do.
The second, (yesterday) I scuttled about so fast that I nearly got warm.
It has been icily cold here as well as with you. The sea had not a chance
of modifying influence. The east wind had the influenza. It was a
draught blowing straight from continental Germany.

As I was saying I went to Blackpool with a business; to find a Trench
Coat for your entreaties helped me to decide. I stand glued to one spot
for just 6 hours. Luckily my attention is also glued, or I should gnaw
my head off. I can of course always gnaw my lunch; and no man smiles
when I shout Sheesh Fire!!! and score a bull with explosive crumbs.
Major Eaton and I tried a shot ourselves this morning, each pretty
nervous of the other. We both scored dead central Bulls with five shots
in a 4 in. group!! (a 12 in. group would Pass). So if we didn't <u>wink</u>
at each other exactly, we certainly smiled in our innards.

Whittaker[2] turned up to see us this morning. I was very glad to see
him. He says the Egyptian Draft is washed out. Did I tell you my name
was down as a Candidate? There is a rumour of India for the whole
Brigade. Whittaker has been offered a (real) Staff <u>Job at Altcar School</u>
of Instruction. Before I left, several wounded but fit officers went on a
Course to Altcar, and I thought they might have returned to take my
old place. But it hasn't happened yet. Meanwhile I am snug enough at

---

[1] Susan Owen's opera glasses.
[2] Major L. A. Whittaker, M C, Manchester Regiment.

Fleetwood, (barring the day-time!) Major Eaton is awfully decent to me. The cooking improves with encouragement. I have a practically perfect orderly, and another willing body-servant on the Range. Best of all I have your letters unfailingly, and feel a sort of desperate joy in delaying answers without being scolded. I feel sick of any sort of prose. On the other hand, I have suddenly seen what I wanted to do with that War Ballad,[1] and indeed finished it on Sunday to my content. You shall have it in our next. I haven't seen 'L'Amour'[2] in print. I don't like Print, now that I see what a dead letter it is to all these living men about me. You shall rather send my stuff to Helen Bowick,[3] for Recitation. They would not have it in Y.M. They'd find it blasphemous, I not doubt. I want to see Leslie's last, but can't get 'Young Men' here. Young men nowadays don't exist, quite right too. We are youths, lads, fellows, pals, chaps, comrades, boys, blokes if you will, but not your Young Men.

I have quite a veneration for Charles Chaplin by the way. Made me laugh almost as much as H. G. Wells. I have not read the books you mention.

Am so glad you quite like the Chair.

If I had missed the S. of France by having a chill I would wear Jaeger's sackcloth ever after. I did indeed venture to put on a rough vest, 6 ins. thick which I rashly bought in Guildford. (Rashly indeed.) I was quite unnerved by it. It seemed to draw the blood to the head.

I am perfectly well, as you have had ample assurance from the post-man's back lately.

                                   Your veriest own lovingest Wilfred x

I do not enquire after you, like a next door neighbour. Nor after our sick neighbours for they are not of my generation, even as Keith Lawrence[4] is not.

472. To Mary Owen

[*Late November 1916*]   *111 Bold St, Fleetwood*

Dearest Mary,

I have seen in Southport a jolly silver Teapot & Sugar Basin & Cream Jug. For the Silver-Wedding Present, must be a Silver Wedding-Present.[5] Don't you think this sort of thing would be the best? Harold is halving the moderate cost with me, if you think it's a good idea. You shall provide the Indigo or Prussian Blue Ribbon which must be arranged to give the silver its full *éclat*. (Not as an indication that the teapot is for Temperance use only)

Write soon, dear, letting me also know how you & Mother are.

                                   Your lovingest Brother Wilfred

[1] Possibly 'To a Comrade in Flanders' (*Poems*, p. 143), which is dated September 1916.
[2] A poem by LG printed in *The Red Triangle*, the YMCA magazine, subsequently included in E. Leslie Gunston, *The Nymph and other poems*, Arthur H. Stockwell, London, 1917.
[3] Unidentified.
[4] See Letter 433.
[5] HO has the teapot now. The sugar basin and cream jug could not be afforded.

473. To Susan Owen

Monday [*9 December 1916*]   *Queen's Hotel, Southport*

We all came down on Sunday Morning. I am back at the Queen's in a rather poor little room at the top.

I am stuck on the new Musketry Party, firing at Crossens, where we march out every morning, about 3 miles, starting at 7.15. It is a bitter change from the good times at Fleetwood. Major Eaton is not our Commandant, but Major Melville,[1] a snotty, acid, scot, impatient, irritated wretch. Nothing will run smoothly while his voice files the air. He is Melville's Scotch Whiskey.

On Sunday I was very miserable for some reason, but I went round to Averys' to tea: and amused myself not badly with their pianola. It is an amusing toy, but not worth a street fiddle for melody.

Mrs. Avery is the type of woman who interests herself in the amatory welfare of her young friends. She has by her own suggestion entirely, arranged a meeting with two girls on Thursday.

All Leave except under exceptional circumstances is stopped by the Brigade until further notice. It may mean a move of the Brigade . . . . abroad??

There is also a rumour of 7 days work a week. Sickening!

Really, you might, some of you come up here for a week-end. Considering how little you are deterred by travelling expenses, the one nuisance with most People, I can't understand why you don't. Stay at the Averys', hospitable folk! 'Sno good, I can't come.

I have Pharyngitis again to a ticklish extent, tho' my throat is not in any way painful or 'swollen'. I am to have it cauterised.

I am sad these days for some reason.

Am I getting fed up with England?

I was today!

Saw Col. Ridge yesterday. He was very nice, and is going to mention the R.F.C. Transfer to the Brigadier.

I knew Father would strafe me about the mutilated Case. I can get a new Revolver at that Rogue's price, in my own Armoury.

                                        Dearest loves to all, Your W.E.O. x x

474. To Susan Owen

[*29 December 1916*]   *Hotel Metropole, Folkestone*

Just put up here. Train was wickedly late. I travelled[2] in Guard's van. Sitting in the Guard's Nook I narrowly escaped being smashed by a passing Goods' train. Some loose timber hit the coach just above my head. It awoke me with a big shock. This caused our train to stop a

---

[1] Major M. G. D. Melvill, MC, 6th Manchesters. He became CO of 2nd/6th Manchesters on 4 November 1917.

[2] After embarkation leave.

long while: I believe in order to telephone about the dangerous goods' train.

I got the Hat Cover and spent half-an-hour finding a suitable pen at Waverley House.

I went an hour early to Charing Cross, in case Harold should be there.

He came quarter of an hour before we started, and made the journey as far as London Bridge.

It was a fine thing to see him. He is translated utterly from the being he was five years ago.

'Tis a glorious fellow.

At Folkestone here I met a Canadian Doctor who seems to be the only other on the train reporting tomorrow. He took me to the best Hotel, where we are sharing a magnificent room.

There is a Boat at 11.30 a.m. More I know not.

Your W.E.O.

THE SOMME AND CRAIGLOCKHART

1917

475. To Susan Owen

1 January 1917   [*France*]

My own dearest Mother,

1.30 p.m. I have just received Orders to take the train at Étaples, to join the 2nd Manchesters. This is a Regular Regiment, so I have come off mighty well. The original Party from the 5th has in the last 2 days got completely dissolved, and as far as I know I am the only one for this Regt. It is a huge satisfaction to be going among well-trained troops and genuine 'real-old' Officers.

I don't pretend it was more than hazard that detailed me to this Battalion; but it is all very mysterious.

I got my Baggage before bed-time.

I have not alas! had any letter from you or anyone.

I think 1/2nd Manchester should find me. But don't send any goods yet.

This is a sort of Hotel Camp where none stay more than 2 or 3 days!

I have not been uncomfortable so far, with a tent to myself, and with a diligent Orderly.

This morning I was hit! We were bombing and a fragment from somewhere hit my thumb knuckle. I coaxed out 1 drop of blood. Alas! no more!!

There is a fine heroic feeling about being in France, and I am in perfect spirits. A tinge of excitement is about me, but excitement is always necessary to my happiness.

I don't think it is the real front I'm going to.

If on my Field Post Card I cross out 'I am being sent down to the base' with a double line ═══════════ then I shall actually be at the Front.

Can't believe it.

Nor must you.

Now I must pack.   Your own Wilfred x x

476. To Susan Owen

4 January 1917   *Address. 2nd Manchester Regt B.E.F.*

My own dear Mother,

I have joined the Regiment, who are just at the end of six weeks' rest.[1]

I will not describe the awful vicissitudes of the journey here. I arrived at Folkestone, and put up at the best hotel. It was a place of luxury—

[1] 2nd Manchesters were at Halloy, near Beaumont Hamel, where they had been resting for six weeks after severe fighting. In the meantime drafts or reinforcements of 527 officers and men had joined, in readiness for an assault on the German salient between the Scarpe and the Ancre by the British Third and Fifth Armies.

inconceivable now—carpets as deep as the mud here—golden flunkeys; pages who must have been melted into their clothes and expanded since; even the porters had clean hands. Even the dogs that licked up the crumbs had clean teeth.

Since I set foot on Calais quays I have not had dry feet.

No one knew anything about us on this side, and we might have taken weeks to get here, and must have, but for fighting our way here.

I spent something like a pound in getting my baggage carried from trains to trains.

At the Base, as I said, it was not so bad. We were in the camp of Sir Percy Cunynghame,[1] who had bagged for his Mess the Duke of Connaught's chef.

After those two days, we were let down, gently, into the real thing, Mud.

It has penetrated now into that Sanctuary my sleeping bag, and that holy of holies my pyjamas. For I sleep on a stone floor and the servant squashed mud on all my belongings; I suppose by way of baptism. We are 3 officers in this 'Room', the rest of the house is occupied by servants and the band; the roughest set of knaves I have ever been herded with. Even now their vile language is shaking the flimsy door between the rooms.

I chose a servant for myself yesterday, not for his profile, nor yet his clean hands, but for his excellence in bayonet work. For the servant is always at the side of his officer in the charge and is therefore worth a dozen nurses. Alas, he of the Bayonet is in the Bombing Section, and it is against Regulations to employ such as a servant. I makeshift with another.

Everything is makeshift. The English seem to have fallen into the French unhappy-go-lucky non-system. There are scarcely any houses here. The men lie in Barns.

Our Mess Room is also an Ante and Orderly Room. We eat & drink out of old tins, some of which show traces of ancient enamel. We are never dry, and never 'off duty'.

On all the officers' faces there is a harassed look that I have never seen before, and which in England, never will be seen—out of jails. The men are just as Bairnsfather[2] has them—expressionless lumps.

We feel the weight of them hanging on us. I have found not a few of the old Fleetwood Musketry party here. They seemed glad to see me, as far as the set doggedness of their features would admit.

I censored hundreds of letters yesterday, and the hope of peace was in every one. The *Daily Mail*[3] map which appeared about Jan 2 will be of extreme interest to you.

[1] Lieutenant-Colonel Sir Percy Cunynghame (1867–1941).
[2] Bruce Bairnsfather (1888–1959), artist and journalist, whose war cartoons were famous. They were published in *Fragments from France, The Better 'Ole, Bullets and Billets, From Mud to Mufti*, etc.
[3] The map showed the St. Quentin front, the British line on the Somme, extending from Gommecourt–Beaumont Hamel–Grandcourt–Le Transloy.

We were stranded in a certain town one night and I saved the party of us by collaring an Orderly in the streets and making him take us to a Sergeants Mess. We were famishing, and a mug of beer did me more good than any meal I ever munched. The place was like a bit of Blighty, all hung with English Greetings and Mistletoe.

As I could I collected accoutrement, some here, some there, and almost am complete: Steel Helmets, & Gas; improved Box Respirator, and cetera.

The badge of the Regt. is some red tabs on the shoulder thus ◇ I scarcely know any of the officers. The senior are old regulars. The younger are, several, Artists! In my room is an Artist of the same school as I passed. He is also a fine water-colour sketcher. I may have time to write again tomorrow. I have not of course had anything from you.

I am perfectly well and strong, but unthinkably dirty and squalid.

I scarcely dare to wash.

Pass on as much of this happy news as may interest people.

The favourite song of the men is

> 'The Roses round the door
> Makes me love Mother more.'

They sing this everlastingly.

I don't disagree.   Your very own W.E.O. x

477. To Susan Owen

Sunday, 7 January 1917   [*2nd Manchester Regt., B.E.F.*]

My dear dear Mother,

It is afternoon. We had an Inspection to make from 9 to 12 this morning. I have wandered into a village cafe where they gave me writing paper. We made a redoubtable March yesterday from the last Camp to this.[1] The awful state of the roads and the enormous weight carried, was too much for scores of men. Officers also carried full packs, but I had a horse part of the way.

It was beginning to freeze through the rain when we arrived at our tents. We were at the mercy of the cold, and, being in health, I never suffered so terribly as yesterday afternoon. I am really quite well, but have sensations kindred to being seriously ill.

As I was making my damp bed, I heard the Guns for the first time. It was a sound not without a certain sublimity. They woke me again at 4 o'clock.

We are two in a tent. I am with the Lewis Gun Officer. We begged stretchers from the doctor to sleep on. Our servant brings our food to

---

[1] The battalion left Halloy on 6 January, marching to Beauval and moving thence by motor-bus to Bertrancourt.

us in our tents. This would not be so bad but for lack of water, and the intense damp cold.

I have had to censor letters by the hundred lately. They don't make inspiring reading.

This morning I have been reading Trench Standing Orders to my Platoon. (Verb. Sap.)

Needless to say I show a cheerier face to them than I wear in writing this letter; but I must not disguise from you the fact that we are at one of the worst parts of the Line.

I have lost no possessions so far; but have acquired a pair of boots and a map case (presents). And of course my valise is heavier by much dirt.

I want a Compass really more than Field Glasses.

My address is
                          2nd Manchester Regt.
                              B.E.F.

I have not a word from England since I left.

I can't tell you any more Facts. I have no Fancies and no Feelings. Positively they went numb with my feet.

Love is not quenched, except the unenduring flickerings thereof. By your love, O Mother, O Home, I am protected from Fatigue of life and the keen spiritual Cold.

                                        Your own W.E.O.

478. To Susan Owen

[*9 January 1917*]   [*2nd Manchester Regt., B.E.F.*]

My own dear Mother,

I forget both the day and the date. It is about the 9th. We moved further up yesterday, most of the way on 'Buses.

I have just had your long-looked-for letter. It seems wrong that even your dear handwriting should come into such a Gehenna as this. There is a terrific Strafe on. Our artillery are doing a 48 hours bombardment.

At night it is like a stupendous thunderstorm, for the flashes are quite as bright as lightning.

When we arrived at this deserted Village[1] last night, there had been no billets prepared for the Battalion—owing to misunderstanding. Imagine the confusion!

For my part I discovered, or rather my new chosen and faithful Servant discovered a fine little hut, with a chair in it! A four-legged chair! The Roof is waterproof, and there is a Stove. There is only one slight disadvantage: there is a Howitzer just 70 or 80 yards away, firing over the top every minute or so. I can't tell you how glad I am you got me the ear-defenders. I have to wear them at night. Every time No. 2 (the nearest gun) fires, all my pharmacopæia, all my boots,

---

[1] Bertrancourt.

candle, and nerves take a smart jump upwards. This phenomena is immediately followed by a fine rain of particles from the roof. I keep blowing them off the page.

From time to time the Village is shelled but just now nothing is coming over. Anyhow there is a good cellar close to.

I am Orderly Officer today and stamp all the Battalion's letters. This has taken an age, and I have only a minute or two before I must despatch the Post.

I chose to spend an hour today behind the guns (to get used to them). The Major commanding the Battery was very pleasant indeed. He took me to his H.Q. and gave me a book of Poems to read as if it were the natural thing to do!!

But all night I shall be hearing the fellow's voice:
                  Number Two—FIRE!

Please send the compass: 2 Manchester Regt. B.E.F. I also need 50 Players Cigarettes & some plain chocolate. There is nothing in all this inferno but mud and thunder.

I am quite incapable of reading anything but your letters; and as you see nearly incapable of writing. Tell me every detail about Colin & Harold that you can; and of course, I long to know everything that happens—or does not happen—at home.

Please tell Leslie & everybody that I really have not time nor wits to write to them from under the cannon's mouth.

But it will lull shortly. I am quite well, and have plenty to eat.

I get more and more used to the cold and wet.

                  Dearest love, my sweet Mother, from your Wilfred
I want a large, soft sleeping helmet and refills for the lamp.

                                                           s.v.p.

479. To Susan Owen

10 January 1917   [*2nd Manchester Regt., B.E.F.*]

My own Mother,

I was censoring letters all afternoon. After tea commenced a big commotion among my friendly neighbours the Howitzers, in the midst of which I wrote a distracted note to Leslie, but the concussion blew out my candle so many times that I lost heart.

I am kept pretty busy, tho' there is only a short 'parade'. The men do practically nothing all day but write letters; but officers have frequent meetings over schemes, maps, instructions, and a thousand cares.

Yesterday I took a tour into the Line which we shall occupy. Our little party was shelled going up across the open country. It was not at all frightful and only one 4.7 got anywhere near, falling plump in the road, but quite a minute after we had passed the spot. I tell you these things because afterwards they will sound less exciting. If I leave all my exploits for recitation after the war without mentioning them now, they will be appearing bomb-shell-bastic.

Now I am not so uncomfortable as last week, for my new servant who has been a chemist's assistant, has turned out not only clean & smart, but enterprising and inventive. He keeps a jolly fire going; and thieves me wood with much cunning.

My Company Commander (A Company) has been out here since the beginning: 'tis a gentleman and an original (!)[1]

Next in command is Heydon,[2] whom I greatly like, and once revered as the assistant Adjutant at Witley & Oswestry.

Then come I, for the remaining subalterns are junior. I chose no. 3 Platoon. I was posted to 2, but one day I took No. 3 in tow when its officer left, because I liked the look of the men.

Even as they prophesied in the Artists, I have to take a close interest in feet, and this very day I knelt down with a candle and watched each man perform his anointment with Whale Oil; praising the clean feet, but not reviling the unclean.

As a matter of fact, my servant and one other, are the only non-verminous bodies in the platoon; not to say Lice-ntious.

Today's letters were rather interesting. The Daddys' letters are specially touching, and the number of x x x to sisters and mothers weigh more in heaven than Victoria Crosses. The Victoria Cross! I covet it not. Is it not Victorian? yah! pah!

I am not allowed to send a sketch, but you must know I am transformed now, wearing a steel helmet, buff jerkin of leather, rubber-waders up to the hips, & gauntlets. But for the rifle, we are exactly like Cromwellian Troopers. The waders are of course indispensable. In $2\frac{1}{2}$ miles of trench which I waded yesterday there was not one inch of dry ground. There is a mean depth of 2 feet of water.

It seems an era since Christmas, Day, and Goose, Carols, Dickens & Mistletoe.

Assuming the war lasts another year I should get leave twice, or three times, for we get it, or should get it every 3 months.[3]

Be sure to have no Chloride of Lime in the house. Our water is overdosed with it enough to poison us. But in the Mess we can get Perrier fortunately.

You need not ask where I am. I have told you as far as I can. These things I need

(1) small pair nail scissors
(2) celluloid hair-pin box from Boots (9d.) with tightfitting lid, & containing boracic powder.
(3) Players Navy Cut
(4) Ink pellets
(5) Sweets (!!) (We shall not be in touch with Supplies by day)

---

[1] Captain (later Major) H. R. Crichton Green (1892–1963), Manchester Regiment. In 1939 he rejoined, and was Camp Commandant at Le Mans until the Dunkirk evacuation. Later he commanded the Regimental Depot of the Manchester Regiment.
[2] Second-Lieutenant A. Heydon. Died of wounds April 1917. See Letter 503.
[3] 'Not so bad' is written in the margin against this paragraph.

Have no anxiety. I cannot do a better thing or be in a righter place. Yet I am not sainted therefore, and so I beg you to annoy . . .[1], for my wicked pleasure.

W.E.O. xxx

480. To Susan Owen

Tues: 16 January 1917   [*2nd Manchester Regt., B.E.F.*]

My own sweet Mother,

I am sorry you have had about 5 days letterless. I hope you had my two letters 'posted' since you wrote your last, which I received tonight. I am bitterly disappointed that I never got one of yours.

I can see no excuse for deceiving you about these last 4 days. I have suffered seventh hell.

I have not been at the front.

I have been in front of it.

I held an advanced post, that is, a 'dug-out' in the middle of No Man's Land.

We had a march of 3 miles over shelled road then nearly 3 along a flooded trench. After that we came to where the trenches had been blown flat out and had to go over the top. It was of course dark, too dark, and the ground was not mud, not sloppy mud, but an octopus of sucking clay, 3, 4, and 5 feet deep, relieved only by craters full of water. Men have been known to drown in them. Many stuck in the mud & only got on by leaving their waders, equipment, and in some cases their clothes.

High explosives were dropping all around out, and machine guns spluttered every few minutes. But it was so dark that even the German flares did not reveal us.

Three quarters dead, I mean each of us $\frac{3}{4}$ dead, we reached the dug-out, and relieved the wretches therein. I then had to go forth and find another dug-out for a still more advanced post where I left 18 bombers. I was responsible for other posts on the left but there was a junior officer in charge.

My dug-out held 25 men tight packed. Water filled it to a depth of 1 or 2 feet, leaving say 4 feet of air.

One entrance had been blown in & blocked.

So far, the other remained.

The Germans knew we were staying there and decided we shouldn't.

Those fifty hours were the agony of my happy life.

Every ten minutes on Sunday afternoon seemed an hour.

I nearly broke down and let myself drown in the water that was now slowly rising over my knees.

Towards 6 o'clock, when, I suppose, you would be going to church, the shelling grew less intense and less accurate: so that I was mercifully helped to do my duty and crawl, wade, climb and flounder over No

[1] Name omitted.

427

Man's Land to visit my other post. It took me half an hour to move about 150 yards.

I was chiefly annoyed by our own machine guns from behind. The seeng-seeng-seeng of the bullets reminded me of Mary's canary. On the whole I can support the canary better.

In the Platoon on my left the sentries over the dug-out were blown to nothing. One of these poor fellows was my first servant whom I rejected. If I had kept him he would have lived, for servants don't do Sentry Duty. I kept my own sentries half way down the stairs during the more terrific bombardment. In spite of this one lad was blown down and, I am afraid, blinded.[1]

This was my only casualty.

The officer of the left Platoon has come out completely prostrated and is in hospital.

I am now as well, I suppose, as ever.

I allow myself to tell you all these things because I am never going back to this awful post. It is the worst the Manchesters have ever held; and we are going back for a rest.

I hear that the officer who relieved me left his 3 Lewis Guns behind when he came out. (He had only 24 hours in). He will be court-martialled.

In conclusion, I must say that if there is any power whom the Soldiery execrate more than another it is that of our distinguished countryman.[2] You may pass it on via Owen, Owen.

Don't pass round these sheets but have portions typed for Leslie etc. My previous letter to you has just been returned. It will be too heavy to include in this.

                                                    Your very own Wilfred x

481. To Susan Owen

Friday, 19 January 1917   [*2nd Manchester Regt., B.E.F.*]

We are now a long way back in a ruined village, all huddled together in a farm. We all sleep in the same room where we eat and try to live. My bed is a hammock of rabbit-wire stuck up beside a great shell hole in the wall. Snow is deep about, and melts through the gaping roof, on to my blanket. We are wretched beyond my previous imagination—but safe.

Last night indeed I had to 'go up' with a party. We got lost in the snow. I went on ahead to scout—foolishly alone—and when, half a mile away from the party, got overtaken by

                                    G A S

---

[1] This incident became the subject of 'The Sentry' (*Poems*, pp. 61–62).
[2] David Lloyd George of Dwyfor, 1st Earl (1863–1945), Minister for War before becoming Prime Minister 1916–22.

It was only tear-gas from a shell, and I got safely back (to the party) in my helmet, with nothing worse than a severe fright! And a few tears. some natural, some unnatural.

Here is an Addition to my List of Wants:
    Safety Razor (in my drawer) & Blades
    Socks (2 pairs)
    6 Handkerchiefs
    Celluloid Soap Box (Boots)
    Cigarette Holder (Bone, 3d. or 6d.)
    Paraffin for Hair.
(I can't wash hair and have taken to washing my face with snow.)

Coal, water, candles, accommodation, everything is scarce. We have not always air! When I took my helmet off last night—O Air it was a heavenly thing!

Please thank Uncle for his letter, and send the Compass. I scattered abroad some 50 Field Post Cards from the Base, which should bring forth a good harvest of letters. But nothing but a daily one from you will keep me up.

I think Colin might try a weekly letter. And Father?

We have a Gramophone, and so musical does it seem now that I shall never more disparage one. Indeed I can never disparage anything in Blighty again for a long time except certain parvenus living in a street of the same name as you take to go to the Abbey.

They want to call No Man's Land 'England' because we keep supremacy there.

It is like the eternal place of gnashing of teeth; the Slough of Despond could be contained in one of its crater-holes; the fires of Sodom and Gomorrah could not light a candle to it—to find the way to Babylon the Fallen.

It is pock-marked like a body of foulest disease and its odour is the breath of cancer.[1]

I have not seen any dead. I have done worse. In the dank air I have perceived it, and in the darkness, felt. Those 'Somme Pictures' are the laughing stock of the army—like the trenches on exhibition in Kensington.

No Man's Land under snow is like the face of the moon chaotic, crater-ridden, uninhabitable, awful, the abode of madness.

To call it 'England'!

I would as soon call my House (!) Krupp Villa, or my child Chlorina-Phosgena.

Now I have let myself tell you more facts than I should, in the exuberance of having already done 'a Bit.' It is done, and we are all going still farther back for a long time. A long time. The people of England needn't hope. They must agitate. But they are not yet agitated even. Let them imagine 50 strong men trembling as with ague for 50 hours!

                    Dearer & stronger love than ever. W.E.O.

[1] CDL points out that 'The Show' (*Poems*, pp. 50–51), probably written in November 1917, is foreshadowed in this letter.

482. To Susan Owen

Sunday, 4 February 1917   [*Advanced Horse Transport Depot*]

My own dear Mother,

I am now indeed and in truth very far behind the Line; sent down to this old Town[1] for a Course in Transport Duties. The Battalion did not get out for a rest, and since my last letter I have had another strong dose of the advanced Front Line.

To begin with, I have come out quite unhurt, except for a touch of dysentery, which is now passed, and a severe cold and cough which keep me in bed today.

I have no mind to describe all the horrors of this last Tour. But it was almost wusser than the first, because in this place my Platoon had no Dug-Outs, but had to lie in the snow under the deadly wind. By day it was impossible to stand up or even crawl about because we were behind only a little ridge screening us from the Bosches' periscope.

We had 5 Tommy's cookers between the Platoon, but they did not suffice to melt the ice in the water-cans. So we suffered cruelly from thirst.

The marvel is that we did not all die of cold.[2] As a matter of fact, only one of my party actually froze to death before he could be got back, but I am not able to tell how many have ended in hospital. I had no real casualties from shelling, though for 10 minutes every hour whizz-bangs fell a few yards short of us. Showers of soil rained on us, but no frag-ments of shell could find us.

I had lost my gloves in a dug-out, but I found 1 mitten on the Field; I had my Trench Coat (without lining but with a Jerkin underneath.) My feet ached until they could ache no more, and so they temporarily died. I was kept warm by the ardour of Life within me. I forgot hunger in the hunger for Life. The intensity of your Love reached me and kept me living. I thought of you and Mary without a break all the time. I cannot say I felt any fear. We were all half-crazed by the buffeting of the High Explosives. I think the most unpleasant reflection that weighed on me was the impossibility of getting back any wounded, a total impossibility all day, and frightfully difficult by night.

We were marooned on a frozen desert.

There is not a sign of life on the horizon and a thousand signs of death.

Not a blade of grass, not an insect; once or twice a day the shadow of big hawk, scenting carrion.

By degrees, day by day, we worked back through the reserve, & support lines to the crazy village where the Battalion takes breath. While

---

[1] Abbeville. The instruction to report to the Advanced Horse Transport Depot there survives. On the back of the message form Wilfred pencilled some lines from Rabindranath Tagore's *Gitanjali*, beginning: 'When I go from hence let this be my parting word, that what I have seen is unsurpassable.' He quoted these words to Susan Owen in August 1918, the day before his last embarkation leave was over.

[2] 'Exposure' (*Poems*, p. 48) is dated February 1916, an evident slip, as EB points out, for February 1917. It must have been written at Abbeville.

in Support we inhabited vast Bosche dug-out (full of all kinds of souvenirs). They are so deep that they seem warm like mines! There we began to thaw. At last I got to the village, & found all your dear precious letters, and the parcel of good and precious things. The Lamp is perfect your Helmet is perfect, everything was perfect.

Then I had the heavenly-dictated order to proceed on a Transport Course. Me in Transports? Aren't you? When I departed, the gloom among the rest of the Subs. and even among Captains, was a darkness that could be felt. They can't understand my luck.

It doesn't necessarily mean a job as Transport Officer straight away, but here I am, in a delightful old town billeted in a house with a young Scotch Officer.

True, we can get no fuel and the very milk freezes in the jug in a few minutes. True, I am sorely bruised by riding. True, this kind of Life is expensive. But I have not been so full of content since the middle of November last.

Tell Colin how we have to ride all manner of horseflesh in the School, cantering round & round for hours, without stirrups, and folding arms and doing all kinds of circus tricks.

It is very amusing—to watch.

Tomorrow I shall send a P.C. of this Town which I must not name in a letter.

Address: R.E. Section
      Advanced Horse Transport Depot
          A.P.O. S1.
             BEF France.

Hope you had numerous Field P.C.'s which I dropped *en route* to here.
The Course should last 1 month!!

Alas! I have missed your last letters. It has taken 3 days to get here.

Fondest love to all, & thanks for all their letters,

                    Your own Wilfred x

P.S. I don't at all deserve the spirited approbation which Father gives me. Though I confess I like to have his kind letters immensely. I shall read them less shame-facedly in dug-outs and trenches, than I do here in this pleasant peaceful town.

Quite 10 years ago I made a study of this town & Cathedral, in the Treasury. It is all familiar now!

Auntie Emma fairly hit it when she 'perceived the awful distaste underlying' my accounts. Dear Aunt was ever a shrewd Doogie.

I suppose I can endure cold, and fatigue, and the face-to-face death, as well as another; but extra for me there is the universal pervasion of Ugliness. Hideous landscapes, vile noises, foul language and nothing but foul, even from one's own mouth (for all are devil ridden), everything unnatural, broken, blasted; the distortion of the dead, whose unburiable bodies sit outside the dug-outs all day, all night, the most execrable sights on earth. In poetry we call them the most glorious. But to sit with them all day, all night . . . and a week later to come back and find them still sitting there, in motionless groups, THAT is what saps the 'soldierly spirit' . . .

Distaste? Distaste, Quotha?

I used to consider Tankerville Street[1] ugly, but now . . .

Well, I easily forget the unpleasant, and, look you, I even have to write it down for the sake of future reminders, reminder of how incomparable is an innocent and quiet life, at home, of work creative or humdrum, with books or without books, moneyed or moneyless, in sunshine or fog, but under an inoffensive sky, that does not shriek all night with flights of shells.

Again I have said too much. But let me repeat that I am mighty snug here, and have a goodly prospect before me now.

I am not sorry you keep in bed from time to time, but I do hope you'll soon get some sunny walks. Are you painting?

The Letter from Lancs. was from Bobby. All the brothers are in college there.[2] Miss de la Touche is as Bobby says 'supposed to be boss' of a Belgian Hospital in London.[3]

Again, dearest love to all. W.E.O.

483. To Susan Owen

[*9 February 1917*]   [*Advanced Horse Transport Depot*]

My own dear Mother,

Your last letter is not numbered—dated Jan. 31. No doubt you have mine from here. No parcel yet. The back of it is all covered with Veterinary Notes which I must try to copy out. The cold almost freezes my eyelids together.

I am in a hut now, because the Scot disturbed me by rolling in every midnight, and when at last he got into our bed, his three sheets did not somehow add to the warmth.

Last night I burnt a petrol lamp under my bed!! I don't know what Risk is, now.

In the morning, the top blanket was stiffish with frost. Don't think I suffer. Every detail of this blessed Life is sweet and precious. 3 more weeks of it yet!

I am putting Colin's letter herein. I'm sorry I was so pretentious as to ask for a typing of my letters. But I really am ashamed of sending such scrawl to Colin. Do have it copied!

I don't think I have told you that I am Mess President of the School Mess! It means a good deal of work. But I am honoured to have it. In the evening I go shopping with the Mess Cart. I am certainly a suitable person to hold the key of our Whisky store! I have fixed the charge of Messing at 25 f. per week!

[1] Shrewsbury.

[2] Bobbie and Johnny de la Touche left Downside in July 1916 and transferred to Stonyhurst College, near Blackburn, Lancashire, where Charles and David had already arrived as pupils from Mérignac.

[3] Miss de la Touche was now in charge of a hospital for Belgian refugees in Surbiton, Surrey.

Sorry I am so busy—for your sake, but no more now but my perfect Love to you.

W.E.O. xxx

484. To Susan Owen

Monday [*12*] *February 1917*   [*Advanced Horse Transport Depot*]

My own dear Mother,

I thought to write yesterday, but we were working all day; sick animals in the morning, and riding in the afternoon. In spite of the hard ground we went out into the country. I had a horse with a reputation of 'warming up'. Sure enough, he would not let me remount after a halt. When at last I swung over, and before I could get the reins properly gathered, he bolted. It was not so much a gallop, as a terrific series of ricochets off the ground, as if we had been fired from a Naval Gun. But the worst part was the sudden checks. Once I found myself with my hands in the brute's mouth; but I was still on top of him somewhere, and never actually touched ground. I was only thoroughly shaken.

Your 3 parcels came within 2 days of each other, 2 actually together. It is so unlucky that they did not reach me up the line, where everything has a tenfold value. Still nothing can take from the preciousness of the presents you send me.

The Cigarettes are the most essential of all, because the stuff sold out here is abominable: except Turkish, which are cheap & good. The Cigarette-holder is the finest imaginable. I am e'en champing it now.

The socks have almost exceeded my need. Withhold Socks for another month or more.

Gingerbreads arrived in fine condition—both lots. They are the most homelike bits in all the parcel

You made a very cunning choice of Biscuits. You overwhelm me with Chocolate. I am keeping it, like most of the sweet-stuff, for going up the Line. Now the potted meat is much too heavy an article, don't you think, especially as it is plentiful, and, even, a Ration. Munchie[1] of course is one of the very best things you could send. Handkerchiefs A.1.

I have not yet come to use the first Lamp Refill. The Lamp is admirable.

Thanks for the Boracic Box, exactly what I desired.

I forget how to use the Quassia.[2] But have had no need.

I get a bath for 1 f. 50. at the Officers' Club, a sumptuous place. But the meals are rather dear. My Mess is succeeding, but the shortage of coal is a terrible nuisance for me.

We have a Canadian, an Australian, various M.G.C's,[3] a S.W.B.[4] a Scot, etc. etc. The S.W. Borderer is in the same Battalion as Merrifield,[5]

[1] The family name for nut, raisin, and chocolate blocks.
[2] Quassia chips, dissolved in water as a disinfectant.
[3] Machine-gun companies.
[4] South Wales Borderer.
[5] Lieutenant S. H. Merfield.

the 'Artist' who mimicked the Colonel at the Holborn. We are all fairly near together on the Line.

What a curious thing about H. Kent! If you care to get the *Morning Post* of Feb. 8 you will see on P. 8 a map[1] (which I should like kept.) The dotted lines represent the exact posts where we lay freezing. I could almost pick out the identical dot where I was. I can't get any news of the Battalion, but the Advance was certainly from the place where I left them.

I brought my servant with me. It is a soft job for him here. I don't know that he is quite worthy of such a holiday. I am not fond of him, because he does nothing off his own bat, and doesn't always 'jump to' my orders!

I must write at once to that lad Browne to go and see you from Wrexham if he can. I think I told you how he stood by me when I was stranded somewhere in F. He had been out over a year and was then on his way home sent back for being under age! He was a Rly. clerk.

I am settling down to a little verse once more, and tonight I want to do Leslie's subject 'Golden Hair' and O.A.J.'s 'Happiness'. Leslie tells me that Miss Joergens considers my Sonnet on 'The End'[2] the finest of the lot. Naturally, because it is, intentionally, in her style! It is in Leslie's possession now. I think hers on 'Golden Hair' very fine indeed. I have lost a bundle of my MSS, together with all the photographs I brought out. They were left out of packing. That's the sort of servant I've got. Please send some photographs. Also would you mind getting an Army Book *Animal Management* pub. by Gale & Polden, Aldershot.

Please thank Mary specially for her dear letters which I read constantly. As for yours, I live by them.

Ever your loving W.E.O. x

485. To Mary Owen

Wed, [*14*] *February 1917*   [*Advanced Horse Transport Depot*]

My dear Mary,

Your letter was one of six, three of mother's, one from Leslie, and one from Kemp, who is now Curate at Watford. He believes it is more than 4 years since we met in his study at Highbury.

I have just come in from driving G.S. Wagons with 4 horses. This hour's work is about all we do in the morning, and this afternoon we are driving out to a Horse Hospital. I tell you, these days are the best I've ever had in the army.

[1] It showed the Beaumont Hamel–Beaucourt area of the front before Grandcourt, just evacuated by the Germans.

[2] Poems were still being exchanged between the three. 'The End' is in *Poems* (p. 89); so is 'Happiness' (p. 93). 'Purple' (p. 135) started as another set subject. There are five BM drafts of 'Golden Hair' and one in HO's possession (dated Abbeville, February 1917); none included in *Poems*. LG's *The Nymph* (see p. 416, note 2) includes *his* poems 'Happiness', 'Golden Hair', and 'Purple'. For Wilfred's further opinion of his own 'Happiness' see Letters 487–8. Olwen Joergens did not include any of these 'set subjects' in her collection, *The Woman and the Sage*.

What a pity about the brooch! but if you saw the enormity of the destruction and loss that goes on out here you would think less seriously of your little breakages.

Do you need a Brooch? I saw an Egyptian one, rather huge, but I am afraid you wouldn't like it.

and an Assyrian. No they wouldn't do since you no longer wear your Ancient British frocks. All the others in this town are either Romish, or non-descript.

One of the officers with me is a lace-designer by profession. You would never guess he spent his days concocting Insertions & Counterpoint, for he is one of the most dashing fellows with the horses.

Do you remember how the Bishop of London said he thought it 'disgraceful for any young man to be fingering lace over a counter, in peace-time or war-time.' Hum-hum! I wonder who loves to wear fine lace about him more than milord Winnie Ingram?[1]

I am so glad you had such good skating. There are no skates of any sort to be had here, so we had no thought of it.

Yesterday we rode not far from the field of Crecy! It was a gallant ride, until we got on some slippery roads where several horses fell. One chap got underneath his beast, but after a modest attempt at fainting, recovered.

I am annoyed that my letters faint so long by the wayside. It is a marvel to me that your parcels come. A very blessed marvel.

Goodbye, sweet sister. I go to preside at Lunch.   W.E.O.

486. To Susan Owen

Sunday, February? [18] *1917*   [*Advanced Horse Transport Depot*]

My own dear Mother,

So little happens that I can't keep up my instalments of blood-and-thunder literature.

I'm glad you got the Picture Post Card. My last letter was to Mary, I think. The Gloves came only yesterday, in an opened envelope, but still containing the ribbon, which is not needed yet. I have now three Sleeping Helmets, but can't make up my mind which to give away. I may need one for waking wear. I found the first one—your make—of great use on a 'Working Party', the very day it came. After a day's work in reserve, Heydon & I were suddenly called to take a fatigue

---

[1] Arthur Foley Winnington-Ingram (1858–1946), Bishop of London 1901–39.

party up to the front. We hadn't time to snatch a cup of tea, but I remembered the Wool Helmet, and after dusk wore it under the steel, which was again reinforced with a layer of ice. We marched, about 10 miles, up to the front and there the men had to dig trenches in ground like granite:—the same men, or rather the survivors of them, who 2 days before had been holding the advanced posts!! The shells were wonderfully few, and we all reached 'Home' about 2 in the morning. They can all march back from the line somehow, I say march, but of course there is no Left-Right-Left, and we got on miserably slowly, because some of the men could not wear boots, but wound their puttees round their frost-bitten feet. It is a good thing no photographs can be taken by night. If they could they would not appear in the *Daily Mirror*, which I see still depicts the radiant smiles of Tommies 'well behind'.

I really thought that night that my Dysentery would soon be bad enough for Hospital, and so it would if next morning I had not been starting for A. By the way Dysentery is not just a polite name. I really had it, but civilised life has soon cured it. I should not have eaten so much Snow. But I still think it better than 'Shell Water'.

Didn't I tell you how I came here? There being no trains at all, I was not likely to go back and wait in the Orderly Room. No! I stopped the first Motor Lorry that came along, without bothering about its direction, and so got a respectable distance from the Battalion. That was a good start. Moreover no shell-holes any more appeared anywhere. That was a very good start. After I had taken 5 different 'buses, I found myself 1/3 of the way here, and in quite a nice little Town, where I stopped the night and had a bath, the first since Shrewsbury. The rest of the distance I was lucky enough to cover in one Bus. only. I put up, the first night, in a café, the Officers' Club being both costly and crowded. Then I billeted with the Scot, canny, and sometimes uncannily 'canned', in the house of a (very) retired old English gentleman, come down in the world.

I did not stay long in the Hut, but soon found a cosy room just outside the camp.

Wed, February? [*21*] *1917*

I kept back the Sunday Letter because the Mails have been held up for 5 days. So that all your letters since the Glove Packet came together this morning.

I am glad enough of the 2 Photographs but should like some more, not excluding one or two of the last of myself. Photography is dear here, but tomorrow we are having a group taken.

I'm jolly glad you have rolled out the Beer-Jug-and-Barrel, and it will be interesting to hear how the next curio behaves.

The Course should end next Sunday. I shall surely be with the Battalion by March 1. I hear from a Staff Officer who came into this Billet last night that 'during Operations' two [*one page missing*] procedure to open any fellows' letters from Paris.

Yes, I was using an Essence last week on my handkerchief, on account of the stenches from the Sick Horses Lines. Certain cases of Thrush, Quitter, and such suppurations go one worse than the battlefield-exhalations.

Yes, once again I shave meticulously, and have re-established a Parting. For in another week I shall again be cleaning my teeth on my sleeve-cuffs and washing my face in my damp pillow.

All the school are desperate nuts in dress: as befits our calling, and immemorial custom of all gallants in a safe place. It is a favourite 'Flash' to trail a violet silk handkerchief! but for my part I consider the colour too noble for such an article.

I hope your next parcel will not reach me until I am up the Line. All I really want is Cigarettes, Munchie, and plain Cadbury's.

I have only received one Identity Disc so far!

I have had all the parcels you made a list of.

You say Father was going to enquire after Brown at Wrexham Stn. but he is still a soldier—in Wrexham Barracks.

No more now, but some more tomorrow.

Your very ownest Wilfred x

487. To Susan Owen

Sunday, 25 February 1917   [*Advanced Horse Transport Depot*]

Mine own Mother,

Just had your letter of Tuesday 20th, enclosing Denny's.[1] I believe it sincere, and value it a good deal more than an acceptance of our proposal. The Salopian applause would be directed to the fine reciter, but here we have the fine reciter applauding. Very thoughtful of you to copy it out for me. Yes, I think Leslie might well see the original. If you write to him you will ask him for my 'Golden Hair' (not a sonnet). It contains about five consecutive lines which I leave as final! My 'Happiness' is dedicated to you. It contains perhaps two good lines. Between you an' me the sentiment is all bilge. Or nearly all. But I think it makes a creditable Sonnet. You must not conclude I have misbehaved in any way from the tone of the poem (though you might infer it if you knew the tone of this Town.) On the contrary I have been a very good boy [*one sheet missing*]

I don't need any more ear-defenders. I don't use these now. The only other thing for Parcels would be some more of those coffee & cocoa cubes. They are A.1.

To demonstrate in concrete form that I am still of my old vain mind, I am going to send over a parcel to you of a cheap copper vase (not 'cheap tin trays')[2] & pot. For cheap modern work, I 'specially approve of this vase. When the field-flowers appear, I foresee that you will fill it with them unto the day of my returning.

[1] Unindentified. It seems unlikely that he was the Artists' Rifles Denny (see Letter 428).
[2] The reference is to John Masefield's 'Cargoes'.

The souvenirs which sell in millions to the soldiers are artistic atrocities: fit signs of the times. This Aluminium Letter Opener which cost
8d. is probably German, judging from the Gretchen-plaits. It is not a
souvenir; and I have no intention of collecting souvenirs of any description. What England will need will be an anti-souvenir. I shall have to
send my parcel as if from the landlady of this house!

As regards your botanical enquiries concerning the prevalence of
parasitic shrubs on apple and oak trees I shall give you information as
the data is acquired.

I have been to the dentist here (Army) and also the Doctor. I have
not much of a cough, but produce an extra-ordinary amount of phlegm,
brown, black, & grey. Fortunately or unfortunately, I feel perfectly
well on it.

Nothing keeps me so cool of mind as knowing you are normally well,
and I keep hoping from all accounts supernormally so.

Goodbye now, sweet Mother. I am like to be 4 or 5 days journeying.

Fondest love to all,

Your very own, Wilfred x

488. To Harold Owen[1]

[27 February 1917]   [2nd Manchester Regt., B.E.F.]

My dear old Harold,

I think I have had more joy from Mother's news of You than chagrin.
Certainly. You are entire. Let all the machinations of the Army crash,
bang, and utterly spifflicate themselves: I rejoice; you are whole[2]
[three lines illegible] yourself to the point of insomnia. I know what
insomnia is. So I won't ask you to write 'all about it' to me yet. How I
admire, & understand, [two lines illegible] stand as an excuse for you,
no other excuse for any wounds going septic in England! [one line
illegible] Did you carry First Field Dressing? NO!

[four lines illegible] with quiet, and al ittle designing—and HOME.

I think less and less of applying to R.F.C. . . . loops and circuits
[one line illegible] and easy soarings of [one word illegible]. Answer
me one question. Did [one line illegible] a sinister attraction on you
[one word illegible]? I hope anyhow you will soon feel right [one page
illegible] As I said, I have no room for commiseration. It is swallowed
up in Congratulation.

I believe I said something nasty about the Navy [two words missing]
I had no notion of what had happened, or was to happen! [one and a
half pages illegible]

It is 10 o'clock; and I must now be turned out of the Café, and will go
and doze on my luggage, probably until Dawn.

I shall dream happily of you at home, where the same Voice that gave

---

[1] This letter survives in fragments only. See Introduction, p. 5.
[2] HO had just survived an aeroplane crash. He was under training as a pilot at the Royal Naval
Air Station, Chingford, Essex, from October 1916 to March 1917. Two crashes were
allowed in training; HO crashed again, and was sent back to sea service.

us ease when we broke a window, will give you the same ease, always.

I think it was your disconsolate mind that wrote my last Sonnet 'Happiness'. You will see.

[*several words illegible*]   Your affectionate, Wilfred

489. To Susan Owen

1 March [*1917*]   *My Dug-Out*

Dearest Mother,

Have just reported at B.H.Q. Dug Out. Find myself posted to B. Coy. of which the Captain is poet Sorrel.[1] There is small chance of doing Transport for a long time if ever. Howsoever, this is a glorious part of the Line[2], new to us, and indeed, to the English (sh!) Most comfortable dug-outs, grass fields, woods, sunshine, quiet. True we are in reserve today, but I hear the very front line is a line, and a quiet one.

My letter to Harold left yesterday by the Army Post. It was in an astonishing way I had your parcel. A man rose up from a hole in a field holding it above his head. It was a fine moment. I soon rushed down & tore it open. Socks most specially valuable, as my servant forgot to put any spare in my Trench Kit. Likewise, I took no Cigarettes, hoping to find 50 in the Parcel. Lo! here are thousands! How good of you all. I smoke Harold's with reverence.

I shall not touch the goodies until the very front line is reached.

The Post is waiting to go.

Yours as ever, but slightly happier than usual.   W.E.O.

490. To Colin Owen

2 March 1917   *B Coy Dug-Out*

My dearest Colin,

This is the first time I have written from a Dug-Out. I am in a French one now. We have straw to sleep on, but it is pretty lousy—after the poilus!

There is a gas-alarm on just now, but I don't really expect it. The air is too still. Just this moment, and since I sat down, a tremendous artillery strafe has opened up. We all remark to each other that it seems there is a war on. I went up to the Front Line with a Fatigue Party for digging. Let me tell you in confidence that I was for the first time a

---

[1] Lieutenant S. Sorrell, M.C., Manchester Regiment, was invalided home a few weeks later with shell-shock. In March 1918 he was a Staff Captain (Assistant Military Landing Officer), and was listed on the Army Reserve in August 1918. We have been unable to identify him as a poet.

[2] On 25 February the brigade of which 2nd Manchesters formed a part had taken over the line from the French near Fresnoy, occupying dug-outs at Bouchoir and billets at Beauvois. They were still on the St. Quentin front. On the same day the Germans were found to have evacuated their positions in front of the Le Transloy–Loupart line and north of the Albert–Bapaume road.

Target.* I ran over the top to get to the head of the Party in the Trench,
& stood a moment to shout an order, when a bullet went Ping, a good
3 ft. over my silly head.

Next day. Where you see the * I left off because the order came 'Stand
to Arms!' What a commotion! We half expected an attack, but nothing
happened. I have no paper to write more, but this letter should be
interesting circumstantially.

Dearest love to you, sweet my Brother.   W.E.O.

You must disinfect your hands, whether sore or not, after stables.

491. To Susan Owen

2 March 1917   *B Coy's Dug-Out*

My dearest Mother,

I am in a good warm Dug-Out, decorated with French postcards,
picturing embraces, medals, roses and mistletoe!

Is it possible I was living civilly no more than 2 days ago? From
letter of last night I hear you have seen the illusory War Films. However, they must hint at the truth, and if done anywhere on this Front,
would not be quite devoid of realism. But, as you know, a just idea of
the First Place could best be got by a tour around Purgatorio.

Did you see any Shell-bursts?

And did they bang tins or whack drums?

Did you see any Red X at the front?

Under no circumstance do we! A good half of their work is done by
S. Bearers of our own Coys. You don't mention Dug-Outs or snipers.
I was marked by one of the Pests yesterday. His 'Direction' was good,
only his 'Elevation' slightly high. A curious thing was who first hissed
'Get down, Sir!'?

One of my old Fleetwood Musketry Party! Quite a few are with me.
One of those to whom I swore I would never tolerate near me at the
Front. I remember his total score was 5!! One of the servants of this
Dug-Out remembers me at Thursley Common, (Witley), and has
photographs of lads I remember, who are now in Egypt, bless 'em.

The Corporal who shared my Coat in the last dug-out (before my
Course), & who was one of them who fell out by the wayside, is now in
hospital, his dysentery having taken a serious form.

I have almost cleared away my cold by means of douches. Thanks
however for the Formamin. Do quick tell me how to use 'Quasha'. Do
I chew it? or suck it? boil it? burn it? or rub it? well in the part affected?
(I have parts affected since last night.)

'Colin's' socks are splendid things.

The Rice fluffy-fluffy makes excellent packing-material.

A Prize for who first solves my conundrum.[1] No knowledge of

[1] If there is a coded place-name in this letter, we have failed to find it.

IX. Officers of the 5th. (Reserve) Battalion, the Manchester Regiment, Milford Camp, Witley, July 1916. Wilfred is second from the right, front row

Xb. Siegfried Sassoon on leave, 1916

Xa. *The Hydra* (Editor, Wilfred Owen)
21 July 1917

<u>French required.</u> I wrote to Harold 3 days ago, & to Colin this afternoon.

Ever your fondest Wilfred x

492. To Susan Owen

Sunday, 4 March 1917   [*2nd Manchester Regt., B.E.F.*]

Dearest Mother,

Just a line at 5.30 today, while you are at Tea. Until I came in from work at 4 o'clock I had no idea it was Sunday. It often happens so. The work was the usual Digging. If anything could give a touch of interest to the work, it was that many of these diggers dug the show-trenches at Thursley, in the days when my stars were bright from their creation by Pope & Bradley.

Some chaps even fired their Course with me at Mytchett. I felt very tempted to take a rifle & do a bit of snapping, but it is forbidden to officers. On bright days like this I begin to be glad of your khaki covers.

For lunch, I had bully-beef, munchie, and flatulent rice. I like this stuff very much.

When I came in, Capt. Sorrel gave me the choice of writing a Sonnet before 7.30. or going with the next Fatigue Party!! I am ever so happy to be with him. He chokes filthiness as summarily as I ever heard a Captain do, or try to do. He is himself an aesthete, and not virtuous according to English standards, perhaps, but no man swears in his presence, nor broaches those pleasantries which so amuse the English officer's mind.

He seems to be one of the few young men who live up to my principle: that Amusement is never an excuse for 'immorality', but that Passion may be so.

I find this Company in a far better state than A, partly, of course, because of good sergeants, but Sorrel has a fine control.

My important letter written yesterday[1] left today, as today's will go tomorrow. How long do they take. It is so quiet here that we have our meals in a shallow dug-out, and only go down deep to sleep.

I sleep well; I eat well; I am well. Surely better than any of you at home. Dear old Harold has not written yet? Did I not warn Colin about his dirty hands? Has the new servant had any effect on your strength? I hope so.

Fondest love to all, Your W.E.O. x

493. To Susan Owen

9 March 1917   *Deserted Village*

My own dearest Mother,

I had no idea your throat was so seriously bad when I last wrote,

---

[1] It has not survived.

3 or 4 days ago from the Dug-Out. But your 2 letters and Mary's came a few hours after dispatching my mail. During these last few days, I have not been able to write at all, nor had I any Field Cards to send. And nothing has come from you since the one telling of how you were sitting up for tea, being a little better. How I hope that by now the pain at least and the Malady of it are gone; and that there is a fair sun healing you!

We have gone back to severe cold and snow. This Village is half destroyed and our billets are not half so cosy as dug-outs.

Another Place
More Deserted Village

11 March

No sooner had I set out my Kit and done a page for you, than I was boosted back nearer the Line on a special job: in charge of a party of Dug-Out Diggers. It is a soft job. I take the men up sometimes by day, sometimes by night, so that (as today) I lie snug in my blankets until lunchtime. We are 4 officers living in this cellar; our servants cook for us. It is a relief to be away from the Battalion for a while. How I hope it will last. It <u>may</u> spin out 3 weeks.

I have just <u>been</u> sweating along a dangerous road to a factory where there is a shower bath. There was no water today! I sweated some more coming back. (Methinks I am becoming something crude in my speech.) 'Tis a crude, vagabondage of a life. While Leslie is theorizing over the art of building, here am I watching a fair old village toppling about my head. I think the wreckage will look even sicklier when the orchard-trees break out, like the souls of infants in Limbo. I am able to read here, but have nothing left now. I receive your *Red* △ with gratitude, but do you think, now, that I am going to read the <u>war-impressions</u> of home-editors? If, here & there, you get a true version of the business— so much the more unreadable. *Punch,* on the other hand takes humour too seriously. From *Punch* you would take a <u>Sentry</u> to be the laughing-stock of Europe.

Spleen!

No, I still tipple *Punch* as hilariously as ever. But don't send any, for some one or other is bound to have one.

What I should like would be a current *Poetry Review.*

Please don't send anything special for my Birthday. You have sent so many specialities lately. For instance, expensive chocolate!

I hope to be able to write again tomorrow, but I have an unwonted amount of official letters to do.

It's now nearly ten days since your Throat started bettering. Surely it is passed off now?

Longing unspeakably to see you, dear Mother, I look forward to Leave in about 3 more months!!

Your own Wilfred x x

494. To Susan Owen

Sunday, [*18*] *March* [*1917*]   [*13th Casualty Clearing Station*]

My dearest Mother,

I am in a hospital bed, (for the first time in life.)

After falling into that hole[1] (which I believe was a shell-hole in a floor, laying open a deep cellar) I felt nothing more than a headache, for 3 days; and went up to the front in the usual way—or nearly the usual way, for I felt too weak to wrestle with the mud, and sneaked along the top, snapping my fingers at a clumsy sniper. When I got back I developed a high fever, vomited strenuously, and long, and was seized with muscular pains. The night before last I was sent to a shanty[2] a bit further back, & yesterday motored on to this Field Hospital, called Casualty Clearing Station 13.[3] It is nowhere in particular that I know, but I may be evacuated to Amiens, if my case lasts long enough. For I began to get right again immediately after getting into these sheets 'that soon smooth away trouble.' The physician handed me over to the surgeon. But my head is not broken or even cut in any way. My temperature etc. may not have had any relation to the knock, and the first doctor said he only hoped it had. Anyhow it was normal yesterday, and below today, and the only abnormal thing about me now is that I don't want a cigarette. That, then, should not worry you. I have now told you everything, and I hope, dear Mother, that you are duly grateful —to me, and concerning the whole circumstance.

Sometimes a Sister blows in to this ward, and flutes a bit on a high voice, or pegs around on a high heel, but we are really attended by orderlies, who are fresh & clean, and much preferable, being not only serener and sensibler, but also private soldiers with no airs of authority about 'em. Rather the other way.

All my kit and belongings have come down with me, including 55 francs, much mud, and Pte. Heath.

Alas! I've had no letter for about 5 days when I had 3 together, and am not likely now to have any for quite a week. I think that for a few days: 2 Man. Regt. with 'Please Forward' will be the best address
[*six lines missing*]   ever, Wilfred x

495. To Colin Owen

Monday, 19 March   *13th Casualty Clearing Station*

My dearest Colin,

I am still kept in bed, though I feel fit for a walk.

---

[1] At Le Quesnoy-en-Santerre, according to E B. A letter dated 14 March 1917—which has not survived—was seen by him when he was writing the Memoir. He quotes from the letter as follows: 'Last night I was going round through pitch darkness to see a man in a dangerous state of exhaustion. I fell into a kind of well, only about 15 ft., but I caught the back of my head on the way down. The doctors (not in consultation!) say I have a slight concussion. Of course I have a vile headache, but I don't feel at all fuddled.'
[2] The Military Hospital at Nesle. See Letter 607, note 1.
[3] This was at Gailly. See Letter 536.

Yesterday I wrote to Mother without knowing it was my birthday! I found out in the evening. It is too bad to be without letters of any sort. It must be a week since I had any. But I lost count of days in that cellar, & even missed the passing of night & daylight, because my only light was a candle.

I know something of the Advances.[1] You will be glad to hear that there has been no undue influx on the hospitals, at least in this area.

Have you met that mighty horse-tamer at Underdale? His picture was in a *Sketch* I saw yesterday.

Always your loving W.E.O.

496. To Susan Owen

21 March [*1917*]   *13th Casualty Clearing Station*

My dearest Mother,

I am getting up today, and perhaps by the time you receive this I shall be starting back to overtake my Battalion, if it is not chasing along too fast.

One of the villages mentioned in the *Daily Mail*, thus: 'we captured a farm so many miles North East of Q[2] . . .' was the one to which I have been going every day or night last week.

We knew what was happening weeks ago, and I saw the smoke of burning behind the Bosche Line on the last day I was up.

I am not moving down to a Base—fortunately, perhaps, because any-one going further back than here becomes detached from his battalion, and is returned somewhere else.

There is no proper village here, and I am miserably in want of Books, not to say Letters. It is not worth writing to the Battalion, which for all I know may be openly warfaring, or perhaps is now already clean wiped out.

One of the sisters brought me some novels, about as palatable as warm water to a starving jaguar. Your remarks on Crocketts' last,[3] remind me that I once said his books were like sawdust—on which an ox has just been slaughtered.

I suppose you did not see Bernard Shaw's accounts of his visit to the front, appearing in the *Glasgow Herald*. He says he put black things like collar-studs into his ears. So very like collar-studs that I have been using mine as such for some time![4]

---

[1] By 10 March it had become clear that the Germans were planning withdrawal to the new positions in the rear known as the Hindenburg Line, and Allied pressure was increasing.

[2] Le Quesnoy-en-Santerre.

[3] Samuel Rutherford Crockett (d. 1914), whose romantic novels included *Princess Penniless* (1908) and *Old Nick and Young Nick* (1910).

[4] A light-hearted article by Shaw in the *Glasgow Herald*, 5 March 1917, entitled 'Joy-Riding at the Front', described his visit as *Daily Chronicle* correspondent to Arras, Ypres, and the Somme front. At Ypres, he wrote, 'I stuck into my ears a pair of seeming black collar-studs, which did not prevent my hearing anything, but did prevent me from overdoing it.'

Yes, I have long missed my Pen, and don't want another. My watch has disappeared since I left the cellar. Left there I think. I was too blind sick to notice anything. In my next parcel I should like some Harrison's Pomade & some more Paraffin.

Fondest Love, Wilfred x

497. To Mary Owen

Wednesday Mng. [*22 March 1917*]   *13th Casualty Clearing Station*

Dearest Mary,

I am now really quite well, but am not getting up yet, as it is snowing and I couldn't go out if I did dress. But we sit round the stove in Kimonos, padded with cotton, very pleasant wear. We are now about ten in the ward. One is an old Artist Rifle, but I never knew him, nor ever want to. They are none of them interesting, from any point of view whatever.

I amuse myself with drawing plans for Country Houses and Bungalows, especially Bungalows. I worked my wits all day on one,[1] and, within the prescribed limits, it is about perfect, for the intended occupant —solitary me.

You see I am thinking of sitting down under my own vine and living for use, some day, and a concrete presentment of the Vine should be incentive.

This passage rather winded me, yea wounded me. Mistress Browning:

> Many fervent souls
> Strike rhyme on rhyme, who would strike steel on steel,
> If steel had offered, in a restless heat
> Of doing something. Many tender hearts
> Have strung their losses on a rhyming thread,
> As children, cowslips. The more pains they take,
> The work more withers. Young men, ay and maids,
> Too often sow their wild oats in tame verse,
> Before they sit down under their own vine,
> And live for use.
>
> Alas, near all the birds,
> Will sing at dawn, and yet we do not take
> The chafering swallow for the holy lark.[2]

Or words to that effect.
Adieu, sweet sister.

Your ever loving W.E.O.

---

[1] HO saw this after the war, and remembers it as a detailed and loving piece of work.

[2] From *Aurora Leigh*, by Elizabeth Barrett Browning (1806–61). A copy of *The Poems of E. B. Browning* (Vol. II, Newnes, London) inscribed 'Bouchoir, Somme, 1917' survives among Wilfred's books.

498. To Colin Owen

24 March   *13th Casualty Clearing Station*

My dear Colin,

In my walk this afternoon, considering at leisure the sunshine and the appearance of peace (I don't mean from the news) I determined what I should do after the war.

I determined to keep pigs.

It occurred to me that after five years development of one pig-stye in a careful & sanitary manner, a very considerable farm would establish itself.

I should like to take a cottage and orchard in Kent Surrey or Sussex, and give my afternoons to the care of pigs. The hired labour would be very cheap, 2 boys could tend 50 pigs. And it would be the abruptest possible change from my morning's work.

If any man mocks me, Remember Paderewski![1]

What do you think of this?

I wonder you do not start with a sow of your own, this year.

Perhaps you will think me clean mad and translated by my knock on the head. How shall I prove that my old form of madness has in no way changed? I will send you my last Sonnet, which I started yesterday. I think I will address it to you.

Adieu, mon petit. Je t'embrasse.   W.E.O.

SONNET—with an Identity Disc[2]

If ever I had dreamed of my dead name
High in the Heart of London; unsurpassed
By Time forever; and the fugitive, Fame,
There taking a long sanctuary at last,

—I'll better that! Yea, now, I think with shame
How once I wished it hidd'n from its defeats
Under those holy cypresses, the same
That mourn around the quiet place of Keats.

Now rather let's be thankful there's no risk
Of gravers scoring[3] it with hideous screed.
For let my gravestone be this body-disc
Which was my yoke. Inscribe no date, nor deed.

But let thy heart-beat kiss it night & day . . .
Until the name grow vague and wear away.

This is private.

I stickle that a sonnet must contain at least 3 clever turns to be good. This has only two.

---

[1] Ignace Jean Paderewski (1860–1941), the pianist and composer who was also President of Poland 1919.

[2] An early draft of 'To My Friend (with an Identity Disc)', *Poems*, p. 106.

[3] 'notching' struck out.

499. To Mary Owen

25 March 1917   *13th Casualty Clearing Station*

My dear Mary,

I went a joy ride on a Motor Ambulance, a Daimler (as pictured in the *Sketch* last week) and so passed a vivid afternoon. The car was going in the direction of the Front, and I stopped at a certain village where refugees from the regained area were just arriving: all hags & children. I had a long talk with a boy of 14, who if he had been 15 would not have been liberated. He could not spell his name, since he has worked on the fields since he was 11. He did not look by any means starving, but had known nothing but scanty food for $2\frac{1}{2}$ years. I plied him with chocolate, and drew the following information. That the Germans carried off all men over 15; left 5 days bread rations for the remainder, set fire to almost every building, choked up the wells with farmyard refuse and disappeared.

Our guns have begun strafing heavily this morning. I can hear, from my bed, the continuous growling.

We are by a Canal, much used by the Army. It looks funny to see a Sergeant Major commanding a Tug, and a Corporal at the helm of the barge.[1] A pleasant life for khaki. Why doesn't Harold try it! The Inland Water Transport Service.

The surgeon says there is no hurry to send me back! I want to go—because of the letters!

Your own W.E.O.

500. To Susan Owen

Wed. Mng., 28 March 1917   [*13th*] *Casualty Clearing Station*

My own dear Mother,

They still keep me here, though I go out every afternoon. I have no letters, but have been able to get a few books from a small town where I motored on Sunday. I also got a cheap watch,—pocket size. I think the usual penalty of loss of property on coming to hospital has been small in my case: my watch. Not the original Brummagem of Clarke's, but a better one which I exchanged for it at a shop in A.[2] I left Colin's there for repairs. It is probably with the Battalion now.

At C.[3] I went into the great Gothic Church, and listened under the nave, as Belloc says, for the voice of the Middle Ages. All I could hear was a voice very much beyond the middle age. However I stayed to vespers; and after leaning my hat and stick up against a piece of the true Cross, I sat and regarded the plants (with their paper flowers wired on them), and St. John in bathing costume looking ruefully at another saint in a gold dressing-gown; and the scarlet urchins holding candles and

[1] See Letter 509.
[2] Probably Amiens. See Letter 501.
[3] Probably Corbie.

chewing,—probably the grease. Indeed it is enough to set the Wykliffe's[1] howling.

I hear that young Boultbee, son of Father Boultbee,[2] one of the prophets, is missing. He was in the R.F.C. and I am told a very wild fellow!

The man in the next bed told me this. We have two cases, pilot & observer, who are terribly smashed. They will both recover, but the pilot has both arms broken, abdominal injuries, both eyes contused, nose cut, teeth knocked in, and skull fractured. It makes me ashamed to be here. But I help to look after him at night. The sister has a wonderful way with him. I like her very much. Constitutionally I am better able to do Service in a hospital than in the trenches. But I suppose we all think that.

Yours as ever W.E.O.

501. To Susan Owen

Picture postcard: Amiens, Le Marché sur l'eau et la Cathédrale. The word
Amiens is underlined. There is no written message.

[Postmark 30 March 1917]   *[Postmark Amiens]*

502. To Susan Owen

4 April 1917[3]   *[2nd Manchester Regt., B.E.F.]*

Dearest Mother,

Know that I have cut my forefinger with a tin of Lobster, and that is why I write shaky. I have been 4 days caravanning from the CCS, & have just found our H.Q. Journeying over the new ground has been most frightfully interesting. The Batt. has just done something great[4] which will find its way into the Communiqué. I am going up to join them in an hour's time. They have lost one officer & many are wounded, Heydon among them.[5] I shall no doubt be in time for the Counter Attack. I have bought an automatic pistol in the town (from which I sent a P.P.C.) By the time you get this we'll be out of the line again. Tonight will be over. . . .

My long rest has shaken my nerve. But after all I hate old age, and there is only one way to avoid it!

Last night I bedded down with a family[6] of refugees, 3 boys, 2 tiny

---

[1] i.e. the reformers.

[2] The Rev. Hugh Edmund Boultbee (d. 1943), Vicar of Greyfriars, Reading, 1905–15, Vicar of Christ Church, Surbiton Hill, 1915–18.

[3] Corrected by Susan Owen from the original 4 March.

[4] A successful but costly brigade attack had been mounted on Savy Wood on 2 April with Selency as its objective. Thereafter A Company (which had suffered heavy losses) probed forward to the outskirts of St. Quentin. See Letter 503.

[5] Altogether, two officers and twelve other ranks were killed, seven officers and fifty-two other ranks wounded.

[6] Perhaps the Lemaire family mentioned in Letter 504.

girls: a good class socially, and of great charm personally. I was treated as a god, and indeed begin to suspect I have a heart as comprehensive as Victor Hugo's, Shakspere's, or your own. In 24 hours I never took so many hugs & kisses in my life, no, not in the first chapter even. They took reliefs at it. It would have astounded the English mind.—While, just the night before I was in blues as deep as the Prussian Blue—not having heard an affectionate spoken word since I left you—or rather since I left A. I am now in the Pink.

No need to tell you where I am going up to fight. It is the town on which the hopes of all England are now turned.[1] I must now dress up in Battle Order.

Your own W.E.O. x x x x x

I find no letters here. Your parcels did not take part in the advance—Too heavy!

Without your Letters I should give in. What to I know not, but I 'sorter' feel I should 'give up the unequal contest!'—without a definite object for carrying on. And that object is not my Motherland, which is a good land, nor my Mother tongue, which is a dear language, but for my Mother, of whom I am not worthy to be called

The Son x x x

I hope this bit of paper is not incriminating[2] to send over but it is all I can find. I must write to Colin & send him some small souvenirs tomorrow. Ah my poor angel! He wants to be with me. He would not live three weeks in this sector of Hades.

503. To Susan Owen

6 [?8] April [1917]   [*2nd Manchester Regt. B.E.F.*]

My own dearest Mother,

We are 'in rest.'[3] I arrived at the Battalion a day too late for the stunt: I am therefore not in the 'we' when I say we captured 6 guns, numerous machine guns, and of course, the Position.

But I am still ME.

I am afraid poor Heydon will not live, and other officers, one of my company, fell on the field. It is interdicted to give any figures at all, but a good number of us are (agreeably) wounded.

When I turned up I went back to A. Coy, where Captain Green was hanging on with only one officer. We stuck to our line 4 days (and

---

[1] St. Quentin.
[2] The last sheet is written on the back of a scrap headed:

AMENDMENT

S.S.143. 'Instructions for the
Training of Platoons in Offensive Action'
Appendix I. NOTES. LINE 6. *After* 'No. 1' *add* 'and No. 2'.

[3] The battalion was relieved on 8 April and withdrew to billets in Beauvois till 12 April, when it returned to Savy Wood. This letter seems to be predated by some two days.

4 nights) without relief, in the open, and in the snow. Not an hour passed without a shell amongst us. I never went off to sleep for those days, because the others were far more fagged after several days of fighting than I fresh from bed. We lay in wet snow. I kept alive on brandy, the fear of death, and the glorious prospect of the cathedral Town[1] just below us, glittering with the morning. With glasses I could easily make out the general architecture of the cathedral: so I have told you how near we have got. The French are on the skirts of the Town, as I could see. It was unknown where exactly the Bosche was lying in front of us. The job of finding out fell upon me. I started out at midnight with 2 corporals & 6 picked men; warning other Regiments on our flanks not to make any mistake about us. It was not very long before the Hun sent up his verilights, but the ground was favourable to us, and I and my Corporal prowled on until we clearly heard voices, and the noises of carrying & digging. When I had seen them quite clearly moving about, and marked the line of their entrenchment it might seem my job was done; but my orders were to discover the force of the enemy. So then I took an inch or two of cover and made a noise like a platoon. Instantly we had at least two machine guns turned on us, and a few odd rifles. Then we made a scramble for 'home'.

Another night I was putting out an Advanced Post when we were seen or heard and greeted with Shrapnel. The man crouching shoulder to shoulder to me gets a beautiful round hole[2] deep in his biceps. I am nothing so fortunate, being only buffeted in the eyes by the shock, and whacked on the calf by a spent fragment, which scarcely tore the puttee.

One day I hung my Trench Coat (which you used to button up for me at Southport) on a bush, & had just jumped down into my hole when a splinter ripped a hole through the chest & back. The tears are not big enough to spoil it for Field use.

I found your Parcel waiting for me here, when we got in at 3 in the morning (all half dead with fatigue & some quite, poor lads.) It was like a look in at Home to burrow into that lovely big box and examine all the loving presents. I opened it in bed (for I found my blankets ready laid out in this cosy cellar) and before I had opened all the boxes fell fast asleep. I am not awake now properly and my letter may appear disjointed. But then I'm not disjointed. I learned with astonishment that you had measles, and selfishly speaking am glad enough I only know it now you are better of it. O darling Mother you can't think how you could secure my peace of mind by being able to tell me you

---

[1] St. Quentin.

[2] The uncompleted poem 'Beauty' (*Poems*, p. 140) was to culminate in 'the beauty of getting a flesh-wound serious enough to send one back to "Blighty".' CDL quotes from the MS pages of attempts at further lines:

> A shrapnel ball
> Just where the wet skin glistened where he swam.
> Like a full-opened sea-anemone.
> We both said 'What a beauty! What a beauty, lad!'
> I knew that in that flower he saw a hope
> Of living on, and seeing again the roses of his home.

are well. Look at me I am nearly screwed to death with cold and nerves one night. Two days later I am in perfect, glowing, brilliant Health.

Tell Mary that Captain Crichton Green is immensely complimentary about her gingerbread.

I will write again tomorrow. Just had yours of 27th. Found Mar. 31st waiting for me. Be sure we shall not go into action again for a long time. It couldn't be done.

Still, always, and ever your very own   Wilfred x x x

504. To Colin Owen

Monday, 9 April 1917   [*2nd Manchester Regt., B.E.F.*]

My dear Colin,

You want Souvenirs? There were plenty of Helmets, Bayonets, Caps, Coats, Shirts, Handkerchiefs, Tobacco, Bread, Soap, Needles & Cotton left by the Hun in the place we took and were holding last week.

I took a Name Patch out of a Coat for you, and a Mark Note, which is specially interesting by reason of its date. 12 August 1914. It looks as if the plant for issuing these war notes was ready before the Declaration of War.

There was nothing of value that I could lay hands on. For I was too occupied with my heavy duties to go scratching around for souvenirs.

Yesterday afternoon, Easter Sunday, we were finishing tea in this Cellar with something like Sunday peace serenity when we were roused by the unexpected shattering sound of machine guns. I rushed up just in time to see a German Aeroplane come shuddering down the sky. With my little pistol in my pocket I dashed over the fields as fast as my sore feet would carry me.

The Machine was a new Albatross[1] No 2234. The Pilot—well I need not horrify you without need. But I took his handkerchief—a rather touching souvenir. You need not show them at home the spatter of blood in the corner. I rather want this handkerchief kept for me. The 3-ply wood is a bit of the body (of the machine).

I could not stay to see the engines & guns dug out of the soil, because I am so frightfully busy. The only other officer of A. Coy has gone sick, and Capt. Green is always in the Battalion Orderly Room fighting so to speak, for V.C.'s, D.C.M.'s etc. for our men. At least one of our Coy. is put in for V.C. and many others for the D.C.M.[2] I think Capt. Green, though not in the action before myself, will get a Military Cross,[3] which he has long deserved—for 2½ years active service.

Between us we are pulling the Company together for we 'go in' again tomorrow! It is rather strange to feel that these heroes feel me as their boss!

[1] German scout plane.
[2] Four Military crosses were awarded for the Savy Wood action, and one D C M (to Private Overton, A. Coy signaller, who had been recommended for the V C).
[3] But he did not.

We had congratulatory telegrams from the Commander in Chief downwards. He himself came[1] . . . sh! 'Ware Censor!

I suppose things were done so well that we are needed again. I had hoped to get down the line as far as V[2] . . . to see my sudden great friend André Lemaire, with whom I lodged on my way up. He has done more damage to the Boche when his fiery soul was under their hated domineering than I ever managed to do:—stretched wires across the high road at night, & upset a Staff Motor Car, threw hundreds of bombs [*letter posted unfinished*]

505. To Susan Owen

25 April 1917   *A. Coy., My Cellar*

My own dearest Mother,

Immediately after I sent my last letter, more than a fortnight ago, we were rushed up into the Line.[3] Twice in one day we went over the top, gaining both our objectives. Our A Company led the Attack, and of course lost a certain number of men. I had some extraordinary escapes from shells & bullets. Fortunately there was no bayonet work, since the Hun ran before we got up to his trench. You will find mention of our fight in the Communiqué; the place happens to be the very village[4] which Father named in his last letter! Never before has the Battalion encountered such intense shelling as rained on us as we advanced in the open.[5] The Colonel sent round this message the next day: 'I was filled with admiration at the conduct of the Battalion under the heavy shell-fire . . . The leadership of officers was excellent, and the conduct of the men beyond praise.' The reward we got for all this was to remain in the Line 12 days. For twelve days I did not wash my face, nor take off my boots, nor sleep a deep sleep. For twelve days we lay in holes, where at any moment a shell might put us out. I think the worst incident was one wet night when we lay up against a railway embankment. A big shell lit on the top of the bank, just 2 yards from my head. Before I awoke, I was blown in the air right away from the bank![6] I passed most of the following days in a railway Cutting, in a hole just big enough to lie in, and covered with corrugated iron. My brother officer of B Coy, 2/Lt Gaukroger[7] lay opposite in a similar hole. But he was covered with earth, and no relief will ever relieve him, nor will his Rest will be a 9 days-Rest. I think that the terribly long time we stayed unrelieved

---

[1] Field-Marshal Douglas Haig, 1st Earl Haig (1861–1928), C-in-C of the British Expeditionary Forces in France and Flanders 1915–19.

[2] Perhaps Villers-Bretonneux, between Amiens and the front.

[3] The battalion had returned to the front at Savy Wood on 12 April to support a new French attack on St. Quentin.

[4] Feyet.

[5] Thirty men were killed in the barrage. See Letter 510; and 'Spring Offensive' (*Poems*, pp. 52–54).

[6] This experience (enlarged on in Letter 508) resulted in Wilfred's shell-shock and invaliding home.

[7] Second-Lieutenant H. Gaukroger, Manchester Regiment.

was unavoidable; yet it makes us feel bitterly towards those in England who might relieve us, and will not.

We are now doing what is called a Rest,[1] but we rise at 6.15 and work without break until about 10 p.m. for there is always a Pow-Wow for officers after dinner. And if I have not written yesterday, it is because I must have kept hundreds of Letters uncensored, and enquiries about Missing Men unanswered [*remainder missing*]

506. To Susan Owen

2 May 1917   *13th Casualty Clearing Station*

Dearest Mother,

Here again! The Doctor suddenly was moved to forbid me to go into action next time the Battalion go, which will be in a day or two. I did not go sick or anything, but he is nervous about my nerves, and sent me down yesterday—labelled Neurasthenia. I still of course suffer from the headaches traceable to my concussion. This will mean that I shall stay here and miss the next Action Tour of Front Line; or even it may mean that I go further down & be employed for a more considerable time on Base Duty or something of the sort. I shall now try and make my French of some avail . . . having satisfied myself that, though in Action I bear a charmed life, and none of woman born can hurt me, as regards flesh and bone, yet my nerves have not come out without a scratch. Do not for a moment suppose I have had a 'breakdown'. I am simply avoiding one.

At the first Ambulance I arrived at in the Car, a Corporal came up to me with a staid air of sleepy dignity that seemed somehow familiar. And when he began to enter in a Note Book my name & age, we knew each other. It was old Hartop of the Technical! Bystanding Tommies were astounded at our fraternity. For the Good old Sort brought back in an instant all the days of study in Shrewsbury, and the years that were better than these, or any years to come. Although married, as you may know to one of the girls who acted with me at the Socials, he has not grown up any more since the last term at the P.T.C. He was reading the same old books that we 'did' there. I was jolly glad to see them again, & to borrow. For he has nothing particular to do but read on his present job of Pack Store Corporal in the R.A.M.C. Davis also is married. How fortunate is Stanley Webb, (not speaking of his engagement, but of his Blighty.)

If I haven't got a Blighty in this war, I will take good care not to get a Blight, as many have done, even from this Regiment. I should certainly have got a bullet wound, if I had not used the utmost caution in wriggling along the ground on one occasion. There was a party of Germans in a wood about 200 yds behind us, and his trench which we had just taken

---

[1] The battalion was relieved on 21 April, and moved to cellar quarters in Quivères. The only draft of 'Le Christianisme' (*Poems*, p. 83) is annotated 'Quivières'.

was only a foot deep in places, & I was obliged to keep passing up & down it. As a matter of fact I rather enjoyed the evening after the Stunt, being only a few hundred yds. from the Town, as you knew, and having come through the fire so miraculously: and being, moreover, well fed on the Bosche's untouched repast!! It was curious and troubling to pick up his letters where he had left off writing in the middle of a word! If we had gone down from the line next day all would have been very well, but we were kept up (in another part of the line) for 9 days after it: under incessant shelling.

I am so glad you got the one Field Card which I was able to work down from there. Your last Parcel has arrived, and I enjoyed the Munchoc right well. I had some compensation for lost parcels in being given a parcel sent to an officer who was wounded the first day he joined us. It is a regimental custom never to send Food Stuffs back after Officers who go down to Hospital! I shall soon want some more Players. Nothing else yet!—Don't omit to address C.C.S.13.

I am more glad than I dare say to know that dear Mary is now all right. I try to imagine that you are really well. How strange that the fact that I am in Hospital means that all cause of uneasiness about me is removed from you! Do not hawk this letter about! Nay, I would rather you told no one I am a Casual again!

Your very own Wilfred

507. To Susan Owen

4 May 1917   *13th Casualty Clearing Station*

My own dear Mother,

I have been expecting every day to be moved from here, but nothing happens; only a great calm happiness. We are a cheery crowd here this time, and I like everyone as a great & interesting fellow. Some of us have been sent down here as a little mad. Possibly I am among them. One man in particular is supposed to be a Brain Case. He is a Trinity College (Oxford) boy, and a nephew of Sir Frederick Treves;[1] and is going to get damages from his C.O. for libel or something of that sort; with Sir Frederick & F. E. Smith to back him up!! The chief arguments of his denouncers are (1) that he had an original Scheme for making a haul of German Prisoners, and (2) he happened to read the Bible. He is, of course, perfectly sane, but may be sent to England!

I have just been writing in French some letters for one Barlow[2] of Typewriter fame, who has given me a personal introduction to old Erskine Macdonald, whom he treats to dinners in Town in return for the literary chat which old Skinny can give him. Also, I shall now have no trouble about Typewriting!

I have no news, but that it has been splendidly hot lately, & we have

---

[1] Sir Frederick Treves (1853–1923), Sergeant-Surgeon to King Edward VII.
[2] Unidentified.

been living the lounging, irresponsible life of a hydro. It will not last long for some of us. I don't care at all if I am not sent back to the same Batt. since the C.O.[1] is leaving, & Sorrel is in England: and I believe we are going to be a Flying Column, rushed about to wherever there is scrapping to be done.

I have, before coming down here, made proper arrangements for your letters to be sent on. Please address everything to 13 C.C.S. who will also send things after me.

Players & the thin Viyella Shirt left in the Drawer are all I want. If you haven't got the Viyella, I must needs have a new one.

Always your lovingest   W.E.O. x

(Leslie has my 'Sunrise'[2] just done here.)

508. To Mary Owen

8 May 1917   *13th Casualty Clearing Station*

My very dear Sister,

I have just re-read your last letter of April 22, which I carry about with me in my Pocket Folio of most valuable papers. Such letters are not received every day—except only from Mother. These papers have had an addition which may be useful—an introductory note to Erskine Macdonald, who edits the Georgy-porgy Verse Books. My new acquaintance Barlow seems to have old Erskine at his beck & call. This Barlow is a Yorkshire man, & knows the Jobsons. Which is more than I do. But I have begun to find that everyone I meet knows someone that I know. There is a 'Neurasthenia Case' here that I remember at H.Q. of the Artists Rifles. He was Mark Hamburg's[3] father's pupil, & Boris Hamburg's secretary. There is an officer of the Welsh Guards who also has news of old friends. I told you how I met old Hartop.

I have also found among French Officers relations of people I knew in Bordeaux!

I saw in the Casualty List about May 1: Major W. Forrest,[4] KOSB International Footballer. I could find no room for doubt about poor old Walter.

I had a most characteristic lovable letter from Dorothy about a week ago. I cannot bear to read the exalted things she exclaims, while I am here, so indolent, & well-looked after.

The Nerve Specialist is a kind of wizard, who mesmerises when he

---

[1] Lieutenant-Colonel L. Luxmore, DSO, commanded the battalion throughout the Somme battles of 1916 till May 1917; he was succeeded as CO by Lieutenant-Colonel Whittaker, MC, Dorsetshire Regiment. In November 1917 Lieutenant-Colonel E. Vaughan, DSO, Manchester Regiment, took over.

[2] See Letter 509.

[3] Mark Hambourg (1879–1960), pianist and composer.

[4] Walter Forrest, Blanche Bulman's fiancé, was killed at Gaza, Palestine, April 1917.

likes: a famous man. He is a friend of Dr. Keeble[1] and the Reading Botany People!

You must not entertain the least concern about me because I am here. I certainly was shaky when I first arrived. But today Dr. Browne was hammering at my knees without any response whatever. (At first I used to execute the High Kick whenever he touched them) i.e. Reflex Actions quite normal. You know it was not the Bosche that worked me up, nor the explosives, but it was living so long by poor old Cock Robin (as we used to call 2/Lt. Gaukroger), who lay not only near by, but in various places around and about, if you understand. I hope you don't!

I have no intimation at all about my next move.

Meanwhile I have superb weather, sociably-possible friends, great blue bowls of yellow Mayflower,[2] baths and bed *ad lib*. Soon I shall have Letters from Home.

Your own W.E.O. x

It is absurd for me to keep saying 'I hope you are well' or even to enquire about Mother. What do you take me for ? ? ?

509. To Susan Owen[3]

10 May 1917   *13th Casualty Clearing Station*

Dearest Mother,

I sent a card yesterday of a place I know very well.[4] When I was with the Dug-Out Making Detachment, we used to pass this village, and every night the whiz-bangs & machine guns exacted their Toll.

---

[1] Professor Sir Frederick William Keeble, CBE, FRS (1870–1952), botanist, was Director of the Royal Horticultural Society's Garden, Wisley, at this time in addition to being Controller of the Horticultural Food Production Department, Board of Agriculture.

[2] His fingers wake and flutter; up the bed.
His eyes come open with a pull of will,
Helped by the yellow may-flowers by his head.
'Conscious', *Poems*, p. 63.

[3] With this letter Wilfred enclosed the following draft of 'A Sunrise' (not included in *Poems*); another draft is in the BM.

A Sunrise

Loomed a pale Pearl more marvellous than the Moon's,
Who thereby waned yet wanner than she was,
Because of the pallor of the Pearl of dawn,—
Her Pearl was whiter than the wan, worn Moon's.

The Pearl cleared Opal; Emerald eftsoons,
And the Emerald trembled peerless for an hour,
Till shower'd with shimmering Sapphires. (Their blue shower
Burst keen and brilliant as the first birds' tunes.)

Then slowly through the shaking jewels of dawn,
Moved the immutable Ruby of the Sun,
Hung the immortal Ruby, huge with morn.

And the Moon was finished like a reel unspun,
She vanished as a Pearl that falls in wine.
She died: like the white Maid that once was mine.

[4] The card has not survived.

This card I found in a shop in Corbie,[1] with the enclosed, a picture taken in Summer 1915, so you can imagine what sort of a billet it made in the Feb. of 1917! It was in this village that I fell, & knocked the good old Nut.[2] I hope you will keep these safe!

I sailed in a steam-tug about 6 miles down the Canal with another 'inmate'.

The heat of the afternoon was Augustan; and it has probably added another year to my old age to have been able to escape marching in equipment under such a sun.

The scenery was such as I never saw or dreamed of since I read the *Fairie Queene*. Just as in the Winter when I woke up lying on the burning cold snow I fancied I must have died & been pitch-forked into the Wrong Place, so, yesterday, it was not more difficult to imagine that my dusky barge was wending up to Avalon, and the peace of Arthur, and where Lancelot heals him of his grievous wound.[3] But the Saxon is not broken, as we could very well hear last night. Later, a real thunderstorm did its best to seem terrible, and quite failed.

The next book for you to read is *A Knight on Wheels*.[4] It is great.

I, with the inherited diffidence of my distinguished Grandma, must say I could never do anything like so great.

I suppose in the million eyes of the Empire I have already done a thing greater than this merry book; but, then, more fools the million eyes . . .

I think it is about time your letters addressed here were turning up. None have been sent down from the Line.

How are you rationing? The French hereabouts subsist chiefly on Dandelion Salad. I am not joking. The young leaves with oil make an excellent supper. Tell me how you find it.

I live mainly on Pine Apple Chunks. There are going to be certain things Afterwards which will be held by all who love me in everlasting TABOO,

One of these is Pine Apple Chunks.

Another is a lead pencil on bad paper.

Another is the smoke of a damp wood fire.

Post is now being cleared.

All Love from your very own   Wilfred x

510. To Colin Owen

14 May 1917   [*13th Casualty Clearing Station*]

Dearest Colin,

Here is some Loot, from a Pocket which I rifled on the Field. I was thinking of you when I was unbuckling the Bugle from the equipment,

[1] Near Amiens.

[2] This card, too, is lost. It must have pictured Le Quesnoy-en-Santerre.

[3] This afternoon on the canal inspired 'Hospital Barge at Cérisy' (*Poems*, p. 97).

[4] *A Knight on Wheels* (1914), by Ian Hay (Major-General John Hay Beith—1876-1952), novelist and playwright.

and being then in a particularly noble frame of mind, meant to present it to you some day. But now I have got too fond of the thing to part with it!

The sensations of going over the top are about as exhilarating as those dreams of falling over a precipice, when you see the rocks at the bottom surging up to you. I woke up without being squashed. Some didn't. There was an extraordinary exultation in the act of slowly walking forward, showing ourselves openly.[1]

There was no bugle and no drum for which I was very sorry. I kept up a kind of chanting sing-song: Keep the Line straight!

Not so fast on the left!

Steady on the Left!

Not so fast!

Then we were caught in a Tornado of Shells. The various 'waves' were all broken up and we carried on like a crowd moving off a cricket-field. When I looked back and saw the ground all crawling and wormy with wounded bodies,[2] I felt no horror at all but only an immense exultation at having got through the Barrage. We were more than an hour moving over the open and by the time we came to the German Trench every Bosche had fled. But a party of them had remained lying low in a wood close behind us, and they gave us a very bad time for the next four hours.

When we were marching along a sunken road, we got the wind up once. We knew we must have passed the German outposts somewhere on our left rear. All at once the cry rang down 'Line the Bank'. There was a tremendous scurry of fixing bayonets, tugging off breach-covers & opening pouches, but when we peeped over, behold one solitary German, haring along towards us, with his head down and his arms stretched in front of him, as if he were going to take a high dive through the earth (which I have no doubt he would like to have done). Nobody offered to shoot him, he looked too funny; that was our only prisoner that day!

Did I tell you that on Easter Sunday evening we brought down a Hun Plane, I took the aviator's handkerchief as a souvenir! It is not permitted to take anything belonging to the machine.

Now write soon something about your new Farm. Sketch me a plan of it. Have you a pleasant room of your own? Most of the gentlemen here seem keen on farming after the war. The musician is going to farm, having not practised the piano since 1914; the aviator is going to farm; the undergraduate is going to farm. Some day I will arise and go unto Mr. Bather,[3] and will say unto him 'Bather, I am no more worthy to be called thy son than Colin; but make me as one of thy hired servants.' But his brother was wrath and would not let him in, and began to beat him and entreat him shamefully. But this Bather came out and said unto

---

[1] The action at Feyet. See Letter 505.
[2] This image is expanded in 'The Show' (*Poems*, pp. 50–51).
[3] The farmer for whom Colin was now working at Cressage, ten miles S W of Shrewsbury.

him 'Why beatest thou the ass? Be gentle with my servant, lest he fall on good soil, and make it like the wilderness of Judea, which is a great wilderness.'

So he departed unto Some Area, and seeing a tree, he also pruned it that it might bring forth more fruit.

After that the tree died also, and he lay down, and slept under the shadow thereof forty days and forty nights; and gathered in his ears in due season, the mustard seed, which is the smallest of all seeds, yet brought forth ten fold, fifty fold, and an hundred fold.

And with the price thereof he bought a field, which is called the Potter's Field, because he pottered there day and night and wrought nothing.

But dined sumptuously every day of locusts and wild asses' milk.

And it came to pass that a woman besought him saying 'Give me, I pray thee, a little water to drink.' Instead of water he gave her the milk. And the same woman was bent double for eighteen years. And went out sorrowful, and wept by the river of Babylon. And all fish that were in the river died.

And he knowing that the time of harvest was near at hand, and of the creeping things that creep upon the earth, went down into that water and washed seven times.

And he was covered with boils from head to foot.

And they put him upon his own ass and took him to an inn.

And in the process of time, he saithe unto him that kept the inn 'I will drink a little wine for my stomach's sake. Fill me seven barrels full.'

And they filled them unto the brim.

And there was silence for the space of half an hour.

And when he understood the meaning of the seven stars, he lifted up his voice, and cried 'Fill them a second time.' So they filled them a second time. Till there was no room for him in the inn.

And his face shone with the brightness of the sun.

And they all looking steadfastly upon his face, said one to another, 'Peradventure he sleepeth.' But he began to belabour them with staves of a new song, so that they all with one accord fled violently down a steep place into the sea.

And there arose a great storm.

For a third part of all the dwellers upon the earth fell into the sea.

But he was asleep.

And he, when he came to himself, saw the stars falling in heaven, like a fig-tree when she casteth her untimely fruits.

But in process of time the devil departed from him, and he arose, and girt up his loins, and sneezed three times, so that the fool said in his heart: It is the coming of a great rain.

But he, stooping down, began to tie the latchet of his shoe. Now because of the new wine and the old leather, it came to pass that the same was rent in twain. And he stood up and cursed them.

And hell followed after.

Then cometh he that kept the inn, grievously tormented, seeking goodly pearls.

But he turned and saithe unto him: Go to! and when I come again I will pay thee.

And he answered and saithe: 'Peradventure thou wilt not return. I will follow thee whithersoever thou goest.'

And he led him up to a pinnacle of the temple; and let him down vehemently through the roof: so that even the stones cried out. And they that saw it were astonied supposing the clouds had dropped this fatness upon the earth. And looking up they beheld the husbandman upon the head-stone of the corner.

And he shook the dust off his feet, and they were all smitten with blindness, because of the things that fell upon the earth.

And he went on his way, rejoicing, and grinning like a dog that licketh the crumbs that the swine would fain have eaten.

And the ass leaped like the hills, even the hill of Basan, which is an high hill. Selah.

CUM PRIVILEGIO.

You can send this to Harold: to be returned to me! I have let my imagination run riot. You must not show these sheets at home. But I hope you will get an innocent laugh out of 'em. I have. It has passed an afternoon very well.

Best love, dear boy. W.E.O. x

511. To Susan Owen

14 May 1917   [*13th Casualty Clearing Station*]

Recv'd your of 9th. Have just written to Colin. There is, as we say, 'nothing to write home about'. I am just waiting for the Post to come in, and the outgoing Post is waiting for me.

Your W.E.O.

512. To Susan Owen

[*?16*] *May 1917*   *41st Stationary Hospital*[1]

My own dear Mother,

Just had yours of Sat. Evening and was astonished to apprehend that the Great Shadow is creeping on towards Colin. What will he be next birthday, seventeen?

I wrote him a wholesome bit of realism in that last letter, as well as a fantasy in the language of the Auth: Ver: of 1611. I have changed my mind and see no reason why you should not have that letter and that fantasia. It was on the model of Leslie's 'Throw her down. So they threw her down. And he said Throw her down again. And they threw

---

[1] 13 CCS was restaffed at this time (see Letter 514, para. 2) and renamed 41st Stationary Hospital.

her down again. And they gathered up of the fragments that remained etc.'

I did it without any reference to the Book, of course; and without any more detraction from reverence, than, say, is the case when a bishop uses modern slang to relate a biblical story. I simply employed seventeenth century English, and was carried away with it.

Incidentally, I think the big number of texts which jogged up in my mind in half-an-hour bears witness to a goodly store of them in my being. It is indeed so; and I am more and more Christian as I walk the unchristian ways of Christendom. Already I have comprehended a light which never will filter into the dogma of any national church: namely that one of Christ's essential commands was: Passivity at any price! Suffer dishonour and disgrace; but never resort to arms. Be bullied, be outraged, be killed; but do not kill. It may be a chimerical and an ignominious principle, but there it is. It can only be ignored: and I think pulpit professionals are ignoring it very skilfully and successfully indeed.

Have you seen what ridiculous figures Frederick & Arthur Wood[1] are cutting? If they made the Great Objection, I should admire them. They have not the courage.

To begin with I think it was puny of Fritz to deny his name. They are now getting up a petition, mentioning their 'unique powers' 'invaluable work' and so on, and wish to carry on their work from 82 Mortimer St. W. as usual. I do not recollect Christ's office address in Jerusalem, but in any case I don't think He spent much time there.

St. Paul's business premises, if I remember, were somewhat cramped, not to say confined.

But I must not malign these Brethren because I do not know their exact Apologia.

And am I not myself a conscientious objector with a very seared conscience?

The evangelicals have fled from a few Candles, discreet incense, serene altars, mysterious music, harmonious ritual to powerful electric-lighting, overheated atmosphere, palm-tree platforms, grand pianos, loud and animated music, extempore ritual; but I cannot see that they are any nearer to the Kingdom.

Christ is literally in no man's land. There men often hear His voice: Greater love hath no man than this, that a man lay down his life—for a friend.

Is it spoken in English only and French?

I do not believe so.

Thus you see how pure Christianity will not fit in with pure patriotism.

I am glad you sent that cutting from Wells' Book. I hope you understood it. I did not. Not a word of it can I make sense of. I would rather we did not read this Book. Now *The Passionate Friends*[2] I found astound-

---

[1] See Letter 111, note 1.
[2] See Letter 468, note.

ing in its realism but like all the great terrible books it is impossible to 'take sides'. It is not meant to be a comfortable book; it is discussional; it refuses to ignore the unpleasant.

(This practice of selective ignorance is, as I have pointed out, one cause of the War. Christians have deliberately cut some of the main teachings of their code.)

At present I am deep in a marvellous work of Hugo's *The Laughing Man*.

By the same post as your letter came two books from Leslie, by O. Henry.[1]

So I am well set up.

I am marked for the next Evacuation!!

So glad my Oak Seedlings are growing. How many are there likely to thrive, out of how many acorns? They have been 'dry', you know, for 6 years. Give them every chance.

This countryside is now superb. But from this we are no longer allowed out of the hospital bounds.

Many thanks for *Punch*. Yes Colin has been very good in writing to me. Keep him up to it. It will do him good, don't-you-know! And as for me: they bring me Shropshire, even as yours bring me Home.

Expect me—before Christmas.

Your—one and only—Wilfred x

513. To Susan Owen

18 May 1917   [*41st Stationary Hospital*]

Dearest Mother,

I had the Parcel (Shirt) last night. Have just awakened—too late to write before the post leaves. Your two letters, with enclosures from Paris, came at the same time. The flowers were quite fresh; & I was very refreshed with them.

No more now. They have just awakened me to know if I have any letters for Post!

Your W.E.O. x

514. To Susan Owen

23 May 1917   [*41st Stationary Hospital*]

Dearest Mother,

I wondered why it was such an effort to write the short notes of a day or two ago. I have discovered that I had a temperature of 102.9, so it was not surprising. I am still feverish but on the right side of 100°. I suppose it is Trench Fever, which has been incubating all this time, but they don't say what it is and I don't think they know.

[1] William Sydney Porter ('O. Henry'), 1862–1910, American journalist and prolific writer of humorous short stories.

I have had a wretched enough time, not from the fever in myself but from the stew that the whole hospital has got into. A completely new staff from England has taken over. The old people cleared off bag and baggage, bed & bedding, before even the new things arrived. They did put us in some sort of beds, but otherwise they stripped the ward stark, taking even the drugs. There was not left one chair, one mug, one tea-pot, one rug, one screen. They took the very ashtrays to which indeed they were welcome, for they are not worth a farthing, and I don't smoke.

No, I could no more smoke a cigarette than any unborn chicken. My servant informed me that I had some Mangee* as he calls it—in my valise. But it does not tempt me at all.

He will not follow me to the Base when—or if—I go.

I repeat the new address of this place:

41st Stationary Hospital.

It is quite likely that I shall appear in the Casualty List, as Neurasthenia is marked W(ound) not S(ick)—not wrongly I think. I know that Capt. Sorrel was mentioned for Shock, and that some persons wear gold stripes for neurasthenia!

Many more are worn for bullet grazes which did not more harm than a needle-scratch.

I am afraid it is quite out of the question to find anything for Mary or even to write for today's post.

Yours ever W.E.O. x

The new staff of the hospital will no doubt start unpacking today.

But I shall never get over my indignation at the manner of the Relief!

* Pronounced Mŭnjy (Lancashire u).

515. To Susan Owen

24 May 1917   *41st Stationary Hospital*

My own dearest Mother,

I feel normal today. Am sitting on the bed in the one Kimono left in this Rag Time Hospital. Have just had your Sat. evening (May 19) Letter, full of gracious truths: the most pleasing being the tales of your gardening. I am sure it will do you good, and I may indeed get Leave before the Summer falls, now that it is likely I am out of the 'Area' of the 2nd Battalion. Some regiments get leave for every officer regularly every 5, 4, or even 3 months, but in the 2nd Man. the minimum seems to have been 7!

x   x   x

The M.O. has just been round—leaving me 5 mins. before the Post goes.

I am astonished at my Balance at Cox's, but not so astonished as you,

463

knowing it is deceptive. There have been a number of Mess Bills, & other cheques drawn lately which are not yet entered at the Bank. Moreover my Military Wardrobe will want renewing if there is another winter campaign.

On the other hand I confess—I mean I profess with pride—that I have not run into any kind of danger of losing moneys. My first Mess Bill for Jan. was £6: which I consider disgraceful for the kind of stuff we got.

I think it will be safe if you send both Cheque Book & Pass Book in registered envelope to 41st Stationary Hospital: (by return)

It is evidently Trench Fever I had, but I feel fine today. I shall send this note & go on writing for tomorrow's post.

Your own W.E.O.

516. To Mary Owen

25 May 1917   *41st Stationary Hospital*

My dearest Mary,

I hope this little note will arrive in time for the Birthday Morning.[1]

I am writing in bed, after an awful breakfast. Enough of those who profess and call themselves Sisters. I have a real sister, and I want her with me!

On one's 21st Birthday, it is better to look forward than back, because that way one cannot see anything at all. It is a good thing—for Father's ethics, and the Bunting, the Majestic One, and the rest—that on my 21st Birthday, when I looked into the Future, I did not see the War coming. I did not. But if I had, I should certainly have borrowed sixpence and bundled over into Spain. In August 1914, when the moon was red, I used to go up at night to a hill-top, and look at Spain. I still do that in dreams. You have your battlefield, my dear sister, to look back upon. You too have walked slowly through many barrages; you have taken trench after trench from resisting Life; and no terror has halted you. You have taken your objective: all that remains is to consolidate. . . .

I've now had all your letters from Alpenrose; they were full of atmosphere. Glad you saw & liked Miss O.A.J. Without wishing to see her myself, I may say that this lady is much to be admired. She has extraordinary power over words. Her power alas sometimes degenerates into tyranny. But she is a woman who has as much poetic worth as Madam Wilcox,[2] the hussy.

It grieves me that I can't send you any present at all yet. I am a prisoner. If they would send me to a Town of some sort I should be cured in a week. Here is the list of places & the amt. of time required to effect complete cure, showing average temperature & pulses.

---

[1] Mary's twenty-first birthday, 30 May 1917.
[2] Ella Wheeler Wilcox (1850–1919), popular American poet and journalist.

Place.	Time Req'd to effect Cure.	Temp. Normal (98.4)	Pulse. Normal 80
St.Q.[1]	10 years after 'Duration'	107° (in the shade)	150
Bordeaux	6 months	98.4	90
Paris	3 months	do.	100
Cressage[2]	10 minutes	do.	normal
H.M.S. *Zealandia*[3]	20 mins.	do.	rather erratic
London	1 hour	perfect	
Alpenrose	½ hour	90°	50
Mahim (Europe)	.01 second	perfect	200 (1st minute only)

There are too many officers here who are quite well. For the last 3 nights the ward has been a midnight pandemonium. It makes me in such a stew that a thermometer if put in my mouth would at once explode. Fortunately, last night an Artillery Colonel came to sleep here. The racket awaked him. He coughs a bit, and kicks the bedclothes up and the mattress down, and the flies all around and about. Then he sits up and opening his eyes to the full extent, bellows: 'Are there N O N E in this ward who wish to sleep.' 'There are, sir,' says I, 'and I am glad you mean to stop the din.' With that he leaps off the bed, & runs out of the ward for the Sister, brings in a wretched trembling maiden just out of England: and cries: 'Look! Madam! Is this a hospital or is it a ——— ——— ——— ? ? ?' And flaps his pyjamas, and tries to stamp, but his bare feet made a poor enough noise.

I wonder what kind of men you get in your wards. I hear that the sisters & nurses are nice people. Did you see anything of 'Missis Gordon'[4] when at Alpenrose?

No more nonsense now, but just my very dearest wishes for the best years of my darling sister. May they be without cloud or ruffle of storm. May they each be long years, that is to say, full, and may they be full of good, filled from Heaven. You will speak for me when you look up to God; and I will stand by you and for you as long as we move among men. In other words, I am, gentle Sister, always your Brother,

Wilfred

[1] St. Quentin.
[2] Where Colin was farming.
[3] The battleship on which H O was now at sea.
[4] Gordon Gunston had recently married.

517. To Susan Owen

Monday, 28 May 1917   [*41st Stationary Hospital*]

Dearest Mother,

Just a note. I was down on the list for evacuation all last week & up to last night. This morning the evacuation takes place—I and another, a Major, are crossed off the list at the last moment. It is sickening, more especially as this place becomes less and less pleasant. I suppose I shall wait for the next batch, but before that I may be turned out elsewhere—to some Line Battalion.

These are the days when last year the army was good to me. The same dreadful uncertainty overhangs me here as on that 'Leave pending Gazette.' Would I had to report at Witley Camp on June —. I came across an old 5 Man. lad a day or two ago. Some of the Witley officers are out near here with the 1/5th. I wish I could rejoin them. I hear that the horrid old Major[1] is now commanding the 2nd Batt. It is not likely that Sorrel will be back for a long time. Hence I hope that I am clear of them, and shall try to avoid rather than find them again. As you may have seen they charged me £6. for my January Mess Bill. I scarcely had anything for it.

I am feeling quite well now, but I keep a sub-normal temp.! Useful enough in this weather.

I hope you will have plenty of picnics in the hay. Have you been to Cressage? *P.R.*[2] arrived last evening before I went to Church. Rather a 'footy' paper as Leslie says. There is a rumour you are going to Alpenrose. Go!

Your lovingest W.E.O. x

518. To Susan Owen

Picture postcard: Amiens,[3] La Cathédrale vue de Saint-Maurice

5 June 1917   [*41st Stationary Hospital*]

Am not here—no move yet—quite happy—you have some erroneous ideas about my state of health! I have a chum here—glorious in my eyes for having hob-nobbed with Ian Hay. You sh'd keep the *Chambers*[4] in which *Knight on Wheels* first appeared. Last evening had your dear letter of May 31.

Things are vastly improving now in the management of this Hydro! Poor Mawkie Morgan! Poor Ragge[5] & no Bones

---

[1] Major, later Lieutenant-Colonel J. F. Dempster, temporarily assumed command of 2nd Manchesters on 18 May 1917. Wilfred encountered him again in London. See Letter 528.

[2] *Poetry Review*.

[3] Against the name is written 'I am not here'.

[4] *Chambers's Journal*, established 1832, regularly taken by Tom Owen.

[5] John Ragge had been invalided home. He later returned to France, where he was killed in September 1918.

519. To Susan Owen

6 June 1917   *41st Stationary Hospital*

Dearest Mother,

I go down today. Where to?—Nobody knows. May be in the Hosp. Train for days.

Health: quite restored.

Mood: highest variety of jinks.

Weather: sub-tropical.

Time: 11 a.m.

Appearance: sun-boiled lobster.

Hair: 8% Grey.

Cash in hand: 5 francs.

Size of Socks: same as previous consignment.

Sole Complaints: Nostalgia
                                Mosquito Bites

Last Book Read: *A picked Company* by Belloc.

Clothing: sparse, almost faun.

Religion: Primitive Christian.

Aim in War: Extinction of Militarism beginning with Prussian.

Aim in Life: Pearls before Swine.

Medicine: Iron

Nerve: Iron—(over?-) wrought.

Favourite Metal: Silver.

Favourite Colour: Sky- violet.

Favourite Drink: Natural Lemon Juice.

Favourite Animal: Children.

  ,, Haunt and which?: Moor—Monk.

Pet Aversion: Pets.

Blood Relations: Unbleedable.

Address of same: Temporal only.
                                Permanent: Unknown & doubtful.

My address: as usual; i.e. unfixed.

Affection: Yours.

Name: W.E.O. or words to that effect.

520. To Susan Owen

8 June [*1917*]   *41st Stationary Hosp!*

Dearest Mother,

Two days ago we started forth in motors for the Railhead: The Train was there, but no accommodation for Officers. The O.C. Train a minute doctor, with many papers and much pince-nez, refused to let us board: especially as a Major who was with us expressed himself thus: 'Aw I decline. I ɐbsolutely decline, to travel in a coach where there are—haw—Men!'

This Major is an unconscionable snob, and consequently suffers something from my humour.

It was slightly too hot that afternoon: they put some twenty Germans into this sumptuous train, and left us stamping on the platform: some indeed lying on stretchers in blankets under the staring sun. When we got back to the Hospital we were the objects of some very ungratifying applause from the unlucky ones left behind. I am still on the List, & the thing may come off more successfully tomorrow or on Monday.

I have not written yesterday, because it is just as well that you should not address any more to the 41st as from the date you heard of my departure. Thus I am getting all you send here up to the last and none will be lost. On the evening we [*remainder missing*].

521. To Susan Owen

Sunday, 10 June 1917   [*41st Stationary Hospital*]

Dearest Mother,

We make another sally this day. On the whole, the rout of our last sortie was fortunate for me, as I have the parcel, and the letters and J. Oxenham's Books.[1]

The *V. Splendid* contains several real poems: those indeed which you have marked. But the majority of the things have no <u>poetic</u> value at all.

The 'Cross Roads' is very very good. Otherwise the work has little <u>Pacific</u> Value, if you understand me.

Except to individual troubles: for he evidently holds the Moslem doctrine—preached by Horatio Bottomley,[2] but not by the Nazarene—of salvation <u>by death in war</u>.

Barbe of Grand Bayou[3] seems a little too idyllic so far. Oxenham's aim seems to be to unsophisticate the reader. It is very pleasant to be reminded of Brittany, which seems not to be of this continent at all.

The book is at the opposite pole from the O. Henry books which Leslie sent me. Impossible to read them together.

At the same time I am at p. 50 of A. & E. Castle's recent book: *The Hope of the House*,[4] which promises well, and which I can recommend.

My man has gone to the neighbouring Town today, so I am in haste to pack. I shall think especially with you this Evening. I crave Travel and shall be pleased like any infant to get into a puff-puff again. Have your letter writ, and post it as soon as you get my address!!

Your W.E.O. x

---

[1] John Oxenham (d. 1941), novelist and poet. *The Vision Splendid* (verse, 1917) contains a poem entitled 'Cross Roads', first published separately in 1903.
[2] Horatio Bottomley (1860–1933), journalist and financier who founded *John Bull* in 1906. Liberal MP 1906–12, Independent MP 1918–22. Twice bankrupt, twice acquitted on fraud charges, he was imprisoned 1922–7. For an example of his style see Letter 667, note 2.
[3] Published 1915.
[4] Published 1915.

522. To Susan Owen
Postcard

[*Postmark 11 June 1917*]

No. 1 General Hospital
Etretat.[1] France.

523. To Susan Owen

Picture postcard: Etretat, Les Roches

[*Postmark 12 June 1917*]   [*No. 1 General Hospital*]

I am sending by same post a Panorama of the Bay. I seem to be in America: the Hospital is staffed with the Amer[n]. Doctors, Orderlies, and Sisters. This is the Officers' Quarter. I live in a Marquee on the front lawn. We are free to walk away thr' this delicious Norman Coast. But so far—all yesterday—and this m'ng we are hanging around waiting for the M.O's interview. I have no idea how long I shall be kept here. Not worth your coming over ! !

W.E.O.

P.S. (later) Shall soon be home on Sick Leave. Vive !

524. To Susan Owen

June 1917   *No. 1 General Hospital*

My dearest Mother,

I think it is very likely that the Americans will send me to England, but we must permit ourselves no jubilations yet. I shall believe it as soon as I find myself within swimming distance of the Suffolk Coast. The usual thing on arrival is a fortnight or more of genuine leave at home!

I am sorry! I can think of nothing else to write about, and if I went on about my expectations this letter would end in a scream. If I go bathing this afternoon it will be to practise swimming in Channel waters.

If I looked all morning at the Northern Horizon it was not because of its infinity of sea, but because of its boundary of cliffs, and the starting of the firm home road.

If I enjoy this place and make the most of it, it is because I believe I am to leave it very soon.

If I seem to be writing a matter of fact letter, it is because I am not too sure that what I am writing about will realize into matter of fact.

I will let you have a card the moment we leave. Don't expect Telegrams. I may be kept some time in London or elsewhere.

Always your W.E.O. x

[1] On the Channel coast, five miles north of Le Havre.

525. To Susan Owen
Postcard

Sunday Mng. [*Postmark 17 June 1917*]   *Welsh Hospital, Netley*[1]
Hampshire

I shall have to stay here a week or so. Visitors are allowed in the afternoons, but you will of course wait till I get my 3 Weeks at home. We are on Southampton Water, pleasantly placed, but not so lovely a coast as Etretat. The Town is not far off, & we are allowed to go in. Hope you had my Telegram. Nothing to write about now. I am in too receptive a mood to speak at all about the other side the seamy side of the *Manche*. I just wander about absorbing Hampshire.

W.E.

526. To Susan Owen

Monday [?18 June 1917]   *Welsh Hospital, Netley*

Dearest of Mothers,

I had your letter this morning—a great delight. This place is very boring, and I cannot believe myself in England in this unknown region. I have just written to Leslie asking him to come and convince me.

It is pleasant to be among the Welsh—doctors, sisters, orderlies.

And nurses.

They kept me in bed all yesterday, but I got up for an hour & went out today, only to be recaught and put back to bed for the inspection of a specialist. He was very nice, and when I said my home was in Shrewsbury he asked if it were in the Town itself or in the country.

I said it was nearer the country. To which he gave the usual specialist reply 'Ha!' I also inwardly said 'Ha!'

There was no choice of Hospitals when we were detailed off from Southampton, tho' I tried to get the Birmingham Train, which those officers who lived hereabouts had to take!

When I get away I shall try to journey through London. There are new clothes I want.

The Voyage was in a luxurious West Indian Liner. I had a cabin to myself, and fared sumptuously at Table.

Here also we fare much better than anywhere in France. I sleep well and show every sign of health, except in the manipulation of this pencil.

Your own W.E.O. x

You may as well prepare Mr. Bather gently for an agricultural slump in labour.

---

[1] The Royal Victoria Hospital, with its imposing façade on Southampton Water, was built in 1863 and demolished, belatedly, in 1966. It was a quarter of a mile long, the world's largest military hospital at its inception, and was severely criticized for its design by Florence Nightingale on her return from the Crimea. The wards were dark and poorly ventilated; and the upkeep a continuous drain on Government finances for a hundred years.

527. To Susan Owen

Picture postcard: Netley Hospital

[*Postmark 22 June 1917*]   [*Postmark Southampton*]

Thanks for your Letters, the last was June 19th. Leslie is coming over this afternoon. I have no idea when I shall get home: hope you had no qualms on Sat., you dears! Now I wd much rather the extra bed removed. There are always my Camp Beds. I do hope you are not overdone by this Bale. Why I should be glad to find you out of doors when I come, but not out of breath. I am sending some goods carriage forward addressed to Father, temporarily. x. W.E.

The 'Welsh' is a hutment behind this Bungalow.

528. To Susan Owen

26 June 1917   *Craiglockhart War Hospital¹, Slateford, Midlothian*

My dearest Mother,

We left Netley at 11 on Monday Morning, & I separated from Captain Robertson at King's Cross about 3 p.m. I got a new hat at Peter Robinson's, and changed into new collar, tie, & pin. I entrusted Peter Robinson to send my old hat to a Cleaner's. It should turn up at home in a week or so. Then I made for Burlington House. This year's show is nothing so good as the last; and I didn't spend very long there. I had tea at the Shamrock Tea Rooms, perhaps the most eminently respectable exclusive and secluded in Town. There was the usual deaf old lady and her Companion holding forth upon the new curate. I happen to know that a few stories higher in the same building is an Opium Den. I have not investigated. But I know. That's London. I met few faces I knew. But Strolling down New Bond Street, I ran into the last person on earth or under the earth that I wished to meet: Major, now Colonel, Dempster, of the 2nd Battalion. We stopped, of course, and he pretended to be very affable and cordial. Yet I know a more thorough-bred Snob does not exist—even in the imagination of Thackeray. To meet him in my first hour in town. Alas! This, also, is London! . . .

I had time to get measured for new Slacks at Pope and Bradley's.

A cheap dinner, and so to King's Cross an hour early to get a Corner Seat.

I read some Israel Zangwill² as far as the Midlands. Then wondering how few miles I was from You, slept. I woke up as we were rounding the Coast by Dunbar. I saw nothing waiting to meet me at the Waverley Station, so I went into the Hotel and breakfasted hugely. I then walked the lovely length of Princes Street. The Castle looked more than ever

---

¹ The Craighlockhart Hydro still stands, in its own grounds, and is now Convent of the Sacred Heart, College of Education.
² Jewish novelist, playwright, and lecturer (1864–1926). *Children of the Ghetto* was his best-known work.

a Hallucination, with the morning sun behind it. Or again it had the appearance of a huge canvas scenic device such as surrounds Earls Court.

A Taxi brought me up here about 2½ miles from the Town.

There is nothing very attractive about the place, it is a decayed Hydro,[1] far too full of officers, some of whom I know.

I shall not see the M.O. till Tomorrow: I am going out now to take the lie of the land.

Has my watch turned up? (Colin's I mean.) It was at a Repairer's when I was called away, but I did not forget it, & an American girl promised to mail it across home right then. Always your lovingest of all,

Wilfred x

529. To Susan Owen

[End June 1917]   *[Craiglockhart]*

[opening missing] The King is said to be coming here next week—coming to see how his thin bullocks are fattening.

The WAAC's[2] now wait on us. It is rather pleasant; a sort of communal home life without parents or children.

My train had just got out of London when the raid began. I suppose I ought to be glad, but a raid is much more thrilling than the daily thunderstorms up here. *[remainder missing]*

530. To Mrs. Bulman

1 July 1917   *Craiglockhart*

Dear Mrs Bulman,

How exceedingly kind of you to send Miss Henderson to see me, and with such a goodly present! A good friend might have sent me straw-

---

[1] Siegfried Sassoon describes Craiglockhart in similar terms in *Sherston's Progress* (Faber and Faber, London, 1936, pp. 86–88), where he calls it Slateford (after the nearest railway station to the Hydro):

'It would be an exaggeration if I were to describe Slateford as a depressing place by daylight. The doctors did everything possible to counteract gloom, and the wretched faces were outnumbered by those who were emerging from their nervous disorders. But the War Office had wasted no money on interior decoration; consequently the place had the melancholy atmosphere of a decayed hydro, redeemed only by its healthy situation and pleasant view of the Pentland Hills. By daylight the doctors dealt successfully with these disadvantages. . . .

'But by night they lost control and the hospital became sepulchral and oppressive with saturations of war experience. One lay awake and listened to feet padding along passages which smelt of stale cigarette smoke; for the nurses couldn't prevent insomnia-ridden officers from smoking half the night in their bedrooms, though the locks had been removed from all doors. One became conscious that the place was full of men whose slumbers were morbid or terrifying . . . by night each man was back in his doomed sector of a horror-stricken front line where the panic and stampede of some ghastly experience was re-enacted among the livid faces of the dead. No doctor could save him then, when he became the lonely victim of his dream disasters and delusions'.

[2] Women's Auxiliary Army Corps.

XIb. Part of a Letter from Scarborough, 18 February 1918

(see Letter 592)

XIa. Draft Letter from Bagnères-de-Bigorre, August 1914

(see Letter 279, note 1)

XIIb. Susan Owen

XIIa. Tom Owen in 1920

berries, but only a very special friend could have remembered the cream!

I have also to thank you for the encouragement of your Letter received in France when encouragement was most needed; but when to answer letters was a physical impossibility. Unfortunately, if I delay an answer for a month, it becomes a moral impossibility! Even this I might have written two days ago; but you will forgive me, my Auntie Nelly, and charitably put it down to my distraught state of mind? (For you are all Charity, and I am beginning to discover the sources of my own Mother's sweetness.)

I am not able to settle down here without seeing Mother. I feel a sort of reserve and suspense about everything I do. Otherwise I am quite well—far better than, say, in the good days at Kelso.

I have endured unnameable tortures in France; but I know that I have not suffered by this war as you have and are suffering.[1] I felt your sympathy with me out there; but now, my dear Auntie Nelly, it is all on my part.

Believe me, very sincerely, and, may I not say affectionately, yours,

Wilfred Owen

531. To Leslie Gunston

1 July 1917   *Craiglockhart*

Dear L.

> Worde is comen unto Edenburrowe
> That you are in Londonne Towne.

You give no address so I forward the *Morals*[2] to Alpenrose. You will like to read it in London. I feel rather limp this morning—couldn't sleep —so read Locke until 3 a.m.

I noticed it never grew quite dark all night; Daylight glimmered through my Northern window even at 2 o'clock.

I have to meet Blanche Bulman in Edinburgh this afternoon.

A pleasaunte streme of letters is flowing in to me: but it must be fed by my own showres swoote.

My Ballad[3] is going strong, finished Fytte 1 at the second sitting. Late last night I very hastily draughted a Fate sonnet. I had an Idea— which is almost my Gospel. Can you get it from this? If so, how would you express it in prose?

Don't—omit to enquire about H. Monro. Your own W.E.O.

---

[1] Her son Bill and her daughter's fiancé, Walter Forrest, had been killed in action. See Letters 370 and 508.

[2] *The Morals of Marcus Ordeyne* (1905), a novel by W. J. Locke (1863–1930). Locke was Secretary to the RIBA 1897–1907. Another of his novels is mentioned in Letter 535.

[3] The BM has thirty-six draft stanzas of an unfinished ballad of Dame Yolande's love for her youthful page, of her jealous husband Baron Oberond, of Sir Lance, and of old Price the Prince. It is a high-spirited, but serious work in the manner of the traditional border ballad.

<u>The Fates. (2nd Draught.)</u>[1]

They watch me, shadowing, to inform the Fates,
   Those constables called Fortune, Chance, and Death;
G. Time, in disguise as one who serves and waits,
   Eternity, as women that have breath:

I know them. Men and boys are in their pay,
And those I hold my perfect friends may prove
Agent of theirs, to take me if I stray
From Fatal[2] ordnance. If I move, they move . . .

<hr/>

Escape? There is one unwatched way: your eyes,
O Beauty! Keep me good that secret gate.[3]
And when the cordon tightens of the spies.
Let the clear iris of your eyes grow great!
Bad So I'll evade the press-gang raid of age
G.   And miss the march of lifetime, stage by stage.

June 2. '17

Your W.E.O.

532. To Susan Owen

Sunday [2 July 1917]   *Craiglockhart*

My dearest Mother,

Your last news was the Note of the 29th. I can't even tell you how long I shall be kept here. I feel pretty sure of another fortnight; but in any case it would be of no interest for you to come just before I am able to get home.

My own plan would be for you to come this week to a lodgement in Edinburgh. (Hotel, Boarding House, Pension, what you will) for two days. Then stay with Mrs. Bulman for a Holiday.[4] It will be very difficult for me to get to Kelso. I should not manage it more than once. I could as easily get right home, I think.

I fancy that having once dislodged you as far as Southport I must not exert you so soon again.

The Stunt Magnificent would have been a semi-surprise expedition to Netley—you and Colin.

I don't want you to travel up alone: taxis & porters require to be hailed with exceeding heavy hailstorms of sticks, bags and umbrellas, nowadays. What about Father? Couldn't he come alone if not with you? Last of all, Send Colin with Tydynges of you all. I will find him a room in the village here, and give him a thundering good time, and he can have my heather suit to come in, and he shall stay four days, and (huf)*

---

[1] A later version is in *Poems*, p. 122. CDL points out that 'June 2' at the end must be a slip for July 2, the poem being drafted 'late last night'.
[2] 'Fate's old' struck out.
[3] 'O Beauty! Keep me ever good that gate' amended to read as above.
[4] Susan Owen followed this proposal. See Letter 533.

I will show him Edinburgh and (huf) the Castle (huf) and Holyrood and (huf) the Zoo, and the fertile fields of Midlothian, and he shall be the incarnation of you all. So shall I be more at rest. For I feel a kind of reservation about all pleasant things I do here. I have made no friends in this place, and the impulse is not in me to walk abroad and find them.

Send therefore Benjamin and inform yourself of me.

I won't write letters. It seems too absurd.

It was good of Leslie to write to you.

Mrs. Bulman sent an ambassadress with strawberries & cream on Friday afternoon: a Miss Henderson, a pleasant young lady, from what I could make out of her Scotch; a trifle nervous of me at first; but I did my best: and was sorry I called her Miss Ferguson so often. We have a fool of a butler-orderly, who comes up to me & says 'Young Lady to see you, Sir!'—no card—no name. So I says 'I don't think, but what's it like?' about a yard from where she was round a corner.

Because the middle of the night before I was wakened up by a kind of monotony in my room, which proved to be an orderly expounding a telegram to me about meeting you or somebody at a certain station next morning. And when I had given thanks, I perceived the telegram was for somebody else.

I therefore turned my face to the wall. But I have yet to deal with that Orderly.

If any of you should just look me up out of friendliness—just a fren'ly aft'noon call—when there's nothin' much doin' at home—please bring plenty of room in your baggage for taking back my surplus stuff.

Personally I don't see what Auntie Bobs[1] has got to do with my seeing my Mother on my return from war. If I had foreseen Auntie Bobs when I was sinking in the mud or coming-to after the Embank-ment-Shell-Shock it would have been the last straw.

I went to a United Free Church this evening, giving up my dinner to do so.

It gave me the indigoes.

Really I am looking so well as to cause remarks to be made as I pass the guid wives in the town. I want you to see me now.

Oh Mother!   x W.E.O.

*Take breath vehemently.

533. To Susan Owen

Saturday, July 1917   [*Craiglockhart*]

My dear, dear Mother,

So good of you to send a note from Yetholm.[2] I had not expected anything before. I am full of activities now. We founded last night a

---

[1] A friend of Mrs. Bulman at Kelso.

[2] Susan Owen had responded to the plea in the previous letter, and come to Edinburgh (see note 4, p. 476). She had travelled on to stay with Mrs. Bulman at Yetholm.

Natural History Club after a first Lecture on the Mosses of the District. I suppose I shall have to revive my Plants, for a Talk on Physiology or something. Few seemed to know what you told me about Sphagnum!

I have done an Essay on the Outlook Tower, to be delivered in privacy to Dr. Brock[1] this afternoon!

On The Hercules-Antaeas[2] Subject—there are only 3 or 4 lines in the Dictionaries. So I shall just do a Sonnet.

I have not seen Dr. Brock's ladies[3] since. The Ballad[4] came 2 days ago. I had even forgotten the title, and had so far forgotten the text that I was deceived in thinking it suitable for the Entertainments Programme.

I went down to Leith as arranged on Thursday. Alas! I had said I must be back by 5.30. The Newboults[5] found it wd. be impossible, unless we started immediately after lunch. So I am to go down to lunch one day next week.

That afternoon I went over the Factory and after that over Munition Works and Brass Foundries.

I am glad you were eye-witness to the instant gravitation of Chubby Cubby[6] into my Spheres. You notice it happened before the Lure of the Sweets came on the Scene. It may be the soldier's clothes: 'that the sweit bairn did win'[7] as the old Ballad says. But I hae me douts.

I spent yesterday morning beating out a plate of Copper into a bowl. That is as near as I can get to those summits of virtuous pursuits: Fretwork, and the taming of Mice.[8]

Leslie is at Hazely Down,[9] not Haslar.

Don't hurry back. There is a difference of environment between Pringle Bank and Somerside Road which must prove a severe trial to your adaptability when you have to return.

Looking forward to some privately conducted tours with you when you get back. Now which of us shall meet you? Tell me the times, & only me.

W.E.O.

Best messages to Auntie Nellie.

---

[1] The doctor in charge of Wilfred at Craiglockhart, who 'took more than common interest in him, regarding him as "a very outstanding figure, both in intellect and in character"' (EB).

[2] 'In order to restore his nerves to serenity, Dr. Brock directed his energies to any peaceful pursuit that could be arranged; he proposed to him the writing of a poem on a classical subject, Antaeus' (EB). 'Antaeus: A Fragment' (*Poems*, p. 120) is taken from the only draft, in Letter 534.

[3] A group of Edinburgh ladies who interested themselves in the rehabilitation of Dr. Brock's patients. See Letter 546.

[4] Probably 'The Ballad of Dame Yolande'.

[5] A Leith family, old friends of the Owens and of Mrs. Bulman. They lived at Bangower, 8 Summerside Place, Leith. Susan Owen had stayed with them for almost two weeks in July. For Miss Mary Newboult's recollections, see Appendix B.

[6] Arthur, the small son of the Newboults. See frontispiece, which was taken about this time, and Letter 553. For Mr. A. K. Newboult's recollections, see Appendix B.

[7] Bishop Percy's *Reliques*, 'The Jew's Daughter', st. 3, l. 4.

[8] Colin's two indoor pursuits.

[9] Near Winchester, where Wilfred later visited LG (who was working at the YMCA there). See Letter 561.

534. To Susan Owen

Tues. [*17 July 1917*]   *Craiglockhart*

Dearest Mother,

Yes: if you came on Friday Morning we would lunch, & have an hour on the Tower: given a fine afternoon.

I have found myself obliged to order a new tunic, to have this old one cleaned, and the other one enlarged by Pope & B. and the longer I leave it, the more extortionate the cost. Already this will be £5: 10! I am to be fitted on Thursday aft. But no reason you sh'd not come on Thurs. if more convenient.

Dorothy's letter aches with fine-feeling. I hope Mary will never write like that. It is too disturbing. Her thoughts are too shockingly unveiled. I mean to write to her, but not as I 'mean' to write to the hundred and one expecters of my letters. I give myself three days to fit it in and no more.

My tiny Notice of the first meeting of our Field Club has gone to press.[1] Old Brock is supposed to have written it. It was better paid than by a pukka Editor's best guineas. He will probably pay me in terms of Months, which is more than Money.

Here is the opening of Antaeas:

> 'So neck to stubborn neck, and obstinate knee to knee,
> Wrestled those two; and peerless Heracles
> Could not prevail, nor get at any vantage . . .
> So those huge hands that, small, had snapped great snakes,
> Let slip the writhing of Antaeas' wrists;
> Those hero's hands that wrenched the necks of bulls,
> Now fumbled round the slim Antaeas' limbs,
> Baffled. Then anger swelled in Heracles,
> And terribly he grappled broader arms,
> And yet more firmly fixed his graspèd feet.
> And up his back the muscles bulged and shone
> Like climbing banks and domes of towering cloud.
> And they who watched that wrestling say he laughed,
> But not so loud as on Eurystheus of old.'

Wilpher d'Oen (!!)

About 50 lines are now done.

535. To Leslie Gunston

Wednesday, July 1917   *Craiglockhart*

Dear L.

Thanks for yours of this morning. I hope you have had my card posted last Monday.

[1] It was written for *The Hydra*, the journal of the Craiglockhart War Hospital, published fortnightly, and appeared in the 21 July issue—by which time Wilfred had become Editor. For the next few months he wrote articles and reviews, as well as editorials: all anonymously. His most distinguished contributor was Siegfried Sassoon, who arrived at Craiglockhart in late July 1917. See Plate Xa.

On Mond. next I lecture the 'Field Club'—a Nat. Hist. association, on the lines of our old Society[1]—Geological, (you & me) & Botanical (Vera). Do you remember: you old Black Moth? Well, the days have come when I am one of the founders of a real learned society.[2] My subject has the rather journalese Title of 'Do Plants Think?'—a study of the Response to Stimuli & Devices for Fertilisation, etc. I have no books yet, but I remember a number of useful points from your big Cassell's (I think it was Cassell's) studied in 1911. Meanwhile I'm beastly bothered with our Mag.[3] (herewith) and I'm [to] take German Lessons at the Berlitz, Edin. Last week I wrote (to order) a strong bit of Blank: on Antaeus v. Heracles. These are the best lines, methinks: (N.B. Antaeus deriving strength from his Mother Earth nearly licked old Herk.)

. . . How Earth herself empowered him with her touch,
Gave him the grip and stringency of winter,
And all the ardour of th' invincible Spring;
How all the blood of June glutted his heart.
And all the glow of huge autumnal storms
Stirred on his face, and flickered from his eyes.

I had seen your Song. May the music be equally happy. You are lucky! You shall have my Locke's *Usurper*[4] if you will. Its now at home.

I see Swinburne also wrote a number of replicas of the olde Ballad! Heigh ho!

Ever Your W.E.O.

536. To Susan Owen

Monday, 30 July 1917, 11 p.m.   [*Craiglockhart*]

My own dear Mother,

The Lecture[5] was a huge success, & went on till 10.20!! At least I was answering cross-questions until that time. My swotting & pottering of the good old Matric. days, and my laborious escapes from Dunsden Vicarage to Reading College have been well crowned tonight. I have only once since getting through the Barrage at Feyet felt such exultation as when winding up to my peroration tonight! The peroration was a [*three words struck out*] (I'm tired) bit from Mrs. Browning which I remembered reading at Gailly:[6]

-----

[1] The AGBS. See Letter 35. LG was known as Black Moth, Wilfred as Carnation.
[2] The Craiglockhart Field Club.
[3] *The Hydra*.
[4] W. J. Locke, *The Usurper* (1901).
[5] To the Field Club: 'Do Plants Think?' The paper survives in HO's possession.
[6] 13 CCS, from which he had written to Mary (Letter 497) quoting from Mrs. Browning's *Aurora Leigh*. He now quotes from the same poem again.

'Earth's crammed with Heaven
And every common bush afire with God;
But only he who sees takes off his shoes;
The rest sit round it and pluck Blackberries,
And daub their natural faces unaware,
More and more from the first similitude.'

The 'only once' was when I saw you gliding up to me, veiled in azure, at the Caledonian. I thought you looked very very beautiful and well, through the veil, and especially on the night of the concert. But without the veil I saw better the supremer beauty of the ashes of all your Sacrifices: for Father, for me, and for all of us. (Even, methought, for Mowgli-Mowlgi of Fiji, or whoever it be that will receive the much fine gold of Israel's literature through your hands.)

Formerly, I should have said I had not time to write to you before. I now (with ever increasing mental vigour) perceive it was that I lacked energy. Not culpably, at all, or lazily. I cannot write to you without intensity, or without all my mind, my soul and heart and—(yes, I forget the Catechism as thoroughly as I remember: 'To him that overcometh, I will give the bright and morning star'. O exquisite words!)

I saw a 1st Edition of Keats' third book[1] this morning. The present price was pencilled on the cover: £56. (I will tell you what dear Mrs. Browning says of Keats next time.) This is a letter of parentheses. It is itself a parenthesis between my work. I must have the Magazine ready by tomorrow morning.

Your own W.E.O. x

P.S. The Concert was a great success. Far better than the one you saw. (I simply made faces.) I looked so sympathetically at poor Antonio by thinking of Portia, who broke down. I was so sorry. She is an old Bensonian,[2] like her husband, who played Shylock. Mrs. Pockett,[3] fresh from the vast London stage, prompted her at the top of her voice! To make a last parenthesis I will add that both these ladies are model wives, no less than model women. And how they love their profession!

537. To Susan Owen

Friday, 3 August 1917   [*Craiglockhart*]

Dearest Mother,

We Field Club were to have excursed to the Pentland Hills this afternoon, but rain prevented it.

By some means, chiefly by swimming in the Public Baths really religiously, for it never fails to give me a Greek feeling of energy and elemental life; by some means, I say, I have managed to have the

---

[1] *Lamia, Isabella & etc.* (1820).

[2] A member of Benson's company. Mrs. Isaacson played Portia; her husband, Second-Lieutenant J. C. Isaacson, RFC, was Shylock.

[3] Mrs. Pockett had acted a fortnight earlier in Alfred Sutro's *The Bracelet*, produced by her husband Lieutenant J. W. G. Pockett. The Pocketts, like the Isaacsons, were professional actors.

Magazine out in plenty of time. You will have your Copy no later than the moment of publication, which is when I plunk the copies outside the Breakfast Room Door tomorrow morning, where they will be given away to all the Club. I am glad my motion has been adopted by the Committee.

The Editorial, with its satires on Trams, the abolition of evening refreshments, the Field Club, a malcontent who sent a letter of evil 'gas' to a previous issue, and so on may read all rubbish to you. In the P. beginning 'For our part' there are six awful puns. But you need to know Musketry, or they will mis-fire.

I have a hand in the Notes & News, but no finger in the pie Peas Blossom has made of the Concert Critique. It was handed to me just as I was dashing away 'to Press'. There is an innuendo about Pockett which I don't like, even if it is unintentional.[1] Had I made the simple change Gratiano instead of Pockett, it would not have carried any innuendo. It is too late.

Thus I learn the awful finality of a corrected proof.

I have had so far one poetical contribution—from a Guards Officer—which he timidly brought up to my room with his own towering person. I was trotting around the room talking to the furniture in German at the moment; but I affected what dignity I could, and tried to look as if I had 10/6 in my pocket, and fifty more contributions on my desk.

Many many dear thanks for your Dorothean letters. This lumbago is a pitiful anticlimax to your holiday and to my Letters. Care should ward it off. You have an infinite capacity for taking Pains! Tut! (or words to that effect) I'm talking like a nasty incapable Doctor! But really I am fretted to hear this trouble, when I imagined you were bettered by being up here.

How is everybody else?   x W.E.O.

538. To Susan Owen

Tues. Night [*8 August 1917*]   [*Craiglockhart*]

Dearest of Mothers,

So pleased to have Father's letter & your note this morning. Letters have been scarce lately. Last week passed unmercifully quickly. The only way to lengthen time is to add more miles to the roads of our journeys. And the only way to lengthen life is to live out several threads at a time and join them up in crucial moments.

At present I am a sick man in hospital, by night; a poet, for quarter of an hour after breakfast; I am whatever and whoever I see while going down to Edinburgh on the tram: greengrocer, policeman, shopping lady, errand boy, paper-boy, blind man, crippled Tommy, bank-clerk, carter, all of these in half an hour; next a German student in

---

[1] 'Mr. Pockett thoroughly convinced us that he was annoyed by the whole business.' *The Hydra.*

earnest; then I either peer over bookstalls in back-streets, or do a bit of a dash down Princes Street,—according as I have taken weak tea or strong coffee for breakfast.

This afternoon I spent with a *Daily Mail* sub-editor, Salmond,[1] and writer to the *B.O.P.*[2] (who is going to talk our Printer into shape.) When we had discussed together many mighty things and men, and an Emersonian silence fell between us, we went upstairs to the Cinema, & so finished a very pleasant afternoon. Tonight Pockett enrôled me as Mr. Wallcomb, in *Lucky Durham*:[3] a fashionable young fellow, whose chief business in the play is introducing people.

Thus I need at once:

1) 1 Green Suit,
2) 2 or 3 Green Shirts,
3) Green Collars (if any)
4) Green Cap.
5) Green Glass Cuff-links: —(on second thoughts,

    I think one of these lies somewhere in the purlieus of Bordeaux.) But didn't Father give me an Indian Silver Pair?
6) The Oil-cloth raincoat.
7) Straw Hat (if any—I think not!)

Pockett, and Mrs. Pockett, Isaacson and Mrs. Isaacson (Portia) are all in it, so I shall know what it really feels like to be 'on the stage'. Only the first 2 Acts are being done next Sat., finishing the following week.

Salmond, the journalist, by the way, knew Walter Forrest, and often wrote his fame; knows also 'Jack' Bulman, the medico!

Yes, you will like to read Mrs. Browning. Having listened so long to her low, sighing voice (which <u>can</u> be <u>heard</u> often through the page,) and having seen her hair, not in a museum case, but palpably in visions, and having received kindness from a boy to whom she was kind (M. Léger—he is still a boy); for these reasons, I say, the Flapper flaps in vain.

---

[1] Second-Lieutenant J. B. Salmond, Black Watch.

[2] *The Boy's Own Paper*. HO has three scribbled pages, dating from the Craiglockhart period, outlining an idea for a short story. The heading is '*B.O.P. Stories for magazines*'.

[3] A comedy by the actor-manager Wilson Barrett (1847–1904), first performed at the King's Theatre, Hammersmith, 28 August 1905. Wilfred's interest in the theatre was considerable (see also p. 551, note 1), and it was known in the family that he drafted a full-length play at Craiglockhart. The MS was never seen, but the following note survives, on headed Craiglockhart paper:

Two Thousand

Act I Scene I The Lord of Europe's Dining Room, London
    Scene II Schoolroom
Act II   (2 days later)
Act III   Secret Meeting House under The Atlantic: reached by private submarine

---

Purpose: To expose war to the criticism of reason.
Plot: The federation of America with Europe by personal violence to the American Emperor.
Interest: Dress: Manners, Machines, References to men of this century.
           e.g. who *was* Lloyd George?

The other day I read a Biography of Tennyson, which says he was unhappy, even in the midst of his fame, wealth, and domestic serenity. Divine discontent! I can quite believe he never knew happiness for one moment such as I have—for one or two moments. But as for misery, was he ever frozen alive, with dead men for comforters. Did he hear the moaning at the bar, not at twilight and the evening bell only, but at dawn, noon, and night, eating and sleeping, walking and working, always the close moaning of the Bar; the thunder, the hissing and the whining of the Bar?

Tennyson, it seems, was always a great child.

So should I have been, but for Beaumont Hamel.

(Not before January 1917 did I write the only lines of mine that carry the stamp of maturity: these:

But the old happiness is unreturning.

Boys have no grief so grievous as youth's yearning;

Boys have no sadness sadder than our hope.[1])

Mayes has just been in, and it is now quarter to one on Wednesday. There is this advantage in being 'one of the ones' at the Hospital, that nurses cease from troubling the weary who don't want rest.

I have a sort of suspicion your note was written in bed; but perhaps it was before nine in the morning.

It is worthy of mention that we have been in mist for 3 days: a gloriously luminous mist at times. I saw Holyrood on Sunday Afternoon (being alone on Salisbury Crags), a floating mirage in gold mist. A sight familiar enough in dreams and poems, but which I never thought possible in these islands. It was the picture of a picture; if you understand. I don't.

It's too late o'night to talk like this. Time I snuggled myself away. Goodnight, dear Mother.

x W.E.O.

539. To Susan Owen

Friday Night [*13 August 1917*]   [*Craiglockhart*]

My own dear Mother,

The Field Club went a long walk over the Pentland foot-hills this afternoon.[2] The Party was:

1) Dr. Brock
2) Mr. Chase, learned (?) in Mosses,
3)   „   Quayle,   „   „ Bees,
4) a Shropshire man, „   „ Birds

----

[1] From 'Happiness', *Poems*, p. 93, where a later version is printed.

[2] The Expedition is described in Wilfred's (unsigned) Field Club article in *The Hydra* for 18 August 1917, in which he also gives an anonymous account of his own paper (read on 31 July), 'Do Plants Think'.

5) Capt. Mackenzie, electrician.
6) his son, aetat 13, learned in nothing.
7) A padre,   „   „   ditto.
8) Me   „   „   very much ditto.

Thus it was a representative body, and between us we managed to observe and philosophize the country to about half the extent that say Belloc would have done, had he taken that walk.

I held my own in the matter of Water Plants, and my ancient chippings at Geology came in useful, not to mention the physical geography I learnt from Miss Jones. (For which lady a fee of fifty guineas would not repay the tuition she gave.) But it is very kind of the Army to provide this free-and-easy Oxford for me. It was a unique walk. We had lunch on the roadside, and tea in a cottage.

But we stayed too long, or went too far, and arrived $\frac{1}{4}$ hour late for dinner, and very fatigued. And immediately after dinner I had to do the last rehearsal of *Lucky Durham*. It is done now, & I must get to bed. I read your letter by a waterfall. The Parcel has not yet come. Many thanks for the considerable trouble of packing it off. Where then is my green cap? So glad you thought of socks. The Expense will be refunded by the Club. I forgot to tell you this.

Yes, I really do wish you could be here tomorrow, for I am fairly confident of my part, and the more so, being with professionals, who can't let one down by any false cues or anything.

Glad you have been to Cressage.

I laughed at your hoping I should learn German during my stay in Edinburgh. It's a vile language to learn. I'm overjoyed that you think of making bandages for the wounded. Leave Black Sambo ignorant of Heaven. White men are in Hell. Aye, leave him ignorant of the civilization that sends us there, and the religious men that say it is good to be in that Hell. (Continued, because important) Send an English Testament to his Grace of Canterbury, and let it consist of that one sentence, at which he winks his eyes:

'Ye have heard that it <u>hath</u> been said: An eye for an eye, and a tooth for a tooth:

But I say that ye resist not evil, but whosoever shall smite thee on thy right cheek, turn to him the other also.'

And if his reply be 'Most unsuitable for the present distressing moment, my dear lady! But I trust that in God's good time . . . etc.' —then there is only one possible conclusion, that there are no more Christians at the present moment than there were at the end of the first century.

While I wear my star and eat my rations, I continue to take care of my Other Cheek; and, thinking of the eyes I have seen made sightless, and the bleeding lad's cheeks I have wiped, I say: Vengeance is mine, I, Owen, will repay.

Let my lords turn to the people when they say 'I believe in . . .

Jesus Christ', and we shall see as dishonest a face as ever turned to the East, bowing, over the Block at Tyburn.

I fear I've written like a converted Horatio Bottomley.

And to you who need no such words.

That is why I want you not to destroy them; for I write so because I see clear at this moment. In my eye there is no mote nor beam, when I look through you across the world.

There is a mote in many eyes, often no other than a tear. It is this: That men are laying down their lives for a friend. I say it is a mote; a distorted view to hold in a general way.

For that reason, if no other, I won't publish in any way the 'Kings and Christs.'

Saturday

Have just got the parcel up from Slateford Station by an Orderly. The Rly. sent me a notification this morning. The suit is not crushed. Everything in order. Wish I were. Shan't wear the ring, or the Emerald!

Have not re-read last night's copy, lest I should cancel it, and you be without a letter of any sort.

Your own W.E.O. x

540. To Susan Owen

15 August 1917   *Scottish Conservative Club, Edinburgh*

Dearest Mother,

I am going to Leith this afternoon; am on the way now. Got up rather late this morning, having had some very bellicose dreams of late.

I really felt most delightfully at ease *en scène* on Sat. Night. The whole Concert was the biggest success our stage has seen. I will send you the Magazine in good time. Mayes wrote 'The Concert' but I rewrote parts and cancelled the reference to myself. I have also had to re-write the field club account of my lecture.

I was very proud of my 'straight make-up' which Isaacson did for me.

How I hankered, a boy, to know the secrets of the glamour of the Shakesperian actors. Well, so it has come about that my first make up was done with the real Bensonian touch. (By Isaacson.)

(Friday)

I found the Newboults out on Wednesday. I thought Wednesday a likely day for a family excursion.

I received a card this morning, which should nerve me for a further attempt at aimless visiting.

I have just been reading Siegfried Sassoon, and am feeling at a very high pitch of emotion. Nothing like his trench life sketches has ever been written or ever will be written. Shakespere reads vapid after these. Not of course because Sassoon is a greater artist, but because of the subjects, I mean. I think if I had the choice of making friends with Tennyson or with Sassoon I should go to Sassoon.

That is why I have not yet dared to go up to him and parley in a casual way. He is here you know because he wrote a letter to the Higher Command which was too plain-spoken. They promptly sent him over here![1] I will send you his book, one day, and tell you what sort of pow-wow we've had.

Your own W.E.O. x

Friday aft. Just had yours. Haven't given it close attention yet.

541. To Leslie Gunston

22 August 1917   *Craiglockhart*

My dear Leslie,

At last I have an event worth a letter. I have beknown myself to Siegfried Sassoon. Went in to him last night (my second call). The first visit was one morning last week.[2] The sun blazed into his room making his purple dressing suit of a brilliance—almost matching my sonnet! He is very tall and stately, with a fine firm chisel'd (how's that?) head, ordinary short brown hair. The general expression of his face is one of boredom. Last night when I went in he was struggling to read a letter from Wells; whose handwriting is not only a slurred suggestion of words, but in a dim pink ink! Wells talks of coming up here to see him and his doctor; not about Sassoon's state of health, but about *God the Invisible King*.[3] After leaving him, I wrote something in Sassoon's style, which I may as well send you, since you ask for the latest.

The Dead-Beat[4] (True—in the incidental)

He dropped, more sullenly, than wearily,
    Became a lump of stench, a clot of meat,
    And none of us could kick him to his feet.
He blinked at my revolver, blearily.

---

[1] Second-Lieutenant Siegfried Sassoon, on convalescent leave from France earlier in the summer, had drawn up and deliberately publicized, through arranging a question in the House of Commons, a statement containing the following key sentence: 'I believe that this war, upon which I entered as a war of defence and liberation, has now become a war of aggression and conquest.' 'The Under-Secretary for War told the House of Commons that I was suffering from a nervous breakdown' (*Siegfried's Journey, 1916–1920*, Faber and Faber, London, 1945, p. 56). Sassoon was sent to Craiglockhart, generally known as the hospital for shell-shocked officers. His first collection of poems, *The Old Huntsman*, had been published earlier in the year.
[2] SS has also described this first meeting, in *Siegfried's Journey*, ch. VI. The whole chapter is an essential part of any account of Wilfred's life.
[3] London, 1917.
[4] A later version is printed in *Poems*, pp. 72–73, where the present draft is also given. See also p. 353, note 1. A version of verses 3 and 4 appeared in Wilfred's editorial in *The Hydra*, 1 September 1917. The same issue also prints SS's 'Dreamers'; and (unsigned) 'Song of Songs' (in the version printed in *Poems*, p.126). See p. 486, note 3, and p. 551, note 3.

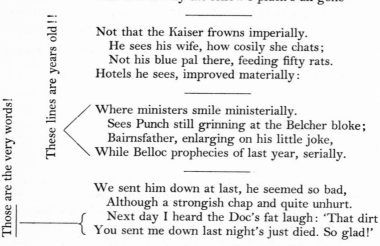

He didn't seem to know a war was on,
  Or see or smell the bloody trench at all . . .
  Perhaps he saw the crowd at Caxton Hall,
And that is why the fellow's pluck's all gone—

———————

Not that the Kaiser frowns imperially.
  He sees his wife, how cosily she chats;
  Not his blue pal there, feeding fifty rats.
Hotels he sees, improved materially:

———————

Where ministers smile ministerially.
  Sees Punch still grinning at the Belcher bloke;
  Bairnsfather, enlarging on his little joke,
While Belloc prophecies of last year, serially.

———————

We sent him down at last, he seemed so bad,
  Although a strongish chap and quite unhurt.
  Next day I heard the Doc's fat laugh: 'That dirt
You sent me down last night's just died. So glad!'

———————

Those are the very words!

These lines are years old!!

Next day

I am going to send you *The Old Huntsman*[1] as a festive gift for the occasion of your First Publication.[2]

'The Death Bed' is the finest poem. I told him my opinion. It is his own. This poem is coming out in the Georgian Anthology. He was struck with the 'Dead Beat', but pointed out that the facetious bit was out of keeping with the first & last stanzas. Thus the piece as a whole is no good. Some of my old Sonnets didn't please him at all. But the 'Antæus' he applauded fervently; and a short lyric which I don't think you know 'Sing me at morn but only with thy Laugh'[3] he pronounced perfect work, absolutely charming, etc. etc. and begged that I would copy it out for him, to show to the powers that be.

So the last thing he said was 'Sweat your guts out writing poetry!' 'Eh?' says I. 'Sweat your guts out, I say!' He also warned me against early publishing: but recommended Martin Secker for a small volume of 10 or 20 poems.

He himself is 30! Looks under 25!

So glad your proofs are done. How long now before I have my copies? That 'Farley Down' occasional verse did not impress me, I am longing to re-read *The Nymph*, & give it to Sassoon!

Would you mind sending me all the MSS verse of mine in your keeping as soon as you can get at them? How I want a confabulation with you in my Room with everything at hand!

[1] *The Old Huntsman and Other Poems,* William Heinemann, London, 1917.
[2] *The Nymph.*
[3] 'Song of Songs.'

Sassoon admires Thos. Hardy more than anybody living. I don't think much of what I've read. Quite potatoey after the meaty *Morals*.

You'll have had enough of Sassoon, what? Just one more tit-bit. Wells said in his last letter: hope you will soon 'devote yourself to the real business of your life, which is poetry only by the way.' Poor Wells! We made some fancy guesses as to what he meant:—Tract-writing? stump-oratory? politics? what?

Cheero! I'm well enough by day, and generally so by night. A better mode of life than this present I could not practically manage.

Yours, with affection, ever, W.E.O.

542. To Susan Owen

Craiglockhart

22 August 1917

My own dear Mother,

I have been waiting for the Address. The most momentous news I have for you is my meeting with Sassoon. He was struggling to read a letter from H. G. Wells when I went in. Wells is thinking of coming up here to see him & his doctor, not about Sassoon's state of health, but about Wells' last book you wot of: *God the Invisible King*.

Sassoon talks about as badly as Wells writes; they accord a slurred suggestion of words only. Certain old sonnets of mine did not please S. at all. But the 'Antæus' he applauded long & fervently, saying So-and-so would like to read this. And a short lyric, done here, he pronounced perfect work, absolutely charming, etc. etc. & begged I would copy it for him, to show to the powers that be. The last thing he said to me was Sweat your guts out writing poetry.

He also warned me against early publishing. He is himself 30. Looks under 25.

I shall be able to tell you much more when I get home.

Saw Harry Lauder the other day, a sincere, goodhearted man, kept one smiling, but never provided a bursting laugh.[1]

The play finished very successfully. Had to do a little gagging with Pockett because Isaacson missed his cue once & didn't come on when expected; a terrible moment.

Was invited to tea last Sunday by Capt. Mackenzie whose wife, boy and girl were at the Concert. (Verb. Sap.) The children, it seems, like me, and contrived a picnic in which I was to play the principal. But the feeling is not reciprocated and I managed to get out of the picnic.

As I said before I have had enough Picnicking to last several lifetimes. I have also a large family: in England, France,—and Ireland.

Bobby writes this morning from Co. Clare saying they are having a good time shooting.

---

[1] Sir Harry MacLennan Lauder (1870–1950), music-hall comedian and singer. His son, Captain J. C. Lauder, Argyll and Sutherland Highlanders, had been killed earlier in the year.

The Field Club are going to the Zoo this afternoon. I missed the last outing.

I am being forced to repeat my Biological paper next Monday.

German is getting on.

Saw Ch. Chaplin again.

Keeping very well, and generally sleeping well. The Barrage'd Nights are quite the exception.

I have been asked to continue a Class of French which has been started. But I don't feel too inclined.

Am anxious about your weather. Beastly up here for Holidays; though I have nothing to complain of; the showers are short; and the mists are delightful. Don't bother about writing till you get back. Forget everything but your new environment.

Forget self in the presence of the sea—I will do all the thinking and remembering of you.

Had a Model Yacht Regatta this morning. Thought how Father would have liked to compete.

Your own Wilfred x

543. To Tom Owen

26 August 1917   [*Craiglockhart*]

My dear Father,

I think this work of Sassoon's will show you to the best possible advantage the tendencies of Modern Poetry. If you don't appreciate these then it's Na-poo. There is nothing better this century can offer you. I've marked the pieces for first reading, and those underlined are specially good. The Old Huntsman was put in as a title piece, to catch the hunting-people, and make 'em read the rest.

'The Death-Bed' is a piece of perfect art.

'Morning Express', page 56 is the kind of thing that makes me despair of myself; everyone says 'I could have done that myself!'

Only no one ever did.

Please send me your Criticisms.

I am beginning to feel uncomfortably editorial again after a fortnight's rest. Nobody is willing to write about our last Concerts, and it looks as if I shall have to fill half the Mag. myself, between now & tomorrow.

I am glad Colin is with you.

Realizing how impossible it is for me to be there has spoilt my holiday here. I was make-believing that I was a free creature here, but it is only that my chain has been let out a little. I should only hurt myself with tugging at it.

Fondest love to all,

Your W.E.O.

544. To Mary Owen

Thursday, 29 August[1] *1917*   *Craiglockhart*

My dear Mary,

I was grieved—almost aggrieved—to hear you had had some bad days at Aberystwyth, and I am still waiting to hear you are all right. This cloud, and a great many other real ones messing about in the heavens and sometimes mooning around the building itself, and generally behaving unbecomingly on the top of us all—and the Russians panicking, and getting out of the war, and ourselves getting deeper and deeper into it, these things, I say, do not make one (eider)—downhearted. So it is not to be wondered at that I was a bit snappy in my Editorial, which you shall have in a day or two.

But a word from Sassoon, though he is not a cheery dog himself, makes me cut capers of pleasure.

My dear, except in one or two of my letters, (alas!) you will find nothing so perfectly truthfully descriptive of war. Cinemas, cartoons, photographs, tales, plays—Na-poo.

Now you see why I have always extolled Poetry.

The 'Redeemer', I have been wishing to write every week for the last three years.

Well, it has been done and I have shaken the greater hand that did it.

'The Death-Bed', my dear sister, should be read seven times, and after that, not again, but thought of only.

Here is a very good brooch, a <u>very</u> good brooch. Unless you like it much, I shall very likely sneak it <u>again</u> for a model of latter-day design! There is no hint of a Board for me yet! I'm going down to make my Evening Tea now. Just a card will tell me how you & dear Mother are.

Your loving Wilfred

545. To Susan Owen

Monday [*2 September 1917*]   [*Craiglockhart*]

My dearest Mother,

It seems you have had unmerciful weather. You will be all the more glad, according to your custom, to be Home again.

Mayes introduced me to some 'modern' people, and I went there yesterday afternoon:—two men and their wives, who share a big house in a fine Georgian Crescent in Edinburgh.

The ladies wear short hair   and decorative

---

[1] 'My Shy Hand' (*Poems*, p. 101) was drafted about this time. C D L notes that L G's draft is dated 29–30 August 1917.

gowns, and think themselves artistic. But yesterday they had to mind their babies, which being self-centred, unmannerly blobs of one to three years bored me utterly.

The drawing room was worth seeing with its black carpetless floor, white walls, solitary superb picture, grand piano, Empire sofa and so on.

I think they are genuine people—the more so because they adore their progeny than because they profess to admire my poetry.

Their picture—a loan—is an Academy Exhibit by the painter of the finest picture now in the Edinburgh Gallery, which you did not see. This last is called Avatar. Bibby[1] of the *Annual* wrote to the artist[2] asking for the same canvas with additions (a wounded soldier). The Artist (forget his name) wrote back: accepted—fee £500. Thus I am specially anxious to see *Bibby's*. Has Father got it? If not I must buy one.

Many thanks for Father's Views (of Aberystwyth). Wish I had his views of S.S. I will copy out one or two of my recent efforts in Sassoon's manner.[3]

I have been doubtful whether to . . . [*four words illegible*] to mine. But now I find it well received by the public and praised by Sassoon with no patronizing manner but as a musical achievement not possible to him. He is sending copies of the *Hydra* to Personages!

Last night I had a consultation with Dr. Brock from 11 to midnight! I asked him (for the first time) when he meant to have me boarded. He said there were no instructions given to him yet; and wasn't I quite happy where I am? Very well . . .

I still have disastrous dreams, but they are taking on a more civilian character, motor accidents and so on.

The Concert last Sat. was nothing very notable. What took the applause of the Faery Mustard Seed was some charming dancing by a girl of 13 or 14. When I see a Ballet Dance, I surrender half my kingdom, lose my head, and put it on a charger. Thus at least I forget the war.

The Field Club Tonight was some stories of Sea-Fishing off the Waterford—Cork Coast—some good yarns.

Nothing more to tell, I think. Horrid weather continues.

Ever your own W.E.O. x

P.S. (1) I should rather like some Typed Copies of these verses.

---

[1] Joseph Bibby (1851–1940), founder of J. Bibby and Sons Ltd., soap manufacturers, writer on economic subjects, and editor of *Bibby's Annual* 1906–22, and 1936.

[2] Henry John Lintott (1877–1965), RSA, ARCA, painter of figure subjects and portraits.

[3] The 29 September issue of *The Hydra* carried (anonymously) 'The Next War'. *Poems* (p. 86) does not list this first printed version, which is identical with the final draft of the six BM drafts except for the last line:

He wars on Death—for Life; not men—for flags.
                                                The Hydra.
He wars on Death—for lives; not men—for flags.
                                                Poems.

See also p. 499, note 1.

(2) Please return at once all MSS. you have—such as were sent on by Leslie.

546. To Susan Owen

7 September 1917   [*Craiglockhart*]

My dearest Mother,

These last two days Thursday and Friday have been the very fullest-happiest of the year—excluding only one or two of the days when you were up here. Went with Mayes to a perfect little dinner at the Grays'[1] and passed an evening of extraordinary fellowship in All the Arts. The men are not of the expansive type—one is a History Honoursman at Oxford, the other owner of a large Munition Works. The ladies have more effusiveness, but are genuine. One is really witty and the other is a sculptor of great power.

They showered books upon me on leaving; and on Monday I am to escort Mrs. Gray on an expedition into the slums to see an old Italian—a street-singer whom she 'took-up' and who says he was once an operatic star! He is probably a fraud, but we shall see that—and we shall see his many children.

Mayes and I crept in at a late hour last night. This is known to the C.O. but he has said nothing to me. Mayes talked it over with him this morning. At midnight, however, a nurse came to me very austerely: 'Dr. Brock will see you at once Mr. Owen!' I went: in pyjamas and perspiration. He said a lady in Edinburgh expected me to lunch today to show me around the Slum Gardens. Goodnight! I retired in stupor.

So I went to lunch at their palatial house with two maiden sisters, The Misses Wyer. One of them took me over the Gardens and I gave my opinions and views. (Dr. Brock is trying to get me in touch with the Edinburgh submerged tenth.) It will never come off while I am in uniform: but I can't tell him that. I went back to a marvellous pleasant Tea with the other Lady, who has travelled far and wide over the continents and the literatures. Then in sailed an enormous old lady of the type of old lady I have but once or twice met—outside Thackeray—intellectual, witty, vigorous: told some good stories and eat a huge tea; an admirer of Alec Waugh's book *Loom of Youth!*[2] Waugh wrote this at 18. But more of this book later. The touches of what I can only call 'kultur' in its universal sense, not English French or German but universal, and the discovery of my own—almost secret—views of such things as sculpture, state-craft, ethics, etc. etc, in these strange beings and places were enough to make the day memorable in itself.

But tonight Sassoon called me in to him; and having condemned some of my poems, amended others, and rejoiced over a few, he read me his

---

[1] An Edinburgh family with whom Wilfred became friendly. Mrs. Gray was one of 'Dr. Brock's ladies'. See Letter 533. Her recollections of Wilfred were included by EB in his Memoir.

[2] Published London, 1917, when Alec Waugh was 19.

very last works, which are superb beyond anything in his Book. Last night he wrote a piece which is the most exquisitely painful war poem of any language or time.[1] I don't tell him so, or that I am not worthy to light his pipe. I simply sit tight and tell him where I think he goes wrong. He is going to alter one passage of this very poem for me.

No wonder I was happy last night, and that tonight I must get it off my chest before I sleep.

The Field Club of 12 members went to the Observatory[2] this afternoon. I forgot I was missing that. But Sassoon as it happens has just asked me to go to tea with the Astronomer Royal tomorrow. So I shall see much more than what I missed! How I shall get a Magazine out this week-end I don't know.

Will you do a sacred task for me? Wrench open the Cupboard of my Desk and withdraw from the top-shelf right-hand side, three port-folios —two are khaki, one is Harold's gilt-stencilled velvet blotter. Upon your unimpeachable honour do not inspect the contents either of the cupboard or of the portfolios. But promptly pack off the portfolios under secure wrappings and plain address. I don't care if you damage the cupboard-door. But don't damage the hinges of your mind by wrenching the secrets of my portfolios. This sounds mysterious; but I am serious. Some of these verses will light my cigarettes, but one or two may light the darkness of the world. It is not a question of wheat and chaff, but of devils and angels. . . .[3]

I have written to Harold. I hope I am not 'feeding' you with this kind of talk, but I write straight from my experiences and heart.

Do thou likewise.

Your own W.E.O. x

547. To Susan Owen

Sunday Evening [*10 September 1917*]   [*Craiglockhart*]

My dearest Mother,

My pen is wet from an amusing contribution to myself: Extracte from the Chronicles of Wilfred de Salope, Knight:[4] describing the Hospital Life in mediæval jargon. I am still 'worried' by lack of matter for my Mag.

Yesterday I lunched with Sassoon at his Golf Club. My discipleship was put to a severe fleshly trial. I had had no breakfast (quite right if invited out to lunch!) choosing to stay in bed till 10; and he did not come in from the Course till quarter past two.

Afterwards I put him to the trial of writing a poem in 3 minutes in

---

[1] SS thinks this must have been 'Dreamers' (Siegfried Sassoon, *Collected Poems 1908–1956*, Faber and Faber, London, 1961, p. 71.)

[2] This visit to the Royal Observatory, Edinburgh, is recorded in *The Hydra*, 15 September 1917. Professor Ralph Allen Sampson (1866–1939), Astronomer-Royal, Scotland, 1910–37, showed the party round and gave them tea. See also *Sherston's Progress*, pp. 62–67.

[3] We have omitted seventeen words.

[4] In the 15 September issue of *The Hydra*.

the manner of those in the *Graphic*, etc. He produced 12 lines in 4 minutes. Absolutely undistinguishable from the style of thing in the Magazines.

Then we walked over to the Observatory, and had a most interesting tea with the Astronomer, his wife and children. The children were dumbfounded with boredom. The only star we talked about was Sir H. Tree,[1] and the only stars Sassoon saw were in the electric-blue eyes of little Tom when I took courage and spoke to him.

S. & I had made a plan to pull the Astronomer's leg, but it didn't come off.

He is a parlous clever man.

There was a pretty good concert that evening.

Tomorrow is the great performance (hinted at by Mustard Seed)[2]

I shall have a busy day with various appointments & am glad I kept out of further play-acting.

Brock wants me to get busy with Scouts now!

Chase wants a Lecture on 'Soil' for the Field Club.

I just want to get home. Would you send around your next letter *Poèmes Elégiaques*,[3] Laurent Tailhade, high shelf of book-case, yellow-backed.

Your lovingest W.E.O.

S. wants to get me a green-tab job[4] in England. I think he could. Fondest love & wishes for Mary, and thanks for her long letter.

548. To Susan Owen

Tuesday [*12*] *September 1917*   [*Craiglockhart*]

My own dear Mother,

Many true thanks for your long letter. I have read it many times. You also find letter writing a fitter mode of intimate communication than speaking.

The enclosed came out of my Parcel of Portfolios rec'vd this evening, together with a stamped letter addressed to Langley, Worcester, which I have duly posted. They had slipped right inside the parcel! Was it a trick of some urchin of Cleveland Street?

The MSS. arrived in perfect order. Did I classify them as Angels & Devils? I meant simply: Live Ones and Duds. I have written no Barrack Room Ballads! You may be a little shocked by Sassoon's language. He is of course, with W.E.O. practically the only one in the place who doesn't swear conversationally. He is simply honest about the war.

---

[1] Sir Herbert Beerbohm Tree (1853–1917), actor-manager and brother of Max Beerbohm. He had died a few weeks earlier, 2 July.

[2] Wilfred's pseudonym (and that of his predecessor) as theatrical and concert critic in *The Hydra*.

[3] 3rd edition, Paris, 1907. This copy survives, with the inscription: 'À Wilfred E. S. Owen, en souvenir de nos belles causeries et des beaux soirs à La Gailleste. Laurent Tailhade, Paris, le 4 Mai, 1916.'

[4] In Military Intelligence.

Your questions concerning him are searching. You will do well to put them on all similar occasions.

For it is very true there are not a few whom I like, say, as a poet only, as an actor only, as a table-companion only, as a trench-mate only, as a servant only, as a statue only, as a marble idol only.

Sassoon I like equally in all the ways you mention, as a man, as a friend, as a poet.

The man is tall and noble-looking. Before I knew him I was told this and by this much only I spotted him! I quote from a publication:[1] 'very slim and shy, with eyes which may be blue or brown when you come to examine them closely.'

He is thirty-one. Let it be thoroughly understood that I nourish no admiration for his nose or any other feature whatever.

The Friend is intensely sympathetic*, with me about every vital question on the planet or off it. He keeps all effusiveness strictly within his pages. In this he is eminently English. It is so restful after the French absurdities, and after Mrs. Gray who gushes all over me. But there is no denying to myself that he is already a closer friend than, say, Leslie. Just as this assertion is not the result of having been with him so much lately, neither is it derogated by the shortness of our acquaintance-time. We have followed parallel trenches all our lives, and have more friends in common, authors I mean, than most people can boast of in a lifetime.

As for the Poet you know my judgement. What's your's? If I ever said anything so ambiguous as 'I wish I had Father's views' I meant 'I wish I knew Father's views'—and had them before me. By the way S. has written two or three pieces 'around' chance things I have mentioned or related! Thus the enclosed scribble[2] is a copy of what he wrote after I had read three Sonnets on 'Beauty' (subject) by E.L.G., O.A.J., and me. . . .[3]

I do think it a pity Leslie is in such a hurry.

I had a jolly afternoon with Mrs. Gray on Saturday. We got ourselves admirably stared at in Lower Edinburgh. I wore a hooligan manner and cap, but unimpeachable gloves, boots and tie. Mrs. Gray wore weird clothes and some priceless rings. Tomaso[4] was out. We left the macaroni, the toffees and so on, in the wrong house at first. We thought the stupefaction of the good woman 'part of the day's work'. However she

---

[1] Saul Kain, *The Daffodil Murderer*, John Richmond Ltd., London, 1913; a skilful parody of Masefield (and an interesting poem in its own right) by SS. Wilfred is quoting from the preface by 'William Butler' (in fact T. W. H. Crosland). The whole paragraph reads: 'I have only to add that Mr. Kain is still a young man, between four and six feet in height, very slim and shy, with eyes which may be blue or brown when you come to examine them closely'. The Preface opens: 'I have read the "Daffodil Murderer" nineteen times. It is, without doubt, the finest literature we have had since Christmas.' Wilfred's copy survives, with an inscription by SS. For a discussion of the poem see Michael Thorpe, *Siegfried Sassoon: a critical study*, Oxford University Press, London, 1966.
[2] This has not survived.
[3] Six words omitted.
[4] The Italian singer. See Letter 546.

discovered our mistake and came after us. We were by then mingling with a crowd following a poor (sober) woman who was being arrested. Tomaso was out, but we found a suitable object of compassion in his (unmistakably Italian) boy who had impaled his leg on a railing-spike. We did not inspect the leg. The smell of carbolic was strong enough under the clothes. Then we rummaged over a delightful dark and filthy curiosity-shop, and I discovered a real Roman Vase which I got for a shilling. But Mrs. Gray bought a real bronze,—doubtful Roman—lamp for 1/6 as a present for me. So I had to give her the vase! For I had another little dinner with them and came up to the Concert in their taxi. Mrs. Steinthal[1] is a mighty clever sculptress. We had great fun in Princes St. buying a laurel-wreath for Mayes for presentation after the play. Poor Mayes overdid himself and has lost his speech. Came up to my room and woke me up this morning with appealing eyes and curious gesturations. I thought he was mad and have yet to get over it! He has been often seized thus, and will soon get right again.

Surely you have some more MSS.—'Purple' for instance. If not, many are lost. I hate losing trifles;—and because they are my only diary, I humbly desire you to keep these letters.

Your very own W.E.O. x

How is Mary?

* sym-pathy = feeling with (Greek)

549. To Susan Owen

Tuesday Aft., 25 September 1917   *Craiglockhart*

My own dear Mother,

Last week has been a pretty full one. I might if I wanted become mildly 'lionized by Edinburgh Society'. The best visit I made was to John Duncan:[2] a pretty great artist, living near the Grays. He is 'one of the ones' in the Academy; but didn't sell his picture this year. It is a thing of many beauties. I have been made very sad by the extreme beauty of the eyelids of one of his Faces. But he used no model for her. It is a sad thought that Nature can't grow a face as old Duncan can. I was to go on to see Lintott, of the Avatar, but I got so comfortable at Duncan's that Mrs. Gray couldn't get me away.

I hear that Lintott's bargain with Bibby took the form of a dying English soldier and four angels carrying off a crystal! Something like that.

One night we had a jolly dinner at the Caledonian Hotel. One of the party was the Librarian[3] of the University, who would be delighted to

---

[1] Another of Dr. Brock's ladies. See Letter 552.

[2] John Duncan (d. 1945), decorative painter who specialized in ecclesiastical work and stained glass.

[3] Frank Nicholson, whose recollections of Wilfred, given to EB, were printed as an Appendix to *The Poems of Wilfred Owen*, Chatto and Windus, London, 1931. See also Osbert Sitwell, *Noble Essences*, Macmillan and Co. Ltd., London, 1950, pp. 95–96.

teach me German. My Berlitz Lessons are now finished. I have learnt enough not to be a nuisance of a pupil to him. I had the first lesson in the University last Friday.

On Sat. we had a Field Day for Boy Scouts.

This morning I gave my first lesson of course of English Literature in a big school[1] in Edinburgh! I had 39 boys, who seemed most intelligently attentive.

I am to be boarded today, and am waiting to be called in at any moment. Dr. Brock says I shall be given an extension.

I had one horrid night since I last wrote.

I send you my two best war Poems.

Sassoon supplied the title 'Anthem':[2] just what I meant it to be. Harold might have them after.

Will write soon again.   Your very own Wilfred x

550. To Susan Owen

Thursday, 10 p.m. [*27 September 1917*]   [*Craiglockhart*]

My own dear Mother,

Glad to have your reproach this morning & to think my letter could not arrive long after your posting. The Result of the Board has not been officially announced, but before it Dr. Brock said I should be kept on. In a few minutes I must go down to a special meeting about the Magazine. We have a new House President now, who is willing to lay out more money for it. At last, moreover, there seem to be people capable of helping to it. Sassoon is too much the great man to be bothered with it, and I wish I had back again the time I have wasted on it. I was cajoled into promising to act in the next big play, but had the fortitude to get out of it again.

I think one of the most humanly useful things I am doing now is the teaching at Tynecastle School. Did I tell you what a great time I had on Tuesday with the 39 boys. Their 'Teacher'[3] is a charming girl,— wife (of course) of an Army Doctor. She had the exquisite tact to offer to leave me alone, but I requested her company for the lesson.

They also have a School Magazine. I was rather struck with this:

'Mr Seaton bought a motor car,
    And had it painted yellow.
In goggles and a big fur coat,
    He looked a handsome fellow.'

Observe the astonishing conciseness of the thing. Three things conjure

---

[1] Tynecastle School. See Letter 550.
[2] 'Anthem for Doomed Youth' (*Poems*, pp. 44–45). The other poem was 'The Next War'. See Letter 550.
[3] Mrs. Edward Fullerton. H O met her after the war.

the complete picture: yellow paint, goggles, big fur coat! And the irony of the last line!

I called for the poet—a wizened little pinch-face, about two feet high! The international idea has already got hold of some of their little imaginations.

Tues. Aft.
2 October 1917

I have rescued these sheets from under a few feet of later accumulations.

I have been quite well all week save for a cold. Nothing has been announced about my Board. Clearly I have another 3 weeks yet—before leaving—or having another board.

Have been to School again. Am going to do *Hiawatha* with them now.

On Friday last I went with a party over the Fleet: inspecting in Detail the longest fighting ship in the world.[1]

Midshipmen showed us round.

Most people knew the *Zealandia*, but I had forgotten the name of Harold's present ship. The officers' cabins are marvels of size & comfort. In the 'Mess Room' an asiatic creature in frowsy livery was hovering behind the table. For a long time I thought it was some waiter or steward, & was astonished when it sat down beside me. It was some Japanese dignitary.

I have been to see the Lintotts. He seems an excellent gentleman, blessed by nature with a clubbed foot, for he is still 'of age', and a boy of about 12.

On Monday I lectured on 'Soil', out of Sheer light-heartedness!

This afternoon I was booked by the Mackenzies to go with them to their son's school. A merciful rainy day and my cold have been my excuse. I think they only want me to see what a magnificent school their kid—a wash out—attends.

Saturday's Concert consisted for me of a series of manoeuvres with the Dancer portrayed on Page 14. It was fluttering about the doors unattended so long that I invited it in. When the lights went up, I thought worse of it; and after a little furious thinking, contrived to steer it safely out of the building, and return to see the Play in peace.

I have before me a letter, (as the novelists say,) from Lady Margaret Sackville[2] to Sassoon, shyly presenting him with her war poems—some of them very fine. She is the great Patroness of Literature, and I am going to ask her for something for the Magazine.

I included my 'Next War' in order to strike a note. I want Colin to read, mark, learn etc. it. This is wretched news of him. If he joins as a private in the R.F.C. very well. But he will never fly with advantage to his Country.

[1] Probably HMS *Repulse* (794 ft.), with the Grand Fleet in 1917.
[2] d. 1963. A copy of her war poems *Pageant of War*, Simpkin, Marshall, Hamilton, Kent & Co., London, 1914, survives among Wilfred's books, inscribed by the author. See Letter 552.

Read Wells' article in today's *Mail*. Most important. I enclose it.[1]

As for myself, I hate washy pacifists as temperamentally as I hate whiskied prussianists. Therefore I feel that I must first get some reputation of gallantry before I could successfully and usefully declare my principles.

I may as well (to make up for so little letter-stuff lately) send you my most lurid war-episode.[2] It is not in a finished state. You had better keep it <u>strictly to yourself</u>, & <u>send it back before</u> you have marked, learnt, & inwardly digested it.

I have been rendered an apathetic maudlin by a cold last week, but it is clearing up now.

Always your own Wilfred x

The figure of the Caliban at Somerside Place affects my imagination even more than the dainty Ariel. I have not been round.

551. To Susan Owen

Sunday, 14 October [*1917*]   *Craiglockhart*

My own dear Mother,

It's getting time I saw you again. Three months without leave would seem long with a Regiment, longer perhaps than it does here; where I am kept amused.

This afternoon, after lunching with Miss Wyer, and a scholastic lady-friend of hers, we went up to Colinton, a village close to here, to see Mr. Blaikie, one of the heads of Constable's, Printers.[3] I was not long discovering that he was a friend of Stevenson's from boyhood. Stevenson's famous old nurse was Blaikie's first. So it was an interesting afternoon; tho' old Blaikie affects a contempt for R.L.S. It is a beautiful thing that children of Tynecastle School,—or of the Birkenhead Institute are able to get nearer to the romantic heart of Stevenson, and really know him in a better way, than this person who played with him before even *Treasure Island* was dreamed of.

On Friday I went to the Lintotts again. Lintott has reason to be proud of his work, which he is not—particularly—; and the beautiful Mrs. Lintott has reason to be proud of her boy, which she is. From there I went to see Mrs. Scott, Mrs. Gray's mother, and her daughter, who has just given up work in the War Office. Miss Scott was out.

---

[1] Wells had written an article asking for peace between pacifists and belligerents, which had aroused opposition. In an article on 22 August 1917 he replied: 'I have always insisted that this war must end not simply in the defeat but in the disappearance of militant imperialism from the world . . . however difficult international controls may be, we have to solve these difficulties. . . . The alternative to the United States of the World is the periodic blood-bath of the world.'

[2] Unidentified.

[3] Walter Biggar Blaikie (1847–1928), Chairman of T. and A. Constable Ltd., University Press, Edinburgh. He lived at Bridgend, Colinton, Midlothian.

On Sat. I met Robert Graves (see last poem of *O.H.*)[1] for Sassoon, whom nothing could keep from his morning's golf; & took Graves over to the Course when he arrived. He is a big, rather plain fellow, the last man on earth apparently capable of the extraordinary, delicate fancies in his books.

No doubt he thought me a slacker sort of sub. S.S. when they were together showed him my longish war-piece 'Disabled'[2] (you haven't seen it) & it seems Graves was mightily impressed, and considers me a kind of Find!![3] No thanks, Captain Graves! I'll find myself in due time.

I think it a rather precious exhibition of esteem that S.S. lends me the MSS. of his next book. On the other hand, when I pointed out a quotation from Shakespere that I intended for my Frontispiece, he collared it by main force, & copied it out for himself!

I don't think of anything else of interest to tell you—even if the above is so. My next board should be a week next Tuesday. They may cast me out the same day,—or give me another month. Both issues are acceptable. I could do a lot with another month here; but I feel a growing homesickness.

I am no longer neurasthenic, though I may be neurotic.

It is high time you started a special course of getting fit so that I may find you all bonny, & so that the exertion of my company may not fatigue you. Time also to get the house swept and garnished, not of dust and cobwebs but of the Webby people that come to spin their yarns there.

Dearest love all round and round   From Wilfred x

552. To Susan Owen

Tuesday [*?16 October 1917*]   [*Craiglockhart*]

Dearest Mother,

I went with Blanche to her Uncles this evening. As you have been I need not describe. They were extremely pleasant, [*half sheet missing*] to see the case tomorrow. Here is a gas poem,[4] done yesterday, (which is not private, but not final).

---

[1] *The Old Huntsman*. The last poem (p. 96) is 'A Letter Home; to Robert Graves'. Wilfred used the last two lines to preface his own poem 'The Next War'. They run:

> War's a joke for me and you
> While we know such dreams are true!

[2] *Poems*, pp. 67–68.

[3] Robert Graves wrote to Wilfred about the poem. In a letter to the present editors (22 February 1966) Mr. Graves writes: 'I met Owen at Craiglockhart when I "escorted" Sassoon there—actually I missed the train and Sassoon got there first; but only occasionally later. Owen came to my wedding, Jan 23 1918, at St. James', Piccadilly & brought me a present of 11 Apostle Spoons. He said the twelfth had been court-martialled for cowardice & was awaiting execution. He sent me a Field Service Postcard from France the day before he was killed.' See Appendix C.

[4] 'Dulce Et Decorum Est' (*Poems*, pp. 55–56). HO's original speculative date for this letter, August 1917, has led to an August dating in *Poems* and in Welland.

The famous Latin tag means of course It is sweet and meet to die for one's country. Sweet! And decorous! [*half sheet missing*] boys to Swanston Cottage—Stevenson's you know. We are reading *St. Ives*; many scenes occur there,[1] and in the Castle, & even on the road just outside the Hydro!

It is horribly cold in my room, but what like out There?

I will enclose this in *The Pageant of War*.[2] I don't know why Lady Margaret has put all those   +   +

Colin might join the Artists' Rifles with about a year's certainty of life; or as a private in the R.F.C. with no danger.

Sassoon came up to me the other night & confessed he didn't know what to do next about his 'show'. He is to be boarded soon, and is getting in a tighter fix than ever.

Wednesday

Here Mayes came up & pow-wowed till after midnight. This afternoon instead of going to Bangower I went to St. Bernards' Crescent,[3] & had my first sitting—about an hour. The charcoal outline was finished in 5 minutes, & before tea the complete rough likeness was done in oils![4] I think it will be a great success—impressionistic rather than finicky. Mrs. S's mother-in-law was there, & did at the same time a small water-colour; it turned out a failure in my opinion.

I proudly record that Pixie, (aged one exactly, & the most exquisite bit of protoplasm of that age I have handled) much preferred me to her grandmother; and would not be taken away from me. I enclose her photograph with her Mother. The fat boy is Martin, Mrs. Steinthal's.

I will help Colin to a motor bike if he will come up here on it.

Ever your lovingest—by many years—of Sons,

Wilfred x

553. To Susan Owen

Thursday, 18 October[5] 1917   *Craiglockhart*

My own Mother,

I think I described to you my meeting with Robert Graves, and how S.S. said of him: he is a man one likes better after he has been with one.

So it turns out with my case. You will be amused with his letter.[6]

---

[1] *St. Ives*, by Robert Louis Stevenson (1850–94), was published in 1898. (Thirty chapters were written at his death; the six final chapters were written by Sir Arthur Quiller-Couch.) The house in which the heroine Flora Gilchrist lived is closely described from Stevenson's memories of Swanston Cottage, a farmhouse on the slopes of the Pentlands, the lease of which his father took in 1867. Family summer holidays were spent there until 1881.

[2] See p. 497, note 2.

[3] Home of the Steinthal family.

[4] Mrs. Steinthal's portrait (which HO remembers) was not liked by Susan Owen, who destroyed it after the war.

[5] 'Winter Song' (*Poems*, p. 103) is dated 18 October 1917.

[6] See Appendix C.

He carried away a Poem, or was carried away with it, without my knowledge. It was only in a <u>Draft</u> State, & I was perfectly aware of all the solecisms.

Yesterday I did go to Newboults—an event you will no doubt hear of. Chubby Cubby had grown, and his face altered. But the old gold and olive ensheath him as in Summer.[1] I should like to pickle his hands for the benefit of mankind in the future.

From there, I went to a *tête-à-tête* dinner with Miss Scott, Mrs. Gray's sister. By the way, you have mixed up the babies of these families—as fairy-godmothers often do. Miss Scott, whose financial means of support are considerable, but whose physical means of support are inadequate, she being some four feet high, became very personal during the meal, & I had hard work to keep the talk on R.L.S. and not L.S.D.

What is the name of Harold's ship? Blanche B. mentioned the Motor Cycle, & I hope to ride home on it. To hear Margaret Bickerton[2] talk physiology gives me the sky-blue shakes. I naturally forget whatever she said . . .[3]

Always your W.E.O. x

Friday

I forgot to mention that yesterday I bought a £5. National Bond; and a Wrist Watch.

Called on Lintott's this afternoon. I notice your last letter wilfully misplaces the adjectives. It is only Lintott's <u>wife</u> that is beautiful, which I say ungrudgingly.

I think quite the best picture in *B.'s Annual* is Lee Hankey's[4] 'Madonna'. Look at it at once!

Lee Hankey the day when . . . [*two words illegible*] the morning after a night-talk with Harold Monro in the Bookshop Days I turned up on parade in Regent's Park without my belt. Lee Hankey gave me an hour's penal drill for this!

I am to meet Lord Guthrie[5] on Sat. at Swanston.

---

[1] It seems clear that 'Sonnet: to a Child' (*Poems*, p. 99) and 'Winter Song' (*Poems*, p. 103) are both addressed to Arthur Newboult. 'Winter Song' is inscribed October 18, 1917, and 'Sonnet: to a Child' is likely to have been written at the same time. 'The old gold and olive ensheath him as in summer', is echoed in 'Sonnet':

> For earlier suns than ours have lent you gold;

and in 'Winter Song':

> The browns, the olives and the yellows died . . .
> From off your face . . .
> The sun-brown and the summer gold are blowing.

[2] One of the two daughters of a Shrewsbury builder. See *JO* II, pp. 8–13, where she is mistakenly called Kathleen.

[3] We have omitted eighteen words.

[4] William Lee-Hankey (1869–1952), ROI, RWS, painter and illustrator. Gazetted lieutenant, Artists' Rifles, November 1916.

[5] Lord Charles John Guthrie (1849–1920), eminent lawyer and antiquarian. He lived at Swanston Cottage; among his publications was *Cummy, R. L. Stevenson's nurse, an Appreciation* (1914).

Somewhere in my Bookshelves, perhaps near the Dressing Table, there is a large boy's-book, pub. by R.T.S.[1] about West Indian Missions. It contains a number of fine photographs of Red Skins. I want all these photographs, if you would please find them and cut them out, and send them. Thanks!

W.E.O.

554. To Susan Owen

Sunday, 21 October 1917   *Craiglockhart*

My dearest Mother,

It was a puzzle and a mystery to many, the party of six that assembled this afternoon at the Braid Hills Tram Terminus, and began a saunter into the Pentland Hills. People saw a married lady, an obviously un-married young man in a reckless soft-cap, a well-dressed boy with violet eyes and tie, (wonder where his mother learnt that?) an ill-dressed thin boy, with an intellect behind his parchment forehead; a fat little knave apparently with a large apple stowed under each cheek in case of emergency; and a tall awkward boy, very nervous of himself. What spirit drove us together? The spirit of Stevenson it was; and he was with us at his gayest all the time.

He caused the finest wind the Pentlands can produce to come and play with us; and October spared us the last of her sun-remnants. When we beheld the Cottage to good advantage, we sat in the lee of a haystack and ate sandwiches. We then sang songs, and told tales, every now and then leaping about and prancing for joy.

It was already darkening when we reached Colinton and had tea, and quite dark when we took the Edinburgh road; and so we took it in good style with songs and dancing, whistling and holloing. Until the meteors showered in heaven; and we fell calm under the winter stars, and some of us saw the pale pathway of the Spirits for the first time.

And seeing it so far above us, and feeling the good road so firm beneath us, we worshipped God in our hearts; and knew we loved one another as no men love for long.[2]

That was my way of spending Sunday.

The boys had each been to church in the morning, and I had been at my travail, for I am not ordained a listener in the temple of life.

Monday

On Sat. I went to Swanston, & fell into a trap. Lord Guthrie wants me to do some historical research work for him in the Edinburgh Libraries. I was not at all keen, & pleaded in vain my ignorance & my hatred of legal matters. But I had to meet him this morning in The Advocates' Library, & have now my work cut out.

---

[1] Religious Tract Society.
[2] These sentences appear again, more or less verbatim, in Letter 557.

In person he is my old idea of a judge, tall, long-faced, with solemn hanging jowls, scrupulously shaven and dazzlingly clean in his tall collar; blue clothes, cravat, and tie-pin.

A most courteous gentleman withal, and no lady has ever given me tea in so fine a manner. We had tea alone in Stevenson's room; but scarcely a word was spoken of him!

I would like you to get his *St. Ives* for 1s. (or 1/3 if you are weak) for I haven't a copy of my own: and read it as quick as you can.

I wrote quite six poems last week, chiefly in Edinburgh; and when I read them to S.S. over a private tea in his room this afternoon, he came round from his first advice of deferred publishing, and said I must hurry up & get what is ready typed. He & his friends will get Heinemann to produce for me. Now it is my judgment alone that I must screw up to printing pitch.

Tell me the date & contents of yr. last letter. Saturday's post didn't arrive owing to the Raid in the South!

I heard from Harold yesterday.

Looking out for the Redskin Photographs, and hoping you will read *St. Ives*,

Yours ever W.E.O. x

You must be prepared for a long period of Post Cards! I find I have put some poetic material on p. 3 for instance which ought to have been economized for my serious workshop.

555. To Susan Owen

Sat. [*29 October 1917*]   *Craiglockhart*

My own dearest Mother,

So relieved by your Card this morning. How good of you to report instantly of your palatial-gorgeous sickness. But it was not a joke to me yesterday.

I hear this morning that I am to be boarded next Tuesday—and sent away. It is not absolutely certain, but Dr. Brock thinks that will be the issue this time. I am rather upset about it. Especially as I am so happy with Sassoon. Spent all day with him yesterday, Breakfast, Lunch, Tea & Dinner, chiefly at the Conservative Club. Hence no letter yesterday!

Today, since 3 o'clock High Jinks reigned at Mrs. Fullerton's Apartments; we gave the boys Tea & Supper; Mrs. F. says she never enjoyed so much any party in her 23 years experience. I can say almost as much. We left the House at 9 p.m. & I have just arrived here.

Strange, if you like, but I am seriously beginning to have aching sensations at being rooted up from this pleasant Region. I wanted to arrange my 3 Weeks around Christmas; but now I can only think of spending the 25th in a detestable Mess Room.

However you will be none too well by Wednesday next, & I may cheer you up, my precious Mother, whose little finger will break all the charm of Edinburgh, and all the love that it has thrown about me.

No more news—or I shall have not enough to gabble about around the Home Fire.

I may not arrive till Thurs. or Friday. Or again I may not come till next year!

S.S. has come in since I started this (2 mins. ago) & is deeply annoyed about this news, and is going to siege his Dr. Rivers about me![1]

Ever your own W.E.O.

556. To Susan Owen

Postcard

Monday [*Postmark 29 October 1917*]   [*Postmark Midlothian*]

It seems really likely that I shall be evacuated on Tuesday. Some time ago the Grays made me promise to stay 2 or 3 days with them before leaving Edinburgh. I am going there this afternoon, & if they ask me again, I may stay one day in order to get my picture done. Sassoon is anxious for me to spend a day or two of my 3 weeks with some people at a Manor near Oxford.[2] I have not made up my mind. We went to the Astronomer's yesterday, & saw the moon.

I wonder how I shall find you all. I shall be in a desperate excited state when I arrive. Make due arrangements for Colin's presence!

So, then, I may turn up on Tues. Night, or Wednesday Morning, or any day until Sat., for I want to stay on here a few days (if it won't shorten the 3 weeks) to be able to return all my borrowed books, & make a graceful exit from these scenes.

W.E.O.

557. To Siegfried Sassoon

5 November 1917   *Mahim, Monkmoor Road, Shrewsbury*

My dear Sassoon,

When I had opened your envelope[3] in a quiet corner of the Club Staircase, I sat on the stairs and groaned a little, and then went up and loosed off a gourd, a Gothic vacuum[4] of a letter, which I 'put by' (as

---

[1] Dr. W. H. R. Rivers. For more about him see *Sherston's Progress*.
[2] Garsington Manor, home of Philip Morrell (1870–1943), Liberal MP for South Oxfordshire, and Lady Ottoline Morrell. SS had first been there in 1916 (see *Siegfried's Journey*). Wilfred never got there.
[3] SS recalls that in saying good-bye at the Conservative Club he gave Wilfred a sealed envelope. It contained a ten-pound note and Robert Ross's address in London.
[4] 'Our final evening together was spent at a quiet Club in Edinburgh. . . . Wilfred was leaving for London by the midnight train. After a good dinner and a bottle of noble Burgundy had put us in good spirits, I produced a volume of portentously over-elaborate verse, recently sent me by the author. From this I began to read extracts—a cursory inspection having assured me that he would find them amusing. It now seems incongruous that my most vivid memory of him, on that last occasion when we were alone together, should be of

you would recommend for such effusions) until I could think over the thing without grame.[1]

I have also waited for this photograph.

Show some rich anger if you will. I thank you; but not on this paper only, or in any writing. You gave—with what Christ, if he had known Latin & dealt in oxymoron, might have called Sinister Dexterity. I imagined you were entrusting me with some holy secret concerning yourself. A secret, however, it shall be until such time as I shall have climbed to the housetops, and you to the minarets of the world.

Smile the penny! This Fact has not intensified my feelings for you by the least—the least grame. Know that since mid-September, when you still regarded me as a tiresome little knocker on your door, I held you as Keats + Christ + Elijah + my Colonel + my father-confessor + Amenophis IV in profile.

What's that mathematically?

In effect it is this: that I love you, dispassionately, so much, so very much, dear Fellow, that the blasting little smile you wear on reading this can't hurt me in the least.

If you consider what the above Names have severally done for me, you will know what you are doing. And you have fixed my Life— however short. You did not light me: I was always a mad comet; but you have fixed me.[2] I spun round you a satellite for a month, but I shall swing out soon, a dark star in the orbit where you will blaze. It is some consolation to know that Jupiter himself sometimes swims out of Ken!

To come back to our sheep, as the French never say, I have had a perfect little note from Robt. Ross,[3] and have arranged a meeting at

---

his surrendering to convulsions of mirth in a large leather-covered armchair. These convulsions I shared until incapable of continuing my recital.

> *What cassock'd misanthrope*
> *Hawking peace-canticles for glory-gain,*
> *Hymns from his rostrum'd height th' epopt of Hate?*

It was, I think, the word "epopt" . . . which caused the climax of our inextinguishable laughter, though the following couplet, evidently "written in dejection" had already scored heavily.

> *O is it true I have become*
> *This gourd, this gothic vacuum?"*
> Siegfried's Journey, pp. 64–65.

The volume of verse was by Aylmer Strong, *A Human Voice*, Elkin Mathews, London, 1917. It survives among Wilfred's books, inscribed to him by SS.

[1] SS cannot explain this word.

[2] 'The ten-stanza poem, of which "This is the Track" originally formed the three last (and only revised) verses, develops an image used in a letter to Sassoon in November 1917 ("I was always a mad comet; but you have fixed me"); in the poem he aspires to be a solitary meteor awakening in men premonitions and intimations of eternity' (Welland). Stanza VII of the BM draft runs:

> To be a meteor, fast, eccentric, lone,
> Lawless; in passage through all spheres,
> Warning the earth of wider ways unknown
> And rousing men with heavenly fears.

[3] Robert Baldwin Ross (1869–1918), Oscar Wilde's friend and editor; critic, authority on art, and patron of young writers. Through him, Wilfred met Osbert Sitwell, Arnold Bennett, H. G. Wells, and others.

12.30 on Nov. 9th. He mentioned staying at Half Moon St., but the house is full.

I have ordered several copies of *Fairies & Fusiliers*,[1] but shall not buy all, in order to leave the book exposed on the Shrewsbury counters! I'm also getting Colvin's new *Life of Keats*,[2] no price advertised, but damn it, I'm to enjoy my Leave!

I am spending happy enough days with my Mother, but I can't get sociable with my Father without going back on myself over ten years of thought.

What I most miss in Edinburgh (not Craiglockhart) is the conviviality of the Four Boys (L. *vivere*—to live). Someday, I must tell how we sang, shouted, whistled and danced through the dark lanes through Colinton; and how we laughed till the meteors showered around us, and we fell calm under the winter stars. And some of us saw the pathway of the spirits for the first time. And seeing it so far above us, and feeling the good road so safe beneath us, we praised God with louder whistling; and knew we loved one another as no men love for long.[3]

Which, if the Bridge-players Craig & Lockhart could have seen, they would have called down the wrath of Jahveh, and buried us under the fires of the City you wot of.

To which also it is time you committed this letter. I wish you were less undemonstrative, for I have many adjectives with which to qualify myself. As it is I can only say I am
Your proud friend, Owen

558. To Susan Owen
Postcard

Thurs. Night [*Postmark 9 November 1917*]   *Regent Palace Hotel, Piccadilly Circus, London W.1*

Woke up at Padd. arriving an hour sooner than expected. Had no difficulty in getting a good room. Looked in at Poetry Bookshop, where I was informed by Miss Klematanski[4] that I had met a friend of hers in Edinburgh. I couldn't recall this friend for some minutes, so shocked at being recognized myself. Monro is in England, but ill.
Your W.E.O.

559. To Susan Owen
Sunday Mng. [*10 November 1917*]   *Regent Palace Hotel*

Had a memorable dinner at the Reform last night, & stayed talking with Ross till one A.M. I and my work are a success. I had already

[1] Robert Graves's second book of poems (William Heinemann, London, 1917). The first was *Over the Brazier* (The Poetry Bookshop, London, 1916).
[2] *John Keats, his Life and Poetry* (London, 1917). Sir Sidney Colvin (1845–1927) had published an earlier Life in the English Men of Letters series (*Keats*, Macmillan and Co. Ltd., London, 1887). Wilfred's copy of the 1909 impression is inscribed 'Torquay, Spring, 1911'.
[3] See Letter 554.
[4] Alida Klemantaski. She married Harold Monro in 1920, his first marriage having been dissolved in 1916.

sent something to the *Nation*[1] which hasn't appeared yet, but it seems the Editor[2] has started talking of me, and Wells told me he had heard of me through that Editor! H.G.W. said some rare things for my edification, & told me a lot of secrets. I only felt ill at ease with him once, and that was when he tried to make me laugh at Arnold Bennett. Wells is easily top dog when it comes to jests, and I'm afraid I took his side, and told Bennett I disapproved of his gaudy silk handkerchief!

Bennett had just had a look round in Ireland, but he had nothing to say outside his *Daily News* Article,[3] which I suppose you read. I didn't. I got Bennett into a corner about Sassoon. I think they 'noticed' me because I <u>stood up to them</u> both politely when they shook hands to go, and <u>argumentatively.</u>

W.E.O.

I've had an imploring card from Leslie, received in a weak moment, namely in a hot bath, and so resolved to go down this afternoon.

[Later]

Dearest Mother,

I have just lunched with Ross, H. G. Wells, & Arnold Bennett. Wells talked exclusively to me for an hour over the coffee, & made jokes at the expense of the Editor of the *Daily News*,[4] who joined us.

I think I can't honestly put more news under one penny stamp!

Your W.E.O.

P.S. Just going up to Gidea Park. I am to have dinner with Ross to-morrow.

560. To Susan Owen
Postcard

Monday [*Postmark 12 November 1917*]   *Winchester P.O.*

I stayed in London till Sunday Evening as I wanted to hear a certain piece at the Queen's Hall. Reached Winchester at about 8.30, & was piloted to the Y.M.C.A. Slept in a Camp Bed. Served the men's coffee this mng. Lunched in Winchester, & spent all afternoon in the Cathedral with Leslie. I have just come out from the Service. Staying tonight w. Leslie. May reach home on Monday Night, or perhaps not before Tuesday.

W.E.O.

561. To Leslie Gunston

16 November 1917   [*? Shrewsbury*]

My dear Leslie,

I did not think to send back a driblet of your Ink so soon, but I have indeed carried off the key.

[1] 'Miners' (*Poems*, p. 91). Published in *The Nation* 16 January 1918.
[2] Henry William Massingham (1860–1924) was Editor 1907–23.
[3] On Irish Home Rule.
[4] Alfred George Gardiner (1865–1946) was Editor 1902–19. He wrote regularly under the pseudonym 'Alpha of the Plough'.

Had it been the key of my box I should surely have left it with you.

As it was I left you the key to many of my poems, which you will guard from rust or soilure. . . .[1]

Good of you to send me the Lyric of Nov. 14th. I can only send my own of the same date,[2] which came from Winchester Downs, as I crossed the long backs of the downs after leaving you. It is written as from the trenches. I could almost see the dead lying about in the hollows of the downs.

I called at the Bookshop during my 3 hours in Town, & had a good chat with Monro, not forgetting to ask him about the *Nymph*. Graves' book just came in while I was there. Haste thee, *Nymph*, and bring with thee Jest & youthful jollity!

Your W.E.O.

562. To Susan Owen
Postcard[3]
[*Postmark 24 November 1917*]   *Victoria Hotel, Scarborough*

At York there was no room at the Station Hotel, no, not on the couches. The whole City is over-full, & the other hotels would not open to my knocking at 4 this morning. So I came on to Sc. and passed the morning at this hotel, which is at the corner of the square where we went to a dentist's[4] once. Went to the Barracks this afternoon, some miles from here. But the officers live at the Clarence Gardens Hotel, where I must now go. This will be my address. Two or three of the old 5th officers have come back before me, & say the Hotel is very comfortable, & they like Scarborough.

W.E.O.

563. To Susan Owen
23 November 1917   *5 (Reserve) Bn. Manchester Regt.,*[5]
                               Northern Cavalry Barracks, Scarborough

Dearest Mother,

I have been put on a species of Light Duty which I little expected: I am Major Domo[6] of the Hotel. There is a Mess President, the Doctor, Capt. Mather,[7] whom I knew at Witley, and like very much; there is also a Food Specialist: under him like me. Capt. Mather then has the responsibility, but will do little but sign his name. I have to control the

[1] We have omitted twenty-two words.
[2] 'Asleep' (*Poems*, p. 57).
[3] Written before Letter 563, despite the earlier postmark.
[4] The Owen family had holidayed at Scarborough c. 1906 (*JO* I, Plate 7b).
[5] Wilfred had left the battalion at Southport in December 1916 to go to France. Shortly after, 3rd/5th, 3rd/6th and 3rd/7th Manchesters were amalgamated into the 5th (Reserve) Battalion, which moved to Scarborough in the summer of 1917. The officers were in the Queen's Hotel and Clarence Gardens Hotel, the men in the large cavalry barracks at Burniston, outside the town. The battalion was filled up in 1918 with boys under 18 who continued training until the Armistice.
[6] Camp Commandant.
[7] Captain J. de V. Mather, RAMC.

Household, which consists of some dozen Batmen, 4 Mess Orderlies, 4 Buglers, the Cook, (a fat woman of great skill,) two female kitcheners, and various charwomen!

They need driving. You should see me scooting the buglers round the dining-room on their knees with dustpan and brush! You should hear me rate the Charwoman for leaving the Lavatory-Basins unclean.

I am responsible for finding rooms for newcomers, which is a great worry, as we are full up. This means however that I have a good room to myself, as well as my Office!

I keep two officers under arrest in their rooms; & spent a dismal hour this morning taking one of these for exercise.

I get up at 6.30. to see that the breakfast is ready in time.

I spent this morning in Correspondence, and Inspection of rooms: working from 8 a.m. to 12. This afternoon I ordered from the Grocers and the Greengrocers vast quantities of food.

I do no parades, and can go out when I like. (This by special ruling of the Colonel.)[1]—Who is not liked among his 70 officers.

I am specially busy at present. There was a guest night yesterday, which meant a gorgeous meal, whose menu I am ashamed to give you. It kept my house-lads sweating till after midnight.

And the Food Expert has gone away for a time.

I am also in charge of the Wine & Tobacco, and took stock in a most business-like manner this afternoon.

It is interesting work but hardly 'lighter' than a Platoon Commander's.

I am pestered by these new officers who are in the first flush of commissionhood, and need to be suppressed.

I shall soon be putting up another pip.

I beg to acknowledge your letter of the 22nd inst. and have noted the facts. Confound this business mood which possesses me! It, as much as the busy-ness of my hours, will prove disastrous to my poems. But things will slack down next week, and so shall my temper.

The C.O. is a terrible old 'Regular', and I am in mortal terror lest one day his bath-water should be cold, or his plates too hot.

There was a Mess Dance the first night I arrived, and I was glad to see several of the old Witley N.C.O.'s. Some had been out & wounded. It was strange to see the change in their expressions. They had been told I was killed. I think I am marked Permanent Home Service: Always your own

                                        W.E.O.

564. To Leslie Gunston

Sunday, 25 November 1917   *Clarence Gardens Hotel, Scarborough*

My dear Leslie,

Received the Books last night, and spent an exciting few minutes looking through the poems.[2] I congratulate you on the Binding & Type.

[1] Lieutenant-Colonel Spencer Mitchell, Manchester Regiment.
[2] *The Nymph.*

The Dedication Page & the Prefatory Note are set perfectly. Yes, it is rather disappointing to have no Back Lettering. I still think many of the Pieces might have enriched themselves with time. I like best

(1) *The Caradoc.* How much better than a photograph does it souvenir that day! I remember talking about the Croziers,[1] and plucking them & uncurling them. What was the date of this June?
(2) *Golden Hair.* This is your very best.
(3) *Sestet of Attar of Roses*
    'red as the dawn of doubtful days' is the best thought in the book.
(4) Ode for A.C.S.
(5) Chopin
(6) The Colloseum!!

I don't like 'Hymn of Love to England', naturally, at this period while I am composing 'Hymns of Hate'.

I wonder you did not include the Bluebottle thing. I liked that ever so well.

And why omit certain Rose Poems which I remember?

It struck me that there was a little too much osculation throughout the book. People will not know that poetry is your only manner of satisfaction, and may draw wrong conclusions.

I think every poem, and every figure of speech should be a matter of experience. That is why I like the first verse of 'Song', and should have omitted the second!

Am looking out for mentions & reviews, and anxious to hear what you know of the Sales.

I am wickedly busy and businesslike now, being Boss of the Hotel, Accommodation, Food, Fires, Lighting, Service, etc. etc. I do no parades, but have not yet allowed myself any free time for walks or reading.

I have no table, & am writing on my knee.

Yours always W.E.O.

565. To Siegfried Sassoon

27 November 1917   *Scarborough*

I sit alone at last, and therefore with you, my dear Siegfried. For which name, as much as for anything in any envelope of your sealing, I give thanks and rejoice.

The 5th have taken over a big Hotel, of which I am Major Domo, which in the vulgar, means Lift Boy. I manage Accommodation, Food, and Service. I boss cooks, housemaids, charwomen, chamber-maids, mess orderlies and—drummers.

---

[1] A description of bracken:

> Like carven croziers are the curled shoots growing
> To bless me as I pass.

There were 80 officers when I came, or 800 grouses daily.

I had a Third Heaven of a time in London, and should have got into a Fourth or Fifth if I had not missed you on Wednesday. Were you there for a 'Reading?' I know nothing of it to this day.

After London, I went to Winchester to see my Cousin, whose fine Book cover with its enclosed pages I dare to send you herewith. ('Here-with' is the staple of my morning's letters, re this and per that.)

In Town, then, R.R. gave me a glorified morning at the Reform, & evening at Half Moon St.—When he had steered me to a lunch-table I found beside me an upstart rodent of a man, who looked astonished to find himself there. But dear Ross sang out with blessed distinctness 'Mister Arnnoldd Bennnettt'. So I stood up and shook hands. Presently I became aware of a pair of bayonet-coloured eyes, threatening at me from over, as it were, a brown sandbag. 'H. G. Wells!' So I stood up and shook hands. I think these men noticed me because I stood up to them—in two senses. Anyhow I got A.B. into a corner about you, as I will tell you someday. And H.G. talked to me exclusively for an hour. I was only ill at ease with him once, and that was when he tried to make me laugh with him at Bennett's gaudy handkerchief.

What sport for my imagination is the idea of your Meeting with R. Nichols.—He is so self-concerned & *vaniteux* in his verse that I thought he must efface himself in a room: even as you who write so acid are so—unsoured; and me, who write so big, am so minuscule.

What is Nichols[1] up to now?

I called at the P. Bookshop the Wednesday you were in Town. A lady was badgering H Monro, trying to discover your age and whereabouts, and so on. Monro proved himself as reticent as his books. But we exchanged some delicious winks. R.G.'s book[2] came in during the hour I was there. I should never stop if I started to rejoice over these poems.

You read many to me: but, wisely, not the best:—or the most charm-ing.

The 'Legion' is too glorious. I tell you I can not believe I rode in a taxi with the man Gracchus. But I did, and he has cursed, battered on the table, over a poor word of mine.[3] Oh! world you are making for me, Sassoon!

---

[1] Robert Malise Bowyer Nichols (1893–1944). He had been invalided home from France (Second-Lieutenant RFA) and was about to join the British Mission (Ministry of Informa-tion) to the U.S.A. At this time he had published two collections: *Invocation: War Poems and Others* (Elkin Mathews, London, 1915) and *Ardours and Endurances* (Chatto and Windus, London, 1917).

[2] *Fairies and Fusiliers.*

[3] 'The Legion' (*Fairies and Fusiliers*) ends with Gracchus speaking:

> The legion is the legion while Rome stands,
> And these same men before the autumn's fall
> Shall bang old Vercingetorix out of Gaul.

Wilfred is quoting:

> The red-faced old centurion started up,
> Cursed, battered on the table . . .

I think I liked reading his Letter[1] to you more than yours to him,[2] but for no better reasons than that I like the future better than the past, and hope you will learn the piccolo.

If These tetrameters aren't enough to bring you to your senses, Mad Jack,[3] what can my drivel effect to keep you from France?

Have you been very sat upon by this Board? Do tell me quick what your movements are.

I have studied and expanded every sentencience of your sole letter to me; until I can make no more out of it, and want some more, please.

Concerning Gunston's book: you might, of your charity, read (1) page 41, because it is the best.

(2) page 49, the sextet, because I asked him to write, on this subject. . . .[4]

(3) Page 11. There is a conceit in v. 3,—a poor thing, but mine own.

My 'Vision'[5] is the result of two hours' leisure yesterday,—and getting up early this morning! If you have objections to make, would you return it? If not, pass it on to R.R.

I trust you'll like the 'Soldier's Dream'[6] well enough to pass it on to the *Nation* or Cambridge?

This was the last piece from Craiglockhart.

Winchester Downs gave me 'Asleep.'

As I do no parades, I shall presently be able to make time for seclusion.

There is no one here whose mind is Truth, or whose body Keats's synonym for Truth.

I'll mind my business, I'm a good worm.

Could you get me another portrait for my room here? I framed the one, and could not pack it.

But don't make it an excuse for delaying a letter.

I hope you will read through this, twice.

I hope you read Graves's Letter to S.S. twice a day, till war ends.

We have had some strong sunshine; and when it strikes anything blue I see you sitting by the bedside as on That Morning in September. You look round,—over my head, which annoys me, so that I go down and rate the kitchen staff of the Hotel, and insult the new subalterns.

> I am Owen; and I am dying.
> I am Wilfred; and I follow the Gleam.[7]

[1] 'Letter to S.S. from Mametz Wood' in which the poet looks forward to travelling with SS after the war:

> Robert will learn the local *bat*
> For billeting and things like that,
> If Siegfried learns the piccolo
> To charm the people as we go.

[2] 'The Next War.' See p. 499, note 1.
[3] SS had this nickname in France.
[4] We have omitted thirty-nine words.
[5] 'A Vision of Whitechapel.' Not in *Poems*. HO has a draft.
[6] *Poems*, p. 84.
[7] *I* am Merlin,
And *I* am dying,
I am Merlin
Who follow The Gleam.
    Tennyson, *Merlin and The Gleam*

566. To Susan Owen

10 p.m. Monday [*27 November 1917*]   *Clarence Gardens, Scarborough*

Dearest my Mother,

I am writing in the uncertain privacy of my Office: to tell you that I did indeed forget to post a card written the hour of arrival in Scarborough. It went only one post before my Letter.

Concerning my re-entrance into the Battalion the thing that is most mentionable was the great unexpected consideration & respect shown me by all ranks. (I had risen from the dead.)

The Colonel is a terrible old misanthrope in the morning. (He has lost two sons) but the evening soothes him, and it is only then that I have dealings with him.

Captain Mather whose hints are my laws of life, is a good sort (i.e. kind and clever.) His father was a friend of Ruskin, and wrote a Ruskin Biography.[1] He has read Sassoon with great appreciation. Our Major is the substantial justification of his name: Major Frank.[2] He lives so courteous & pleasant to all that I knew he valued War Poetry before he told me so!

(This may seem a strange inference but it is worth thinking over.)

Have just been interrupted by two drummers who've been stavying[3] here with dish-washing working all day since 6, who need a note to pass the Barrack Sentry.

I was working all Sunday Evening with Mess Bills for 25 officers 'going out' in a few days.

The wind has been glorious for me as annoying for you. The sea was— not a thing for this notepaper to tell of. Much love to all at Alpenrose. I am well pleased with this job.

Dearest of my love. W.E.O.

Thanks for Boots.

567. To Susan Owen

Sunday [*3 December 1917*]   [*Scarborough*]

Dearest Mother,

I wrote in the middle of the week. Did you get a complete letter? For I have discovered a page of writing to you among my papers. This afternoon I had a fire in my grate, which smokes horribly in the wind. Thus I finished an important poem this afternoon,[4] in the right atmosphere. I also drafted three others. I'm going to get up at dawn tomorrow to do a dawn piece which I've had in mind since those dismal hours at York, 3 to 7 a.m.! All dressed up, and nowhere to go.

[1] James Marshall Mather (1851–1916) *Life and Teachings of John Ruskin,* Warne, London, 1883.
[2] Major N. G. Frank, 6th Manchesters.
[3] *sic.*
[4] 'Wild with all Regrets.' See Letter 568, note 1.

I don't want to see York again. No use to me. Worse than Crewe.
Here I have a certain amount of what might degenerate into worry, but
it doesn't with me. I think my chief trouble is watching that hundreds
of windows are shaded at 4 p.m. And no unnecessary lights burning. I
think I have hereditary aptitudes for this. I housekeep on a scale that
would fairly stagger you and Mary, don't you know.

Engaged two chamber-maids yesterday to polish furniture—or we
shall have a big depreciation bill.

The men however do excellent work, and learn as quickly as a female
forgets.

I took a joy-walk into Scarboro' yesterday, & discovered 3 genuine
'Hepplethwaite' Chairs. I think I must have 'em.

Did I tell you the Hotel stands on the edge of the North Cliff; just
where we played cricket once?

The whole bay is white as milk, the wind being contrary to the
breakers.

I was really very sorry not to be able to call at Alpenrose. But it was
on your account, wasn't it?

I hope you'll see Dunsden & the Vicar.

Mary wrote the other day, enclosing my Edinburgh Mails. One of
my Waiters here lives under the shadow of Holyrood. He's the best
lad for work I've got—wounded in the leg. Our old Bar Corporal was
at Bangower, & Blanche has written to him since! I wonder if you heard
from H. today? I suppose he mustn't write to me yet. Give my messages
to him.

Ever your boy Wilfred

Am writing on my knee.

568. To Siegfried Sassoon

6 December 1917   *Scarborough*

My friend,

I shall continue to poop off heavy stuff at you, till you get my range
at Scarborough, and so silence me, for the time. This 'Wild with all
Regrets'[1] was begun & ended two days ago, at one gasp. If simplicity,
if imaginativeness, if sympathy, if resonance of vowels, make poetry
I have not succeeded. But if you say 'Here is poetry,' it will be so for me.
What do you think of my Vowel-rime stunt in this, and 'Vision'? Do
you consider the hop from Flea to Soul too abrupt?

Wouldn't our Theosophist[2] like the Thought Form of this piece? I

---

[1] An early draft, dated December 5, 1917, of 'À Terre' (*Poems*, p. 64, where this draft is
printed as Appendix Two).

[2] A fellow patient at Craiglockhart. '. . . I was fool enough to begin grumbling about the
war. . . . The Theosophist responded by assuring me that we were all only on the great
stairway which conducts us to higher planes of existence, and when I petulantly enquired
what he thought about conscripted populations slaughtering one another, on the great
stairway, in order to safeguard democracy and liberty, he merely replied: "Ah, Sherston,
that is the Celestial Surgeon at work upon humanity".' (*Sherston's Progress*, pp. 29–30.)

quite see the origin of Theosophy. It's the same as that of heaven, and Abraham's bosom, and of the baby that sucked Abraham's bosom, (supposing he lived long enough ago) : desperate desire.

Your W.E.O.

569. To Susan Owen[1]

Friday Night [*9 December 1917*]   [*Scarborough*]

Dearest Mother,

I wanted Colin to come, hoping I should be in Billets. He could only have tea with me here. There are rooms vacant, but as the Hotel is quite taken over by the Gov't he couldn't sleep. I have made no friends even of the most temporary nature in the Town, but I could easily find him a lodgement, which I would offer him as a Christmas Present. I should be able to be with him either morning or afternoon for hours.

I think he could disport himself very well between times. I went to an Auction yesterday, & got an antique side table[2] wondrous cheap. It will arrive addressed to Father at Station. A beautiful old piece,—to be my Cottage sideboard. There were none but Dealers at this sale! They would double the price in their shop, I was told.

So glad to hear you feel weller. I'm all right. Best wishes to Uncle & Auntie.

Your W.E.O.

Tuesday.!!!

4 p.m.

My own Mother,

I wonder how you are disporting yourself at Alpenrose. Life here is a mixture of wind, sand, crumbs on carpets, telephones, signatures, clean sheets, shortage of meat, and too many money-sums. But I like it. For one thing I fell so suddenly into mental preoccupations that there was no dallying with regrets for leaving Home. I have not even written to Sassoon or anyone.

We are getting four maidservants and a page, as these boys are being overworked at present. You would love to see me 'keeping an eye on the charwoman.'

Gen. Lovatt[3] called yesterday but didn't come in as I thought he would—to see that no fire was burning in my office, and generally look up the kitchen-taps.

I was flurrying round like any Mrs. Smith de Smith when 'Company' is expected.

I 'get out' for an hour or two daily, if only to promenade the 'arrested' subaltern, who is a *ci-devant* Sergeant Major, under arrest for laying hands on an A.P.M.,[4] a big fellow, and a gruff. On our first walk I kept on the landward side of the cliff. There is also a Major under arrest for striking a private. I have to keep looking them up.

---

[1] Two letters in one.
[2] HO now has this, as well as the chest-of-drawers mentioned in Letter 590.
[3] Major-General Lord Lovat (1871–1933).
[4] Assistant Provost Marshal.

The Hotel is a pleasanter place even than the Queen's at Southport, well furnished & commodious. My room has hideous furniture, but a comfortable bed—and fireplace. My personal servant had a bad shell shock in Gallipoli, while lying sun-stricken. He was about a year in hospital, but has all his wits about him now. . . .[1]

I must now go and see that every blind is drawn, aye and double-drawn.

Always your own W.E.O.

570. To Susan Owen

13 December 1917   *Scarborough*

Dearest Mother,

It is the quarter of an hour after lunch. The coffee has given me satisfaction and everybody else. (I serve coffee after lunch as well as dinner.) So I sit in the middle of my five-windowed turret, and look down upon the sea. The sun is valiant in its old age. I draw the Venetian blinds, so that the shadow of the lattices on the table gives an illusion of great heat.

———

I thought Arnold Bennett's article of yesterday showed how much he wants Peace, but how little he knows of war.[2] I hope you read it. How do you find that book about the Fusiliers?

Yesterday I was sent the Tynecastle School Magazine, very amusing. Mrs. Fullerton writes again this morning, reminding me how I promised to go up there for my first leave.

'You can imagine our welcome better than I can write' they say. Now, I find that Leave from Friday Night to Monday Night is granted every month! But Mrs. Fullerton is leaving the school for ever on the 21st. in order to be with her husband who will soon get sent out again.

There is much talk of Education for the 'A 4's' of the Battalion, that is the tender younglings. I have been 'approached' on the subject, but I shall not consent to lecture on Militarian subjects. The scheme either comes of a desperate feeling that the race is going to perdition intellectually or else it is a Jesuitical movement to catch 'em young, & prepare them for the Eucharist of their own blood.

Dearest love from W.E.O.

571. To Susan Owen

[18 December 1917]   *Scarborough*

My dearest Mother,

Glad to hear from Mary as well as you this morning. I hope she is not made to work too hard at that job, and wish she could get something in the Hospital less crockish.

———

[1] Seventy-seven words omitted.
[2] 'That Inconclusive Peace' (*Daily News*, 13 December 1917).

If you hold to giving me a present this is what I most want:

Tides, Poems by John Drinkwater:

Sidwick and Jackson. 2/6.[1]

Siegfried is going out next week, but may stay in Ireland on the way. He feels like a condemned man, with just time to put things straight. One of his last deeds here is causing Robert Nichols (of the *Ardours & Endurances*) to write to me, and befriend me. I await Nichols's letter with much wonder.

Enclosed is an article[2] in which I am quoted pretty freely.

I feel immensely glad that Harold is at ease [*remainder missing*]

572. To Susan Owen
Postcard

Wed. Aft. [*Postmark 19 December 1917*]   [*Scarborough*]

Am just scurrying off to Edinburgh, leaving in an hour's time. If you write on Thurs. let it be to 21 St. Bernard's Crescent. The Grays wrote this mng. begging me to go up & see them; so that decided me.

Am sending a Registered Box in Parcel, to be opened 'on Christmas'.

Your W.E.O. x

573. To Susan Owen
Picture postcard: York, Royal Station Hotel

[*Postmark 19 December 1917*]   *York, 8 p.m.*

Had the best dinner here a Rly Hotel ever provided possibly because Sir A. Yapp[3] also dined here tonight. Am going on at 10.45 arr. Ed. 4.45! Am still feeling amazed at the ease with which I obtained Leave.

Your W.E.O.

574. To Susan Owen

20 December [*1917*]   *North British Station Hotel, Edinburgh*

Dearest Mother,

Train was an hour late at York. There had been an accident in front I believe. Thus I got in after 6 a.m. to Waverley—fortunately—for there was no bedroom vacant at all. But I had a big bath & big breakfast. Then went straight to Craiglockhart—mainly after my Chesterton Drawing Originals,[4] which had not yet been returned to me, & which it seems one Salmond has carried off. I saw Dr. Brock, whose first word was 'Antaeas!' which they want immediately for the next Mag! Shall

---

[1] Published 1917. Wilfred's copy survives.
[2] Which has not survived.
[3] Sir Arthur Keysall Yapp (1869–1936), National Secretary of the YMCA and Assistant Controller, Ministry of Food.
[4] A page of sketches by G. K. Chesterton appeared under the title of 'Profiteers' in *The Hydra* (No. 1, New Series) November 1917.

have to spin it off again while up here. Crowds of the men I knew are still at the Hydro, and thought I had come back relapsed (N.B. I had very little sleep last night.)

Then I went off to Tynecastle. They were in the act of writing Christmas Letters to me! My address was on the Blackboard. And 'original' Christmas Cards were all over the room! I am going to see the Grays this afternoon & may stay with them tomorrow. Am feeling <u>very</u> fit, in spite of the wretched weather, & journey.

Hope your parcel comes all right—

—And my table!   Always your lovingest W.E.O.

575. To Susan Owen

Sunday [23 December 1917]   *Scarborough*

My own Mother,

Came back last night for Supper, leaving Ed. at quarter to two. A good journey, and as a show well worth the money in itself. The sun began to think of setting about two o'clock and so there was a three hours' winter sunset over the Northumberland moors. I liked what I saw of Berwick on Tweed.

Monday

I was interrupted here. Have now had your lovely parcel, & opened it but not broken into the scrumshies.

The Scotch boys gave me 100 Players Cigarettes. It was most touching, for I had given most of them nothing—beyond *Hiawatha*. We had a great time in Minnehaha's Wigwam on Thursday. Dined with the Grays and Mrs. Steinthal on Friday: stayed in digs of my own.

I can think of nothing at the moment but Robert Graves' letter,[1] which came by the same post as the parcel.

He says 'Don't make any mistake, Owen, you are a —— fine poet already, & are going to be more so. I won't have the impertinence to criticize . . .

Puff out your chest a little, and be big for you've more right than most of us . . .

You must help S.S. & R.N. & R.G. to revolutionize English Poetry. So outlive this war.

Yours ever, *Robert Graves.*'

I have never yet written to him!

This aft. I am appointed to tea with Cousin May. This will give a Christmas feeling.

The weather is Septemberish.[2]

I little expected so large a parcel. I am upset in soul that no present will arrive to Mary or Father in time.

[1] See Appendix C.
[2] 'Mayish' struck out.

I left the tea-pot unpolished to emphasize its antiquity. So looking forward to see you pour out—early in Feby.

I shall gather round tomorrow with you in what Bob Cratchit calls a circle round the fire. This was in one of the many home made Christmas cards I got:

> The thoughts of love are long long thoughts
>   But memories sweet are longer.
> The bonds of wealth are strong, strong bonds
>   But friendship's ties are stronger!

Pity it's not more banal than it is.   x W.E.O.

576. To Mary Owen

27 December 1917   *Scarborough*

My dear Mary,

I left Scarboro' so suddenly that there was no time to review the shops for your present. Is there anything you wish?

The Brilliantine is both useful <u>and</u> ornamental when used. Thank you, dear, for this surprise.

Mother's letter was a treasure for me this morning.

I went to tea with Cousin May again, & had a German lesson from a lady staying there!

Would you please send me (1) Berlitz German Book: in the shelf opposite the window.

(2) The 12th Nocturne (tear it out of the book.)

(3) The Article concerning R. Graves in *Chambers*.[1] (I think Father keeps *Chambers*?), Or if not, some extracts?

I must now write to Uncle John.

I'm sorry Mother didn't keep a few of those photographs!

We had a very mopish Christmas. The C.O. held an orderly Room for punishments in the morning—a thing forbidden in King's Regulations on Christmas Day—and strafed right & left, above & below.

Did you get any Christmas Cards? I got crowds.

Always your loving Wilfred

Has my Table arrived?

577. To Leslie Gunston

30 December 1917   *Scarborough*

My dear Leslie,

It is overlong since I wrote; but now, composed by my bedroom fire this Sunday afternoon, my thoughts impel themselves after you, & wish

---

[1] *Chambers's Journal* for 13 October 1917 carried an article by E. B. Osborn, 'Soldier Poets', in which Graves, Sassoon, and F. W. Harvey were singled out for praise.

you were here to read a little Swinburne, whom I find particularly fine on Sundays.

Have you yet got Gosse's life of A.G.S. ?[1]

I had a longish letter from Sassoon recently, saying he will get Robert Nichols to write to me, for he likes him much. Nichols' *Ardours & Endurances* you know, are in the 3rd or 4th Edition.

Graves also wrote to me, telling me to 'puff out my chest & look big', for I have as much right as most of Them.

Some poems of mine sent him by S.S. he is passing on to Nichols.

They believe in me, these Georgians, and I suffer a temptation to be satisfied that they read me; and to remain a poet's poet!

S.S. who has your book, (for the letter which he acknowledges, was in it,) says not a word of the book. He may have unfortunately read the 'Nations' Debt' first, and taken offence. Remember Poetry with him is become a mere vehicle of propaganda.

Already, by now, I believe he is in France.

I have had some good inspirations in Scarboro', but my need is to revise now, rather than keep piling up 'first drafts'. My duties, as you know, are in your Line, and I like 'em. Went to the most atrocious bad play ever witnessed, the other night: low melodrama shocking bad acting.

But there were a dozen girls who danced & sang by way of Interlude; & they being only 14 to 18 had adorable slender bare legs, nude as you could wish. What's more some of them came outside the Hotel next day. I waved and blew kisses from the window, but didn't speak to them. Anyhow it was better than overhearing conversation in a motor-car!

An old Bordeaux friend[2] of mine is now Interpreter in the American Y.M.C.A. near Bordeaux. Will write again soon.

Always your W.E.O.

578. To Susan Owen

31 December 1917[3]   *Scarborough*

My own dear Mother,

Just a short note to thank you for the message enclosed with forwarded letters. I guess you saw the Cards, from Johnny & Bobby; characteristic cards: pictures of monkeys & the motto: 'Times change, & we with Time, but not in ways of Friendship.' So they are unchanged—from the old shallow waggery, and the old deep affection. I haven't written to them since my arrival in England.

The other letter was from my *cher ami* in Bordeaux who, unlike

---

[1] Sir Edmund Gosse (1849–1928), *The Life of Algernon Charles Swinburne* (London, 1917).
[2] Pierre Berthaud.
[3] In a list of eighteen 'Books read at Scarborough, Dec. 1917' appear H. Barbusse, *Under Fire*; Wilfrid Gibson, *Battle*; Robert Nichols, *Ardours and Endurances*; John Masefield, *Lollingdown Downs* and *The Daffodil Fields*; Stopford Brooke, *Studies in Poetry*; Theocritus; Bion; and Moschus.

Raoul, persists in his expressions of fidelity. What I taught him of English has got him a post as Interpreter to the <u>American</u> Y.M.C.A. at Bordeaux. (*verb. sap.*) I think Bordeaux is first on my post-war Visiting List. Many & various, strange & multitudinous are the friends that befriend me in this world. Yet I never found one false, or that did not surpass me in some virtue.

Some are very young, and some are already old, but none are middling.

And there are no dogs among my friends.

No dogs, no sorcerers, nor the other abominations on that list. For I have been bitten by the dogs of the world; and I have seen through the sorceries and the scarlet garments.

And so I have come to the true measure of man.

I am not dissatisfied with my years. Everything has been done in bouts:

Bouts of awful labour at Shrewsbury & Bordeaux; bouts of amazing pleasure in the Pyrenees, and play at Craiglockhart; bouts of religion at Dunsden; bouts of horrible danger on the Somme; bouts of poetry always; of your affection always; of sympathy for the oppressed always.

I go out of this year a Poet, my dear Mother, as which I did not enter it. I am held peer by the Georgians; I am a poet's poet.

I am started. The tugs have left me; I feel the great swelling of the open sea taking my galleon.[1]

Last year, at this time, (it is just midnight, and now is the intolerable instant of the Change) last year I lay awake in a windy tent in the middle of a vast, dreadful encampment. It seemed neither France nor England, but a kind of paddock where the beasts are kept a few days before the shambles. I heard the revelling of the Scotch troops, who are now dead, and who knew they would be dead. I thought of this present night, and whether I should indeed—whether we should indeed—whether you would indeed—but I thought neither long nor deeply, for I am a master of elision.

But chiefly I thought of the very strange look on all faces in that camp; an incomprehensible look, which a man will never see in England, though wars should be in England; nor can it be seen in any battle. But only in Étaples.

It was not despair, or terror, it was more terrible than terror, for it was a blindfold look, and without expression, like a dead rabbit's.

It will never be painted, and no actor will ever seize it. And to describe it, I think I must go back and be with them.

We are sending seven officers straight out tomorrow.

I have not said what I am thinking this night, but next December I will surely do so.

I know what you are thinking, and you know me   Wilfred.

[1] See p. 326, note.

RETURN TO FRANCE

1918

579. To Mary Owen

4 January 1918   *Scarborough*

My dear Mary,

Many, many thanks for the Parcel, and your charming little letter. I have seen the last of Cousin May, but her friend, an uncommonly plain lady, is going to continue her German lessons. It is very kind, & I shall make the best of my rare opportunities.

I hear *John Bull* has published an aspersion on the Officers of the 5th Manchester Regt. implying that their men get only ¼ hour for breakfast but the officers get more.[1] I met the C.O.'s train with a taxi this afternoon, and as we were riding together, he asked me what I would do about this lie of Bottomley's. I hoped he would prosecute.

My servant, a deplorable 'shock' case, is run down, & I am giving him a rest, and I think changing him for a secondary-school-educated youth, who has fought at Beaumont Hamel, and at Serre, and all those places, if they can be called places.

He was badly wounded, and his leg has been badly set. He still wears the shell-torn boots.

Lt. Whittaker has just arrived here, for a week's 'training' before going out. Most of our old Musketry Instructors at Oswestry etc. are now killed, he says. But we've got stacks of men, as Sassoon says.

Your cheery Brother

Please send Sassoon's *Daffodil Murderer*[2]—in Bookcase.

580. To Susan Owen

10.30 p.m. 5 January 1918   [*Scarborough*]

My dear dear Mother,

This has been a day of continuous work from 7 a.m. to 9 p.m.!! not excluding meals!

True I went out to tea to Miss Bennett,[3] but I worked at German Conversation all the time there and walking back—'home'.

We have dismissed the Mess Corporal, & I have all the sundry items as well. And winding up last year's accounts for the Auditors! O my!

On such days I always write to you—as you notice. Because on such days I have no time to settle down to my art. For it is an art, & will need the closest industry. Consider that I spend—what?—three hours a week

---

[1] '*A Damnable order*. How long do the officers of the 5th Manchesters spend over their meals? Rather longer, we fancy, than the time granted to the men by a recent order—Tommy being allowed only a ¼ hr. for breakfast, and the same for dinner. Such haste is hardly conducive to digestion, even with rations on Lord Rhondda's scale' (*John Bull*, 5 January 1918).
[2] See p. 494, note 1.
[3] Who was giving him German lessons.

at it, which means one fruitful half-hour, when I ought to be doing SIX hours a day by all precedents.

Leslie has been unfavourably reviewed by the *Times Literary Supplement*. Not attacked of course: one does not attack harmless civilians—They say he rimes with ease but has no originality or power.

I rime with wicked difficulty, but a power of five men, four women, three children, two horses, and one candle is in me.

I see I am hand-writing like a sick man. Indeed I am in pyjamas & my fleece, lying before my fire, airing my toes,—which have not yet forgotten Beaumont Hamel; and have turned septic in a mortifying manner (interpret this as you will) & cause my left ankle and knee to ache. The doctor applies iodine but he has not seen the 'breaking-out' up the leg. I am not lame enough to stop stair-climbing; but I think I shall rest tomorrow.

Much wondering how you are feeling.   Your own Wilfred x

581. To Leslie Gunston

8 January 1918   [*Scarborough*]

My dear Leslie,

I was glad to find you take up a strong attitude with regard to your poetry & mine.

You ask me if I saw the Reviews of S.S. I have read every word of them—in his huge book of Press Cuttings. The vast majority are entirely appreciative. As for Graves, have you seen *Chambers' Journal* lately, or the Sat. *Westminster*?[1] And remember the *Edinburgh Review*:[2] fame itself!

But these men are not out for fame.

They simply say what Everyman most needs. And everyman is glad.

Graves's technique is perfect. Did Poetry ever stand still? You can hark back if you like, and be deliberately archaic, but don't make yourself a lagoon, salved from the ebbing tide of the Victorian Age.

The *Times* is just in what it says. But you have only to go on with your quiet unassuming graceful style, and presently everybody else will so scream themselves hoarse that you will be the only happy voice remaining, then you will be indeed original, and a haven for many.

The more I think of your ease & rapidity in writing, the more I hope for an inimitable book next time. But not within five years.

We Georgians are all so old.

Tell me all the Reviews you get.

I am much in doubt whether to put forth any poems next Spring or not.

Someday I'll lend you my *Georgian Poetry* 1917.[3] If you would like it soon I'll send it.

---

[1] The *Westminster Review* (est. 1824).

[2] The *Edinburgh Review* for October 1917 carried enthusiastic reviews by Edmund Gosse of Robert Graves, *Over the Brazier*, and *The Old Huntsman*.

[3] SS, Graves, Nichols, and Monro were well represented. See Letter 585, note 1.

I don't forget I am in debt to you for 3/- isn't it?

I've been reading Wells' *What is coming*.[1]

Hazlitt's *Essays*,

and a glorious book of critical essays by A. K. Thompson, called *The Greek Tradition*.[2]

I read no fiction. Wells' *Wife of Sir Isaac Harman*[3] which I've just finished isn't fiction.

Ever your affectionate Wilfred

582. To Susan Owen

17 January 1918   [*Scarborough*]

My own dear Mother,

Just had your lovely letter, together with an invitation to Robt. Graves's Wedding[4] at St. James' Piccadilly, and afterwards at 11 Apple-Tree Yard,

St. James's Square.

on Jan. 23rd.

Suppose I got leave for this, would you be very sad? Nichols will no doubt be there, and a host of others. Graves is marrying Miss Nicholson, daughter of the Painter.[5]

I send you the Coal Poem.[6]—don't want it back. Yes, I got the Georgian Anthology while in London.

I suppose you saw how Subalterns are now getting 10/6 a day. I should soon be getting 11/6.

Foot's better.

Love to all.   Your W.E.O.

583. To Susan Owen

19 January 1918   *Scarborough*

My dear darling Mother,

That was a naughty tentative letter of mine. I meant to call at Home on the way. If I can get away on Tuesday Morning, I shall arrive Shrewsbury a few minutes to 5 p.m. There surely will be an early morning train to London, arriving noon or one p.m.

The wedding is at 2.30.

With your beautiful letter came a proof from the *Nation* of my 'Miners'. This is the first poem I have sent to the *Nation* myself, and it has evidently been accepted. It was scrawled out on the back of a note to the Editor; and no penny stamp or addressed envelope was enclosed for return! That's the way to do it.

[1] *What is Coming? A Forecast of Things after the War*. Cassell, 1916.
[2] Not listed in the BM catalogue; nor does Wilfred's copy survive.
[3] London, 1914.
[4] See p. 499, note 3.
[5] Sir William Newzam Prior Nicholson (1871–1949).
[6] 'Miners'.

'Miners' will probably appear next Saturday, but don't order a copy. Will Colin be over on Tuesday Night?

Of course the Leave is not absolutely certain. It is a kind of duty both to myself and Graves to go to the Wedding. You know how hard it will be to start away on Wednesday Morning.

Always your W.E.O.

584. To Susan Owen

Thursday, 24 January 1918   *Scarborough*

Just five minutes and half a sheet of paper left to tell you what a good, full, & profitable 24 hours I had in London.

Lunched with Ross. Wells was there, but at another table, whence he waved to me from afar. Had a few words after lunch, but we were in a hurry to drive off. The wedding was nothing extraordinary. Not a great crowd of people, but a very mixed one. Some were dressed in the dowdiest unfashion. Possibly these were celebrities in their way?

George Belcher[1] was the greatest surprise: togged up in 1870 costume, a very striking figure. Max Beerbohm[2] was also at the reception.

Graves was pretty worked up, but calm. The Bride, 18 years old, was pretty, but nowise handsome.

Heinemann[3] was there. He is jibbing at Sassoon's new book, because of the 'violent' poems.

Dined at the Reform again with Roderick Meiklejohn[4] of the Liquor Control Board. (Lord Rhondda[5] was the nearest person to me at lunch!)

Then repaired to Half Moon St. with Meiklejohn, & passed the evening with Ross and two Critics.

At 2 a.m. found my way to Imperial Hotel, and started up this morning by the 10 a.m. from King's Cross.

Feel much refreshed.   Dearest love. W.E.O.

585. To Leslie Gunston

Saturday Night [26 January 1918]   *[Scarborough]*

Dear L.

Great thanks for your letter. I can't identify your 'A. & E.' without applying the method of superposition, coordinating the figures each to each, and so on.

---

[1] Artist and caricaturist (1875–1937).
[2] Sir Max Beerbohm (1872–1956).
[3] William Heinemann (1863–1920), who founded the publishing house.
[4] Sir Roderick Sinclair Meiklejohn (1876–1962), Private Secretary to Mr. Asquith 1905–11, at this time Deputy Controller of Supply Services in the Treasury. A poem in *The Old Huntsman*, 'Liquor-Control', is dedicated to him.
[5] David Alfred Thomas, 1st Viscount Rhondda (1856–1918), was Food Controller at this time.

Went up to Town for Robert Graves's Wedding last Tuesday, calling Home on the way. Arrived at Padd. on Wed. Mng. I hired a bath room, but had no time to get in the water as the page announced my taxi before I had finished shaving. So I arrived punctually at the Reform to lunch with Robert Ross.

Wells was there, but at a different table. But he waved to me from afar, and we had a few words on going out.

Lord Rhondda sat within reaching distance of me!

To you, Max Beerbohm and George Belcher will be the most interesting people at the Reception. Belcher appeared as a dandy of the 1870 period!—Very long Frock coat, very tall dull hat, Cravat, Choker Collar, Side whiskers, and a pole of a walking stick.

Max B. dressed fairly ordinarily, but when he looked at me, I felt my nose tip-tilting in an alarming manner; my legs warped; my chin became a mere pimple on my neck.

Heinemann was there; and Edward Marsh,[1] the Georgian Anthologist tho' I did not know him as such till afterwards. I was introduced as 'Mr. Owen, Poet' or even 'Owen, the poet'.

You may feel keen enough to buy this week's *Nation*. I have at last a poem in it, which I sent off on the same evening as writing!!

Don't yet ask Matthews for *Keats* thanks very much, as Boots Ltd. may lend it me. I subscribe for 3 months.

Always your W.E.O.

586. To Susan Owen

28 January 1918   [*Scarborough*]

Here then is the *Nation*.

I hope you'll not hawk it about or make much of it to anybody who-ever.

I'm proud of one thing and that's the decent amount of room they give under the impressive title **POETRY**!

Last night I went to Church, & afterwards to see those friends of Cousin May—called Horseley.

There is nothing to tell you.

I am put in charge of a Café we have opened for the men: but a Sergeant manages the stock: and there is a baby-corporal; and a cook who makes pastries; and various fatigue urchins.

As soon as I took over I was disgusted by the thick brown irremovable fungus stuff in all the mugs. So I had it cleaned off with Spirit of Salt, and was rather nervous that evening if it might poison the Battalion, so first I drank of most mugs myself!

---

[1] Sir Edward Marsh (1872–1963). At this time Private Secretary to Winston Churchill, he was also publishing with William Heinemann *Georgian Poetry*, anthologies of contemporary verse, five of which appeared between 1912–1921. Wilfred also met C. K. Scott Moncrieff (see Letter 619) at the wedding. In a letter of 1 February 1918, in HO's possession, Robert Graves wrote 'I hope you found Marsh and Scott Moncrieff worth talking to'.

The 'Wind' from Industrial Centres has blown over.

Eleven more officers tomorrow: must now go and find accommodation.

I thought you looked not unwell, my dear Mother, but the left eye was noticeable somehow.

Always your W.E.O.

587. To Susan Owen

8 February 1918   *Scarborough*

Dearest Mother,

I forget how much I borrowed for my travelling money last month; but I think it was less than this Cheque, which is fortunately on your Bank. For half an hour's work I think Two Guineas is good pay. I played with the poem afterwards a little, but the work was done in 30 minutes.

Leslie's 'musical ear' is offended by my rimes. Isn't that delicious?

I am sorry: there is nothing to tell you of my military destiny.

My foot showed improvement last week, but is now as bad as ever.

I have 'put up' my blue chevron for Foreign Service. You will no doubt see two or three chevrons on Officers in Shrews: each additional one means a year's service.

The 'Women' have not turned up, so things go on as before except that the dinner is slightly better cooked by two kitchen lads than by our late she-cooks who cost £10. a month: not including Beer.

Many thanks for all your letters. I heard from Harold yesterday and replied.

Still waiting for Colin's 'Story'.   Dearest Love, W.E.O.

588. To Susan Owen

[11 February 1918]   *Scarborough*

[*first sheet missing*] and with plenty to sing about. 'But few have the courage, or the consistency, to go their own way, to their own ends.'

It all depends what manner of opening I, or my friends, can wedge open for me in England, that is, London.

Yesterday, I had tea in the Club in Scarborough, and taking up *Who's Who* was amazed to find that Roderick Meiklejohn who invited me to dinner at the Reform was Mr. Asquith's private secretary while Mr. Asquith was in office.

The unpleasant Major Mess President has left, and Priestley[1] is now P.M.C. We are good friends.

Priestley is mad on old furniture, and buys it too. But he buys Walnut,[2] so I am not jealous, but only supercilious about his 'finds'.

[1] Lieutenant H. Priestley, 7th Manchesters.
[2] Wilfred bought oak.

Tues. Morning.

I never finished off my letter last night, and now here is Father's handwriting to scare me. I plucked the letter off the rack in a manner that startled beholders. But I was glad to read it, and how glad to find your little message in the corner.

The medicine mixture was quite funny. I wonder if Colin is staying with you still. He ought to.

The £1: 1: 0., my first proud earnings, <u>must</u> be used on superb coal-fires in your room. It is only poetic justice. Stoke up!

I have 'written' profusely last week, but nothing of a topical nature.

I am well enough; and the foot forgetteth its crimson anger in gentle tears.

Number of officers are sick. The bar-corporal swooned away under a load of drinks the other day. The same day a little Scot who somehow got into the Battalion and the Mess, fainted away like any Mrs. Bardell.[1]

We get exactly enough to eat. I still doubt if you nourish yourself in the completest possible way.

Hoping for just a card from you tomorrow.

Father's letter has cheered me up a lot, where it speaks of me. Of yourselves I can only pretend not to worry, and pretend to advise.

Your own Wilfred

589. To Leslie Gunston

Picture postcard addressed **Y.M.C.A. Hazely Down Camp**, Near Winchester
The card bears the following verse, as amended by Wilfred:

A Little Health, A Little Wealth, A Little
House, and Freedom—and at The End,
I'd Like a Friend, And *Every* Cause to Need Him.

[*Postmark 12 February 1918*]   [*Postmark Scarborough*]

Quite as delighted to have your blunt criticism as your first postcard. I suppose I am doing in poetry what the advanced composers are doing in music. I am not satisfied with either. Still I am satisfied with the Two Guineas that half-hour's work brought me. Got the Cheque this m'ng!

Your W.E.O.

590. To Susan Owen

Wednesday [*14 February 1918*]   *Scarborough*

My own dear Mother,

How shall I cheer you up? This afternoon is all blanketed in sea-fog, but it is not at all desolate but quite a cosy kind of fog. All the same Scarborough is a moribund place. I would rather the back of behind Edinburgh than all the Front of Scarboro'.

[1] In *Pickwick Papers.*

Priestley took me to a secret Old Shop where they sell to dealers more than to the public.

There I saw in a very frowsy condition something like the perfect chair; and, what's more, a filthy old Chest of Drawers of lovely proportions and precious oak.

I think I have found what I want at last.

It occurs to me that I should make a really workmanlike Dealer in Antiques. If I could get a shop in London and some experienced Hands I should be not uncontent. Colin might manage the business while I go foraging in Bagdad, Peru, Ceylon, Pompeii, or Market Drayton.

Tonight I am 'dining out' with Bainbrigge.[1] It is amusing to think of myself in the Masters' Rooms at Shrewsbury, as one who deigns not to enter the classrooms, being above these things—as no doubt I shall be—after the war.

How is Mary keeping?

But I want you to write about yourself. I feel particularly fit today. Can it have been the Antique Shop?

Always your loving W.E.O.

591. To Susan Owen

[? 16 February 1918]   Scarborough

My own Mother,

What happiness was in your card & letter for me. Your joke did me good, because I think it did you good.

For light reading there is nothing like Arnold Bennett. So I send you *The Card*.[2] It is notable among my books as the only novel I've read in which I did not in some manner identify myself with the hero.

It is because I loathe Machin that I consider A.B. a wonderful writer, for I read the book with avidity. And it was because I loathed Machin this book has done me so much good.

I consider Mrs. Machin as good a portrait as any novel contains.

It's hard to think of any books you would specially like from my hoard.

Try the *Life of Tennyson* in the Bureau-Case: and, in conjunction, read some of *The Idylls of the King*.

Ross has got the majority of my war poems in his keeping, in order to study and ruminate them.

[1] P. G. Bainbrigge was a master at Shrewsbury School 1913–17; his death is reported in Letter 666. 'A tall, weedy man with very thick glasses in his spectacles' (Nevil Shute, *Slide Rule*, London, 1954), he had great academic ability and a notable sense of humour. He was the author of a clerihew singled out for praise by the inventor of this testing verse form, E. C. Bentley:

> The Emperor Pertinax
> Kept a certain axe
> With which he used to strike
> Men whom he did not like.

Quoted by Philip Cowburn, editor, *A Salopian Anthology*, Macmillan, London, 1964.

[2] London, 1911.

I am going to reconsider the Chair and Chest tomorrow.

I suppose I may get leave in a fortnight or so; but there is a new rumour of my going to a Command Depot; which is where most Light Duty Officers 'end up', doing physical drill, to fit them for serious warfare.

Our patrols shot a man last night, supposed to be a spy. I know nothing more.

Ever your own W.E.O.

592. To Susan Owen

18 February 1918   *Scarborough*

My dear, dear Mother,

Yours was the letter among five others. I will send you Mrs. Gray's, for so you will learn much about her, and about myself!

You did not remark on the incidence that while you were writing to ask me whose 'Life' to read, I was writing to you the reply—Tennyson's.

I have a life of R.L.S. somewhere. I think on the Biography Shelf in the Bureau, by Graham Balfour.[1] Not a wonderfully good one.

I could make you like Scarborough. I could make you like anywhere I wished.

Last night I took an artist johnny—called Claus[2] (!) (exhibits & sells at the Carfax,[3] does Italian peasants in Italy, studio in London; reveres the name of Robert Ross, as one who with a word could raise him to eminence—). I took old Claus, (a fat old tub, with round spectacles, and a conical head)—took old Claus to the Scarborough, where there's not a house built since 1780, not a street much wider than Claus, and miles of it, mind you, miles of glorious eighteenth century. It was twilight and the Sunday evening bell.

Not a soul in the alleys.

Not a lamp lit. A dim moon—and the Past.

And we got excited. What excited us, who shall say? We jumped about, we bumped about, we sang praises, we cursed Manchester; we looked in at half open doors and blessed the people inside. We saw Shakespere in a lantern, and the whole of Italy in a Balcony. A tall chimney became a Greek Column; and in the inscriptions on the walls we read romances and philosophies.

It was a strange way of getting drunk. I wonder if the people in the officers' bar suspected that evening, how much more cheaply a man can get fuddled on fresh air and old winding passages?

I am sorry you have disturbing and daylight-lingering dreams. It is possible to avoid them: by proper thinking before sleep. I confess I

---

[1] Sir Graham Balfour (1858–1929), *Life of Robert Louis Stevenson*, London, 1901.
[2] Emile Claus (1849–1924), Belgian painter.
[3] In Bury Street, W.1. Robert Ross was a Director of Carfax and Co. Ltd., picture dealers, 1900–8.

bring on what few war dreams I now have, entirely by <u>willingly</u> considering war of an evening. I do so because I have my duty to perform
towards War.

I will copy out the best bit of <u>Compression</u> I have accomplished—
P.T.O.

You know with what feelings I think of you—well or unwell. They are
such, when I hear you are at least bettering, as make me a better creature,
and my dreams younger. So must you think of me, and Harold and
Colin.

If I do not read hymns, and if Harold marks no Bible, or Colin sees
no life-guide in his prayer-book, it is no bad sign. I have heard the
cadences of harps not audible to Sankey, but which were strung by God;
and played by mysteries to Him, and I was permitted to hear them.

There is a point where prayer is indistinguishable from blasphemy.
There is also a point where blasphemy is indistinguishable from prayer.
As in this first verse:

Last Words[1]

> 'O Jesus Christ!' one fellow sighed.
> And kneeled, and bowed, tho' not in prayer, and died.
> > And the Bullets sang—'In vain'
> > Machine Guns chuckled 'Vain'
> > Big Guns guffawed 'In vain'
>
> 'Father and Mother!' one boy said.
> Then smiled—at nothing like a small child; being dead.
> > And the Shrapnel Cloud
> > Slowly gestured 'Vain!'
> > The falling Splinters muttered 'Vain'.
>
> 'My Love!' another cried, 'My love, my bud!'
> Then, gently lowered, his whole face kissed the mud.
> > And the Flares gesticulated, 'Vain'
> > The Shells hooted, 'In vain'
> > And the Gas hissed, 'In vain'.

593. To Susan Owen

Midnight, 21 February 1918   [*Scarborough*]

My own dear Mother,

My purple slippers & enchanter's fleece are on, and off is the brisk
soldierly authority, which is such a hindrance to my writings to you.

All day I've been hoping you've had weather like to ours. The
Elements left nothing to be desired except a mild fire at half past four.

Which I had.

In truth, I am very comforted in Scarboro'. 'For everything' that

---

[1] Early draft of 'The Last Laugh' (*Poems*, p. 59). See also Plate XIb.

Solomon mentions, 'there is time' except the singing and dancing. I cut the Local Concerts and the Select Bachelor Dances. Yet I do dance, privately in my room, to the music of good news from you. I dance when the melody of a good line comes into my noddle; I dance also when I dash my bad foot against a stone.

I am looking forward to seeing some good Boxing on Sat. night.

Last week I went to an excellent play, a really charming Comedy— *Quinney's*, by Vachell.[1] Am now reading a book by Vachell *The Hill*,[2] a tale of Harrow, and the hills on which I never lay, nor shall lie: heights of thought, heights of friendship, heights of riches, heights of jinks.

Lovely and melancholy reading it is for me.

Still, was there not Broxton Hill for my uplifting, whose bluebells it may be, more than Greek Iambics, fitted me for my job.

Midnight, 22 February 1918

I got so thoughtful last night that I could not go on writing. I hope I did not Harrow you too much.

That 'Last Words' seems to have rather a harrowing effect on you. I have shown it to no one else as it is not chastened yet. It baffles my critical spirit.

What can I talk about tonight?

Priestley bought some wonderful large Ranunculi this morning; and they are so fine that nothing would do but he must buy a fine bowl to set them in. So we are winning at least the 'Warness' of War.

Things look stupefyingly catastrophic on the Eastern Front. Bainbrigge of Shrewsbury, (over some oysters we consumed in our little oyster-bar this afternoon) opined that the whole of civilization is extremely liable to collapse.

Let us therefore think of more enduring things, my lovely Mother. Such as the February flowers. These are they whose whiteness I have not yet suffered enough to buy. They are what I prayed to when Colin had Scarlet Fever. I could not buy them then for poverty. Now I cannot buy them for shame: For to my extraordinary thinking, it is a wicked traffic, this of grabbing up the Mediterranean Narcissi, and vending them to the rich. Still they are to be seen in the shop-windows of Grange Road West;[3] in Birkenhead; and in Scarborough, and I suppose in Bermondsey, Stockport, Dudley, and perhaps in the uttermost parts of Lybia about Berlin.

For that we must be thankful.

Their odour is disinfectant of souls, as Carbolic is of mortal breath. Narcissi and Carbolic: that is all Life. The Field Daffodils and the Field Dressing Station: these are the best ideas of Heaven and Hell for the senses.

[1] Horace Annesley Vachell (1861–1955). *Quinney's* is the best-known play by this prolific novelist and playwright. It was first written as a novel (1914).
[2] London, 1905.
[3] Shrewsbury.

You will notice that Christ is never represented with the Syrian Lilies in His hand. That is to be expected: for as one says 'There were many Christians before Christ; The astonishing thing is: there have been none since.'[1]

One Spring, Carbolic may have saved you and me. Every Spring the Narcissus is enough to save a man's soul, if it be worth saving.

Show now therefore the Narcissus to Colin at this time.

The immensity of our devotion to Childe Colin has yet to be achieved. A fever more scarlet is already inculcating in his veins; and you must take him apart to yourself, wash him with pure words of truth, feed him with the best, and that according to his desires. In the strangeness of his fever he will push you from him; and all your thought will not be able to quench his thirst. Deny him not the thing he craves, as I was denied; for I was denied, and the appeal which, if you watched, you must have seen in my eyes, you ignored. And because I knew you resisted, I stretched no hand to take the Doll that would have made my contentment.

And my nights were terrible to be borne.

For I was a child, and you laughed at my Toys, so that I loved them beyond measure; but never looked at them.

Yet no man is ashamed of his first doll.

With Harold it has been otherwise. He was always insensible to laughter.

Make easy, I say, the pillow of Colin's fever, for it will be soon; and let us draw aside and think together for him; and tremble before this thing of life and death.

I had meant this to be a consoling kind of letter, and if you read it rightly, it will prove so:—In spite of this Latest News: Leave only once in 3 months (8 days)!

Always your own loving Wilfred x

594. To Susan Owen

Afternoon, 28 February 1918   *Scarborough*

My own Mother,

So by now you are really in Llanduddno! I never pay much attention to anybody's Movements, least of all my own, till the cab is at the very door. You should find the Irish Sea all milky and the Welsh air crystal, as here the German Ocean are and the Yorkshire air.

Be not apprehensive of my Leave. None is possible for me, as I said, within 7 weeks, unless for urgent reasons.

For your health you might just as well have come here. That Scarborough is bleak is a figment of imagination; Even whenever it's dull & rainy, it is warm.

---

[1] We have failed to find the source of this.

Won't you make the regulation 14 days' Cure, and spend a week with me. It would pack you with health; for I am in great spirits, and wouldn't talk about War. I've been twice interrupted since I started this note five minutes ago, and now here is a new officer come, & I must fix him up with a room. There are between seventy and eighty officers here now.

Tuesday

So delighted with your Card this morning.

Give my gratitude to your Hostess.

At Llanduddno you will think of Denry![1] And the Bird Man,[2] whose trumpet Leslie & I could never blow!

I noticed the very crimson sunset last night which you speak of. How quickly we can talk nowadays through the post!

I resolutely forget the anniversaries of last year's miseries. I have now, I think, nothing positive to complain of!

Apparently three months anywhere are enough to make me attached. Tho' I have no friends in Scarboro' outside the Army. Bainbrigge is going to Shrewsbury on Mar. 1st staying at a School House. Claus is gone into a quiet part of Yorks. country—spy-hunting. You mustn't mention this.

Your own W.E.O. x

---

595. To Susan Owen

Postcard

Wed. [*Postmark 6 March 1918*]   [*Postmark Scarborough*]

Your letter of the 4th needs no answer. It was itself an answer which I had tried for a long time to get.

We want Corresponse, not correspondence.

Do you know where my Chinese Wall Scrolls are? I want the best two to give Priestley. You'll be hard put to choose the pictures so please send the best in condition of paper etc. Address to Lieut. Henry Priestley, Clarence Gardens, etc. Thank you, dear Mother, for careful packing!

How many scrolls are there?

Am no forrader with my Chest of Drawers. The man won't sell as it is, & says he has no time yet to work on it. Am sending a card to Rhoslan in hopes.

W.E.O.

Could Owen Owen get me a good 'Education Job?'

---

[1] Denry Machin in Arnold Bennett's *The Card*.
[2] LG recalls that an Italian with trained birds regularly announced the opening of his sea-front performance with blasts on a trumpet.

596. To Susan Owen
Postcard

Sat. [*Postmark 11 March 1918*]   *Scarborough*

Just heard I've got to go to <u>Northern Command Depôt Ripon</u>—as a result of my last Medical Board. There I shall do physical drill and so on, till I am quite fit. Not a bad idea even if I be demobilized! Am glad it's not to Manchester I'm going. Shall be glad to explore this part of Yorkshire. I start on Tues. and the above is all my Address. Have tried to get home for this weekend, but Priestley is away, and they won't let me go. You might come & stay at Harrogate!

Am sending a big box of books & winter clothes home—to be left unopened. I did so want to see you getting well; and Colin before he left. Am writing to Colin tonight.

W.E.O.

597. To Susan Owen
Postcard

Tuesday [*Postmark 12 March 1918*]   *Officers Command Depot
32 Lines, Ripon*

An awful Camp—huts—dirty blankets—in fact W A R once more. Farewell Books, Sonnets, Letters, friends, fires, oysters, antique-shops. Training again!

Your W.E.O.

Scroll arrived just in time to see Priestley open it. Thank you!

598. To Susan Owen
Postcard

Wednesday [*13 March 1918*]   *Ripon P.O.*

Off duty at 3 p.m.! Glorious weather. So strolled into the Town, & was just going into Cathedral when I met Isaacson the actor coming out. He is now very much the Actor, having been discharged from Craiglockhart. Benson is giving *The Merry Wives of Windsor* in the Garrison Theatre tonight. I am going round to be introduced to B. & Lucy Benson. I feel much bucked after a tea with an old Craiglockhartian!

599. To Susan Owen

Friday [*15 March 1918*]   *Address to Officers Command Depot
B. Coy., Ripon*

Dearest my Mother,

As you foretold, this place has made me completely ill. I am now in an Isolation Hut, sweating under Army Blankets and the disappointment of not seeing the Bensons. Don't know the name of my Complaint, but a

538

staggering headache came on yesterday, accompanied by pains in limbs, sore throat, fever etc. etc. It's not influenza, and I am very much better today, (after a perfectly ghastly night.)

But don't be bothered about me now. I am getting as suddenly better as I fell suddenly ill. It was rather curious to have a bad sore throat for an hour or so, and then—quite all right again.

I think the Disorder is traceable to my extreme disgust of the life here—and the badly served cold food. Will write tomorrow.

Am in for a good night.

Your W.E.O. x

600. To Susan Owen

Sat. Morning [*16 March 1918*]   [*Ripon*]

This is a sorry Birthday Letter, my darling Mother, but I can assure you that this morning I already feel better than you—alas! Ate my breakfast egg, even without salt, and thirsted for the tea though without sugar. I am now able to be amused at the bad style of my attendance.

It is only the style that is bad: I was put into sheets stippled with somebody's blood, and blankets caked with mud, like a cow's flank.

The Doctor has just been in. He says this fever has no connection with previous fevers of mine, but is one which often attacks newcomers to this Camp.

I shall be going back to my hut tomorrow as I am not bad enough for hospital.

There are 14 officers in that hut and 13 too many. Most of them are privates & sergeants in masquerade (as were half the officers at Clarence Gdns.) I'd prefer to be among honest privates than these snobs.

It was something to have seen Isaacson and to be made welcome by the merry company of Shakesperians.

Just after I left Craiglockhart a great wave of Discharges swept in, and floated off Isaacson and crowds of others. I am left here 'bound in shallows & in miseries'.[1]

Please do let me have Mrs. A—'s[2] address. I know nothing more of her than of her association—I will not risk the word friendship—with the Gunstons.

I will now think about Colin. If I were his age, with his obvious disqualifications for

1. steady business,
2. or a learned profession,
3. or pictorial or literary Art,

and with

1. great emotional faculties
2. the promise of great good looks in a year or two
3. high ideals

---

[1] *Julius Caesar*, IV. iii. 210.   [2] Name omitted. Wilfred visited her. See Letter 603.

I should join the Benson Company. He has been given an excess of emotional faculty, and that excess he must turn to account in the form of bread & butter. But must I suppose he has only 3 months' liberty?

Then send him to school.

Or if pride forbids, call it an agricultural college.

Say, to Reading or the Shropshire College. You couldn't make a better investment.

Yes, this is my advice.

I will make another suggestion if this won't do.

Tell me how you all exactly 'are'.

Your lovingest Wilfred x

601. To Susan Owen

Picture postcard: Fountains Abbey

18 March [*1918*]   [*Postmark Ripon*]

Thank you, dearest Mother, & Mary & Colin for your Birthday Letters. Got up yesterday & walked to Fountains Abbey: but came back too tired to write. But the adventuring on Fountains Abbey by chance did me a world of good. I think of going to Harrogate tomorrow for a joy-day. Had a quiet afternoon in Ripon Cathedral today. Came 'home' in taxi!

x W.E.O.

602. To Susan Owen

Picture postcard: Fountains Abbey, Nave East

20 March 1918   *Ripon*

Just going out to find Mrs. A.'s with help of a map. Thanks for the fairly excellent gingerbread! I was gladdest of the apples. There is talk of Easter Leave!

Had enough of Harrogate in the afternoon I spent there yesterday.

Dearest Love W.E.O.

603. To Susan Owen

10 a.m., 21 March 1918   *Ripon*

My own dear Mother,

We should be at a Lecture this hour, but have all been told to go and hide!

I think that Fever did me good. For one thing it has left me with no desire to smoke. Also I have made a vow not to imbibe Alcohol in this Camp at all. (It is pleasant to make vows which cost one nothing at all.)

I get up at seven to have a hot and cold Shower. From nine to about 3 p.m. we do physical, short walks, & Lectures. We are thus free all evening. I shall not know what to do unless I get a Room where I can use my big spectacles to advantage.

540

Wending 'home' from Fountains Abbey last Sunday I noticed a kind of Watchtower[1] or chapel on the top of a hill. It arrested attention as all such towers do, and I climbed up, and finding inhabitants in it, desired tea of them. Only half the old chapel is occupied by peasants; the other is vacant. The rent would be about 2s. a week! I wish it weren't so far from here. The windows have a marvellous view (for this part of the world) & I could spend my spring evenings very pleasantly up there. Anyhow, will Colin need the Bicycle now? I should be very glad of it here. It is almost necessary if I am to get away from huts ever.

Mrs. A. lives in the country about 2 miles away. Her son, a Lieut. in the 'Wavy Navy' was at home. The daughter, in a Bank, had her affianced Bank Clerk there, doing the gardening.

Miss A. (I steadily refused to use any other name) is a young person with teeth like a pianoforte keyboard. The rest of her face is like nothing whatever. No doubt an amiable creature. Philip is what you would call 'nice-quiet'. A corporal & a gunner turned up for an evening's music, both of them piano-players. Mrs. A. can click the piano quite quickly: about as musically as Miss Carr. I wonder these people buy pianos at all, when a good typewriter is so much cheaper, and makes almost the same noise. Mrs. A. makes a good bun or pastry, so I ate two, and was able to say I had a very pleasant evening.

I wonder if it would be much trouble to you to pack off the rest of the Chinese Scrolls to Lieut. H. Priestley. I don't much like these scrolls, & Priestley has spent pounds on me (oysters etc.) and he is looking after my bargaining at the Antique Shop. For I wasn't able to get a price either for the Chair or the Chest. The Dealer says they don't belong to him, & he must get permission to sell, from someone he can't find!

So good of dear Mary to write for my Birthday, & to send me chocolate. The parcel came the day before yesterday. It reminded me of war again; the more so because the tin box had been crushed in, and there was blood splashed on the label & wrapping!

I am trying for Easter Leave.

Sorry to have so had the wind up about my health!

Always your loving Wilfred x

604. To Susan Owen

Picture postcard: Fountains Hall

[*Postmark 23 March 1918*]   [*Postmark Ripon*]

Wonderful weather these days. Went to service at Cathedral again. Discovered a Room in a Cottage close to camp: the very thing. Fountains Hall[2] is a glorious house—uninhabited too! Almost worth fighting for!.

W.E.O.

[1] Probably How Hill Tower, a mile beyond Fountains Abbey. Now derelict, but still picturesque.
[2] A Tudor building, built with materials from Fountains Abbey.

605. To Mary Owen

Wed. [? *25 March 1918*]   *7 Borage Lane, Ripon*[1]

My dearest Mary,

So glad to have your cheery letter. You know, we scramble for letters, twice a day, almost as eagerly as when on Active Service Abroad. Many of the officers here have been wounded over and over again. People with crippled arms do <u>special</u> physical exercises. It is rather pitiful. The Senior M.O. is a Harley St. Heart Specialist. He put me in the 6th and Lowest Class of Fitness! But I shall be moved up any day. No leave longer than 48 hours is possible yet. Is it worth while? Every battalion, I understand, has sent two companies of A 4 (boys) on Draft Leave: in consequence of our <u>Straits</u>. (Don't see the joke, I didn't mean it.) It is specially cruel for <u>me</u> to hear of all <u>we</u> gained by St. Quentin having been lost. They are dying again at Beaumont Hamel, which already in 1916 was cobbled with skulls.[2]

Meanwhile I think less of leaving the Army: and more of getting fit.

My realest thanks to dear Mother for her packing of the Chinese Scrolls. Priestley (before he could have received the parcel) sent me some lovely Mediterranean Flowers . . . That's how we keep our war-weary spirits up!

I don't like the charwoman idea. I think I shall postpone my Leave till I hear you've a regular servant, what?

Your loving old Brother

606. To Colin Owen

[*Circa 30 March 1918*]   *Ripon*

My dear Colin,

I send you a rather well-composed photograph of the village-city. You'll see that it's quite pleasant, though not beautiful.

Note the grooved tiles of the roofs.

The five minutes walk from Camp to my Cottage is by a happy little stream—tributary of the Ure. There is boating of a kind on the Ure; but much better at Knaresborough on the Ouse itself, I think. How I look forward to your Invitation to a Pengwern[3] boat. Didn't know you were a member of the Club.

Evidently you need the bicycle more than I. Ripon is only a mile from my hut, and through Borage Lane (my lane) it is an interesting walk;—especially this morning when the buds all made a special spurt between dawn and noon, and all the Lesser Celandines opened out together.

---

[1] The cottage is now No.23. Borrage Lane is the current spelling.
[2] The last German offensive of the war, the Second Somme Battle, was launched in March on a fifty-mile front against the British 3rd and 4th Armies. British losses were heavy, and included 100,000 prisoners. The tide turned on 1 May. The striking phrase 'cobbled with skulls' gives a clue to the dating of 'Insensibility' (*Poems*, pp. 37–38), line 5 of which runs: 'Sore on the alleys cobbled with their brothers.'
[3] The Shrewsbury Rowing Club.

I don't think there is the least probability of demobilization now. On the contrary, I am trying to get fit.

Our Physical Exercises are varied by tricks like doing the opposite of the order, or on the command <u>Do This</u>! you do what the instructor does, but on the command <u>Do That!</u> you don't move. It's really an old parlour game, but frightfully difficult done quickly. Last time we played this mental game I was the last man out, or rather I was never caught out. So I consider myself completely restituted now from Shell Shock.

Do tell me about your Farm, & farmers, and also what your arrangements are for joining the Royal Air Force.

Your dearly loving Wilfred

What have you read during March?

607. To Susan Owen

Easter Sunday [*31 March 1918*]   *The Ante-Room, O.C.D., Ripon*

My Mother Dear,

I am writing crouched up in one of the good easy chairs with which we have stocked our Common Room Hut. We have also a good piano, which helps to drown the chinkling of silver on the Bridge Tables. I scarcely have spoken to any of this crowd of 'gentlemen' except to decline to make a Four at bridge.

I find myself growing more conventional in the matter of 'Proper Introductions' as I grow older. There are no less than five people made aware of my presence in Ripon, by friends who tell me I must go and see them

1) Mrs. A.—done.
2) A Major, friend of Bainbrigge of Shrewsbury—not done.
3) A friend and relation of Priestley's—not done.
4) A great friend of the Grays of Edinburgh—not done yet.
5) Two maiden ladies, benefactresses when he was in Ripon of the Scottie in Clarence Gardens (who faints and has undiscoverable parents). These old dears as I had been advised provide a mighty good tea to anything in khaki that strays into their house. They have also some inklings of breeding, and traces of Accent, having been in the service of the Marchioness of Ripon for 37 years. I shall go there again the next time there's a bad lunch in Camp.

Outside my cottage-window children play soldiers so piercingly that I've moved up into the attic, with only a skylight. It is a jolly Retreat. There I have tea and contemplate the inwardness of war, and behave in an owlish manner generally.

One poem have I written there; and thought another. I have also realized many defectuosities in older compositions.

The enormity of the present Battle numbs me. Because I perfectly foresaw these days, it was that I said it would have been better to make peace in 1916. Or even last Autumn. It certainly is 'impossible' now.

What did I say about America?

Why did I denounce them?

Fancy the old 13th C.C.S. being in German hands! Even Nesle,[1] a town hospital where I paused 3 days, is occupied. On Good Friday I believe the most frightful fighting was round about the Canal where I used to board the barges.

The Mystery Gun of St. Gobain Wood is about as romantic an episode as the whole war has provided. Paris, after all, has so many ugly buildings and unnecessary civilians . . . 160 casualties in a second or two, and that in the heart of the enemy country, is pretty work.[2]

I wonder how many a *frau, fraulein, knabe und madchen* Colin will kill in his time?

Johnny de la Touche leaves school this term, I hear, and goes to prepare for the Indian Army.

He must be a creature of killable age by now.

God so hated the world that He gave several millions of English-begotten sons, that whosoever believeth in them should not perish, but have a comfortable life.

I could face the world-facts better if I could be sure of at least your health and peacefulness at home. Don't let your fire burn low; don't leave off winter-clothing; don't eat pickles; and don't read newspapers. Thus you'll keep well.

I meant, when I said you must get a servant before I get leave, that it will be a severe discomfort to me,—not otherwise than as thus:—

That I will not eat from plates which you must needs wash. The moral discomfort, I say, will drive me to the Crown, aye the Britannia, aye the Oyster Bar, and finally the Cop Fried Fish Shop.

Now you know.

Your lovingest old Wilfred

608. To Leslie Gunston

[*Circa 1 April 1918*]   *Ripon*

Opening sheets missing

are enjoying your pleasaunce of Alpenrose.

All the joy of this good weather is for me haunted by the vision of the lands about St. Quentin crawling with wounded. If the Line was as thinly held as when we held it, I don't wonder at the Breakage. Our Staff is execrable.

Was awakened yesterday by this sentence: long range guns firing on Paris.

Isn't it stupendous?

I must buck up and get fit!   'Yours to a cinder'* W.E.O.

*Borrowed this expression from a letter from *mon petit ami* in Scarboro!

[1] See Letter 494, note 2.
[2] Paris had been shelled on Good Friday, 29 March. One shell hit the church of St. Gervais, killing seventy-five and wounding ninety.

609. To Susan Owen

[*April 1918*]   *The Ante-Room* [*Ripon*]

Mine own Mother,

Your portrait is certainly slightly camouflaged. I should tell the merchant to do <u>less</u> retouching, but you will never persuade him to let go a photograph purely *au naturel*, you know. I think the result will be <u>most</u> satisfactory, if you say you will not accept the present rendering. <u>Only</u>, don't they retouch the negative itself? I am loath to let this charming picture away—all the same. Hope he won't be long finishing off.

This afternoon I was retouching a 'photographic representation' of an officer dying of wounds—[1]

Thus:

> Sit on the bed; I'm just a mass of shell:
> Don't touch me—can't shake hands now—never shall.
> My arms have mutinied against me—brutes.
> My fingers fidget like ten idle brats.
> I tried to pop out soldierly—no use!
> I'm dying of war like any old disease.
> This bandage feels like pennies on my eyes.
> My death won't cut much figure in your book.
>
> A short life and a merry one, my buck!
> We used to say we'd hate to live dead-old,—
> But, now, not to live old seems—* (were you told
> How long I've got?) etc.

I hear that of the 100 officers now in Clarence Gns. *53* are going out immediately, and practically the whole of the <u>men</u> (so <u>called</u>).

How curious that Warne[2] is there. Had I <u>been</u> there I might have got him a good job with me in the hotel, unless he be too very countrified?

Is he very 'superior'?

Immensely glad Colin is so content.

Numbers of officers have bunked away from here as far as London even—<u>without leave</u>. They have been discovered, poor chaps. There is to be a solemn assembly tomorrow.

A fair goodnight to all.

W.E.O. x

Piano, Flute & Violin are making most lovely music. I can't scarcely read, it's so fine. I am not ill pleased with Ripon generally.

*I can't find a word strong enough here.

---

[1] 'À Terre.'
[2] Son of a Shrewsbury estate agent. His sister Mary was a friend of Mary Owen.

610. To Susan Owen
Postcard

Friday [*Postmark 6 April 1918*]   [*Postmark Ripon*]

Am trying to get off on Monday or Tues. It will be for only 48 hours. If I don't succeed, Harold <u>must</u> come up here.[1] Trust me to do my best. I may telegraph for a telegram from him, to help my case.   Your W.E.O.

611. To Leslie Gunston
21 April 1918   *Ripon*

My dear Leslie,

I address to Alpenrose, though I believe you to be at Worple Road. Your job[2] seems to me the limit of good fortune. And what are the increments withal, excuse me?

Will this manner of war work in itself exempt you from encountering common foe, dam Hun, excuse me?*

See also p. 54 *Sphere* for a good peep at Swinburne.[3] Dam disgusting, excuse me. How do you like the Prize Plaque Memorial?[4] Had I adjudicated I should have chosen this; yet, for my own name, I should prefer Sapper MacDougall's beautiful grief, among the realistic forests of wooden crosses. To me, the British Lion in the Prize looks a thoroughly nasty animal; and the breasts of Britannia are somehow not the breasts of a chaste woman, excuse me.

Have you seen Arnold Bennett's *Pretty Lady*. Fortunately I just secured my copy before circulation was prohibited.[5] The book is one which the century needs, as much as the Victorians needed *Oliver Twist*. As an amusing narrative it is unsurpassed, in spite of its being a collection of pieced-together idylls. If you can't get it I will send you my copy.

Or shall I bring it. I am due for a long week-end leave!! My 48 hours, (which I considerably overstayed) at home were an emergency affair. Since then Leave has been granted, as from the W.O., for 15% of the Camp weekly. I should like to spend some of it in Town: not of course Wimbledon. I have now risen to the 4th (of 6 Divisions) of Fitness. There is no doubt—from the elaborate soundings to which I'm subjected—that my heart is shock-affected.

Have you read Gilbert Frankau?[6] I have not. (See *Sphere*.)

In my Chaumbers under the roof of a cottage (7 Borage Lane, Ripon)

---

[1] They saw each other at Shrewsbury, for the last time. See *JO* III, pp. 161–74.

[2] LG was engaged on architectural work at the Albert Dock, London.

[3] An account by G. B. Burgin, the novelist, of a depressing lunch with Swinburne at The Pines, Putney, at which the poet spoke once only to complain that the beer was flat.

[4] *The Sphere* carried a photograph of E. Carter Preston's prize-winning design for a Memorial Plaque for the Fallen, to be given to next-of-kin.

[5] Published 1918. The book was not withdrawn; but there were objections from Roman Catholic sources (the central figure is a prostitute who is an RC) and W. H. Smith decided not to stock the work in their bookshops.

[6] The writer (1884–1952) whose war poems, *The Judgement of Valhalla* (Chatto and Windus, London, 1918), received a favourable review in the same issue of *The Sphere*.

I have written, I think, two poems: one an Ode which, considering my tuneless tendencies, may be called dam good, excuse me.[1]

It is a very parfit Bowre this Cottage of mine. I wish you could look in for a cup of tea and half a cigarette sometimes. No one here knows of my retreat. If I lived in London I should take two empty chambers somewhere in the Cardiac Region and furnish them with Camp kit.

Sorry you could not find the Word I wanted.

Did you or did you not receive the letter[2] I once wrote from this Hut? It contained some wild statements, and I should like to be reassured that it's not lost.

Looking forward to a highly interesting account of your occupations.

Your affectionate W.E.O.

Harold has had some terrific adventures: but chiefly on land: & not connected with the war.

* See p. 46. *Sphere*, Ap. 20.[3]

612. To Susan Owen

Sunday Aft. [*22 April 1918*]   O.C.D. [*Ripon*]

My dearest Mother,

Have had another lapse from letter writing, lasting a week or more.

The only news is that I am re-graded into Division 4. So it's a long way yet to the top: and a longer time before I shall go over it; again.

This date is somewhere near the Anniversary of my Shock.

I hear from Paris that Amiens is '*complètement évacué*'; and that the school-children of Paris are all being removed into the provinces.

Dr & Mme. Horteloup are both well. My old pupil and disciple Pierre of Bordeaux was not taken for Military Service when his *Classe* was called up; so he is still with the American Y.M.C.A.

This afternoon I am going over to the Officers' Y.M. to meet someone Mrs. A. wants me to meet.

We have a new padre, and his sermon this morning was as bad as they make 'em.

You will love to read (1) Thomas Hardy's *Under the Greenwood Tree* in my Novel Shelf. A most reposing book. Arnold Bennett's new book[4] has caused some stir, and has been withdrawn from circulation, but not before I secured my copy. It deals with nothing but truth, however; and is as much needed today as *Oliver Twist* was to the Victorians.

---

[1] The Ode was possibly 'Insensibility'; the other the final version of 'À Terre' or 'The Send-Off', at this time called 'The Draft' (*Poems*, pp. 46–47). See Letter 616.

[2] Possibly Letter 608, of which the opening sheets have been lost.

[3] A war-weary poem on this page by Robert Nichols, *The Automaton*, is perhaps referred to. It closes:

> When once I lie down nor seek nor find me!
> I have endured but not endured blindly.
> Batter the drum. I must never awake!

[4] *The Pretty Lady.*

Possibly it was withdrawn owing to a slighting reference to the King.

I shall be very interested to know how you take to *The Greenwood Tree*.

Of Poetry there is no lack on the Poetry Shelf of the Bookcase.

I will write in a day or two: though to quote myself cynically 'Nothing happens.'[1] A certain gloom was, however, noticeable as I travelled from town to town. There was a hint of war.

Dearest Love to all. W.E.O.

613. To Susan Owen

Saturday [*28 April 1918*]   *Crown Hotel, Boroughbridge*

Dearest Mother,

I walked over here to see the land, how it lies around Ripon. Have been further than Boroughbridge to Aldborough where there are Roman Remains, and the finest tessellated pavement in Britain. It is in a cottage![2] I suppose the house has been used ever since the Romans.

I am much too footsore to walk back, so I am now waiting for train to take me to Harrogate.

The weather is superb, and I have spent an afternoon of great 'elation' in these fine old villages.

Many, many thanks for your last letter.

I thought of poor Stanley Webb when I was among the 'Remains'.

If in 1913 I used to wish to have lived in the 4th Century, how much more now!

Your own W.E.O.

614. To Susan Owen

Tues., 29 April 1918   *Hut 23* [*Ripon*]

Dearest Mother,

I read your letter during the 'stand-easies' of 'Physical'.

I know what would improve your eye. I. Abstain from all reading & needlework for a month, as Doctor says, but what is more important cultivate your long range vision in the open air. II. Don't look at near objects more than necessary. As a regular exercise, sit at your open window and study the contours of the Wrekin, and count the trees on Haughmond.

This for one hour a day.

Here is a course for 1st week.

1st day: fix objects within 100 yds. and describe them to yourself. Time $\frac{1}{4}$ hour.

2nd day: objects at 500 yds.

3rd   ,,   follow moving objects at 1 mile distance.

4th   ,,   objects within 2 miles and so on.

[1] The refrain in 'Exposure' (*Poems*, pp. 48–49).
[2] Near Boroughbridge. Three pavements, all now removed to the museum, represent the she-wolf suckling Romulus and Remus, a lion awaiting its prey, and the Muses.

III. Obtain a proper civilized shade for Dining Room Light. The present glare is enough to make a blind-worm turn. (Joke)

In your blessed simplicity you think it's your Candle that injures your sight. Nothing of the sort. It's that execrable German invention the Welsbach Mantle.

I once said you took things too seriously. My light sallies you often do. But on the other hand you take my most serious advice as a joke. There is no joke at all about my Prescription above.

Will you please buy & put away for me a box of 12 tablets Pears Soap (6/-?) It will soon be taxed I think. So will pyjamas! Now you see the wisdom of my large stock! Stow the soap in my drawers! [*several words illegible*] I send 10s., the rest to go in something you know Mary would like. No, it is too near her birthday. Use the 4s. for an efficient lamp-shade, thus

I will talk books and literature next time.   Ever your W.E.O. x

615. To Susan Owen

Thursday [*? 2 May 1918*]   *7 Borage Lane, Ripon*

My dearest Mother,

So Harold was not in this Zeebrugge Show.[1] What does he say about it? Its success will not be measured before a month or so. The secret was well kept, especially by Harold.

We had a Surgeon-General inspecting today, the same was responsible for the ghastly medical deficiencies & mismanagement on the Peninsula. In spite of the revelations of the Mesop: Commission, here he is still at large,—spoiling a fine afternoon for us.[2]

This morning we had a lecture from a captain from the War Office, designed to stimulate our fighting instincts.

Two 5th Manchester Officers are here; one 'went out' with me on my ship.

I am feeling very well.

I shall have to smoke less (as soon as my pre-Budget stock of cigarettes is exhausted.)

Leave is now possible from Friday to Tuesday, since our Commandant has been to the War Office about it. I could obtain it next week end, or the following. I should like to go to London with some MSS. What do you say?

[1] On 23 April a British naval force under Sir Roger Keyes (Vice-Admiral Dover Patrol) destroyed the mole and temporarily blocked Zeebrugge Harbour (one of the main U-boat bases) by sinking three concreted old cruisers at its mouth. HO was on the short list for this operation; but through the luck of the draw did not take part.
[2] Major-General W. G. Birrell (1859–1950), Director of Medical Services in the Gallipoli campaign. He came under criticism in *Final Report of the Dardanelles Commission: Part II, Conduct of Operations* (Cmd. 371, 1919).

If you are not very well I shall come home, go round to the Salop Orphanage, and try the power of my glamour on some of its inmates. Seriously have you tried the Orphanage?

Tell me how you really are.   Your lovingest Wilfred

616. To Susan Owen

Sat., 4 May [*1918*]   *Hut 23* [*Ripon*]

Dearest my Mother,

Just a note for your Sunday. I discovered that one of my teeth wanted mending, so on Friday I stayed in my flea-bag till the Dr. came round to the Hut (to see 3 others who've now gone to hospital with influenza.)

I went to the Dentist in the afternoon.

The Army will do nothing.

It is interesting to note that by thinking of my tooth, I brought on slight toothache.

Have been to two of Hall Cain's[1] plays this week. How badly written they were! I can't stand Hall Cain. But then was he not my imagined rival in love, when he used to give presents of jewels, when I had not even nuts and apples to give.

I can recommend to you *Tides* by John Drinkwater: (on poetry shelf).

I have long 'waited' for a final stanza to 'the Draft'[2] (which begins.

I

'Down the deep, darkening lanes they sang their way
To the waiting train,
And filled its doors with faces grimly gay,
And heads & shoulders white with wreath & spray,
As men's are, slain.')

*   *   *   *

IV

Will they return, to beatings of great bells,
In wild train-loads?
—A few, a few, too few for drums and yells,
May walk back, silent, to their village wells,
Up half-known roads.

Today is pouring wet.

I hope to hear from Colin soon.

I can't get any Gillette Blades in Ripon. Will you please buy 1 dozen ready to send me at any moment? I forgot the 10/- note last letter! I

-----

[1] Sir Thomas Henry Hall Caine (1853–1931), whose novels won wide popularity, some being dramatized. The reference to 'my rival in love' is unexplained.
[2] Subsequently 'The Send-Off'. See p. 547, note 1.

know why I had no letter today! You are carrying out my Prescription and forbid yourself pen & paper as well as books!

Is there any improvement?   Your own W.E.O.[1]

617. To Susan Owen
Postcard
[Postmark 10 May 1918]   *[Postmark Ripon]*

Thank you for dear letters. Hope this weather will draw you out. Please send Gillette blades, and obtain a reserve of 12! Have just read a wonderful book by R. H. Benson: *Where no Fear Was,* a collection of spiritual Essays.[2] Why not order it for Mary's birthday from me? I am now in Div. 3. I think of getting leave on the 17th.

Always your W.E.O.

618. To Susan Owen
Monday [13 May 1918]   *[Ripon]*

My dearest Mother,

Made a careful study of your letter, but for the life of me can't make any real conclusions how you are. Still, it is something to know names, and to have the complaints located.

I look forward to your holiday in Torquay as much as you do. You must try for that Hotel. Hotel would suit you better than boarding house: tho' I have no liking for either myself. I am lucky to get a room in London near Mr. Ross's flat. Leslie sends a card today saying he'll be at Alpenrose for Whitsun. Rather unlucky, but he may change his mind (!) There is also a danger that H. G. Wells etc. may be out of town. I particularly want to see him. But with the Landlady expecting me, as I divine from Mr. Ross's letter (I will enclose it) I won't try the impossible effort of changing the dates of my hard-earned Leave—precarious as the promise of it is.

Leslie informs me I've won a prize in the *Bookman.* (My first try.) I omitted to get a copy, so don't know what it is.[3]

If there's nothing much doing in London, on Sunday, I may drop in to you on Monday just for a little pow-wow and x.

W.E.O.

---

[1] On the following day he jotted down the following:
     Projects: (5 May, 1915. Ripon)
1. To write blank-verse plays on old Welsh themes. Models: Tennyson, Yeats, 1920.
2. Collected Poems (1919)
3. Perseus
4. Idylls in Prose.
There is a BM fragment of a poem on Perseus. See also Letter 340.

[2] *Where no Fear Was: a Book about Fear,* Smith Elder and Co., London, 1914. The author was not RH, but Arthur Christopher Benson (1862–1925), Master of Magdalene College, Cambridge. Wilfred's copy survives.

[3] It was 'Song of Songs', one of three winners in a Lyric competition in the May 1918 issue. Curiously, an inferior version to that printed in *The Hydra,* 1 September 1917. See p. 485, note 4. This may explain the disparaging comment in Letter 624. See also Welland, p. 129.

619. To Susan Owen
Postcard
Frid. [*Postmark 17 May 1918*]   *Piccadilly*

Having a glorious time. Spent all aft. at War Office, Scott-Moncrieff[1] is trying to find me a job in England—lecturer to a Cadet Batt. Arrived last night. Report back on Sunday.   W.

620. To Susan Owen
Monday [*20 May 1918*]   *Ripon*
My Mother,

You'll excuse a short letter yet awhile: it is hot; and I'm sleepy this afternoon. In 2 nights & days I have slept only 3 hours. I always have a week of freedom from the need of sleep somewhere about May; fortunately it has occurred during last week.

My 'reception' in London has been magnificent. The upshot is that I am to have my work typed at once, and send it to Heinemann, who is certain to send it to Ross to read for him!! This is very subtle. Ross first meant to take it himself but we thought this independent idea a great joke.

Judging from my own diffidence, and the state of the paper supply a book is not likely to appear before next Spring. I am rather proud—to have got so far on one published poem. Almost an unparalleled case, what! How far I have got, learn from this extract in the *New Witness* (Chesterton's weekly).[2] It is a criticism of an American Anthology of English Verse:[3] 'The book is curiously dull & undistinguished. Our younger fame seems not to have reached him: there is nothing by Robert Nichols, Robert Graves, Siegfried Sassoon, W. J. Turner, Wilfred Owen, Osbert Sitwell, or any of their contemporaries junior to Rupert Brooke . . .' Osbert Sitwell was 'phoned round to Half-Moon St. 'to meet me!'[4] I had a whole flat above Ross's for 7/6 with breakfast! And I had more invitations to lunch & dinner than I could manage!

More tomorrow. Shrewsbury as you saw was impossible.   x

621. To Susan Owen
Postcard
Tues. [*Postmark 21 May 1918*]   [*Postmark Ripon*]

I am much enjoying the hot weather: which, as weather, is pleasanter here than in London. All I can tell you about my worldly schemes (or rather the schemes of my friends) is: I have every chance of becoming

[1] Charles Kenneth Scott Moncrieff (1889–1930), later to become the translator of Proust. A captain in the KOSB, with an MC, he had been invalided home and now had a staff job.
[2] Cecil Chesterton was editor until his death in 1919, when his brother G. K. Chesterton took it over and renamed it *G.K.'s Weekly*.
[3] The book reviewed in *The New Witness* was W. Reginald Wheeler (ed.), *A Book of Verse of the Great War*, Yale University Press, 1918. The reviewer was Scott Moncrieff.
[4] Sir Osbert Sitwell has described the meeting. See Appendix D.

Instructing Staff Officer to a Cadet Battalion.[1] I would rather work in the W.O. itself and that seems not impossible either. Really I would like most to go to Egypt or Italy, but that is not entertained by Scott-Moncrieff. Scott-Moncrieff, is a lamed captain, related to General[2] of that name, known as the 'Father of the War Office', who has just died.
I am now in Div. 2 awaiting Board, before W.O. friends can do anything.

622. To Susan Owen

Saturday [*25 May 1918*]   *Borage Lane* [*Ripon*]
Dearest Mother,

I've been 'busy' this evening with my terrific poem (at present) called 'The Deranged.'[3] This poem the Editor of the *Burlington Magazine*—(a 2/6 Arts Journal which takes no poetry)—old More Adey,[4] I say, solemnly prohibited me from sending to the *English Review*, on the grounds that 'the *English Review* should not be encouraged'.!!!!

Five years ago this would, as you suggest, have turned my head—but nowadays my head turns only in shame away from these first flickers of the limelight. For I am old already for a poet, and so little is yet achieved.

And I want no limelight, and celebrity is the last infirmity I desire.
Fame is the recognition of one's peers.

I have already more than their recognition: I have the silent and immortal friendship of Graves and Sassoon and those. Behold are they not already as many Keatses?

As I looked out into the untravelled world over the hedges of Dunsden Garden, I saw them in the dawn and made ready to go out and meet them.

And they were glad and rejoiced, though I am the gravest and least witty of that grave, witty company.

Today I climbed back over the hedges into Dunsden again and wandered round the parish for hours. (For this ordinary [*remainder missing*]

623. To Susan Owen
Postcard
Tues. [*Postmark 29 May 1918*]   [*Postmark Ripon*]
Have you got a Tennis Racket in pretty good condition? If so please send at once to Camp. Had a splendid game this afternoon, but can't go

---

[1] 'Graves's brother [turned up] yesterday, who wants to go and be a cadet at Oxford. We might send you to teach him.' Letter from Scott Moncrieff, headed War Office, 26 May 1918, now in H O's possession.
[2] Major-General Sir George Kenneth Scott Moncrieff (1855–1924), Director of Fortifications and Works, War Office, 1911–18. Wilfred was anticipating his death.
[3] This became 'Mental Cases' (*Poems*, pp. 69–70).
[4] William More Adey (1858–1942), Joint Editor of the *Burlington Magazine* 1911–19. A description of him as an old man is given in *Siegfried's Journey*, pp. 35–36.

on borrowing rackets. Hope you will often get out to the Farm during this weather. Yorkshire is surprisingly florescent about here. This is the pleasantest camp I know.

Yours W.E.O.

624. To Susan Owen

[*29 May 1918*]   *Ripon P.O.*

Came into Town to find something for Mary & Father,[1] but the effort & responsibility are too great.

Will you yourself or Colin do the shopping?

Thanks for news this morning.

The heat is most enjoyable—am going bathing in river this afternoon.

The *Bookman* affair about which you are so kindly importunate was a mere idle joke, an old lyric I condescended to send from Scarboro'.[2]

It gained me only a book. The Bookman people are hopeless bad literary people.

You shall see 'Deranged'[3] some fine day when you feel strenuous enough.

Dearest love to Mary, and congratulations to dear Father.

What about a pipe for him?

So Colin is aware that such things as letters are written? Even perhaps he reads them sometimes? [*remainder missing*]

625. To Mary Owen

Wednesday Night. 11 p.m. to Midnight [*29 May 1918*]   [*Ripon*]

My dear Little Sister,

I am rather weary now, having Swum this afternoon, and—in consequence of the exercise—, having written a promising poem this evening. I can now write so much better than a year ago that for every poem I add to my list I subtract one from the beginning of it. You see I take myself solemnly now, and that is why, let me tell you, once for all, I refrain from indecent haste in publishing. So much for myself.

A pity and shame to myself that I was not able to choose you a present. To speak truth, it baffles me to know what you really are interested in; beyond Mother.

This is beautiful in itself, but I wish I knew there was some Sphere of human activity you played or worked at. Music—no bon! Painting—nah pooh! Literature—taboo! Horticulture, likewise, Medical work, ditto. Why not, then, specialise in Embroidery or some such craft,—design something remarkable, and produce something astonishing.

My dear I am as serious as I am rude. Chiefly for your own benefit I am saying this,—To give you some tie to Mother Earth. I feel that a

---

[1] Mary's birthday was the following day. Tom Owen's was 31 May.

[2] See p. 551, note 3.

[3] An early draft of 'Mental Cases' (*Poems*, p. 69).

light wind of grief, to say nothing of a storm, might blow you off your innocent feet.

Nor entirely for your benefit do I suggest these Interests. So many Activities that Matter are in the hands of non-good people.

Possibly I am quite wrong in asking you to hook on to something Material. You will wistfully wonder if I am a Pagan. It would be good if you would arise, and in a loud voice, <u>tell me so</u>. I am not, but such a discussion would get us to the bedrock <u>of things</u>. The bedrock of things should be—well, Who should it be?

My religion consists in a sort of beautiful and Christ-like Intervention between the disputing parties Paul of Tarsus and the ruined but skilful silversmiths of Ephesus. Very gently I should make some clever remark which should send the silversmiths contentedly back to their beautiful work, and give Paul a contract for as many tents as the army required for subjugating the Gauls, and exiling the soldiery.

My religion says it is better to design a church than sit and look at its design once a week.

Forgive the exuberance of this letter. It comes of my recent baptism in the pleasant waters of this River. It was an amusing afternoon. After toiling many miles to the bathing place I found it reserved for the Civilian Population on Wednesdays! However the civilian population were not dismayed to share the water with Officers. Anyone seeing these civilians (or rather in their father's old clothes, which they wore) would have kept well upstream of them. An Artist Cadet there, losing his head with joy, dived into 2 feet of water, and nearly lost it again. He cut it open, but as there was no brandy, he decided not to faint, and I got him safe into a cab.

This letter, writ with much rubbing of mine eyes, is my Birthday present, and <u>not</u> John Bradbury's little note.[1] God bless you as you are a blessing to <u>us</u>, and reward you from the treasury where your great heart is.

Wilfred

626. To Mary Owen

1 June 1918   *Ripon*

My dear dear Sister,

I did not let myself go in my letter, and did not let go the letter to the post, without much consideration. It was not written to gratify you, but to inure you a little. Don't bother to answer textually. There is no answer. It did not seem to you a cheerful piece of reading? It was too cheerful. I was so horribly cheerful that I overlooked your fallible health as if it didn't count. Yet one would almost think by your own cheeriness and the amount of work you do that health were now working all on your side?

[1] John Swanwick Bradbury, 1st Baron (1872–1950), Joint Permanent Secretary to the Treasury 1913–19, whose name became a popular synonym for a treasury note.

Many times I have mentioned to you Ruskin's *Sesame and Lilies* or *Of King's Treasuries and Queen's Gardens*.[1] (I have two copies there.)

Until you have absolutely digested these two Lectures, I vow I will neither lend, recommend, give, offer, proffer, refer, or thrust or foist, or hint any other book to you.

But before the Moon of Strawberries is out you must also have read every line of *Hiawatha*. (Longfellow). That is not a book: it is a dream —Price one penny!

All thanks for Mother's letter this morning. The racket has not arrived, that is, the tennis-racket. I promise not to be solemn again in letters till this time next year.

Your dearly loving brother Wilfred

4 June

Withheld this pending Board today, which passed me Fit. I go to Scarboro' tomorrow.

627. To Susan Owen

Thursday [*6 June 1918*]   *5th Manchester Regt., Cavalry Barracks,*
Scarborough

Had a rather pleasant arrival. Priestley is still P.M.C. & has two apartments in the Barracks, where he gave me a private tea—fine China tea,—in priceless porcelain.

Most of the officers here in March are 'gone' and a new crowd are here—junior to me fortunately.

The last of my old Mess Staff went yesterday. The W.A.A.C.'s do everything now.

I live in a tent with a cinder floor, a yard or two from the Main Entrance to Camp; so it is inundated with vile dust. Thus it is not necessary to try to grit my teeth: it is done without effort.

We get up at six, and work furiously till 6 p.m., after which we are too tired to move.

Priestley is powerless to give me a room in Barracks as all A officers must sleep under canvas.

I have informed the War Office of my Category & address. I cannot keep alive here long. Here one does not live at all. One eats, (badly) sleeps, (well) and works like a demented piece of clockwork.

We call the recruits Rookies because they are so thin.

The padre is going to find Warne as I don't know his Company.

My Company is B.

Drummer George of Dunsden wept when I said goodbye. (I had seen him 3 times!) This you must not tell anybody. Such things are not for this generation of vipers.

All thanks to dear Mary for her beautiful letters.

W.E.O. x

---

[1] Two lectures by John Ruskin, published together in one volume, *Sesame and Lilies*, in 1865.

628. To Susan Owen

[*Circa 9 June 1918*]   [*Scarborough*]
First sheet missing

were brought back to this place, all thick, as it was, with the dust we had shaken off our feet. I had the blessed compensation of your parcel. The Cake travelled perfectly: and the gingerbreads likewise have journeyed yet further to their appointed place. The destiny of the cake is now half accomplished.

I wonder if its nutriment went to succour the white corpuscles so put about by insect-bites, or whether it went to swell the grey matter so diminished by the war.

There is an excellent article on Nerves in the *Daily Mail*, June 5th 6th or 7th; 6th I think.

You need study to observe none of these precautions concerning me: except to respect my strange solitude when I resort to it, and stranger friends if I resort to them. And except the following:—

Preserve me scrupulously from old women without dignity, wit, or wisdom.

Preserve me from young women with gush and no beauty.

Preserve me from women of beauty and no charm; but take not measures against women of charm and no beauty, for they are the sugar of the earth.

Preserve me from dogs.

Preserve me from ugly children.

Preserve me from varnished wood, powdered women, dusty plants, plated silver, antimacassars, wigs, and all false hair.

Preserve me from men in waistcoats shirt cuffs and braces of a Sunday afternoon; (and preserve them from me for I would tear their waistcoats from them, and cut their throats (open at the neck) and belt them into noble creatures.)

Preserve me from the man who sits in stocking feet of an evenin', and scratches his big toe with his heel.

Preserve me from the youth who carries a pencil on the lobe of his right ear; (but preserve the cigarette in the ear of a Tommy for it is his last.)

Preserve this letter.

Preserve me from irritant underclothes.

Preserve me from the unclean bath.

Preserve me from billiards, whist, and football, and all talk of the same.

Preserve me from people who eat eggs when I don't want any.

Preserve me from the person who sneezes like a bomb bursting in water.

Preserve me from the player who in the same chord strikes the bass before the treble.

Preserve me from all rag-time.

557

Preserve me from *Answers*,[1] *Pearsons*,[2] and all but Page 1 of *Tit-Bits*.[3]
Preserve me from Pennyman.[4]
Preserve me from Morris.[5]
Preserve me from the exposition of all instruments of war in chambers, all ships in glass-bottles, plush chairs, group-photographs, flowers under glass-shades, shell-pictures-frames, scene-painted boulders, and all the arts and deceitful devices of Victoria.

_____

This will be as much as you can memorize for the moment.
I have not finished.
                                                    Your very own W.E.O.

Great thanks for Book: *Barbe*,[6] which I had read in ancient days—in Torquay—borrowing from the library: but have quite forgotten & shall be so glad to read again.

629. To Susan Owen
Postcard
11 June 1918   *Scarborough*

Am wondering a little why no letter at all since I arrived here. Am earning my pay again with a vengeance. But a short bout of this work is not unpleasant. Have got a habitable tent now. Am going on Musketry for a few days, thanks to Whittaker, who is still here. What company is Warne? Letter from W.O. says I'll probably be sent to Artists. Tell Colin the R.A.F. are asking Infantry Officers to transfer to flying. Numbers of ones have gone for approval today.
Thanks: Letter received.

630. To Susan Owen

Saturday Morning [*15 June 1918*]   *Priestley's Rooms in Barracks*
                                                    [*Scarborough*]
Dearest Mother,
    Have just been inoculated, so will write while able, and before I begin to roll about. Was working yesterday till 8 p.m. with 1 hr. for lunch, & ¼ hr. for tea. Spent 2 solid hours seeing that the Rookies

_____

[1] A light weekly journal containing fiction, topical articles, and competitions. Founded in 1888, it continued, in a modified form, until 1956.
[2] *Pearson's Weekly* contained articles on general topics, fiction, and humour. Founded in 1890, it was incorporated with *Tit-Bits* in 1939.
[3] The first page was composed entirely of jokes.
[4] The Rev. William Geoffrey Pennyman (d. 1942) was Vicar of St. Mary the Virgin, Shrewsbury, 1910–13, and author of *The War's Challenge to the Church*: possibly the cause of Wilfred's antipathy.
[5] Unidentified; unless, as the next paragraph condemns Victoriana, William Morris is referred to.
[6] *Barbe of Grand Bayou* by John Oxenham. See Letter 521.

bathed themselves properly & washed their toes—especially the con-
scripts who came the same day from the Mills, awful specimens, almost
green-pale, another Race altogether from the mahogany swashbucklers
who have finished their training.

I found Warne, and interviewed him. He looks very well-treated, a
little too strapping ponderous and bumpkinish a fellow for my much
liking.

My week-end is wrecked. But it should not be many days before I
am called to the W.O. and so to Berkhampstead for a month's pre-
paratory course with the Inns of Court O.T.C.

It must not be thought I am unhappy here, meanwhile. I have now
a waterproof tent with long grass & buttercups all round to act as
dustscreens. Mine is the only single tent, thanks to Priestley, who also
puts his apartments at my disposal when I have time to come here,
which is this morning for the first time. I had magnificently resolved
not to unpack my books or papers while in camp; when lo! an urgent
request from the Sitwells in London for more of my poems for their 1918
Anthology[1] which is coming out immediately. This is on the strength of
'The Deranged', which S. Moncrieff showed them the other day. I know
not what to do. For one thing I want to see the Sitwells' etc. works
before I decide to co-appear in a book!

I suppose I must congratulate Colin.[2] Hope very much to see him at
Hampstead.

I may have big expenses at the end of the month, but you must decide
what Colin should have, & I'll do my fondest.

631. To Susan Owen

Friday Evg. [*21 June 1918*]   [*Scarborough*]

Weary though I be, I must yet let you know before I sleep that I am
well, & in humour with the life about me. The effects of inoculation
wore off about Wednesday, & I do full duty. Today have been Revolver
Shooting, & it may be a final proof of my normality (for Father's
satisfaction)[3] that I shot better than most. We go on with this Course
tomorrow.

I see my 'Hospital Barge' and another poem[4] appear in this week's
Nation. I'll send you the Editor's cheque early in July, helping to launch
Colin into Extravagance.

My Immortal Innocent has rather let himself down in my estimation

---

[1] *Wheels*, the annual miscellany of contemporary poetry founded and edited by Edith Sitwell
with the assistance of her brother Osbert. In *Wheels*, 1919 (dedicated to Wilfred's memory),
were included 'Strange Meeting', 'The Show', 'À Terre', 'The Sentry', 'Disabled', 'The
Dead-Beat', and 'The Chances'.

[2] He had become a cadet in the R.A.F., and was undergoing initial training at Swiss Cottage,
London. His birthday (24 July) was approaching.

[3] See Letter 634, closing lines.

[4] 'Futility' (*Poems*, p. 58). Published in *The Nation* on 15 June 1918.

by going to the Bing Boys[1] when he swore his first Theatre should be Shakespere. The Regent Palace is no longer the Hotel it was when I used to stay years ago. My last visit was most unfavourable, and in the light of recommending it to a younger brother, alarming.

Was so pleased to get a letter from Father. Will write to him to Torquay—when will that be?

Will send a Card to Chubbie Cubbie. And to Colin. Have not seen again Warne, but have found under my care other Shropshire lads whose speech bewrayed them to me. These, and some Welsh chappies we have are indeed, look you, I am prout to say, the muscle, as well as the voice, look you, of the company.

The Lancashire Mill Hands are weeds, why, Weeds.

Nothing to report from War Office. Have been interrupted even at this hour, so Goodnight, my darling Mother.

x

632. To Susan Owen

Monday [*24 June 1918*]   *My Tent* [*Scarborough*]

STAND BACK FROM THE PAGE! and disinfect yourself.

Quite $\frac{1}{3}$ of the Batt. and about 30 officers are smitten with the Spanish Flu.

The hospital overflowed on Friday, then the Gymnasium was filled, and now all the place seems carpeted with huddled blanketed forms. Only the very bad cases have beds. The boys are dropping on parade like flies in number. Priestley and the Adjutant are the two latest cases.

The thing is much too common for me to take part in. I have quite decided not to!

Scottie, whom I still see sometimes, went under today, & my servant yesterday.

Imagine the work that falls on the unaffected officers. Yesterday, I was Orderly Officer for the Battalion, & was not able to take off my frown for five minutes on end between Reveille & midnight. My temperature is normal, so don't be alarmed. I'm afraid my new servant,—a Herefordshire gardener's-boy, with the garden still lying in loamy beds about his ears—will 'drop' tomorrow.

There is no panic; most are already convalescent.

As no call has come from the W.O. has reached me, I shall likely be here another month—unless drafted out, which is not probable.

War Dreams have begun again; but that is because of the flapping of the canvas all night in the high winds; or else the hideous faces of the Advancing Revolver Targets I fired at last week. It is not because I am G.S. as I will prove to you another day.

Ever your W.E.O. x

[1] *The Bing Boys are Here*, which opened at the Alhambra in 1916, marked the first appearance in revue of George Robey (1869–1954). An enormous success, it was followed by *The Bing Boys on Broadway*.

633. To Susan Owen
Postcard

Sunday [Postmark 1 July 1918]   *[Postmark Scarborough]*

I wondered if Colin would be infected, and am now only hoping he won't carry it to you. I am quite immune—to everybody's amazement. Went a Cross Country Run last Wednesday, from which my calves are still suffering. Have seldom enjoyed any exercise so much.

Refereeed a Football Match yesterday!!

Had 2 long belated letters from Siegfried (in France). One letter had twice been sent from Craiglockhart to Dublin after some other Owen.

Siegfried sends a poem which I'll copy for you some day. Osbert Sitwell wrote to me yesterday, also sending a poem on the latest news 'M. Clemenceau is fully satisfied with the conditions at the front'.[1] O's father, Sir George is a magnate in Scarborough & his own estimation.

634. To Osbert Sitwell[2]

July[3] 1918   *[Scarborough]*

Dear Osbert Sitwell,

I rehearsed your very fine epigram upon our Mess President—rather a friend of mine. He did not immediately recognize Jesus. The rest of the Mess would not of course know the name of Monsieur Clemenceau. (To my mind this would be no indication of any man's ignorance of affairs.) May I send 'Ill Winds' to a French youth who might translate and circulate it where it would be appreciated?

---

[1] 'I had sent him an epigram I had composed on Clemenceau, at the time French Premier. Whenever catastrophe threatened to overwhelm the Allied Cause, as it frequently did in 1917 and '18, and whatever the extent of human suffering involved, inevitably in the English papers some such reassuring sentence as this would appear: "On being informed of these happenings, Monsieur Clemenceau announced that he was fully satisfied" . . . "Ill Winds", as the epigram was called, remained unpublished.
    It ran—

> "Up on the Cross, in ugly agony,
> The Son of Man hung dying—and the roar
> Of earthquakes rent the solemn sky
> Already thundering its wrath, and tore
> The dead from out their tombs . . . then Jesus died—
> But Monsieur Clemenceau is fully satisfied!" '   *Noble Essences.*

[2] We reproduce the text from *Noble Essences.*
[3] At some time in July he listed the poems that would be included in his first collection. The list included all the poems known to have been written in June ('Training', 'Futility', 'Arms and the Boy', 'The Calls', 'The Roads Also'), but excluded 'The Kind Ghosts', dated 30 July. The proposed title was *Disabled and Other Poems*, in preference to two other possibilities, *With Lightning and with Music* and *English Elegies*. On the same sheet of paper (in HO's possession) he wrote down the names of those to receive copies. The list reads: 'S.S., R. Graves, Leslie, P. B. [Poetry Bookshop], Mrs. Gray, Mrs. Fullerton, Dr. Sampson, Dr. Brock, Miss Wyer (?), R. Meiklejohn, Dr. Rayner, Laurent Tailhade, A. Bennett, H. G. Wells, Johnny de la Touche, Bainbrigge, Lady Margaret Sackville, R. Nichols, W. B. Yeats, J. Drinkwater?'

Always hoping to find an hour in which to copy out and generally denebulize a few poems acceptable to you either as Editor or—may I not say—friend—I have delayed this letter so long. Tonight there is only time for a tedious brief speech with you before the mind wakes up for its only amusement these days—dreams.

For 14 hours yesterday I was at work—teaching Christ to lift his cross by numbers, and how to adjust his crown; and not to imagine he thirst till after the last halt; I attended his Supper to see that there were no complaints; and inspected his feet to see that they should be worthy of the nails. I see to it that he is dumb and stands to attention before his accusers. With a piece of silver I buy him every day, and with maps I make him familiar with the topography of Golgotha.

Last week I broke out of camp to order *Wheels*, 1917. Canning[1] refused to stock copies. I persisted so long that the Young Lady loudly declared she knew all along that I was 'Osbert himself'. This caused a consternation throughout the crowded shop; but I got the last laugh by— 'No, Madam; the book is by a friend of mine, Miss Sitwell.'

Rigby's[1] people would not order a single copy without deposit!

Is the 1918 vol. designed to go on the caterpillar wheels of Siegfried's Music Hall Tank ?[2] If so I might help with the ammunition. Would you like some short War Poems, or what? Please give me a final date for submitting them to you.

I very much look forward to meeting you again, and if it be in Scarborough the pleasure will be that of all snatched joys. I am incarcerated more strictly than you imagine. Westborough[3] is now a weekly ambition. The Spa is beyond my hopes. This is the beginning of decadence. As is proved by my Father's message on hearing I was G.S.: 'gratified to know you are normal again.'—Very sympathetically yours,
                                                              W. E. S. Owen

635. To Mary Owen

Tues. [?*5 July 1918*]   *Scarborough*

My dear Mary,

I have just read your letter over a little snack of strawberries which Priestley provided me in his Apartments after tea.

On Sunday Aft. we went to a large empty house near the Camp, and

---

[1] Scarborough bookshop, no longer in existence.
[2] 'Blighters', from *The Old Huntsman:*

> The House is crammed: tier beyond tier they grin
> And cackle at the Show, while prancing ranks
> Of harlots shrill the chorus, drunk with din;
> 'We're sure the Kaiser loves the dear old Tanks!'

> I'd like to see a Tank come down the stalls,
> Lurching to rag-time tunes, or 'Home, sweet Home,'—
> And there'd be no more jokes in Music-Halls
> To mock the riddled corpses round Bapaume.

[3] The principal street in Scarborough.

the Lodge people provided tea in the garden. This was the sole recreation of any sort in 7 days. I dare not go out in the evening (we are not free till 8.30 or 9 p.m.) for fear of getting to bed late, which would mean disastrous inability to get up on the Bugle. For the same reason I dare not begin to read earnestly or write earnestly in the evening. I am haunted by bugles and startled by drums and perturbed by the tramp of feet every moment of the daylight hours.

So glad to hear from Mother & you that you had such a nice picnic. I scarcely find time for an ordinary Tub, let alone a sea bathe. (There goes the 5.30 bugle for Cleaning Parade!)

You'll be glad to hear that all our boys have recovered from the Influenza. I am one of the four or five officers who disdained it. I think I must have had it in Ripon, you remember.

Have you finished *Sesame & Lilies* and *Hiawatha*?

A ship was sunk on Friday just off here. I heard some tremendous explosions, but (such is the spirit of the Army) was only too glad we were not called out to gape at the sea over the cliffs. It happened about 10 p.m.

Sunday Mng.

I've passed several days under the impression I had sent this letter, but I must have been called away before finishing off. Spent all my letter-writing time yesterday (about 30 mins.) in cheering up old Siegfried, who is in the forefront of the battle. His new book[1] is to appear any day now. I advise Leslie to secure a copy early. Will write to him soon. In addition to duties, I've had a Gas Course last week, with Exam. all Sat. Mng.

On Sat. Aft. had to pay the Coast Patrols stationed a dozen miles away. Stiebel[2] very kindly took me on the back of his Motor Bike. They seem to have a perfect Life each patrol officer & his men. I must try for this. They complain of Loneliness. My stars!

Most of the officers here are glorified N.C.O.'s but there is an element of gentlemen left.

I am to be awaked at 5.15 tomorrow so must get some sleep in somewhere today.

Will just copy out Osbert Sitwell's poem.   Yours ever, W

How are Mother's eyes improving?

636. To Susan Owen

Friday [*15 July 1918*]   [*Scarborough*]

Dearest of Mothers,

I started a letter on Tues. but didn't get far, so I'll abandon it altogether, & begin again. Since Tues. I have been Messing Officer to the

---

[1] *Counter-Attack, and other poems*, Heinemann, London, 1918.
[2] Lieutenant J. S. Stiebel, 7th Manchesters.

Battalion in place of Stiebel who is away at Torquay for 10 days. This means that I am 'on my own', responsible to the Colonel & my conscience for the feeding of a thousand 'souls'. (I wish men's Souls were as hungry as these Bodies.)

My new job means no diminution of work but it is more interesting. I have a dozen brawny W.A.A.C.s to do the cooking, two boy stokers, & 3 men Night Cooks.

The Rationing is a tremendous affair, but the reckoning & much of the ordering is done by 2 Corporals, skilled ledger-men both. The washing up is done by a little army of W.A.A.C.s in charge of a man-sergeant. When I scold, which is regularly every hour, you might recognize some of your own voice-tones such as you used when Phyllis was unusually 'trying'. I have never in my life had to appear so omniscient & omnipotent. Nor have I ever struggled so desperately or so vainly against dirt & disorder. I put on overalls & whitewashed the cookhouse myself this morning!

Time goes cruelly fast. The army seems to be a vast digestive apparatus, with hunger as eternal as the cookhouse fires.

To dip for a moment into more savoury things, let me remind you that because I am sacrificing my Thought and Time to the bellies of the multitude is no reason why no letters should be written to me. I've had a miserable Post all week. Leslie no doubt is influenced by the $1\frac{1}{2}$ post, but it is a sad fact, that people want an i for an i and a t for a t. (Except such people as Siegfried.) I've got his new book of the things I looked over at Craiglockhart.

Priestley has obtained a fair price for my Chest of Drawers, & accordingly it will be sent on Monday next addressed to Father. I hope Father will get the Carriage Refunded. The drawers may be packed with books or other refuse in the form of valuable candlesticks.

I still wear one pip because nobody knows whether I am Lieut. or not.

Harold—where is he? Does he consider it fortunate to be sent to the Tropics—I think he should. I'd rather be sent to the North Pole—and going out into the blizzard like a gallant gentleman than go and get spattered with the blood I am trying here to enrichen [*five words illegible*]

W.E.O.

637. To Susan Owen

Tuesday, 17 July   [*Scarborough*]

My dearest Mother,

Now that you have had a quiet holiday at Alpenrose I'll make my grouse. Why didn't you come to Scarborough for a few days? I could not have seen much of you, but it would have shortened the time of my long wait for Leave.

I should get Leave within or almost within a month; & come home, of course. Next week when Stiebel comes back I must be inoculated all

over again, because my first dose has lost effect, & my second must not
be given now for fear of taking me from my duties.

If I said before that Battalion Messing was a big job, I now say it is
an enormous job; and I shall be glad when it's over. I've had a special
rumpus because I had to separate the Under 19's from the Over 19's,
the lads being allowed more meat & bread. Heretofore it was all
equalized; and the task of re-apportioning has been laborious.

I keep well, but the smell of the Cookhouse & Meat Store is rather
nauseating this hot weather.

Will you please send my bicycle; I think it a shame, I do, that I have
to race about over the Camp and in to Scarborough when I possess a
bicycle.

I hope the Chest of Drawers will please you; and that its reception
into the house won't cause you bother.

So glad Father is bettered by his holiday.

Aren't you? You don't say so. Did you speak your mind about the
War at Alpenrose?

Hope you saw the note about Siegfried in today's *News*.[1]

Your W.E.O. x

638. To Susan Owen

Saturday [*21 July 1918*]   [*Scarborough*]

Dear, dear Mother,

Wonderful of you to write so bravely of your cares. I think of these
things at night because I must not by day. The only comfort from my
quarter is the Statement that I am well and all my anxiety here is what
I share from you.

Your card came this morning.

Stiebel came back tonight.

Priestley leaves tomorrow for hospital & wants me to take on his job
permanently. I am not too keen. I am glad to Have Done with the
W.A.A.C's. It is almost impossible to control them. They either weep
or take flight when reprimanded. 2 of Priestley's deserted today. One of
'mine' 'cries' several times every day.

Their work it is true is terribly hard; but I was responsible for the
men's food, and had to 'slave' them. Tell Mary I overheard one
W.A.A.C. say after me 'I'd like to smack 'is brown face forrim.'

I wish I could get my Leave now to be with you. Would you like me
to exaggerate matters (if indeed it is possible) and come. Colonel
Mitchell is away and the acting C.O. is a Major with whom I am quite
friendly & informal.

More tomorrow.

Your own W.E.O.

[1] The *Daily News* of 16 July 1917 carried an unsigned review of *Counter-Attack*, calling it 'a
book of the protests of a tortured spirit'.

639. To Susan Owen

Sunday [*22 July 1918*]   [*Scarborough*]

Dearest Mother,

Yes, I like these portraits[1] much better. I like them entirely. There is a very fine softness about them which, whether retouching or no, is true art because it is veri-symbolic representation. In plain words, both photographs are very <u>like</u>, & I must keep them both.

We must be took together when I arrive next.

It would only increase your difficulties if I came before a few weeks yet-awhile.

Priestley has now handed over to me the affairs of the Mess Presidency so I find myself in that eminent position usually held by a Major! Possibly the C.O. will not approve of the nomination when he returns, but I'm going to move into Priestley's flat of 3 rooms as soon as P. goes.

I shall no doubt find my bicycle at the Station. It's a necessity now; I shall go shopping almost every morning!

Has the Chest come? I hope Mary will be well enough to inspect it.

I have no unused boots with me, but I left a delicate middle-aged pair in the Kitchen Cupboard or somewhere. Can you find them? and will they do?

Colin <u>should</u> not really wear any but ammunition-boots at his Rank.

I see an old Diet Sheet on the table so will put it in for Mary's instruction.

I do so long to hear that she is well again.

I have just been playing a little cricket with the lads. It bores me beyond toleration to walk in Scarborough on Sunday Nights.

Love to all. W.E.O. x

640. To Susan Owen

Friday [*27 July 1918*]   *Scarborough*

Dearest Mother,

Just a short Thank you for your last news. Hope Mary will soon be writing to me.

As I expect the Major acting C.O. while the Colonel was away has been made P.M.C.; so after today I return to my musketry & my tent. It has been quite a holiday to live in rooms again, and go out into Scarborough.

The beach is not very populous, but the sea-side feeling has begun, in spite of <u>daily</u> thunderstorms.

My bicycle arrived, in no worse state than Colin left it. I am glad, though, he found it so useful. What about the brown boots? Is Colin <u>allowed</u> to wear brown boots? How does he dress? In the admirable clothes of a simple private or the detestable rig-out of an unfledged officer?

[1] One is reproduced as Plate XIIb.

Did Father have to pay for the Bicycle carriage? In any case here is 10/-, the surplus however small for Mary to spend forthwith.

No Cheque from the *Nation* yet, so I enclose £1. for Colin's present.

Did Harold [*several words illegible*]? I suppose so, poor old boy. Say please, once more, where he is now.

'Siegfried is in London, the victim of a British Sniper.'[1] That's all I know. If only you'd come to Scarborough I might see him.

Am putting in for Leave about Aug. 9.

Yours ever W.E.O.

641. To Susan Owen

[*Circa 30 July*[2] *1918*]   *Scarborough*

My own Mother,

I send you a precious letter, from the Greatest friend I have.

I was inoculated again on Sat. but it was Siegfried's condition and not my own that made me so wretched. This time surely he has done with war.

The most encouraging thing is that he is writing already again.

Now must I throw my little candle on his torch, and go out again.

There are rumours of a large draft of officers shortly.

Sorry I only sent 10/- when the expenses were altogether about 14/-. Here is the residue for Mary.

Will try & get the books you mention, & also send you Siegfried's.

Dearest wishes to Mary,

Your lovingest W.E.O. x

642. To Susan Owen

Thursday, 7.30 a.m. [*8 August 1918*]   *Scarborough*

Dearest Mother,

Am just about to start out for the day's work,—on the Butts today.

Have had another black week, alarms calling us out at 4 in the morning, & since Sat. continuous Rain, so that my tent floor was half under water for 2 days.

I shall be on Range Duty up to Friday Night, so my Leave will not start before Friday week, if then.

So sorry I've missed Colin, but if I go to London I'll see him there. Yes, with Colin and S.S. in London I really must pass 1 day there.

I send you S.S's last note. The first sentence refers to a poem I wrote last week and sent him.

I can tell by many signs that Siegfried has been really unnerved this time.

---

[1] Returning from a dawn patrol on 13 July, SS was taken for a German and received a bullet wound in the head from one of his own NCOs. He was invalided home. See *Sherston's Progress*, pp. 264–7.

[2] 'The Kind Ghosts' (*Poems*, p. 102) is dated 30 July 1918, and is probably the poem referred to in Letter 642.

All thanks for the news you've sent from time to time of yourself, Colin, & Mary. Harold sent the Refund this week. I hope he was quite well able. I don't understand your exclamations about the Boots.

Will pay that Dentist's Bill of course.

How are your eyes now?   Always your W.E.O. x

643. To Susan Owen

Saturday [*10 August 1918*]   *Scarborough*

Dearest Mother,

Tomorrow I am for a medical inspection with 21 others, to be declared fit for draft. This means we may be sent on draft leave tomorrow, & I may reach you even before this letter! I know not. I am glad. That is I am much gladder to be going out again than afraid. I shall be better able to cry my outcry, playing my part.[1]

The secondary annoyances & discomforts of France behind the line can be no worse than this Battalion. On Friday we were called up at 3 a.m. and had the usual day's work. The Adjutant is ill, & Stiebel is ill. I did Stiebel's job on the Stunt, & am still doing it.

These are only mock alarms of course. But this morning at 8.20 we heard a boat torpedoed in the bay about a mile out, they say who saw it. I think only 10 lives were saved. I wish the Bosche would have the pluck to come right in & make a clean sweep of the Pleasure Boats, and the promenaders on the Spa, and all the stinking Leeds & Bradford War-profiteers now reading *John Bull* on Scarborough Sands.

Siegfried is being moved to Berwick on Tweed next week. Am trying to find which day. Imagine what wretched uncertainty I'm in tonight. All I feel sure of is my excellent little servant Jones, who'll pack my stuffs in quarter of an hour, night or day.

Let me thank Mary for her Boat Letter. Hope we'll all have a River Afternoon in spite of my wished-for torpedoes-nearer-home.

I like poor Doris better now I hear she understands *The Old Huntsman* Book.

My mind is a cobweb of lines radiating to Shrewsbury, London, Hastings,[2] Berwick, London, Shrewsbury, Berwick, Edinburgh, Portsmouth[3] - - -

Ever, W.E.O.

644. To Susan Owen[4]

Monday [*19 August 1918*]   *Scarborough*

Dearest dear Mother,

Arrived on Sat. Night about 9 in Barracks—plenty of time for Church Parade next morning. Was Patrol Officer all last night. Only had half

---

[1] 'You have cried your cry, you have played your part' (Letter 647, note).
[2] Colin had been posted to Hastings.
[3] HO had been on a gunnery course at Portsmouth earlier in the year.
[4] Embarkation leave is over.

an hour's sleep in clothes; so I am half-asleep now. Will write proper letter tomorrow.

Have you ordered your Claret or Wincarnis yet? Don't waste a day! I'll send the necessary.

Small hope of getting all the MSS. off which I want to.

Ever W.E.O. x

645. To Susan Owen

Monday Night [*19 August 1918*]   *My Tent, Scarborough*

I rushed off a note in time for this evening's post, which may seem very mingy. Work has not fallen hard on me yet; I have done nothing today because my trench feet are so bad I can't walk; & the Patrol last night was altogether enjoyable, and the Dawn this morning.

Still, I am quite wretched tonight, missing you so much. Oh so much!

Taking the world as it really is, not everybody of my years can boast, (or as many would say, confess) that their Mother is absolute in their affections.

But I believe it will always be so with me, always.

There is nothing in heaven or earth like you, and that is why I can't write a poem for you.

Next time I come, we must have a very long and very deep talk.

Meanwhile, eat, drink, and be merry. Here is for half a dozen bottles of red wine, which must be finished before I'll look at you again. I sometimes wonder if you are still haunted by the horror of wine 'taking hold' of me!! You are too absurd! That transgression at least will never bring a blush to my nose.

Eat, Drink, and Be Merry, for tomorrow we live, and the day after tomorrow live, live, live. Even in Scarborough I must live; though I feel dead to all these people.

I have done something towards my Contribution to *Wheels*, but the night watch has rather muddled me.

Strange how suddenly my toes went wrong! It is the old frostbite 'playing on' me again as Jones says. Because I said I was sad, little Jones is prattling to me now, & I am talking volubly while I write.

I am also thinking wildly and crying a little for only you to hear.

Wilfred x

646. To Susan Owen

Postcard

Sat. Mng. [*Postmark 31 August 1918*]   [*Postmark Folkestone*]

Am writing in a hairdresser's shop waiting for a shave. Found no room in Hotels so got put up in an Officers' Club, thanks to S. Moncrieff's knowledge of the region. Got up at 5.30 this mng. & caught train in good time. On the train I was astonished to meet Major Fletcher, the

P.M.C. you remember, who settled up my accounts last Monday, not dreaming he himself would be pushed off on Tuesday. But here he is, & I am very glad & shall try to keep with him; he used to be 2nd in command of the 5th in France.

We go on board at 3 p.m. Will write from Boulogne.

Love and good cheer W.E.O. x

647. To Susan Owen

Sat., 31 August 1918   *E.F.C., Officers Rest House and Mess*

[*half page missing*] Arriving at Victoria I had to wheel my own baggage down the platform & through the streets to the Hotel, which was full. But I got a bed (as I [*half page missing*] My last hours in England were brightened by a bathe in the fair green Channel, in company of the best piece of Nation left in England—a Harrow boy, of superb intellect & refinement, intellect because he detests war more than Germans, and refinement because of the way he spoke of my going away; and the way he spoke of the Sun; and of the Sea, and the Air; and everything. In fact the way he spoke.

And now I go among cattle to be a cattle-driver . . .

I am now fairly and reasonably tired & must go to my tent, without saying the things which you will better understand unsaid.

> O my heart,
> Be still; You have cried your cry, you played your part.

Did I ever send you Siegfried's poem which he wrote on the boat:

> For the last time I say War is not glorious;
> Tho' lads march out superb & die victorious,
> And crowned by peace, the sunlight on their graves;
>   You say we crush the Beast; I say we fight
>   Because men lost their landmarks in the night,
>   And met in gloom to grapple, stab, & kill.
> Yelling the fetish names of Good & Ill
> Which have been shamed in history.

> O my heart,
> Be still; you have cried your cry, you have played your part![1]

Goodnight, goodnight.
You are at home; yet you are home;
Your love is my home, and I cannot feel abroad.   Wilfred x

---

[1] SS did not publish this. The closing lines, slightly modified, appear in 'To Leonide Massine in "Cleopatra" ' (*Collected Poems*).

> O mortal heart
> Be still; you have drained the cup; you have played your part.

648. To Siegfried Sassoon

Sat., 31 August 1918   *E.F.C., Officers Rest House and Mess*

Goodbye—
    dear Siegfried—
I'm much nearer to you here than in Scarborough, and am by so much happier.

I have been incoherent ever since I tried to say goodbye on the steps of Lancaster Gate.[1] But everything is clear now: & I'm in hasty retreat towards the Front. Battle is easier here; and therefore you will stay and endure old men & women to the End, and wage the bitterer war and more hopeless.

When you write, please address to Mahim,
Monkmoor Rd.
Shrewsbury.

What more is there to say that you will not better understand unsaid.
Your W.E.O.

649. To Siegfried Sassoon

Sunday, 1 September 1918   *A Depot, A.P.O. S.17, B.E.F. France*

Dearest of all Friends,
    Here is an address which will serve for a few days.

The sun is warm, the sky is clear, the waves are dancing fast & bright . . . But these are not Lines written in Dejection.[2] Serenity Shelley never dreamed of crowns me. Will it last when I shall have gone into Caverns & Abysmals such as he never reserved for his worst daemons?

Yesterday I went down to Folkestone Beach and into the sea, thinking to go through those stanzas & emotions of Shelley's to the full. But I was too happy, or the Sun was too supreme. Moreover there issued from the sea distraction, in the shape, Shape I say, but lay no stress on that, of a Harrow boy, of superb intellect & refinement; intellect because he hates war more than Germans; refinement because of the way he spoke of my Going, and of the Sun, and of the Sea there; and the way he spoke of Everything. In fact, the way he spoke—

And now I am among the herds again, a Herdsman; and a Shepherd of sheep that do not know my voice.

Tell me how you are.

With great & painful firmness I have not said you goodbye from England. If you had said In the heart or brain you might have stabbed me, but you said only in the leg;[3] so I was afraid.

---

[1] SS was in the American Women's Hospital, Lancaster Gate, overlooking Hyde Park.
[2] The opening lines of Shelley's 'Stanzas, written in dejection, near Naples'.
[3] SS annotates this letter: 'I had told him I would stab him in the leg if he tried to return to the Front.'

Perhaps if I 'write' anything in dug-outs or talk in sleep a squad of riflemen will save you the trouble of buying a dagger.

Goodbye W.E.O.

650. To Susan Owen
Postcard

Aft. of Sunday, 1 September [1918]   *Address: H Depot, A.P.O. S17, B.E.F., France*

Have here caught up a number of our officers drafted out before me. This place is vastly more habitable than in 1917. Impossible to feel depressed. All Auguries are of good fortune. How blessedly different from last year!

All love. W.E.O.

651. To Susan Owen

2 September 1918   [*H. Depot, A.P.O. S17*]

My own sweet Mother,
The sun still shines, & everything is little more warlike than in Scarboro. Except that large numbers of wounded were being rushed down the road as I marched a party this morning.

I went to the sea-side by tram yesterday afternoon but there was nothing to do.

I am now in a Y.M.C.A. quite vacant of custom, which is the reason I came, and also to see the gentleman in charge, a man of letters whose name I know, but whose works are not much known, Mr. O'Riordan.[1] He has just come in—, an extraordinary hunch-backed little Irishman, of very pleasant manners.

I sent a card to you for Colin which you'll forward to Hastings.
Here is a list of things which sent at once should reach me here.
Paraffin, Toilet, Boots, small bottle.
1 pair pyjamas, flannelette.
1 lozenge-shaped identity disc;
Keys, 3 or 4 small, if found.
2 small towels now in wash.

No more now. Hoping to hear in 2 or 3 days.   Ever W x

652. To Susan Owen

Saturday [7 *September 1918*]   H. Depot, A.P.O. S17

My own Mother,
Still here, but may go up the Line any hour. Orders have come through

---

[1] Conal Holmes O'Connell O'Riordan (1874–1948), Irish man of letters who succeeded J. M. Synge as Director of the Abbey Theatre Dublin in 1909. He ran the YMCA Rest Hut at the Base Camp, Étaples, until the end of the war. He wrote under the pen name of Norreys Connell. See Letter 652.

that I rejoin the 2nd Battalion, so that will be my address.

2nd Batt.

The Manchester Regt.

B.E.F.

France.

Was out all day yesterday, & came in too late for post.

It was a fine bold idea of yours to address a letter here, without waiting for my version of the address. I had that letter two days ago, and had great joy of it. Yours & Mary's came last night. Mary's must have a very long answer when I find one.

I have been seeing O'Riordan daily, 'O'Riordan', as G. K. Chesterton writes, 'whom all of us know and love as Norries Connell.'—'All of us' means the whole clan of English writers.

I sleep in a Dormitory, not a Tent, and discovered near by last night one of Erskine Macdonald's little Georgian Poets. He is, really, a big Scotchman,[1] of no genius, but useful as an audience.

The Staff here think they are doing me a favour by sending me back to my old Unit. It's certainly better than any other Lancs crowd, and there is no possibility of a Welsh Regt. from this Camp. If I can't transfer to anything better, I shall perhaps transfer to the 2nd to avoid the prospect of passing the rest of my days with the Scarborough mob.

My parcel will be sent on if I leave before it comes. Will write again tonight or tomorrow.   Ever W.E.O.

653. To Susan Owen

Saturday [*7 September 1918*]   [*H Depot, A.P.O. S17*]

My dearest Mother,

Just a memorandum that I start 'hence' tomorrow morning, with a body of troops as well as my luggage to pull after me. When I'll have delivered the troops to their destination, I make my way straight to my own battalion which, I repeat, is the 2nd.

O'Riordan will be at the station to see me off. I've just spent three hours in his hut, talking, not books, but life & people, as is the way between Authors. Especially authors who haven't read each other!

Thus my mind has been amused, & I must not allow this letter to bemuse it.

If I see around me other officers whose faces bitterness is changing from their complacent English expressions, I laugh them to scorn.

You would not know me for the poet of sorrows.   Wilfred x

---

[1] Second-Lieutenant Murray McClymont, 2nd/10th (Scottish) KLR, who had three poems in *More Songs by the Fighting Men* (Erskine Macdonald, London, 1917). A copy of the book in HO's possession is annotated by Susan Owen: 'This came back with Wilfred's kit. Dec. 1918.' McClymont had inscribed it (7 September 1918):

> A little book and a little song,
> The first all right and the last all wrong;
> Which is but meet, let it be known,
> Since mine's the song, and the book's for Owen!

573

654. To Susan Owen

Monday, 9 September 1918   [*France*]

My own Mother,

I am at a Reception Depot, where I rest, having safely delivered my party of men, who behaved excellently. Our Reception here was not very warm, as we detrained in pitch darkness, & no one had the faintest idea where to go. Guides, however, turned up at last; & led on to billets in this now ruinous old town[1] which I've often spoken & written about.

It was frightfully nice of Haig to allow the French to be shelled out of it, & so leave us any amount of room & household goods. I have a good room in a large house, with a young officer,—quite bearable,— bound also for the 2nd. Man. There are no window panes, but the valuable hand-lace-curtains remain. I sleep on a table, for which a kind Kiltie has just found me a mattress. It's huge fun looting for furniture, & I sleep on my table in a serenity far different from, let us say, at Hastings.

I calculate I'll find several of your letters, & other's, waiting my arrival at the Battalion. In about a week (but I'll tell you again with details) I'd like a parcel with re-fill battery, cigarettes, & chocolate.

I enclose letter explaining the gloves, which I should like included in next parcel, please.

Send me such of Harold's and Colin's letters as you may.

Tell them, and them only, how peculiarly unreluctant I am to be back here with the Nation, & to have the Channel between me and all that the . . .[2] typify.

Your Wilfred x

655. To Susan Owen

Thursday [*12 September 1918*]   *Y.M.C.A.,*
                                                  With The Australian Imperial Force

No move yet; and no news to better that news.

How many of your letters, I wonder are amassing in the Man. Regimental Postbags.

You might chance one card here to tell me you're well.

Because I may stay here indefinitely.

The weather is wet & cold, but my temper, it is proved, keeps independent of sunlight.

This afternoon I went forth in search of adventure, & took a joy ride in a tank.

I was accosted in the Australian Y.M. by an old Runner of mine who shared the miseries of the—Rly. Banks.[3] He has never had so frightful a time since.

---

[1] Amiens.
[2] Names omitted.
[3] See p. 452, note 6.

Just as I was moving off at the Base, a private rushed out from the crowd & shook my hand. I just was able to recognize him as a drummer at Southport—he looks a middle-aged man now.

The augury was good, and I think the incident put my draft in a confident mood.

Potts[1] is good solid companion, not without wit, & full of wisdom.

I hear the C.O. of the 2nd. is the Major or Colonel mentioned in all the papers the other day as wounded for the tenth time.[2]

I don't know where they are.

Literary Cuttings, and others from the news, would amuse me. At present I read Stevenson's Essays, & do not want any books.

Do not inform friends & relations that I pass my hours reading, sleeping, conversing, & gathering roses from bewildered gardens. But so it is, and I'm getting fat upon it.

I assure you the difference is noticeable when I come to shave my face, (about 11 in the morning).

I kiss your hand.   W.E.O.

656. To Susan Owen

Tues. 10 September 1918   *Y.M.C.A.,*
                          With The Australian Imperial Force

My own Mother,

I'm sitting in my Camel Hair Coat at my bed-table, by the light of 2 candles. Tomorrow, it seems, will be spent here like today—no duties, no cares, but no letters.

Plenty of French books, plenty of cigarettes, plenty of magnificent life about me, and—enough to eat. No wounded pass through here; as for the poor battered houses they make me merry at heart, for they were all in bad style. And since probably by now the soldiers whose these houses were or were to have been are Unreturning, no pity whatever for their destruction moves me.

I kick joyfully about the debris, and only feel a twinge of sadness when a little child's copy-book or frock or crumpled little hat is laid bare.

Near the Cathedral I picked up a delightful wee lace-surplice, my only souvenir so far.

Potts, that is my comrade—in billets—, chose a Toby Jug,—in very bad taste.

Potts is a science student at Manchester; only 20; book learned in certain 'Subjects', but not without ideas. Indeed we talked 3 good hours last night.

It is a pleasure to find someone worth disagreeing with, nowadays, and here-a-placed.

---

[1] Second-Lieutenant F. Potts, Manchester Regiment, was wounded on 1 October 1918.
[2] Major J. N. Marshall, MC, Irish Guards, had joined 2nd Manchesters on 1 June 1918 as Second-in-Command. He had been wounded (for the tenth time) on 11 August.

I think we are fond of each other, moreover, & will do each other much good.

The Australian Y.M. is a shack of a cottage, near a little place where I once had tea last year, & which Sassoon also knew.

It was strange to wander again by the Canal where the 'Hospital Barge' passed. . . .

I had a strong poetical experience in a wrecked garden this afternoon, not an ordinary garden, but full of conservatories of tropical plants, aviaries, fish-ponds, palms & so on. I can't make a poem of it, because of Shelley's 'Sensitive Plant'[1] which you might turn up if you want the effect I enjoyed. I say enjoyed . . .

Here is a list for next parcel which you might send as soon as convenient after receiving this:

1 Pears Soap.
1 Euthymol Toothpaste.
1 Refill Battery.
2 Boxes Non Safety Matches.
2 pair Madoxes 2/6 socks.
The gloves.
20 Players Navy Cut or more if possible.
Horlicks Tablets.
No Chocolate, unless room is left.
? Handkerchiefs.

Goodnight; and may your peace be as divine as mine is tonight.

Your son, your son, your son . . .

657. To Susan Owen

Friday, 13 September [*1918*]   *Y.M.C.A.,*
With The Australian Imperial Force

Dear, dear Mother,

News today that the Batt. is coming down here, instead of my going Hence. Excellent. I have been billeting troops today. Write to the 2nd. Man., not this Recep. Camp as I'll be joining about Sunday.

It is funny to think of your letters being brought down from the Front!

Do not, (as I afore-asked) undeceive the world which thinks I'm having a bad time, if it thinks at all. But take to yourself the fact that I've an amusing little holiday here; and know that nowhere in the universe, and at no time, can I experience anything again like—and—in 1917.

Ever your W.E.O. x

[1] Written in 1820, it describes an idyllic garden tended by a fair lady, on whose death it falls into neglect, becoming a wilderness. Its plants are finally ravaged by a cruel winter.

> That garden sweet, that lady fair,
> And all sweet shapes and colours there,
> In truth have never passed away;
> 'Tis we, 'tis ours, are changed! not they.

658. To Susan Owen

Sunday, 15 September 1918   *With the 2nd. Batt., The Manchester Regt.*[1]

My dear dear Mother,

I reported to the Adjutant at 9 this morning, & am now in D Coy.—which is part of my address. Your letter of Sept. 10 (unnumbered) (with the photograph), was on the table at lunch. After lunch, I went round to B.H.Q. for the rest, but found none, & could get nothing out of the post-corporal.

I hung about interrogating people till the Terrible Major, (he of the 10 wounds fame) asked me if he could help me! I departed. Mysteriously, at dinner, eight more letters were brought to me, including only one of yours, The No. 3. None from S.S. It is possible that his correspondence is specially censored—and intercepted.

All thanks for the parcels—in anxious anticipation!

Cigarettes are scarcer and scarcer. *Verb. Sap.* The poor Boys were smoking grass in envelopes in the line last week. I wish I could tell you what they have done in the making of last month's News.

Yesterday I had the honour (!) of preparing the Brigadier's Quarters: & supervising Guides for various units of the Brigade. I watched The Manchesters 'march in' and great cheer it was to see at least two lads instantly recognize me as they went by. They were, strangely enough, the very two I most hoped had survived. Almost they are the only survivors in the ranks. . . .

Many of the N.C.O.'s I remember.

I like my Coy. Commander:[2] & the other four Coy. Officers are anything but blighters. Three, I believe are junior to me.

But Potts has been put in another Coy.

We billet together, nevertheless.

Of our billets (in a village close adjacent to where I was last week) I will write more next time—tomorrow, I hope.

By the writing you may judge I am not yet very comfortable.

W.E.O. xx

659. To Susan Owen

Saturday [*21 September 1918*]   [*2nd Manchester Regt.*]

Just a tiny note as a sign of life, & to say that both your Parcels have reached me, one yesterday and one today! Tomorrow—Sunday—I will thank you in detail.

All news is told when I say I am still in the same billet, & no doubt shall be for long after you get this letter.

---

[1] The Germans were now in retreat; but were hitting back strongly as they withdrew. 2nd Manchesters had been heavily engaged about Vermandovillers, Ablaincourt, and Cizancourt in the last days of August, and had been withdrawn to Berny, then to the Neuville area, on 6 September. Wilfred rejoined them at Corbie on 15 September.

[2] Captain Hugh Somerville, M C and Bar, commanding D Coy. See p. 586, note 1.

I have been appointed Bombing Officer to the Battalion. N.B. I know nothing specially about bombs. I told the Adjutant so, & he said something about making me Gas Officer; or 'some Battalion job'. I am flattered.

The Adjutant is a fine pleasant man.

My Captain is an Honours Student of Eng. Literature. Need I say more? (Yes, I need: he is not a producer).

The Colonel[1] is an agreeable non-ferocious gentleman. But the Major of the 12 wounds loves Soldiering & has passed his life wherever he could find any fighting. Need I say more?

Your W.E.O. x

660. To Siegfried Sassoon

22 September 1918   *D Coy. 2nd Manchester Regt.*

My dear Siegfried,

Here are a few poems to tempt you to a letter. I begin to think your correspondence must be intercepted somewhere. So I will state merely

I have had no letter from you ⎰lately
⎱for a long time,

and say nothing of my situation, tactical or personal.

You said it would be a good thing for my poetry if I went back.

That is my consolation for feeling a fool. This is what shells scream at me every time: Haven't you got the wits to keep out of this?

———

Did you see what the Minister of Labour[2] said in the *Mail* the other day? 'The first instincts of the men after the cessation of hostilities will be to return home.' And again—

'All classes acknowledge their indebtedness to the soldiers & sailors . . .'

About the same day, Clemenceau is reported by the *Times* as saying: 'All are worthy . . . yet we should be untrue to ourselves if we forgot that the greatest glory will be to the splendid poilus, who, etc.'

I began a Postcript to these Confessions, but hope you will already have lashed yourself, (lashed yourself!) into something . . .

———

O Siegfried, make them Stop![3]

W.E.O.

P.S. My Mother's address is Mahim

Monkmoor Rd. Shrewsbury.

I know you would try to see her, if ——— I failed to see her again.

---

[1] Lieutenant-Colonel G. McM. Robertson, DSO, North Staffs., had become CO on 18 May 1918.
[2] George Henry Roberts (1869–1928), Minister of Labour 1917–19.
[3] The last words of 'Attack' (*Counter-Attack*) are: 'O Jesus, make it stop!'

661. To Susan Owen

Sat. 28 September 1918   *Same Address*

Dearest Mother,

Am still sitting on straw under our Tamboo,[1] for it is raining again. These few days have been dry & not really cold. You must not suppose I have been uncomfortable. Though I left the last vestige of civilization, in the Civil sense, behind at ————, there is here all but all that a man wants fundamentally; clean air, enough water to wash once a day; plain food and plentiful; letters from Home of good news, shelter from the rain & cold; an intellectual gentleman for Captain; 3 bright & merry boys for my corporals; & stout grizzled old soldiers in my platoon. My Sergeant is a tiny man. We get on very well together.

Major Marshall of the 10 wounds is the most arrant utterly soldierly soldier I ever came across. I have not 'come across' his path yet, & hope not to. Bold, robust, dashing, unscrupulous, cruel, jovial, immoral, vast-chested, handsome-headed, of free, coarse speech, I am not surprised he figures in a book. I don't know which book; must find out.

The Colonel is a mild, honourable gentleman, who lets us alone to do our work.

Two at least of the officers in D. Coy. are quite temporary gentlemen. They call me The Ghost, (which is a point in favour of their latent imaginations.)

So delighted with all your news of Harold.[2] Didn't I tell you it was 'A Good Thing.' You don't say where Colin is, after having left Hastings.

As I hope I said, I had his letter, but at present I'm borrowing note paper, of which a quire is not to be found in the Company.

The forthcoming news should be of intense interest to you.[3]

Here is my lunch; roast beef & baked potatoes! I'm hungry!

Ever your W.E.O. x

---

[1] Bivouac.

[2] HO had reached Simonstown to join the light cruiser *Astraea* as sub-lieutenant. See *JO* III, ch. 12.

[3] Later the same day the battalion moved (with its Brigade, the 96th) to Vendelles, crossing the St. Quentin Canal, and took up positions east of Magny-la-Fosse, near Bellenglise, on 29 September in preparation for a brigade attack on Joncourt to gain the Beaurevoir-Fonsomme Line round Chataignies Wood.

662. To Susan Owen

4th (or 5th) October 1918   *In the Field*

Strictly private

My darling Mother,

As you must have known both by my silence and from the news-papers which mention this Division—and perhaps by other means & senses—I have been in action for some days.[1]

I can find no word to qualify my experiences except the word SHEER. (Curiously enough I find the papers talk about sheer fighting!) It passed the limits of my Abhorrence. I lost all my earthly faculties, and fought like an angel.

If I started into detail of our engagement I should disturb the censor and my own Rest.

You will guess what has happened when I say I am now Command-ing the Company, and in the line had a boy lance-corporal as my Sergeant-Major.

With this corporal who stuck to me and shadowed me like your prayers I captured a German Machine Gun and scores of prisoners.

I'll tell you exactly how another time. I only shot one man with my revolver (at about 30 yards!); The rest I took with a smile. The same thing happened with other parties all along the line we entered.

I have been recommended for the Military Cross;[2] and have recom-mended every single N.C.O. who was with me!

My nerves are in perfect order.

I came out in order to help these boys—directly by leading them as well as an officer can; indirectly, by watching their sufferings that I may speak of them as well as a pleader can. I have done the first.

Of whose blood lies yet crimson on my shoulder where his head was— and where so lately yours was—I must not now write.

It is all over for a long time. We are marching steadily <u>back</u>.

Moreover

The War is nearing an end.

Still,

Wilfred and more than Wilfred

---

[1] The brigade had attacked on 1 October and had gained its objectives. The Manchesters attacked with great gallantry, broke through the Beaurevoir-Fonsomme Line, and after stiff hand-to-hand fighting cleared 1,400 yards of the line, capturing 210 prisoners. Repeated counter-attacks were made during the following night. Five officers were killed, six wounded (including Potts); eighty-five other ranks were killed or wounded. On 3 October the battalion was relieved and pulled back to dug-outs on the banks of the St. Quentin Canal near Lehancourt; and on 5 October moved to Hancourt in the Vendelles area to rest. Wilfred writes during the march back to Hancourt.

[2] The award was immediate. The citation runs: 'For conspicuous gallantry and devotion to duty in the attack on the Fonsomme Line on 1st/2nd October 1918. On the Company Commander becoming a casualty, he assumed command and showed fine leadership and resisted a heavy counter-attack. He personally captured an enemy Machine Gun in an isolated position and took a number of prisoners. Throughout he behaved most gallantly.'

663. To Susan Owen

[8 October 1918]   [2nd Manchester Regt.]

It is 5 o'clock this Sunday Evening. You will be sitting at tea. I fear you are without news, and a little wondering . . .

You will understand I could not write—when you think of us for days all but surrounded by the enemy. All one day (after the battle) we could not move from a small trench, though hour by hour the wounded were groaning just outside. Three stretcher-bearers who got up were hit, one after one. I had to order no one to show himself after that, but remembering my own duty, and remembering also my forefathers the agile Welshmen of the Mountains I scrambled out myself & felt an exhilaration in baffling the Machine Guns by quick bounds from cover to cover. After the shells we had been through, and the gas, bullets were like the gentle rain from heaven.

My servant was wounded in the first hour of the attack. My new servant has just gone on leave this afternoon, carrying with him some books & binoculars[1] of mine, with instructions to call on you as he passes through Shrewsbury (to Manchester.) This Howarth is a 'scratch' servant not my choice; but I rather hope he'll call on you & tell you what he can.

So strange to read your letters again! And so good to hear you are at least trying to keep quite well. Glad you find your Help worth accommodating.

Must now write to hosts of parents of Missing, etc.

Your W.E.O. x

664. To Siegfried Sassoon

10 October 1918   [2nd Manchester Regt.]

Very dear Siegfried,

Your letter reached me at the exact moment it was most needed— when we had come far enough out of the line to feel the misery of billets; and I had been seized with writer's cramp after making out my casualty reports. (I'm O.C. D Coy).

The Batt. had a sheer time last week. I can find no better epithet: because I cannot say I suffered anything; having let my brain grow dull: That is to say my nerves are in perfect order.

It is a strange truth: that your *Counter-Attack* frightened me much more than the real one: though the boy by my side, shot through the head, lay on top of me, soaking my shoulder, for half an hour.

Catalogue? Photograph? Can you photograph the crimson-hot iron as it cools from the smelting? That is what Jones's blood looked like, and felt like. My senses are charred.

I shall feel again as soon as I dare, but now I must not. I don't take the cigarette out of my mouth when I write Deceased over their letters.

[1] A German pair, now in HO's possession.

But one day I will write Deceased over many books.

I'm glad I've been recommended for M.C., & hope I get it, for the confidence it may give me at home. Full of confidence after having taken a few machine guns (with the help of one seraphic lance corporal,) I held a most glorious brief peace talk in a pill box. You would have been *'en pamoisons'*.

I found one of your poems in another L. Cpl's possession! The Theosophist[1] one it was: containing, let me tell you, the one line I resent.

In bitter safety I awake unfriended.

Please apologise—now.

Yes, there is something you can send me: 2 copies of *C. Attack*, one inscribed. One is for the Adjutant,—who begged a book of Erskine MacD's Soldier-Poets which I had with me—because I met one of these amalgamations at the Base. And liked him for his immediate subjugation to my principles and your mastery.

But he is now sending me V.A.D. love poems,[2] so he will remain a private in my section of poets.

Was so interested about Prewett.[3]

At the Base I met O'Riordan (of the Irish Theatre, & collaborator with Conrad.) A troll of a man; not unlike Robbie for unexpected shocks. It was easy, & as I reflect, inevitable to tell him everything about oneself.

I have nothing to tell you except that I'm rather glad my servant was happily wounded: & so away from me. He had lived in London, a Londoner.

While you are apparently given over to wrens,[4] I have found brave companionship in a poppy, behind whose stalk I took cover from five machine-guns and several howitzers.

I desire no more exposed flanks of any sort for a long time.

Of many who promised to send me literary magazines no one has succeeded, except the Ed. of *Today*[5] who sent me (by whose request?) Mais's[6] article & the picture, which I have at last managed to stick to the corrugated iron wall of my Tamboo. For mercy's sake send me

---

[1] 'Sick Leave' (*Counter-Attack*).

[2] McClymont had written on 11 September: ' I have altered the sonnet as below. Sorry to trouble you, but I want your criticism.' The love poem followed. On the back of this letter, Wilfred drafted 'Smile, Smile, Smile' (*Poems*, p. 77).

[3] SS was now convalescing at Lennel, near Coldstream in Berwickshire, the home of Lady Clementine Waring. Among his fellow convalescents was a Canadian poet, Frank Prewett, who published a volume of poems, *The R al Scene*, some years later, thereafter abandoning poetry for farming. See *Siegfried's Journey*.

[4] 'I had described how, early one morning, a golden-crested wren had appeared in my bedroom and perched on my pillow, thereby affording me the innocent pleasure of releasing it at the open window. Reading his rejoinder to this almost maiden-auntlike piece of news, I probably told myself that war experience was mainly composed of acute contrasts, of which this—in conjunction with his—seemed a classic example' (*Siegfried's Journey*).

[5] Holbrook Jackson (1874–1948), author and bookman, editor of *T.P.'s Weekly* 1911–14 and of *To-day* 1917–23.

[6] The writer S. P. B. Mais (1885–   ), at this time a schoolmaster, was also literary critic on the *Evening News*.

something to read which may help to neutralize my present stock of literature. I send you the choicest of specimens.[1]

Ever your W.E.O.

665. To Susan Owen

10 October 1918   [*2nd Manchester Regt.*]

My own Mother,

I think all your dear letters have now reached me. By Oct. 3, your last, we had got out of the danger zone.

At five in the mng. I led the Company out, by the stars, through an air mysterious with faint gas. Such was our state that when dawn broke some of us were surprised, and for half an hour I had myself thought it was five in the evening! Since then I have been pretty busy with the Company, still in my charge, with 2 junior officers. At three this morning, a big number of lads from Scarborough turned up, several of them outgrown drummers, once my waiters in Clarence Gdns!

Nearly all have come to my Company, & from my company in Scarborough. Luck again! I'm in the horrible position of not having enough food for them, as they left their rations some ten miles away!

Some of them look pretty scared already, poor victims. Tonight I must stand before them & promulgate this General Order:

'Peace talk in any form is to cease in Fourth Army.

All ranks are warned against the disturbing influence of dangerous peace talk.' And so on.

_____

It is amusing to think of anyone being upset by a friend's arm-amputation in hospital[2] . . .

How would Father like—No, I will spare you.

Father would like to see me on my Charger; or sitting at my Orderly Room Table, where I can inflict Field Punishment! In a few days a senior officer will no doubt turn up from Leave or somewhere.

Am looking out with hungry eyes for your parcel. None of my rich relations consider 20 cigarettes worth my life. They'll have a murderer's curse; if I should curse them. Meanwhile you have a martyr's blessing.

W.E.O.

666. To Susan Owen

11 October 1918   [*2nd Manchester Regt.*]

Not for circulation as a whole.

Dearest of Mothers,

No letter from you today, and no parcel. The great concerns which

_____

[1] A Special Order of the Day from the 4th Army Commander, quoted in Letter 665.

[2] Tom Owen's superior, Mr. Williams, Chief Superintendent of the West Region, London North-Eastern and Great Western Railways, had undergone the operation; and Tom Owen became Acting Chief Superintendent, a position he held until his retirement several years later. Williams refusing to retire, the much-increased pension Tom Owen would have received on his retirement was not forthcoming.

take my time have prevented me from properly thanking you for the many little blessings of your last parcel. The Munchie I ate over a period of several days & nights; and the fact that it was once eaten under a particularly nasty & accurate bombardment—(shells so close that they thoroughly put the wind up a Life Guardsman in the trench with me—so that he shook as the Guards shake on parade) these circumstances, I say, have not taken the good savour from Munchie-munchie.

The New Food[1] served me one night when we lay drenched to the bone, and the awful Cold had begun to paralyse my stomach. I don't like this Food.

On that night both officers & men lay in the mud utterly despondent; but a lance-corporal spread half his blanket (not supposed to be carried) over me, and the warmth came like the rising of the May-day sun. So I was saved from the nearest approach to the excruciation of my First Campaign. That time on the Somme in 1917 was so infinitely worse than this for cold, privation, and fatigue that nothing daunts me now.

The Sergeant, now acting my Coy. Sgt. Major, was a corporal with me in the first dug-out where the Sentry was blinded, you remember. He remembers it . . .

I still command D. Coy, and have now four junior officers.

It is delightful to have the Scarborough Drums to fill the Vacant Ranks. Censoring letters today I came across this: 'Do you know that little officer called Owen who was at Scarborough; he is commanding my Company, and he is a toff I can tell you. No na-poo. Compree?' Interpreted: 'a fine fellow, no nonsense about him!'

I record this because it is more pleasing than military medals with many bars.

———

Returning to the unpacking of my parcels: cigarettes: arrived just in time: sweets & (good) chocolate always welcome.

You see I live between the extremes of gross materialism—feeding savagely & sleeping doggishly—and of high spirituality—suffering & sacrificing.

                                                                    Wilfred

Next day

Together with your last letter came one from S. Moncrieff, now in France supervising or piloting Beach Thomas[2] and Philip Gibbs.[3]

He hopes to motor over to see me some day. His letter told me the very sad news of Robert Ross;[4] and also of P. Bainbrigge of Shrewsbury School, my friend of Scarborough; killed.

I am glad you are finding courage to speak. In a previous letter you

[1] New Food Committees had been set up on 8 October 1918 to fix compulsory percentages of potatoes in bread, meat in sausages, etc.
[2] Sir William Beach-Thomas (1868–1957), journalist and writer on the countryside. He was War Correspondent of the *Daily Mail* at this time.
[3] Sir Philip Gibbs (1877–1962), author and journalist, was War Correspondent for the *Daily Chronicle* and other papers throughout the war.
[4] Robert Ross died on 5 October 1918, aged 49.

said you kept quiet. I was not proud of that. The 4th Army General has had to issue an Order:

'Peace Talk must cease in the Fourth Army.'

From another Letter to Scarboro'—Mr. Owen is my Coy. Commander, and his such a desent chap.

667. To Susan Owen

15 October [*1918*]   [*2nd Manchester Regt.*]

Dearest Mother,

No change of situation, except that I now live in a tent, & a change of weather has made the place more miserable. On the night when the news was officially sent us of the German 'Acceptance' we spent a merry enough night; I even discovered I could sing. We still hope something may be concluded by the Mixed Commission before we go into the line again. By we, I mean every officer & man left, of the legions who have suffered and are dust.[1]

I am not depressed even by Bottomley's 'NO! NO! NO!'..[2]

It has had the effect of turning the whole army against its John Bull at last. My heart has been warmed by the curses I have heard levelled at the *Daily Mail*.

Robbie Ross's death is more affecting to me, almost, than many of the deaths that took place at my side. Thank you so much for the paragraph from the *Times*. It was marvellously true of him, and kind, considering the *Times* was never his friend.

_____

A Senior Lieutenant has turned up from Leave so I am now only Second in Command of D. Coy. He has returned from his first visit to London utterly disgusted with England's indifference to the real meaning of the war as we understand it.

_____

The Parcel came all right; my only grouse is that it was too big. Suppose it had reached me nearer the line I should have had to dump most of it: as every ounce tells on the back after the tenth muddy mile and the fourth sleepless night.

Please note, once more, that I don't want old, shrunk, darned socks. No use at all. I must have new ones if my feet are to remain 'beautiful on the mountains' of victory. Nothing now lacks—but in, say, a week's time, you might send only

_____

[1] The closing lines of SS's 'Prelude: The Troops' in *Counter-Attack* run:

> The unreturning army that was youth:
> The legions who have suffered and are dust.

[2] 'I have no intention, as far as I have any power, of allowing the Gentlemen of Whitehall to come to an arrangement with the Kaiser. I don't want any more talk of not being out to destroy the German nation—that is just what I am out for . . .' Bottomley, 'I shall be there' (*John Bull*, 12 October 1918).

(1 small writing pad.
(1 small Toilet Paraffin.
(2 Munchies.

———

We have had cigarettes from Capt. Somerville's[1] parcels. His wound in the thigh has got him to Bristol now. Only Lt. Gregg[2] died of wounds. I had known him in Scarborough. He had been very fond of his wife, and proud of his little daughter.

I suppose the child will be told she should be proud of Daddie, now.

I don't like the new Coy. Officers.

I have sent one of my corporals away for a Commission: such was my august pleasure.

I would, if I could, send many of these officers away (to a secondary school) to train for corporals.

I await Colin's fate with great hope. Thank you for passing on news to Harold.

. . .[3] Numbers have really bad chests from gas; but it is their own fault. They would not put on their masks, when I did. My health is perfect.

Later

Your letters of Oct. 10th & 11th & Mary's have just come.

Mary's hopes for Peace Next Summer are sanguine, not to say sanguinary. Next Summer! When Christmas is the Limit of our Extreme Patience! Time gets marvellously lengthened out between the first rustle of a shell coming down & the VRACH! It seems, when at night a plane over you shuts off its engines for a moment in order to drop a bomb, hours.

———

I have just been given this enclosed Cutting. The 4 p.m. was timed on my wrist-watch! I hope Pte. Howarth will have told you all he can. My letters are written under such disjointed circumstances that they must read disjointedly. Admire at least my soldierly braggadoccio to Father.

Ever Wilfred

668. To Susan Owen

Sat. 19 October 1918   [*2nd Manchester Regt.*]

My dearest Mother,

We left the Corrugated Iron & Red Tent Billet in a hurry early yesterday morning.[4] For future Reference I will call this the False Floor Dug Out. It goes down some 50 ft. but the Bosche has covered it in at a depth of 5 ft.—no doubt because he was having so many prisoners taken from the tunnels. I need not say these are not yet The Trenches.

---

[1] Wounded in the Fonsomme Line battle, Wilfred taking over command.
[2] Second-Lieutenant R. A. Gregg, Manchester Regiment.
[3] Twenty-two words omitted.
[4] The battalion moved to Bohain and Bussigny, still rear areas, in the second half of October.

We have the *Times* of Thursday, and the strange news makes us feel that the Rumble on the horizon may cease any hour.[1] I'm listening now, but it still goes on, a gigantic carpet-beating.

I wonder has my servant called on you, or has he sent the Binoculars.

In the hurry of our departure yesterday, I left behind my Boracic Powder & Perm. of Potash! Please include small quantities, with writing pad & Mixed Fruit & Nut! It is now six weeks since I saw a shop, or decent habitation.

Thank you indeed for the *Punch*. Parts were very good; though much was dastardly. Would you please send me the next *New Statesman*?— around a letter.

I'm afraid I leave many things in your letters unanswered.

All that I might say to Mary & Colin & Father (& you)— if I had a fair table to write on,—or even if there were not so many dead horses corrupting the wind—you must imagine for me.

Ever your own Wilfred

669. To Susan Owen

20 October 1918   [*2nd Manchester Regt.*]

Dearest Mother,

After a very heavy march on which I had the painful duty of collecting & goading along the stragglers, we have come upon the vestiges of civilization again: civilians, just liberated, still continue here. It is just like March 1917. We have a fairly good billet, but may move any hour. We have only been 'in' 4 hours. After a 7 hours march, (without food on the way), I fed, and revived, & questioned civilians,—instead of writing a longer letter than this is to be.

Please send Colin's address so that I can write direct to Hastings.

About a week ago, a letter of 2 Lt. Foulkes[2] was opened and examined by the Base Censor. If any of mine have received his attentions, tell me. So little of interest I may tell you and so ill I tell it, all letters are Private.

Did I tell you S. Moncrieff is now with B. Thomas? Siegfried is thinking of Parliament (a Labour Seat!) A *Daily News* round your letter would be very welcome.

You write just seldom enough to avoid 3 letters coming together, & just often enough to keep me serene. I am conscious of your prayers. Please say more about your own restoration to health. Though I have read the opening chapters of *Little Dorrit* (& carefully enough to remember them after marching umpteen miles) still I say Will is the best medicine.

Ever Wilfred

---

[1] The news was the break-up of the Dual Monarchy. Hungary separated from Austria, and Austria was proclaimed a Federation of Germans, Austrians, Czechs, Ukrainians, and Yugoslavs.

[2] Lieutenant J. Foulkes, M C, Manchester Regiment, the only other D Coy. officer to come out of the Fonsomme Line battle unscathed. He won his M C at the same time. For his recollections of Wilfred, see E B's *Memoir*.

670. To Susan Owen

Tues. Mng., 22 October 1918   (*Same kitchen*) [*2nd Manchester Regt.*]

Dearest Mother,

Your last letter before going to Alpenrose, & the one from Alpenrose and the parcel reached me together yesterday. Two days ago I was thinking a great deal of your Restoration to health, and even managed to mention it, I believe! This is fine news of your visit to Dr. Armitage. Let nothing waver you from your treatment, however incommodious to other people (or yourself.) How happily I think of you always in bed. About the end of November you will start to move about your room. Your room must be arranged. All my Articles of Vertue which you like are to represent me there. My Jacobean Chest; (why not?) my carpets; my tall candlesticks; my pictures; my tables: have them all in.

About Christmas you will start the hardening processes. You will lengthen your walks and your paces. You will grow keen with the keenness of frost and cold, blue sunlight. So you will be ready, early in February, for my Leave. We will walk to Haughmond, and while you are resting on the top, I will run round the Wrekin and back, to warm my feet.

For even were Prussianism removed from London & Berlin and Peace happened before Christmas, I should not get home before January or February.

We move from here in a few hours, not for the front. Communication is frightfully difficult with the Base. It passes my wits how letters arrive so soon! Now the rain has begun, the roads are increasingly baffling: and though my letters cease for a week or more you must not conclude I am in the fighting zone. It is unlikely for a considerable time, time even for the British Government & its accomplices to save their Nations.

W.E.O. x

P.S. Thank you for everything in parcel, except socks which I had spared & exempted as unfit last August.

671. To Leslie Gunston

25 October 1918   *2nd Manchester Regt., France.*

Dear Leslie

I rejoice with you over your success with the *Nation*. Certainly that Roundel meant more to me than all the *Nymph* poems put together. Now you are recognized by Massingham, Sassoon will want to see your work: I'll tell him. He wrote to me on the 16th a letter which I got yesterday, telling how he was with dear Robbie Ross on the evening before our inestimable friend suddenly died.[1] Siegfried mentions that A. Bennett offered him a job under Beaverbrook, but that S.S. wrote to

[1] The evening is described in *Siegfried's Journey*, pp. 82–84.

Beaver's Pte. Sec. saying he had no qualifications for War Propaganda except that he had been wounded in the head: that repartee deserves eternal fame.[1]

You must not imagine when you hear we are 'resting' that we lie in bed smoking. We work or are on duty always. And last night my dreams were troubled by fairly close shelling. I believe only civilians in the village were killed (Thank God). In this house where I stay five healthy girls died of fright when our guns shelled the place last fortnight. You & I have always been open with each other: and therefore I must say that I feel sorry that you are neither in the flesh with us nor in the spirit against War.

There are two French girls in my billet, daughters of the Mayor, who (I suppose because of my French) single me for their joyful gratitude for *La Déliverance*. Naturally I talk to them a good deal; so much so that the jealousy of other officers resulted in a Subalterns' Court Martial being held on me! The dramatic irony was too killing, considering certain other things, not possible to tell in a letter.

Until last night though I have been reading Swinburne, I had begun to forget what a kiss was.

I have found in all these villages no evidence of German atrocities. The girls here were treated with perfect respect. All the material ruin has been wrought by our guns. Do you still shake your befoozled head over the *Daily Mail* & the *Times*?

Love W.E.O.

P.S. I shall be glad of any literary literature.

672. To Susan Owen

29 October 1918   [*2nd Manchester Regt.*]

Dearest Mother,

Through so much marching I have not been able to write for a day or two. I don't want to send Field Cards in case you suppose they mean in the Line. In future, however, a F. Card will be no proof that I am actually there.

Last night I slept in a cottage, but in an hour or two we move on: not to fight.[2]

Your last letters were the two with the Permang: & the Boric. Many many thanks for sending this so quickly.

Yesterday evening I hear the post corporal fell into a river; I understand the letters are all right; but haven't got any yet.

Howarth came back a day or two ago, but I did not take him back to me. My present one is Pte. Roberts, whom I knew in Scarborough.

[1] See *Siegfried's Journey*, p. 71.
[2] The battalion moved into the line at St. Souplet on the evening of the same day, 29 October, taking over the line west of the Sambre-Oise Canal, north of Ors, on the following night, 30–31 October. An attack over and beyond the canal was to be mounted.

The civilians here are a wretched, dirty crawling community, afraid of us, some of them, and no wonder after the shelling we gave them 3 weeks go.

Did I tell you that five healthy girls died of fright in one night at the last village. The people in England and France who thwarted a peaceable retirement of the enemy from these areas are therefore now sacrificing aged French peasants and charming French children to our guns. Shells made by women in Birmingham are at this moment burying little children alive not very far from here.

It is rumoured that Austria has really surrendered.[1] The new soldiers cheer when they hear these rumours, but the old ones bite their pipes, and go on cleaning their rifles, unbelieving.

A little gleam of good news I discovered in your note which said already you felt rested by being in bed.

I wonder what your diet is?

For my next parcel, will Mary please get:

    (1 small bottle Tatcho
    (1 ,,   Oatine
    (1 pair cork boot-socks, size 6.
    (20 Players.
    (Chocolate.

There is a pair of breeches too narrow in the knees left in a drawer. Would Father get the Tailor who made my last pair to enlarge the knees ? & dispatch to me ? I will send a cheque soon.

Thank Father very much for his last letter.

The cutting from the *News*, & especially Gardiner's article[2] was appreciated by us all.

Siegfried sent me a little book which he had in France. Offered a job in War Propaganda under Beaverbrook he wrote to B's private sec. saying he had no qualifications for such work, except that he had been wounded in the head.

So glad you liked Tolstoy.

All my dearest love, my darling Mother.   W.E.O.

673. To Susan Owen

Thurs. 31 October [*1918*] *6.15 p.m.*   [*2nd Manchester Regt.*]

Dearest Mother,

I will call the place from which I'm now writing 'The Smoky Cellar of the Forester's House'. I write on the first sheet of the writing pad which came in the parcel yesterday. Luckily the parcel was small, as it

---

[1] An armistice was signed with the Italians on 3 November 1918.

[2] The article by A. G. Gardiner, the Editor, in the 19 October issue of the *Daily News*, entitled 'The Victory and its Uses', in which ways of making final peace terms were discussed with notable level-headedness.

reached me just before we moved off to the line. Thus only the paraffin was unwelcome in my pack. My servant & I ate the chocolate in the cold middle of last night, crouched under a draughty Tamboo, roofed with planks. I husband the Malted Milk for tonight, & tomorrow night. The handkerchief & socks are most opportune, as the ground is marshy,[1] & I have a slight cold!

So thick is the smoke in this cellar that I can hardly see by a candle 12 ins. away, and so thick are the inmates that I can hardly write for pokes, nudges & jolts. On my left the Coy. Commander snores on a bench: other officers repose on wire beds behind me. At my right hand, Kellett, a delightful servant of A Coy. in The Old Days radiates joy & contentment from pink cheeks and baby eyes. He laughs with a signaller, to whose left ear is glued the Receiver; but whose eyes rolling with gaiety show that he is listening with his right ear to a merry corporal, who appears at this distance away (some three feet) nothing [but] a gleam of white teeth & a wheeze of jokes.

Splashing my hand, an old soldier with a walrus moustache peels & drops potatoes into the pot. By him, Keyes, my cook, chops wood; another feeds the smoke with the damp wood.

It is a great life. I am more oblivious than alas! yourself, dear Mother, of the ghastly glimmering of the guns outside, & the hollow crashing of the shells.

There is no danger down here, or if any, it will be well over before you read these lines.[2]

I hope you are as warm as I am; as serene in your room as I am here; and that you think of me never in bed as resignedly as I think of you always in bed. Of this I am certain you could not be visited by a band of friends half so fine as surround me here.

Ever Wilfred x

---

[1] The Ors Canal was some 70 feet wide bank to bank, except at the locks, with an average depth of 6–8 feet. All bridges had been demolished or prepared for demolition. Low ground on both sides of the canal had been inundated by the Germans; most of it was swamp. The Germans held the eastern bank.

[2] Strong patrolling continued till zero hour for the IX Corps attack, 5.45 a.m. 4 November. 14 Brigade crossed; 96 Brigade, which included 2nd Manchesters, was not successful. The engineers got a bridge across, but the area was swept with shell and machine-gun fire. Two platoons made the crossing, but the bridge was then destroyed. The remainder of the battalion crossed at Ors, where 1st Dorsets had secured a crossing. Wilfred Owen was killed on the canal bank on 4 November. One other officer (Second-Lieutenant Kirk, posthumously awarded the VC) and twenty-two other ranks were also killed; three officers and eighty-one other ranks were wounded; eighteen other ranks missing. A week later, the war was over.

APPENDIX A

From Edmund Blunden's Memoir, prefaced to the 1931 edition of the poems.

One warm day in December 1911 he wrote a letter in verse, from somewhere in Oxfordshire.

> Full springs of Thought around me rise
> Like Rivers Four to water my fair garden.
> Eastwards, where lie wide woodlands, rich as Arden,
> From out the beechen solitudes hath sprung
> A stream of verse from aerial Shelley's tongue,
> While, as he drifted on between the banks
> Of happy Thames, the waters 'neath the planks
> Of his light boat gurgled contentedly
> And ever with his dreams kept company.
> To-day, the music of the slow, turmoiling river,
> The music of the rapid vision-giver,
> To me are vocal both.
>   To eastward, too,
> A churchyard sleeps, and one infirm old yew,
> Where in the shadows of the fading day,
> Musing on faded lives, sate solemn Gray.
> There to majestic utterance his soul was wrought,
> And still his mighty chant is fraught
> With golden teaching for the world, and speaks
> Strong things with sweetness unto whoso seeks.
> Yet can I never sit low at his feet
> And, questioning, a gracious answer meet.
> For he is gone, and his high dignity
> Lost in the past (tho' he may haply be
> Far in Futurity as well).
>   To North
> Are hills where Arnold wandered forth
> Which, like his verse, still undulate in calm
> And tempered beauty.
>   And the marriage-psalm
> Was sung o'er Tennyson, small space away.

This rhyming letter has something still more intimate, for, towards its close, Owen declares his longing for a new great poet—for all of us, and himself:

> Let me attain
> To talk with him, and share his confidence.

His loneliness as a young poet breaks out; he may read even Keats and 'still', he appeals, 'I am alone among the Unseen Voices'.

APPENDIX B

Recollections of Mary and Arthur Newboult (*see p. 476, notes 4 and 5*)

Miss Mary Newboult writes (*26 February 1967*):

I knew Wilfred was coming to Edinburgh and the first time he came to see us was on a broiling hot Wednesday afternoon. Mother was at a church work party and it fell to me to entertain him. In those days I was a very shy and inarticulate girl but I do remember how very easy Wilfred was to talk to. He had the gift of drawing people out of themselves . . . I think my most vivid memory is of the times we—Mother, Auntie Sue and myself—sat in the garden and Wilfred read his poems to us, the beautiful cadence of his voice held me spellbound. I can hear it still. I remember too how he helped me with my homework. I loved reading the classics but it was the way in which Wilfred made the authors come alive. Even today . . . I am very conscious of the personality of the author and it is the picture Wilfred painted on my mind . . . Running through all this was his very great interest in and his *deep compassion* for other people. Looking back now I think I would say that Wilfred was nervy and highly strung during the time he was with us. But at the age of 14 I suppose I would not be interested in understanding that side of him. It was just wonderful for me to find someone like Wilfred to be interested in a raw, awkward schoolgirl such as I was.

Mr. Arthur Newboult writes (*1 February 1967*):

. . . my recollection of Wilfred Owen is rather dim now . . . but there are three things which do stick out in my memory. Firstly he was the person who gave me my first penknife, and I well remember the excitement when he told me outside the shop that we were to go in and purchase one for my very own use. When we returned home he said to my mother that he did hope she would not mind me having this knife . . . On another occasion he took me to the Edinburgh Zoo. We travelled part of the way by train to Murrayfield and there transferred to a train to take us to Corstorphine. At the changeover point there was a small sweetshop and I was told to go in and get some sweets, which I did. At the time I had a great liking for liquorice sticks, and I came out armed with these and boy-like proceeded to eat them. I well remember Wilfred asking me to kindly put those dirty things in my pocket before we boarded the train. I can see now looking back over the years the reason for this as he was so smartly turned out and to have a small boy eating liquorice with him must have offended his good taste. The third thing happened when he was playing with me in the kitchen. He used to pick me up and swing me round and round to my great delight. Whilst he was doing this of course I was laughing and shouting. At the time we had a fox terrier . . . whether he thought Wilfred was hurting me or not I didn't know but he suddenly flew at us, and I got quite a nasty bite on the wrist. I remember my father and mother telling me in later years how very upset Wilfred had been. . . . At the time the photo was taken [*see frontispiece*] I would be 7 years old, and would just have joined the Wolf Cubs—hence Chubby Cubby.

That is all . . . apart from the grief there was when we learned of his death. I can see my mother now standing in the kitchen crying when she heard either by letter or wire that he had been killed in action.

APPENDIX C

Two Letters from Robert Graves (See Letters 553 and 575)

[*Circa 17 October 1917*]   3rd Garr. Batt., R.W.F., Kinmel Park,
Rhyl, N. Wales

Do you know, Owen, that's a damn fine poem of yours, that 'Disabled.'
Really damn fine!

So good the general sound and weight of the words that the occasional
metrical outrages are most surprising. It's like seeing a golfer drive onto the
green in one and then use a cleek instead of a putter, & hole out in twelve.

For instance you have a foot too much in

    In the old days before he gave away his knees
& in He wasn't bothered much by Huns or crimes or guilts
&   They cheered him home but not as they would cheer a goal
&   Now he will spend a few sick years in institutes

There is an occasional jingle

                Voices of boys
       & Voices of play and pleasure after day

And an occasional cliché

                Girls glanced lovelier
                Scanty suit of grey

I wouldn't worry to mention all this if it wasn't for my violent pleasure at
some of the lines like the one about 'the solemn man who brought him fruits'
& the 'jewelled hilts of daggers in plaid socks' & the 'Bloodsmear down his
leg after the matches'.

Owen, you have seen things; you are a poet; but you're a very careless one
at present. One can't put in too many syllables into a line & say 'Oh, it's all
right. That's my way of writing poetry'. One has to follow the rules of the
metre one adopts. Make new metres by all means, but one must observe the
rules where they are laid down by custom of centuries. A painter or musician
has no greater task in mastering his colours or his musical modes & harmonies,
than a poet.

It's the devil of a sweat for him to get to know the value of his rhymes,
rhythms or sentiments. But I have no doubt at all that if you turned seriously
to writing, you could obtain Parnassus in no time while I'm still struggling
on the knees of that stubborn peak.

Till then, good luck in the good work. Yours Robert Graves.

Love to Sassoon.

[*Circa 22 December 1917*]   R.W.F.

My dear Owen,

'Scuse pencil—lazy—Saw old Sassoon yesterday & he showed me your
poems—Don't make any mistake, Owen, you are a damned fine poet already
& are going to be more so—I wont have the impertinence to criticize—you
have found a new method and must work it yourself—those assonances instead

of rhymes are fine—Did you know that it was a trick of Welsh poetry or was it instinct?

Two things however you'll forgive. Best thing, I find, is never to marry two colloquialisms in the same line, put a stray one in here and there but always mate it with better quality words & make it seem meritable & so poetic. S.S. often overdoes it: he started sparingly but its a temptingly easy path to run down to bathos by—

For God's sake cheer up and write more optimistically—The war's not ended yet but a poet should have a spirit above wars—Thanks awfully for cheering S.S. up: he actually talked of *aprés la guerre* yesterday & looks as fit as your soulful flea [*in 'À Terre': see Letter 568*]—I will send your poems to R.N. with instructions to return them to you later. Robert is a ripping fellow really but any stupid person would easily mistake him for an insufferable bounder. This sounds funny, but true—I am devoted to him. Puff out your chest a little, Owen, & be big—for you've more right than most of us. I am getting married in Jan. to a girl called Nancy, daughter of W. Nicholson the painter, & I'm frightfully busy as O.C. detachment of 500 men and 80 officers. But I find time for this for I don't want to lose sight of you—You must help S.S. and R.N. and R.G. to revolutionize English Poetry—So outlive this War.

Yours ever Robert Graves.

My address is 3rd. G.B. Rw Fus, Kinmel Park, Rhyl.

APPENDIX D

Sir Osbert Sitwell on Wilfred Owen

The younger men who would be found at Robbie's were usually writers and often poets, and he would often ask me to come and meet them. I was not surprised, therefore, when in September 1917,[1] he telephoned to me and invited me to come round to his rooms in Half-Moon Street the next evening after dinner. He said it was very important, and when I enquired why, he told me that a newly-discovered poet called Wilfred Owen, a friend whom Siegfried had met at Craiglockhart, was dining with him at the Reform, and that he wanted me to meet him. He gave promise of being a remarkable poet, Robert Ross added, and he asked me especially 'not to frighten him'—oddly enough, a thing I have often been asked—, for he was the most diffident and sensitive of men.

Accordingly I went round at the hour named, and there, in the comfortable warmth of Robbie's sitting-room, I saw a young officer of about my age—he was three months younger than myself—, of sturdy, medium build, and wearing a khaki uniform. His face was rather broad, and I think its most unusual characteristics were the width of eye and forehead, and the tawny, rather sanguine skin, which proclaimed, as against the message of his eyes—deep in colour and dark in their meaning—, a love of life and a poet's enjoyment of air and light. His features were mobile but determined, and his hair short and of a soft brown. His whole appearance, in spite of what he had been through, gave the impression of being somewhat young for his age, and, though he seemed perfectly sure of himself, it was easy to perceive that by nature he was shy. He had the eager, supple good manners of the sensitive, and was eager and receptive, quick to see a point and smile. His voice—what does his voice sound like across the years? A soft modulation, even-toned, but with a warmth in it (I almost hear it now), a well-proportioned voice that signified a sense of justice and of compassion. With his contemporaries he talked at ease. Only in the presence of such literary nabobs of the period as Wells and Bennett could he scarcely bring himself to speak; and this silence, apart from being rooted in his natural modesty and good manners, was due, I think, to the immense esteem in which he held literature and those who practised the profession of author. His residence in France may have deepened this attitude of respect, and almost awe, which had in it nothing of the Englishman's casual approach to books. To him they were all-important, while poetry was the very crown of life, and constituted its meaning. (*Noble Essences*, pp. 103–4)

[1] We now know from Letter 620 that their first meeting was in May 1917.

INDEX

Compiled by R. E. Thompson

INDEX

601

Long Mynd, 46
Longfellow, H. W., 'The Arrow and the Song', 107–8; *Hiawatha*, 320, 497, 518, 556, 563
Lost Property Office, unclaimed field glasses lent to W., 413; owner turns up, 413–15, 417
Lott, Mrs. (housekeeper), 101–2, 104–5, 113, 124–7, 133, 146, 153, 157–9, 172, 177, 190; a river trip, 142–5
Loughrey, Kathleen (cousin), 101
Loughrey, May (aunt), 22, 101
Loughrey, Dr. Richard (uncle), 341
Loupart, 439
Lourdes, 269
Lovat, Major-General Lord, 515
Love, 'I ought to be in love and am not', 295; W. on 'love one another as no men love for long', 502, 506
Lovell, (education officer), 286
Lowell, James Russell, quoted, 160
Lubbock, Sir John, 356
Lurton-Burke, Rev. J. W., 208–9, 216
Luxmore, Lieutenant-Colonel L., 452, 455
Lyth Hill, 71–72

Mabel (maid), 167, 168
Macaulay's history, volumes of, 62
McClymont, Second-Lieutenant Murray, 573, 582
Macdonald, Mr. (clergyman), 43
Macdonald, Erskine, 344, 454–5, 573, 582
MacDougall, Sapper, 546
Machine-gun companies, 433
McHutchon, Colin, 23
Mackenzie, Captain (and son), 483, 487, 497
Mackenzie, Ian, 344
'Mad Jack' (nickname for Sassoon), 512
Maddock-Jones, Mrs. (Aunt Clara), 63
Magny-la-Fosse, 579
Mahim, Shrewsbury (house of Owen family), Owens move to, 58; house built opposite, 210; attitude to paying guests at, 237, 241, 263; neighbours, 240; origin of name, 58; school at, 88, 97, 210; tent in garden, 131; mentioned, 122, 168, 222, 272, 277–8, 369, 465 (and *passim*)
Mais, S. P. B., 582
Maitland, Miss Crichton-, 162
Maitland, F. E., 355
Major Domo of Officers' Mess, W. as, 508–16, 519, 525, 530
'Man' (word), meaning of, 43–44
Manchester, 391, 533, 538, 581
Manchester Regiment, 2nd, W. with in France, 421 *et seq.*; badge, 423; W. posted to B. Company, 439; battalion takes over new positions, 439; W. rejoins after accident, 448*ff*; successful attack towards St. Quentin, 448–52; heavy losses, 448; further operations, 452; Commanding Officers, 455, 466,

575, 578–9; W. invalided home, 470; W. rejoins in France, 573–7 *et seq.*; appointed Bombing Officer, 578; operations, 577, 579–91; W. in command of Company, 580–1, 583–6; hands over to returned officer, 585
Manchester Regiment, 5th, history, 377; W. commissioned in, 377–8; W. with, 394–418; officers 'go out', 401, 408; drafts from, 402, 406, 409, 412, 415, 421; rumours of move, 405; win Sports Cup, 408; W. put down for new battalion, 407–9; amalgamation of battalions, 409; W. on Musketry course, 409, 417; moves north, 410–13; Firing Party, 412–13; W. embarks for France, 417–18; news of former officers, 466, 549
Manchester Regiment, 5th (Reserve), history, 508; W. reports to and is put on light duty, 508; W. made Major Domo of Officers' Mess, 508–16, 519, 525, 530; Commanding Officer, 509; time spent over meals, 525; W. in charge of café for the men, 529; W. moved to Ripon, 538; W. rejoins after being passed fit, 556; Messing Officer, 563–5, 570; uncertainty of W's rank, 564; W. returns to France, 569 *et seq.*
Manchester Regiment, 8th, 413
Manoel II, ex-King, 403
Mansell's (bookshop), 41
Mapledurham, 158
Marconi, G., 92
Marine insurance agent, pupil of W., 298, 303, 315
Markowski, Mlle, 221, 226, 258–9
Marlow, Shelley's house at, 106
Marmion, 405
Marriage in France, W. on, 253
Marsh, Sir Edward, *Georgian Poetry*, 526, 529
Marshall, Major J. N., 575, 577–9
Martin, Miss (art mistress), 255
Martin, André, 288, 356
Martin-Harvey, Sir John, 393
Mary, Queen, 84
Masefield, John, 437, 494, 520
Massine, Leonide, 570
Massingham, H. W., 507, 588
Matches, scarce in Bordeaux, 200; and customs, 223
Mathematics, examination, 81
Mather, Captain J. de V., 508, 513
Mather, James Marshall, 513
Mathews, Dr., 203, 379
Matriculation examination, London University, 77–81, 83, 85–87; W's 'mere pass', 80, 254
Matthews, 529
Maud'huy, Viscount, 290, 293, 295–6, 343
Maud'huy, Viscountess, 289
'Maundy Thursday', 10
May, Cousin, *see* Davies

Printed in Great Britain by
W. & J. Mackay & Co. Ltd, Chatham, Kent